The Ernst & Young Tax Guide 2012

D1401653

Years of critical acclaim for America's no. 1 tax guide ...

"This is the best tax guide of the bunch ... the most up-to-date guide."

USA Today

"Hard to beat ... [Ernst & Young professionals] elucidate each point, giving examples, definitions and strategies that you won't learn about from the IRS."

Money

"This book ... has more up-to-date information on tax changes than its competitors—or even the IRS."

Chicago Sun-Times

"Best of the commercially available guides."

New York Daily News

"Destined to become the 'old standard,' all written in plain English .... If you can afford just one tax book, this could be the one."

Seattle Post-Intelligencer

"The text-with-commentary approach makes the book both authoritative and easy-to-use."

People

"The simplest tax guide to understand."

CBS This Morning

"The explanations, examples, and planning advice are top-drawer."

Orlando Sentinel

"Exceptionally detailed."

The Sunday Denver Post

"An excellent book, full of clear explanations, planning hints, tax savers and sample forms."

Atlanta Journal Constitution

"Our brand-name choice for filers with lots of questions for filing and planning situations."

Fort Worth Star-Telegram

"... a veritable fountain of information."

Milwaukee Sentinel

"... the best of the bunch for return preparation."

Des Moines Register

2012 tax calendar

Date in 2012	Action required

January

17 ☐ Final estimated tax payment for 2011 due if you did not pay your income tax (or enough of your income tax) for that year through withholding. Use Form 1040-ES.

31 ☐ If you did not pay your last installment of estimated tax by January 17, file your income tax return for 2011 on this date, thereby avoiding any penalty for late payment of the last installment. Use Form 1040 or 1040A.

February

15 ☐ File a new Form W-4 if you can claim exemption from withholding.

March

1 ☐ Farmers and fishermen must file their 2011 income tax return (Form 1040) to avoid an underpayment penalty for the last quarter of 2011 if they were required to but did not pay estimated tax on January 17.

April

17 ☐ File your income tax return for 2011 (Forms 1040, 1040A, or 1040EZ) and pay any tax due.

☐ Make your 2011 IRA contribution.

☐ If you are not extending your return, make your Keogh or SEP-IRA contribution if you have self-employment income.

☐ For an automatic 6-month extension, file Form 4868 and pay any tax that you estimate will be due. Then file Form 1040 or 1040A by October 15. If you get an extension, you can't file Form 1040EZ. (You can use one Form 4868 to file for both your income tax and gift tax extensions.)

☐ Pay the first installment of your 2012 estimated tax if you are not paying your 2012 income tax (or enough of it) through withholding tax.

☐ If you made any taxable gifts during 2011 (more than $13,000 per donee), file a gift tax return for that year (Form 709 or 709-A) and pay any tax due.

June

15 ☐ Pay the second installment of 2012 estimated tax.

☐ If you are a U.S. citizen or resident alien living and working (or on military duty) outside the United States and Puerto Rico, file Form 1040 and pay any tax, interest, and penalties due. Otherwise, see April 17.

30 ☐ Individuals who have signature authority or other authority over certain bank, securities, or other financial accounts in a foreign country must file Form TD F 90-22.1. The form must be received on or before June 30.

September

17 ☐ Pay the third installment of your 2012 estimated tax.

☐ Last day to make a required minimum contribution to a defined benefit or money purchase Keogh plan.

October

15 ☐ If you requested an automatic 6-month extension to file your 2011 income tax return, file Form 1040 or Form 1040A and pay any tax, interest, and penalty due, and file any gift tax return if due.

☐ Last day to make a Keogh or SEP-IRA contribution deductible for calendar year 2011 if you requested a 6-month extension of time to file your tax return.

December

31 ☐ Last day to establish a Keogh plan for 2012.

The Ernst & Young Tax Guide 2012

By the Tax Partners and Professionals of Ernst & Young LLP

Peter W. Bernstein, Editor

ERNST & YOUNG

Quality In Everything We Do

The Ernst & Young Tax Guide Editorial Board 2012

Special thanks to:

James S. Turley, Chair and Chief Executive Officer–Ernst & Young Global Network; Stephen R. Howe, Americas Area Managing Partner; Gary L. Belske, Senior Vice Chair, Chief Operating Officer; Kathryn J. Barton, Americas Vice Chair–Tax Services; James L. Henderson, Americas Chief Operating Officer–Tax; Eric Solomon, Director of National Tax; Charles R. Kowal, Global Director of Personal Tax Services; David A. Boyle, Americas Director of Personal Financial Services

Special acknowledgments:

Thanks to Donald Batting, James Gaynor, Ellen Lee, Ingrid McGuire, Peter McKinley, Amy Rhodes, Julia Sonnhalter, Michael Sords, and Glenn Terrell.

The Ernst & Young global network of member firms has more than 20,000 tax practitioners worldwide, with more than 6,500 practitioners in the United States. This book draws upon the experience of many of those professionals for its content.

To Order
Ingram Publisher Services (IPS) accepts orders in a variety of ways, including through Ingram's ordering tools ipage® and companion®, phone, fax, and e-mail. Terms on IPS orders are the same regardless of ordering method.

ipage: ipage.ingrambook.com
Phone: (866) 767-8797
Fax: (800) 838-1149
E-mail: customer.service@ingrampublisherservices.com
ACCESS (automated stock check and ordering line): (800) 961-8031

Visit **ingrampublisherservices.com/ordering** for full details on our electronic ordering capabilities–including instructions on how to order via your POS system.

This book contains portions of Internal Revenue Service Publication 17, *Your Federal Income Tax* (rev. Dec. 2010), the author's 2011 updates, and portions of other pertinent Internal Revenue Service publications.

ISBN
978-1-879161-02-3

Printed in the United States of America
10 9 8 7 6 5 4 3 2 1

Notice: In the preparation of this book, every effort has been made to offer the most current, correct, and clearly expressed information available prior to publication: the Internal Revenue Code as of September 2011, the 2010 version of Internal Revenue Service Publication 17, *Your Federal Income Tax* (rev. Dec. 2010), updated by the author for 2011, and portions of other pertinent Internal Revenue Service publications. Readers may obtain the 2011 version of Publication 17 at *www.irs.gov*. Note also that inadvertent errors can occur, and tax rules and regulations often change.

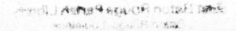

How to use this guide

The *Ernst & Young Tax Guide 2012* is an easy-to-use, step-by-step guide to preparing your own tax return. It has been designed with you in mind, and its format should help highlight information to save you time and money.

The book explains, in clear and simple English, important aspects of the tax laws that affect you. It covers what you need to know about your taxes—from how to file your return to how to lower the tax you'll pay next year. Throughout the book, you will find hundreds of examples illustrating how the tax laws work. Sample tax forms and schedules show you how to fill out your return line by line. Here are some of the book's special features and how to use them:

- **Two Books in One.** The *Ernst & Young Tax Guide 2012* is really two books. The first book is the 2010 version of the official Internal Revenue Service tax guide, Publication 17, *Your Federal Income Tax,* which is reproduced here. Published annually, it contains the IRS's position on many of the tax questions taxpayers face. To make the *Ernst & Young Tax Guide 2012* available to the public as quickly as possible, we have updated the text of the 2010 version of IRS Publication 17 to take into account developments during 2011. These updates are noted throughout the text. Upon release, the 2011 IRS Publication 17 can be found at *www.irs.gov*. The second book is the Ernst & Young guide. Here are comments, explanations, and tax-saving tips on what the IRS tells you—and doesn't tell you. It's no surprise that the IRS doesn't tell you everything, and what it does say often favors the U.S. government. Courts and tax professionals frequently differ with IRS opinions. The Ernst & Young text provides you with this additional material. The two books have been spliced together to give you the most well-rounded tax guide on the market. To distinguish between the two perspectives, the original IRS text appears in black throughout the book, our updates of the IRS text are underlined, and Ernst & Young's comments appear in the green boxes.

- **TaxSavers, TaxPlanners, TaxAlerts, and TaxOrganizers.** Among this book's biggest attractions are the more than 400 *TaxSavers, TaxPlanners, TaxAlerts,* and *TaxOrganizers* that you'll find appropriately placed throughout the text. *TaxSavers* are tips that help you slash your tax bill this year and next—legally. *TaxPlanners* outline ideas that help you plan better for the upcoming year. *TaxAlerts* point out tax rules and regulations that have just changed or may change in the near future; they give you important current filing advice about issues you will want to consider as you prepare your return. *TaxOrganizers* point out steps you can take now to make it easier to file your taxes later.

- **Tax Breaks and Deductions You Can Use Checklists.** You will find a checklist of key tax breaks and deductions for which you may be eligible at the beginning of each chapter, immediately following the Introduction. You should review each checklist to make sure you are taking all the deductions and tax breaks that you deserve.

- **Companion Website.** Purchase of this guide includes access throughout the 2011 tax return filing season to *ey.com/EYTaxGuide*. This website contains up-to-date information you need about changes in the tax laws that occur throughout the year.

- **Special Contents.** We've taken great pains to ensure that this book is clearly organized for easy access. If you can't find the section you want in the regular Contents, check the **Special Contents.** All told, there are eight of these—one each for families, homeowners, investors in stocks and bonds, investors in real estate, self-employed entrepreneurs, business executives, senior citizens, and members of the Armed Forces. Each **Special Contents** section contains a listing of the major tax issues for members of that group and tells where you can find the answers in the book. In addition, we have a table of contents at the beginning of each chapter to help you find what you need.

We have drawn from the tax experience of scores of Ernst & Young LLP partners, professionals, and staff from all parts of the United States to create this tax guide. Among the major accounting firms, only Ernst & Young LLP publishes a complete tax guide that is available to the general public. It provides the most complete and up-to-date tax information of any tax guide published.

Contents

Special contents

Real estate investors' tax guide

Self-employed entrepreneurs' tax guide

Business executives' tax guide

Senior citizens' tax guide

Members of the Armed Forces' tax guide

(Including Veterans)

Changes in the tax law you should know about

In the face of a struggling economy, a deeply divided Congress was finally able to compromise on their differences long enough to pass the Tax Relief, Unemployment Insurance Reauthorization, and Job Creation Act (the 2010 Tax Act) on December 17, 2010. The 2010 Tax Act extended the so-called Bush tax cuts through 2012, and extended for two more years (through 2011) multiple tax provisions that expired at the end of 2009. The Republicans fought hard to permanently extend the Bush tax cuts, while the Democrats favored eliminating the tax cuts for taxpayers with income over $200,000 ($250,000 if married filing jointly). In the end, both sides settled on maintaining the status quo–through 2012.

The battle over future tax rates, deductions, and overall tax reform continues to rage, and has been thrust into the larger, highly divisive debate over the federal budget deficit, the climbing national debt, and overall economic policy. The fight over extending the debt ceiling in the summer of 2011 culminated with President Obama's signing the Debt Control Act of 2011 on August 2, 2011. The Debt Control Act of 2011 raised the federal debt ceiling to prevent the United States from defaulting on its debt, cut spending, and provided for the creation of a bipartisan joint committee to review further proposals to either cut spending, raise taxes, or some combination of the two. While any tax law changes most likely will not impact the preparation of your 2011 tax return, they may have an impact on your tax planning for future years.

For updated information on new tax legislation that is enacted after this book is published, see our website, *ey.com/EYTaxGuide*.

Tax Changes Effective for 2011

Tax Benefits Extended Through 2011

The following tax benefits were set to expire at the end of 2009, but were extended for two more years by the 2010 Tax Act. If no new legislation is passed, these provisions will expire on December 31, 2011. (For updated information on this and any other tax law changes that occur after this book is published, see our website, *ey.com/EYTaxGuide*.)

- Deduction for state and local general sales taxes. See chapter 23.
- Deduction for certain expenses of elementary and secondary school teachers (educator expenses). See chapter 19.
- Deduction for qualified tuition and related expenses. See chapters 19 and 36.
- Contributions of capital gain real property made for conservation purposes. See chapters 25 and 48.
- District of Columbia first-time homebuyer credit.
- Premiums for mortgage insurance deductible as interest that is qualified residence interest. See chapter 24.
- Tax-free distributions from individual retirement plans for charitable purposes. See chapter 17. Since the 2010 Tax Act was passed so late in 2010, taxpayers were allowed to make charitable contributions in January 2011, and treat them as if they were made in 2010. This provision enables the contribution to count toward satisfying the taxpayer's minimum distribution requirement from IRAs for 2010. Such qualified charitable distributions count against the 2010 $100,000 limitation on the exclusion.

Reductions in Individual Income Tax Rates

As a result of the extension of the so-called Bush tax cuts, which were first enacted in 2001 and 2003, the 10%, 25%, 28%, 33%, and 35% individual income tax brackets are extended through December 31, 2012. Unless new tax legislation is passed, beginning in 2013, tax rates are scheduled to increase to 15%, 28%, 31%, 36%, and 39.6%, respectively. These same rates also apply to income taxes paid by trusts and estates.

Zero Tax Rate on Qualified Dividends and Long-Term Capital Gains for Taxpayers in Lower Brackets

For 2011 (and 2012), the tax rate on qualified dividends and long-term capital gains continues at zero for taxpayers taxed in the 10% and 15% tax brackets for ordinary income. The maximum rate for taxpayers in higher brackets remains at 15% through the end of 2012. These provisions are scheduled to expire at the end of 2012.

Personal Exemption Limitation Eliminated

The complete elimination of the personal exemption phaseout that began in 2010 continues for 2011 and 2012. As a result, higher-income taxpayers will be able to deduct the full amount of their personal exemptions. After 2012, the old phaseout rules are scheduled to be fully reinstated.

Limitation on Itemized Deductions Eliminated

The complete elimination of the itemized deduction phaseout that began in 2010 continues for 2011 and 2012. Under prior law, taxpayers with adjusted gross income (AGI) over specified levels (e.g., in 2009, greater than $166,800 or $83,400 if married filing separately) were required to reduce their itemized deductions. In 2011 and 2012, higher-income taxpayers will *not* have to reduce their total itemized deductions based on an AGI limitation. For 2013, the old phaseout rule is scheduled to be fully reinstated.

Marriage Penalty Relief

The marriage penalty relief for the standard deduction and the 15% bracket range is extended through 2012.

Although married couples may elect to file separate returns, the tax rate schedules and other tax provisions are structured so that a married couple filing separate returns usually has a higher combined tax than when filing a joint return. Different rate schedules and tax provisions apply to single taxpayers. A "marriage penalty" is said to exist when the tax liability of a married couple filing jointly is greater than the sum of the tax liabilities that would apply if each taxpayer were single.

A 2003 tax law pegged the standard deduction amount for joint filers at twice the standard deduction amount for single filers. This 2003 law also provided relief for the marriage penalty that resulted due to the fact that the upper band on the 15% tax bracket was considerably lower for married filing jointly taxpayers than it was for unmarried taxpayers. Two unmarried individuals thus could have a greater amount of income taxed at the lower 15% tax rate than a married couple with similar income. This 2003 law extended the range of the 15% rate bracket for joint returns to twice the size of the corresponding rate bracket for single returns. Both of these provisions were scheduled to expire at the end of 2010, but have been extended through 2012. See chapter 2, *Filing status*, for more information.

Temporary Reduction in Employee-Paid Payroll Taxes

Under current law, employees pay a 6.2% social security tax on all wages earned up to $106,800 in 2011, and self-employed individuals pay a 12.4% social security self-employment tax on all their self-employment income up to the same $106,800 threshold. The 2010 Tax Act provides a payroll/self-employment tax holiday during 2011 of two percentage points. This means employees pay only 4.2% on wages, and self-employed individuals pay only 10.4% on their self-employment income up to the $106,800 threshold. As of the date this book went to press, President Obama had indicated he wants to see this benefit extended through 2012, but Congress had not yet acted. If no action is taken, this tax rate reduction will expire after 2011.

Standard Mileage Rates

The standard mileage rate for the cost of operating your car increased to 51 cents a mile for all business miles driven from January 1, 2011, through June 30, 2011, and 55.5 cents a mile for all business miles driven during the rest of 2011. See chapter 27, *Car expenses and other employee business expenses.*

The standard mileage rate allowed for the use of your car for medical reasons or a qualified move is 19 cents per mile during the first 6 months of 2011, and 23.5 cents a mile from July 1, 2011, through the end of the year. See chapter 22, *Medical and dental expenses,* and chapter 20, *Moving expenses.*

The standard mileage rate allowed for charitable purposes remains at 14 cents per mile for 2011. See chapter 25, *Contributions.*

Alternative Minimum Tax (AMT) Changes

AMT exemption increased for 2011. The tax laws give preferential treatment to certain kinds of income and allow special deductions and credits for certain kinds of expenses. The alternative minimum tax (AMT) attempts to ensure that anyone who benefits from these tax advantages pays at least a minimum amount of tax. The AMT is a separately computed tax that eliminates many deductions and credits that are allowed in computing your regular tax liability.

The AMT is the government's mechanism through which taxpayers with a large amount of deductions still pay some income tax. The tentative minimum tax rates on ordinary income are 26% and 28%. The 15% maximum tax rate (0% for those taxpayers who are otherwise in the 10% and 15% marginal tax brackets for ordinary income in 2011) on qualified dividends and capital gains for regular tax purposes also applies when calculating the AMT. If your taxable income for regular tax purposes, plus any adjustments and preference items you have, total more than the exemption amount, then you may have to pay the AMT.

The exemption amount provided in the original AMT legislation passed in 1986 is not indexed for inflation. As a result, many taxpayers have found themselves subject to the AMT. In recognition of this problem, Congress has repeatedly enacted temporary measures that significantly raised the applicable exemption amounts above the levels that last applied in 2000. The 2010 Tax Act continued this trend and provided some relief through 2011. The exemption amounts for 2011 are as follows:

1. $74,450 for married filing jointly/qualified widow or widower.
2. $48,450 for single or head of household.
3. $37,225 for married filing separately.

If Congress does not take action to increase the exemption amount for 2012, the AMT exemption amount will revert back to the levels that existed prior to 2001 as follows:

1. $45,000 for married filing jointly/qualified widow or widower.
2. $33,750 for single or head of household.
3. $22,500 for married filing separately.

For updated information on this and any other tax law changes that occur after this book is published, see our website, *ey.com/EYTaxGuide.*

For an explanation of the AMT, see chapter 31, *How to figure your tax.*

Certain credits allowed to offset AMT through 2011. The ability to offset both your regular tax liability and your AMT liability with specific nonrefundable personal credits—including the credit for child and dependent care expenses, credit for the elderly or the disabled, American opportunity credit, lifetime learning credit, nonbusiness energy property credit, D.C. first-time homebuyer credit, and mortgage interest credit—was extended through 2011 by the 2010 Tax Act. If legislation is not passed to extend this benefit beyond 2011, then these credits will be allowed only to the extent that your regular income tax liability exceeds your tentative minimum tax, determined without regard to the minimum tax foreign tax credit. For updated information on this and any other tax law changes that occur after this book is published, see our website, *ey.com/EYTaxGuide.*

General business credit subject to AMT. Generally, taxpayers may claim allowable general business credits only to the extent that their regular tax liability exceeds their AMT liability. The Small Business Jobs Act of 2010 allowed certain small businesses to use all types of general business credits against their AMT, but this provision was only available for 2010, and was not extended. This applied to general business credits for those sole proprietorships, partnerships, and nonpublicly traded corporations with $50 million or less in average annual gross receipts for the prior three years. For companies that have a fiscal year end, the provision applied for the first tax year beginning after December 31, 2009.

Accelerated recovery of AMT refundable credit. You are allowed a refundable credit for AMT you paid in past years to the extent that your AMT liability was attributable to the exercise of incentive stock options and other deferral adjustments. Eligible long-term unused minimum tax credits may be refunded over two years (50% per year). Since the credit is refundable, you can receive a refund even if the refund exceeds your total tax liability for the year. For 2011, a portion of any unused minimum tax credit carryforward from 2007 or earlier years may be refunded. Since this provision expires after 2012 for calendar year taxpayers, only those unused credits that arose before 2009 can be eligible for recovery as a refundable credit. Unused credits realized after 2008 can only be claimed under the preexisting rules for claiming minimum tax credits. See *Refundable Credit for Prior Year Minimum Tax* in chapter 37, *Other credits including the earned income credit,* for more information on how to claim this credit and receive a refund—even when the refund exceeds your total tax liability for the year.

Income to Be Reported Related to 2010 and 2011 Roth IRA Conversions

For 2010 and beyond, any taxpayer with a traditional IRA account or a 401(k) or other deferral plan from a former employer can elect to convert the plan to a Roth IRA, regardless of the amount of their adjusted gross income (AGI). If the conversion is made in 2011, any taxable amounts will be included in income in 2011. If the conversion was made in 2010, any taxable amounts are included in income in equal amounts in 2011 and 2012, unless you opted to make an election to report the entire amount as income in 2010. For more information, see *Rollovers to Roth IRAs* in chapter 10, *Retirement plans, pensions, and annuities,* and *Conversions* in chapter 17, *Individual retirement arrangements (IRAs).*

Income to Be Reported Related to Converting Elective Deferral Plan to a Designated Roth Account

The Small Business Jobs Act of 2010 contains a provision that allows 401(k), 403(b), and governmental 457(b) plans to permit participants to roll their pretax account balances into a designated Roth account within the same plan, if the plan so allows. (457(b) plans can establish Roth designated accounts beginning in 2011.) Rollovers to a designated Roth account are only allowed, however, in the event of a permitted distributable event such as separation from service or attaining age 59½. Just like a conversion to a Roth IRA, the amount rolled over is includible in taxable income except to the extent it includes a return of after-tax contributions. If the rollover to a designated Roth account in a 401(k) or 403(b) plan is made in 2011, any taxable amounts are included in income in 2011. If the rollover was made in 2010, any taxable amounts would be included in income in equal amounts in 2011 and 2012, unless you made an election to report the entire amount as income in 2010. For more information, see *Rollovers to Roth Designated Accounts* in chapter 10, *Retirement plans, pensions, and annuities.*

First-Time Homebuyer Credit Not Available for Most Taxpayers

You generally cannot claim the credit for a home you bought after April 30, 2010. However, certain members of the Armed Forces and certain other federal employees had until April 30, 2011, to buy a home and take the credit. For more information, see *First-Time Homebuyer Credit* in chapter 37, *Other credits including the earned income credit.*

Recapture of First-Time Homebuyer Credit for Homes Purchased in 2008

If you claimed the first-time homebuyer credit for a home you bought in 2008, you were required to begin repaying the credit in 2010. Your second installment will be due with your 2011 tax return. You generally must repay the credit over a 15-year period in 15 equal installments. Each installment is reported as additional tax on your tax return. However, if you sold or stopped using your home as your principal residence before the 15-year period is up, you must include all remaining annual installments as additional tax on the return for the tax year that happens. See *Recapturing (Paying Back) the First-Time Homebuyer Credit* in chapter 15, *Selling your home,* for additional information.

Recapture of First-Time Homebuyer Credit for Homes Purchased After 2008

If you claimed the first-time homebuyer credit for a home purchased after 2008, you generally must repay the credit if, during the 36-month period beginning on the purchase date and after the year for which you claim the credit, you dispose of the home or it ceases to be your main home. This includes situations where you sell the home; you convert the entire home to business or rental property; the home is destroyed, condemned, or disposed of under threat of condemnation; or the lender forecloses on the mortgage. You repay the credit by including it as additional tax on the return for the year the home ceases to be your main home. If the home continues to be your main home for at least 36 months beginning on the purchase date, you do not have to repay any of the credit. See *Recapturing (Paying Back) the First-Time Homebuyer Credit* in chapter 15, *Selling your home,* for additional information.

Exclusion from Gross Income of Certain Discharged Mortgage Debt

Legislation passed in 2008 allows you to exclude from your gross income, income realized from the discharge of qualified principal residence indebtedness through 2012. Up to $2 million ($1 million if married filing separately) of qualified principal residence indebtedness may be forgiven, and no income would have to be recognized related to the cancellation of debt. However, your basis in your principal residence would be reduced by the amount excluded from income.

Qualified principal residence indebtedness is defined as acquisition indebtedness with respect to your principal residence. Acquisition indebtedness generally means debt you incurred in the acquisition, construction, or substantial improvement of your principal residence that is secured by the residence. It also includes the refinancing of such debt to the extent the new loan balance is attributable to qualified principal residence indebtedness.

Itemized Deduction for Mortgage Insurance Premiums

Premiums you paid during 2011 for "qualified mortgage insurance" may be deductible as an itemized deduction. The deduction applies only to mortgage insurance contracts issued after 2006.

The amount you can deduct is reduced by 10% (.10) for every $1,000 ($500 if your filing status is married filing separately) by which your adjusted gross income exceeds $100,000 ($50,000 if your filing status is married filing separately). Since the calculation rounds up to the nearest $1,000 increment, the deduction is not allowed if your adjusted gross income exceeds $110,000 ($55,000 in the case of a married individual filing a separate return).

American Opportunity Credit

The 2010 Tax Act extended the benefits of the American opportunity credit through 2012. This education credit is available to a broad range of taxpayers, including those with higher incomes and those who owe no tax. The terms of the credit include:

1. A maximum credit of $2,500 per student. The credit is phased out if your modified adjusted gross income (AGI) is between $80,000 and $90,000 ($160,000 and $180,000 if you file a joint return). See chapter 36, *Education credits and other education tax benefits,* for additional information.

2. The credit can be claimed for the first four years of postsecondary education.

3. Generally, 40% of the credit is refundable, which means that you can receive up to a $1,000 refund, even if you do not have a tax liability. There are a few circumstances that limit the refundability of the credit.

4. The term "qualified tuition and related expenses" has been expanded to include expenditures for "course materials." For this purpose, the term "course materials" means books, supplies, and equipment needed for a course of study whether or not the materials are purchased from the educational institution as a condition of enrollment or attendance.

Unless Congress acts, the American opportunity credit will expire at the end of 2012, and the provisions of the Hope credit will be reinstated beginning in 2013. See chapter 36, *Education credits and other education tax benefits,* for more information on the American opportunity credit.

Computers No Longer Qualify as Qualified Education Expenses in Section 529 Education Plans

Section 529 Education Plans are tax-advantaged savings plans that cover all qualified education expenses, including tuition, room and board, mandatory fees, and books. Under a 2009 tax law, the cost of computers and computer technology were allowed as qualified education expenses if the computer or technology was used for college work. This benefit expired at the end of 2010 and was not extended.

Student Loan Interest Deduction Benefits Extended Through 2012

Taxpayers who have paid interest on qualified education loans may claim an above-the-line deduction from their gross income for the interest paid up to $2,500. The deduction is phased out for taxpayers with modified adjusted gross income in excess of $60,000 ($120,000 if married filing jointly), and is completely phased out for taxpayers with modified adjusted gross income of $75,000 or more ($150,000 or more if married filing jointly). Beginning in 2013, this benefit will only be allowed for the first 60 months that interest payments are required, and the income phaseout ranges will be cut to $40,000 to $55,000 ($60,000 to $75,000 if married filing jointly).

Coverdell Account Benefits Extended Through 2012

Coverdell Education Savings Accounts are tax-exempt savings accounts used to pay the higher education expenses of a designated beneficiary. Tax legislation passed during the Bush administration increased the annual contribution amount from $500 to $2,000, and expanded the definition of education expenses to include elementary and secondary school expenses. The 2010 Tax Act extends these benefits through 2012.

Section 179 Small Business Expensing Increased and Expanded for 2010 and 2011

Section 179 of the tax code allows you to elect to deduct all or part of the cost—up to specified yearly limits—of certain qualifying property in the year in which the property is purchased and placed in service, rather than capitalizing the cost and depreciating it over its life. This means that you can deduct all or part of the cost up front in one year rather than take depreciation deductions spread out over many years. You must decide for each item of qualifying property whether to deduct, subject to the yearly limit, or capitalize and depreciate its cost. Qualifying property is property purchased for use in your trade or business and property that would have qualified for the investment tax credit.

Under the Small Business Jobs Act of 2010, the maximum Section 179 deduction available for qualifying property placed into service during taxable years beginning in 2011 (and 2010) is $500,000. This limit is reduced dollar for dollar once the cost of qualifying property placed in service during the year exceeds $2 million. Within those thresholds, this 2010 tax law also allows taxpayers to expense up to $250,000 of the cost of qualified leasehold improvement property, qualified restaurant property, and qualified retail improvement property placed into service during taxable years beginning in 2011 (and 2010).

In 2012, the maximum Section 179 deduction will be reduced to $125,000 ($25,000 after 2012) with an investment ceiling of $500,000 ($200,000 after 2012). After 2012, the maximum Section 179 deduction is scheduled to drop to $25,000, with an investment ceiling of $200,000. After 2011, qualified property no longer includes qualified leasehold improvement property, qualified restaurant property, or qualified retail improvement property.

Special Depreciation Allowance

The 2010 Tax Act provided that qualified property placed in service after September 8, 2010, and before January 1, 2012, is eligible for 100% first-year depreciation. (Tax laws enacted in 2009 and 2010 allowed an additional first-year depreciation deduction equal to 50% of the adjusted basis of qualified property placed in service after December 31, 2007, and before September 9, 2010.) For 2012, the bonus depreciation allowed for investments placed into service generally drops from 100% to 50% of the depreciable basis of qualified property. The types of property that qualify for the 100% special depreciation allowance are Section 168 (tangible) property with a recovery period of 20 years or less, off-the-shelf computer software, water utility property, and qualified leasehold improvement property. The rules for claiming the special depreciation allowance are complex. See Publication 946, *How to Depreciate Property*, for more information. You should also consider consulting your tax advisor prior to claiming this benefit.

Decreased Deduction for Start-Up Expenditures

The Small Business Jobs Act of 2010 temporarily increased the amount of start-up expenditures that may be deducted to $10,000 for 2010 only. This benefit was not extended for 2011. Consequently, the amount of start-up expenditures that may be deducted for 2011 is now $5,000 (down from $10,000 in 2010). This deduction is reduced by the amount by which start-up expenditures exceed $50,000 (decreased from $60,000 in 2010). Start-up expenditures are defined as expenses paid or incurred in connection with investigating or creating an active trade or business, which would be deductible if paid or incurred in connection with the operation of an existing trade or business.

Health Insurance Deduction No Longer Available for Purposes of Calculating Self-Employment Tax

The Small Business Jobs Act of 2010 permitted self-employed individuals to deduct the cost of health insurance for themselves, their spouses, and children who had not attained age 27 as of the end of 2010 in the calculation of their 2010 self-employment income subject to self-employment tax. This benefit was not extended for 2011 and is no longer available. Self-employed taxpayers can continue to deduct 100% of their cost of health insurance for themselves, their spouses, and children who have not attained age 27 as of the end of the taxable year in the calculation of their adjusted gross income, subject to certain limits. See chapter 38, *Self-employment income: How to file Schedule C*, for more information on the calculation of self-employment tax.

100% Exclusion of Small Business Capital Gains

Generally, noncorporate taxpayers may exclude 50% of the gain from the sale of certain small business stock acquired at original issue and held for more than five years. Qualifying small business stock is from a C corporation with gross assets that do not exceed $50 million (including the proceeds received from the issuance of the stock). The corporation must also meet a specific active business requirement. The amount of gain eligible for the exclusion is limited to the greater of ten times the taxpayer's basis in the stock or $10 million of gain from stock in that corporation.

For stock acquired after February 17, 2009, and before September 28, 2010, the exclusion was increased to 75%. (At the time of sale, however, 28% of the excluded gain is treated as a tax preference item subject to the alternative minimum tax (AMT).)

Two tax laws (including the 2010 Tax Act) enacted in 2010 temporarily increased the amount of the exclusion to 100% of the gain from the sale of qualifying small business stock that is acquired at original issue after September 27, 2010, and before January 1, 2012. There is also no AMT preference item attributable for that sale. For more information, see *Gain on Qualified Small Business Stock*, in chapter 16, *Reporting gains and losses*.

Temporary Reduction in Recognition Period for S Corporation Built-In Gains

Prior to enactment of the American Recovery and Reinvestment Tax Act of 2009, when a C corporation elected to become an S corporation, all gains that were built-in at the time of the election (or were attributable to property received by the S corporation from a C corporation in a transaction when basis carried over) were taxed if they were recognized during the first 10 years of S corporation status. The built-in gains tax is assessed at the highest corporate rate, currently 35%. This tax does not include gains that were created after the election or gains that are offset by losses. The 2009 law reduced the built-in gain holding period from 10 to 7 years for tax years that begin in 2009 and 2010, thereby reducing the period when S corporation shareholders may distribute built-in gains.

The Small Business Jobs Act of 2010 further reduces the built-in gain holding period from 7 to 5 years for taxable years beginning in 2011. Unless Congress changes the law, the holding period will increase back to 10 years for taxable years beginning in 2012 and thereafter.

General Business Credit Can No Longer Be Carried Back Five Years

The Small Business Jobs Act of 2010 extended the one-year carryback for general business credits to five years for certain small businesses. This applied to general business credits for those sole proprietorships, partnerships, and nonpublicly traded corporations with $50 million or less in average annual gross receipts for the prior three years. This change in the law was applicable for 2010 only. For fiscal year filers, the effective tax year is the first tax year beginning after December 31, 2009. For 2011 and future years, unused general business credits may generally be carried back to offset taxes paid in the previous year, and the remaining amount may be carried forward for 20 years to offset future tax liabilities.

2011 Disaster Area Tax Relief

A number of areas throughout the country are entitled to disaster tax relief for 2011. For the most up-to-date listing of the areas receiving relief, see *Disaster Assistance and Emergency Relief for Individuals and Businesses* at www.irs.gov for additional details.

Making Work Pay Credit No Longer Available

The American Recovery and Reinvestment Act of 2009 provided for a refundable tax credit of up to $400 for working individuals and $800 for working families. This tax credit was calculated at a rate of 6.2% of earned income, and was phased out for taxpayers with adjusted gross income in excess of $75,000 ($150,000 for married couples filing jointly). This benefit was available for 2009 and 2010, but was not extended for 2011 and future years.

Nonbusiness Energy Property Credit

This credit has been extended for one year with a reduced rate of 10%. Amounts provided by subsidized federal, state, or local energy financing do not qualify for the credit. The energy-efficiency standards for qualified natural gas, propane, and oil furnaces and hot water boilers have been increased. For 2011, the credit is limited as follows.

- A total combined credit limit of $500 for all tax years after 2005 (Form 5695, Part I).
- A combined credit limit of $200 for windows for all tax years after 2005.
- A maximum credit for residential energy property costs of $50 for any advanced main air circulating fan; $150 for any qualified natural gas,

propane, or oil furnace or hot water boiler; and $300 for any item of energy-efficient building property.

See chapter 37, *Other credits including the earned income credit,* for additional information.

Benefits of Refundable Portion of the Child Tax Credit Extended Through 2012

The 2010 Tax Act extends the current "enhanced" child tax credit through 2012. The maximum credit allowed is $1,000 for each qualifying child under age 17, and applies against both regular tax and alternative minimum tax (AMT) provided the taxpayer is under certain income thresholds. The phaseout of the credit begins at $75,000 ($110,000 for married filing jointly, and $55,000 for married filing separately). The credit continues to be refundable to the extent of 15% of the taxpayer's earned income in excess of $3,000. For more information, see chapter 35, *Child tax credit.*

Tax Benefits for Adoption

The adoption credit and the maximum exclusion from income of benefits under an employer's adoption assistance program are increased to $13,360 for 2011. These benefits are phased out for taxpayers with AGI between $185,210 and $225,210. The credit is fully refundable. As a result, you can receive a refund for the full amount of the credit you claim, even when your credit exceeds your tax liability. Unless Congress acts, the increased credit and exclusion amounts, as well as "refundability" expire after 2012. See *Adoption Credit* in chapter 37, *Other credits including the earned income credit.*

Penalty and Information Return Reporting Changes

The Small Business Jobs Act of 2010 increased penalties for failure to file information returns to the IRS. These provisions apply with respect to information returns required to be filed on or after January 1, 2011. For "small filers," including most individuals, the first-tier penalty is increased from $15 to $30, and the calendar year maximum is increased from $25,000 to $75,000. The second-tier penalty is increased from $30 to $60, and the calendar year maximum is increased from $50,000 to $200,000. The third-tier penalty is increased from $50 to $100, and the calendar year maximum is increased from $100,000 to $500,000. Higher maximum amounts apply if you are not a small filer. Further, the minimum penalty for each failure due to intentional disregard of the law is increased from $100 to $250. The penalty amounts are adjusted every five years for inflation.

The Small Business Jobs Act of 2010 also required that, beginning in 2011, individuals receiving rental income from real property file information returns (generally Form 1099-MISC) to the IRS and to service providers reporting payments of $600 or more during the year for rental property expenses. This provision was repealed and is no longer applicable.

Increase in Earned Income Credit

The American Recovery and Reinvestment Act of 2009 temporarily increased the earned income credit (EIC) for working families with three or more children. The act extended these benefits through 2011 and 2012. See chapter 37, *Other credits including the earned income credit,* for additional information.

Advance Payment of Earned Income Credit (EIC) No Longer Available After 2010

A 2010 tax law eliminated the ability for taxpayers to elect to receive advance payments through their paychecks of their refundable portion of the EIC. Beginning in 2011, taxpayers eligible for the refundable portion of the EIC will need to wait to claim a refund on their tax return filed by April 15 of the following year. You can still effectively receive the nonrefundable portion of the EIC through your paycheck, by adjusting withholding, to the extent you otherwise have positive tax liability.

Estate, Gift, and Generation-Skipping Transfer Taxes

The 2010 Tax Act made numerous changes to the estate, gift, and generation-skipping transfer (GST) tax provisions. To understand the implications of these changes, a little history about gift and estate tax law in recent years is helpful.

Under the law in effect through 2009, specified amounts of taxable gifts you made during your life and taxable transfers of property held in your estate at your death were exempted from gift and estate taxes. Before 2004, the estate and gift taxes were fully unified, such that a single graduated tax rate schedule and a single total exemption amount applied for purposes of determining the tax on cumulative taxable transfers made during your lifetime and at death. From 2004 through 2009, the gift tax and the estate tax continued to be determined using a single graduated tax rate schedule, but the specified exemption amounts allowed for estate tax purposes was higher than the effective exemption amount allowed for gift tax purposes. In 2009, the highest estate and gift tax rate was 45%. The exemption amount was $3.5 million for estate tax purposes and $1 million for gift tax purposes. The tax basis in property your heirs inherited from you was generally "stepped up" to equal the fair market value of the property as of the date of your death.

Under the so-called Bush tax cuts, the estate and generation-skipping transfer taxes were repealed for decedents dying and generation-skipping transfers made during 2010. The gift tax remained in effect, however, during 2010 with a $1 million exemption amount and a top gift tax rate of 35%. New complex rules also went into effect for determining the basis in property inherited from a decedent who died in 2010. Such inherited property did not get a "stepped-up" basis. Instead, the basis equaled the lesser of the fair market value of the property on the decedent's date of death or the decedent's adjusted basis in the property. This is commonly referred to as "carryover basis." There is also an exception to this rule. A decedent's executor can increase the basis of assets transferred by a total of $1.3 million plus any unused capital losses, net operating losses, and certain "built-in" losses of the decedent. An additional $3 million basis increase is allowed for property transferred to a surviving spouse, which means that property transferred to a spouse was allowed a basis increase of $4.3 million. Certain types of assets were not eligible for this increase in basis. Nonresident aliens were only allowed an increase in basis of $60,000. For more information, see *Property Inherited From a Decedent Who Died During 2010* in chapter 44, *Estate and gift planning.*

Estate and generation-skipping transfer taxes reinstated retroactively for 2010. The 2010 Tax Act reinstated the estate and GST taxes effective for decedents dying and transfers made after December 31, 2009. The estate and gift tax exemption amounts are reunified for 2011 and increased to $5 million. The maximum tax rate on transfers of property subject to gift, estate, and GST tax is 35% (although the tax rate applicable to GST transfers is zero for decedents who died in 2010). These higher exemptions and lower tax rates are effective for 2011 and 2012. Beginning in 2013, the gift, estate, and GST tax laws are scheduled to revert to what they were before 2001—meaning that the top tax rate climbs to 55% and cumulative exemption amount drops to $1 million.

Special election for decedents who died during 2010. In conjunction with reinstating the estate and GST taxes for 2010, the 2010 Tax Act also generally allows the executor of an estate of a person who died during 2010 to elect not to have reinstated estate tax apply, but instead have the special carryover basis rules apply to inherited property (rather than the stepped-up basis rules that apply if the estate tax is in effect). There are many complex rules and considerations to balance if this election is available. Executors considering this election should seek the advice of their tax advisor. For more information about these tax changes, see chapter 44, *Estate and gift tax planning.*

Gift tax applicable for 2011. The annual exclusion remains at $13,000 for 2011 per donee for gifts. As described above, the 2010 Tax Act increased the gift tax exemption in 2011 to $5 million. The maximum tax rate on taxable gifts made during 2011 (and 2012) is capped at 35%. Unless Congress acts, the higher exemption and lower tax rate are scheduled to expire after 2012. See *The Fundamentals of the Gift Tax* in chapter 44, *Estate and gift tax planning.*

Inflation Adjustments for 2011

Each year a number of tax benefits and income limitations for tax benefits are adjusted for inflation. In recent years these changes, if any, were very small due to the low rate of inflation—and this is true for 2011 as well. The adjustments for 2011 are as follows:

- Tax Rate Tables: The income bracket for each tax rate has been increased slightly. See chapter 49, *Tax rate schedules*.
- Personal Exemption: The personal exemption amount increased from $3,650 to $3,700 in 2011. See chapter 3, *Personal exemptions and dependents*.
- Standard Deduction: The standard deduction increased for 2011 to $11,600 (up from $11,400) for married individuals filing joint returns and surviving spouses, $8,500 (up from $8,400) for heads of household, and $5,800 (up from $5,700) for unmarried individuals and married individuals filing separate returns. The additional standard deduction for blind people and senior citizens is $1,150 (up from $1,100) for married individuals, and $1,450 (up from $1,400) for singles and heads of household. See chapter 21, *Standard deduction*.
- Pension Plan Limitations: Most of the contribution limits and income limitations remain the same. However, there were a few minor changes, including:
  1. For married couples filing jointly, in which the spouse who makes the IRA contribution is an active participant in an employer-sponsored retirement plan, the income phaseout range is $90,000 to $110,000 for 2011, up from $89,000 to $109,000.
  2. For an IRA contributor who is not an active participant in an employer-sponsored retirement plan and is married to someone who is an active participant, the deduction is phased out if the couple's income is between $169,000 and $179,000 for 2011, up from $167,000 and $177,000.
  3. The AGI phaseout range for 2011 for taxpayers making contributions to a Roth IRA is $169,000 to $179,000 for married couples filing jointly, up from $167,000 to $177,000; for singles and heads of household, the income phaseout range is $107,000 to $122,000, up from $105,000 to $120,000; and the phaseout range for married taxpayers filing separately remains unchanged at $0 to $10,000. See chapter 17, *Individual retirement arrangements (IRAs)*.
- Saver's Credit Limitations: The AGI limit for the saver's credit (also known as the retirement savings contributions credit) in 2011 is $56,500 for married couples filing jointly, up from $55,500. For heads of household, the AGI limit is $42,375, up from $41,625, and for married individuals filing separately and for singles, the AGI limit is $28,250, up from $27,750. See chapter 37, *Other credits including the earned income credit*.
- Earned Income Credit: The maximum earned income credit (EIC) rises to $5,751 for 2011, up from $5,666 in 2010. The maximum income limit for the EIC rises to $49,078 for 2011, up from $48,362 in 2010.

The credit varies by family size, filing status, and other factors, with the maximum credit going to joint filers with three or more qualifying children. See chapter 37, *Other credits including the earned income credit*.

- Lifetime Learning Credit Limitation: The modified adjusted gross income threshold at which the lifetime learning credit begins to phase out in 2011 is $102,000 for joint filers, up from $100,000, and $51,000 for singles and heads of household, up from $50,000. The limitation for the American opportunity credit remains unchanged. See chapter 36, *Education credits and other education tax benefits*.
- Alternative Minimum Tax (AMT) Exemption for a Child Subject to the Kiddie Tax: For purposes of determining the AMT tax on a child subject to the "kiddie tax," the exemption amount increased for 2011 to the sum of the child's earned income for the taxable year, plus $6,800 (up from $6,700). See chapter 31, *Figuring your tax*.
- Education Savings Bond Program Limitations: The exclusion of interest income from savings bonds for taxpayers who pay qualified higher education expenses begins to phase out in 2011 for modified adjusted gross income (MAGI) above $106,650 (up from $105,100) for joint returns, and $71,100 (up from $70,100) for other returns. The exclusion is completely phased out for MAGI of $136,650 (up from $135,100) or more for joint returns, and $86,100 (up from $85,100) or more for other returns. See chapter 36, *Education credits and other education tax benefits*.
- Long-Term Care Premium Deduction: The long-term care premium deduction has increased slightly in 2011 for each age group. For taxpayers age 40 or less, the amount that can be claimed as a medical expense deduction is $340 (up from $330); for taxpayers age 41–50, the deduction is $640 (up from $620); for taxpayers age 51–60, the deduction is $1,270 (up from $1,230); for taxpayers age 61–70, the deduction is $3,390 (up from $3,290); and for taxpayers more than 70 years old, the deduction is $4,240 (up from $4,110). See chapter 22, *Medical and dental expenses*.
- Medical Savings Account Limitations: The minimum and maximum annual deductible for self-only and family coverage, and the annual out-of-pocket expenses required to be paid for covered benefits has been increased slightly. See IRS Publication 969, *Health Savings Accounts and Other Tax-Favored Health Plans*, for more information on these limits.

Planning Ahead for 2012 and Beyond

See chapter 47 for a discussion of tax developments and issues in 2012 and after.

Changes in the tax law you should know about

Summary of expiring provisions

Over the past several years, multiple tax laws have been enacted which extended multiple tax benefits and modified others, as well as effectively allowing others to lapse. With all the tax laws, it can be hard to keep up with all the various provisions and expiration dates. This table provides a brief summary of the tax provisions, the expiration date of the provision, and the chapter where additional information can be found.

Tax Provision	Expiration Date	Chapter Reference
Impacting Tax Rates		
Lower individual tax rates of 10%, 25%, 28%, 33%, and 35%	December 31, 2012	Chapters 47 and 48
Lower long-term capital gains tax rates of 0% and 15%	December 31, 2012	Chapters 16 and 47
Lower qualified dividend tax rates of 0% and 15%	December 31, 2012	Chapters 8 and 47
Marriage penalty relief	December 31, 2012	Chapters 2 and 47
Impacting Income		
Exclusion from income certain discharged mortgage debt	December 31, 2012	Chapters 15 and 47
100% exclusion of small business capital gains	December 31, 2011	Chapter 14
Temporary reduction in recognition period for S corporation built-in gains	December 31, 2011	Chapter 16
Exclusion from income of benefits under an employer's adoption assistance program	December 31, 2012	Chapter 5
Impacting Deductions		
No limit on personal exemption	December 31, 2012	Chapters 3 and 47
No limit on itemized deductions	December 31, 2012	Chapters 30 and 47
Increased AMT exemption amount	December 31, 2011	Chapters 31 and 47
100% bonus depreciation deduction	December 31, 2011	Chapter 38
50% bonus depreciation deduction (starting on January 1, 2012)	December 31, 2012	Chapters 38 and 47
Increase in expensing under Section 179	December 31, 2011, for $500,000 limit; December 31, 2012, for $125,000 limit	Chapters 38 and 47
Deduction for state and local general sales taxes	December 31, 2011	Chapter 23
Above-the-line deduction for certain expenses of elementary and secondary school teachers	December 31, 2011	Chapter 19
Above-the-line deduction for qualified tuition and related expenses	December 31, 2011	Chapters 19 and 36
Tax-free distributions from IRAs for charitable purposes	December 31, 2011	Chapter 17
Premiums for mortgage insurance deductible as qualified residence interest	December 31, 2011	Chapter 24
Temporary reduction in employee-paid payroll taxes	December 31, 2011	Changes in the Law You Should Know About
Increased deduction for student loan interest deduction	December 31, 2012	Chapters 19 and 36
Increased contribution limit for Coverdell accounts	December 31, 2012	Chapter 36
Increased deduction for start-up expenditures	December 31, 2010	Chapter 38
Health insurance deduction for purposes of calculating self-employment tax	December 31, 2010	Chapter 38
Increased charitable deduction limit for qualified conservation contributions	December 31, 2011	Chapters 25 and 47
Impacting Tax Credits		
AMT refundable credit	December 31, 2012	Chapters 37 and 47
Certain credits allowed to offset AMT	December 31, 2011	Chapters 31 and 47
Additional child tax credit	December 31, 2012	Chapters 35 and 47
Tax credit for first-time DC homebuyers	December 31, 2011	Chapter 47
American opportunity credit	December 31, 2012	Chapters 36 and 47
Making work pay credit	December 31, 2010	Chapter 37
Credit for residential energy property and alternative energy equipment	December 31, 2011	Chapter 37
Increase in adoption credit	December 31, 2012	Chapters 37 and 47
Increase in earned income tax credit	December 31, 2012	Chapters 37 and 47
Retirement savings contributions credit	Made permanent—no expiration date	Chapter 37
Increased dependent care credit and phaseout range	December 31, 2012	Chapter 33
Other Tax Provisions		
Lower estate and gift tax rate	December 31, 2012	Chapters 44 and 47
Unified credit exemption of $5 million	December 31, 2012	Chapters 44 and 47
Portability of unused credit exemption of spouse for estate tax purposes	December 31, 2012	Chapters 44 and 47

Important 2011 tax reminders

Listed below are important reminders and other items that may help you file your 2011 tax return. Many of these items are explained in more detail later in this publication.

- **Write in your social security number.**
  To protect your privacy, social security numbers (SSNs) are not printed on the peel-off label that comes in the mail with your tax instruction booklet. This means you must enter your SSN in the space provided on your tax form. If you filed a joint return for 2010 and are filing a joint return for 2011 with the same spouse, enter your names and SSNs in the same order as on your 2010 return. See chapter 1.

- **Taxpayer identification numbers.**
  You must provide the taxpayer identification number for each person for whom you claim certain tax benefits. This applies even if the person was born in 2011. Generally, this number is the person's social security number (SSN). See chapter 1.

- **Individual retirement arrangements (IRAs).**
  For purposes of taking an IRA deduction, earned income includes any nontaxable combat pay received by a member of the U.S. Armed Forces.

- **Qualified joint venture.**
  A qualified joint venture conducted by you and your spouse may not be treated as a partnership if you file a joint return for the tax year. See chapters 12 and 38.

- **Recordkeeping requirements for cash contributions.**
  You cannot deduct a cash contribution, regardless of the amount, unless you keep as a record of the contribution a bank record (such as a canceled check, a blank copy of a canceled check, or a bank statement containing the name of the charity, the date, and amount) or a written communication from the charity. The written communication must include the name of the charity and the date and amount of the contribution. See chapter 25.

- **Foreign source income.**
  If you are a U.S. citizen with income from sources outside the United States (foreign income), you must report all such income on your tax return unless it is exempt by U.S. law. This is true whether you reside inside or outside the United States and whether or not you receive a Form W-2 or 1099 from the foreign payer. This applies to earned income (such as wages and tips) as well as unearned income (such as interest, dividends, capital gains, pensions, rents, and royalties).

  If you reside outside the United States, you may be able to exclude part or all of your foreign source earned income. For details, see IRS Publication 54, *Tax Guide for U.S. Citizens and Resident Aliens Abroad.*

- **Automatic six-month extension to file tax return.**
  You can use Form 4868, Application for Automatic Extension of Time To File U.S. Individual Income Tax Return, to obtain an automatic 6-month extension of time to file your tax return. See chapter 1.

- **Tax Computation Worksheet.**
  If your taxable income is $100,000 or more, figure your tax using the Tax Computation Worksheet, which can be found at the IRS website (*www.irs.gov*). The Tax Rate Schedules in chapter 49 are shown so you can see the tax rate that applies to all levels of taxable income. Do not use the Tax Rate Schedules to figure your tax. Instead, see chapter 31.

- **Joint return responsibility.**
  Generally, both spouses are responsible for the tax and any interest or penalties on a joint tax return. In some cases, one spouse may be relieved of that responsibility for items of the other spouse that were incorrectly reported on the joint return. See chapter 2.

- **Include your phone number on your return.**
  To promptly resolve any questions the IRS has in processing your tax return, they would like to be able to call you. Please enter your daytime telephone number on your tax form next to your signature.

- **Third party designee.**
  You can check the "Yes" box in the "Third Party Designee" area of your return to authorize the IRS to discuss your return with a friend, family member, or any other person you choose. This allows the IRS to call the person you identified as your designee to answer any questions that may arise during the processing of your return. It also allows your designee to perform certain actions. See chapter 1.

- **Frivolous tax submissions.**
  The IRS has published a list of positions that are identified as frivolous. The penalty for filing a frivolous tax return is $5,000. Also, the $5,000 penalty will apply to other specified frivolous submissions. See chapter 1.

- **Filing erroneous claim for refund or credit.**
  You may have to pay a penalty if you file an erroneous claim for refund or credit. See chapter 1.

- **Payment of taxes.**
  Make your check or money order payable to "United States Treasury." You can pay your taxes by credit card (a convenience fee will be charged if paying by credit card) or debit card, using the Electronic Federal Tax Payment System (EFTPS), or, if you file electronically, by electronic funds withdrawal. See chapter 1.

- **Faster ways to file your return.**
  The IRS offers fast, accurate ways to file your tax return information without filing a paper tax return. You can use IRS *e-file* (electronic filing). See chapters 1 and 46.

- **Free electronic filing.**
  You may be able to file your 2011 taxes online for free thanks to an electronic filing agreement. See chapter 1.

- **Change of address.**
  If you change your address, you should notify the IRS. See *Change of Address*, under *What Happens After I File*, in chapter 1.

- **Private delivery services.**

  You may be able to use a designated private delivery service to mail your tax returns and payments. See chapter 1.

- **Refund on a late filed return.**

  If you were due a refund but you did not file a return, you generally must file your return within 3 years from the date the return was due (including extensions) to get that refund. See chapter 1.

- **Customer service for taxpayers expanded.**

  The IRS has expanded customer service for taxpayers. You can set up a personal appointment at the most convenient Taxpayer Assistance Center, on the most convenient business day.

- **Secure your tax records from identity theft.**

  Identity theft occurs when someone uses your personal information, such as your name, SSN, or other identifying information, without your permission, to commit fraud or other crimes. An identity thief may use your SSN to get a job or may file a tax return using your SSN to receive a refund. To reduce your risk:
  - Protect your SSN,
  - Ensure your employer is protecting your SSN, and
  - Be careful when choosing a tax preparer.

  If your tax records are affected by identity theft and you receive a notice from the IRS, respond right away to the name and phone number printed on the IRS notice or letter. If your tax records are not currently affected by identity theft but you think you are at risk due to a lost or stolen purse or wallet, questionable credit card activity or credit report, etc., contact the IRS Identity Protection Specialized Unit at 1-800-908-4490 or submit Form 14039. For more information, see Publication 4535, *Identity Theft Prevention and Victim Assistance*. Victims of identity theft who are experiencing economic harm or a systemic problem, or are seeking help in resolving tax problems that have not been resolved through normal channels, may be eligible for Taxpayer Advocate Service (TAS) assistance. You can reach TAS by calling the National Taxpayer Advocate helpline toll-free case intake line at 1-877-777-4778 or TTY/TDD 1-800-829-4059.

  Protect yourself from suspicious emails or phishing schemes. Phishing is the creation and use of email and websites designed to mimic legitimate business emails and websites. The most common form is the act of sending an email to a user falsely claiming to be an established legitimate enterprise in an attempt to scam the user into surrendering private information that will be used for identity theft. The IRS does not initiate contacts with taxpayers via emails. Also, the IRS does not request detailed personal information through email or ask taxpayers for the PIN numbers, passwords, or similar secret access information for their credit card, bank, or other financial accounts. If you receive an unsolicited email claiming to be from the IRS, forward the message to: *phishing@ irs.gov*. You may also report misuse of the IRS name, logo, forms, or other IRS property to the Treasury Inspector General for Tax Administration toll-free at 1-800-366-4484. You can forward suspicious emails to the Federal Trade Commission at: *spam@uce.gov* or contact them at *www.ftc.gov/ idtheft* or 1-877-IDTHEFT (1-877-438-4338). Visit *www.irs .gov* and enter "identity theft" in the search box to learn more about identity theft and how to reduce your risk.

Ordering forms and publications. Visit *www.irs.gov/formspubs* to download forms and publications, or call 1-800-829-3676 to request forms and publications by mail. If the forms and publications are requested by mail, it generally takes 7 to 15 business days to receive the information.

Tax questions. If you have a tax question, visit *www.irs.gov* or call 1-800-829-1040. For TTY/TDD, call 1-800-829-4059.

How to avoid 25 common errors

1. Most importantly, check your math.

2. Double-check that your social security number has been correctly written on the return. If you are married, check that your spouse's social security number is properly listed, whether filing a joint or separate return.

3. Include your social security number on each page of the return so that if a page is misplaced by the IRS, it can be reattached.

4. Check that you have claimed all of your dependents, such as elderly parents who may not live with you. See chapter 3, *Personal exemptions and dependents*.

5. Include on the return the social security numbers for all dependents, including those born during 2011. In addition, for each child under age 17 who is a qualifying child for the child tax credit, make sure you checked the box beside the child's name indicating the child is a qualifying child for the child tax credit.

6. If you are single and have a dependent who lives with you, check to see if you qualify for the lower tax rates available to a head of household or surviving spouse.

7. You may be eligible for the earned income credit if you do NOT file as married filing separately. If you have one qualifying child and your earned income and modified adjusted gross income for 2011 are less than $36,052 ($41,132 if married filing jointly), you may qualify. If you have two qualifying children, you may qualify for the earned income credit if your earned income and modified adjusted gross income for 2011 are less than $40,964, or $46,044 if married filing jointly. If you have three or more qualifying children, you may qualify for the earned income credit if your earned income and modified adjusted gross income for 2011 are less than $43,998 ($49,078 if married filing jointly). If you do not have a qualifying child, but are over age 24 and under age 65, and your earned income for 2011 and modified adjusted gross income are less than $13,660 ($18,740 if filing jointly), you may qualify as well. See chapter 37, *Other credits including the earned income credit*.

8. If you are married, check to see if filing separate returns rather than a joint return is more beneficial.

9. Attach all copies B of your W-2 forms to your return in order to avoid correspondence with the IRS. If you received a Form 1099-R showing federal income tax withheld, attach copy B of that form as well.

10. You may be eligible to claim the additional standard deductions if you are blind or 65 years of age or older.

11. Be sure to sign your check and write your social security number, the form number, and the tax year on the face of any checks made out to the United States Treasury. (Example: "000-00-000–2011 Form 1040.")

12. Be sure that your Form W-2 and all Form 1099s are correct. If they're wrong, have them corrected as soon as possible so that the IRS's records agree with the amounts you show on your return.

13. If you worked for more than one employer, be sure to claim a credit for any overpaid social security taxes withheld from your wages.

14. If you received a state tax refund or a refund of interest you paid on a mortgage in an earlier year, make sure you have not included too much of your refund in your income. These refunds may not be taxable if you did not get a tax benefit from deducting them. If, for example, you used the standard deduction in the year in which the taxes or interest were paid, you do not have to include the refund in income this year. In addition, if you were subject to the alternative minimum tax in the prior year, a portion, or all, of your state income tax refund may not be taxable.

15. Deductible real property taxes should be distinguished from assessments paid for local benefits, such as repair of streets, sidewalks, sewers, curbs, gutters, and other improvements that tend to benefit specific properties. Assessments of this type generally are not deductible.

16. Make sure that you sign and date your return and enter your occupation. If you are filing a joint return, be sure that your spouse also signs as required.

17. Only a portion of your social security benefits may be taxable. If your income does not exceed a certain amount, none of it may be taxable.

18. Check last year's tax return to see if there are any items that carry over to this year, such as charitable contributions or capital losses that exceeded the amount you were previously able to deduct.

19. If you can be claimed as a dependent on someone else's return, do not claim a personal exemption on your return. Your standard deduction may be limited as well. See chapter 21, *Standard deduction*.

20. Fill out Form 8606, Nondeductible IRA Contributions, for your contributions to an IRA account, if you don't claim any deduction for the contribution.

21. Recheck your basis in the securities that you sold during the year, particularly shares of a mutual fund. Income and capital gains dividends that were automatically reinvested in the fund over the years increase your basis in the mutual fund and thus reduce a gain or increase a loss that you have to report. Also, any "front-end" or purchase fees are still considered part of your cost basis for tax purposes, even though they reduce your investment in a mutual fund.

22. Recheck that you have used the correct column in the Tax Rate Table or the right Tax Rate Schedule for your filing status.

23. Don't miss deadlines: December 31–set up a Keogh plan; April 17–make your IRA contribution; April 17–file your return or request an extension. Check the tax calendar periodically. See the *2012 Tax Calendar*.

24. If you regularly get large refunds, you're having too much withheld and, in effect, giving the IRS an interest-free loan. Increasing the number of allowances you claim on Form W-4 will increase your take-home pay.

25. Keep copies of all documents you send to the IRS. Use certified mail for all important correspondence to the IRS. Don't forget to keep your records in good shape so that you can find answers to any IRS questions about your return.

50 of the most easily overlooked deductions

The following list will serve as a reminder of some deductions you can easily overlook when you prepare your return. It is not intended to be all-inclusive, nor applicable to everyone. The circumstances of your situation will determine whether you qualify. See the chapter reference following each item for a complete explanation.

1. Accounting fees for tax preparation services and IRS audits (chapter 29)
2. Alcoholism and drug abuse treatment (chapter 22)
3. Amortization of premium on taxable bonds (chapter 29)
4. Appraisal fees for charitable donations or casualty losses (chapters 25 and 26)
5. Appreciation on property donated to a charity (chapter 25)
6. Casualty or theft losses (chapter 26)
7. Cellular telephones (chapter 29)
8. Cleaning and laundering services when traveling (chapter 27)
9. Commissions and closing costs on sale of property (chapter 14)
10. Contact lenses, eyeglasses, and hearing devices (chapter 22)
11. Contraceptives, if bought with a prescription (chapter 22)
12. Costs associated with looking for a new job in your present occupation, including fees for résumé preparation and employment of outplacement agencies (chapter 29)
13. Depreciation of home computers (chapter 29)
14. Dues to labor unions (chapter 29)
15. Education expenses to the extent required by law or your employer or needed to maintain or improve your skills (chapters 28 and 29)
16. Employee contributions to a state disability fund (chapter 23)
17. Employee's moving expenses (chapter 20)
18. Federal estate tax on income with respect to a decedent (chapter 29)
19. Fees for a safe-deposit box to hold investments (e.g., stock certificate) (chapter 29)
20. Fees paid for childbirth preparation classes if instruction relates to obstetrical care (chapter 22)
21. Fifty percent of self-employment tax (chapter 38)
22. Foreign taxes paid (chapter 23)
23. Foster child care expenditures (chapter 25)
24. Gambling losses to the extent of gambling winnings (chapter 29)
25. Hospital services fees (laboratory work, therapy, nursing services, and surgery) (chapter 22)
26. Impairment-related work expenses for a disabled individual (chapter 29)
27. Improvements to your home (chapter 15)
28. Investment advisory fees (chapter 29)
29. IRA trustee's administrative fees billed separately (chapter 29)
30. Lead paint removal (chapter 22)
31. Legal fees incurred in connection with obtaining or collecting alimony (chapter 29)
32. Long-term care insurance premiums (chapter 22)
33. Margin account interest expense (chapter 24)
34. Medical transportation, including standard mileage deduction (chapter 22) and lodging expenses incurred for medical reasons while away from home (chapter 22)
35. Mortgage prepayment penalties and late fees (chapter 24)
36. Out-of-pocket expenses relating to charitable activities, including the standard mileage deduction (chapter 25)
37. Health insurance premiums if self-employed (chapter 38)
38. Penalty on early withdrawal of savings (chapter 7)
39. Personal liability insurance for wrongful acts as an employee (chapter 29)
40. Points on a home mortgage and certain refinancings (chapter 24)
41. Protective clothing required at work (chapter 29)
42. Real estate taxes associated with the purchase or sale of property (chapter 23)
43. Seller-paid points on the purchase of a home (chapter 24)
44. Special equipment for the disabled (chapter 22)
45. Special schools and separately stated fees for medical care included in tuition (chapter 22)
46. State personal property taxes on cars and boats (chapter 23)
47. Subscriptions to professional journals (chapter 29)
48. Theft or embezzlement losses (chapter 26)
49. Trade or business tools with life of 1 year or less (chapter 29)
50. Worthless stock or securities (chapter 16)

Individual tax organizer

The following schedules should help you organize the data you need to prepare your 2011 federal income tax return. They are intended only to provide general guidelines and should not be regarded as all-inclusive.

Taxpayer information

Personal data

Your name:

Your spouse's name:

Social security number: | Spouse's social security number:

Marital status at year end: ☐ Married ☐ Single ☐ Widowed after 2009 with qualifying child ☐ Divorced ☐ Married but separated

Dependent children

(Qualifying children) Name (address if different from yours)	Social security number	Date of birth	Did you provide more than half of support?	Married filing a joint return?	Full-time student for 5 months or more?

Other dependents

(Qualifying relative) Name (address if different from yours)	Social security number	Relationship	Months lived in your home	Is dependent's income over $3,700?	Did you provide more than half of support?

Payments and refunds of income taxes

	FEDERAL		STATE		CITY	
	Date paid	Amount	Date paid	Amount	Date paid	Amount
2011 estimated payments, including overpayment credited from 2010 return						
Tax refunds received in 2011[1]						

[1] Do not include interest received on refunds. Detail these amounts in the interest income section of this organizer.

Compensation

Indicate recipient: H=Husband; W=Wife

H W	Employer name	Gross earnings	Federal income tax withheld	Social security tax withheld	Medicare tax withheld	State tax withheld	City tax withheld

Interest income

Indicate ownership: H=Husband; W=Wife; J=Joint.

Report all interest received by you or for your account on Forms 1099-INT or other statements of total interest received. Failure to record any such income could result in notice from the IRS.

If the amount of interest reported on Forms 1099-INT includes interest accrued on bonds at the time of purchase, adjustments can be made.
If you invested in a tax-exempt municipal bond fund, note the fund's schedule of percentage income related to each state.

H W J		Amount
	Savings accounts, credit unions, and certificates of deposit	$
	U.S. savings bonds and other U.S. government securities	$
	Corporate bonds	$
	Other interest[1]	$
	Tax exempt interest	$
	Interest received on tax refunds	$

[1] If you received interest income from seller-financial mortgages, you will need the payer's name, address, and social security number.

Dividend income

Indicate ownership: H=Husband; W=Wife; J=Joint.

Report all dividends received by you for your account on Forms 1099-DIV or other information statements received.
Failure to record any such income could result in a notice from the IRS.

H W J	Name of corporation [identify foreign corporation with (F)]	Indicate: T (taxable) C (capital gain) N (nontaxable) U (U.S. obligation) X (exempt) Q (qualified)	Dividends received	U.S. taxes withheld

Sale of residence

Did you sell your residence during the year or within the last two years? If you answered "Yes," see chapter 15, *Selling your home.*	☐ Yes	☐ No

Sale of stocks and bonds

Indicate ownership: H=Husband; W=Wife; J=Joint.

Note: Gross proceeds from sales reported here should reconcile with Forms 1099-B received from your broker. You should explain any discrepancies to prevent an IRS inquiry stemming from their matching program.

H W J	Description (including numbers of shares, common or preferred, and par value of bonds)	Date		Gross sales price[1]	Cost or other basis plus expenses of sale[2]	Gain or (loss)[3]
		Acq.	Sold			

[1] List proceeds of sale or cash received in lieu of fractions on receipt of stock rights or stock dividends.

[2] The basis of stock should be decreased by all nontaxable dividends and increased by any reinvested dividends. See chapter 13, Basis of property.

[3] Have you acquired stock, securities, contracts, or options to sell or acquire stock or securities substantially identical to stock or securities sold at a loss within a period beginning 30 days prior to and ending 30 days after the date of sale? ☐ Yes ☐ No
If "Yes," see the discussion of "Wash Sale" in chapter 14, Sale of property.

Other transactions

Did you exchange securities for other securities or exchange any investment property for any other property? Did any security held by you or any amounts due to you become worthless during the year? Did you sell your vacation home or other property during the year? Did you realize a gain or a loss on property, in whole or part, by destruction, theft, seizure, or condemnation (including the threat or imminence thereof)? Did you engage in any commodity transactions (including open positions on December 31) during the year? Did you engage in any transactions involving traded options?

If you answered "Yes" to any of these questions, read the applicable portions of this book.

Sale of other property

H W J	Description	Date		Gross sales price	Cost or other basis plus expenses of sale	Depreciation or depletion	Gain or (loss)
		Acq.	Sold				

Installment sales

Did you make sales during the year for which the receipt of all or part of the sales price was deferred until future years?	☐ Yes	☐ No
If "Yes," discuss with your tax advisor.		
Did you collect on any installment obligations from sales made prior to 2011?	☐ Yes	☐ No
For more information, see chapter 14, *Sale of property*.		

Rent and royalty income

	Property A	Property B
Did you actively participate in the operation of the rental activity during the year? For more information on active participation, see chapter 9, *Rental income and expenses*.	☐ Yes ☐ No	☐ Yes ☐ No
Location and description of property[1]		
Gross rents and royalties received		
Expenses		

[1] If property has been used by you or your family as a personal residence, indicate the total days held for rent but not rented, days rented, and days used by you or your family.

Partnerships (P), small business corporations (S), and estates and trusts (E/T)

Retain all Forms K-1 or other information relating to entity listed below.

P S E/T	H W J	Name	Tax shelter registration number	I.D. number	Income or (loss)

Pension and annuity income

Did you receive any payments from a retirement plan?	☐ Yes	☐ No
If yes, write in the amount received during the year and any taxes withheld.	$	
Did you roll over a profit-sharing or retirement plan distribution into another plan?	☐ Yes	☐ No
What was the starting date of your annuity?		
What is the amount received in the current taxable year?	$	
Did you receive any IRA distributions during the year?	☐ Yes	☐ No
Retain all Forms 1099-R or other information relating to each distribution.		
Did you convert all or any part of a regular IRA into a Roth IRA during 2011?	☐ Yes	☐ No
If yes, write in the amount converted.	$	
Did you convert all or any part of a regular IRA into a Roth IRA during 2010?	☐ Yes	☐ No
If yes, write in the amount converted.	$	
Did you elect to report all of the distribution as income in 2010?	☐ Yes	☐ No

Other income

Description	Amount
Alimony or legal separation payments received	$
Disability payments	$
Other tax refunds not shown elsewhere	$
Unemployment insurance compensation	$
Social security benefits	$
Other[1] (described)	$

[1] The types of other income include, but are not limited to, net income from self-employment, director's fees, prizes, cancellation of debts, gambling winnings, jury fees, punitive damages (unless awarded in a wrongful death action where state law so provides), and receiver's fees. Also, include gross income from oil and gas working interests, as well as any expenses relating to them. For more information see chapter 12, Other income.

			Amount
Did you receive any income from a foreign source?	☐ Yes	☐ No	$
Did you own shares in a mutual fund that retained your share of capital gains and paid the tax on it?	☐ Yes	☐ No	$
Did you have any income from farm property?	☐ Yes	☐ No	$
Did you have any bartering income?	☐ Yes	☐ No	$

Deductions

Adjustments to income

			Amount
Alimony or legal separation payment made in current year			
Recipient's last name _____	Social security no. _____		
Penalties for early withdrawal of savings			$ _____
Education-related expenses			
☐ Student loan interest			$ _____
☐ Educator expenses			$ _____
☐ Tuition and fees deduction			$ _____
Individual retirement arrangements (IRAs)[1]			
Did you contribute to your own IRA?	☐ Yes	☐ No	$ _____
Type:			
☐ Regular			$ _____
☐ Roth			$ _____
Did you participate in a retirement plan maintained by your employer?	☐ Yes	☐ No	$ _____
Did your spouse contribute to his/her own IRA?	☐ Yes	☐ No	$ _____
Did your spouse participate in a retirement plan maintained by his/her employer?	☐ Yes	☐ No	
Did your and your spouse contribute to a spousal IRA?	☐ Yes	☐ No	$ _____

Self-employed Keogh (HR-10) plan	Yours	Spouse's
Amount contributed	$ _____	$ _____
Self-employed health insurance[2]	$ _____	$ _____

Have you incurred moving expenses in connection with starting work at a new permanent location? See chapter 20, Moving expenses.	☐ Yes	☐ No	
Did you or your spouse receive any disability payments?	☐ Yes	☐ No	
Health Savings Account (amount contributed)			$ _____

[1] Depending on your (and your spouse's) income level and whether you (or your spouse) are an active participant in an employer-maintained retirement plan, your IRA deduction may be limited.

[2] If you were self-employed and had a net profit for the year, were a general partner (or a limited partner receiving guaranteed payments), or if you received wages from an S corporation in which you were a more than 2% shareholder, you may be able to deduct the amount paid for health insurance on behalf of yourself, your spouse, and dependents.

Medical expenses

Note: You will qualify for a federal deduction only if your total unreimbursed medical expenses exceed 7.5% of your adjusted gross income.

List even if reimbursed	Amount
Medical or health insurance premiums (including amounts paid by payroll deductions)	$
Medicare premiums	$
Premiums paid for long-term health care[1]	
For you	$
For your spouse	$
Prescription drugs and insulin	$
Doctors and dentists	$
Hospitals	$
Other medical expenses (eyeglasses, contact lenses, hearing aids, travel and lodging expenses)	$
Reimbursements for medical expenses through insurance or other sources	( )

Note: If you are divorced or separated, have a child, and paid medical expenses for that child, include these amounts whether or not you are entitled to the dependency exemption. For more information, see chapter 22, Medical and dental expenses.

[1] *See chapter 22 for limitations on deduction.*

Taxes

Item	Amount
Real estate taxes	$
Personal property	$
Vehicle licenses (allowed in some states). State of:	$
State or local income taxes	$
State disability tax	$
State and local sales taxes	$
Foreign income taxes[1]	$

[1] *Generally, you can take either a deduction or a credit for income taxes imposed on you by a foreign country or a U.S. possession. For more information on deducting foreign income taxes, see Foreign Income Taxes in chapter 23, Taxes you may deduct. For more information on claiming a credit for such taxes paid, see Foreign Tax Credit in chapter 37, Other credits including the earned income credit.*

Interest expenses

Item	Payee	Amount
Home mortgage paid to financial institutions		$
Home mortgage paid to individuals[1]		$
Mortgage points on principal residence[2]		$
Prepayment penalty on loans		$
Mortgage insurance premiums[3]		$
Brokerage accounts		$
Investment interest		$
Other (itemize)		$

[1] *You need name(s) and social security number(s).*

[2] *Include only points, including loan organization fees, on the purchase or improvement of your principal residence. If you paid points to refinance your mortgage, see chapter 24, Interest expense.*

[3] *Premiums you paid or accrued during 2011 for qualified mortgage insurance may be deductible. For more information, see chapter 24, Interest expense.*

Charitable contributions

In addition to outright gifts of cash or property, deductible contributions also include out-of-pocket expenses incurred for charity, for example, transportation, meals and lodging away from home, and cost and upkeep of special uniforms and equipment required in the performance of donated services. Contributions of cash, regardless of the amount, are allowed only if you have appropriate substantiation such as a canceled check, credit card statement, or receipt from the charity. In addition, you need a contemporaneous written acknowledgment from the charity to which a contribution or contributions of $250 or more was made during the year. A canceled check does not constitute adequate substantiation for contributions in excess of $250.

If you have sold any property to a charity for less than the property's fair market value, you will need details. For more information, see chapter 25, *Contributions*.

Cash Contributions

Recipient	Amount

If total noncash contributions have a value in excess of $500, you may need the following information:

The name and address of the donee; the date of the gift; a description of the property; how it was acquired by you, and when it was acquired by you; your tax basis; its value at the time of the donation and how the value was ascertained. Indicate (✓) if any property was held by you one year or less.

If you made noncash contributions of property in excess of $5,000 in value, use Form 8283, Noncash Charitable Contributions, with Section B, *Appraisal Summary,* completed.   ☐ Yes   ☐ No

If you contributed a motor vehicle to charity, see chapter 25, *Contributions*.

Casualty losses

Note: You will qualify for a deduction for a personal casualty loss only if it exceeds 10% of your adjusted gross income and only for the amount not covered by insurance reimbursements. However, special rules apply if you are in a federally declared disaster area. See chapter 26, *Casualty and theft losses*, for details.

Casualty losses include such items as losses from automobile collisions; damage from storms, fires, and floods; and damage from vandalism, theft, and other casualties.

A disaster loss is a loss that occurred in an area determined by the President of the United States to warrant federal disaster assistance. See chapter 26, *Casualty and theft losses*.

Describe the casualty and loss and its approximate date and location:

Indicate (✓) type of property: ☐ business   ☐ investment   ☐ personal

Other deductions

Note: In general, you will qualify for a federal deduction only if your total other miscellaneous deductions exceed 2% of your adjusted income.

Item	Amount	Item	Amount
Investment expenses		Educational expense (to maintain or improve skills required by employer)	
Automobile expenses			
Investment counsel fees		Meals and entertainment[1]	
Safe-deposit box		Tax advice/return fees	
Subscriptions		Union dues	
Telephone		Dues for professional organizations	
IRA fees		Business publications	
Other		Office-in-home expenses[2]	

[1] *Generally, only 50% of meals and entertainment expenses are deductible.*
[2] *See* chapter 29, Miscellaneous deductions.

Employee business expenses

Were you reimbursed for any business expenses incurred in connection with the performance of services for your employer?	☐ Yes	☐ No
If yes, answer the following questions:		
A. Are you required to return reimbursement to the extent it exceeds expenses?	☐ Yes	☐ No
B. Are you required to submit itemized supporting documentation to your employer?	☐ Yes	☐ No

If you answered "Yes" to the above questions and your reimbursement does not exceed your expenses, you are generally not required to report the reimbursement and expenses on your return. However, if your reimbursement does not equal your expenses, or if you answered "No" to questions A and/or B, report below the total reimbursements and expenses for the year. Certain other business expenses, even if not reimbursed, may also be deductible.

Does your employer have an accountable reimbursement plan? See chapter 27, *Car Expenses and Other Employee Business Expenses*.	☐ Yes	☐ No

Employee business expenses:	Amount
	$
	$
Total amount reimbursed. (Do not include any amounts that were reported to you as wages in box 1 of Form W-2.)	$

Do you have substantiation (described below) for travel and entertainment expenses?	☐ Yes	☐ No

Information that must be available includes:
- Amounts spent
- Dates of departure and return for each trip and the number of days spent on business
- Dates of entertainment
- Places of entertainment or travel
- Dates and descriptions of business gifts
- Business purposes of the travel, entertainment, or business gifts
- Business relationships with the persons entertained or to whom gifts were made

Automobile expenses

Mileage	Automobile 1	Automobile 2
Number of months used for business during the year	$	$
Total mileage (include personal miles)	$	$
Business mileage portion of the total mileage	$	$
Commuting mileage portion of the total mileage	$	$
Original cost	$	$
Annual lease payments	$	$
Total actual expenses (business and personal for months used for business)		

Automobile Depreciation

Year, make, model	Cost	Date Acquired
Automobile:	$	$
Do you have adequate or sufficient evidence to justify the deduction for the vehicles?	☐ Yes ☐ No	
If yes, is the evidence written?	☐ Yes ☐ No	

Child care credit

If you incurred any expenses for child or dependent care so that you and your spouse could be gainfully employed or attend an educational institution as a full-time student, complete the table below.

Did your employer provide or reimburse you for the cost of child or dependent care?	☐ Yes	☐ No

If so, the qualifying expenses for calculating the credit must be reduced by the amount excluded from your income through your employer's dependent care assistance program. See chapter 33, *Child and dependent care credit*.

Name of child or dependent	Name, address, and social security number or FEIN of person or organization providing care	Relationship, if any	Period of care		Amount paid
			From	To	

Foreign taxes

List foreign source income and foreign income taxes paid or withheld[1]

Country	Income		Taxes Paid	
	Type	Amount	Date Paid	Amount

[1] *Generally, you can take either a credit or a deduction for income taxes imposed on you by a foreign country or a U.S. possession. For more information on claiming a credit for such taxes paid, see* Foreign Tax Credit *in chapter 37,* Other credits including the earned income credit. *For more information on deducting foreign income taxes, see* Foreign Income Taxes *in chapter 23,* Taxes you may deduct.

Employing domestic help

Did you employ domestic help?	☐ Yes	☐ No
Did you pay more than $1,700 during the year to an individual for services provided in your home?	☐ Yes	☐ No
If so, you may be required to pay employment taxes (see chapter 40, *What to do if you employ domestic help*).		

Income and expense records you should keep in addition to your income tax return

Some Suggestions That Could Come in Handy

Income	Records
☐ **Wages, salaries**	✓ Form W-2
☐ **Interest income**	✓ 1099-INT, 1099-OID, or Substitute 1099, such as broker statement or year-end account summary
☐ **Dividend income**	✓ 1099-DIV or Substitute 1099, such as broker statement or year-end account summary
☐ **State tax refunds**	✓ Form 1099-G, state income tax return
☐ **Self-employment income**	✓ Sales slips, invoices, receipts, sales tax reports, business books and records, 1099-MISC
☐ **Capital gains and losses**	✓ 1099-B or Substitute 1099, such as broker statement or year-end account summary showing proceeds from sales of securities or other capital assets. Records must also show your cost or other basis and the expenses of the sale. Your records must show when and how an asset was acquired (including property received as a gift or inheritance), how the asset was used, and when and how it was disposed of. To support the basis of securities, you should keep old account statements, buy/sell execution records, stock dividend and stock split information, and dividend reinvestment records (see chapter 14, *Sale of property*).
☐ **IRA distributions**	✓ 1099-R, year-end account summary, Form 8606
☐ **Pension and annuities**	✓ 1099-R, records of contributions
☐ **Rents**	✓ Checkbook, receipts and canceled checks, and other books and records, 1099-MISC
☐ **Partnerships, S corporations**	✓ Schedule K-1, record of unused passive activity losses
☐ **Estates, trusts**	✓ Schedule K-1, copies of last will and testament including codicils, Form 56–Notice Concerning Fiduciary Relationship, Form 1310–Statement of Person Claiming Refund Due a Deceased Taxpayer, including death certificate or letters of office, Form 4810–Request for Prompt Assessment Under IRC Section 6501(d), Tax Worksheets showing pre- and post-death income allocation, including copies of all 1099s received for the year of death, copies of prior three years' Forms 1040, and copies of all prior-year gift tax returns
☐ **Social security benefits**	✓ Form SSA-1099
☐ **Royalties**	✓ 1099-MISC
☐ **Unemployment compensation**	✓ 1099-G
☐ **Alimony**	✓ Divorce settlement papers
☐ **Miscellaneous income**	✓ 1099-MISC and other records of amounts received

Expense	Records
☐ **Domestic employee expense**	✓ Canceled checks, state unemployment tax payments; see chapter 40, *What to do if you employ domestic help*
☐ **Self-employment expense**	✓ Bills, canceled checks, receipts, bank statements, all business books and records
☐ **IRA contribution**	✓ Year-end account summary, deposit receipt
☐ **Keogh contribution**	✓ Year-end account summary, deposit receipt
☐ **Alimony**	✓ Divorce settlement papers, canceled alimony checks
☐ **Medical and dental expense**	✓ Bills, canceled checks, receipts, pay stubs if employer withholds medical insurance from wages
☐ **Taxes**	✓ Canceled checks, mortgage statements, receipts, Form W-2
☐ **Interest expense**	✓ Bank statements, mortgage statements (Form 1098), canceled checks
☐ **Charitable contributions**	✓ Canceled checks, receipts, detailed description of noncash property contributed (see chapter 25)
☐ **Miscellaneous deductions**	✓ Receipts, canceled checks, or other documentary evidence (see chapters 27 through 29)
☐ **Casualty and theft losses**	✓ Description of property, photograph of damaged property, receipts, canceled checks, policy and insurance reports
☐ **Exemptions**	✓ Birth certificates, social security numbers, signed Form 8332, divorce decree

Credits	Records
☐ **Child and dependent care**	✓ Receipts, canceled checks, and name, address, and identification number of care provider
☐ **Estimated taxes**	✓ Canceled checks
☐ **Foreign taxes**	✓ Form 1099-DIV or Substitute 1099 such as broker statement or year-end account summary
☐ **Withheld taxes**	✓ Forms W-2 and 1099 (including SSA-1099)
☐ **First-time homebuyer**	✓ Closing statement

Part 1

The income tax return

ey.com/EYTaxGuide

The four chapters in this part provide basic information on the tax system. They take you through the first steps of filling out a tax return—such as deciding what your filing status is, how many exemptions you can take, and what form to file. They also discuss recordkeeping requirements, IRS *e-file* (electronic filing), certain penalties, and the two methods used to pay tax during the year: withholding and estimated tax. You can find additional information about electronic filing in chapter 45, *Everything you need to know about e-filing*.

Chapter 1	Filing information
Chapter 2	Filing status
Chapter 3	Personal exemptions and dependents
Chapter 4	Tax withholding and estimated tax

Chapter 1
Filing information

Introduction

This chapter provides the basic framework you need to know for filing your federal income tax return. It explains when you must file your tax return and what to do if you are unable to get it prepared on time. The chapter also answers many of the most frequently asked questions about procedures and calculations used to determine your income tax.

The chapter discusses such items as who is required to file a return and who should file a return even though he or she is not required to do so. It tells you which tax forms to use, how to go about preparing your tax return once you have obtained the correct forms, and where to mail your tax return once it has been completed. In addition, the chapter reviews the penalties that may be imposed if you do not pay your taxes on time and instructs you on what to do if you discover that a previous tax return contains errors. It also explains what the different accounting methods are and which method may be used in preparing your return.

What's New

Due date of return. File your 2011 income tax return by April 17, 2012. The due date is April 17, instead of April 15, because of the Emancipation Day holiday in the District of Columbia even if you do not live in the District of Columbia.

Who must file. Generally, the amount of income you can receive before you must file a return has been increased. See Table 1-1, Table 1-2, and Table 1-3 for the specific amounts.

Mailing your return. You may be mailing your return to a different address this year because the IRS has changed the filing location for several areas. See *Where Do I File*, later in this chapter.

Reminders

Alternative filing methods. Rather than filing a return on paper, you may be able to file electronically using IRS *e-file*. Create your own personal identification number (PIN) and file a completely paperless tax return. For more information, see *Does My Return Have To Be on Paper*, later.

Change of address. If you change your address, you should notify the IRS. See *Change of Address*, later, under *What Happens After I File*.

Enter your social security number. You must enter your social security number (SSN) in the spaces provided on your tax return. If you file a joint return, enter the SSNs in the same order as the names.

Direct deposit of refund. Instead of getting a paper check, you may be able to have your refund deposited directly into your account at a bank or other financial institution. See *Direct Deposit* under *Refunds*, later. If you choose direct deposit of your refund, you may be able to split the refund among two or three accounts.

Alternative payment methods. If you owe additional tax, you may be able to pay electronically. See *How To Pay*, later.

Installment agreement. If you cannot pay the full amount due with your return, you may ask to make monthly installment payments. See *Installment Agreement*, later, under *Amount You Owe*. You may be able to apply online for a payment agreement if you owe federal tax, interest, and penalties.

Automatic 6-month extension. You can get an automatic 6-month extension to file your tax return if, no later than the date your return is due, you file Form 4868, Application for Automatic Extension of Time To File U.S. Individual Income Tax Return. See *Automatic Extension*, later.

Service in combat zone. You are allowed extra time to take care of your tax matters if you are a member of the Armed Forces who served in a combat zone, or if you served in the combat zone in support of the Armed Forces. See *Individuals Serving in Combat Zone*, later, under *When Do I Have To File*.

Adoption taxpayer identification number. If a child has been placed in your home for purposes of legal adoption and you will not be able to get a social security number for the child in time to file your return, you may be able to get an adoption taxpayer identification number (ATIN). For more information, see *Social Security Number*, later.

Taxpayer identification number for aliens. If you or your dependent is a nonresident or resident alien who does not have and is not eligible to get a social security number, file Form W-7, Application for IRS Individual Taxpayer Identification Number, with the IRS. For more information, see *Social Security Number*, later.

Frivolous tax submissions. The IRS has published a list of positions that are identified as frivolous. The penalty for filing a frivolous tax return is $5,000. Also, the $5,000 penalty will apply to other specified frivolous submissions. For more information, see *Civil Penalties*, later.

This chapter discusses the following topics.
- **Whether you have to file a return.**
- **Which form to use.**
- **How to file electronically.**

- When, how, and where to file your return.
- What happens if you pay too little or too much tax.
- What records you should keep and how long you should keep them.
- How you can change a return you have already filed.

Do I Have To File a Return?

You must file a federal income tax return if you are a citizen or resident of the United States or a resident of Puerto Rico and you meet the filing requirements for any of the following categories that apply to you.

1. Individuals in general. (There are special rules for surviving spouses, executors, administrators, legal representatives, U.S. citizens and residents living outside the United States, residents of Puerto Rico, and individuals with income from U.S. possessions.)
2. Dependents.
3. Certain children under age 19 or full-time students.
4. Self-employed persons.
5. Aliens.

The filing requirements for each category are explained in this chapter.

The filing requirements apply even if you do not owe tax.

Individuals—In General

If you are a U.S. citizen or resident, whether you must file a return depends on three factors:

1. Your gross income,
2. Your filing status, and
3. Your age.

To find out whether you must file, see Table 1-1, Table 1-2, and Table 1-3. Even if no table shows that you must file, you may need to file to get money back. (See *Who Should File*, later.)

Gross income. This includes all income you receive in the form of money, goods, property, and services that is not exempt from tax. It also includes income from sources outside the United States

Tip

Even if you do not have to file a return, it may be to your advantage to do so. See Who Should File, later.

Caution

File only one federal income tax return for the year regardless of how many jobs you had, how many Forms W-2 you received, or how many states you lived in during the year. Do not file more than one original return for the same year, even if you have not gotten your refund or have not heard from the IRS since you filed.

Table 1-1. **2011 Filing Requirements for Most Taxpayers**

IF your filing status is...	AND at the end of 2011 you were...*	THEN file a return if your gross income was at least...**
single	under 65	$ 9,500
	65 or older	$10,950
married filing jointly***	under 65 (both spouses)	$19,000
	65 or older (one spouse)	$20,150
	65 or older (both spouses)	$21,300
married filing separately	any age	$ 3,700
head of household	under 65	$12,200
	65 or older	$13,650
qualifying widow(er) with dependent child	under 65	$15,300
	65 or older	$16,450

*If you were born on January 1, 1947, you are considered to be age 65 at the end of 2011.

**Gross income means all income you received in the form of money, goods, property, and services that is not exempt from tax, including any income from sources outside the United States or from the sale of your main home (even if you can exclude part or all of it). Do not include any social security benefits unless (a) you are married filing a separate return and you lived with your spouse at any time during 2011 or (b) one-half of your social security benefits plus your other gross income and any tax-exempt interest is more than $25,000 ($32,000 if married filing jointly). If (a) or (b) applies, see the instructions for Form 1040 or 1040A or Publication 915 to figure the taxable part of social security benefits you must include in gross income.

***If you did not live with your spouse at the end of 2011 (or on the date your spouse died) and your gross income was at least $3,700, you must file a return regardless of your age.

or from the sale of your main home (even if you can exclude all or part of it). Include part of your social security benefits if:

1. You were married, filing a separate return, and you lived with your spouse at any time during 2011; or
2. Half of your social security benefits plus your other gross income and any tax-exempt interest is more than $25,000 ($32,000 if married filing jointly).

If either (1) or (2) applies, see the instructions for Form 1040 or 1040A, or Publication 915, *Social Security and Equivalent Railroad Retirement Benefits*, to figure the social security benefits you must include in gross income.

Common types of income are discussed in *Part Two* of this publication.

Community income. If you are married and your permanent home is in a community property state, half of any income described by state law as community income may be considered yours. This affects your federal taxes, including whether you must file if you do not file a joint return with your spouse. See Publication 555, *Community Property*, for more information.

California, Nevada, and Washington domestic partners. A registered domestic partner in California, Nevada, or Washington must report half the combined community income earned by the individual and his or her domestic partner. See Publication 555.

Self-employed individuals. If you are self-employed, your gross income includes the amount on line 7 of Schedule C (Form 1040), Profit or Loss From Business; line 1 of Schedule C-EZ (Form 1040), Net Profit From Business; and line 11 of Schedule F (Form 1040), Profit or Loss From Farming. See *Self-Employed Persons*, later, for more information about your filing requirements.

Filing status. Your filing status depends on whether you are single or married and on your family situation. Your filing status is determined on the last day of your tax year, which is December 31 for most taxpayers. See chapter 2 for an explanation of each filing status.

Age. If you are 65 or older at the end of the year, you generally can have a higher amount of gross income than other taxpayers before you must file. See Table 1-1. You are considered 65 on the day before your 65th birthday. For example, if your 65th birthday is on January 1, 2012, you are considered 65 for 2011.

EXAMPLE
You are 65 years old and earned $11,000 of taxable income last year. Your husband, who is 66 years old, received a pension of $6,000, all of which was taxable income. You and your husband legally separated on December 28. If you had been living together at the end of the year, you would not have had to file an income tax return, because your combined income was less than $21,300. But, because you are living apart and your gross income was more than $10,950, you must file a return.

Surviving Spouses, Executors, Administrators, and Legal Representatives
You must file a final return for a decedent (a person who died) if both of the following are true.
- You are the surviving spouse, executor, administrator, or legal representative.
- The decedent met the filing requirements at the date of death.

For more information on rules for filing a decedent's final return, see Publication 559, *Survivors, Executors, and Administrators*.

U.S. Citizens and Residents Living Outside the United States
If you are a U.S. citizen or resident living outside the United States, you must file a return if you meet the filing requirements. For information on special tax rules that may apply to you, see Publication 54, *Tax Guide for U.S. Citizens and Resident Aliens Abroad*. It is available at most U.S. embassies and consulates. *Text intentionally omitted.*

EXPLANATION
For more information about U.S. citizens living abroad, see chapter 41, *U.S. citizens working abroad: Tax treatment of foreign earned income.*

Residents of Puerto Rico
Generally, if you are a U.S. citizen and a resident of Puerto Rico, you must file a U.S. income tax return if you meet the filing requirements. This is in addition to any legal requirement you may have to file an income tax return for Puerto Rico.

If you are a resident of Puerto Rico for the entire year, gross income does not include income from sources within Puerto Rico, except for amounts received as an employee of the United States or a U.S. agency. If you receive income from Puerto Rican sources that is not subject to U.S. tax, you must reduce your standard deduction. As a result, the amount of income you must have before you are required to file a U.S. income tax return is lower than the applicable amount in Table 1-1 or Table 1-2. For more information, see Publication 570, *Tax Guide for Individuals With Income From U.S. Possessions.*

Individuals With Income From U.S. Possessions

If you had income from Guam, the Commonwealth of the Northern Mariana Islands, American Samoa, or the U.S. Virgin Islands, special rules may apply when determining whether you must file a U.S. federal income tax return. In addition, you may have to file a return with the individual island government. See Publication 570 for more information.

Table 1-2.   **2011 Filing Requirements for Dependents**

See chapter 3 to find out if someone can claim you as a dependent.

If your parents (or someone else) can claim you as a dependent, and any of the situations below apply to you, you must file a return. (See Table 1-3 for other situations when you must file.)

In this table, earned income includes salaries, wages, tips, and professional fees. It also includes taxable scholarship and fellowship grants. (See *Scholarships and fellowships* in chapter 12.) Unearned income includes investment-type income such as taxable interest, ordinary dividends, and capital gain distributions. It also includes unemployment compensation, taxable social security benefits, pensions, annuities, cancellation of debt, and distributions of unearned income from a trust. Gross income is the total of your earned and unearned income.

Single dependents—Were you either age 65 or older or blind?

☐ **No.**   You must file a return if any of the following apply.
- Your unearned income was more than $950.
- Your earned income was more than $5,800.
- Your gross income was more than the larger of:
  - $950, or
  - Your earned income (up to $5,500) plus $300.

☐ **Yes.**   You must file a return if any of the following apply.
- Your unearned income was more than $2,400 ($3,850 if 65 or older and blind).
- Your earned income was more than $7,250 ($8,700 if 65 or older and blind).
- Your gross income was more than the larger of:
  - $2,400 ($3,850 if 65 or older and blind), or
  - Your earned income (up to $5,500) plus $1,750 ($3,200 if 65 or older and blind).

Married dependents—Were you either age 65 or older or blind?

☐ **No.**   You must file a return if any of the following apply.
- Your unearned income was more than $950.
- Your earned income was more than $5,800.
- Your gross income was at least $5 and your spouse files a separate return and itemizes deductions.
- Your gross income was more than the larger of:
  - $950, or
  - Your earned income (up to $5,500) plus $300.

☐ **Yes.**   You must file a return if any of the following apply.
- Your unearned income was more than $2,100 ($3,250 if 65 or older and blind).
- Your earned income was more than $6,950 ($8,100 if 65 or older and blind).
- Your gross income was at least $5 and your spouse files a separate return and itemizes deductions.
- Your gross income was more than the larger of:
  - $2,100 ($3,250 if 65 or older and blind), or
  - Your earned income (up to $5,500) plus $1,450 ($2,600 if 65 or older and blind).

Dependents

If you are a dependent (one who meets the dependency tests in <u>chapter 3</u>), see <u>Table 1-2</u> to find whether you must file a return. You also must file if your situation is described in <u>Table 1-3</u>.

Responsibility of parent. Generally, a child is responsible for filing his or her own tax return and for paying any tax on the return. But if a dependent child who must file an income tax return cannot file it for any reason, such as age, then a parent, guardian, or other legally responsible person must file it for the child. If the child cannot sign the return, the parent or guardian must sign the child's name followed by the words "By (your signature), parent for minor child."

Child's earnings. Amounts a child earns by performing services are his or her gross income. This is true even if under local law the child's parents have the right to the earnings and may actually have received them. If the child does not pay the tax due on this income, the parent is liable for the tax.

EXPLANATION
For more details about dependents, see <u>chapter 3</u>, *Personal exemptions and dependents.*

Certain Children Under Age 19 or Full-Time Students

If a child's only income is interest and dividends (including capital gain distributions and Alaska Permanent Fund dividends), the child was under age 19 at the end of 2011 or was a full-time student under age 24 at the end of 2011, and certain other conditions are met, a parent can elect to include the child's income on the parent's return. If this election is made, the child does not have to file a return. See *Parent's Election To Report Child's Interest and Dividends* in chapter 31.

TAXALERT
The unearned income of children under age 19, or under age 24 if a full-time student, is taxed at the parent's rate. Unearned income includes interest, dividends, and capital gains distributions.

If a child's interest, dividends, capital gains distributions, and other investment income total more than $1,900, part of that income is taxed at the marginal tax rate to which the child's parent is subject, rather than the child's own marginal rate. In effect, such income is treated as if the parent had received the income.

Children who are age 18 by the end of 2011, or between ages 19 and 23 and a full-time student, are not subject to the so-called kiddie tax if they have earned income that exceeds one-half of the amount of support they receive.

See <u>chapter 32</u>, *Tax on investment income of certain minor children*, for more information.

Self-Employed Persons

You are self-employed if you:
- Carry on a trade or business as a sole proprietor,
- Are an independent contractor,
- Are a member of a partnership, or
- Are in business for yourself in any other way.

Self-employment can include work in addition to your regular full-time business activities, such as certain part-time work you do at home or in addition to your regular job.

EXAMPLES
A person who delivers newspapers would be subject to self-employment tax. A person working at home in a cottage industry—woodworking or furniture making, for example—would be subject to self-employment tax. In some instances, it is to your advantage to report income from self-employment, because if you do not already qualify, you will then become eligible for social security benefits. For more information on self-employed persons, see <u>chapter 38</u>, *Self-employment income: How to file Schedule C.*

You must file a return if your gross income is at least as much as the filing requirement amount for your filing status and age (shown in Table 1-1). Also, you must file Form 1040 and Schedule SE (Form 1040), Self-Employment Tax, if:

1. Your net earnings from self-employment (excluding church employee income) were $400 or more, or
2. You had church employee income of $108.28 or more. (See Table 1-3.)

Use Schedule SE (Form 1040) to figure your self-employment tax. Self-employment tax is comparable to the social security and Medicare tax withheld from an employee's wages. For more information about this tax, see Publication 334, *Tax Guide for Small Business*.

> ### TAXSAVER
> You are able to deduct one-half of your self-employment tax for the year in calculating your adjusted gross income. For details see chapter 23, *Taxes you may deduct*.

> ### TAXALERT
> For 2010, self-employed individuals were allowed to deduct the cost of health insurance for themselves, their spouses, dependents, and children who had not attained age 27 as of the end of the taxable year in the calculation of their 2010 self-employment income subject to self-employment tax. Beginning in 2011, no such deduction is allowed for figuring the amount of your self-employment income subject to self-employment tax. However, amounts paid for such health insurance premiums are still deductible as an adjustment for figuring adjusted gross income subject to income tax on line 29 of Form 1040.

> ### TAXALERT
> Self-employment tax has two parts: old age, survivor, and disability insurance (OASDI) and Medicare hospital insurance (HI). (The comparable social security tax withheld on an employee's wages consists of these same two parts.) In 2011, the cap on self-employment income subject to OASDI is $106,800. There is no limit on the amount of self-employment income subject to the HI portion of the self-employment tax. More information about the social security contribution and benefit base is available at *www.socialsecurity.gov/OA CT/ COLA/cbb.html*.

Employees of foreign governments or international organizations. If you are a U.S. citizen who works in the United States for an international organization, a foreign government, or a wholly owned instrumentality of a foreign government, and your employer is not required to withhold social security and Medicare taxes from your wages, you must include your earnings from services performed in the United States when figuring your net earnings from self-employment.

Ministers. You must include income from services you performed as a minister when figuring your net earnings from self-employment, unless you have an exemption from self-employment tax. This also applies to Christian Science practitioners and members of a religious order who have not taken a vow of poverty. For more information, see Publication 517, *Social Security and Other Information for Members of the Clergy and Religious Workers*.

Aliens

Your status as an alien—resident, nonresident, or dual-status—determines whether and how you must file an income tax return.

The rules used to determine your alien status are discussed in Publication 519, *U.S. Tax Guide for Aliens*.

Resident alien. If you are a resident alien for the entire year, you must file a tax return following the same rules that apply to U.S. citizens. Use the forms discussed in this publication.

Nonresident alien. If you are a nonresident alien, the rules and tax forms that apply to you are different from those that apply to U.S. citizens and resident aliens. See Publication 519 to find out if U.S. income tax laws apply to you and which forms you should file.

Dual-status taxpayer. If you are a resident alien for part of the tax year and a nonresident alien for the rest of the year, you are a dual-status taxpayer. Different rules apply for each part of the year. For information on dual-status taxpayers, see Publication 519.

Who Should File

Even if you do not have to file, you should file a federal income tax return to get money back if any of the following conditions apply.

1. You had federal income tax withheld or made estimated tax payments.
2. You qualify for the earned income credit. See chapter 37 for more information.
3. You qualify for the additional child tax credit. See chapter 35 for more information.
4. You qualify for the health coverage tax credit. See chapter 37 for more information.
5. You qualify for the refundable credit for prior year minimum tax.
   Text intentionally omitted.
6. You qualify for the first-time homebuyer credit See chapter 37 for more information.
7. You qualify for the American opportunity credit. See chapter 36 for more information.
8. You qualify for the credit for federal tax on fuels. See chapter 37 for more information.
9. You qualify for the adoption credit. See chapter 37 for more information.

Tip

See *the discussion under* Form 1040 *for when you must use that form.*

Which Form Should I Use?

You must use one of three forms to file your return: Form 1040EZ, Form 1040A, or Form 1040. (But also see *Does My Return Have To Be on Paper*, later.)

Form 1040EZ

Form 1040EZ is the simplest form to use.

You can use Form 1040EZ if all of the following apply.

1. Your filing status is single or married filing jointly. If you were a nonresident alien at any time in 2011, your filing status must be married filing jointly.

Table 1-3. **Other Situations When You Must File a 2011 Return**

If any of the four conditions listed below applies, you must file a return, even if your income is less than the amount shown in Table 1-1 or Table 1-2.

1. You owe any special taxes, including any of the following.

   - Social security or Medicare tax on tips you did not report to your employer. (See chapter 6.)
   - Social security or Medicare tax on wages you received from an employer who did not withhold these taxes.
   - Uncollected social security, Medicare, or railroad retirement tax on tips you reported to your employer. (See chapter 6.)
   - Uncollected social security, Medicare, or railroad retirement tax on your group-term life insurance. This amount should be shown in box 12 of your Form W-2.
   - Alternative minimum tax. (See chapter 30.)
   - Additional tax on a qualified retirement plan, including an individual retirement arrangement (IRA). (See chapter 17.)
   - Additional tax on an Archer MSA or health savings account. (See Publication 969, *Health Savings Accounts and Other Tax-Favored Health Plans*.)
   - Additional tax on a Coverdell ESA or qualified tuition program. (See Publication 970, *Tax Benefits for Education*.)
   - Recapture of an investment credit or a low-income housing credit. (See the Instructions for Form 4255, Recapture of Investment Credit, or Form 8611, Recapture of Low-Income Housing Credit.)
   - Recapture tax on the disposition of a home purchased with a federally subsidized mortgage. (See chapter 15.)
   - Recapture of the qualified electric vehicle credit. (See chapter 37.)
   - Recapture of an education credit. (See chapter 35.)
   - Recapture of the Indian employment credit. (See the Instructions for Form 8845, Indian Employment Credit.)
   - Recapture of the new markets credit. (See Form 8874, New Markets Credit.)
   - Recapture of alternative motor vehicle credit. (See Form 8910, Alternative Motor Vehicle Credit.)
   - Recapture of first-time homebuyer credit.
   - Household employment taxes. (See Schedule H (Form 1040), Household Employment Taxes.)

2. You received any advance earned income credit (EIC) payments from your employer. This amount should be shown in box 9 of your Form W-2. (See chapter 36.)

3. You had net earnings from self-employment of at least $400. (See *Self-Employed Persons* earlier in this chapter.)

4. You had wages of $108.28 or more from a church or qualified church-controlled organization that is exempt from employer social security and Medicare taxes. (See Publication 334.)

---

2. You (and your spouse if married filing a joint return) were under age 65 and not blind at the end of 2011. If you were born on January 1, 1947, you are considered to be age 65 at the end of 2011.
3. You do not claim any dependents.
4. Your taxable income is less than $100,000.
5. Your income is only from wages, salaries, tips, unemployment compensation, Alaska Permanent Fund dividends, taxable scholarship and fellowship grants, and taxable interest of $1,500 or less.
6. You did not receive any advance earned income credit (EIC) payments.
7. You do not claim any adjustments to income, such as a deduction for IRA contributions or student loan interest.
8. You do not claim any credits other than the earned income credit. *Text intentionally omitted.*
9. You do not owe any household employment taxes on wages you paid to a household employee.
10. You are not claiming the additional standard deduction.

You must meet all of these requirements to use Form 1040EZ. If you do not, you must use Form 1040A or Form 1040.

Figuring tax. On Form 1040EZ, you can use only the tax table to figure your tax. You cannot use Form 1040EZ to report any other tax.

Form 1040A

If you do not qualify to use Form 1040EZ, you may be able to use Form 1040A.

You can use Form 1040A if all of the following apply.

1. Your income is only from wages, salaries, tips, IRA distributions, pensions and annuities, taxable social security and railroad retirement benefits, taxable scholarship and fellowship grants, interest, ordinary dividends (including Alaska Permanent Fund dividends), capital gain distributions, and unemployment compensation.
2. Your taxable income is less than $100,000.
3. Your adjustments to income are for only the following items.
   a. IRA deduction.
   b. Student loan interest deduction.
4. You do not itemize your deductions.
5. Your taxes are from only the following items.
   a. Tax Table.
   b. Alternative minimum tax. (See chapter 31.)
   c. Advance earned income credit (EIC) payments, if you received any. (See chapter 37.)
   d. Recapture of an education credit. (See chapter 36.)
   e. Form 8615, Tax for Certain Children Who Have Investment Income of More Than $1,900.
   f. Qualified Dividends and Capital Gain Tax Worksheet.
6. You claim only the following tax credits.
   a. The credit for child and dependent care expenses. (See chapter 33.)
   b. The credit for the elderly or the disabled. (See chapter 34.)
   c. The child tax credit. (See chapter 35.)
   d. The additional child tax credit. (See chapter 35.)
   e. The education credits. (See chapter 36.)
   f. The retirement savings contributions credit. (See chapter 37.)
   g. The earned income credit. (See chapter 37.)
   Text intentionally omitted.
7. You did not have an alternative minimum tax adjustment on stock you acquired from the exercise of an incentive stock option. (See Publication 525, *Taxable and Nontaxable Income.*)

You must meet all of the above requirements to use Form 1040A. If you do not, you must use Form 1040.

Form 1040

If you cannot use Form 1040EZ or Form 1040A, you must use Form 1040. You can use Form 1040 to report all types of income, deductions, and credits.

You may pay less tax by filing Form 1040 because you can take itemized deductions, some adjustments to income, and credits you cannot take on Form 1040A or Form 1040EZ.

You must use Form 1040 if any of the following apply.

1. Your taxable income is $100,000 or more.
2. You itemize your deductions.
3. You had income that cannot be reported on Form 1040EZ or Form 1040A, including tax-exempt interest from private activity bonds issued after August 7, 1986.
4. You claim any adjustments to gross income other than the adjustments listed earlier under *Form 1040A*.
5. Your Form W-2, box 12, shows uncollected employee tax (social security and Medicare tax) on tips (see chapter 6) or group-term life insurance (see chapter 5).
6. You received $20 or more in tips in any 1 month and did not report all of them to your employer. (See chapter 6.)
7. You were a bona fide resident of Puerto Rico and exclude income from sources in Puerto Rico.
8. You claim any credits other than the credits listed earlier under *Form 1040A*.
9. You owe the excise tax on insider stock compensation from an expatriated corporation.
10. Your Form W-2 shows an amount in box 12 with a code Z.
11. You had a qualified health savings account funding distribution from your IRA.
12. You are an employee and your employer did not withhold social security and Medicare tax.
13. You have to file other forms with your return to report certain exclusions, taxes, or transactions.
14. You are a debtor in a bankruptcy case filed after October 16, 2005.
15. *Text intentionally omitted.* You must recapture the first-time homebuyer credit.

Text intentionally omitted.

Does My Return Have To Be on Paper?

You may be able to file a paperless return using IRS *e-file* (electronic filing). If your 2011 adjusted gross income (AGI) is $58,000 or less, you are eligible for Free File. If you do not qualify for Free File, then you should checkout *www.irs.gov* for low-cost *e-file* options or Free File Fillable Forms.

> **TAXPLANNER**
> As of the date this book went to press, the maximum amount of adjusted gross income (AGI) that qualified for free filing had not yet been announced. In 2010, the maximum AGI was $58,000. For more information about e-filing and the IRS's Free File program, see chapter 45, *Everything you need to know about e-filing.*

IRS *e-file*

Table 1-4 lists the benefits of IRS *e-file*. IRS *e-file* uses automation to replace most of the manual steps needed to process paper returns. As a result, the processing of *e-file* returns is faster and more accurate than the processing of paper returns. However, as with a paper return, you are responsible for making sure your return contains accurate information and is filed on time. Using *e-file* does not affect your chances of an IRS examination of your return.

> **TAXPLANNER**
> You expect a $3,000 refund. A refund check related to an electronically filed return should be issued within three weeks of the date the IRS acknowledges receipt of the return. But, if you elect to have your refund directly deposited when you electronically file your return, your refund could be deposited into your designated account in as few as ten days. Both of these methods can enable you to receive your refund much sooner than you would by filing a paper return. (If you file a paper return, it could take six weeks to receive a refund check.)
> Filing an electronic return could allow you to receive a refund sooner and invest the amount you receive. However, some companies charge a separate fee for electronically filing a return, so you will need to weigh the advantage of investing your refund earlier against additional costs you may incur.

Table 1-4. **Benefits of IRS *e-file***

- Free File allows qualified taxpayers to prepare and *e-file* their own tax returns for free.
- Free File is available in English and Spanish.
- Free File is available online 24 hours a day, 7 days a week.
- Get your refund in as few as 10 days with Direct Deposit.
- Sign electronically with a secure self-selected PIN number and file a completely paperless return.
- Receive an acknowledgement that your return was accepted.
- If you owe, you can *e-file* and authorize an electronic funds withdrawal or pay by credit card. You can also file a return early and pay the amount you owe by the due date of your return.
- Save time by preparing and e-filing federal and state returns together.
- IRS computers quickly and automatically check for errors or other missing information.
- Help the environment, use less paper, and save taxpayer money—it costs less to process an e-filed return than a paper return.

Free File Fillable Forms. If you do not need the help of a tax preparer, then Free File Fillable Forms may be for you. These forms:
- Do not have an income requirement so everyone is eligible,
- Are easy to use,
- Perform basic math calculations,
- Are available only at *www.irs.gov*, and
- Apply only to a federal tax return.

Electronic return signatures. To file your return electronically, you must sign the return electronically using a personal identification number (PIN). If you are filing online, you must use a Self-Select PIN. If you are filing electronically using a tax practitioner, you can use a Self-Select PIN or a Practitioner PIN.

Self-Select PIN. The Self-Select PIN method allows you to create your own PIN. If you are married filing jointly, you and your spouse will each need to create a PIN and enter these PINs as your electronic signatures.

A PIN is any combination of five digits you choose except five zeros. If you use a PIN, there is nothing to sign and nothing to mail—not even your Forms W-2.

To verify your identity, you will be prompted to enter your adjusted gross income (AGI) from your originally filed 2010 federal income tax return, if applicable. Do not use your AGI from an amended return (Form 1040X) or a math error correction made by the IRS. AGI is the amount shown on your 2010 Form 1040, line 38; Form 1040A, line 22; or Form 1040EZ, line 4. If you do not have your 2010 income tax return, you can quickly request a transcript by using our automated self-service tool. Visit us at *www.irs.gov* and click on "Order a Transcript" or call 1-800-908-9946 to get a free transcript of your return. (If you filed electronically last year, you may use your prior year PIN to verify your identity instead of your prior year AGI. The prior year PIN is the five digit PIN you used to electronically sign your 2010 return.) You will also be prompted to enter your date of birth (DOB). Make sure your DOB is accurate and matches the information on record with the Social Security Administration by checking your annual social security statement.

Practitioner PIN. The Practitioner PIN method allows you to authorize your tax practitioner to enter or generate your PIN. The practitioner can provide you with details.

Form 8453. You must send in a paper Form 8453 if you are attaching or filing Appendix A of Revenue Procedure 2009-20, Forms 1098-C, 2848 (for an electronic return signed by an agent), 3115, 3468 (if attachments are required), 4136 (if certificate or statement required), 5713, 8283 (if a statement is required for Section A or if Section B is completed), 8332 (or certain pages from a decree or agreement that went into effect after 1984 and before 2009), 8858, 8864 (if certification or statement required), 8885, *text intentionally omitted,* or 8949.

For more details, visit *www.irs.gov/efile* and click on "Individual Taxpayers."

Caution

You cannot use the Self-Select PIN method if you are a first-time filer under age 16 at the end of 2011.

Caution

If you cannot locate your prior year AGI or prior year PIN use the Electronic Filing PIN Request. This can be found at www.irs.gov. Click on "Request Electronic Filing PIN" under "I Need To." Or you can call 1-866-704-7388.

Power of attorney. If an agent is signing your return for you, a power of attorney (POA) must be filed. Attach the POA to Form 8453 and file it using that form's instructions. See *Signatures*, later for more information on POAs.

State returns. In most states, you can file an electronic state return simultaneously with your federal return. For more information, check with your local IRS office, state tax agency, tax professional, or the IRS website at *www.irs.gov/efile*.

Refunds. You can have a refund check mailed to you, or you can have your refund deposited directly to your checking or savings account or split among two or three accounts. With *e-file,* your refund will be issued faster than if you filed on paper.

As with a paper return, you may not get all of your refund if you owe certain past-due amounts, such as federal tax, state tax, a student loan, or child support. See *Offset against debts* under *Refunds*, later.

TAXALERT
The IRS will allow you to deposit your refund into up to three accounts. See Form 8888, Allocation of Refund (including Savings Bond Purchases), for more information.

TAXPLANNER
Some banks do not allow a joint refund to be deposited into an individual account. You should check with your bank to make sure your direct deposit will be accepted.

EXPLANATION
Direct Deposit Refunds
Direct deposit refunds will usually be issued within ten days from the date the electronic return is accepted. However, the Treasury Department does not guarantee that a refund will be issued by a specific date or for the anticipated amount. Direct deposit is quickest when used in conjunction with *e-filing*; however, it can be used regardless of the method used to file your return.

TAXALERT
You can use the "Where's My Refund?" feature at *www.irs.gov* to determine the status of your return.
  The following conditions may delay refunds and/or change refund amounts. Direct deposit elections generally will not be honored in these cases:
1. You owe back taxes, either individual or business.
2. You owe delinquent child support.
3. You have certain delinquent debts, such as student loans.
4. The last name and social security number of the primary taxpayer are not the same as on last year's return. If this is the case, the return will be delayed at least 1 week for rematching.
5. The estimated tax payments reported on the return do not match the estimated tax payments recorded on the IRS master file. This generally occurs when:
    a. The spouse made separate payments and filed a joint return, or vice versa; or
    b. The return was filed before the last estimated tax payment was credited to the taxpayer's account (i.e., before January 17, 2012).
6. You have a Schedule E claiming a deduction for a questionable tax shelter.
7. You are claiming a blatantly unallowable deduction.

TAXPLANNER
A refund anticipation loan (RAL) is a loan made to you based on your expected refund. The loan is a contract between you and a financial institution. Generally, the financial institution will require that you sign an authorization that permits the institution to debit your account after

the refund has been credited to it. You can expect to pay a fee to the electronic return origina-tor, who, with your permission, submits information to the financial institution, and a fee to the financial institution. These fees are in addition to the tax preparation fee and electronic filing fee. However, if you file your return electronically and select the direct deposit option for your refund, you could receive your refund in just a few days. This method would be faster and could cost less than using an RAL.

The IRS has recently made changes to the type of information that will be provided to return preparers and financial institutions providing RALs. Beginning with the 2011 tax year, RAL pro-viders will no longer receive an indication of whether an individual taxpayer will have any portion of the refund offset for delinquent tax or other debts, such as unpaid child support or delinquent federally funded student loans. This acknowledgment, which is known as the *debt indicator,* was used as a tool to help RAL providers determine the portion of a taxpayer's refund that would be available as an RAL. Because the information will no longer be given to an RAL provider, taxpay-ers and their return preparers will likely turn to the "Where's My Refund?" service on *www.irs. gov* to access information about their tax refunds and any offsets. Since the information posted to the "Where's My Refund?" site is available at nearly the same time as a taxpayer's refund could be deposited to their bank account through the Direct Deposit program, it is expected that the number of RALs issued to taxpayers will decline.

Although an RAL could speed up the time for you to receive your refund by a week or more, there is often a relatively high "interest cost." For example, if your expected refund is $1,000 and the loan fee charged is $30, the "interest cost" to you for 2 weeks' use of the money comes to nearly three-quarters the amount of the loan cost, figured on an annualized basis. E-filing your return and requesting the refund via direct deposit may be just as fast as setting up an RAL, and may ultimately cost you less in fees and interest. This is especially likely for taxpayers with income under $58,000 who qualify for the IRS Free File program.

Another alternative to using the RAL is to have your annual withholding adjusted during the year by filing a Form W-4. This could enable you to keep more of your income throughout the year, instead of waiting to receive a large refund after filing your tax return. See chapter 4, *Tax withholding and estimated tax.*

Explanation
Composition of an Electronic Return
In total, an electronic return contains the same information as a comparable return filed entirely on paper documents. An electronic return consists of:
1. Electronic portion of return—Data transmitted to the IRS electronically
2. Nonelectronic portion of return—Paper documents (filed with the IRS within three days of the IRS acceptance of the electronic portion of the return) that contain in-formation that cannot be electronically transmitted, such as documents prepared by third parties

Electronic Portion of Return
For 2011 returns, most forms and schedules, including Form 1040 and Form 1040A, can be transmitted electronically and are considered the "electronic portion" of the return.

Nonelectronic Portion of Return
If you have portions of your tax return that cannot be submitted electronically, you will need to mail them in with Form 8453, U.S. Individual Income Tax Transmittal for an IRS e-file Return. See chapter 45, *Everything you need to know about e-filing,* for more information.

TAXALERT
The IRS and many states have mandated that tax practitioners e-file the returns they prepare. Subject to certain requirements, the IRS and the following states have imposed mandatory e-filing: Alabama, California, Connecticut, Georgia, Indiana, Kansas, Louisiana, Maine, Maryland, Massachusetts, Michigan, Minnesota, Nebraska, New Jersey, New Mexico, New York, Ohio, Okla-homa, Rhode Island, South Carolina, Utah, Virginia, West Virginia, and Wisconsin. Individuals who file their own returns can file on paper or electronically. For details on states that provide filing directly via their website and other information about e-filing, see chapter 45, *Everything you need to know about e-filing.*

Refund inquiries. You can go online to check the status of your refund 72 hours after the IRS acknowledges receipt of your e-filed return; see *Refund Information*, later.

Amount you owe. To avoid late-payment penalties and interest, pay your taxes in full by April 17, 2012. You can make your payment electronically by credit or debit card or by scheduling an electronic funds withdrawal from your checking or savings account.

See *How To Pay*, later, for information on how to pay the amount you owe.

Using Your Personal Computer

You can file your tax return in a fast, easy, and convenient way using your personal computer. A computer with Internet access and tax preparation software are all you need. Best of all, you can *e-file* from the comfort of your home 24 hours a day, 7 days a week.

IRS approved tax preparation software is available for online use on the Internet, for download from the Internet, and in retail stores.

For information, visit *www.irs.gov/efile*.

Through Employers and Financial Institutions

Some businesses offer free *e-file* to their employees, members, or customers. Others offer it for a fee. Ask your employer or financial institution if they offer IRS *e-file* as an employee, member, or customer benefit.

Free Help With Your Return

Free help in preparing your return is available nationwide from IRS-trained volunteers. The Volunteer Income Tax Assistance (VITA) program is designed to help low to moderate income taxpayers and the Tax Counseling for the Elderly (TCE) program is designed to assist taxpayers age 60 or older with their tax returns. Many VITA sites offer free electronic filing and all volunteers will let you know about the credits and deductions you may be entitled to claim. To find a site near you, call 1-800-906-9887. Or to find the nearest AARP TaxAide site, visit AARP's website at *www.aarp.org/taxaide* or call 1 -888-227-7669. For more information on these programs, go to *www.irs.gov* and enter keyword "VITA" in the upper right-hand corner.

TAXPLANNER

The U.S. military also has a strong Volunteer Income Tax Assistance (VITA) program to provide free tax advice, tax preparation, and assistance to Army, Air Force, Navy, Marine Corps, and Coast Guard personnel. This special worldwide tax program is overseen by the Armed Forces Tax Council (AFTC). The AFTC, in coordination with the IRS, trains and equips volunteers for serving military-specific tax issues, such as combat zone tax benefits and the Earned Income Tax Credit.

More information can be found via *www.irs.gov* by entering the keyword "AFTC" in the upper right-hand corner.

Using a Tax Professional

Many tax professionals electronically file tax returns for their clients. You may personally enter your PIN or complete Form 8879, IRS *e-file* Signature Authorization, to authorize the tax professional to enter your PIN on your return.

Note. Tax professionals may charge a fee for IRS *e-file*. Fees can vary depending on the professional and the specific services rendered.

When Do I Have To File?

April 17, 2012, is the due date for filing your 2011 income tax return if you use the calendar year. For a quick view of due dates for filing a return with or without an extension of time to file (discussed later), see Table 1-5.

Table 1-5. **When To File Your 2011 Return**

For U.S. citizens and residents who file returns on a calendar year.

	For Most Taxpayers	For Certain Taxpayers Outside the U.S.
No extension requested	April 17, 2012	June 15, 2012
Automatic extension	October 15, 2012	October 15, 2012

If you use a fiscal year (a year ending on the last day of any month except December, or a 52-53-week year), your income tax return is due by the 15th day of the 4th month after the close of your fiscal year.

When the due date for doing any act for tax purposes—filing a return, paying taxes, etc.—falls on a Saturday, Sunday, or legal holiday, the due date is delayed until the next business day.

Filing on time. Your paper return is filed on time if it is mailed in an envelope that is properly addressed, has enough postage, and is postmarked by the due date. If you send your return by registered mail, the date of the registration is the postmark date. The registration is evidence that the return was delivered. If you send a return by certified mail and have your receipt postmarked by a postal employee, the date on the receipt is the postmark date. The postmarked certified mail receipt is evidence that the return was delivered.

Private delivery services. If you use a private delivery service designated by the IRS to send your return, the postmark date generally is the date the private delivery service records in its database or marks on the mailing label. The private delivery service can tell you how to get written proof of this date.

The following are designated private delivery services.

- DHL Express (DHL): Same Day Service.
- Federal Express (FedEx): FedEx Priority Overnight, FedEx Standard Overnight, FedEx 2Day, FedEx International Priority, and FedEx International First.
- United Parcel Service (UPS): UPS Next Day Air, UPS Next Day Air Saver, UPS 2nd Day Air, UPS 2nd Day Air A.M., UPS Worldwide Express Plus, and UPS Worldwide Express.

Electronically filed returns. If you use IRS *e-file*, your return is considered filed on time if the authorized electronic return transmitter postmarks the transmission by the due date. An authorized electronic return transmitter is a participant in the IRS *e-file* program that transmits electronic tax return information directly to the IRS.

The electronic postmark is a record of when the authorized electronic return transmitter received the transmission of your electronically filed return on its host system. The date and time in your time zone controls whether your electronically filed return is timely.

Filing late. If you do not file your return by the due date, you may have to pay a failure-to-file penalty and interest. For more information, see *Penalties*, later. Also see *Interest* under *Amount You Owe*.

If you were due a refund but you did not file a return, you generally must file within 3 years from the date the return was due (including extensions) to get that refund.

Nonresident alien. If you are a nonresident alien and earn wages subject to U.S. income tax withholding, your 2011 U.S. income tax return (Form 1040NR or Form 1040NR-EZ) is due by:

- April 17, 2012, if you use a calendar year, or
- The 15th day of the 4th month after the end of your fiscal year if you use a fiscal year.

If you do not earn wages subject to U.S. income tax withholding, your return is due by:

- June 15, 2012, if you use a calendar year, or
- The 15th day of the 6th month after the end of your fiscal year, if you use a fiscal year.

See Publication 519 for more filing information.

For a decedent. If you must file a final income tax return for a taxpayer who died during the year (a decedent), the return is due by the 15th day of the 4th month after the end of the decedent's normal tax year. See Publication 559.

Extensions of Time To File

You may be able to get an extension of time to file your return. Special rules apply for those who were:

- Outside the United States, or
- Serving in a combat zone.

Automatic Extension

If you cannot file your 2011 return by the due date, you may be able to get an automatic 6-month extension of time to file.

Example. If your return is due on April 17, 2012, you will have until October 15, 2012, to file.

How to get the automatic extension. You can get the automatic extension by:

1. Using IRS *e-file* (electronic filing), or
2. Filing a paper form.

E-file options. There are two ways you can use *e-file* to get an extension of time to file. Complete Form 4868, Application for Automatic Extension of Time To File U.S. Individual Income Tax Return, to use as a worksheet. If you think you may owe tax when you file your return, use *Part*

Caution

Private delivery services cannot deliver items to P.O. boxes. You must use the U.S. Postal Service to mail any item to an IRS P.O. box address.

Caution

If you do not pay the tax due by the regular due date (generally, April 15), you will owe interest. You may also be charged penalties, discussed later.

II of the form to estimate your balance due. If you *e-file* Form 4868 to the IRS, do not also send a paper Form 4868.

E-file using your personal computer or a tax professional. You can use a tax software package with your personal computer or a tax professional to file Form 4868 electronically. You will need to provide certain information from your tax return for 2010. If you wish to make a payment by electronic funds withdrawal, see *Electronic payment options*, under *How To Pay*, later in this chapter.

E-file and pay by credit or debit card. You can get an extension by paying part or all of your estimate of tax due by using a credit or debit card. You can do this by phone or over the Internet. You do not file Form 4868. See *Electronic payment options*, under *How To Pay*, later in this chapter.

Filing a paper Form 4868. You can get an extension of time to file by filing a paper Form 4868. Mail it to the address shown in the form instructions.

If you want to make a payment with the form, make your check or money order payable to the "United States Treasury." Write your SSN, daytime phone number, and "2011 Form 4868" on your check or money order.

TAXPLANNER
The IRS offers some relief to taxpayers unable to pay the amount owed with the filing of Form 4868. The IRS permits Form 4868 to be filed and an automatic 6-month extension obtained even though the tax properly estimated to be due is not paid in full when the form is filed. No late filing penalty will be assessed under these circumstances. However, it is still required that the tax liability shown on Form 4868 be properly estimated based on the information available to the taxpayer. Furthermore, unless at least 90% of the taxpayer's actual tax liability was paid prior to the original due date of the return through withholding or estimated payments, a late payment penalty of 0.5% per month will be assessed for each month from the original due date to the date of payment plus the regular rate of interest on underpayments.

When to file. You must request the automatic extension by the due date for your return. You can file your return anytime before the 6-month extension period ends.

TAXSAVER
An extension of time to file will not be valid if it does not show a "proper" estimate of tax liability. A proper estimate is based on all the facts and information you have at the time of filing. If your estimate is found to be improper, your extension will be invalid and you will be subject to failure-to-file penalties. See *Penalties,* later. Some tax experts contend that you should request an extension to file your return, arguing that your chances of an audit are reduced, because IRS field agents will have less time to conduct the audit. Other tax experts contend that you're better off filing on April 15, because that way you get lost in the crowd. Both theories are gross oversimplifications of IRS procedures.

When you file your return. Enter any payment you made related to the extension of time to file on Form 1040, line 68. If you file Form 1040EZ or Form 1040A, include that payment in your total payments on Form 1040EZ, line 10, or Form 1040A, line 44. Also enter "Form 4868" and the amount paid in the space to the left of line 10 or line 44.

TAXPLANNER
An extension of time to file is not an extension of time to pay. If you are unable to pay the full amount of tax due with your tax return because of financial hardship, you should still file the tax return along with a "good faith" payment of as much of the tax due as you can afford to pay. If you can pay in full within 120 days, you should call 1-800-829-1040 to establish the request. Alternatively, you can apply online by going to *www.irs.gov* and entering the keyword "OPA" in the upper right-hand corner to locate the link for the "Online Payment Agreement Application." If you cannot pay within 120 days, you should complete Form 9465 to request the privilege of paying the remaining tax in installments. This form should be attached to the front of the return when it is filed. However, the IRS will impose a fee of $105 ($52 if you make your payments by electronic funds withdrawal) for entering into an installment agreement. (If your income is below a certain level, you may qualify to pay a reduced fee of $43.) You can expect a decision back from the IRS within 30 days regarding your installment request, but you still will be subject to interest and the failure-to-pay penalty on the unpaid tax.

The IRS will continue to send you a bill for the unpaid tax, interest, and penalty until the total amount is paid. After the tax is completely paid, you can request in writing that the penalty be waived due to reasonable cause because of financial hardship. The IRS has total discretion in waiving penalties and may require you to prove your financial hardship.

If your tax return is already in the formal collection process (i.e., you have been contacted by an IRS official regarding a delinquent tax liability) and you are unable to pay the tax due, you may request an installment agreement with the IRS officer. If he or she agrees, the installment agreement is made using Form 433-D, and you will be required to provide financial information. You may need to seek professional tax advice if this is the case.

Individuals Outside the United States

You are allowed an automatic 2-month extension (until June 15, 2012, if you use the calendar year) to file your 2011 return and pay any federal income tax due if:

1. You are a U.S. citizen or resident, and
2. On the due date of your return:
   a. You are living outside the United States and Puerto Rico, and your main place of business or post of duty is outside the United States and Puerto Rico, or
   b. You are in military or naval service on duty outside the United States and Puerto Rico.

However, if you pay the tax due after the regular due date (generally, April 15), interest will be charged from that date until the date the tax is paid.

If you served in a combat zone or qualified hazardous duty area, you may be eligible for a longer extension of time to file. See _Individuals Serving in Combat Zone_, later, for special rules that apply to you.

Married taxpayers. If you file a joint return, only one spouse has to qualify for this automatic extension. If you and your spouse file separate returns, this automatic extension applies only to the spouse who qualifies.

How to get the extension. To use this automatic extension, you must attach a statement to your return explaining what situation qualified you for the extension. (See the situations listed under (2), earlier.)

Extensions beyond 2 months. If you cannot file your return within the automatic 2-month extension period, you may be able to get an additional 4-month extension, for a total of 6 months. File Form 4868 and check the box on line 8.

No further extension. An extension of more than 6 months will generally not be granted. However, if you are outside the United States and meet certain tests, you may be granted a longer extension. For more information, see _When To File and Pay_ in Publication 54.

Individuals Serving in Combat Zone

The deadline for filing your tax return, paying any tax you may owe, and filing a claim for refund is automatically extended if you serve in a combat zone. This applies to members of the Armed Forces, as well as merchant marines serving aboard vessels under the operational control of the Department of Defense, Red Cross personnel, accredited correspondents, and civilians under the direction of the Armed Forces in support of the Armed Forces.

Combat zone. For purposes of the automatic extension, the term "combat zone" includes the following areas.

1. The Persian Gulf area, effective January 17, 1991.
2. The qualified hazardous duty area of the Federal Republic of Yugoslavia (Serbia/ Montenegro), Albania, the Adriatic Sea, and the Ionian Sea north of the 39th parallel, effective March 24, 1999.
3. Afghanistan, effective September 19, 2001.

See Publication 3, _Armed Forces' Tax Guide_, for information about other tax benefits available to military personnel serving in a combat zone.

TAXPLANNER

In addition to the three combat zones listed above, certain areas that support active military operations receive the same combat zone tax benefits (for example, Qualified Hazardous Duty Areas). These areas are listed at _www.irs.gov_ and can be found by entering the keyword "Combat Zone" in the upper right-hand corner. Military operations that are part of Operation Enduring Freedom and Operation Iraqi Freedom are included on the list.

Extension period. The deadline for filing your return, paying any tax due, and filing a claim for refund is extended for at least 180 days after the later of:

1. The last day you are in a combat zone or the last day the area qualifies as a combat zone, or
2. The last day of any continuous qualified hospitalization for injury from service in the combat zone.

In addition to the 180 days, your deadline is also extended by the number of days you had left to take action with the IRS when you entered the combat zone. For example, you have 3½ months (January 1–April 15) to file your tax return. Any days left in this period when you entered the combat zone (or the entire 3½ months if you entered it before the beginning of the year) are added to the 180 days. See *Extension of Deadlines* in Publication 3 for more information.

The above rules on the extension for filing your return also apply when you are deployed outside the United States (away from your permanent duty station) while participating in a designated contingency operation.

How Do I Prepare My Return?

This section explains how to get ready to fill in your tax return and when to report your income and expenses. It also explains how to complete certain sections of the form. You may find Table 1-6 helpful when you prepare your return.

Substitute tax forms. You cannot use your own version of a tax form unless it meets the requirements explained in Publication 1167, *General Rules and Specifications for Substitute Forms and Schedules*.

EXPLANATION
You may obtain tax forms via the Internet by visiting the IRS site at *www.irs.gov*.

Form W-2. If you are an employee, you should receive Form W-2 from your employer. You will need the information from this form to prepare your return. See *Form W-2* under *Credit for Withholding and Estimated Tax* in chapter 4.

Your employer is required to provide or send Form W-2 to you no later than January 31, 2012. If it is mailed, you should allow adequate time to receive it before contacting your employer. If you still do not get the form by February 15, the IRS can help you by requesting the form from your employer. When you request IRS help, be prepared to provide the following information.

- Your name, address (including ZIP code), and phone number.
- Your SSN.
- Your dates of employment.
- Your employer's name, address (including ZIP code), and phone number.

Form 1099. If you received certain types of income, you may receive a Form 1099. For example, if you received taxable interest of $10 or more, the payer is required to provide or send Form 1099 to you no later than January 31, 2012 (or by February 15, 2012, if furnished by a broker). If it is mailed, you should allow adequate time to receive it before contacting the payer. If you still do not get the form by February 15 (or by March 3, 2012, if furnished by a broker), call the IRS for help.

When Do I Report My Income and Expenses?

You must figure your taxable income on the basis of a tax year. A "tax year" is an annual accounting period used for keeping records and reporting income and expenses. You must account for your income and expenses in a way that clearly shows your taxable income. The way you do this is called an accounting method. This section explains which accounting periods and methods you can use.

Table 1-6.   **Six Steps for Preparing Your Return**

1 – Get your records together for income and expenses.
2 – Get the forms, schedules, and publications you need.
3 – Fill in your return.
4 – Check your return to make sure it is correct.
5 – Sign and date your return.
6 – Attach all required forms and schedules.

Accounting Periods

Most individual tax returns cover a calendar year—the 12 months from January 1 through December 31. If you do not use a calendar year, your accounting period is a fiscal year. A regular fiscal year is a 12-month period that ends on the last day of any month except December. A 52-53-week fiscal year varies from 52 to 53 weeks and always ends on the same day of the week.

You choose your accounting period (tax year) when you file your first income tax return. It cannot be longer than 12 months.

TAXPLANNER

To operate on a fiscal year accounting basis, you must keep your books and records based on that fiscal year. Because most individual taxpayers keep their personal financial records on a calendar year basis, it is easier to use a calendar year period. It is virtually impossible for an individual to obtain approval from the IRS to change to a fiscal year accounting period without justification. Usually, the justification must be that you are involved in a cyclical business from which self-employment or partnership income flows. Furthermore, in most cases, that income has to be your sole or principal source of income.

More information. For more information on accounting periods, including how to change your accounting period, see Publication 538, *Accounting Periods and Methods*.

Accounting Methods

Your accounting method is the way you account for your income and expenses. Most taxpayers use either the cash method or an accrual method. You choose a method when you file your first income tax return. If you want to change your accounting method after that, you generally must get IRS approval.

Cash method. If you use this method, report all items of income in the year in which you actually or constructively receive them. Generally, you deduct all expenses in the year you actually pay them. This is the method most individual taxpayers use.

EXPLANATION

Accounting methods are important because they determine when you recognize income and when you deduct expenses for tax purposes. The cash method allows you more flexibility and control over your tax liability. Individuals who do not own and operate their own business must use the cash method. However, the IRS generally will not permit you to use the cash method if you own your own business and cash method accounting doesn't clearly show your income. The cash method is generally not permitted if your business maintains inventory, or production materials are on hand at the end of the year. See IRS Publication 538, *Accounting Periods and Methods*, for more information.

TAXALERT

IRS officials have expressed the view that you may not use the cash method for any substantial business activity, even one providing only personal or professional services. The law does not support this view. Nevertheless, in conducting audits, the IRS has been aggressive in urging taxpayers to change to the accrual method of accounting.

TAXPLANNER

Generally, most taxpayers who expect to be in the same tax bracket from one year to the next and who want to reduce their current tax bill as much as possible should attempt to defer income to a subsequent year and to take deductions in the current year. If you suspect you might be in a higher tax bracket in a subsequent year, however, you would want to do just the opposite. Under current law, tax rates are scheduled to rise starting in 2013. (As of the date this book was published in October 2011, the future direction for income tax rates after the so-called Bush Tax Cuts expire at the end of 2012 have been a topic of vigorous debate within Congress and between the President and Congressional Republicans. For updated information on this and any other tax law changes that occur after publication, see our website, *ey.com/EYTaxGuide*.)

If you find yourself facing higher tax rates next year, it may make sense for you to rethink traditional tax strategies. For such taxpayers, it may be beneficial to accelerate and recognize income in an earlier year, while deferring deductions to a later year. This approach may allow you to pay tax on the accelerated income at a lower tax rate. Deductions deferred until future years could produce a greater tax benefit for you. Whether you decide to accelerate deductions into 2011, or defer them until 2012, keep in mind that in some states and cities, you may pay property, state, and local income taxes in either December or January, giving you the opportunity to pay 2 years' worth of these taxes in a single calendar year. You can also control when you make charitable contributions. To some extent, you can also control when you make interest payments on a mortgage.

For more information about tax law changes that are scheduled to take effect in 2012 and thereafter, see chapter 47, *Planning ahead for 2012 and beyond*. We also recommend that you consult your tax advisor for planning assistance in anticipation of forthcoming tax law changes.

Constructive receipt. Generally, you constructively receive income when it is credited to your account or set apart in any way that makes it available to you. You do not need to have physical possession of it. For example, interest credited to your bank account on December 31, 2011, is taxable income to you in 2011 if you could have withdrawn it in 2011 (even if the amount is not entered in your passbook or withdrawn until 2012).

TAXALERT
Profits from a brokerage account, or similar account, are fully taxable in the year you earn them. This is true even if:
1. You do not withdraw the earnings,
2. You automatically reinvest your earnings (i.e., a dividend reinvestment plan),
3. The credit balance in the account may be reduced or eliminated by losses in later years, or
4. Current profits are used to reduce or eliminate a debit balance from a prior year.

Example
You sold your ABC Company stock on December 20, 2011, realizing a gain of $5,000. You did not withdraw the cash in your account until January 5, 2012. The gain is taxable income to you for 2011.

Garnished wages. If your employer uses your wages to pay your debts, or if your wages are attached or garnisheed, the full amount is constructively received by you. You must include these wages in income for the year you would have received them.

Debts paid for you. If another person cancels or pays your debts (but not as a gift or loan), you have constructively received the amount and generally must include it in your gross income for the year. See *Canceled Debts* in chapter 12 for more information.

EXAMPLE
Your new employer pays the balance of the mortgage due on your home that is not covered by the selling price so you can move to Florida to work for him. The payments are not intended to be a gift or a loan to you. The amount your employer pays on the mortgage is income to you in the year that it is paid off.

Payment to third party. If a third party is paid income from property you own, you have constructively received the income. It is the same as if you had actually received the income and paid it to the third party.

Payment to an agent. Income an agent receives for you is income you constructively received in the year the agent receives it. If you indicate in a contract that your income is to be paid to another person, you must include the amount in your gross income when the other person receives it.

Check received or available. A valid check that was made available to you before the end of the tax year is constructively received by you in that year. A check that was "made available to you" includes a check you have already received, but not cashed or deposited. It also includes, for example, your last paycheck of the year that your employer made available for you to pick up at the office before the end of the year. It is constructively received by you in that year whether or not you pick it up before the end of the year or wait to receive it by mail after the end of the year.

No constructive receipt. There may be facts to show that you did not constructively receive income.

Example. Alice Johnson, a teacher, agreed to her school board's condition that, in her absence, she would receive only the difference between her regular salary and the salary of a substitute teacher hired by the school board. Therefore, Alice did not constructively receive the amount by which her salary was reduced to pay the substitute teacher.

More information. For more information on the determination of medical and dental expenses, see chapter 22, *Medical and dental expenses*, and Publication 502, *Medical and Dental Expenses*.

Exception

Individual Retirement Arrangements. If you qualify for a tax-deductible contribution, you may take a deduction for a contribution to an individual retirement arrangement (IRA) in one year, even though you do not make the actual cash contribution to your account until the following year; that is, you may file your tax return showing a deduction for a contribution to your IRA, although you have not yet made the contribution. The deduction is valid as long as you make the contribution on or before April 15 of the following year, even if you get a filing extension. For example, you can make a contribution to an IRA for tax year 2011 on or before April 17, 2012. For more information, see chapter 17, *Individual retirement arrangements (IRAs)*, and Publication 590, *Individual Retirement Arrangements (IRAs)*.

Accrual method. If you use an accrual method, you generally report income when you earn it, rather than when you receive it. You generally deduct your expenses when you incur them, rather than when you pay them.

Income paid in advance. An advance payment of income is generally included in gross income in the year you receive it. Your method of accounting does not matter as long as the income is available to you. An advance payment may include rent or interest you receive in advance and pay for services you will perform later.

A limited deferral until the next tax year may be allowed for certain advance payments. See Publication 538 for specific information.

Additional information. For more information on accounting methods, including how to change your accounting method, see Publication 538.

Social Security Number

You must enter your social security number (SSN) in the space provided on your return. Be sure the SSN on your return is the same as the SSN on your social security card. If you are married, enter the SSNs for both you and your spouse, whether you file jointly or separately.

If you are filing a joint return, write the SSNs in the same order as the names. Use this same order in submitting other forms and documents to the IRS.

Name change. If you changed your name because of marriage, divorce, etc., be sure to report the change to your local Social Security Administration (SSA) office before filing your return. This prevents delays in processing your return and issuing refunds. It also safeguards your future social security benefits.

Dependent's social security number. You must provide the SSN of each dependent you claim, regardless of the dependent's age. This requirement applies to all dependents (not just your children) claimed on your tax return.

Exception. If your child was born and died in 2011 and you do not have an SSN for the child, enter "DIED" in column (2) of line 6c (Form 1040 or 1040A) and attach a copy of the child's birth certificate, death certificate, or hospital records.

No social security number. File Form SS-5, Application for a Social Security Card, with your local SSA office to get an SSN for yourself or your dependent. It usually takes about 2 weeks to get an SSN. If you or your dependent is not eligible for an SSN, see *Individual taxpayer identification number (ITIN)*, later.

If you are a U.S. citizen or resident alien, you must show proof of age, identity, and citizenship or alien status with your Form SS-5. If you are 12 or older and have never been assigned an SSN, you must appear in person with this proof at an SSA office.

Form SS-5 is available at any SSA office, on the Internet at *www.socialsecurity.gov*, or by calling 1-800-772-1213. If you have any questions about which documents you can use as proof of age, identity, or citizenship, contact your SSA office.

If your dependent does not have an SSN by the time your return is due, you may want to ask for an extension of time to file, as explained earlier under *When Do I Have To File*.

If you do not provide a required SSN or if you provide an incorrect SSN, your tax may be increased and any refund may be reduced.

Adoption taxpayer identification number (ATIN). If you are in the process of adopting a child who is a U.S. citizen or resident and cannot get an SSN for the child until the adoption is final, you can apply for an ATIN to use instead of an SSN.

File Form W-7A, Application for Taxpayer Identification Number for Pending U.S. Adoptions, with the IRS to get an ATIN if all of the following are true.

- You have a child living with you who was placed in your home for legal adoption.
- You cannot get the child's existing SSN even though you have made a reasonable attempt to get it from the birth parents, the placement agency, and other persons.
- You cannot get an SSN for the child from the SSA because, for example, the adoption is not final.
- You are eligible to claim the child as a dependent on your tax return.

After the adoption is final, you must apply for an SSN for the child. You cannot continue using the ATIN.

See Form W-7A for more information.

Nonresident alien spouse. If your spouse is a nonresident alien, your spouse must have either an SSN or an ITIN if:

- You file a joint return,
- You file a separate return and claim an exemption for your spouse, or
- Your spouse is filing a separate return.

If your spouse is not eligible for an SSN, see the next discussion.

Tip

If you are applying for an ITIN for yourself, your spouse, or a dependent in order to file your tax return, attach your completed tax return to your Form W-7. See the Form W-7 instructions for how and where to file.

Individual taxpayer identification number (ITIN). The IRS will issue you an ITIN if you are a nonresident or resident alien and you do not have and are not eligible to get an SSN. This also applies to an alien spouse or dependent. To apply for an ITIN, file Form W-7 with the IRS. It usually takes about 6 weeks to get an ITIN. Enter the ITIN on your tax return wherever an SSN is requested.

Penalty for not providing social security number. If you do not include your SSN or the SSN of your spouse or dependent as required, you may have to pay a penalty. See the discussion on *Penalties*, later, for more information.

SSN on correspondence. If you write to the IRS about your tax account, be sure to include your SSN (and the name and SSN of your spouse, if you filed a joint return) in your correspondence. Because your SSN is used to identify your account, this helps the IRS respond to your correspondence promptly.

Caution

An ITIN is for tax use only. It does not entitle you or your dependent to social security benefits or change the employment or immigration status of either of you under U.S. law.

Presidential Election Campaign Fund

This fund helps pay for Presidential election campaigns. The fund reduces candidates' dependence on large contributions from individuals and groups and places candidates on an equal financial footing in the general election. If you want $3 to go to this fund, check the box. If you are filing a joint return, your spouse can also have $3 go to the fund. If you check a box, your tax or refund will not change.

Computations

The following information on entering numbers on your tax return may be useful in making the return easier to complete.

Rounding off dollars. You may round off cents to whole dollars on your return and schedules. If you do round to whole dollars, you must round all amounts. To round, drop amounts under 50 cents and increase amounts from 50 to 99 cents to the next dollar. For example, $1.39 becomes $1 and $2.50 becomes $3.

If you have to add two or more amounts to figure the amount to enter on a line, include cents when adding the amounts and round off only the total.

Example. You receive two Forms W-2: one showing wages of $5,000.55 and one showing wages of $18,500.73. On Form 1040, line 7, you would enter $23,501 ($5,000.55 + $18,500.73 = $23,501.28), not $23,502 ($5,001 + $18,501).

Equal amounts. If you are asked to enter the smaller or larger of two equal amounts, enter that amount.

Example. Line 1 is $500. Line 3 is $500. Line 5 asks you to enter the smaller of line 1 or 3. Enter $500 on line 5.

Negative amounts. If you need to enter a negative amount, put the amount in parentheses rather than using a minus sign. To combine positive and negative amounts, add all the positive amounts together and then subtract the negative amounts.

Attachments

Depending on the form you file and the items reported on your return, you may have to complete additional schedules and forms and attach them to your return.

Form W-2. Form W-2 is a statement from your employer of wages and other compensation paid to you and taxes withheld from your pay. You should have a Form W-2 from each employer. Be sure to attach a copy of Form W-2 in the place indicated on the front page of your return. Attach it only to the front page of your return, not to any attachments. For more information, see Form W-2 in chapter 4.

If you received a Form 1099-R, Distributions From Pensions, Annuities, Retirement or Profit-Sharing Plans, IRAs, Insurance Contracts, etc., showing federal income tax withheld, attach a copy of that form in the place indicated on the front page of your return.

Form 1040EZ. There are no additional schedules to file with Form 1040EZ.

Form 1040A. Attach any forms and schedules behind Form 1040A in order of the "Attachment Sequence Number" shown in the upper right corner of the form or schedule. Then arrange all other statements or attachments in the same order as the forms and schedules they relate to and attach them last. Do not attach items unless required to do so.

Form 1040. Attach any forms and schedules behind Form 1040 in order of the "Attachment Sequence Number" shown in the upper right corner of the form or schedule. Then arrange all other statements or attachments in the same order as the forms and schedules they relate to and attach them last. Do not attach items unless required to do so.

> **TAXPLANNER**
>
> If you fail to organize your return according to the prescribed sequence numbers, the IRS, upon receipt of your return, will disassemble it and put it back together in the proper order. This procedure may result in the loss of a page of your return, causing some delay in its processing. To avoid this problem, you can electronically file your return. See chapter 45, *Everything you need to know about e-filing.*

Third Party Designee

You can authorize the IRS to discuss your return with your preparer, a friend, family member, or any other person you choose. If you check the "Yes" box in the *Third party designee* area of your 2011 tax return and provide the information required, you are authorizing:

1. The IRS to call the designee to answer any questions that arise during the processing of your return, and
2. The designee to
   a. Give information that is missing from your return to the IRS,
   b. Call the IRS for information about the processing of your return or the status of your refund or payments,
   c. Receive copies of notices or transcripts related to your return, upon request, and
   d. Respond to certain IRS notices about math errors, offsets (see *Refunds*, later), and return preparation.

The authorization will automatically end no later than the due date (without any extensions) for filing your 2012 tax return. This is April 15, 2013, for most people.

See your form instructions for more information.

Signatures

You must sign and date your return. If you file a joint return, both you and your spouse must sign the return, even if only one of you had income.

If you are due a refund, it cannot be issued unless you have signed your return.

Enter your occupation in the space provided in the signature section. If you file a joint return, enter both your occupation and your spouse's occupation. Entering your daytime phone number may help speed the processing of your return.

Tip

You may be able to file a paperless return using IRS e-file. There's nothing to sign, attach, or mail, not even your Forms W-2.

Caution

If you file a joint return, both spouses are generally liable for the tax, and the entire tax liability may be assessed against either spouse. See chapter 2.

Tip

If you e-file *your return, you can use an electronic signature to sign your return. See* <u>Does My Return Have To Be on Paper</u>, *earlier.*

When someone can sign for you. You can appoint an agent to sign your return if you are:
1. Unable to sign the return because of disease or injury,
2. Absent from the United States for a continuous period of at least 60 days before the due date for filing your return, or
3. Given permission to do so by the IRS office in your area.

Power of attorney. A return signed by an agent in any of these cases must have a power of attorney (POA) attached that authorizes the agent to sign for you. You can use a POA that states that the agent is granted authority to sign the return, or you can use Form 2848, Power of Attorney and Declaration of Representative. Part I of Form 2848 must state that the agent is granted authority to sign the return.

Unable to sign. If the taxpayer is mentally incompetent and cannot sign the return, it must be signed by a court-appointed representative who can act for the taxpayer.

If the taxpayer is mentally competent but physically unable to sign the return or POA, a valid "signature" is defined under state law. It can be anything that clearly indicates the taxpayer's intent to sign. For example, the taxpayer's "X" with the signatures of two witnesses might be considered a valid signature under a state's law.

Spouse unable to sign. If your spouse is unable to sign for any reason, see *Signing a joint return* in chapter 2.

Child's return. If a child has to file a tax return but cannot sign the return, the child's parent, guardian, or another legally responsible person must sign the child's name, followed by the words "By (your signature), parent for minor child."

Paid Preparer

Generally, anyone you pay to prepare, assist in preparing, or review your tax return must sign it and fill in the other blanks, including their Preparer Tax Identification Number (PTIN), in the paid preparer's area of your return.

A paid preparer can sign the return manually or use a rubber stamp, mechanical device, or computer software program. The preparer is personally responsible for affixing his or her signature to the return.

If the preparer is self-employed (that is, not employed by any person or business to prepare the return), he or she should check the self-employed box in the *Paid Preparer Use Only* space on the return.

The preparer must give you a copy of your return in addition to the copy filed with the IRS.

If you prepare your own return, leave this area blank. If another person prepares your return and does not charge you, that person should not sign your return.

If you have questions about whether a preparer must sign your return, contact any IRS office.

EXPLANATION
Paid preparer authorization. In the signature area of your 2011 tax return, you are asked whether the IRS can discuss the return with the paid preparer who signed the return. If you check the "Yes" box, you are authorizing:
1. The IRS to call the paid preparer to answer any questions that arise during the processing of your return, and
2. The paid preparer to:
   a. Give information that is missing from your return to the IRS,
   b. Call the IRS for information about the processing of your return or the status of your refund or payments, and
   c. Respond to certain IRS notices that you have shown the preparer. IRS notices about math errors, offsets (see *Refunds*, later), and return preparation will be sent to you, not the preparer.

The authorization cannot be revoked. However, for your 2011 tax return, it will automatically end no later than the due date (without any extensions) for filing your 2012 tax return. This is April 15, 2013, for most people. See your form instructions for more information.

TAXALERT
A person who is paid to prepare all or a substantial portion of your income tax return must sign it. In addition, the IRS says that a tax consultant who is paid to review a tax return that you have already prepared and signed is also considered a tax return preparer and must sign it.

If an individual who prepares your return refuses to sign it, you are probably dealing with someone you should not rely on. While you could still file the return, you should probably consider using another tax preparer. If you have to pay the first preparer, you should report the matter to the IRS.

Refunds

When you complete your return, you will determine if you paid more income tax than you owed. If so, you can get a refund of the amount you overpaid or, if you file Form 1040 or Form 1040A, you can choose to apply all or part of the overpayment to your next year's (2012) estimated tax. You cannot have your overpayment applied to your 2012 estimated tax if you file Form 1040EZ.

Follow the form instructions to complete the entries to claim your refund and/or to apply your overpayment to your 2012 estimated tax.

> ### EXPLANATION
> If you choose to apply all or part of your overpayment to your next year's estimated tax, the estimated tax installment payment is considered made on April 15. Your first installment may be reduced accordingly. For more information, see chapter 4, *Tax withholding and estimated tax*, and Publication 505, *Tax Withholding and Estimated Tax*.

Instead of getting a paper check you may be able to have your refund deposited directly into your checking or savings account, including an individual retirement arrangement. Follow the form instructions to request direct deposit.

If the direct deposit cannot be done, the IRS will send a check instead.

TreasuryDirect®. You can request a deposit of your refund to a TreasuryDirect® online account to buy U.S. Treasury marketable securities and savings bonds. For more information, go to *www.treasurydirect.gov*.

Split refunds. If you choose direct deposit, you may be able to split the refund and have it deposited among two or three accounts or you can use it to buy up to $5,000 in paper series I savings bonds. Complete Form 8888, Allocation of Refund (Including Savings Bond Purchases), and attach it to your return.

Overpayment less than one dollar. If your overpayment is less than one dollar, you will not get a refund unless you ask for it in writing.

Cashing your refund check. Cash your tax refund check soon after you receive it. Checks not cashed within 12 months of the date they are issued will be canceled and the proceeds returned to the IRS.

If your check has been canceled, you can apply to the IRS to have it reissued.

Refund more or less than expected. If you receive a check for a refund you are not entitled to, or for an overpayment that should have been credited to estimated tax, do not cash the check. Call the IRS.

If you receive a check for more than the refund you claimed, do not cash the check until you receive a notice explaining the difference.

If your refund check is for less than you claimed, it should be accompanied by a notice explaining the difference. Cashing the check does not stop you from claiming an additional amount of refund.

If you did not receive a notice and you have any questions about the amount of your refund, you should wait 2 weeks. If you still have not received a notice, call the IRS.

Offset against debts. If you are due a refund but have not paid certain amounts you owe, all or part of your refund may be used to pay all or part of the past-due amount. This includes past-due federal income tax, other federal debts (such as student loans), state income tax, and child and spousal support payments. You will be notified if the refund you claimed has been offset against your debts.

Joint return and injured spouse. When a joint return is filed and only one spouse owes a past-due amount, the other spouse can be considered an injured spouse. An injured spouse should file Form 8379, Injured Spouse Allocation, if both of the following apply and the spouse wants a refund of his or her share of the overpayment shown on the joint return.

1. You are not legally obligated to pay the past-due amount.
2. You made and reported tax payments (such as federal income tax withheld from your wages or estimated tax payments), or claimed a refundable tax credit (see the credits listed under *Who Should File*, earlier).

Note. If the injured spouse's residence was in a community property state at any time during the tax year, then the injured spouse must only meet (1) above.

Caution

If you choose to have a 2011 overpayment applied to your 2012 estimated tax, you cannot change your mind and have any of it refunded to you after the due date (without extensions) of your 2011 return.

Tip

If your refund for 2011 is large, you may want to decrease the amount of income tax withheld from your pay in 2012. See chapter 4 for more information.

An injured spouse claim is different from an innocent spouse relief request. An injured spouse uses Form 8379 to request the division of the tax overpayment attributed to each spouse. An innocent spouse uses Form 8857, Request for Innocent Spouse Relief, to request relief from joint liability for tax, interest, and penalties on a joint return for items of the other spouse (or former spouse) that were incorrectly reported on the joint return. For information on innocent spouses, see <u>Relief from joint responsibility</u> *under* Filing a Joint Return *in chapter 2.*

Caution

If you do not pay your tax when due, you may have to pay a failure-to-pay penalty. See Penalties, *later. For more information about your balance due, see Publication 594,* The IRS Collection Process.

Tip

If the amount you owe for 2011 is large, you may want to increase the amount of income tax withheld from your pay or make estimated tax payments for 2012. See <u>chapter 4</u> *for more information.*

Tip

You do not have to pay if the amount you owe is less than $1.

If you have not filed your joint return and you know that your joint refund will be offset, file Form 8379 with your return. You should receive your refund within 14 weeks from the date the paper return is filed or within 11 weeks from the date the return is filed electronically.

If you filed your joint return and your joint refund was offset, file Form 8379 by itself. When filed after offset, it can take up to 8 weeks to receive your refund. Do not attach the previously filed tax return, but do include copies of all Forms W-2 and W-2G for both spouses and any Forms 1099 that show income tax withheld. The processing of Form 8379 may be delayed if these forms are not attached, or if the form is incomplete when filed.

A separate Form 8379 must be filed for each tax year to be considered.

Amount You Owe

When you complete your return, you will determine if you have paid the full amount of tax that you owe. If you owe additional tax, you should pay it with your return.

If the IRS figures your tax for you, you will receive a bill for any tax that is due. You should pay this bill within 30 days (or by the due date of your return, if later). See *Tax Figured by IRS* in chapter 30.

How To Pay

If you have an amount due on your tax return, you can pay by check, money order, credit or debit card. If you filed electronically, you also may be able to make your payment electronically.

Check or money order. If you pay by check or money order, make it out to the "United States Treasury." Show your correct name, address, SSN, daytime phone number, and the tax year and form number on the front of your check or money order. If you are filing a joint return, enter the SSN shown first on your tax return.

For example, if you file Form 1040 for 2011 and you owe additional tax, show your name, address, SSN, daytime phone number, and "2011 Form 1040" on the front of your check or money order. If you file an amended return (Form 1040X) for 2010 and you owe tax, show your name, address, SSN, daytime phone number, and "2010 Form 1040X" on the front of your check or money order.

Enclose your payment with your return, but do not attach it to the form. If you filed Form 1040 or Form 1040A, complete Form 1040-V, Payment Voucher, and enclose it with your payment and return. Although you do not have to use Form 1040-V, doing so allows us to process your payment more accurately and efficiently. Follow the instructions that come with the form.

Do not mail cash with your return. If you pay cash at an IRS office, keep the receipt as part of your records.

Payment not honored. If your check, money order, or any other commercial instrument for payment is not honored by your bank (or other financial institution) and the IRS does not receive the funds, you still owe the tax. In addition, you may be subject to a dishonored payment penalty.

Electronic payment options. Electronic payment options are convenient, safe, and secure methods for paying individual income taxes. There's no check to write, money order to buy, or voucher to mail. Payments can be made 24 hours a day, 7 days a week.

Credit or debit card. For information on paying your taxes with a credit or debit card, go to *www.irs.gov/e-pay*.

TAXPLANNER

Be careful about paying your taxes by credit card. Most of the payment options demand that you pay a "convenience fee" for using your card. Also, use caution if you won't be paying off your balance right away. The interest your credit card charges may be much higher than the interest the IRS charges for late payment. The IRS e-pay service providers are listed below. As of the date this book went to press, the convenience fee for paying by credit card for both Link2Gov and Official Payments Corporation was 2.35% of the payment made, and the fee for RBS WorldPay was 1.95% of the payment made. If you choose to pay your tax liability with a debit card, each provider charges a flat fee per transaction rather than a convenience fee. This flat fee ranges from $3.89 to $3.95 per transaction. Since both the convenience fee and the flat fee are subject to change, you should contact the service providers for the most up-to-date information before deciding if paying by credit or debit card makes sense for you. For additional information, go to the IRS website at *www.irs.gov* and type in "pay taxes by credit card" in the search box in the upper right-hand corner of the screen.

Electronic funds withdrawal. You can *e-file* and pay in a single step by authorizing an electronic funds withdrawal from your checking or savings account. If you select this payment option, you will need to have your account number, your financial institution's routing transit number, and account type (checking or savings). You can schedule the payment for any future date up to and including the return due date.

Electronic Federal Tax Payment System (EFTPS). EFTPS is a free tax payment system that all individual and business taxpayers can use. You can make payments online or by phone.

Here are just a few of the benefits of this easy-to-use system.

- Convenient and flexible. You can use it to schedule payments in advance. For example, you can schedule estimated tax payments (Form 1040-ES) or installment agreement payments weekly, monthly, or quarterly.
- Fast and accurate. You can make a tax payment in minutes. Because there are verification steps along the way, you can check and review your information before sending it.
- Safe and secure. It offers the highest available levels of security. Every transaction receives an immediate confirmation.

For more information or details on enrolling, visit *www.irs.gov/e-payor* or *www.eftps.gov* or call EFTPS Customer Service at 1-800-316-6541 (individual) or 1-800-555-4477 (business). TTY/TDD help is available by calling 1-800-733-4829.

Estimated tax payments. Do not include any 2012 estimated tax payment in the payment for your 2011 income tax return. See chapter 4 for information on how to pay estimated tax.

Interest

Interest is charged on tax you do not pay by the due date of your return. Interest is charged even if you get an extension of time for filing.

Interest on penalties. Interest is charged on the failure-to-file penalty, the accuracy-related penalty, and the fraud penalty from the due date of the return (including extensions) to the date of payment. Interest on other penalties starts on the date of notice and demand, but is not charged on penalties paid within 21 calendar days from the date of the notice (or within 10 business days if the notice is for $100,000 or more).

Interest due to IRS error or delay. All or part of any interest you were charged can be forgiven if the interest is due to an unreasonable error or delay by an officer or employee of the IRS in performing a ministerial or managerial act.

A ministerial act is a procedural or mechanical act that occurs during the processing of your case. A managerial act includes personnel transfers and extended personnel training. A decision concerning the proper application of federal tax law is not a ministerial or managerial act.

The interest can be forgiven only if you are not responsible in any important way for the error or delay and the IRS has notified you in writing of the deficiency or payment. For more information, see Publication 556, *Examination of Returns, Appeal Rights, and Claims for Refund*.

Interest and certain penalties may also be suspended for a limited period if you filed your return by the due date (including extensions) and the IRS does not provide you with a notice specifically stating your liability and the basis for it before the close of the 36-month period beginning on the later of:

- The date the return is filed, or
- The due date of the return without regard to extensions.

For more information, see Publication 556.

> **Caution**
>
> *Be sure to check with your financial institution to make sure that an electronic funds withdrawal is allowed and to get the correct routing and account numbers.*

> **Tip**
>
> *If the IRS figures your tax for you, interest cannot start earlier than the 31st day after the IRS sends you a bill. For information, see* Tax Figured by IRS *in chapter 30.*

TAXPLANNER

If you owe additional tax, it is not a good idea to file your return by January 31. As long as you have planned well and have paid enough in estimated taxes to avoid a penalty, you would be better off keeping any other tax you owe in your savings account, where it will earn interest for 2½ months, rather than paying your tax bill early.

Installment Agreement

If you cannot pay the full amount due with your return, you can ask to make monthly installment payments for the full or a partial amount. However, you will be charged interest and may be charged a late payment penalty on the tax not paid by the date your return is due, even if your request to pay in installments is granted. If your request is granted, you must also pay a fee. To limit the interest and penalty charges, pay as much of the tax as possible with your return. But before requesting an installment agreement, you should consider other less costly alternatives, such as a bank loan.

To ask for an installment agreement, use Form 9465, Installment Agreement Request. You should receive a response to your request within 30 days. But if you file your return after March 31, it may take longer for a reply.

In addition to paying by check or money order, you can use a credit or debit card or EFTPS to make installment agreement payments. See *How To Pay*, earlier.

TAXPLANNER

An extension of time to file is not an extension of time to pay. If you are unable to pay the full amount of tax due with your tax return because of financial hardship, you should still file the tax return along with a "good faith" payment of as much of the tax due as you can afford to pay. If you can pay in full within 120 days, you should call 1-800-829-1040 to establish the request. Alternatively, you can apply online by going to *www.irs.gov* and entering the keyword "OPA" in the upper right-hand corner to locate the link for the "Online Payment Agreement Application." If you cannot pay within 120 days, you should complete Form 9465 to request the privilege of paying the remaining tax in installments. This form should be attached to the front of the return when it is filed. However, the IRS will impose a fee of $105 ($52 if you make your payments by electronic funds withdrawal) for entering into an installment agreement. (If your income is below a certain level, you may qualify to pay a reduced fee of $43.) You can expect a decision back from the IRS within 30 days regarding your installment request, but **you still will be subject to interest and the failure-to-pay penalty on the unpaid tax.**

The IRS will continue to send you a bill for the unpaid tax, interest, and penalty until the total amount is paid. After the tax is completely paid, you can request in writing that the penalty be waived due to reasonable cause because of financial hardship. The IRS has total discretion in waiving penalties and may require you to prove your financial hardship.

If your tax return is already in the formal collection process (i.e., you have been contacted by an IRS official regarding a delinquent tax liability) and you are unable to pay the tax due, you may request an installment agreement with the IRS officer. If he or she agrees, the installment agreement is made using Form 433-D, and you will be required to provide financial information. You may need to seek professional tax advice if this is the case.

Guaranteed availability of installment agreement. The IRS must agree to accept the full payment of your tax liability in installments if, as of the date you offer to enter into the agreement:
1. Your total taxes (not counting interest, penalties, additions to the tax, or additional amounts) do not exceed $10,000,
2. In the last 5 years, you (and your spouse if the liability relates to a joint return) have not:
   a. Failed to file any required income tax return,
   b. Failed to pay any tax shown on any such return, or
   c. Entered into an installment agreement for the payment of any income tax,
3. You show you cannot pay your income tax in full when due,
4. The tax will be paid in full in 3 years or less, and
5. You agree to comply with the tax laws while your agreement is in effect.

Online payment agreement (OPA) application. You may be able to apply online for a payment agreement if you owe federal tax, interest, and penalties. If you have received a balance due notice from the IRS and you cannot pay in full, you may request a payment agreement. The OPA application allows you, or your authorized representative, to self-qualify for and apply for a payment agreement, receive notification of approval, and arrange a payment schedule.

To use the OPA application, you must have filed all required tax returns. You should also have the following information available:
- Balance due notice from the IRS.
- Social security number or individual taxpayer identification number.
- Personal identification number, which can be established online using the caller identification number from the balance due notice.

For more information, go to *www.irs.gov*, use the pull-down menu under "I need to..." and select "Set Up a Payment Plan." If you just want to go to the OPA application, click on it under the section on *Online Services*.

Gift To Reduce Debt Held by the Public

You can make a contribution (gift) to reduce debt held by the public. If you wish to do so, make a separate check payable to "Bureau of the Public Debt." Send your check to:

Bureau of the Public Debt
ATTN: Department G
P.O. Box 2188
Parkersburg, WV 26106-2188.

Or, enclose your separate check in the envelope with your income tax return. Do not add this gift to any tax you owe.

You can deduct this gift as a charitable contribution on next year's tax return if you itemize your deductions on Schedule A (Form 1040).

Name and Address

After you have completed your return, fill in your name and address in the appropriate area of the Form 1040, Form 1040A, or Form 1040EZ.

P.O. box. If your post office does not deliver mail to your street address and you have a P.O. box, print your P.O. box number on the line for your present home address instead of your street address.

Foreign address. If your address is outside the United States or its possessions or territories, enter the information on the line for "City, town or post office, state, and ZIP code" in the following order:
1. City,
2. Province or state, and
3. Name of foreign country. (Do not abbreviate the name of the country.)

Follow the country's practice for entering the postal code.

> ### TAXALERT
> You are not excused from filing a return because you have not received the proper forms from the IRS. The IRS has free tax forms and publications on a wide variety of topics. If you need IRS forms or information, try one of these easy options:
> - **Internet:** You can access forms and publications on the IRS website 24 hours a day, 7 days a week, at *www.irs.gov*.
> - **Phone:** Call 1-800-TAX-FORM (800-829-3676) to order current year forms, instructions, and publications, and prior year forms and instructions. You should receive your order within 10 days.
> - **Locations in your community:** During the tax-filing season, many libraries and post offices offer free tax forms to taxpayers. Some libraries also have copies of commonly requested publications. Braille materials may also be available. Many large grocery stores, copy centers, and office supply stores have forms you can photocopy or print from a CD.
> - **Mail:** Order your tax forms and publications from the IRS National Distribution Center, 1201 N. Mitsubishi Motorway, Bloomington, IL, 61705-6613. You should receive your products 10 days after receipt of your order.

Where Do I File?

After you complete your return, you must send it to the IRS. You can mail it or you may be able to file it electronically. See *Does My Return Have To Be on Paper*, earlier.

Mailing your return. Mail your return to the address shown in your instructions.

What Happens After I File?

After you send your return to the IRS, you may have some questions. This section discusses concerns you may have about recordkeeping, your refund, and what to do if you move.

What Records Should I Keep?

You must keep records so that you can prepare a complete and accurate income tax return. The law does not require any special form of records. However, you should keep all receipts, canceled checks or other proof of payment, and any other records to support any deductions or credits you claim.

If you file a claim for refund, you must be able to prove by your records that you have overpaid your tax.

How long to keep records. You must keep your records for as long as they are important for the federal tax law.

Keep records that support an item of income or a deduction appearing on a return until the period of limitations for the return runs out. (A period of limitations is the period of time after which no legal action can be brought.) For assessment of tax you owe, this generally is 3 years from the date you filed the return. For filing a claim for credit or refund, this generally is 3 years from the date you filed the original return, or 2 years from the date you paid the tax, whichever is later. Returns filed before the due date are treated as filed on the due date.

If you did not report income that you should have reported on your return, and it is more than 25% of the income shown on the return, the period of limitations does not run out until 6 years after you filed the return. If a return is false or fraudulent with intent to evade tax, or if no return is filed, an action can generally be brought at any time.

You may need to keep records relating to the basis of property longer than the period of limitations. Keep those records as long as they are important in figuring the basis of the original or replacement property. Generally, this means for as long as you own the property and, after you dispose of it, for the period of limitations that applies to you. See chapter 13 for information on basis.

Note. If you receive a Form W-2, keep Copy C until you begin receiving social security benefits. This will help protect your benefits in case there is a question about your work record or earnings in a particular year. Review the information shown on your annual (for workers over age 25) Social Security Statement.

Copies of returns. You should keep copies of tax returns you have filed and the tax forms package as part of your records. They may be helpful in amending filed returns or preparing future ones.

If you need a copy of a prior year tax return, you can get it from the IRS. Use Form 4506, Request for Copy of Tax Return. There is a charge for a copy of a return, which you must pay with Form 4506. It may take up to 60 calendar days to process your request.

Transcript of tax return. If you just need information from your return, you can quickly request transcripts by using our automated self-service tools. Visit us at *www.irs.gov* and click on "Order a Transcript" or call 1-800-908-9946. You can also use Form 4506-T, Request for Transcript of Tax Return, or Form 4506T-EZ, Short Form Request for Transcript of Tax Return. There is no fee for a transcript.

More information. For more information on recordkeeping, see Publication 552, *Record-keeping for Individuals*.

Special rules allow for basis to be stepped up to specified limits on certain property inherited from a decedent who died during 2010. When receiving property as a gift, the taxpayer must know the donor's adjusted basis as well as the fair market value at the time of the gift in order to properly determine the basis used in calculating the gain or loss upon disposition. For more information, see chapter 44, *Estate and gift tax planning*.

Knowing the donor's basis, you can easily determine your gain or loss when you sell the property. See chapter 13, *Basis of property*, for more details on determining gains and losses from the sale of property.

Example

Your parents buy a house for you as a wedding present. You sell the house 10 years later. The only record of the initial transaction is in the county real estate records. You believe there were other costs associated with the purchase but you cannot find any records of them. If you claim the additional unsupported costs and the IRS examines your return for the year of the sale, it's likely that those costs will not be allowed. If you claim the additional costs and do not disclose on your return the lack of records to substantiate them, you could be subject to a penalty.

Refund Information

You can go online to check the status of your 2011 refund 72 hours after IRS acknowledges receipt of your e-filed return, or 3 to 4 weeks after you mail a paper return. If you filed Form 8379 with your return, allow 14 weeks (11 weeks if you filed electronically) before checking your refund status. Be sure to have a copy of your 2011 tax return available because you will need to know the filing status, the first SSN shown on the return, and the exact whole-dollar amount of the refund. To check on your refund, do one of the following.

- Go to *www.irs.gov*, and click on "Where's My Refund?"
- Call 1-800-829-4477 24 hours a day, 7 days a week for automated refund information.
- Call 1-800-829-1954 during the hours shown in your form instructions.

Interest on Refunds

If you are due a refund, you may get interest on it. The interest rates are adjusted quarterly.

If the refund is made within 45 days after the due date of your return, no interest will be paid. If you file your return after the due date (including extensions), no interest will be paid if the refund is made within 45 days after the date you filed. If the refund is not made within this 45-day period, interest will be paid from the due date of the return or from the date you filed, whichever is later.

Accepting a refund check does not change your right to claim an additional refund and interest. File your claim within the period of time that applies. See *Amended Returns and Claims for Refund*, later. If you do not accept a refund check, no more interest will be paid on the overpayment included in the check.

Interest on erroneous refund. All or part of any interest you were charged on an erroneous refund generally will be forgiven. Any interest charged for the period before demand for repayment was made will be forgiven unless:

1. You, or a person related to you, caused the erroneous refund in any way, or
2. The refund is more than $50,000.

For example, if you claimed a refund of $100 on your return, but the IRS made an error and sent you $1,000, you would not be charged interest for the time you held the $900 difference. You must, however, repay the $900 when the IRS asks.

Change of Address

If you have moved, file your return using your new address.

If you move after you filed your return, you should give the IRS clear and concise notification of your change of address. The notification may be written, electronic, or oral. Send written notification to the Internal Revenue Service Center serving your old address. You can use Form 8822, Change of Address. If you are expecting a refund, also notify the post office serving your old address. This will help in forwarding your check to your new address (unless you chose direct deposit of your refund). For more information, see Revenue Procedure 2010-16, 2010-19 I.R.B. 664, available at *www.irs.gov/irb/2010-19_IRB/ar07.html*.

Be sure to include your SSN (and the name and SSN of your spouse, if you filed a joint return) in any correspondence with the IRS.

What If I Made a Mistake?

Errors may delay your refund or result in notices being sent to you. If you discover an error, you can file an amended return or claim for refund.

Amended Returns and Claims for Refund

You should correct your return if, after you have filed it, you find that:

1. You did not report some income,
2. You claimed deductions or credits you should not have claimed,
3. You did not claim deductions or credits you could have claimed, or
4. You should have claimed a different filing status. (Once you file a joint return, you cannot choose to file separate returns for that year after the due date of the return. However, an executor may be able to make this change for a deceased spouse.)

If you need a copy of your return, see *Copies of returns* under *What Records Should I Keep*, earlier in this chapter.

Form 1040X. Use Form 1040X, Amended U.S. Individual Income Tax Return, to correct a return you have already filed. An amended tax return cannot be filed electronically under the e-file system.

Completing Form 1040X. On Form 1040X, enter your income, deductions, and credits as you originally reported them on your return, the changes you are making, and the corrected amounts. Then figure the tax on the corrected amount of taxable income and the amount you owe or your refund.

If you owe tax, pay the full amount with Form 1040X. The tax owed will not be subtracted from any amount you had credited to your estimated tax.

If you cannot pay the full amount due with your return, you can ask to make monthly installment payments. See *Installment Agreement*, earlier.

If you overpaid tax, you can have all or part of the overpayment refunded to you, or you can apply all or part of it to your estimated tax. If you choose to get a refund, it will be sent separately from any refund shown on your original return.

Filing Form 1040X. After you finish your Form 1040X, check it to be sure that it is complete. Do not forget to show the year of your original return and explain all changes you made. Be sure to attach any forms or schedules needed to explain your changes. Mail your Form 1040X to the Internal Revenue Service Center serving the area where you now live (as shown in the instructions to the form). However, if you are filing Form 1040X in response to a notice you received from the IRS, mail it to the address shown on the notice.

File a separate form for each tax year involved.

Time for filing a claim for refund. Generally, you must file your claim for a credit or refund within 3 years after the date you filed your original return or within 2 years after the date you paid the tax, whichever is later. Returns filed before the due date (without regard to extensions) are considered filed on the due date (even if the due date was a Saturday, Sunday, or legal holiday). These time periods are suspended while you are financially disabled, discussed later.

If the last day for claiming a credit or refund is a Saturday, Sunday, or legal holiday, you can file the claim on the next business day.

If you do not file a claim within this period, you may not be entitled to a credit or a refund.

Protective claim for refund. Generally, a protective claim is a formal claim or amended return for credit or refund normally based on current litigation or expected changes in tax law or other legislation. You file a protective claim when your right to a refund is contingent on future events and may not be determinable until after the statute of limitations expires. A valid protective claim does not have to list a particular dollar amount or demand an immediate refund. However, a valid protective claim must:

- Be in writing and signed,
- Include your name, address, SSN or ITIN, and other contact information,
- Identify and describe the contingencies affecting the claim,
- Clearly alert the IRS to the essential nature of the claim, and
- Identify the specific year(s) for which a refund is sought.

Mail your protective claim for refund to the address listed in the instructions for Form 1040X, under *Where To File*.

Generally, the IRS will delay action on the protective claim until the contingency is resolved.

Limit on amount of refund. If you file your claim within 3 years after the date you filed your return, the credit or refund cannot be more than the part of the tax paid within the 3-year period (plus any extension of time for filing your return) immediately before you filed the claim. This time period is suspended while you are financially disabled, discussed later.

Tax paid. Payments, including estimated tax payments, made before the due date (without regard to extensions) of the original return are considered paid on the due date. For example, income tax withheld during the year is considered paid on the due date of the return, April 15 for most taxpayers.

Example 1. You made estimated tax payments of $500 and got an automatic extension of time to October 15, 2009, to file your 2008 income tax return. When you filed your return on that date, you paid an additional $200 tax. On October 15, 2012, you filed an amended return and claimed a refund of $700. Because you filed your claim within 3 years after you filed your original return, you can get a refund of up to $700, the tax paid within the 3 years plus the 6-month extension period immediately before you filed the claim.

Example 2. The situation is the same as in *Example 1*, except you filed your return on October 30, 2009, 2 weeks after the extension period ended. You paid an additional $200 on that date. On October 30, 2012, you filed an amended return and claimed a refund of $700. Although you filed your claim within 3 years from the date you filed your original return, the refund was limited to $200, the tax paid within the 3 years plus the 6-month extension period immediately before you filed the claim. The estimated tax of $500 paid before that period cannot be refunded or credited.

If you file a claim more than 3 years after you file your return, the credit or refund cannot be more than the tax you paid within the 2 years immediately before you file the claim.

Example. You filed your 2008 tax return on April 15, 2009. You paid taxes of $500. On November 3, 2010, after an examination of your 2008 return, you had to pay an additional tax of $200. On May 14, 2012, you file a claim for a refund of $300. However, because you filed your claim more than 3 years after you filed your return, your refund will be limited to the $200 you paid during the 2 years immediately before you filed your claim.

Financially disabled. The time periods for claiming a refund are suspended for the period in which you are financially disabled. For a joint income tax return, only one spouse has to be financially disabled for the time period to be suspended. You are financially disabled if you are unable to manage your financial affairs because of a medically determinable physical or mental impairment which can be expected to result in death or which has lasted or can be expected to last for a continuous period of not less than 12 months. However, you are not treated as financially disabled during any period your spouse or any other person is authorized to act on your behalf in financial matters.

To claim that you are financially disabled, you must send in the following written statements with your claim for refund.

1. A statement from your qualified physician that includes:
   a. The name and a description of your physical or mental impairment,
   b. The physician's medical opinion that the impairment prevented you from managing your financial affairs,
   c. The physician's medical opinion that the impairment was or can be expected to result in death, or that its duration has lasted, or can be expected to last, at least 12 months,
   d. The specific time period (to the best of the physician's knowledge), and
   e. The following certification signed by the physician: "I hereby certify that, to the best of my knowledge and belief, the above representations are true, correct, and complete."
2. A statement made by the person signing the claim for credit or refund that no person, including your spouse, was authorized to act on your behalf in financial matters during the period of disability (or the exact dates that a person was authorized to act for you).

Exceptions for special types of refunds. If you file a claim for one of the items listed below, the dates and limits discussed earlier may not apply. These items, and where to get more information, are as follows.

- Bad debt. (See *Nonbusiness Bad Debts* in chapter 14.)
- Worthless security. (See *Worthless securities* in chapter 14.)
- Foreign tax paid or accrued. (See Publication 514, *Foreign Tax Credit for Individuals*.)
- Net operating loss carryback. (See Publication 536, *Net Operating Losses (NOLs) for Individuals, Estates, and Trusts*.)
- Carryback of certain business tax credits. (See Form 3800, General Business Credit.)
- Claim based on an agreement with the IRS extending the period for assessment of tax.

Processing claims for refund. Claims are usually processed 8-12 weeks after they are filed. Your claim may be accepted as filed, disallowed, or subject to examination. If a claim is examined, the procedures are the same as in the examination of a tax return.

If your claim is disallowed, you will receive an explanation of why it was disallowed.

Taking your claim to court. You can sue for a refund in court, but you must first file a timely claim with the IRS. If the IRS disallows your claim or does not act on your claim within 6 months after you file it, you can then take your claim to court. For information on the burden of proof in a court proceeding, see Publication 556.

The IRS provides a direct method to move your claim to court if:

- You are filing a claim for a credit or refund based solely on contested income tax or on estate tax or gift tax issues considered in your previously examined returns, and
- You want to take your case to court instead of appealing it within the IRS.

When you file your claim with the IRS, you get the direct method by requesting in writing that your claim be immediately rejected. A notice of claim disallowance will be sent to you.

You have 2 years from the date of mailing of the notice of claim disallowance to file a refund suit in the United States District Court having jurisdiction or in the United States Court of Federal Claims.

Interest on refund. If you receive a refund because of your amended return, interest will be paid on it from the due date of your original return or the date you filed your original return, whichever is later, to the date you filed the amended return. However, if the refund is not made within 45 days after you file the amended return, interest will be paid up to the date the refund is paid.

Reduced refund. Your refund may be reduced by an additional tax liability that has been assessed against you.

Also, your refund may be reduced by amounts you owe for past-due child support, debts to another federal agency, or for state income tax. If your spouse owes these debts, see _Offset against debts_, under _Refunds_, earlier, for the correct refund procedures to follow.

Effect on state tax liability. If your return is changed for any reason, it may affect your state income tax liability. This includes changes made as a result of an examination of your return by the IRS. Contact your state tax agency for more information.

TAXPLANNER
The IRS routinely shares information with most states that have state income taxes. If you file an amended federal tax return showing a balance due, you may avoid interest on tax due to the state and any penalties by taking the initiative and filing amended state tax returns when that is appropriate.

Penalties
The law provides penalties for failure to file returns or pay taxes as required.

Civil Penalties
If you do not file your return and pay your tax by the due date, you may have to pay a penalty. You may also have to pay a penalty if you substantially understate your tax, understate a reportable transaction, file an erroneous claim for refund or credit, file a frivolous tax submission, or fail to supply your SSN or individual taxpayer identification number. If you provide fraudulent information on your return, you may have to pay a civil fraud penalty.

Filing late. If you do not file your return by the due date (including extensions), you may have to pay a failure-to-file penalty. The penalty is usually 5% for each month or part of a month that a return is late, but not more than 25%. The penalty is based on the tax not paid by the due date (without regard to extensions).

Fraud. If your failure to file is due to fraud, the penalty is 15% for each month or part of a month that your return is late, up to a maximum of 75%.

Return over 60 days late. If you file your return more than 60 days after the due date or extended due date, the minimum penalty is the smaller of $135 or 100% of the unpaid tax.

Exception. You will not have to pay the penalty if you show that you failed to file on time because of reasonable cause and not because of willful neglect.

Paying tax late. You will have to pay a failure-to-pay penalty of 1/2 of 1% (.50%) of your unpaid taxes for each month, or part of a month, after the due date that the tax is not paid. This penalty does not apply during the automatic 6-month extension of time to file period if you paid at least 90% of your actual tax liability on or before the due date of your return and pay the balance when you file the return.

The monthly rate of the failure-to-pay penalty is half the usual rate (.25% instead of .50%) if an installment agreement is in effect for that month. You must have filed your return by the due date (including extensions) to qualify for this reduced penalty.

If a notice of intent to levy is issued, the rate will increase to 1% at the start of the first month beginning at least 10 days after the day that the notice is issued. If a notice and demand for immediate payment is issued, the rate will increase to 1% at the start of the first month beginning after the day that the notice and demand is issued.

This penalty cannot be more than 25% of your unpaid tax. You will not have to pay the penalty if you can show that you had a good reason for not paying your tax on time.

Combined penalties. If both the failure-to-file penalty and the failure-to-pay penalty (discussed earlier) apply in any month, the 5% (or 15%) failure-to-file penalty is reduced by the failure-to-pay penalty. However, if you file your return more than 60 days after the due date or extended due date, the minimum penalty is the smaller of $135 or 100% of the unpaid tax.

Accuracy-related penalty. You may have to pay an accuracy-related penalty if you underpay your tax because:

1. You show negligence or disregard of the rules or regulations,
2. You substantially understate your income tax,
3. You claim tax benefits for a transaction that lacks economic substance, or
4. You fail to disclose a foreign financial asset.

The penalty is equal to 20% of the underpayment. The penalty is 40% of any portion of the underpayment that is attributable to an undisclosed noneconomic substance transaction or an undisclosed foreign financial asset transaction. The penalty will not be figured on any part of an underpayment on which the fraud penalty (discussed later) is charged.

Negligence or disregard. The term "negligence" includes a failure to make a reasonable attempt to comply with the tax law or to exercise ordinary and reasonable care in preparing a return. Negligence also includes failure to keep adequate books and records. You will not have to pay a negligence penalty if you have a reasonable basis for a position you took.

The term "disregard" includes any careless, reckless, or intentional disregard.

TAXPLANNER

The IRS has a comprehensive program to compare the amounts of income reported as paid by payers on Form 1099 series information returns with the amounts of income reported by the payees on their income tax returns. If this document-matching program discloses apparently underreported income, you will receive a notice of additional tax due that may include imposition of a 20% negligence penalty. If you receive an information return showing income paid to you that, through no fault of your own, you did not receive in 2011 or that for some reason is not taxable to you, you should nevertheless report as income on your return the entire amount shown by the information return and subtract from that the amount you believe to be erroneous. Following this procedure usually will avoid automatic generation of the IRS notice and the inconvenience and frustration of corresponding with the IRS to get the matter resolved.

TAXALERT

The penalty in the case of a gross valuation misstatement is 40% of the portion of the underpayment attributable to the misstatement. A gross valuation misstatement is a misstatement with respect to which either the value or adjusted basis claimed on the return for any property is 150% (200% for returns filed prior to August 18, 2006) or more of the correct value or adjusted basis. You should keep the necessary documentation in order to avoid the valuation misstatement penalty.

Example

Ted and Joan contributed property to a charity and claimed a charitable contribution deduction of $120,000 on their joint return. The property is actually worth only $54,000. Since the value of the property claimed on the return is more than 150% of the correct value, they are subject to a penalty of 40% on the difference between the amount of tax they should have paid if they claimed only $54,000 as a charitable contribution and the amount of tax they actually paid.

Adequate disclosure. You can avoid the penalty for disregard of rules or regulations if you adequately disclose on your return a position that has at least a reasonable basis. See *Disclosure statement*, later.

This exception will not apply to an item that is attributable to a tax shelter. In addition, it will not apply if you fail to keep adequate books and records, or substantiate items properly.

Substantial understatement of income tax. You understate your tax if the tax shown on your return is less than the correct tax. The understatement is substantial if it is more than the larger of 10% of the correct tax or $5,000. However, the amount of the understatement may be reduced to the extent the understatement is due to:

1. Substantial authority, or
2. Adequate disclosure and a reasonable basis.

If an item on your return is attributable to a tax shelter, there is no reduction for an adequate disclosure. However, there is a reduction for a position with substantial authority, but only if you reasonably believed that your tax treatment was more likely than not the proper treatment.

Substantial authority. Whether there is or was substantial authority for the tax treatment of an item depends on the facts and circumstances. Some of the items that may be considered are court opinions, Treasury regulations, revenue rulings, revenue procedures, and notices and announcements issued by the IRS and published in the Internal Revenue Bulletin that involve the same or similar circumstances as yours.

Disclosure statement. To adequately disclose the relevant facts about your tax treatment of an item, use Form 8275, Disclosure Statement. You must also have a reasonable basis for treating the item the way you did.

In cases of substantial understatement only, items that meet the requirements of Revenue Procedure 2010-15 (or later update) are considered adequately disclosed on your return without filing Form 8275.

Use Form 8275-R, Regulation Disclosure Statement, to disclose items or positions contrary to regulations.

Transaction lacking economic substance. For more information on economic substance, see section 7701 (o).

Foreign financial asset. For more information on undisclosed foreign financial assets, see section 6662(j).

Reasonable cause. You will not have to pay a penalty if you show a good reason (reasonable cause) for the way you treated an item. You must also show that you acted in good faith.

This does not apply to a transaction that lacks economic substance.

EXPLANATION

The IRS's explanation of the penalty for substantial understatement and how to avoid it oversimplifies a very complex situation.

Under regulations issued by the IRS, the following items may generally be considered substantial authority:

- Internal Revenue Code and other statutory provisions
- Temporary and final IRS regulations
- Court cases
- Administrative pronouncements (including revenue rulings and revenue procedures)
- Tax treaties and regulations issued as a result of a treaty
- Congressional intent as reflected in committee reports, joint explanatory statements of managers included in conference committee reports, and statements made in Congress by one of a bill's managers prior to enactment of a bill
- General explanations of tax legislation prepared by the Joint Committee on Taxation (the Blue Book)
- Proposed IRS regulations
- Information or press releases, notices, announcements, and any other similar documents published by the IRS in the Internal Revenue Bulletin
- Private letter rulings, technical advice memoranda, actions on decisions, and general counsel memoranda after they have been released to the public, if they are dated after March 12, 1981

Filing erroneous claim for refund or credit. You may have to pay a penalty if you file an erroneous claim for refund or credit. The penalty is equal to 20% of the disallowed amount of the claim, unless you can show a reasonable basis for the way you treated an item. The penalty will not be figured on any part of the disallowed amount of the claim that relates to the earned income credit or on which the accuracy-related or fraud penalties are charged.

Frivolous tax submission. You may have to pay a penalty of $5,000 if you file a frivolous tax return or other frivolous submissions. A frivolous tax return is one that does not include enough information to figure the correct tax or that contains information clearly showing that the tax you reported is substantially incorrect. For more information on frivolous returns, frivolous submissions, and a list of positions that are identified as frivolous, see Notice 2010-33, 2010-17 I.R.B. 609, available at *www.irs.gov/irb/2010-17_IRB/ar13.html*.

You will have to pay the penalty if you filed this kind of return or submission based on a frivolous position or a desire to delay or interfere with the administration of federal tax laws. This includes altering or striking out the preprinted language above the space provided for your signature.

This penalty is added to any other penalty provided by law.

Fraud. If there is any underpayment of tax on your return due to fraud, a penalty of 75% of the underpayment due to fraud will be added to your tax.

Joint return. The fraud penalty on a joint return does not apply to a spouse unless some part of the underpayment is due to the fraud of that spouse.

Failure to supply social security number. If you do not include your SSN or the SSN of another person where required on a return, statement, or other document, you will be subject to a penalty of $50 for each failure. You will also be subject to a penalty of $50 if you do not give your SSN to another person when it is required on a return, statement, or other document.

For example, if you have a bank account that earns interest, you must give your SSN to the bank. The number must be shown on the Form 1099-INT or other statement the bank sends you. If you do not give the bank your SSN, you will be subject to the $50 penalty. (You also may be subject to "backup" withholding of income tax. See chapter 4.)

You will not have to pay the penalty if you are able to show that the failure was due to reasonable cause and not willful neglect.

Criminal Penalties

You may be subject to criminal prosecution (brought to trial) for actions such as:
1. Tax evasion,
2. Willful failure to file a return, supply information, or pay any tax due,
3. Fraud and false statements, or
4. Preparing and filing a fraudulent return.

Chapter 2
Filing status

Note

IRS Publication 17 (*Your Federal Income Tax*) has been updated by Ernst & Young LLP for 2011. Dates and dollar amounts shown are for 2011. Underlined type is used to indicate where IRS text has been updated. Places where text has been removed are indicated by the sentence: *Text intentionally omitted*.

ey.com/EYTaxGuide
Ernst & Young LLP will update the *Ernst & Young Tax Guide 2012* website with relevant taxpayer information as it becomes available. You can also sign up for email alerts to let you know when changes have been made.

Introduction

One of the first things to determine in preparing your income tax return is your filing status. There are five possible choices: single, married filing jointly, married filing separately, unmarried head of household, and qualifying widow or widower with a dependent child. Your choice of filing status dictates which Tax Table or Tax Rate Schedule to use in calculating your tax liability; whether you may claim an exemption for a dependent; whether you may be claimed as a dependent; and how much income you can have before you are taxed at all.

This chapter helps you determine which filing status to use. There are five filing statuses.
- Single.
- Married Filing Jointly.
- Married Filing Separately.
- Head of Household.
- Qualifying Widow(er) With Dependent Child.

Tip

If more than one filing status applies to you, choose the one that will give you the lowest tax.

EXPLANATION

If your filing status changes during the year, you may not file under one status for one part of that year and under a second status for the remainder of the year. The law requires that your filing status for the entire year be determined by your status on the last day of the tax year. For example, even if you get married on December 31, you are treated as married for the entire year and you may either file as married filing jointly or married filing separately. Choose the one that will produce the lowest tax. (Note: If your spouse or a qualifying person died during the year, see the IRS explanation below.)

You must determine your filing status before you can determine your filing requirements (chapter 1), standard deduction (chapter 20), and correct tax (chapter 31). You also use your filing status in determining whether you are eligible to claim certain deductions and credits.

Useful Items

You may want to see:

Publication
- ☐ **501** Exemptions, Standard Deduction, and Filing Information
- ☐ **519** U.S. Tax Guide for Aliens
- ☐ **555** Community Property

Marital Status

In general, your filing status depends on whether you are considered unmarried or married. For federal tax purposes, a marriage means only a legal union between a man and a woman as husband and wife.

TAXPLANNER

Same-sex marriages, civil unions, and registered domestic partnerships. Under federal law, same-sex marriages are not recognized for tax purposes even though such marriages may be valid for state purposes. An individual who is married in a same-sex marriage or has entered into a civil union or registered domestic partnership can only select single filing status, or if qualified, the head of household filing status when filing their own federal income tax return.

In addition, a registered domestic partner (RDP), in Nevada, Washington, or California (or a person in California who is married to a person of the same sex) generally must follow state community property laws and report half the combined community income of the individual and his or her RDP (or California same-sex spouse) on their individual federal income tax returns, according to the IRS (see IRS Publication 555, *Community Property*, for more details). Each taxpayer is also entitled to half of any taxes withheld since the RDP is the recipient of one-half of the couple's community property income. These rules apply to RDPs in Nevada, Washington, and California because they have full community property rights in 2011. RDPs in California attained these rights as of January 1, 2007. Nevada RDPs attained them as of October 1, 2009, and Washington RDPs attained them as of June 12, 2008.

For years prior to 2011, RDPs who reported income without regard to the community property laws may file amended returns to report half of the community income of the RDPs for the applicable periods, but are not required to do so. If one of the RDPs files an amended return to report half of the community income, the other RDP must report the other half.

Although federal law does not recognize same-sex marriage for tax purposes, a number of states do so and allow married filing status to be selected when filing state income tax forms. Some states also may recognize same-sex marriages or RDPs that were entered into in another state.

If you are in a registered domestic partnership, civil union, or a same-sex marriage recognized under state law, you should consult with a professional tax advisor for advice on preparing your federal and state tax returns, as these rules are very complex and are constantly evolving.

Example

John and Mark are RDPs in California. In 2011, John earned wages of $20,000 and Mark earned wages of $100,000. When applying the community property rules discussed above, John and Mark file separate Federal income tax returns, however, their income is split equally with each reporting income of $60,000 (one-half of their community income of $120,000), rather than John reporting income of $20,000 and Mark reporting income of $100,000 on their respective 2011 Federal income tax returns. Each is also entitled to claim credit for half of the income tax withheld on their combined wages of $120,000.

Unmarried persons. You are considered unmarried for the whole year if, on the last day of your tax year, you are unmarried or legally separated from your spouse under a divorce or separate maintenance decree. State law governs whether you are married or legally separated under a divorce or separate maintenance decree.

Divorced persons. If you are divorced under a final decree by the last day of the year, you are considered unmarried for the whole year.

Divorce and remarriage. If you obtain a divorce in one year for the sole purpose of filing tax returns as unmarried individuals, and at the time of divorce you intended to and did remarry each other in the next tax year, you and your spouse must file as married individuals.

Annulled marriages. If you obtain a court decree of annulment, which holds that no valid marriage ever existed, you are considered unmarried even if you filed joint returns for earlier years. You must file Form 1040X, Amended U.S. Individual Income Tax Return, claiming single or head of household status for each tax year affected by the annulment that is not closed by the statute of limitations for filing a tax return. The statute of limitations generally does not end until 3 years after your original return was filed.

Tax Breaks and Deductions You Can Use Checklist

Married Filing Separately. If you're married it's usually more beneficial for you to file a joint return. But there are circumstances where filing a separate return might be a better idea. For example, if one spouse has substantial medical or employee business expenses, you may be able to reduce your combined tax liability by filing separate tax returns. Other reasons to file separate returns are if one spouse does not want to be exposed to any unknown tax liability of the other or if one spouse refuses to provide the information necessary to file a joint return to the other spouse.

Married Filing Jointly. Jointly filed returns typically result in a lower tax liability for married couples versus filing separately. Other advantages to filing jointly are (1) a nonworking spouse is eligible to contribute to a spousal IRA even though he or she may not have any earned income, (2) it is generally less costly and time consuming to complete one return instead of two, (3) you can reduce your taxable income by the highest standard deduction if you don't itemize, and (4) certain tax credits such as the child and dependent care credit, adoption credit, American opportunity credit, and lifetime learning credit are only available to married couples if they file a joint return. A qualified widow or widower may also be eligible to file a joint return for two tax years following the death of their spouse if certain requirements are met.

Head of Household. A special filing status called "Head of Household" can save you a significant amount of taxes. If you qualify, you can use the lower rates and other benefits available for this status, such as potential eligibility for the Earned Income Credit, a higher standard deduction than single or married filing separately, and additional personal exemptions that reduce your taxable income.

In order to qualify you must meet these requirements:

1. You must be unmarried or "considered unmarried" on the last day of the year,
2. You paid more than half the cost of keeping up a home for the year, and
3. A "qualifying person" lived with you in the home for more than half the year (except for temporary absences, such as school). If the "qualifying person," however, is your dependent parent, he or she does not have to live with you.

EXPLANATION

Invalid divorces. This is a very confusing subject because courts in different geographic locations disagree with each other. Furthermore, the courts and the IRS have interpreted the law differently.

Generally, the law in your state of residence determines whether you are legally married. The marital laws in every state require you to be unmarried before being allowed to get married. Therefore, you may not file a joint return with your second spouse unless the marital relationship with your first spouse has been severed. Only a few states recognize common law marriage, and only residents of those states may file as married filing jointly if they are in a common law marriage relationship.

While terminating a marriage is usually a matter of obtaining a divorce from a domestic or foreign court, it is not always that straightforward. When a particular state's law does not recognize the validity of a divorce decree acquired in another jurisdiction, the IRS and the courts disagree over the status of the divorce.

The Second and Third Circuit Courts of Appeals adhere to the so-called rule of validation. Basically, this rule specifies that a divorce in any court's jurisdiction must be recognized for the purposes of tax law. Consequently, under the rule of validation, a valid joint return may be filed with a second spouse. However, the IRS, the Tax Court, and the Ninth Circuit Court of Appeals do not support the rule of validation. Instead, they maintain that a second court possessing jurisdiction may declare a prior divorce invalid. Thus, a return filed jointly by a party of the invalid divorce and a subsequent marriage partner may not be valid. Nevertheless, neither these courts nor the IRS will challenge the validity of a divorce decree until a court of competent jurisdiction has declared the divorce invalid.

Prisoners of war. You are still considered to be married if your spouse is a prisoner of war (POW) or is listed as missing in action (MIA). Even if you subsequently discover that your spouse died in action or in captivity in a prior year, you cannot alter your married filing status on prior income tax returns.

TAXSAVER

When to get divorced. December is the better month to get divorced if spouses have similar incomes. In this way, you can file single returns for the entire year. January is the better month to get divorced if one spouse has considerably more income than the other and you both want to save on taxes.

The IRS contends that actions that are designed to control an individual's marital status at the close of the year for tax purposes, such as a year-end tax-motivated divorce followed by immediate remarriage, are shams and should be disregarded for tax purposes. According to the IRS, individuals retain their married status when:

1. A divorce under the laws of a foreign jurisdiction is obtained late in the year.
2. At the time of the divorce the parties intend to remarry.
3. The remarriage occurs in January of the next year.

However, a divorce followed by cohabitation is not necessarily a sham. The IRS has recognized such arrangements and has allowed individuals to claim single filing status as long as they say that they intend to remain divorced and not remarry each other.

TAXPLANNER

If you are getting a divorce, you should consider the impact of the alternative minimum tax (AMT) on special types of income. Accelerating these types of income or deferring related deductions may provide a greater benefit while still filing as married filing jointly. See chapter 31, *How to figure your tax*, for additional discussion of the AMT.

Head of household or qualifying widow(er) with dependent child. If you are considered unmarried, you may be able to file as a head of household or as a qualifying widow(er) with a dependent child. See *Head of Household* and *Qualifying Widow(er) With Dependent Child* to see if you qualify.

Married persons. If you are considered married for the whole year, you and your spouse can file a joint return, or you can file separate returns.

Considered married. You are considered married for the whole year if on the last day of your tax year you and your spouse meet any one of the following tests.

1. You are married and living together as husband and wife.
2. You are living together in a common law marriage that is recognized in the state where you now live or in the state where the common law marriage began.
3. You are married and living apart, but not legally separated under a decree of divorce or separate maintenance.
4. You are separated under an interlocutory (not final) decree of divorce. For purposes of filing a joint return, you are not considered divorced.

Spouse died during the year. If your spouse died during the year, you are considered married for the whole year for filing status purposes.

If you did not remarry before the end of the tax year, you can file a joint return for yourself and your deceased spouse. For the next 2 years, you may be entitled to the special benefits described later under *Qualifying Widow(er) With Dependent Child*.

If you remarried before the end of the tax year, you can file a joint return with your new spouse. Your deceased spouse's filing status is married filing separately for that year.

Married persons living apart. If you live apart from your spouse and meet certain tests, you may be considered unmarried. If this applies to you, you can file as head of household even though you are not divorced or legally separated. If you qualify to file as head of household instead of as married filing separately, your standard deduction will be higher. Also, your tax may be lower, and you may be able to claim the earned income credit. See *Head of Household*, later.

Single

Your filing status is single if, on the last day of the year, you are unmarried or legally separated from your spouse under a divorce or separate maintenance decree, and you do not qualify for another filing status. To determine your marital status on the last day of the year, see *Marital Status*, earlier.

Widow(er). Your filing status may be single if you were widowed before January 1, 2011, and did not remarry before the end of 2011. However, you might be able to use another filing status that will give you a lower tax. See *Head of Household* and *Qualifying Widow(er) With Dependent Child*, later, to see if you qualify.

How to file. You can file Form 1040EZ (if you have no dependents, are under 65 and not blind, and meet other requirements), Form 1040A, or Form 1040. If you file Form 1040A or Form 1040, show your filing status as single by checking the box on line 1. Use the *Single* column of the Tax Table or Section A of the Tax Computation Worksheet to figure your tax.

Married Filing Jointly

You can choose married filing jointly as your filing status if you are married and both you and your spouse agree to file a joint return. On a joint return, you report your combined income and deduct your combined allowable expenses. You can file a joint return even if one of you had no income or deductions.

If you and your spouse decide to file a joint return, your tax may be lower than your combined tax for the other filing statuses. Also, your standard deduction (if you do not itemize deductions) may be higher, and you may qualify for tax benefits that do not apply to other filing statuses.

How to file. If you file as married filing jointly, you can use Form 1040 or Form 1040A. If you have no dependents, are under 65 and not blind, and meet other requirements, you can file Form 1040EZ. If you file Form 1040 or Form 1040A, show this filing status by checking the box on line 2. Use the *Married filing jointly* column of the Tax Table or Section B of the Tax Computation Worksheet to figure your tax.

> **Tip**
>
> *If you and your spouse each have income, you may want to figure your tax both on a joint return and on separate returns (using the filing status of married filing separately). Choose the method that gives the two of you the lower combined tax.*

> **EXPLANATION**
> **Marriage tax penalty.** Marriage partners who earn approximately the same income may pay more tax if they file a joint return or file separate married returns than they would if they filed two single returns. This is known as "the marriage tax penalty."

Spouse died during the year. If your spouse died during the year, you are considered married for the whole year and can choose married filing jointly as your filing status. See _Spouse died during the year_, earlier, for more information.

Divorced persons. If you are divorced under a final decree by the last day of the year, you are considered unmarried for the whole year and you cannot choose married filing jointly as your filing status.

Filing a Joint Return
Both you and your spouse must include all of your income, exemptions, and deductions on your joint return.

Accounting period. Both of you must use the same accounting period, but you can use different accounting methods. See _Accounting Periods_ and _Accounting Methods_ in chapter 1.

Joint responsibility. Both of you may be held responsible, jointly and individually, for the tax and any interest or penalty due on your joint return. One spouse may be held responsible for all the tax due even if all the income was earned by the other spouse.

Divorced taxpayer. You may be held jointly and individually responsible for any tax, interest, and penalties due on a joint return filed before your divorce. This responsibility may apply even if your divorce decree states that your former spouse will be responsible for any amounts due on previously filed joint returns.

Relief from joint responsibility. In some cases, one spouse may be relieved of joint liability for tax, interest, and penalties on a joint return for items of the other spouse that were incorrectly reported on the joint return. You can ask for relief no matter how small the liability.

There are three types of relief available.
1. Innocent spouse relief.
2. Separation of liability, which applies to joint filers who are divorced, widowed, legally separated, or have not lived together for the 12 months ending on the date election of this relief is filed.
3. Equitable relief.

You must file Form 8857, Request for Innocent Spouse Relief, to request any of these kinds of relief. Publication 971, Innocent Spouse Relief, explains these kinds of relief and who may qualify for them.

Signing a joint return. For a return to be considered a joint return, both husband and wife generally must sign the return.

Spouse died before signing. If your spouse died before signing the return, the executor or administrator must sign the return for your spouse. If neither you nor anyone else has yet been appointed as executor or administrator, you can sign the return for your spouse and enter "Filing as surviving spouse" in the area where you sign the return.

Spouse away from home. If your spouse is away from home, you should prepare the return, sign it, and send it to your spouse to sign so that it can be filed on time.

Injury or disease prevents signing. If your spouse cannot sign because of disease or injury and tells you to sign, you can sign your spouse's name in the proper space on the return followed by the words "By (your name), Husband (or Wife)." Be sure to also sign in the space provided for your signature. Attach a dated statement, signed by you, to the return. The statement should include the form number of the return you are filing, the tax year, the reason your spouse cannot sign, and that your spouse has agreed to your signing for him or her.

Signing as guardian of spouse. If you are the guardian of your spouse who is mentally incompetent, you can sign the return for your spouse as guardian.

Spouse in combat zone. If your spouse is unable to sign the return because he or she is serving in a combat zone (such as the Persian Gulf Area, Yugoslavia, or Afghanistan), and you do not have a power of attorney or other statement, you can sign for your spouse. Attach a signed statement to your return that explains that your spouse is serving in a combat zone. For more information on special tax rules for persons who are serving in a combat zone, or who are in missing status as a result of serving in a combat zone, see Publication 3, Armed Forces' Tax Guide.

Other reasons spouse cannot sign. If your spouse cannot sign the joint return for any other reason, you can sign for your spouse only if you are given a valid power of attorney (a legal document giving you permission to act for your spouse). Attach the power of attorney (or a copy of it) to your tax return. You can use Form 2848, Power of Attorney and Declaration of Representative.

TAXALERT

Contrary to the IRS's assertion, the failure of one spouse to sign a return will not prevent a finding that the return was a joint return. If the facts of the case support the conclusion that the nonsigning spouse gave tacit consent to a joint filing, then a valid joint return exists.

Even when a spouse's signature is forged, a valid joint return can exist. In one case, the IRS challenged the return of a husband who, due to marital difficulties, had an unknown person forge his wife's signature. Even though his wife testified in court that she would not have signed a joint return under any circumstances, the court ruled that the joint return was valid. The court reasoned that the wife's refusal to sign was unrelated to the joint filing status claim. Furthermore, because the couple had always filed jointly in the past and the wife did nothing to indicate her disapproval of her husband's intention to continue to file jointly, the court said she had no grounds to complain after the filing was made. The court's message is: The presence or absence of an authentic signature does not constitute conclusive evidence of the intent to file jointly or singly. In addition, the refusal to sign does not necessarily mean that the intent to file a joint return was nonexistent.

Nonresident alien or dual-status alien. A joint return generally cannot be filed if either spouse is a nonresident alien at any time during the tax year. However, if one spouse was a nonresident alien or dual-status alien who was married to a U.S. citizen or resident alien at the end of the year, the spouses can choose to file a joint return. If you do file a joint return, you and your spouse are both treated as U.S. residents for the entire tax year. For information on this choice, see chapter 1 of Publication 519.

TAXPLANNER

You may file a joint return and use the more beneficial joint tax rates if you fall into either of the following two categories:

1. As of the close of the tax year, you are a nonresident alien married to a citizen or resident of the United States.
2. You are a nonresident alien at the beginning of the tax year but a resident of the United States at the close of the tax year (i.e., a dual-status taxpayer) and you are married to a citizen or resident of the United States at the end of the tax year.

The catch is that a joint return requires that the worldwide income of both spouses for the entire year be included in taxable income.

Generally, not filing jointly means that separate returns are required. Only the worldwide income of a U.S. citizen and the worldwide income of an alien while a U.S. resident would be included in each person's taxable income. As a result, the alien spouse's income while a nonresident would be excluded. However, the more burdensome married filing separately tax rates must be used.

Married Filing Separately

You can choose married filing separately as your filing status if you are married. This filing status may benefit you if you want to be responsible only for your own tax or if it results in less tax than filing a joint return.

If you and your spouse do not agree to file a joint return, you may have to use this filing status unless you qualify for head of household status, discussed next.

You may be able to choose head of household filing status if you live apart from your spouse, meet certain tests, and are considered unmarried (explained later, under *Head of Household*). This can apply to you even if you are not divorced or legally separated. If you qualify to file as head of household, instead of as married filing separately, your tax may be lower, you may be able to claim the earned income credit and certain other credits, and your standard deduction will be higher. The head of household filing status allows you to choose the standard deduction even if your spouse chooses to itemize deductions. See *Head of Household*, later, for more information.

How to file. If you file a separate return, you generally report only your own income, exemptions, credits, and deductions on your individual return. You can claim an exemption for your spouse if your spouse had no gross income and was not the dependent of another person. However, if your spouse had any gross income or was the dependent of someone else, you cannot claim an exemption for him or her on your separate return.

If you file as married filing separately, you can use Form 1040A or Form 1040. Select this filing status by checking the box on line 3 of either form. You also must enter your spouse's full name in the space provided and must enter your spouse's SSN or ITIN in the space provided unless your spouse does not have and is not required to have an SSN or ITIN. Use the *Married filing separately* column of the Tax Table or Section C of the Tax Computation Worksheet to figure your tax.

Special Rules

If you choose married filing separately as your filing status, the following special rules apply. Because of these special rules, you will usually pay more tax on a separate return than if you used another filing status that you qualify for.

1. Your tax rate generally will be higher than it would be on a joint return.
2. Your exemption amount for figuring the alternative minimum tax will be half that allowed to a joint return filer.
3. You cannot take the credit for child and dependent care expenses in most cases, and the amount that you can exclude from income under an employer's dependent care assistance program is limited to $2,500 (instead of $5,000 if you filed a joint return). For more information about these expenses, the credit, and the exclusion, see chapter 33.
4. You cannot take the earned income credit.
5. You cannot take the exclusion or credit for adoption expenses in most cases.
6. You cannot take the education credits (the American opportunity credit and lifetime learning credit) or the deduction for student loan interest.
7. You cannot exclude any interest income from qualified U.S. savings bonds that you used for higher education expenses.
8. If you lived with your spouse at any time during the tax year:
   a. You cannot claim the credit for the elderly or the disabled, and
   b. You will have to include in income more (up to 85%) of any social security or equivalent railroad retirement benefits you received.
9. The following credits are reduced at income levels that are half those for a joint return:
   a. The child tax credit, and
   b. The retirement savings contributions credit.
10. Your capital loss deduction limit is $1,500 (instead of $3,000 if you filed a joint return).
11. If your spouse itemizes deductions, you cannot claim the standard deduction. If you can claim the standard deduction, your basic standard deduction is half the amount allowed on a joint return.

Adjusted gross income (AGI) limits. If your AGI on a separate return is lower than it would have been on a joint return, you may be able to deduct a larger amount for certain deductions that are limited by AGI, such as medical expenses.

Individual retirement arrangements (IRAs). You may not be able to deduct all or part of your contributions to a traditional IRA if you or your spouse were covered by an employee retirement plan at work during the year. Your deduction is reduced or eliminated if your income is more than a certain amount. This amount is much lower for married individuals who file separately and lived together at any time during the year. For more information, see *How Much Can You Deduct* in chapter 17.

Rental activity losses. If you actively participated in a passive rental real estate activity that produced a loss, you generally can deduct the loss from your nonpassive income, up to $25,000. This is called a special allowance. However, married persons filing separate returns who lived together at any time during the year cannot claim this special allowance. Married persons filing separate returns who lived apart at all times during the year are each allowed a $12,500 maximum special allowance for losses from passive real estate activities. See *Limits on Rental Losses* in chapter 9.

Community property states. If you live in Arizona, California, Idaho, Louisiana, Nevada, New Mexico, Texas, Washington, or Wisconsin and file separately, your income may be considered separate income or community income for income tax purposes. See Publication 555.

Joint Return After Separate Returns
You can change your filing status by filing an amended return using Form 1040X.

If you or your spouse (or both of you) file a separate return, you generally can change to a joint return any time within 3 years from the due date of the separate return or returns. This does not include any extensions. A separate return includes a return filed by you or your spouse claiming married filing separately, single, or head of household filing status.

Separate Returns After Joint Return
Once you file a joint return, you cannot choose to file separate returns for that year after the due date of the return.

> ### EXPLANATION
> If a husband and wife fail to file for a particular year, they may still file a joint return for that period, even if the return is as much as 3 years overdue. However, once the IRS has notified each spouse individually that he or she has not filed a return that is more than 3 years overdue, they cannot file a joint return.

Exception. A personal representative for a decedent can change from a joint return elected by the surviving spouse to a separate return for the decedent. The personal representative has 1 year from the due date of the return (including extensions) to make the change. See Publication 559, *Survivors, Executors, and Administrators*, for more information on filing a return for a decedent.

Head of Household
You may be able to file as head of household if you meet all the following requirements.
1. You are unmarried or "considered unmarried" on the last day of the year.
2. You paid more than half the cost of keeping up a home for the year.
3. A "qualifying person" lived with you in the home for more than half the year (except for temporary absences, such as school). However, if the "qualifying person" is your dependent parent, he or she does not have to live with you. See *Special rule for parent*, later, under *Qualifying Person*.

Kidnapped child. A child may qualify you to file as head of household even if the child has been kidnapped. For more information, see Publication 501.

How to file. If you file as head of household, you can use either Form 1040A or Form 1040. Indicate your choice of this filing status by checking the box on line 4 of either form. Use the *Head of household* column of the Tax Table or Section D of the Tax Computation Worksheet to figure your tax.

Considered Unmarried
To qualify for head of household status, you must be either unmarried or considered unmarried on the last day of the year. You are considered unmarried on the last day of the tax year if you meet all the following tests.
1. You file a separate return (defined earlier under *Joint Return After Separate Returns*).
2. You paid more than half the cost of keeping up your home for the tax year.
3. Your spouse did not live in your home during the last 6 months of the tax year. Your spouse is considered to live in your home even if he or she is temporarily absent due to special circumstances. See *Temporary absences*, under *Qualifying Person*, later.
4. Your home was the main home of your child, stepchild, or foster child for more than half the year. (See *Home of qualifying person*, under *Qualifying Person*, later, for rules applying to a child's birth, death, or temporary absence during the year.)
5. You must be able to claim an exemption for the child. However, you meet this test if you cannot claim the exemption only because the noncustodial parent can claim the child using the rules described in *Children of divorced or separated parents or parents who live apart*

under *Qualifying Child* in chapter 3, or in <u>*Support Test for Children of Divorced or Separated Parents or Parents Who Live Apart*</u> under *Qualifying Relative* in chapter 3. The general rules for claiming an exemption for a dependent are explained under <u>*Exemptions for Dependents*</u> in chapter 3.

Nonresident alien spouse. You are considered unmarried for head of household purposes if your spouse was a nonresident alien at any time during the year and you do not choose to treat your nonresident spouse as a resident alien. However, your spouse is not a qualifying person for head of household purposes. You must have another qualifying person and meet the other tests to be eligible to file as a head of household.

Earned income credit. Even if you are considered unmarried for head of household purposes because you are married to a nonresident alien, you are still considered married for purposes of the earned income credit (unless you meet the five tests listed earlier under <u>*Considered Unmarried*</u>). You are not entitled to the credit unless you file a joint return with your spouse and meet other qualifications. See <u>chapter 37</u> for more information.

Choice to treat spouse as resident. You are considered married if you choose to treat your spouse as a resident alien.

Keeping Up a Home

To qualify for head of household status, you must pay more than half of the cost of keeping up a home for the year. You can determine whether you paid more than half of the cost of keeping up a home by using the worksheet shown on this page.

Caution

If you were considered married for part of the year and lived in a community property state (listed earlier under <u>Married Filing Separately</u>*), special rules may apply in determining your income and expenses. See Publication 555 for more information.*

Cost of Keeping Up a Home

 Keep for Your Records

	Amount You Paid	Total Cost
Property taxes	$ _____	$ _____
Mortgage interest expense	_____	_____
Rent	_____	_____
Utility charges	_____	_____
Repairs/maintenance	_____	_____
Property insurance	_____	_____
Food consumed on the premises	_____	_____
Other household expenses	_____	_____
Totals	$ _____	$ _____
Minus total amount you paid		(_____)
Amount others paid		$ _____

If the total amount you paid is more than the amount others paid, you meet the requirement of paying more than half the cost of keeping up the home.

Costs you include. Include in the cost of upkeep expenses such as rent, mortgage interest, real estate taxes, insurance on the home, repairs, utilities, and food eaten in the home.

If you used payments you received under Temporary Assistance for Needy Families (TANF) or other public assistance programs to pay part of the cost of keeping up your home, you cannot count them as money you paid. However, you must include them in the total cost of keeping up your home to figure if you paid over half the cost.

Costs you do not include. Do not include in the cost of upkeep expenses such as clothing, education, medical treatment, vacations, life insurance, or transportation. Also, do not include the rental value of a home you own or the value of your services or those of a member of your household.

TAXPLANNER
If you are providing some support for your parents–but less than half of their total support–you should investigate targeting your support payments so that you can qualify as a head of household by establishing one of your parents as a dependent. For example, when you are providing funds to your parents for their support, some type of notation should be made on your check that specifically states for whom the money is being provided. In this fashion, you can clearly demonstrate that the 50% support requirement has been satisfied for at least one of your parents.

Qualifying Person

See <u>Table 2-1</u> to see who is a qualifying person.

Any person not described in <u>Table 2-1</u> is not a qualifying person.

Example 1—child. Your unmarried son lived with you all year and was 18 years old at the end of the year. He did not provide more than half of his own support and does not meet the tests to be a qualifying child of anyone else. As a result, he is your qualifying child (see *Qualifying Child*, in chapter 3) and, because he is single, is a qualifying person for you to claim head of household filing status.

Example 2—child who is not qualifying person. The facts are the same as in *Example 1* except your son was 25 years old at the end of the year and his gross income was $5,000. Because he does not meet the age test (explained under *Qualifying Child* in chapter 3), your son is not your

Table 2-1.   **Who Is a Qualifying Person Qualifying You To File as Head of Household?**[1]

IF the person is your ...	AND ...	THEN that person is ...
qualifying child (such as a son, daughter, or grand-child who lived with you more than half the year and meets certain other tests)[2]	he or she is single	a qualifying person, whether or not you can claim an exemption for the person.
	he or she is married <u>and</u> you can claim an exemption for him or her	a qualifying person.
	he or she is married <u>and</u> you cannot claim an exemption for him or her	not a qualifying person.[3]
qualifying relative[4] who is your father or mother	you can claim an exemption for him or her[5]	a qualifying person.[6]
	you cannot claim an exemption for him or her	not a qualifying person.
qualifying relative[4] other than your father or mother (such as a grandparent, brother, or sister who meets certain tests)	he or she lived with you more than half the year, <u>and</u> he or she is related to you in one of the ways listed under *Relatives who do not have to live with you* in chapter 3 <u>and</u> you claim an exemption for him or her[5]	a qualifying person.
	he or she did not live with you more than half the year	not a qualifying person.
	he or she is not related to you in one of the ways listed under *Relatives who do not have to live with you* in chapter 3 and is your qualifying relative only because he or she lived with you all year as a member of your household	not a qualifying person.
	you cannot claim an exemption for him or her	not a qualifying person.

[1]A person cannot qualify more than one taxpayer to use the head of household filing status for the year.

[2]The term "qualifying child" is defined in chapter 3. **Note.** If you are a noncustodial parent, the term "qualifying child" for head of household filing status does not include a child who is your qualifying child for exemption purposes only because of the rules described under *Children of divorced or separated parents or parents who live apart* under *Qualifying Child* in chapter 3. If you are the custodial parent and those rules apply, the child generally is your qualifying child for head of household filing status even though the child is not a qualifying child for whom you can claim an exemption.

[3]This person is a qualifying person if the only reason you cannot claim the exemption is that you can be claimed as a dependent on someone else's return.

[4]The term "*qualifying relative*" is defined in chapter 3.

[5]If you can claim an exemption for a person only because of a multiple support agreement, that person is not a qualifying person. See *Multiple Support Agreement* in chapter 3.

[6]See *Special rule for parent* for an additional requirement.

qualifying child. Because he does not meet the gross income test (explained later under *Qualifying Relative* in chapter 3), he is not your qualifying relative. As a result, he is not your qualifying person for head of household purposes.

Example 3—girlfriend. Your girlfriend lived with you all year. Even though she may be your qualifying relative if the gross income and support tests (explained in chapter 3) are met, she is not your qualifying person for head of household purposes because she is not related to you in one of the ways listed under *Relatives who do not have to live with you* in chapter 3. See Table 2-1.

Example 4—girlfriend's child. The facts are the same as in *Example 3* except your girlfriend's 10-year-old son also lived with you all year. He is not your qualifying child and, because he is your girlfriend's qualifying child, he is not your qualifying relative (see *Not a Qualifying Child Test*, in chapter 3). As a result, he is not your qualifying person for head of household purposes.

Home of qualifying person. Generally, the qualifying person must live with you for more than half of the year.

Special rule for parent. If your qualifying person is your father or mother, you may be eligible to file as head of household even if your father or mother does not live with you. However, you must be able to claim an exemption for your father or mother. Also, you must pay more than half the cost of keeping up a home that was the main home for the entire year for your father or mother. You are keeping up a main home for your father or mother if you pay more than half the cost of keeping your parent in a rest home or home for the elderly.

TAXALERT

Married child. Your child who is married at the end of the year generally cannot be your qualifying person unless you can claim the child as a dependent. However, the child is a qualifying person if all three of the following requirements are met.

- The child is your qualifying child (as defined under *Exemptions for Dependents* in chapter 3, *Personal exemptions and dependents*).
- The child does not file a joint return, unless the return is filed only as a claim for refund and no tax liability would exist for either spouse if they had filed separate returns.
- The child is a U.S. citizen or resident, or a resident of Canada or Mexico. (This requirement is met if you are a U.S. citizen and the child is an adopted child who lived with you all year as a member of your household.)

Temporary absences. You and your qualifying person are considered to live together even if one or both of you are temporarily absent from your home due to special circumstances such as illness, education, business, vacation, or military service. It must be reasonable to assume that the absent person will return to the home after the temporary absence. You must continue to keep up the home during the absence.

EXAMPLES

One court has held that a man still qualified for head of household status even though he temporarily moved out of his home after becoming legally separated. The court believed that the man had always intended to return to his home (and, in fact, he did return). The court was also aware that he had been awarded custody of his child.

Another court has held that a man could not claim that he was the head of the household that he maintained for his son where he himself did not live because of fear of his son.

Note: If your child or stepchild is absent from the home less than 6 months under a custody agreement, the absence is considered temporary.

Death or birth. You may be eligible to file as head of household if the individual who qualifies you for this filing status is born or dies during the year. You must have provided more than half of the cost of keeping up a home that was the individual's main home for more than half the year or, if less, the period during which the individual lived.

Example. You are unmarried. Your mother, for whom you can claim an exemption, lived in an apartment by herself. She died on September 2. The cost of the upkeep of her apartment for the year until her death was $6,000. You paid $4,000 and your brother paid $2,000. Your brother made no other payments toward your mother's support. Your mother had no income. Because you paid more than half the cost of keeping up your mother's apartment from January 1 until her death, and you can claim an exemption for her, you can file as a head of household.

Except when you are supporting and maintaining your parents, who do not have to live with you, the IRS says that you cannot qualify as head of household unless you live in the home that you are supporting and maintaining. However, some courts have said that you can maintain more than one home and still claim head of household status. The household that qualifies you as a head of household need not be your principal place of abode, but it must be the home where you and members of your household live for an adequate period of time.

Example 1
A woman who owned two homes, hundreds of miles apart, could still claim to be head of household at the home that was the principal place of residence of her adopted son, though she spent only 40% of her time there. For both homes, however, she paid more than half the cost of upkeep.

Example 2
A man could not claim to be head of household, although he paid 80-90% of the household expenses and was a member of a nearby church, because he did not spend a substantial amount of time at the house. He only visited his sisters at the house, either when he was in town on business during the week or when he stopped by for Sunday dinner. The house was owned by his sisters.

Example 3
A woman who spent 85% of her time in one house and 15% in another house that was the principal residence of her daughter and grandchildren was not allowed to claim head of household status. In this case, the houses were less than 2 miles apart and the woman stayed over at her daughter's only when either she or her daughter were ill. Besides, the daughter, not her mother, rented the house, although the daughter used money given to her by her mother to pay the rent.

Example 4
The case of the two-family house. In this case, a husband, wife, and their children lived in one of the house's units and the wife's mother and unwed sister lived in the other unit. The home contained some common areas but also some partitioned areas for the private use of each family unit. A court upheld the wife's mother's claim of head of household status based on her support of her unwed daughter. Even though the mother paid less than half of the total household expenses, she did pay more than half of the expenses attributable to her and her daughter.

Qualifying Widow(er) With Dependent Child

If your spouse died in 2011, you can use married filing jointly as your filing status for 2011 if you otherwise qualify to use that status. The year of death is the last year for which you can file jointly with your deceased spouse. See *Married Filing Jointly*, earlier.

You may be eligible to use qualifying widow(er) with dependent child as your filing status for 2 years following the year your spouse died. For example, if your spouse died in 2010, and you have not remarried, you may be able to use this filing status for 2011 and 2012.

This filing status entitles you to use joint return tax rates and the highest standard deduction amount (if you do not itemize deductions). This status does not entitle you to file a joint return.

How to file. If you file as qualifying widow(er) with dependent child, you can use either Form 1040A or Form 1040. Indicate your filing status by checking the box on line 5 of either form. Use the *Married filing jointly* column of the Tax Table or Section B of the Tax Computation Worksheet to figure your tax.

Eligibility rules. You are eligible to file your 2011 return as a qualifying widow(er) with dependent child if you meet all of the following tests.
- You were entitled to file a joint return with your spouse for the year your spouse died. It does not matter whether you actually filed a joint return.
- Your spouse died in 2009 or 2010 and you did not remarry before the end of 2011.
- You have a child or stepchild for whom you can claim an exemption. This does not include a foster child.
- This child lived in your home all year, except for temporary absences. See *Temporary absences*, earlier, under *Head of Household*. There are also exceptions, described later, for a child who was born or died during the year, and for a kidnapped child.
- You paid more than half the cost of keeping up a home for the year. See *Keeping Up a Home*, earlier, under *Head of Household*.

Example. John Reed's wife died in 2009. John has not remarried. During 2010 and 2011, he continued to keep up a home for himself and his child, who lives with him and for whom he can claim

Caution

As mentioned earlier, this filing status is available for only 2 years following the year your spouse died.

an exemption. For 2009 he was entitled to file a joint return for himself and his deceased wife. For 2010 and 2011, he can file as qualifying widower with a dependent child. After 2011 he can file as head of household if he qualifies.

Death or birth. You may be eligible to file as a qualifying widow(er) with dependent child if the child who qualifies you for this filing status is born or dies during the year. You must have provided more than half of the cost of keeping up a home that was the child's main home during the entire part of the year he or she was alive.

Kidnapped child. A child may qualify you for this filing status even if the child has been kidnapped. See Publication 501.

Chapter 3

Personal exemptions and dependents

ey.com/EYTaxGuide

Note

IRS Publication 17 (*Your Federal Income Tax*) has been updated by Ernst & Young LLP for 2011. Dates and dollar amounts shown are for 2011. Underlined type is used to indicate where IRS text has been updated. Places where text has been removed are indicated by the sentence: *Text intentionally omitted.*

ey.com/EYTaxGuide
Ernst & Young LLP will update the *Ernst & Young Tax Guide 2012* website with relevant taxpayer information as it becomes available. You can also sign up for email alerts to let you know when changes have been made.

Introduction

In 2011, you are entitled to a $3,700 deduction for yourself, your spouse, and each person you support who otherwise qualifies as a dependent. This is a $50 increase over the personal exemption amount of $3,650 that was effective for 2010. The amount of the personal exemption generally increases over time because of the statutory requirement to adjust the amount annually for inflation. This chapter tells you what specific qualifications you have to meet to take this deduction. This chapter also informs you about the special rules and procedures that apply to divorced and separated couples with children, widows and widowers, and residents of community property states. Perhaps most important, this chapter suggests when it might not be a good idea to take a deduction, even though you could qualify for it.

There are two types of dependents: a qualifying child and a qualifying relative.

First, a word about a qualifying child. A uniform definition of a "qualifying child" applies to all of the following tax benefits:

1. Dependency exemption
2. Child tax credit
3. Earned income credit
4. Child and dependent care credit
5. Head of household filing status
6. The exclusion from income for dependent care benefits

In order to claim an exemption for a qualifying child, the following four tests must be met:

1. Relationship test
2. Residency test
3. Age test
4. Support test

In addition to these four tests, the child must not file a joint return, unless the return was filed only as a claim for refund. In addition, special rules apply if the child is a qualifying child of more than one person. These tests are discussed in greater detail later on in this chapter. You should be aware, however, that a child who is not a qualifying child might still be a dependent as a qualifying relative. Other rules apply in determining whether someone is a "qualifying relative." These rules are also discussed in detail in this chapter.

The original intent of personal *exemptions* for dependents was to provide tax relief so that even the poorest citizen would be left with enough money after taxes to support themselves and their family. Obviously, a $3,700 deduction can save the taxpayer only a small portion of the income necessary to live. Ironically, the higher your income level and the higher your marginal tax rate, the greater economic benefit you derive from these deductions. A $3,700 deduction is worth $555 to a married couple filing a joint return with a taxable income of $50,000 and a marginal tax rate of 15%. The same $3,700 deduction is worth $1,036 to a married couple filing a joint return with a taxable income over $139,350 and a marginal tax rate of 28%. Figuring out who should claim whom as a dependent can be a difficult matter. For example, when parents are divorced, the custodial parent may sign a declaration permitting the noncustodial parent to claim the exemption for the dependent child. Consequently, if the noncustodial parent is in a higher tax bracket, a greater tax benefit can be obtained. Either parent is entitled to claim the medical expenses paid for the child, even if that parent cannot claim the child as a dependent.

What's New

Personal Exemption increased. The amount you can deduct for each exemption in 2011 is $3,700—up slightly from the 2010 exemption amount of $3,650.

Limits on personal exemptions ended. For 2011, you will not lose part of your deduction for personal exemptions, regardless of the amount of your adjusted gross income.

> **TAXPLANNER**
> This repeal of this limitation on personal exemptions also applies for 2012. After 2012, the old phaseout rule is scheduled to return in full force unless Congress intervenes. For updated information on these proposals and any other tax law changes that occur after this book was published, see our website, *ey.com/EYTaxGuide*.)

This chapter discusses exemptions. The following topics will be explained.
- Personal exemptions—You generally can take one for yourself and, if you are married, one for your spouse.
- Exemptions for dependents—You generally can take an exemption for each of your dependents. A dependent is your qualifying child or qualifying relative. If you are entitled to claim an exemption for a dependent, that dependent cannot claim a personal exemption on his or her own tax return.
- Social security number (SSN) requirement for dependents—You must list the social security number of any dependent for whom you claim an exemption.

Deduction. Exemptions reduce your taxable income. You can deduct $3,700 for each exemption you claim in 2011.

How to claim exemptions. How you claim an exemption on your tax return depends on which form you file.

If you file Form 1040EZ, the exemption amount is combined with the standard deduction amount and entered on line 5.

If you file Form 1040A or Form 1040, follow the instructions for the form. The total number of exemptions you can claim is the total in the box on line 6d. Also complete line 26 (Form 1040A) or line 42 (Form 1040).

Useful Items

You may want to see:

Publication
- □ **501** Exemptions, Standard Deduction, and Filing Information

Form (and Instructions)
- □ **2120** Multiple Support Declaration
- □ **8332** Release/Revocation of Release of Claim to Exemption for Child by Custodial Parent

Exemptions

There are two types of exemptions you may be able to take:
- Personal exemptions for yourself and your spouse, and
- Exemptions for dependents (dependency exemptions).

While each is worth the same amount ($3,700 for 2011), different rules apply to each type.

Personal Exemptions

You are generally allowed one exemption for yourself. If you are married, you may be allowed one exemption for your spouse. These are called personal exemptions.

Your Own Exemption

You can take one exemption for yourself unless you can be claimed as a dependent by another taxpayer. If another taxpayer is entitled to claim you as a dependent, you cannot take an exemption for yourself even if the other taxpayer does not actually claim you as a dependent.

Your Spouse's Exemption

Your spouse is never considered your dependent.

Tax Breaks and Deductions You Can Use Checklist

Personal Exemption. You can claim a deduction for yourself, called a personal exemption. You can claim a deduction for your spouse on a joint return. And you can claim a deduction for each of your dependents. In 2011, the exemption amount is $3,700 (each year it is indexed for inflation).

Phasedown of Personal Exemption Deduction. In 2009, the deduction for personal exemptions was phased down (and used to be entirely phased out) if your adjusted gross income (AGI) was too high. For 2010, 2011, and 2012, the personal exemption phaseout has been repealed and higher-income taxpayers can now deduct the full amount of their personal exemptions. After 2012, the old phaseout rule will return in full force, unless Congress intervenes and extends the current law or perhaps even permanently repeals the personal exemption phaseout. But remember that if you have to pay the alternative minimum tax (AMT), the personal exemption deduction is disallowed.

Joint return. On a joint return you can claim one exemption for yourself and one for your spouse.

Separate return. If you file a separate return, you can claim an exemption for your spouse only if your spouse had no gross income, is not filing a return, and was not the dependent of another taxpayer. This is true even if the other taxpayer does not actually claim your spouse as a dependent. This is also true if your spouse is a nonresident alien.

Death of spouse. If your spouse died during the year and you file a joint return for yourself and your deceased spouse, you generally can claim your spouse's exemption under the rules just explained under *Joint return.* If you file a separate return for the year, you may be able to claim your spouse's exemption under the rules just described in *Separate return.*

If you remarried during the year, you cannot take an exemption for your deceased spouse.

If you are a surviving spouse without gross income and you remarry in the year your spouse died, you can be claimed as an exemption on both the final separate return of your deceased spouse and the separate return of your new spouse for that year. If you file a joint return with your new spouse, you can be claimed as an exemption only on that return.

Divorced or separated spouse. If you obtained a final decree of divorce or separate maintenance by the end of the year, you cannot take your former spouse's exemption. This rule applies even if you provided all of your former spouse's support.

Exemptions for Dependents

You are allowed one exemption for each person you can claim as a dependent. You can claim an exemption for a dependent even if your dependent files a return.

The term "dependent" means:

- A qualifying child, or
- A qualifying relative.

The terms *"qualifying child"* and *"qualifying relative"* are defined later.

> ## EXPLANATION
> Oddly enough, a qualifying child does not have to be your child and your child may be a qualifying relative and not a qualifying child.

You can claim an exemption for a qualifying child or qualifying relative only if these three tests are met.

1. Dependent taxpayer test.
2. Joint return test.
3. Citizen or resident test.

These three tests are explained in detail later.

All the requirements for claiming an exemption for a dependent are summarized in Table 3-1.

Housekeepers, maids, or servants. If these people work for you, you cannot claim exemptions for them.

Child tax credit. You may be entitled to a child tax credit for each qualifying child who was under age 17 at the end of the year if you claimed an exemption for that child. For more information, see chapter 35.

Dependent Taxpayer Test

If you could be claimed as a dependent by another person, you cannot claim anyone else as a dependent. Even if you have a qualifying child or qualifying relative, you cannot claim that person as a dependent.

If you are filing a joint return and your spouse could be claimed as a dependent by someone else, you and your spouse cannot claim any dependents on your joint return.

Joint Return Test

You generally cannot claim a married person as a dependent if he or she files a joint return.

Exception. An exception to the joint return test applies if your child and his or her spouse file a joint return merely as a claim for refund and no tax liability would exist for either spouse on separate returns.

Example 1. You supported your 18-year-old daughter, and she lived with you all year while her husband was in the Armed Forces. The couple files a joint return. You cannot take an exemption for your daughter.

Example 2. Your 18-year-old son and his 17-year-old wife had $800 of interest income and no earned income. Neither is required to file a tax return. Taxes were taken out of their interest income due to backup withholding so they filed a joint return only to get a refund of the withheld taxes. The exception to the joint return test applies, so you are not disqualified from claiming their exemptions just because they file a joint return. You can claim their exemptions if you meet all the other requirements to do so.

Text intentionally omitted.

Citizen or Resident Test

You cannot claim a person as a dependent unless that person is a U.S. citizen, U.S. resident alien, U.S. national, or a resident of Canada or Mexico. However, there is an exception for certain adopted children, as explained next.

> ## EXPLANATION
> Residents of Puerto Rico do not meet the citizenship test unless they are also U.S. citizens.

Caution

Dependent not allowed a personal exemption. If you can claim an exemption for your dependent, the dependent cannot claim his or her own personal exemption on his or her own tax return. This is true even if you do not claim the dependent's exemption on your return.

Table 3-1. **Overview of the Rules for Claiming an Exemption for a Dependent**
Caution. This table is only an overview of the rules. For details, see the rest of this chapter.

• You cannot claim any dependents if you, or your spouse if filing jointly, could be claimed as a dependent by another taxpayer.
• You cannot claim a married person who files a joint return as a dependent unless that joint return is only a claim for refund and there would be no tax liability for either spouse on separate returns.
• You cannot claim a person as a dependent unless that person is a U.S. citizen, U.S. resident alien, U.S. national, or a resident of Canada or Mexico.[1]
• You cannot claim a person as a dependent unless that person is your **qualifying child** or **qualifying relative.**

Tests To Be a Qualifying Child	Tests To Be a Qualifying Relative
1. The child must be your son, daughter, stepchild, foster child, brother, sister, half brother, half sister, stepbrother, stepsister, or a descendant of any of them.	1. The person cannot be your qualifying child or the qualifying child of any other taxpayer.
2. The child must be (a) under age 19 at the end of the year and younger than you (or your spouse, if filing jointly), (b) under age 24 at the end of the year, a full-time student, and younger than you (or your spouse, if filing jointly), or (c) any age if permanently and totally disabled.	2. The person either (a) must be related to you in one of the ways listed under *Relatives who do not have to live with you,* or (b) must live with you all year as a member of your household[2] (and your relationship must not violate local law).
3. The child must have lived with you for more than half of the year.[2]	3. The person's gross income for the year must be less than $3,700.[3]
4. The child must not have provided more than half of his or her own support for the year.	4. You must provide more than half of the person's total support for the year.[4]
5. The child is not filing a joint return for the year (unless that return is filed only as a claim for refund)	
If the child meets the rules to be a qualifying child of more than one person, only one person can actually treat the child as a qualifying child. See the *Special Rule for Qualifying Child of More Than One Person* to find out which person is the person entitled to claim the child as a qualifying child.	

[1]There is an exception for certain adopted children.
[2]There are exceptions for temporary absences, children who were born or died during the year, children of divorced or separated parents or parents who live apart, and kidnapped children.
[3]There is an exception if the person is disabled and has income from a sheltered workshop.
[4]There are exceptions for multiple support agreements, children of divorced or separated parents or parents who live apart, and kidnapped children.

Exception for adopted child. If you are a U.S. citizen or U.S. national who has legally adopted a child who is not a U.S. citizen, U.S. resident alien, or U.S. national, this test is met if the child lived with you as a member of your household all year. This exception also applies if the child was lawfully placed with you for legal adoption.

Child's place of residence. Children usually are citizens or residents of the country of their parents.

If you were a U.S. citizen when your child was born, the child may be a U.S. citizen even if the other parent was a nonresident alien and the child was born in a foreign country. If so, this test is met.

EXAMPLE
The IRS has ruled that a U.S. citizen living in England since the age of 9, who subsequently married an Englishwoman, could not claim their son, who was born in England, as a dependent. The foreign-born child of a U.S. citizen and a nonresident alien is not a citizen or resident of the United States unless the American parent lived in the United States for 10 years before the child's birth. At least 5 of those 10 years must have been subsequent to age 14.

Foreign students' place of residence. Foreign students brought to this country under a qualified international education exchange program and placed in American homes for a temporary period generally are not U.S. residents and do not meet this test. You cannot claim an exemption for them. However, if you provided a home for a foreign student, you may be able to take a charitable contribution deduction. See *Expenses Paid for Student Living With You* in chapter 25.

> ## EXPLANATION
> For more information about taxes for aliens, see chapter 42, *Foreign citizens living in the United States.*

U.S. national. A U.S. national is an individual who, although not a U.S. citizen, owes his or her allegiance to the United States. U.S. nationals include American Samoans and Northern Mariana Islanders who chose to become U.S. nationals instead of U.S. citizens.

Qualifying Child

There are five tests that must be met for a child to be your qualifying child. The five tests are:

1. Relationship,
2. Age,
3. Residency,
4. Support, and
5. Joint return.

These tests are explained next.

Relationship Test

To meet this test, a child must be:

- Your son, daughter, stepchild, foster child, or a descendant (for example, your grandchild) of any of them, or
- Your brother, sister, half brother, half sister, stepbrother, stepsister, or a descendant (for example, your niece or nephew) of any of them.

Adopted child. An adopted child is always treated as your own child. The term "adopted child" includes a child who was lawfully placed with you for legal adoption.

Foster child. A foster child is an individual who is placed with you by an authorized placement agency or by judgment, decree, or other order of any court of competent jurisdiction.

> ## EXAMPLE
> Enrique and Lisa are married. Emma, a 5-year-old orphan, is placed by an authorized adoption agency in their home in July 2011. She is a member of the household for the rest of the year. Even though Emma was not a resident of their household for 12 months during 2011, and even though she was not legally adopted by Enrique and Lisa until 2012, she may be claimed as Enrique and Lisa's dependent for 2011. However, if Emma had not been placed in Enrique and Lisa's home by an authorized adoption agency, Enrique and Lisa would not be able to claim her as a dependent.

Age Test

To meet this test, a child must be:

- Under age 19 at the end of the year and younger than you (or your spouse, if filing jointly),
- A full-time student under age 24 at the end of the year and younger than you (or your spouse, if filing jointly), or
- Permanently and totally disabled at any time during the year, regardless of age.

Example. Your son turned 19 on December 10. Unless he was permanently and totally disabled or a full-time student, he does not meet the age test because, at the end of the year, he was not **under** age 19.

Child must be younger than you or spouse. To be your qualifying child, a child who is not permanently and totally disabled must be younger than you. However, if you are married filing jointly, the child must be younger than you or your spouse but does not have to be younger than both of you.

Example 1—child not younger than you or spouse. Your 23-year-old brother, who is a full-time student and unmarried, lives with you and your spouse. He is not disabled. Both you and

---

Caution

If a child meets the five tests to be the qualifying child of more than one person, a special rule applies to determine which person can actually treat the child as a qualifying child. See Special Rule for Qualifying Child of More Than One Person, *later.*

your spouse are 21 years old, and you file a joint return. Your brother is not your qualifying child because he is not younger than you or your spouse.

Example 2—child younger than your spouse but not younger than you. The facts are the same as in Example 1 except that your spouse is 25 years old. Because your brother is younger than your spouse and you and your spouse are filing a joint return, your brother is your qualifying child, even though he is not younger than you.

Full-time student. A full-time student is a student who is enrolled for the number of hours or courses the school considers to be full-time attendance.

Student defined. To qualify as a student, your child must be, during some part of each of any 5 calendar months of the year:

1. A full-time student at a school that has a regular teaching staff, course of study, and a regularly enrolled student body at the school, or
2. A student taking a full-time, on-farm training course given by a school described in (1), or by a state, county, or local government agency.

The 5 calendar months do not have to be consecutive.

School defined. A school can be an elementary school, junior or senior high school, college, university, or technical, trade, or mechanical school. However, an on-the-job training course, correspondence school, or school offering courses only through the Internet does not count as a school.

Vocational high school students. Students who work on "co-op" jobs in private industry as a part of a school's regular course of classroom and practical training are considered full-time students.

EXPLANATION

In order to qualify for the full-time student exemption, the child must be enrolled in an institution in which education is the primary purpose.

Example

A hospital providing programs for interns and residents does not qualify. However, a division of the hospital whose primary purpose is the education of students rather than on-the-job training may qualify.

EXPLANATION

For full-time students under the age of 24, the parents must continue to provide over half of the child's support to take the deduction as a qualifying child.

Example

Mr. and Mrs. Wong's 22-year-old unmarried son, Robert, graduated from college in June 2011 and got a job for the remainder of the year that paid him $10,000 in taxable income. Because Robert was a full-time student for at least 5 months during 2011 and he is under the age of 24, he meets the age test under the definition of qualifying child. Nevertheless, Mr. and Mrs. Wong will not be able to take a $3,700 deduction for Robert as their dependent unless they can prove that they provided over half of Robert's support during the entire year. If they are entitled to take the deduction for him, Robert is not entitled to claim an exemption for himself on his return.

Assuming the exemption for Robert is more valuable on his parents' return than on Robert's own return, Robert's parents should document that they did furnish over half their son's support during the year by paying for his tuition and room and board while he was in school. Robert should have used as large a portion of his income as possible for things that did not constitute support. The more money he saved and invested in 2011, the better. Then Mr. and Mrs. Wong would be entitled to claim Robert as a dependent and take a $3,700 deduction.

On the other hand, if Mr. and Mrs. Wong are subject to the alternative minimum tax (AMT), claiming Robert as a dependent may not offer any tax savings. Personal exemptions are not deductible for purposes of calculating the AMT.

Permanently and totally disabled. Your child is permanently and totally disabled if both of the following apply.

- He or she cannot engage in any substantial gainful activity because of a physical or mental condition.
- A doctor determines the condition has lasted or can be expected to last continuously for at least a year or can lead to death.

Residency Test

To meet this test, your child must have lived with you for more than half of the year. There are exceptions for temporary absences, children who were born or died during the year, kidnapped children, and children of divorced or separated parents.

Temporary absences. Your child is considered to have lived with you during periods of time when one of you, or both, are temporarily absent due to special circumstances such as:

- Illness,
- Education,
- Business,
- Vacation, or
- Military service.

Death or birth of child. A child who was born or died during the year is treated as having lived with you all year if your home was the child's home the entire time he or she was alive during the year. The same is true if the child lived with you all year except for any required hospital stay following birth.

Child born alive. You may be able to claim an exemption for a child who was born alive during the year, even if the child lived only for a moment. State or local law must treat the child as having been born alive. There must be proof of a live birth shown by an official document, such as a birth certificate. The child must be your qualifying child or qualifying relative, and all the other tests to claim an exemption for a dependent must be met.

> **TAXPLANNER**
> You can take a dependency exemption for 2011 for a child born on or before December 31, 2011, but not for a baby born January 1, 2012. Plan accordingly!

> **TAXPLANNER**
> In addition to the personal exemption, a tax credit may be available for each qualifying child under age 17. The per child credit for 2011 remains constant at $1,000. See chapter 35, *Child tax credit*, for additional information.

Stillborn child. You cannot claim an exemption for a stillborn child.

Kidnapped child. You can treat your child as meeting the residency test even if the child has been kidnapped, but both of the following statements must be true.

1. The child is presumed by law enforcement authorities to have been kidnapped by someone who is not a member of your family or the child's family.
2. In the year the kidnapping occurred, the child lived with you for more than half of the part of the year before the date of the kidnapping.

This treatment applies for all years until the child is returned. However, the last year this treatment can apply is the earlier of:

1. The year there is a determination that the child is dead, or
2. The year the child would have reached age 18.

Children of divorced or separated parents or parents who live apart. In most cases, because of the residency test, a child of divorced or separated parents is the qualifying child of the custodial parent. However, the child will be treated as the qualifying child of the noncustodial parent if all four of the following statements are true.

1. The parents:
   a. Are divorced or legally separated under a decree of divorce or separate maintenance,
   b. Are separated under a written separation agreement, or
   c. Lived apart at all times during the last 6 months of the year, whether or not they are or were married.
2. The child received over half of his or her support for the year from the parents.
3. The child is in the custody of one or both parents for more than half of the year.
4. Either of the following statements is true.
   a. The custodial parent signs a written declaration, discussed later, that he or she will not claim the child as a dependent for the year, and the noncustodial parent attaches this

written declaration to his or her return. (If the decree or agreement went into effect after 1984 and before 2009, see *Post-1984 and pre-2009 divorce decree or separation agreement*, later. If the decree or agreement went into effect after 2008, see *Post-2008 divorce decree or separation agreement*, later.)

   b. A pre-1985 decree of divorce or separate maintenance or written separation agreement that applies to 2011 states that the noncustodial parent can claim the child as a dependent, the decree or agreement was not changed after 1984 to say the noncustodial parent cannot claim the child as a dependent, and the noncustodial parent provides at least $600 for the child's support during the year.

Custodial parent and noncustodial parent. The custodial parent is the parent with whom the child lived for the greater number of nights during the year. The other parent is the noncustodial parent.

If the parents divorced or separated during the year and the child lived with both parents before the separation, the custodial parent is the one with whom the child lived for the greater number of nights during the rest of the year.

A child is treated as living with a parent for a night if the child sleeps:

- At that parent's home, whether or not the parent is present, or
- In the company of the parent, when the child does not sleep at a parent's home (for example, the parent and child are on vacation together).

Equal number of nights. If the child lived with each parent for an equal number of nights during the year, the custodial parent is the parent with the higher adjusted gross income.

December 31. The night of December 31 is treated as part of the year in which it begins. For example, December 31, 2011, is treated as part of 2011.

Emancipated child. If a child is emancipated under state law, the child is treated as not living with either parent. See Examples 5 and 6.

Absences. If a child was not with either parent on a particular night (because, for example, the child was staying at a friend's house), the child is treated as living with the parent with whom the child normally would have lived for that night, except for the absence. But if it cannot be determined with which parent the child normally would have lived or if the child would not have lived with either parent that night, the child is treated as not living with either parent that night.

Parent works at night. If, due to a parent's nighttime work schedule, a child lives for a greater number of days but not nights with the parent who works at night, that parent is treated as the custodial parent. On a school day, the child is treated as living at the primary residence registered with the school.

Example 1—child lived with one parent greater number of nights. You and your child's other parent are divorced. In 2011, your child lived with you 210 nights and with the other parent 155 nights. You are the custodial parent.

Example 2—child is away at camp. In 2011, your daughter lives with each parent for alternate weeks. In the summer, she spends 6 weeks at summer camp. During the time she is at camp, she is treated as living with you for 3 weeks and with her other parent, your ex-spouse, for 3 weeks because this is how long she would have lived with each parent if she had not attended summer camp.

Example 3—child lived same number of days with each parent. Your son lived with you 180 nights during the year and lived the same number of nights with his other parent, your ex-spouse. Your adjusted gross income is $40,000. Your ex-spouse's adjusted gross income is $25,000. You are treated as your son's custodial parent because you have the higher adjusted gross income.

Example 4—child is at parent's home but with other parent. Your son normally lives with you during the week and with his other parent, your ex-spouse, every other weekend. You become ill and are hospitalized. The other parent lives in your home with your son for 10 consecutive days while you are in the hospital. Your son is treated as living with you during this 10-day period because he was living in your home.

Example 5—child emancipated in May. When your son turned age 18 in May 2011, he became emancipated under the law of the state where he lives. As a result, he is not considered in the custody of his parents for more than half of the year. The special rule for children of divorced or separated parents does not apply.

Example 6—child emancipated in August. Your daughter lives with you from January 1, 2011, until May 31, 2011, and lives with her other parent, your ex-spouse, from June 1, 2011, through the end of the year. She turns 18 and is emancipated under state law on August 1, 2011. Because she is treated as not living with either parent beginning on August 1, she is treated as living with you the greater number of nights in 2011. You are the custodial parent.

Written declaration. The custodial parent may use either Form 8332 or a similar statement (containing the same information required by the form) to make the written declaration to release the exemption to the noncustodial parent. The noncustodial parent must attach a copy of the form or statement to his or her tax return.

The exemption can be released for 1 year, for a number of specified years (for example, alternate years), or for all future years, as specified in the declaration.

Post-1984 and pre-2009 divorce decree or separation agreement. If the divorce decree or separation agreement went into effect after 1984 and before 2009, the noncustodial parent may be able to attach certain pages from the decree or agreement instead of Form 8332. The decree or agreement must state all three of the following.

1. The noncustodial parent can claim the child as a dependent without regard to any condition, such as payment of support.
2. The custodial parent will not claim the child as a dependent for the year.
3. The years for which the noncustodial parent, rather than the custodial parent, can claim the child as a dependent.

The noncustodial parent must attach all of the following pages of the decree or agreement to his or her tax return.

• The cover page (write the other parent's social security number on this page).
• The pages that include all of the information identified in items (1) through (3) above.
• The signature page with the other parent's signature and the date of the agreement.

Post-2008 divorce decree or separation agreement. The noncustodial parent can no longer attach pages from the decree or agreement instead of Form 8332 if the decree or agreement went into effect after 2008. The custodial parent must sign either Form 8332 or a similar statement whose only purpose is to release the custodial parent's claim to an exemption for a child, and the noncustodial parent must attach a copy to his or her return. The form or statement must release the custodial parent's claim to the child without any conditions. For example, the release must not depend on the noncustodial parent paying support.

Revocation of release of claim to an exemption. The custodial parent can revoke a release of claim to exemption that he or she previously released to the noncustodial parent on Form 8332 or a similar statement. If the custodial parent provided, or made reasonable efforts to provide, the noncustodial parent with written notice of the revocation in 2010, the revocation can be effective no earlier than 2011. The custodial parent can use Part III of Form 8332 for this purpose and must attach a copy of the revocation to his or her return for each tax year he or she claims the child as a dependent as a result of the revocation.

Remarried parent. If you remarry, the support provided by your new spouse is treated as provided by you.

Parents who never married. This special rule for divorced or separated parents also applies to parents who never married and lived apart at all times during the last 6 months of the year.

Support Test (To Be a Qualifying Child)

To meet this test, the child cannot have provided more than half of his or her own support for the year.

This test is different from the support test to be a qualifying relative, which is described later. However, to see what is or is not support, see *Support Test (To Be a Qualifying Relative)*, later. If you are not sure whether a child provided more than half of his or her own support, you may find Worksheet 3-1 helpful.

Example. You provided $4,000 toward your 16-year-old son's support for the year. He has a part-time job and provided $6,000 to his own support. He provided more than half of his own support for the year. He is not your qualifying child.

Foster care payments and expenses. Payments you receive for the support of a foster child from a child placement agency are considered support provided by the agency. Similarly, payments you receive for the support of a foster child from a state or county are considered support provided by the state or county.

If you are not in the trade or business of providing foster care and your unreimbursed out-of-pocket expenses in caring for a foster child were mainly to benefit an organization qualified to receive deductible charitable contributions, the expenses are deductible as charitable contributions but are not considered support you provided. For more information about the deduction for charitable contributions, see chapter 25. If your unreimbursed expenses are not deductible as charitable contributions, they are considered support you provided.

If you are in the trade or business of providing foster care, your unreimbursed expenses are not considered support provided by you.

Example 1. Lauren, a foster child, lived with Mr. and Mrs. Smith for the last 3 months of the year. The Smiths cared for Lauren because they wanted to adopt her (although she had not been

Funds Belonging to the Person You Supported

1. Enter the total funds belonging to the person you supported, including income received (taxable and nontaxable) and amounts borrowed during the year, plus the amount in savings and other accounts at the beginning of the year. Do not include funds provided by the state; include those amounts on line 23 instead .... **1.** _____
2. Enter the amount on line 1 that was used for the person's support .... **2.** _____
3. Enter the amount on line 1 that was used for other purposes .... **3.** _____
4. Enter the total amount in the person's savings and other accounts at the end of the year .... **4.** _____
5. Add lines 2 through 4. (This amount should equal line 1.) .... **5.** _____

Expenses for Entire Household (where the person you supported lived)

6. Lodging (complete line 6a or 6b):
   6a. Enter the total rent paid .... **6a.** _____
   6b. Enter the fair rental value of the home. If the person you supported owned the home, also include this amount in line 21.. **6b.** _____
7. Enter the total food expenses.. **7.** _____
8. Enter the total amount of utilities (heat, light, water, etc. not included in line 6a or 6b) .... **8.** _____
9. Enter the total amount of repairs (not included in line 6a or 6b) .... **9.** _____
10. Enter the total of other expenses. Do not include expenses of maintaining the home, such as mortgage interest, real estate taxes, and insurance................................ **10.** _____
11. Add lines 6a through 10. These are the total household expenses..................... **11.** _____
12. Enter total number of persons who lived in the household........................... **12.** _____

Expenses for the Person You Supported

13. Divide line 11 by line 12. This is the person's share of the household expenses .... **13.** _____
14. Enter the person's total clothing expenses....................................... **14.** _____
15. Enter the person's total education expenses .... **15.** _____
16. Enter the person's total medical and dental expenses not paid for or reimbursed by insurance.... **16.** _____
17. Enter the person's total travel and recreation expenses............................. **17.** _____
18. Enter the total of the person's other expenses.................................... **18.** _____
19. Add lines 13 through 18. This is the total cost of the person's support for the year .... **19.** _____

Did the Person Provide More Than Half of His or Her Own Support?

20. Multiply line 19 by 50% (.50) .... **20.** _____
21. Enter the amount from line 2, plus the amount from line 6b if the person you supported owned the home. This is the amount the person provided for his or her own support .... **21.** _____
22. Is line 21 more than line 20?

   ☐ **No.** You meet the support test for this person to be your qualifying child. If this person also meets the other tests to be a qualifying child, stop here; do not complete lines 23-26. Otherwise, go to line 23 and fill out the rest of the worksheet to determine if this person is your qualifying relative.

   ☐ **Yes.** You do not meet the support test for this person to be either your qualifying child or your qualifying relative. **Stop here.**

Did You Provide More Than Half?

23. Enter the amount others provided for the person's support. Include amounts provided by state, local, and other welfare societies or agencies. Do not include any amounts included on line 1 .... **23.** _____
24. Add lines 21 and 23 .... **24.** _____
25. Subtract line 24 from line 19. This is the amount you provided for the person's support .... **25.** _____
26. Is line 25 more than line 20?

   ☐ **Yes.** You meet the support test for this person to be your qualifying relative.

   ☐ **No.** You do not meet the support test for this person to be your qualifying relative. You cannot claim an exemption for this person unless you can do so under a multiple support agreement, the support test for children of divorced or separated parents, or the special rule for kidnapped children. See *Multiple Support Agreement*, *Support Test for Children of Divorced or Separated Parents Who Live Apart*, or *Kidnapped Child* under *Qualifying Relative*.

placed with them for adoption). They did not care for her as a trade or business or to benefit the agency that placed her in their home. The Smiths' unreimbursed expenses are not deductible as charitable contributions but are considered support they provided for Lauren.

Example 2. You provided $3,000 toward your 10-year-old foster child's support for the year. The state government provided $4,000, which is considered support provided by the state, not by the child. See *Support provided by the state (welfare, food stamps, housing, etc.)*, later. Your foster child did not provide more than half of her own support for the year.

> ### EXPLANATION
> Unlike prior law, the current tax law does not consider the person who provides over half the support of the child as relevant for determining who is a qualifying child. What is relevant is that the child cannot provide over half of his or her own support during the year.

Scholarships. A scholarship received by a child who is a full-time student is not taken into account in determining whether the child provided more than half of his or her own support.

Joint Return Test (To Be a Qualifying Child)
To meet this test, the child cannot file a joint return for the year.

Exception. An exception to the joint return test applies if your child and his or her spouse file a joint return merely as a claim for refund.

Example 1. You supported your 18-year-old daughter, and she lived with you all year while her husband was in the Armed Forces. The couple files a joint return. Because your daughter filed a joint return, she is not your qualifying child.

Example 2. Your 18-year-old son and his 17-year-old wife had $800 of interest income and no earned income. Neither is required to file a tax return. Taxes were taken out of their interest income due to backup withholding so they filed a joint return only to get a refund of the withheld taxes. The exception to the joint return test applies, so your son may be your qualifying child if all the other tests are met.
Text intentionally omitted.

Special Rule for Qualifying Child of More Than One Person

> ### TAXALERT
> **Children of divorced or separated parents.** If a parent may claim the child as a qualifying child then no other person may claim such child as a qualifying child unless (1) the parents do not claim the child as a qualifying child, (2) the other person is eligible to claim the child as a qualifying child, and (3) the adjusted gross income of the other person is higher than the highest adjusted gross income of any parent of the child.

Sometimes, a child meets the relationship, age, residency, support, and joint return tests to be a qualifying child of more than one person. Although the child meets the conditions to be a qualifying child of each of these persons, only one person can actually treat the child as a qualifying child to take all of the following tax benefits (provided the person is eligible for each benefit).
1. The exemption for the child.
2. The child tax credit.
3. Head of household filing status.
4. The credit for child and dependent care expenses.
5. The exclusion from income for dependent care benefits.
6. The earned income credit.

The other person cannot take any of these benefits based on this qualifying child. In other words, you and the other person cannot agree to divide these tax benefits between you. The other person cannot take any of these tax benefits unless he or she has a different qualifying child.

Tiebreaker rules. To determine which person can treat the child as a qualifying child to claim these six tax benefits, the following tie-breaker rules apply.
- If only one of the persons is the child's parent, the child is treated as the qualifying child of the parent.

> **Tip**
>
> *If your qualifying child is not a qualifying child of anyone else, this special rule does not apply to you and you do not need to read about it. This is also true if your qualifying child is not a qualifying child of anyone else except your spouse with whom you file a joint return.*

> **Caution**
>
> *If a child is treated as the qualifying child of the non-custodial parent under the rules for children of divorced or separated parents or parents who live apart, described earlier, see* Applying this special rule to divorced or separated parents or parents who live apart, *later.*

- If the parents do not file a joint return together but both parents claim the child as a qualifying child, the IRS will treat the child as the qualifying child of the parent with whom the child lived for the longer period of time during the year. If the child lived with each parent for the same amount of time, the IRS will treat the child as the qualifying child of the parent who had the higher adjusted gross income (AGI) for the year.
- If no parent can claim the child as a qualifying child, the child is treated as the qualifying child of the person who had the highest AGI for the year.
- If a parent can claim the child as a qualifying child but no parent does so claim the child, the child is treated as the qualifying child of the person who had the highest AGI for the year, but only if that person's AGI is higher than the highest AGI of any of the child's parents who can claim the child. If the child's parents file a joint return with each other, this rule can be applied by dividing the parents' combined AGI equally between the parents. See *Example 6*.

Subject to these tiebreaker rules, you and the other person may be able to choose which of you claims the child as a qualifying child.

EXPLANATION

The table below summarizes the tiebreaker rules:

When More Than One Person Files a Return Claiming the Same Qualifying Child (Tiebreaker Rule)

Caution. If a child is treated as the qualifying child of the noncustodial parent under the rules for children of divorced or separated parents, see Applying this special test to divorced or separated parents or parents who live apart.

IF more than one person files a return claiming the same qualifying child and . . .	THEN the child will be treated as the qualifying child of the . . .
only one of the persons is the child's parent,	parent.
two of the persons are parents of the child and they do not file a joint return together,	parent with whom the child lived for the longer period of time during the year.
two of the persons are parents of the child, they do not file a joint return together, and the child lived with each parent the same amount of time during the year,	parent with the higher adjusted gross income (AGI).
none of the persons are the child's parent,	person with the highest AGI.
the parents of the child can claim the child as a qualifying child, but no parent claims the child.	no one else can claim the child as a qualifying child, unless that person's AGI is higher than the highest AGI of any parent of the child.*

*If the child's parents file a joint return with each other, this rule can be applied by dividing the parents' combined AGI equally between the parents.

Example 1—child lived with parent and grandparent. You and your 3-year-old daughter Jane lived with your mother all year. You are 25 years old, unmarried, and your AGI is $9,000. Your mother's AGI is $15,000. Jane's father did not live with you or your daughter. The rule explained earlier for children of divorced or separated parents or parents who live apart does not apply. Jane is a qualifying child of both you and your mother because she meets the relationship, age, residency, support, and joint return tests for both you and your mother. However, only one of you can claim her. Jane is not a qualifying child of anyone else, including her father. You agree to let your mother claim Jane. This means your mother can claim Jane as a qualifying child for the dependency exemption, child tax credit, head of household filing status, credit for child and dependent care expenses, exclusion for dependent care benefits, and the earned income credit, if she qualifies for each of those tax benefits (and if you do not claim Jane as a qualifying child for any of those tax benefits).

Example 2—parent has higher AGI than grandparent. The facts are the same as in *Example 1* except your AGI is $18,000. Because your mother's AGI is not higher than yours, she cannot claim Jane. Only you can claim Jane.

Example 3—two persons claim same child. The facts are the same as in *Example 1* except that you and your mother both claim Jane as a qualifying child. In this case, you as the child's parent will be the only one allowed to claim Jane as a qualifying child. The IRS will disallow your mother's claim to the six tax benefits listed earlier unless she has another qualifying child.

Example 4—qualifying children split between two persons. The facts are the same as in _Example 1_ except you also have two other young children who are qualifying children of both you and your mother. Only one of you can claim each child. However, if your mother's AGI is higher than yours, you can allow your mother to claim one or more of the children. For example, if you claim one child, your mother can claim the other two.

Example 5—taxpayer who is a qualifying child. The facts are the same as in _Example 1_ except you are only 18 years old and did not provide more than half of your own support for the year. This means you are your mother's qualifying child. If she can claim you as a dependent, then you cannot claim your daughter as a dependent because of the _Dependent Taxpayer Test_ explained earlier.

Example 6—child lived with both parents and grandparent. The facts are the same as in _Example 1_ except that you and your daughter's father are married to each other, live with your daughter and your mother, and have AGI of $20,000 on a joint return. If you and your husband do not claim your daughter as a qualifying child, your mother can claim her instead. Even though the AGI on your joint return, $20,000, is more than your mother's AGI of $15,000, for this purpose each parent's AGI can be treated as $10,000, so your mother's $15,000 AGI is treated as higher than the highest AGI of any of the child's parents who can claim the child.

Example 7—separated parents. You, your husband, and your 10-year-old son lived together until August 1, 2011, when your husband moved out of the household. In August and September, your son lived with you. For the rest of the year, your son lived with your husband, the boy's father. Your son is a qualifying child of both you and your husband because your son lived with each of you for more than half the year and because he met the relationship, age, support, and joint return tests for both of you. At the end of the year, you and your husband still were not divorced, legally separated, or separated under a written separation agreement, so the rule for children of divorced or separated parents or parents who live apart does not apply.

You and your husband will file separate returns. Your husband agrees to let you treat your son as a qualifying child. This means, if your husband does not claim your son as a qualifying child, you can claim your son as a qualifying child for the dependency exemption, child tax credit, and exclusion for dependent care benefits, if you qualify for each of those tax benefits. However, you cannot claim head of household filing status because you and your husband did not live apart for the last 6 months of the year. As a result, your filing status is married filing separately, so you cannot claim the earned income credit or the credit for child and dependent care expenses.

Example 8—separated parents claim same child. The facts are the same as in _Example 7_ except that you and your husband both claim your son as a qualifying child. In this case, only your husband will be allowed to treat your son as a qualifying child. This is because, during 2011, the boy lived with him longer than with you. If you claimed an exemption, the child tax credit, or the exclusion for dependent care benefits for your son, the IRS will disallow your claim to all these tax benefits, unless you have another qualifying child. In addition, because you and your husband did not live apart for the last 6 months of the year, your husband cannot claim head of household filing status. As a result, his filing status is married filing separately, so he cannot claim the earned income credit or the credit for child and dependent care expenses.

Example 9—unmarried parents. You, your 5-year-old son, and your son's father lived together all year. You and your son's father are not married. Your son is a qualifying child of both you and his father because he meets the relationship, age, residency, support, and joint return tests for both you and his father. Your AGI is $12,000 and your son's father's AGI is $14,000. Your son's father agrees to let you claim the child as a qualifying child. This means you can claim him as a qualifying child for the dependency exemption, child tax credit, head of household filing status, credit for child and dependent care expenses, exclusion for dependent care benefits, and the earned income credit, if you qualify for each of those tax benefits (and if your son's father does not, in fact, claim your son as a qualifying child for any of those tax benefits).

Example 10—unmarried parents claim same child. The facts are the same as in _Example 9_ except that you and your son's father both claim your son as a qualifying child. In this case, only your son's father will be allowed to treat your son as a qualifying child. This is because his AGI, $14,000, is more than your AGI, $12,000. If you claimed an exemption, the child tax credit, head of household filing status, credit for child and dependent care expenses, exclusion for dependent care benefits, or the earned income credit for your son, the IRS will disallow your claim to all these tax benefits, unless you have another qualifying child.

Example 11—child did not live with a parent. You and your 7-year-old niece, your sister's child, lived with your mother all year. You are 25 years old, and your AGI is $9,300. Your mother's AGI is

$15,000. Your niece's parents file jointly, have an AGI of less than $9,000, and do not live with you or their child. Your niece is a qualifying child of both you and your mother because she meets the relationship, age, residency, support, and joint return tests for both you and your mother. However, only your mother can treat her as a qualifying child. This is because your mother's AGI, $15,000, is more than your AGI, $9,300.

Applying this special rule to divorced or separated parents or parents who live apart. If a child is treated as the qualifying child of the noncustodial parent under the rules described earlier for children of divorced or separated parents or parents who live apart, only the noncustodial parent can claim an exemption and the child tax credit for the child. However, the custodial parent, if eligible, or other eligible person can claim the child as a qualifying child for head of household filing status, the credit for child and dependent care expenses, the exclusion for dependent care benefits, and the earned income credit. If the child is the qualifying child of more than one person for these benefits, then the tiebreaker rules will determine which person can treat the child as a qualifying child.

Example 1. You and your 5-year-old son lived all year with your mother, who paid the entire cost of keeping up the home. Your AGI is $10,000. Your mother's AGI is $25,000. Your son's father did not live with you or your son. Under the rules explained earlier for children of divorced or separated parents or parents who live apart, your son is treated as the qualifying child of his father, who can claim an exemption and the child tax credit for him. Because of this, you cannot claim an exemption or the child tax credit for your son. However, your son's father cannot claim your son as a qualifying child for head of household filing status, the credit for child and dependent care expenses, the exclusion for dependent care benefits, or the earned income credit. You and your mother did not have any child care expenses or dependent care benefits, but the boy is a qualifying child of both you and your mother for head of household filing status and the earned income credit because he meets the relationship, age, residency, support, and joint return tests for both you and your mother. (Note: The support test does not apply for the earned income credit.) However, you agree to let your mother claim your son. This means she can claim him for head of household filing status and the earned income credit if she qualifies for each and if you do not claim him as a qualifying child for the earned income credit. (You cannot claim head of household filing status because your mother paid the entire cost of keeping up the home.)

Example 2. The facts are the same as in *Example 1* except that your AGI is $25,000 and your mother's AGI is $21,000. Your mother cannot claim your son as a qualifying child for any purpose because her AGI is not higher than yours.

Example 3. The facts are the same as in *Example 1* except that you and your mother both claim your son as a qualifying child for the earned income credit. Your mother also claims him as a qualifying child for head of household filing status. You as the child's parent will be the only one allowed to claim your son as a qualifying child for the earned income credit. The IRS will disallow your mother's claim to the earned income credit and head of household filing status unless she has another qualifying child.

Qualifying Relative

There are four tests that must be met for a person to be your qualifying relative. The four tests are:
1. Not a qualifying child test,
2. Member of household or relationship test,
3. Gross income test, and
4. Support test.

Age. Unlike a qualifying child, a qualifying relative can be any age. There is no age test for a qualifying relative.

Kidnapped child. You can treat a child as your qualifying relative even if the child has been kidnapped, but both of the following statements must be true.
1. The child is presumed by law enforcement authorities to have been kidnapped by someone who is not a member of your family or the child's family.
2. In the year the kidnapping occurred, the child met the tests to be your qualifying relative for the part of the year before the date of the kidnapping.

This treatment applies for all years until the child is returned. However, the last year this treatment can apply is the earlier of:
1. The year there is a determination that the child is dead, or
2. The year the child would have reached age 18.

Not a Qualifying Child Test

A child is not your qualifying relative if the child is your qualifying child or the qualifying child of any other taxpayer.

Example 1. Your 22-year-old daughter, who is a full-time student, lives with you and meets all the tests to be your qualifying child. She is not your qualifying relative.

Example 2. Your 2-year-old son lives with your parents and meets all the tests to be their qualifying child. He is not your qualifying relative.

Example 3. Your son lives with you but is not your qualifying child because he is 30 years old and does not meet the age test. He may be your qualifying relative if the gross income test and the support test are met.

Example 4. Your 13-year-old grandson lived with his mother for 3 months, with his uncle for 4 months, and with you for 5 months during the year. He is not your qualifying child because he does not meet the residency test. He may be your qualifying relative if the gross income test and the support test are met.

Child of person not required to file a return. A child is not the qualifying child of any other taxpayer and so may qualify as your qualifying relative if the child's parent (or other person for whom the child is defined as a qualifying child) is not required to file an income tax return and either:
- Does not file an income tax return, or
- Files a return only to get a refund of income tax withheld or estimated tax paid.

Example 1—return not required. You support an unrelated friend and her 3-year-old child, who lived with you all year in your home. Your friend has no gross income, is not required to file a 2011 tax return, and does not file a 2011 tax return. Both your friend and her child are your qualifying relatives if the member of household or relationship test, gross income test, and support test are met.

Example 2—return filed to claim refund. The facts are the same as in *Example 1* except your friend had wages of $1,500 during the year and had income tax withheld from her wages. She files a return only to get a refund of the income tax withheld and does not claim the earned income credit or any other tax credits or deductions. Both your friend and her child are your qualifying relatives if the member of household or relationship test, gross income test, and support test are met.

Example 3—earned income credit claimed. The facts are the same as in *Example 2* except your friend had wages of $8,000 during the year and claimed the earned income credit on her return. Your friend's child is the qualifying child of another taxpayer (your friend), so you cannot claim your friend's child as your qualifying relative.

Child in Canada or Mexico. A child who lives in Canada or Mexico may be your qualifying relative, and you may be able to claim the child as a dependent. If the child does not live with you, the child does not meet the residency test to be your qualifying child. If the persons the child does live with are not U.S. citizens and have no U.S. gross income, those persons are not "taxpayers," so the child is not the qualifying child of any other taxpayer. If the child is not your qualifying child or the qualifying child of any other taxpayer, the child is your qualifying relative if the gross income test and the support test are met.

You cannot claim as a dependent a child who lives in a foreign country other than Canada or Mexico, unless the child is a U.S. citizen, U.S. resident alien, or U.S. national. There is an exception for certain adopted children who lived with you all year. See *Citizen or Resident Test,* earlier.

Example. You provide all the support of your children, ages 6, 8, and 12, who live in Mexico with your mother and have no income. You are single and live in the United States. Your mother is not a U.S. citizen and has no U.S. income, so she is not a "taxpayer." Your children are not your qualifying children because they do not meet the residency test. Also, they are not the qualifying children of any other taxpayer, so they are your qualifying relatives and you can claim them as dependents if all the tests are met. You may also be able to claim your mother as a dependent if all the tests are met, including the gross income test and the support test.

Member of Household or Relationship Test

To meet this test, a person must either:
1. Live with you all year as a member of your household, or
2. Be related to you in one of the ways listed under *Relatives who do not have to live with you.*

If at any time during the year the person was your spouse, that person cannot be your qualifying relative. However, see *Personal Exemptions*, earlier.

Relatives who do not have to live with you. A person related to you in any of the following ways does not have to live with you all year as a member of your household to meet this test.
- Your child, stepchild, foster child, or a descendant of any of them (for example, your grandchild). (A legally adopted child is considered your child.)
- Your brother, sister, half brother, half sister, stepbrother, or stepsister.
- Your father, mother, grandparent, or other direct ancestor, but not foster parent.
- Your stepfather or stepmother.
- A son or daughter of your brother or sister.
- A brother or sister of your father or mother.
- Your son-in-law, daughter-in-law, father-in-law, mother-in-law, brother-in-law, or sister-in-law.

Any of these relationships that were established by marriage are not ended by death or divorce.

Example. You and your wife began supporting your wife's father, a widower, in 2004. Your wife died in 2010. In spite of your wife's death, your father-in-law continues to meet this test, even if he does not live with you. You can claim him as a dependent if all other tests are met, including the gross income test and support test.

Foster child. A foster child is an individual who is placed with you by an authorized placement agency or by judgment, decree, or other order of any court of competent jurisdiction.

Joint return. If you file a joint return, the person can be related to either you or your spouse. Also, the person does not need to be related to the spouse who provides support.

For example, your spouse's uncle who receives more than half of his support from you may be your qualifying relative, even though he does not live with you. However, if you and your spouse file separate returns, your spouse's uncle can be your qualifying relative only if he lives with you all year as a member of your household.

Temporary absences. A person is considered to live with you as a member of your household during periods of time when one of you, or both, are temporarily absent due to special circumstances such as:
- Illness,
- Education,
- Business,
- Vacation, or
- Military service.

If the person is placed in a nursing home for an indefinite period of time to receive constant medical care, the absence may be considered temporary.

Death or birth. A person who died during the year, but lived with you as a member of your household until death, will meet this test. The same is true for a child who was born during the year and lived with you as a member of your household for the rest of the year. The test is also met if a child lived with you as a member of your household except for any required hospital stay following birth.

If your dependent died during the year and you otherwise qualified to claim an exemption for the dependent, you can still claim the exemption.

Example. Your dependent mother died on January 15. She met the tests to be your qualifying relative. The other tests to claim an exemption for a dependent were also met. You can claim an exemption for her on your return.

Local law violated. A person does not meet this test if at any time during the year the relationship between you and that person violates local law.

Example. Your girlfriend lived with you as a member of your household all year. However, your relationship with her violated the laws of the state where you live, because she was married to someone else. Therefore, she does not meet this test and you cannot claim her as a dependent.

Adopted child. An adopted child is always treated as your own child. The term "adopted child" includes a child who was lawfully placed with you for legal adoption.

Cousin. Your cousin meets this test only if he or she lives with you all year as a member of your household. A cousin is a descendant of a brother or sister of your father or mother.

A dependent must be either a relative as described above or a full-time resident in your principal residence. Your child qualifies as a relative, even if the child is illegitimate.

While your stepchild, stepfather, and stepmother all qualify as relatives, their blood relations do not. Even so, their blood relations may qualify as your dependents if they are full-time residents in your home.

While your spouse's brother and/or sister qualify as relatives to you, their spouses do not.

Example

Amy is married to Oliver. Amy's sister Laura, along with Laura's husband, Stephen, are relatives of Amy, but only Laura is a relative of Oliver. If Amy and Oliver file a joint tax return, Laura and Stephen may both be claimed as dependents (as relatives) if they otherwise qualify. But if Amy and Oliver file as married filing separately, Stephen would not be considered a relative of Oliver and could only be claimed as a dependent by Oliver if Stephen was a full-time resident in Oliver's personal residence.

Gross Income Test

To meet this test, a person's gross income for the year must be less than $3,700.

You are not allowed an exemption for a child who is age 24 or older whose gross income is not less than the exemption amount ($3,700 for 2011). The term "dependent" means that the individual is either a qualifying child or a qualifying relative. A 24-year-old child does not meet the age requirement under the uniform definition of a qualifying child. The 24-year-old child is also not a qualifying relative because the child's income is greater than the exemption amount of $3,700 (for 2011). However, all is not lost if you can't claim an exemption for your child because of this rule. The child can still claim the exemption on his or her return.

Gross income defined. Gross income is all income in the form of money, property, and services that is not exempt from tax.

In a manufacturing, merchandising, or mining business, gross income is the total net sales minus the cost of goods sold, plus any miscellaneous income from the business.

Gross receipts from rental property are gross income. Do not deduct taxes, repairs, etc., to determine the gross income from rental property.

Gross income includes a partner's share of the gross (not a share of the net) partnership income.

Jamal's father retired 5 years ago and receives over half of his support from Jamal. The father is a partner in a real estate partnership, and his share of gross rental income from the partnership is $3,800 before expenses. After expenses, his net rental income is $200. Jamal may not claim his father as a dependent because his father's share of the partnership's gross rental income exceeds the $3,700 exemption amount.

Gross income also includes all taxable unemployment compensation and certain scholarship and fellowship grants. Scholarships received by degree candidates that are used for tuition, fees, supplies, books, and equipment required for particular courses may not be included in gross income. For more information about scholarships, see chapter 12.

Tax-exempt income, such as certain social security benefits, is not included in gross income.

Gross income also includes (1) gross profit from self-employment, (2) the full gain from the sale of stock or real estate, and (3) the gain on the sale of a personal residence.

Gross income does not include (1) tax-free municipal bond interest and (2) gifts received from others.

Disabled dependent working at sheltered workshop. For purposes of this test (the gross income test), the gross income of an individual who is permanently and totally disabled at any time during the year does not include income for services the individual performs at a sheltered workshop. The availability of medical care at the workshop must be the main reason for the individual's presence there. Also, the income must come solely from activities at the workshop that are incident to this medical care.

A "sheltered workshop" is a school that:
- Provides special instruction or training designed to alleviate the disability of the individual, and
- Is operated by certain tax-exempt organizations, or by a state, a U.S. possession, a political subdivision of a state or possession, the United States, or the District of Columbia.

"Permanently and totally disabled" has the same meaning here as under *Qualifying Child*, earlier.

Support Test (To Be a Qualifying Relative)
To meet this test, you generally must provide more than half of a person's total support during the calendar year.

However, if two or more persons provide support, but no one person provides more than half of a person's total support, see *Multiple Support Agreement*, later.

How to determine if support test is met. You figure whether you have provided more than half of a person's total support by comparing the amount you contributed to that person's support with the entire amount of support that person received from all sources. This includes support the person provided from his or her own funds.

You may find Worksheet 3-1 helpful in figuring whether you provided more than half of a person's support.

Person's own funds not used for support. A person's own funds are not support unless they are actually spent for support.

Example. Your mother received $2,400 in social security benefits and $300 in interest. She paid $2,000 for lodging and $400 for recreation. She put $300 in a savings account.

Even though your mother received a total of $2,700 ($2,400 + $300), she spent only $2,400 ($2,000 + $400) for her own support. If you spent more than $2,400 for her support and no other support was received, you have provided more than half of her support.

Child's wages used for own support. You cannot include in your contribution to your child's support any support that is paid for by the child with the child's own wages, even if you paid the wages.

EXPLANATION

The gross income of a married couple residing in a community property state is generally split equally between each spouse for the purposes of the dependency deduction.

Example

Henry Smith provides more than 50% of the support for his son Jim and his daughter-in-law Jan, both of whom are over 19. Jim has no income and is not a student during 2011. Jan earns $8,000. Assuming that the other dependency tests are met, Henry Smith may claim his son Jim as a dependent in a common-law state. In a community property state, however, Henry could not claim Jim as a dependent, because each spouse is treated as having gross income of $4,000 (half of $8,000).

A qualifying relative with income greater than the exemption amount ($3,700 for 2011) cannot be claimed as a dependent. But this income test does not apply to the determination of the exemption allowed for a qualifying child.

Example

Casey Burns provides more than 50% of the support for her child and mother during 2011. Casey's child, Alexis, has a part-time job that pays her $3,850 during 2011. Alexis was under the age of 19 at the end of 2011. Casey's mother, Christina, earned $2,300 in babysitting income and $2,500 from the sale of home-baked goods during 2011. Assuming that Alexis meets all the requirements of qualifying child classification and the other dependency tests, Casey may claim her as a dependent on her 2011 return. Even though Alexis had $150 in income in excess of her exemption amount ($3,850–$3,700), her gross income does not come into play when determining whether she is a dependent of Casey's for 2011. Casey cannot claim her mother as a dependent, even though she meets the support and other tests of dependency, because her mother earned $1,100 more than her exemption amount ($2,300 babysitting income plus $2,500 from the sale of home-baked goods minus $3,700 exemption).

Year support is provided. The year you provide the support is the year you pay for it, even if you do so with borrowed money that you repay in a later year.

EXPLANATION

Only the amount actually spent on support is relevant to the support test. The funds made available for support purposes are not relevant until actually used.

Example 1

The income of a trust for the benefit of a minor was not spent for the minor's support. The parent who provided the funds for the child's support may claim the dependency deduction.

Example 2

According to a court ruling, an individual could claim a dependency deduction for his grandmother even though she received state old-age assistance payments that exceeded the amounts spent by the grandson. The grandmother did not spend all of the payments received from the state for her support. The amount of the state payments that she did spend for her support was less than what was provided to her by her grandson.

If you use a fiscal year to report your income, you must provide more than half of the dependent's support for the calendar year in which your fiscal year begins.

TAXPLANNER

You should maintain complete records of expenditures made to support anyone whom you intend to claim as a dependent. Take particular pains to maintain records of support for children of divorced parents and for children who are attending college.

The IRS has established guidelines so that members of a community property state can determine who is entitled to deduct whom as a dependent. For additional information, see IRS Publication 555.

Armed Forces dependency allotments. The part of the allotment contributed by the government and the part taken out of your military pay are both considered provided by you in figuring whether you provide more than half of the support. If your allotment is used to support persons other than those you name, you can take the exemptions for them if they otherwise qualify.

Example. You are in the Armed Forces. You authorize an allotment for your widowed mother that she uses to support herself and her sister. If the allotment provides more than half of each person's support, you can take an exemption for each of them, if they otherwise qualify, even though you authorize the allotment only for your mother.

Tax-exempt military quarters allowances. These allowances are treated the same way as dependency allotments in figuring support. The allotment of pay and the tax-exempt basic allowance for quarters are both considered as provided by you for support.

Tax-exempt income. In figuring a person's total support, include tax-exempt income, savings, and borrowed amounts used to support that person. Tax-exempt income includes certain social security benefits, welfare benefits, nontaxable life insurance proceeds, Armed Forces family allotments, nontaxable pensions, and tax-exempt interest.

Example 1. You provide $4,000 toward your mother's support during the year. She has earned income of $600, nontaxable social security benefits of $4,800, and tax-exempt interest of $200. She uses all these for her support. You cannot claim an exemption for your mother because the $4,000 you provide is not more than half of her total support of $9,600.

Example 2. Your brother's daughter takes out a student loan of $2,500 and uses it to pay her college tuition. She is personally responsible for the loan. You provide $2,000 toward her total support. You cannot claim an exemption for her because you provide less than half of her support.

Social security benefits. If a husband and wife each receive benefits that are paid by one check made out to both of them, half of the total paid is considered to be for the support of each spouse, unless they can show otherwise.

If a child receives social security benefits and uses them toward his or her own support, the benefits are considered as provided by the child.

Support provided by the state (welfare, food stamps, housing, etc.). Benefits provided by the state to a needy person generally are considered support provided by the state. However, payments based on the needs of the recipient will not be considered as used entirely for that person's support if it is shown that part of the payments were not used for that purpose.

Home for the aged. If you make a lump-sum advance payment to a home for the aged to take care of your relative for life and the payment is based on that person's life expectancy, the amount of support you provide each year is the lump-sum payment divided by the relative's life expectancy. The amount of support you provide also includes any other amounts you provided during the year.

EXAMPLE
Selena's mother resides in a senior citizens' home that is supported and operated by a church. It cost the church $6,000 last year to support Selena's mother. For Selena to claim her mother as a dependent, she must prove that she has provided more than $6,000 additional support for her mother, over and above the $6,000 provided by the church.

Total Support
To figure if you provided more than half of a person's support, you must first determine the total support provided for that person. Total support includes amounts spent to provide food, lodging, clothing, education, medical and dental care, recreation, transportation, and similar necessities.

EXPLANATION
Money that is not included in gross income, such as certain social security benefits, veterans' benefits, and so on, must be considered in determining support. For example, an amount borrowed by the person, or by you, and spent for support must be included in total support.

Generally, the amount of an item of support is the amount of the expense incurred in providing that item. For lodging, the amount of support is the fair rental value of the lodging.

Expenses that are not directly related to any one member of a household, such as the cost of food for the household, must be divided among the members of the household.

Example 1. Grace Brown, mother of Mary Miller, lives with Frank and Mary Miller and their two children. Grace gets social security benefits of $2,400, which she spends for clothing, transportation, and recreation. Grace has no other income. Frank and Mary's total food expense for the household is $5,200. They pay Grace's medical and drug expenses of $1,200. The fair rental value of the lodging provided for Grace is $1,800 a year, based on the cost of similar rooming facilities. Figure Grace's total support as follows:

Fair rental value of lodging	$ 1,800
Clothing, transportation, and recreation	2,400
Medical expenses	1,200
Share of food (1/5 of $5,200)	1,040
Total support	$6,440

The support Frank and Mary provide ($1,800 lodging + $1,200 medical expenses + $1,040 food = $4,040) is more than half of Grace's $6,440 total support.

Example 2. Your parents live with you, your spouse, and your two children in a house you own. The fair rental value of your parents' share of the lodging is $2,000 a year ($1,000 each), which includes furnishings and utilities. Your father receives a nontaxable pension of $4,200, which he spends equally between your mother and himself for items of support such as clothing, transportation, and recreation. Your total food expense for the household is $6,000. Your heat and utility bills amount to $1,200. Your mother has hospital and medical expenses of $600, which you pay during the year. Figure your parents' total support as follows:

Support provided	Father	Mother
Fair rental value of lodging	$1,000	$1,000
Pension spent for their support	2,100	2,100
Share of food (1/6 of $6,000)	1,000	1,000
Medical expenses for mother		600
Parents' total support	$4,100	$4,700

You must apply the support test separately to each parent. You provide $2,000 ($1,000 lodging, $1,000 food) of your father's total support of $4,100 – less than half. You provide $2,600 to your mother ($1,000 lodging, $1,000 food, $600 medical) – more than half of her total support of $4,700. You meet the support test for your mother, but not your father. Heat and utility costs are included in the fair rental value of the lodging, so these are not considered separately.

Lodging. If you provide a person with lodging, you are considered to provide support equal to the fair rental value of the room, apartment, house, or other shelter in which the person lives. Fair rental value includes a reasonable allowance for the use of furniture and appliances, and for heat and other utilities that are provided.

Fair rental value defined. This is the amount you could reasonably expect to receive from a stranger for the same kind of lodging. It is used instead of actual expenses such as taxes, interest, depreciation, paint, insurance, utilities, cost of furniture and appliances, etc. In some cases, fair rental value may be equal to the rent paid.

If you provide the total lodging, the amount of support you provide is the fair rental value of the room the person uses, or a share of the fair rental value of the entire dwelling if the person has use of your entire home. If you do not provide the total lodging, the total fair rental value must be divided depending on how much of the total lodging you provide. If you provide only a part and the person supplies the rest, the fair rental value must be divided between both of you according to the amount each provides.

Example. Your parents live rent free in a house you own. It has a fair rental value of $5,400 a year furnished, which includes a fair rental value of $3,600 for the house and $1,800 for the furniture. This does not include heat and utilities. The house is completely furnished with furniture belonging to your parents. You pay $600 for their utility bills. Utilities are not usually included in rent for houses in the area where your parents live. Therefore, you consider the total fair rental value of the lodging to be $6,000 ($3,600 fair rental value of the unfurnished house, $1,800 allowance for the furnishings provided by your parents, and $600 cost of utilities) of which you are considered to provide $4,200 ($3,600 + $600).

Person living in his or her own home. The total fair rental value of a person's home that he or she owns is considered support contributed by that person.

Living with someone rent free. If you live with a person rent free in his or her home, you must reduce the amount you provide for support of that person by the fair rental value of lodging he or she provides you.

TAXSAVER
If your dependent is living in his or her own home, it may be to your mutual advantage for you to acquire a partial interest in the home and thereby become jointly liable for the mortgage and real estate taxes. By doing this, you can include 50% of the mortgage expense and real estate taxes you incur as part of your support calculation.

TAXPLANNER
If your mother lives alone in her own home and you pay the mortgage and real estate taxes for her, no one is entitled to the deduction for mortgage interest expenses or real estate taxes. You pay them, but because you are not personally liable for them, you may not deduct them. Conversely, your mother is personally responsible for them, but she does not pay them and so she may not deduct them.

If you give your mother the cash and she pays the mortgage interest expenses and real estate taxes, she would be entitled to the deductions. However, if you are in a higher tax bracket than your mother, it would be more advantageous for you to take the deductions than for your mother to do so. The higher your tax bracket, the more a deduction is worth.

If the house were transferred into joint ownership and you also became obligated for the mortgage, you could deduct the mortgage interest and real estate taxes you paid. In addition, you could claim your mother as a dependent. Arranging things in this manner may realize the greatest tax savings. To take full advantage of the deduction for mortgage interest, you would have to meet the special rules for qualified residence mortgages. See chapter 24, *Interest expense.*

Property. Property provided as support is measured by its fair market value. Fair market value is the price that property would sell for on the open market. It is the price that would be agreed upon between a willing buyer and a willing seller, with neither being required to act, and both having reasonable knowledge of the relevant facts.

Capital expenses. Capital items, such as furniture, appliances, and cars, that are bought for a person during the year can be included in total support under certain circumstances.

The following examples show when a capital item is or is not support.

Example 1. You buy a $200 power lawn mower for your 13-year-old child. The child is given the duty of keeping the lawn trimmed. Because the lawn mower benefits all members of the household, you cannot include the cost of the lawn mower in the support of your child.

Example 2. You buy a $150 television set as a birthday present for your 12-year-old child. The television set is placed in your child's bedroom. You can include the cost of the television set in the support of your child.

Example 3. You pay $5,000 for a car and register it in your name. You and your 17-year-old daughter use the car equally. Because you own the car and do not give it to your daughter but merely let her use it, you cannot include the cost of the car in your daughter's total support. However, you can include in your daughter's support your out-of-pocket expenses of operating the car for her benefit.

Example 4. Your 17-year-old son, using personal funds, buys a car for $4,500. You provide all the rest of your son's support—$4,000. Since the car is bought and owned by your son, the car's fair market value ($4,500) must be included in his support. Your son has provided more than half of his own total support of $8,500 ($4,500 + $4,000), so he is not your qualifying child. You did not provide more than half of his total support, so he is not your qualifying relative. You cannot claim an exemption for your son.

Medical insurance premiums. Medical insurance premiums you pay, including premiums for supplementary Medicare coverage, are included in the support you provide.

Medical insurance benefits. Medical insurance benefits, including basic and supplementary Medicare benefits, are not part of support.

Tuition payments and allowances under the GI Bill. Amounts veterans receive under the GI Bill for tuition payments and allowances while they attend school are included in total support.

Example. During the year, your son receives $2,200 from the government under the GI Bill. He uses this amount for his education. You provide the rest of his support—$2,000. Because GI benefits are included in total support, your son's total support is $4,200 ($2,200 + $2,000). You have not provided more than half of his support.

Child care expenses. If you pay someone to provide child or dependent care, you can include these payments in the amount you provided for the support of your child or disabled dependent, even if you claim a credit for the payments. For information on the credit, see chapter 33.

Other support items. Other items may be considered as support depending on the facts in each case.

Do Not Include in Total Support

The following items are not included in total support.

1. Federal, state, and local income taxes paid by persons from their own income.
2. Social security and Medicare taxes paid by persons from their own income.
3. Life insurance premiums.
4. Funeral expenses.
5. Scholarships received by your child if your child is a full-time student.
6. Survivors' and Dependents' Educational Assistance payments used for the support of the child who receives them.

Multiple Support Agreement

Sometimes no one provides more than half of the support of a person. Instead, two or more persons, each of whom would be able to take the exemption but for the support test, together provide more than half of the person's support.

When this happens, you can agree that any one of you who individually provides more than 10% of the person's support, but only one, can claim an exemption for that person as a qualifying relative. Each of the others must sign a statement agreeing not to claim the exemption for that year. The person who claims the exemption must keep these signed statements for his or her records. A multiple support declaration identifying each of the others who agreed not to claim the exemption must be attached to the return of the person claiming the exemption. Form 2120, Multiple Support Declaration, can be used for this purpose.

You can claim an exemption under a multiple support agreement for someone related to you or for someone who lived with you all year as a member of your household.

Example 1. You, your sister, and your two brothers provide the entire support of your mother for the year. You provide 45%, your sister 35%, and your two brothers each provide 10%. Either you or your sister can claim an exemption for your mother. The other must sign a statement agreeing not to take an exemption for your mother. The one who claims the exemption must attach Form 2120, or a similar declaration, to his or her return and must keep the statement signed by the other for his or her records. Because neither brother provides more than 10% of the support, neither can take the exemption and neither has to sign a statement.

Example 2. You and your brother each provide 20% of your mother's support for the year. The remaining 60% of her support is provided equally by two persons who are not related to her. She does not live with them. Because more than half of her support is provided by persons who cannot claim an exemption for her, no one can take the exemption.

Example 3. Your father lives with you and receives 25% of his support from social security, 40% from you, 24% from his brother (your uncle), and 11% from a friend. Either you or your uncle can take the exemption for your father if the other signs a statement agreeing not to. The one who takes the exemption must attach Form 2120, or a similar declaration, to his return and must keep for his records the signed statement from the one agreeing not to take the exemption.

Support Test for Children of Divorced or Separated Parents or Parents Who Live Apart

In most cases, a child of divorced or separated parents will be a qualifying child of one of the parents. See *Children of divorced or separated parents or parents who live apart* under *Qualifying Child*, earlier. However, if the child does not meet the requirements to be a qualifying child of either parent, the child may be a qualifying relative of one of the parents. In that case, the following rules must be used in applying the support test.

A child will be treated as being the qualifying relative of his or her noncustodial parent if all four of the following statements are true.

1. The parents:
   a. Are divorced or legally separated under a decree of divorce or separate maintenance,
   b. Are separated under a written separation agreement, or
   c. Lived apart at all times during the last 6 months of the year, whether or not they are or were married.
2. The child received over half of his or her support for the year from the parents (and the rules on multiple support agreements, explained earlier, do not apply).
3. The child is in the custody of one or both parents for more than half of the year.
4. Either of the following statements is true.
   a. The custodial parent signs a written declaration, discussed later, that he or she will not claim the child as a dependent for the year, and the noncustodial parent attaches this written declaration to his or her return. (If the decree or agreement went into effect after 1984 and before 2009, see *Post-1984 and pre-2009 divorce decree or separation agreement*, later. If the decree or agreement went into effect after 2008, see *Post-2008 divorce decree or separation agreement*, later.)
   b. A pre-1985 decree of divorce or separate maintenance or written separation agreement that applies to 2011 states that the noncustodial parent can claim the child as a dependent, the decree or agreement was not changed after 1984 to say the noncustodial parent cannot claim the child as a dependent, and the noncustodial parent provides at least $600 for the child's support during the year.

Custodial parent and noncustodial parent. The custodial parent is the parent with whom the child lived for the greater number of nights during the year. The other parent is the noncustodial parent.

If the parents divorced or separated during the year and the child lived with both parents before the separation, the custodial parent is the one with whom the child lived for the greater number of nights during the rest of the year.

A child is treated as living with a parent for a night if the child sleeps:
- At that parent's home, whether or not the parent is present, or
- In the company of the parent, when the child does not sleep at a parent's home (for example, the parent and child are on vacation together).

Equal number of nights. If the child lived with each parent for an equal number of nights during the year, the custodial parent is the parent with the higher adjusted gross income.

December 31. The night of December 31 is treated as part of the year in which it begins. For example, December 31, 2011, is treated as part of 2011.

Emancipated child. If a child is emancipated under state law, the child is treated as not living with either parent.

Absences. If a child was not with either parent on a particular night (because, for example, the child was staying at a friend's house), the child is treated as living with the parent with whom the child normally would have lived for that night, except for the absence. But if it cannot be determined with which parent the child normally would have lived or if the child would not have lived with either parent that night, the child is treated as not living with either parent that night.

Parent works at night. If, due to a parent's nighttime work schedule, a child lives for a greater number of days but not nights with the parent who works at night, that parent is treated as the custodial parent. On a school day, the child is treated as living at the primary residence registered with the school.

Written declaration. The custodial parent may use either Form 8332 or a similar statement (containing the same information required by the form) to make the written declaration to release the exemption to the noncustodial parent. The noncustodial parent must attach a copy of the form or statement to his or her tax return.

The exemption can be released for 1 year, for a number of specified years (for example, alternate years), or for all future years, as specified in the declaration.

Post-1984 and pre-2009 divorce decree or separation agreement. If the divorce decree or separation agreement went into effect after 1984 and before 2009, the noncustodial parent may be able to attach certain pages from the decree or agreement instead of Form 8332. The decree or agreement must state all three of the following.

1. The noncustodial parent can claim the child as a dependent without regard to any condition, such as payment of support.
2. The custodial parent will not claim the child as a dependent for the year.
3. The years for which the noncustodial parent, rather than the custodial parent, can claim the child as a dependent.

The noncustodial parent must attach all of the following pages of the decree or agreement to his or her tax return.

- The cover page (write the other parent's social security number on this page).
- The pages that include all of the information identified in items (1) through (3) above.
- The signature page with the other parent's signature and the date of the agreement.

Post-2008 divorce decree or separation agreement. The noncustodial parent can no longer attach pages from the decree or agreement instead of Form 8332 if the decree or agreement went into effect after 2008. The custodial parent must sign either Form 8332 or a similar statement whose only purpose is to release the custodial parent's claim to an exemption for a child, and the noncustodial parent must attach a copy to his or her return. The form or statement must release the custodial parent's claim to the child without any conditions. For example, the release must not depend on the noncustodial parent paying support.

Revocation of release of claim to an exemption. The custodial parent can revoke a release of claim to an exemption that he or she previously released to the noncustodial parent on Form 8332 or a similar statement. If the custodial parent provided, or made reasonable efforts to provide, the noncustodial parent with written notice of the revocation in 2010, the revocation can be effective no earlier than 2011. The custodial parent can use Part III of Form 8332 for this purpose and must attach a copy of the revocation to his or her return for each tax year he or she claims the child as a dependent as a result of the revocation.

Remarried parent. If you remarry, the support provided by your new spouse is treated as provided by you.

Child support under pre-1985 agreement. All child support payments actually received from the noncustodial parent under a pre-1985 agreement are considered used for the support of the child.

Example. Under a pre-1985 agreement, the noncustodial parent provides $1,200 for the child's support. This amount is considered support provided by the noncustodial parent even if the $1,200 was actually spent on things other than support.

Alimony. Payments to a spouse that are includible in the spouse's gross income as either alimony, separate maintenance payments, or similar payments from an estate or trust, are not treated as a payment for the support of a dependent.

Parents who never married. This special rule for divorced or separated parents also applies to parents who never married and lived apart at all times during the last 6 months of the year.

Caution

The noncustodial parent must attach the required information even if it was filed with a return in an earlier year.

TAXPLANNER

Due to the education credits (see chapter 36, *Education credits and other education tax benefits*, for information about the American opportunity credit, a temporary modification of the Hope Credit, and the lifetime learning credit), there are situations where the parent may not want to claim an eligible dependent. Under the provisions of the American opportunity credit, education credits phaseout for single taxpayers with modified adjusted gross income between $80,000 and $90,000 and for couples filing jointly with modified adjusted gross income between $160,000 and $180,000. The credits are not available to married taxpayers filing separately.

The student may claim the credits, even if the parents paid the expenses, but no one may claim the student as a dependent. The parent must not include the student on his or her tax return, and if the parent is allowed to take a dependency exemption for the student, the student may not claim a dependency exemption on his or her own tax return.

You should not claim your child as your dependent if the education tax credit will provide a greater tax benefit for your child than your tax benefit from the $3,700 exemption amount. The maximum tax benefit for a married couple, in the 28% tax bracket, to claim a child as a dependent is $1,036.

TAXPLANNER

Generally, the parent in the higher tax bracket should be designated as the parent to claim the dependency exemption for a child, assuming that the parent meets all the tests for claiming the dependency deduction. However, if the person with the highest tax bracket is subject to alternative minimum tax, that person receives no tax benefit for claiming a dependency deduction. In that case, it will be more beneficial for the parent in the lower tax bracket to claim the child as a dependent.

Consider the deduction for higher education expenses. You may be able to deduct qualified tuition and related expenses paid during the year on behalf of a dependent, even if you do not itemize. However, since income limitations apply, it may be more beneficial for the parent in the lower tax bracket to claim the child as a dependent.

Note: The child and dependent care credit and medical expense deductions may be claimed whether or not you can claim the child as a dependent. For more information on the child and dependent care credit, see chapter 33, *Child and dependent care credit*. For more information on the medical expense deduction, see chapter 22, *Medical and dental expenses*.

Multiple support agreement. If the support of the child is determined under a multiple support agreement, this special support test for divorced or separated parents or parents who live apart does not apply.

Limits on personal exemptions ended. For 2011, you will not lose part of your deduction for personal exemptions, regardless of the amount of your adjusted gross income.

TAXALERT

In December 2010, the President and Congress agreed to extend the so-called Bush Tax Cuts. Among the provisions extended is the continuing repeal of the phaseout of personal exemptions for both 2011 and 2012. As a result, taxpayers at all income levels can deduct the full amount of their personal exemptions. Beginning in 2013, however, the old phaseout rules are scheduled to return.

Social Security Numbers for Dependents

You must show the social security number (SSN) of any dependent for whom you claim an exemption in column (2) of line 6c of your Form 1040 or Form 1040A.

No SSN. If a person for whom you expect to claim an exemption on your return does not have an SSN, either you or that person should apply for an SSN as soon as possible by filing Form SS-5, Application for a Social Security Card, with the Social Security Administration (SSA). You can get Form SS-5 online at *www.socialsecurity.gov* or at your local SSA office.

It usually takes about 2 weeks to get an SSN. If you do not have a required SSN by the filing due date, you can file Form 4868 for an extension of time to file.

Caution

If you do not show the dependent's SSN when required or if you show an incorrect SSN, the exemption may be disallowed.

Born and died in 2011. If your child was born and died in 2011, and you do not have an SSN for the child, you may attach a copy of the child's birth certificate, death certificate, or hospital records instead. The document must show the child was born alive. If you do this, enter "DIED" in column (2) of line 6c of your Form 1040 or Form 1040A.

Alien or adoptee with no SSN. If your dependent does not have and cannot get an SSN, you must list the individual taxpayer identification number (ITIN) or adoption taxpayer identification number (ATIN) instead of an SSN.

Taxpayer identification numbers for aliens. If your dependent is a resident or nonresident alien who does not have and is not eligible to get an SSN, your dependent must apply for an individual taxpayer identification number (ITIN). Write the number in column (2) of line 6c of your Form 1040 or Form 1040A. To apply for an ITIN, use Form W-7, Application for IRS Individual Taxpayer Identification Number.

Taxpayer identification numbers for adoptees. If you have a child who was placed with you by an authorized placement agency, you may be able to claim an exemption for the child. However, if you cannot get an SSN or an ITIN for the child, you must get an adoption taxpayer identification number (ATIN) for the child from the IRS. See Form W-7A, Application for Taxpayer Identification Number for Pending U.S. Adoptions, for details.

Chapter 4
Tax withholding and estimated tax

Note

IRS Publication 17 (*Your Federal Income Tax*) has been updated by Ernst & Young LLP for 2011. Dates and dollar amounts shown are for 2011. Underlined type is used to indicate where IRS text has been updated. Places where text has been removed are indicated by the sentence: *Text intentionally omitted.*

ey.com/EYTaxGuide

Ernst & Young LLP will update the *Ernst & Young Tax Guide 2012* website with relevant taxpayer information as it becomes available. You can also sign up for email alerts to let you know when changes have been made.

Introduction

April 15 is the date by which most people file their income tax return for the previous year, but it is not the day most people actually pay their taxes. The bulk of your tax liability is paid during the year, either through money withheld from your paycheck by your employer or through payment of estimated taxes every quarter. The tax system operates on a pay-as-you-go policy, which generally requires that at least 90% of your tax liability be paid during the year.

The tax law imposes severe penalties if you underwithhold or underpay your estimated taxes. Yet, it is clearly not in your best interest to overwithhold or overpay estimated taxes, as the U.S. government does not pay interest on such overpayments. Therefore, it is essential that you estimate your tax liability as accurately as possible so you neither underpay nor overpay your taxes. This chapter helps you do just that.

Salaries and wages are subject to withholding by your employer regardless of the amount you are paid, the frequency of payment, or the form of payment. Nevertheless, you are entitled to reduce the amount of withholding by filing a completed Form W-4 with your employer. This form takes into account not only your marital status, personal exemptions, and dependents, but also your estimated deductions and tax credits. Form W-4 may prove especially beneficial if you have large mortgage interest deductions.

Estimated tax payments cover sources of income not subject to withholding; for example, income from partnerships, S-corporations, rental property, royalties, self-employment, trusts and estates, interest, dividends, and capital gains. While generally your tax withholding and estimated payments have to cover 90% of your tax liability for you to avoid paying some stiff penalties, this is not always the case. This chapter discusses all the important exceptions.

What's New for 2012

Tax law changes for 2012. When you figure how much income tax you want withheld from your pay and when you figure your estimated tax, consider tax law changes effective in 2012. For information on the status of expiring tax benefits for 2012, go to *www.irs.gov*.

TAXALERT

When calculating how much income tax to withhold from your wages or other sources, or computing your estimated tax payments each quarter, it is important to keep in mind any changes in the tax law. Several tax provisions that could affect your withholding or estimated tax payment calculations expired in 2011, including:

- The making work pay credit
- The self-employed health insurance deduction when calculating self-employment tax
- The exclusion from income of benefits provided to volunteer firefighters and emergency medical responders
- Computer technology and equipment allowed as expenses for higher education qualified tuition programs (i.e., section 529 plans)
- The exemption from AMT treatment for certain tax-exempt bonds
- The advance earned income credit

TAXPLANNER

After 2012, the tax cuts enacted in 2001 and 2003 (the so called "Bush tax cuts"), which were extended in 2010, are set to expire. At that time, the tax brackets and tax rates will revert to pre-2001 levels. This includes the elimination of the 10% tax bracket for low income filers and the top bracket increasing from 35% to 39.6%. Further, the long-term capital gains rates will increase from 15% to 20%, and the special rate on qualified dividends is scheduled to be eliminated. You should keep these changes in mind and also stay abreast of any new tax law changes enacted in 2012 as you plan for your 2013 estimated tax payments and withholding obligations.

Reminders

Estimated tax safe harbor for higher income taxpayers. If your 2011 adjusted gross income was more than $150,000 ($75,000 if you are married filing a separate return), you must deposit the smaller of 90% of your expected tax for 2012 or 110% of the tax shown on your 2011 return to avoid an estimated tax penalty.

This chapter discusses how to pay your tax as you earn or receive income during the year. In general, the federal income tax is a pay-as-you-go tax. There are two ways to pay as you go.

- *Withholding.* If you are an employee, your employer probably withholds income tax from your pay. Tax also may be withheld from certain other income, such as pensions, bonuses, commissions, and gambling winnings. The amount withheld is paid to the IRS in your name.
- *Estimated tax.* If you do not pay your tax through withholding, or do not pay enough tax that way, you may have to pay estimated tax. People who are in business for themselves generally will have to pay their tax this way. Also, you may have to pay estimated tax if you receive income such as dividends, interest, capital gains, rent, and royalties. Estimated tax is used to pay not only income tax, but self-employment tax and alternative minimum tax as well.

This chapter explains these methods. In addition, it also explains the following.

- *Credit for withholding and estimated tax.* When you file your 2011 income tax return, take credit for all the income tax withheld from your salary, wages, pensions, etc., and for the estimated tax you paid for 2011. Also take credit for any excess social security or railroad retirement tax withheld (discussed in chapter 37).
- *Underpayment penalty.* If you did not pay enough tax during the year, either through withholding or by making estimated tax payments, you may have to pay a penalty. In most cases, the IRS can figure this penalty for you. See *Underpayment Penalty for 2011* at the end of this chapter.

Useful Items

You may want to see:

Publication

- ☐ **505** Tax Withholding and Estimated Tax
- ☐ **919** How Do I Adjust My Tax Withholding?

Form (and Instructions)

- ☐ **W-4** Employee's Withholding Allowance Certificate
- ☐ **W-4P** Withholding Certificate for Pension or Annuity Payments
- ☐ **W-4S** Request for Federal Income Tax Withholding From Sick Pay
- ☐ **W-4V** Voluntary Withholding Request
- ☐ **1040-ES** Estimated Tax for Individuals
- ☐ **2210** Underpayment of Estimated Tax by Individuals, Estates, and Trusts
- ☐ **2210-F** Underpayment of Estimated Tax by Farmers and Fishermen

Tax Withholding for 2012

This section discusses income tax withholding on:

- Salaries and wages,
- Tips,
- Taxable fringe benefits,
- Sick pay,
- Pensions and annuities,
- Gambling winnings,
- Unemployment compensation, and
- Certain federal payments, such as social security.

This section explains the rules for withholding tax from each of these types of income.

This section also covers backup withholding on interest, dividends, and other payments.

Salaries and Wages

Income tax is withheld from the pay of most employees. Your pay includes your regular pay, bonuses, commissions, and vacation allowances. It also includes reimbursements and other expense allowances paid under a nonaccountable plan. See *Supplemental Wages*, later, for more information about reimbursements and allowances paid under a nonaccountable plan.

If your income is low enough that you will not have to pay income tax for the year, you may be exempt from withholding. This is explained under *Exemption From Withholding*, later.

You can ask your employer to withhold income tax from noncash wages and other wages not subject to withholding. If your employer does not agree to withhold tax, or if not enough is withheld, you may have to pay estimated tax, as discussed later under *Estimated Tax for 2012*.

Military retirees. Military retirement pay is treated in the same manner as regular pay for income tax withholding purposes, even though it is treated as a pension or annuity for other tax purposes.

Household workers. If you are a household worker, you can ask your employer to withhold income tax from your pay. A household worker is an employee who performs household work in a private home, local college club, local fraternity or sorority chapter.

Tax is withheld only if you want it withheld and your employer agrees to withhold it. If you do not have enough income tax withheld, you may have to pay estimated tax, as discussed later under *Estimated Tax for 2012*.

Farmworkers. Income tax generally is withheld from your cash wages for work on a farm unless your employer both:

- Pays you cash wages of less than $150 during the year, and
- Has expenditures for agricultural labor totaling less than $2,500 during the year.

> don't know what their tax liability will be in the coming year, the law allows them to base their estimated tax payments on the previous year's tax liability. See this chapter for more details on how to calculate the amount of estimated taxes you need to pay in order to avoid underpayment penalties.

EXPLANATION

Generally, withholding is required on wages, regardless of the amount of wages paid, the frequency of payment, the form of payment (cash, check, stock, or other property), or the manner in which the wage is computed (hourly, weekly, yearly, or even as a percentage of employer profits).

For more information about household workers, see chapter 40, *What to do if you employ domestic help*.

Differential wage payments. When employees are on leave from employment for military duty, some employers may make up the difference between the military pay and civilian pay. Payments made after December 31, 2008, to an employee who is on active duty for a period of more than 30 days, will be subject to income tax withholding, but not subject to social security or Medicare taxes. The wages and withholding will be reported on Form W-2, Wage and Tax Statement.

Determining Amount of Tax Withheld Using Form W-4

The amount of income tax your employer withholds from your regular pay depends on two things.
- The amount you earn in each payroll period.
- The information you give your employer on Form W-4.

Form W-4 includes four types of information that your employer will use to figure your withholding.
- Whether to withhold at the single rate or at the lower married rate.
- How many withholding allowances you claim (each allowance reduces the amount withheld).
- Whether you want an additional amount withheld.
- Whether you are claiming an exemption from withholding. See *Exemption From Withholding*, later.

New Job

When you start a new job, you must fill out Form W-4 and give it to your employer. Your employer should have copies of the form. If you need to change the information later, you must fill out a new form.

If you work only part of the year (for example, you start working after the beginning of the year), too much tax may be withheld. You may be able to avoid overwithholding if your employer agrees to use the part-year method. See *Part-Year Method* in chapter 1 of Publication 505 for more information.

Employee also receiving pension income. If you receive pension or annuity income and begin a new job, you will need to file Form W-4 with your new employer. However, you can choose to split your withholding allowances between your pension and job in any manner. See Publication 919 for more information.

Changing Your Withholding

During the year changes may occur to your marital status, exemptions, adjustments, deductions, or credits you expect to claim on your tax return. When this happens, you may need to give your employer a new Form W-4 to change your withholding status or number of allowances.

If the changes reduce the number of allowances you are claiming or changes your marital status from married to single, you must give your employer a new Form W-4 within 10 days.

Generally, you can submit a new Form W-4 whenever you wish to change the number of your withholding allowances for any other reason.

Changing your withholding for 2013. If events in 2012 will decrease the number of your withholding allowances for 2013, you must give your employer a new Form W-4 by December 1, 2012. If the event occurs in December 2012, submit a new Form W-4 within 10 days.

> ### EXPLANATION
> You must file a new Form W-4 when it becomes reasonable for you to expect that the estimated deductions or credits you claim on your existing Form W-4 will be less than you anticipated. Conversely, you may file a new Form W-4 when it becomes reasonable to expect that your estimated deductions or credits will be more than you claim on your existing form. Examples of situations that might warrant that you file a new Form W-4 include (1) buying or selling a house, (2) refinancing or paying off a home mortgage, (3) moving to a different city, (4) a substantial increase in medical costs, (5) change in filing status, or (6) change in number of dependents.

Checking Your Withholding

After you have given your employer a Form W-4, you can check to see whether the amount of tax withheld from your pay is too little or too much. See *Publication 919*, later. If too much or too little tax is being withheld, you should give your employer a new Form W-4 to change your withholding.

Completing Form W-4 and Worksheets

Form W-4 has worksheets to help you figure how many withholding allowances you can claim. The worksheets are for your own records. Do not give them to your employer.

Note

You must specify a filing status and a number of withholding allowances on Form W-4. You cannot specify only a dollar amount of withholding.

Note

You cannot give your employer a payment to cover withholding on salaries and wages for past pay periods or a payment for estimated tax.

Multiple jobs. If you have income from more than one job at the same time, complete only one set of Form W-4 worksheets. Then split your allowances between the Forms W-4 for each job. You cannot claim the same allowances with more than one employer at the same time. You can claim all your allowances with one employer and none with the other(s), or divide them any other way.

> ### EXAMPLE
> Bill and Alice are married. Both are employed and expect to file a joint return. When they combine their expected salary and other income and then total their expected deductions and credits on a Form W-4 worksheet, they determine that they are entitled to claim 26 allowances. Bill and Alice must both file separate W-4 forms with their respective employers but may allocate the 26 allowances any way they like. Bill could claim 24 allowances and Alice could claim 2, for example, or each could claim 13 allowances.

Married individuals. If both you and your spouse are employed and expect to file a joint return, figure your withholding allowances using your combined income, adjustments, deductions, exemptions, and credits. Use only one set of worksheets. You can divide your total allowances any way, but you cannot claim an allowance that your spouse also claims.

If you and your spouse expect to file separate returns, figure your allowances using separate worksheets based on your own individual income, adjustments, deductions, exemptions, and credits.

Alternative method of figuring withholding allowances. You do not have to use the Form W-4 worksheets if you use a more accurate method of figuring the number of withholding allowances. For more information, see *Alternative method of figuring withholding allowances* under *Completing Form W-4 and Worksheets* in Publication 505, chapter 1.

Personal Allowances Worksheet. Use the Personal Allowances Worksheet on page 1 of Form W-4 to figure your withholding allowances based on exemptions and any special allowances that apply.

> ### EXAMPLE
> John and Mary are married and plan to file a joint return. John's wages from his only employer are $55,000. Mary's wages from her only employer are $1,000. Because Mary's wages are $1,000 or less, John may claim a special allowance.

Deductions and Adjustments Worksheet. Use this worksheet if you plan to itemize your deductions, claim certain credits, or claim adjustments to the income on your 2012 tax return and you want to reduce your withholding. Also, complete this worksheet when you have changes to these items to see if you need to change your withholding.

The Deductions and Adjustments Worksheet is on page 2 of Form W-4. Chapter 1 of Publication 505 explains this worksheet.

Two-Earners/Multiple Jobs Worksheet. You may need to complete this worksheet if you have more than one job, a working spouse, or are also receiving a pension. Also, on line 8 of this worksheet you can add any additional withholding necessary to cover any amount you expect to owe other than income tax, such as self-employment tax.

Getting the Right Amount of Tax Withheld
In most situations, the tax withheld from your pay will be close to the tax you figure on your return if you follow these two rules.
- You accurately complete all the Form W-4 worksheets that apply to you.
- You give your employer a new Form W-4 when changes occur.

But because the worksheets and withholding methods do not account for all possible situations, you may not be getting the right amount withheld. This is most likely to happen in the following situations.
- You are married and both you and your spouse work.
- You have more than one job at a time.
- You have nonwage income, such as interest, dividends, alimony, unemployment compensation, or self-employment income.
- You will owe additional amounts with your return, such as self-employment tax.

- Your withholding is based on obsolete Form W-4 information for a substantial part of the year.
- Your earnings are more than the amount shown under *Check your withholding* in the instructions at the top of page 1 of Form W-4.
- You work only part of the year.
- You change the number of your withholding allowances during the year.

EXAMPLE

Tom is a bachelor living in an apartment. His annual income is $35,000, and he claims the standard deduction when he files his income tax return. He is currently claiming two allowances on his Form W-4. In March 2012, Tom buys a house. As a result of the increased deductions resulting from the purchase, he will itemize his deductions on his 2012 federal income tax return. He estimates that the deductions will total $13,200 and will be made up of mortgage interest, points, real estate tax, and state income tax. He revises his Form W-4 to reflect the change in his status to claim four allowances for the remainder of the year.

Cumulative wage method. If you change the number of your withholding allowances during the year, too much or too little tax may have been withheld for the period before you made the change. You may be able to compensate for this if your employer agrees to use the cumulative wage withholding method for the rest of the year. You must ask your employer in writing to use this method.

To be eligible, you must have been paid for the same kind of payroll period (weekly, biweekly, etc.) since the beginning of the year.

TAXPLANNER

The tax withheld from your salary or wages based on the revised Form W-4 that you file with your employer should be appropriate for your circumstances on an annual basis. However, the new withholding is effective only for pay periods after you file the form, and the total tax withheld for any given year may be significantly less than your actual tax liability. You should estimate your annual tax, as explained later in this chapter, and compare that estimate to the year-to-date tax withheld plus the amounts expected to be withheld based on your revised Form W-4. If that comparison shows a substantial gap, it would be appropriate to file a new Form W-4, claiming fewer allowances or requesting a larger additional amount to be withheld in order to narrow that gap.

TAXPLANNER

You are liable for severe penalties if you complete a Form W-4 with false information in an attempt to reduce your withholding below the amount you are legally allowed. The form should be filled out carefully and accurately so that the amount of your withholding is the least you are legally allowed but enough to avoid underpayment penalties.

On the other hand, contrary to the belief of many taxpayers, there is not a penalty for over-withholding.

So much emphasis has been put on the accuracy of various worksheets that some taxpayers may have increased their withholding more than they actually want. If you are more comfortable claiming fewer exemptions than you are entitled to so that you can get a nice refund when you file your return, feel free to do so, but remember, it is like giving the government an interest-free loan during the year.

TAXPLANNER

Your Form W-4 should be reviewed periodically as your sources and levels of income change and as your deductible expenses and credits increase or decrease.

Example 1

You have an estimated net loss from a partnership of $2,000, which you would report on Schedule E of your Form 1040. You are not required to make any payments of estimated tax. You may use your $2,000 partnership loss to figure the number of withholding allowances you may claim on your Form W-4.

Example 2

In addition to wages, you have alimony income of $5,000 and an estimated net loss from business of $3,000, which you would report on Schedule C. If you did not have the estimated business loss, you would have been required to make payments of estimated tax on your alimony income of $5,000. The business loss can be netted against the alimony income in order to figure the amount of net income on which you would be required to pay estimated tax–$2,000 in this case. You may not use your business loss to figure your withholding allowances since the loss is already used to offset the alimony income.

Example 3

You have an estimated net loss from your farm of $5,000, which you would report on Schedule F. You would otherwise be required to make payments of estimated tax on rental income of $4,000. To figure your withholding allowances, you may include only $1,000 of your farm loss ($5,000 estimated net loss minus $4,000 income subject to estimated tax).

Example 4

You expect to have itemized deductions of $15,000, which you would report on Schedule A. You also expect to have $9,000 of self-employment income on which you would otherwise have to pay estimated tax. To figure your withholding allowances for Form W-4, you should include only $6,000 of your itemized deductions ($15,000 total itemized deductions minus the $9,000 self-employment income subject to estimated tax). This will, in effect, allow you to withhold through your salary any estimated tax due on your self-employment income. However, you will still be subject to self-employment tax on the $9,000 income.

Rules relating to when you may properly claim withholding allowances. For the purpose of figuring your withholding allowances for estimated deductions and estimated tax credits, *estimated* means the dollar amount of each item you reasonably expect to claim on your 2012 return. That dollar amount should be no more than the sum of the following:

1. The amount of each item shown or expected to be shown on your 2011 return that you also reasonably expect to show on your 2012 return
2. Additional amounts that you can determine for each item for 2012

Additional amounts that can be determined. These are amounts that are not included in (1) and that can be shown to result from identifiable events in 2011 or 2012. Amounts can be shown to result from identifiable events if the amounts relate to payments already made during 2012, to binding obligations to make payments (including payments of taxes) during 2012, and to other events or transactions that have been started and that you can prove at the time you file your Form W-4.

Amounts disallowed by the Internal Revenue Service. Generally, to figure your withholding allowances for 2012, you should not include any amount shown on your 2011 return that has been disallowed by the IRS. If you have not yet filed your 2011 return, you should not include any amount shown on your 2010 return that has been disallowed by the IRS.

Publication 919

To make sure you are getting the right amount of tax withheld, get Publication 919. It will help you compare the total tax to be withheld during the year with the tax you can expect to figure on your return. It also will help you determine how much additional withholding, if any, is needed each payday to avoid owing tax when you file your return. If you do not have enough tax withheld, you may have to pay estimated tax, as explained under *Estimated Tax for 2012*, later.

TAXPLANNER

In essence, overwithholding is equivalent to giving the government a portion of your salary as an interest-free loan. Nevertheless, underwithholding may subject you to stiff non-deductible penalties. It is therefore essential that you estimate your tax liability as accurately as possible so that you neither underwithhold nor overwithhold.

Rules Your Employer Must Follow

It may be helpful for you to know some of the withholding rules your employer must follow. These rules can affect how to fill out your Form W-4 and how to handle problems that may arise.

New Form W-4. When you start a new job, your employer should give you a Form W-4 to fill out. Beginning with your first payday, your employer will use the information you give on the form to figure your withholding.

If you later fill out a new Form W-4, your employer can put it into effect as soon as possible. The deadline for putting it into effect is the start of the first payroll period ending 30 or more days after you turn it in.

No Form W-4. If you do not give your employer a completed Form W-4, your employer must withhold at the highest rate, as if you were single and claimed no withholding allowances.

Repaying withheld tax. If you find you are having too much tax withheld because you did not claim all the withholding allowances you are entitled to, you should give your employer a new Form W-4. Your employer cannot repay any of the tax previously withheld. Instead, claim the full amount withheld when you file your tax return.

However, if your employer has withheld more than the correct amount of tax for the Form W-4 you have in effect, you do not have to fill out a new Form W-4 to have your withholding lowered to the correct amount. Your employer can repay the amount that was withheld incorrectly. If you are not repaid, your Form W-2 will reflect the full amount actually withheld, which you would claim when you file your tax return.

> ### TAXPLANNER
> Before April 14, 2005, if you claimed 10 or more allowances on your Form W-4, your employer was required to send a copy of the form to the IRS. Your employer is no longer required to do so. Instead, the IRS relies on a process it has developed to use information already reported on Forms W-2 to effectively identify workers having withholding compliance problems. You should not be concerned if, by all reasonable expectations, your deductions and credits entitle you to 10 or more allowances. If you are entitled to 10 or more allowances, you should claim them.

Exemption From Withholding
If you claim exemption from withholding, your employer will not withhold federal income tax from your wages. The exemption applies only to income tax, not to social security or Medicare tax.

You can claim exemption from withholding for 2012 only if both of the following situations apply.
- For 2011 you had a right to a refund of all federal income tax withheld because you had no tax liability.
- For 2012 you expect a refund of all federal income tax withheld because you expect to have no tax liability.

Students. If you are a student, you are not automatically exempt. See chapter 1 to find out if you must file a return. If you work only part time or only during the summer, you may qualify for exemption from withholding.

Age 65 or older or blind. If you are 65 or older or blind, use Worksheet 1-1 or 1-2 in chapter 1 of Publication 505, to help you decide if you qualify for exemption from withholding. Do not use either worksheet if you will itemize deductions, claim exemptions for dependents, or claim tax credits on your 2012 return. Instead, see *Itemizing deductions or claiming exemptions or credits* in chapter 1 of Publication 505.

Claiming exemption from withholding. To claim exemption, you must give your employer a Form W-4. Do not complete lines 5 and 6. Enter "Exempt" on line 7.

If you claim exemption, but later your situation changes so that you will have to pay income tax after all, you must file a new Form W-4 within 10 days after the change. If you claim exemption in 2012, but you expect to owe income tax for 2013, you must file a new Form W-4 by December 1, 2012.

Your claim of exempt status may be reviewed by the IRS.

An exemption is good for only 1 year. You must give your employer a new Form W-4 by February 15 each year to continue your exemption.

Supplemental Wages
Supplemental wages include bonuses, commissions, overtime pay, vacation allowances, certain sick pay, and expense allowances under certain plans. The payer can figure withholding on supplemental wages using the same method used for your regular wages. However, if these payments are identified separately from your regular wages, your employer or other payer of supplemental wages can withhold income tax from these wages at a flat rate.

Expense allowances. Reimbursements or other expense allowances paid by your employer under a nonaccountable plan are treated as supplemental wages.

Reimbursements or other expense allowances paid under an accountable plan that are more than your proven expenses are treated as paid under a nonaccountable plan if you do not return the excess payments within a reasonable period of time.

For more information about accountable and nonaccountable expense allowance plans, see _Reimbursements_ in chapter 26.

Penalties
You may have to pay a penalty of $500 if both of the following apply.

- You make statements or claim withholding allowances on your Form W-4 that reduce the amount of tax withheld.
- You have no reasonable basis for those statements or allowances at the time you prepare your Form W-4.

There is also a criminal penalty for willfully supplying false or fraudulent information on your Form W-4 or for willfully failing to supply information that would increase the amount withheld. The penalty upon conviction can be either a fine of up to $1,000 or imprisonment for up to 1 year, or both.

These penalties will apply if you deliberately and knowingly falsify your Form W-4 in an attempt to reduce or eliminate the proper withholding of taxes. A simple error or an honest mistake will not result in one of these penalties. For example, a person who has tried to figure the number of withholding allowances correctly, but claims seven when the proper number is six, will not be charged a W-4 penalty.

Tips

The tips you receive while working on your job are considered part of your pay. You must include your tips on your tax return on the same line as your regular pay. However, tax is not withheld directly from tip income, as it is from your regular pay. Nevertheless, your employer will take into account the tips you report when figuring how much to withhold from your regular pay.

See chapter 6 for information on reporting your tips to your employer. For more information on the withholding rules for tip income, see Publication 531, *Reporting Tip Income*.

How employer figures amount to withhold. The tips you report to your employer are counted as part of your income for the month you report them. Your employer can figure your withholding in either of two ways.
- By withholding at the regular rate on the sum of your pay plus your reported tips.
- By withholding at the regular rate on your pay plus a percentage of your reported tips.

Not enough pay to cover taxes. If your regular pay is not enough for your employer to withhold all the tax (including income tax and social security and Medicare taxes (or the equivalent railroad retirement tax)) due on your pay plus your tips, you can give your employer money to cover the shortage. See *Giving your employer money for taxes* in chapter 6.

Allocated tips. Your employer should not withhold income tax, social security tax, Medicare tax, or railroad retirement tax on any allocated tips. Withholding is based only on your pay plus your reported tips. Your employer should refund to you any incorrectly withheld tax. See *Allocated Tips* in chapter 6 for more information.

TAXSAVER
Many students and retired persons who expect to have no federal income tax liability work part time in occupations in which they receive tips. To avoid unnecessary income tax withholding, you may file a Form W-4 with your employer, certifying that you had no federal income tax liability last year and expect to have none this year as well. Keep in mind that the exemption only applies to income tax withholding, not to social security or Medicare tax.

Taxable Fringe Benefits

The value of certain noncash fringe benefits you receive from your employer is considered part of your pay. Your employer generally must withhold income tax on these benefits from your regular pay.

For information on fringe benefits, see *Fringe Benefits* under *Employee Compensation* in chapter 5.

Although the value of your personal use of an employer-provided car, truck, or other highway motor vehicle is taxable, your employer can choose not to withhold income tax on that amount. Your employer must notify you if this choice is made.

For more information on withholding on taxable fringe benefits, see chapter 1 of Publication 505.

Sick Pay

Sick pay is a payment to you to replace your regular wages while you are temporarily absent from work due to sickness or personal injury. To qualify as sick pay, it must be paid under a plan to which your employer is a party.

If you receive sick pay from your employer or an agent of your employer, income tax must be withheld. An agent who does not pay regular wages to you may choose to withhold income tax at a flat rate.

However, if you receive sick pay from a third party who is not acting as an agent of your employer, income tax will be withheld only if you choose to have it withheld. See _Form W-4S_, below.

If you receive payments under a plan in which your employer does not participate (such as an accident or health plan where you paid all the premiums), the payments are not sick pay and usually are not taxable.

Union agreements. If you receive sick pay under a collective bargaining agreement between your union and your employer, the agreement may determine the amount of income tax withholding. See your union representative or your employer for more information.

Form W-4S. If you choose to have income tax withheld from sick pay paid by a third party, such as an insurance company, you must fill out Form W-4S. Its instructions contain a worksheet you can use to figure the amount you want withheld. They also explain restrictions that may apply.

Give the completed form to the payer of your sick pay. The payer must withhold according to your directions on the form.

Estimated tax. If you do not request withholding on Form W-4S, or if you do not have enough tax withheld, you may have to make estimated tax payments. If you do not pay enough tax, either through estimated tax or withholding, or a combination of both, you may have to pay a penalty. See _Underpayment Penalty for 2011_ at the end of this chapter.

Pensions and Annuities

Income tax usually will be withheld from your pension or annuity distributions unless you choose not to have it withheld. This rule applies to distributions from:
- A traditional individual retirement arrangement (IRA);
- A life insurance company under an endowment, annuity, or life insurance contract;
- A pension, annuity, or profit-sharing plan;
- A stock bonus plan; and
- Any other plan that defers the time you receive compensation.

The amount withheld depends on whether you receive payments spread out over more than 1 year (periodic payments), within 1 year (nonperiodic payments), or as an eligible rollover distribution (ERD). Income tax withholding from an ERD is mandatory.

EXPLANATION
A part of your pension or annuity may not be taxable. See chapter 10, _Retirement plans, pensions, and annuities,_ for information on figuring the nontaxable part. Income tax will not be withheld from the part of your pension or annuity that is nontaxable. Therefore, the tax withheld will be figured on, and cannot be more than the taxable part.

TAXALERT
A distribution that is eligible for direct rollover treatment (see chapter 10, _Retirement plans, pensions, and annuities_) but is not directly rolled over is subject to mandatory 20% withholding, unless the participant's eligible rollover distributions for the year are expected to be less than $200.

If a participant elects to have a portion of a distribution transferred in a direct rollover and the remainder distributed to him or her, only the portion that is distributed to him or her will be subject to the 20% withholding. A plan administrator will not be liable for tax, interest, or penalties for failure to withhold if he or she reasonably relied on information about the participant's plan received from the participant.

TAXPLANNER
If _property other than cash_ is distributed, such property is subject to 20% withholding. If all of the property distributed is company stock, no withholding is actually due. However, if, in addition to company stock, the distribution consists of cash or other property, the actual amount withheld need not exceed the sum of the cash and fair market value of such other property received, though the 20% withholding factor will be applied to the entire distribution including the value of company stock distributed.

TAXALERT

A written explanation of the direct rollover option and related rules (including the rules governing withholding) must generally be provided to participants not more than 90 days and not less than 30 days before the distribution date. For a series of periodic payments that are eligible for direct rollover, an initial timely notice must be given and an additional notice must be provided at least annually for as long as the payments continue.

Failure to provide such notice could cause the plan to become disqualified under the Internal Revenue Code. The IRS has issued a model notice that plan administrators are allowed to customize by deleting any portions that do not apply to the plan and adding additional information that is not inconsistent with the model notice.

Periodic Payments

Withholding from periodic payments of a pension or annuity is figured in the same way as withholding from salaries and wages. To tell the payer of your pension or annuity how much you want withheld, fill out Form W-4P, Withholding Certificate for Pension or Annuity Payments, or a similar form provided by the payer. Follow the rules on withholding discussed under *Salaries and Wages*, earlier, to fill out your Form W-4P.

The withholding rules for pensions and annuities differ from those for salaries and wages in the following ways:

1. If you do not fill out a withholding certificate, tax will be withheld as if you were married and were claiming three withholding allowances.
2. Your certificate will not be sent to the IRS regardless of the number of allowances you claim on it.
3. You can choose not to have tax withheld, regardless of how much tax you owed last year or expect to owe this year. You do not have to qualify for exemption. See *Choosing Not to Have Income Tax Withheld*, later.
4. Tax will be withheld as if you were single and claiming no withholding allowances if:
   a. You do not give the payer your social security number (in the required manner), or
   b. The IRS notifies the payer, before any payment or distribution is made, that you gave it an incorrect social security number.

Note: Military retirement pay generally is treated in the same manner as wages and not as a pension or annuity for income tax withholding purposes. Military retirees should use Form W-4, not Form W-4P.

TAXALERT

If a series of periodic payments began prior to January 1, 1993, you determine whether post-December 31, 1992, payments are a series of substantially equal periodic payments over a specified period by taking into account all payments, including payments made before January 1, 1993. If the post-December 31, 1992, payments are not a series of substantially equal periodic payments, they will be subject to the direct rollover rules, including mandatory 20% withholding.

Nonperiodic Payments

Tax will be withheld at a 10% rate on any nonperiodic payments you receive.

Because withholding on nonperiodic payments does not depend on withholding allowances or whether you are married or single, you cannot use Form W-4P to tell the payer how much to withhold. However, you can use Form W-4P to specify that an additional amount be withheld. You can also use Form W-4P to choose not to have tax withheld or to revoke a choice not to have tax withheld. See *Choosing Not to Have Income Tax Withheld*, later.

Eligible Rollover Distributions (ERDs)

Distributions you receive that are eligible to be rolled over tax-free into qualified retirement or annuity plans are subject to a 20% withholding tax.

An eligible rollover distribution (ERD) is any distribution of all or any part of the balance to your credit in a qualified retirement plan except:

1. Any of a series of substantially equal distributions paid at least once a year over:
   a. Your lifetime or life expectancy,
   b. The joint lives or life expectancies of you and your beneficiary, or
   c. A period of 10 years or more.
2. A required minimum distribution (discussed in Publication 575, *Pension and Annuity Income*, under *Tax on Excess Accumulation*),

3. Hardship distributions,
4. Corrective distributions of excess contributions or excess deferrals, and any income allocable to these distributions, or of excess annual additions and any allocable gains (see *Corrective distributions of excess plan contributions*, at the beginning of *Taxation of Nonperiodic Payments* in Publication 575),
5. A loan treated as a distribution because it does not satisfy certain requirements either when made or later (such as upon default), unless the participant's accrued benefits are reduced (offset) to repay the loan (see *Loans Treated as Distributions*, in Publication 575),
6. Dividends paid on employer securities, and
7. The cost of life insurance coverage.

In addition, a distribution to the plan participant's beneficiary generally is not treated as an eligible rollover distribution. However, see *Qualified domestic relations order, Rollover by surviving spouse*, and *Rollovers by nonspouse beneficiary*, later.

For more information about eligible rollover distributions, see Publication 575, *Pension and Annuity Income*.

Explanation

The withholding rules for non-ERD distributions are discussed earlier under Periodic Payments and Nonperiodic Payments.

A distribution is subject to withholding if it is not substantially equal to the periodic payments.

For example, upon retirement you receive 30% of your accrued pension benefits in the form of a single sum distribution with the balance payable in annuity form. The 30% distribution is an ERD subject to 20% withholding. The annuity payments are periodic payments subject to withholding only if you choose to have withholding taken out.

The payer of a distribution must withhold at a 20% rate on any part of an ERD that is not rolled over directly to another qualified plan. You cannot elect not to have withholding on these distributions.

If tax is withheld on the ERD, it will be withheld only on the taxable portion of the distribution. You must either:

1. Contribute to the new plan (within 60 days from the date of the distribution) an amount equal to the taxable part of the total ERD, including the amount withheld, to avoid including the distribution as taxable income on your 2012 tax return or
2. Include in your income for the year of the distribution any amount withheld for which you did not make a matching contribution to the new plan.

The matching contribution to cover the withheld amount, as explained in 1 above, must be in addition to the rollover of the net amount that you actually received. If all or any portion of an amount equal to the amount withheld is not contributed as a rollover, it must be included in your income to the extent of the difference between the taxable part of the distribution and the actual rollover amount.

Exception to withholding rule. The only way to avoid withholding on an ERD is to have it directly rolled over from the employer's plan to a qualified plan or IRA. This direct rollover is made only at your direction. You must first make sure that the receiving trustee agrees to accept a direct rollover. The transferor or trustee must allow you to make such a rollover and provide to you, within a reasonable period of time, written instructions on how to do so. You must also follow spousal consent and other participant and beneficiary protection rules.

TAXSAVER

If you receive an eligible rollover distribution from which the mandatory 20% withholding tax has been withheld, and you then decide you wish to roll the distribution over to an IRA within the allowed 60 days, you must come up with the 20% that was withheld from other funds within the 60-day period in order to roll the entire balance over. Otherwise the 20% that has been withheld will be treated as a taxable distribution and ineligible for rollover.

Choosing Not to Have Income Tax Withheld

You can choose not to have income tax withheld from your pension or annuity, whether the payments are periodic or nonperiodic. This rule does not apply to eligible rollover distributions. The payer will tell you how to make this choice. If you use Form W-4P, check the box on line 1 to make this election. Your choice will stay in effect until you decide you want withholding. The payer will ignore your request not to have income tax withheld if:

1. You do not give the payer your social security number (in the required manner), or
2. The IRS notifies the payer, before any payment or distribution is made, that you gave it an incorrect social security number.

More information. For more information on taxation of annuities and distributions (including ERDs) from qualified retirement plans, see chapter 10. For information on IRAs, see chapter 17. For more information on withholding on pensions and annuities, including a discussion of Form W-4P, see *Pensions and Annuities* in chapter 1 of Publication 505.

Gambling Winnings

Income tax is withheld at a flat 25% rate from certain kinds of gambling winnings.

Gambling winnings of more than $5,000 from the following sources are subject to income tax withholding.

- Any sweepstakes; wagering pool, including payments made to winners of poker tournaments; or lottery.
- Any other wager, if the proceeds are at least 300 times the amount of the bet.

It does not matter whether your winnings are paid in cash, in property, or as an annuity. Winnings not paid in cash are taken into account at their fair market value.

Exception. Gambling winnings from bingo, keno, and slot machines generally are not subject to income tax withholding. However, you may need to provide the payer with a social security number to avoid withholding. See *Backup withholding on gambling winnings* in chapter 1 of Publication 505. If you receive gambling winnings not subject to withholding, you may need to pay estimated tax. See *Estimated Tax for 2012*, later.

If you do not pay enough tax, either through withholding or estimated tax, or a combination of both, you may have to pay a penalty. See *Underpayment Penalty for 2011* at the end of this chapter.

Form W-2G. If a payer withholds income tax from your gambling winnings, you should receive a Form W-2G, Certain Gambling Winnings, showing the amount you won and the amount withheld. Report the tax withheld on line 62 of Form 1040.

Unemployment Compensation

You can choose to have income tax withheld from unemployment compensation. To make this choice, fill out Form W-4V (or a similar form provided by the payer) and give it to the payer.

All unemployment compensation is taxable. So, if you do not have income tax withheld, you may have to pay estimated tax. See *Estimated Tax for 2012*, later.

If you do not pay enough tax, either through withholding or estimated tax, or a combination of both, you may have to pay a penalty. For information, see *Underpayment Penalty for 2011* at the end of this chapter.

Federal Payments

You can choose to have income tax withheld from certain federal payments you receive. These payments are:

1. Social security benefits,
2. Tier 1 railroad retirement benefits,
3. Commodity credit corporation loans you choose to include in your gross income, and
4. Payments under the Agricultural Act of 1949 (7 U.S.C. 1421 et. seq.), as amended, or title II of the Disaster Assistance Act of 1988, that are treated as insurance proceeds and that you receive because:
   a. Your crops were destroyed or damaged by drought, flood, or any other natural disaster, or
   b. You were unable to plant crops be cause of a natural disaster described in (a).

To make this choice, fill out Form W-4V (or a similar form provided by the payer) and give it to the payer.

If you do not choose to have income tax withheld, you may have to pay estimated tax. See *Estimated Tax for 2012*, later.

If you do not pay enough tax, either through withholding or estimated tax, or a combination of both, you may have to pay a penalty. For information, see *Underpayment Penalty for 2011* at the end of this chapter.

More information. For more information about the tax treatment of social security and railroad retirement benefits, see chapter 11. Get Publication 225, *Farmer's Tax Guide*, for information about the tax treatment of commodity credit corporation loans or crop disaster payments.

Backup Withholding

Banks or other businesses that pay you certain kinds of income must file an information return (Form 1099) with the IRS. The information return shows how much you were paid during the year. It also includes your name and taxpayer identification number (TIN). TINs are explained in chapter 1 under *Social Security Number*.

These payments generally are not subject to withholding. However, "backup" withholding is required in certain situations. Backup withholding can apply to most kinds of payments that are reported on Form 1099.

The payer must withhold at a flat 28% rate in the following situations.

- You do not give the payer your TIN in the required manner.
- The IRS notifies the payer that the TIN you gave is incorrect.
- You are required, but fail, to certify that you are not subject to backup withholding.
- The IRS notifies the payer to start with holding on interest or dividends because you have underreported interest or dividends on your income tax return. The IRS will do this only after it has mailed you four notices over at least a 210-day period.

See *Backup Withholding* in chapter 1 of Publication 505 for more information.

Penalties. There are civil and criminal penalties for giving false information to avoid backup withholding. The civil penalty is $500. The criminal penalty, upon conviction, is a fine of up to $1,000 or imprisonment of up to 1 year, or both.

Estimated Tax for 2012

Estimated tax is the method used to pay tax on income that is not subject to withholding. This includes income from self-employment, interest, dividends, alimony, rent, gains from the sale of assets, prizes, and awards. You also may have to pay estimated tax if the amount of income tax being withheld from your salary, pension, or other income is not enough.

Estimated tax is used to pay both income tax and self-employment tax, as well as other taxes and amounts reported on your tax return. If you do not pay enough tax, either through withholding or estimated tax, or a combination of both, you may have to pay a penalty. If you do not pay enough by the due date of each payment period (see *When To Pay Estimated Tax*, later), you may be charged a penalty even if you are due a refund when you file your tax return. For information on when the penalty applies, see *Underpayment Penalty for 2011* at the end of this chapter.

Figure 4-A. **Do You Have To Pay Estimated Tax?**

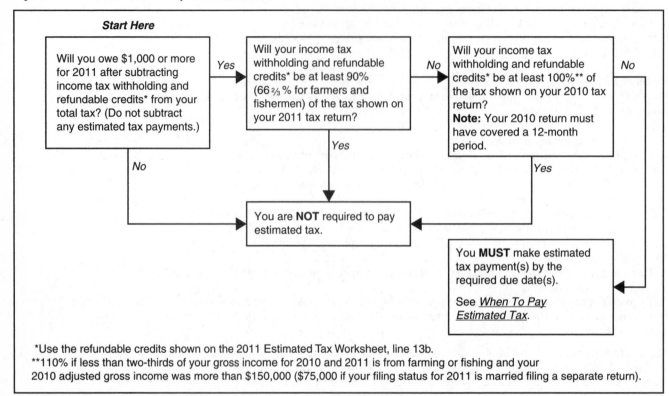

*Use the refundable credits shown on the 2011 Estimated Tax Worksheet, line 13b.
**110% if less than two-thirds of your gross income for 2010 and 2011 is from farming or fishing and your
2010 adjusted gross income was more than $150,000 ($75,000 if your filing status for 2011 is married filing a separate return).

Who Does Not Have To Pay Estimated Tax

If you receive salaries or wages, you can avoid having to pay estimated tax by asking your employer to take more tax out of your earnings. To do this, give a new Form W-4 to your employer. See chapter 1 of Publication 505.

Estimated tax not required. You do not have to pay estimated tax for 2012 if you meet all three of the following conditions.
- You had no tax liability for 2011.
- You were a U.S. citizen or resident for the whole year.
- Your 2011 tax year covered a 12-month period.

You had no tax liability for 2011 if your total tax was zero or you did not have to file an income tax return. For the definition of "total tax," see *Total tax for 2011—line 14b* in Publication 505, chapter 2.

Who Must Pay Estimated Tax

If you owe additional tax for 2011, you may have to pay estimated tax for 2012.

You can use the following general rule as a guide during the year to see if you will have enough withholding, or if you should increase your withholding or make estimated tax payments.

General rule. In most cases, you must pay estimated tax for 2012 if both of the following apply.
1. You expect to owe at least $1,000 in tax for 2012, after subtracting your withholding and refundable credits.
2. You expect your withholding plus your refundable credits to be less than the smaller of:
   a. 90% of the tax to be shown on your 2012 tax return, or
   b. 100% of the tax shown on your 2011 tax return (but see *Special rules for farmers, fishermen, and higher income taxpayers* below). Your 2011 tax return must cover all 12 months.

TAXPLANNER

If you receive a considerable amount of taxable income on which no tax is withheld, you might need to make quarterly estimated tax payments to the IRS.

Some of the most common sources of income not subject to withholding are:
1. Income from self-employment
2. Alimony
3. Interest, dividends, and capital gains
4. Rent
Even if most or all of your income is subject to withholding, you might not be having enough tax withheld to satisfy the IRS—and you might need to pick up the slack by increasing withholding, making estimated tax payments, or both.

TAXALERT

For 2012, you can avoid underpayment penalties by calculating your estimated payments as 100% of your 2011 tax if your adjusted gross income (AGI) was $150,000 or less. If your AGI for 2011 was greater than $150,000, you must have 110% of your 2011 tax paid in. All taxpayers can avoid penalties for underpayment of tax if at least 90% of their current tax liability is paid through withholding and estimated tax payments.

Example

Hope Lane's 2012 income tax liability is $45,000. Her adjusted gross income in 2011 was $140,000, while her 2011 tax liability was $30,000. Lane will avoid an underpayment penalty in 2009 if the total amount of tax withheld and estimated tax payments made for 2009 are at least 100% of her 2011 liability, or $30,000.

Each quarter, the calculation for estimated payment purposes may differ depending on which method yields the lesser tax liability. Therefore, the estimated payment for the 1st quarter may be based on your 2011 tax liability while the 2nd quarter estimated payment may be based on 90% of your current year tax liability.

Special rules for farmers, fishermen, and higher income taxpayers. If at least two-thirds of your gross income for 2011 or 2012 is from farming or fishing, substitute 662/3% for 90% in (2a) under the *General rule*, earlier. If your AGI for 2011 was more than $150,000 ($75,000 if your filing status for 2012 is married filing a separate return), substitute 110% for 100% in (2b) under *General rule*, earlier. See Figure 4-A and Publication 505, chapter 2, for more information.

Aliens. Resident and nonresident aliens also may have to pay estimated tax. Resident aliens should follow the rules in this chapter unless noted otherwise. Nonresident aliens should get Form 1040-ES (NR), U.S. Estimated Tax for Nonresident Alien Individuals.

You are an alien if you are not a citizen or national of the United States. You are a resident alien if you either have a green card or meet the substantial presence test. For more information about the substantial presence test, see Publication 519, *U.S. Tax Guide for Aliens*.

Married taxpayers. If you qualify to make joint estimated tax payments, apply the rules discussed here to your joint estimated income.

You and your spouse can make joint estimated tax payments even if you are not living together. However, you and your spouse cannot make joint estimated tax payments if:
- You are legally separated under a decree of divorce or separate maintenance,
- You and your spouse have different tax years, or
- Either spouse is a nonresident alien (unless that spouse elected to be treated as a resident alien for tax purposes (see chapter 1 of Publication 519)).

If you do not qualify to make joint estimated tax payments, apply these rules to your separate estimated income. Making joint or separate estimated tax payments will not affect your choice of filing a joint tax return or separate returns for 2012.

2011 separate returns and 2012 joint return. If you plan to file a joint return with your spouse for 2012, but you filed separate returns for 2011, your 2011 tax is the total of the tax shown on your separate returns. You filed a separate return if you filed as single, head of household, or married filing separately.

2011 joint return and 2012 separate returns. If you plan to file a separate return for 2012 but you filed a joint return for 2011, your 2011 tax is your share of the tax on the joint return. You file a separate return if you file as single, head of household, or married filing separately.

Caution

As mentioned earlier, this filing status is available for only 2 years following the year your spouse died.

To figure your share of the tax on the joint return, first figure the tax both you and your spouse would have paid had you filed separate returns for 2011 using the same filing status as for 2012. Then multiply the tax on the joint return by the following fraction.

$$\frac{\text{The tax you would have paid had you filed a separate return}}{\text{The total tax you and your spouse would have paid had you filed separate returns}}$$

Example. Joe and Heather filed a joint return for 2011 showing taxable income of $48,500 and a tax of $6,425. Of the $48,500 taxable income, $40,100 was Joe's and the rest was Heather's. For 2012, they plan to file married filing separately. Joe figures his share of the tax on the 2011 joint return as follows.

Tax on $40,100 based on a separate return	$6,150
Tax on $8,400 based on a separate return	840
Total	$6,990
Joe's percentage of total ($6,150 ÷ $6,990)	87.98%
Joe's share of tax on joint return ($6,425 × 87.98%)	$5,653

How To Figure Estimated Tax

To figure your estimated tax, you must figure your expected adjusted gross income (AGI), taxable income, taxes, deductions, and credits for the year.

When figuring your 2012 estimated tax, it may be helpful to use your income, deductions, and credits for 2011 as a starting point. Use your 2011 federal tax return as a guide. You can use Form 1040-ES to figure your estimated tax. Nonresident aliens use Form 1040-ES (NR) to figure estimated tax (see chapter 8 of Publication 519 for more information).

You must make adjustments both for changes in your own situation and for changes in the tax law. For a discussion of changes in tax law, visit *www.irs.gov*.

Form 1040-ES includes a worksheet to help you figure your estimated tax. Keep the worksheet for your records.

For more complete information and examples of how to figure your estimated tax for 2012, see chapter 2 of Publication 505.

TAXPLANNER

A convenient way to figure your estimated tax is to list all your sources of income from last year. Then enter the estimated income from each source for this year. Add to this list all new sources of income that you expect this year. Repeat this procedure for all deductions and exemptions. If your itemized deductions are more than the standard deduction, use your itemized deductions. Then compute your estimated tax liability for 2012 based on your estimated taxable income.

After you have calculated your estimated tax liability, add any additional taxes, including self-employment taxes, household employment taxes, and alternative minimum taxes, that you expect to pay for the current year. Then subtract the various tax credits you expect to claim for the current year, and also subtract the income tax you expect to have withheld. The remaining tax liability is your estimated tax.

If your estimated tax exceeds $1,000, equal estimated tax payments generally have to be made on April 15, June 15, September 15, and January 15. Special exceptions, described later in this chapter, may reduce or eliminate this requirement.

When To Pay Estimated Tax

For estimated tax purposes, the tax year is divided into four payment periods. Each period has a specific payment due date. If you do not pay enough tax by the due date of each payment period, you may be charged a penalty even if you are due a refund when you file your income tax return. The payment periods and due dates for estimated tax payments are shown next.

For the period:	Due date:
Jan. 1–March 31	April 17, 2012*
April 1–May 31	June 15, 2012
June 1–Aug. 31	Sept. 17, 2012*
Sept. 1–Dec. 31	Jan. 15, 2013**

*See *Saturday, Sunday, holiday rule* below.
**See *January payment* below.

Saturday, Sunday, holiday rule. If the due date for an estimated tax payment falls on a Saturday, Sunday, or legal holiday, the payment will be on time if you make it on the next day that is not a Saturday, Sunday, or legal holiday.

In 2012, April 15 is Sunday and Monday is a holiday in the District of Columbia; therefore, the payment is due Tuesday, April 17th. Also, in 2012, the September 15th payment is due Monday, September 17, because September 15 is a Saturday.

January payment. If you file your 2012 Form 1040 or Form 1040A by January 31, 2013, and pay the rest of the tax you owe, you do not need to make the payment due on January 15, 2013.

Fiscal year taxpayers. If your tax year does not start on January 1, see the Form 1040-ES instructions for your payment due dates.

When To Start

You do not have to make estimated tax payments until you have income on which you will owe the tax. If you have income subject to estimated tax during the first payment period, you must make your first payment by the due date for the first payment period. You can pay all your estimated tax at that time, or you can pay it in installments. If you choose to pay in installments, make your first payment by the due date for the first payment period. Make your remaining installment payments by the due dates for the later periods.

No income subject to estimated tax during first period. If you do not have income subject to estimated tax until a later payment period, you must make your first payment by the due date for that period. You can pay your entire estimated tax by the due date for that period or you can pay it in installments by the due date for that period and the due dates for the remaining periods. The following chart shows when to make installment payments.

> ### EXAMPLE
> In April 2012, John figured that his estimated tax for 2012 would be $12,000. Accordingly, he made his first 2012 quarterly estimated payment of $3,000 on April 17, 2012, and his second quarterly estimated payment of $3,000 on June 15, 2012. In August, John purchased a new home, and his monthly mortgage payments increased dramatically. Because John could deduct his mortgage interest payments, he reduced his third and fourth quarterly estimated payments due on September 17, 2012, and January 15, 2013, respectively.

If you first have income on which you must pay estimated tax:	Make a payment by:*	Make later installments by:*
Before April 1	April 15	June 15 Sept. 15 Jan. 15 next year
April 1–May 31	June 15	Sept. 15 Jan. 15 next year
June 1–Aug. 31	Sept. 15	Jan. 15 next year
After Aug. 31	Jan. 15 next year	(None)

*See *January payment* and *Saturday, Sunday, holiday rule*, earlier.

How much to pay to avoid a penalty. To determine how much you should pay by each payment due date, see *How To Figure Each Payment*, next.

> ### EXPLANATION
> The discussion that follows shows in detail how to compute your annualized income installment. Figure your installment for each payment period as follows:
> 1. Figure your adjusted gross income (AGI), alternative minimum taxable income (AMTI), and adjusted self-employment income (SEI) for the months in 2012 ending before the due date of the payment period. (Your AGI is your actual total income minus your actual adjustments to income for the months in the period.) See chapter 31, *How to figure your tax,* for more information on AMTI. Also, see chapter 38, *Self-employment income: How to file Schedule C,* for more information on SEI.

2. Multiply each of the amounts in step (1) by
   a. 4, if the payment due date is April 17.
   b. 2.4, if the payment due date is June 15.
   c. 1.5, if the payment due date is September 17.
   d. 1, if the payment due date is January 15, 2013. These amounts are your annualized AGI, AMTI, and SEI.
3. Determine the greater of your
   a. Actual allowable itemized deductions for the months in the period multiplied by the same figure used in step (2), or
   b. Standard deduction for the year.
4. Multiply your exemptions by the 2012 exemption amount (see chapter 3, *Personal exemptions and dependents*).
5. Add the amounts from steps (3) and (4), and subtract the total from your annualized AGI determined in step (2). This amount is your annualized taxable income.
6. Figure the appropriate tax on your annualized taxable income [from step (5)], the alternative minimum tax on your annualized AMTI, and self-employment tax on SEI [from step (2)].
7. Total the amounts figured in step (6).
8. Add any additional taxes that you may owe because of events that occurred during the months in 2012 ending before the due date of the payment period. "Other Taxes" are the ones listed on lines 56–60 of the 2011 Form 1040.
9. Subtract from this total any nonrefundable credits that you may be able to claim because of events that occurred during the months in 2012 ending before the due date of the payment period. These are the credits that make up the total on line 54 of the 2011 Form 1040. If these credits are more than the total of step (7) plus additional taxes figured in step (8), use zero as the result and go on to the next step.
10. Add to the result of step (9) any of the taxes listed below that you may owe because of events that occurred during the months in 2012 ending before the due date of the payment period:
    a. Uncollected social security and Medicare tax or RRTA tax on tips or group term life insurance.
    b. Excise tax on golden parachute payments.
    c. Plus the tax from Form 4952, Tax on Lump Sum Distributions, Form 8814, Parent's Election to report Report Child's Interest and Dividends, and alternative minimum tax.
11. Subtract the following credits that apply to your situation for the months in 2012 ending before the due date of the payment period:
    a. Credit for federal tax on gasoline and special fuel.
    b. Earned income credit.
    c. American opportunity credit.
    d. Adoption credit.
    e. Etc.
12. Multiply the result of step (11) by
    a. 22.5%, if the payment due date is April 17.
    b. 45%, if the payment due date is June 15.
    c. 67.5%, if the payment due date is September 17.
    d. 90%, if the payment due date is January 15, 2013.
13. Figure the total estimated tax you had to pay by the due date of each of the preceding payment periods. This is the total of the lower of the required installment or the annualized income installment for each payment period.
14. Subtract the step (13) amount from the step (12) amount.

If the annualized income installment for the payment period is less than the required installment, you only need to pay the annualized income installment.

When you pay the annualized income installment for the next payment period, you must add the difference between the required installment for that subsequent payment period (as increased) and the annualized income installment for the previous payment period to the required installment for the next payment period.

How To Figure Each Payment

You should pay enough estimated tax by the due date of each payment period to avoid a penalty for that period. You can figure your required payment for each period by using either the regular installment method or the annualized income installment method. These methods are described in chapter 2 of Publication 505. If you do not pay enough during each payment period, you may be charged a penalty even if you are due a refund when you file your tax return.

If the earlier discussion of _No income subject to estimated tax during first period_ or the later discussion of _Change in estimated tax_ applies to you, you may benefit from reading _Annualized Income Installment Method_ in chapter 2 of Publication 505 for information on how to avoid a penalty.

Underpayment penalty. Under the regular installment method, if your estimated tax payment for any period is less than one-fourth of your estimated tax, you may be charged a penalty for underpayment of estimated tax for that period when you file your tax return. Under the annualized income installment method, your estimated tax payments vary with your income, but the amount required must be paid each period. See chapter 4 of Publication 505 for more information.

Change in estimated tax. After you make an estimated tax payment, changes in your income, adjustments, deductions, credits, or exemptions may make it necessary for you to refigure your estimated tax. Pay the unpaid balance of your amended estimated tax by the next payment due date after the change or in installments by that date and the due dates for the remaining payment periods.

Estimated Tax Payments Not Required

You do not have to pay estimated tax if your withholding in each payment period is at least as much as:

- One-fourth of your required annual payment, or
- Your required annualized income installment for that period.

You also do not have to pay estimated tax if you will pay enough through withholding to keep the amount you owe with your return under $1,000.

How To Pay Estimated Tax

There are five ways to pay estimated tax.

Credit an overpayment on your 2011 return to your 2012 estimated tax.

- Send in your payment (check or money order) with a payment voucher from Form 1040-ES.
- Pay electronically using the Electronic Federal Tax Payment System (EFTPS).
- Pay by electronic funds withdrawal if you are filing Form 1040 or Form 1040A electronically.
- Pay by credit or debit card using a pay-by-phone system or the Internet.

Credit an Overpayment

If you show an overpayment of tax after completing your Form 1040 or Form 1040A for 2011, you can apply part or all of it to your estimated tax for 2012. On line 75 of Form 1040, or line 44 of Form 1040A, enter the amount you want credited to your estimated tax rather than refunded. Take the amount you have credited into account when figuring your estimated tax payments.

You cannot have any of the amount you credited to your estimated tax refunded to you until you file your tax return for the following year. You also cannot use that overpayment in any other way.

EXPLANATION

An overpayment that is applied to your estimated tax payment for the current year is considered to have been paid on time even if you are granted an extension and file your previous year's tax return after April 15.

Example

If you get a legal extension on your tax return from April 15 to October 15 and you actually file your return in July, you can apply any overpayment you may have made in the previous year to your estimated tax payments that were due first on April 15 and then on June 15.

Pay by Check or Money Order Using the Estimated Tax Payment Voucher

Each payment of estimated tax by check or money order must be accompanied by a payment voucher from Form 1040-ES. If you made estimated tax payments last year and did not use a paid preparer to file your return, you should receive a copy of the 2012 Form 1040-ES in the mail. It will contain payment vouchers preprinted with your name, address, and social security number. Using the preprinted vouchers will speed processing, reduce the chance of error, and help save processing costs.

Use the window envelopes that came with your Form 1040-ES package. If you use your own envelopes, make sure you mail your payment vouchers to the address shown in the Form 1040-ES instructions for the place where you live.

If you did not pay estimated tax last year, you can order Form 1040-ES from the IRS (see inside back cover of this publication) or download it from *www.irs.gov*. Follow the instructions in the package to make sure you use the vouchers correctly.

If you file a joint return and are making joint estimated tax payments, enter the names and social security numbers on the payment voucher in the same order as they will appear on the joint return.

Change of address. You must notify the IRS if you are making estimated tax payments and you changed your address during the year. Send a clear and concise written statement to the Internal Revenue Service Center where you filed your last return and provide all of the following.

- Your full name (and spouse's full name).
- Your signature (and spouse's signature).
- Your old address (and spouse's old address if different).
- Your new address.
- Your social security number (and spouse's social security number).

You can use Form 8822, Change of Address, for this purpose.

Pay Electronically

If you want to make estimated payments by using EFTPS, by electronic funds withdrawal, or by credit or debit card, go to *www.irs.gov/e-pay*.

Credit for Withholding and Estimated Tax for 2011

When you file your 2011 income tax return, take credit for all the income tax and excess social security or railroad retirement tax withheld from your salary, wages, pensions, etc. Also take credit for the estimated tax you paid for 2011. These credits are subtracted from your tax. Because these credits are refundable, you should file a return and claim these credits, even if you do not owe tax.

Two or more employers. If you had two or more employers in 2011 and were paid wages of more than $106,800, too much social security or tier 1 railroad retirement tax may have been withheld from your wages. You may be able to claim the excess as a credit against your income tax when you file your return. See *Credit for Excess Social Security Tax or Railroad Retirement Tax Withheld* in chapter 37.

Withholding

If you had income tax withheld during 2011, you should be sent a statement by January 31, 2012, showing your income and the tax withheld. Depending on the source of your income, you should receive:

- Form W-2, Wage and Tax Statement,
- Form W-2G, Certain Gambling Winnings, or
- A form in the 1099 series.

Forms W-2 and W-2G. Always file Form W-2 with your income tax return. File Form W-2G with your return only if it shows any federal income tax withheld from your winnings.

You should get at least two copies of each form you receive. Attach one copy to the front of your federal income tax return. Keep one copy for your records. You also should receive copies to file with your state and local returns.

EXAMPLE

Ted Jones is employed by ABC Company, Inc. His Form W-2, box 2, reflects that he had $10,675.50 in federal tax withheld by ABC Company on wages of $46,958.

His state income tax of $2,817.48 withheld for the state of Georgia is reflected in box 17 on the same amount of wages. Box 12 (Code D—code definitions can be found on the back of the W-2 form) indicates that Ted contributed $2,546.21 to his company's 401(k) plan. That amount of income was not included in the federal or state wages, but it is included in determining how much was withheld from Ted's income for social security and Medicare purposes. Refer to boxes 3 and 5. The social security tax withheld is in box 4, and the Medicare tax withheld is in box 6. The retirement plan box is checked in box 13 and lets Ted (and the IRS) know that he is covered by a retirement plan and therefore may be limited in his ability to make deductible IRA contributions.

22222	**a** Employee's social security number	OMB No. 1545-0008	Safe, accurate, FAST! Use	IRS *e-file* — Visit the IRS website at www.irs.gov/efile

b Employer identification number (EIN)	**1** Wages, tips, other compensation **44,958.00** / **2** Federal income tax withheld **10,675.00**
c Employer's name, address, and ZIP code **ABC Company, Inc.**	**3** Social security wages **49,504.21** / **4** Social security tax withheld **2,079.18**
	5 Medicare wages and tips **49,958.00** / **6** Medicare tax withheld **717.81**
	7 Social security tips / **8** Allocated tips
d Control number	**9** / **10** Dependent care benefits
e Employee's first name and initial Last name Suff. **Ted Jones**	**11** Nonqualified plans / **12a** See instructions for box 12 Code **D** **2546.21**
	13 Statutory employee ☐ Retirement plan ☒ Third-party sick pay ☐ / **12b** Code
	14 Other / **12c** Code
f Employee's address and ZIP code	**12d** Code

15 State	Employer's state ID number	16 State wages, tips, etc.	17 State income tax	18 Local wages, tips, etc.	19 Local income tax	20 Locality name
GA		46,958.00	2,817.48			

Form **W-2** Wage and Tax Statement   **2011**   Department of the Treasury—Internal Revenue Service

Copy B—To Be Filed With Employee's FEDERAL Tax Return.
This information is being furnished to the Internal Revenue Service.

Form W-2

Your employer is required to provide or send Form W-2 to you no later than January 31, 2012. You should receive a separate Form W-2 from each employer you worked for.

If you stopped working before the end of 2011, your employer could have given you your Form W-2 at any time after you stopped working. However, your employer must provide or send it to you by January 31, 2012.

If you ask for the form, your employer must send it to you within 30 days after receiving your written request or within 30 days after your final wage payment, whichever is later.

If you have not received your Form W-2 on time, you should ask your employer for it. If you do not receive it by February 15, call the IRS.

Form W-2 shows your total pay and other compensation and the income tax, social security tax, and Medicare tax that were withheld during the year. Include the federal income tax withheld (as shown in box 2 of Form W-2) on:

- Line 62 if you file Form 1040,
- Line 36 if you file Form 1040A, or
- Line 7 if you file Form 1040EZ.

In addition, Form W-2 is used to report any taxable sick pay you received and any income tax withheld from your sick pay.

Form W-2G

If you had gambling winnings in 2011, the payer may have withheld income tax. If tax was withheld, the payer will give you a Form W-2G showing the amount you won and the amount of tax withheld.

Report the amounts you won on line 21 of Form 1040. Take credit for the tax withheld on line 62 of Form 1040. If you had gambling winnings, you must use Form 1040; you cannot use Form 1040A or Form 1040EZ.

The 1099 Series

Most forms in the 1099 series are not filed with your return. These forms should be furnished to you by January 31, 2012 (or, for Forms 1099-B, 1099-S, and certain Forms 1099-MISC, by February 15, 2012). Unless instructed to file any of these forms with your return, keep them for your records. There are several different forms in this series, including:

- Form 1099-B, Proceeds From Broker and Barter Exchange Transactions;
- Form 1099-C, Cancellation of Debt;
- Form 1099-DIV, Dividends and Distributions;
- Form 1099-G, Certain Government Payments;
- Form 1099-INT, Interest Income;
- Form 1099-MISC, Miscellaneous Income;
- Form 1099-OID, Original Issue Discount;
- Form 1099-Q, Payments From Qualified Education Programs;
- Form 1099-R, Distributions From Pensions, Annuities, Retirement or Profit-Sharing Plans, IRAs, Insurance Contracts, etc.;
- Form 1099-S, Proceeds From Real Estate Transactions;
- Form SSA-1099, Social Security Benefit Statement; and
- Form RRB-1099, Payments by the Railroad Retirement Board.

If you received the types of income reported on some forms in the 1099 series, you may not be able to use Form 1040A or Form 1040EZ. See the instructions to these forms for details.

Form 1099-R. Attach Form 1099-R to your return if box 4 shows federal income tax withheld. Include the amount withheld in the total on line 62 of Form 1040 or line 36 of Form 1040A. You cannot use Form 1040EZ if you received payments reported on Form 1099-R.

Backup withholding. If you were subject to backup withholding on income you received during 2011, include the amount withheld, as shown in box 4 of your Form 1099, in the total on line 62 of Form 1040, line 36 of Form 1040A, or line 7 of Form 1040EZ.

Form Not Correct

If you receive a form with incorrect information on it, you should ask the payer for a corrected form. Call the telephone number or write to the address given for the payer on the form. The corrected Form W-2G or Form 1099 you receive will have an "X" in the "CORRECTED" box at the top of the form. A special form, Form W-2c, Corrected Wage and Tax Statement, is used to correct a Form W-2.

In certain situations, you will receive two forms in place of the original incorrect form. This will happen when your taxpayer identification number is wrong or missing, your name and address are wrong, or you received the wrong type of form (for example, a Form 1099-DIV instead of a Form 1099-INT). One new form you receive will be the same incorrect form or have the same incorrect information, but all money amounts will be zero. This form will have an "X" in the "CORRECTED" box at the top of the form. The second new form should have all the correct information, prepared as though it is the original (the "CORRECTED" box will not be checked).

Form Received After Filing

If you file your return and you later receive a form for income that you did not include on your return, you should report the income and take credit for any income tax withheld by filing Form 1040X, Amended U.S. Individual Income Tax Return.

Separate Returns

If you are married but file a separate return, you can take credit only for the tax withheld from your own income. Do not include any amount withheld from your spouse's income. However, different rules may apply if you live in a community property state.

Community property states are listed in chapter 2. For more information on these rules, and some exceptions, see Publication 555, *Community Property*.

Fiscal Years

If you file your tax return on the basis of a fiscal year (a 12-month period ending on the last day of any month except December), you must follow special rules to determine your credit for federal income tax withholding. For a discussion of how to take credit for withholding on a fiscal year return, see *Fiscal Years (FY)* in chapter 3 of Publication 505.

Estimated Tax

Take credit for all your estimated tax payments for 2011 on line <u>63</u> of Form 1040 or line <u>37</u> of Form 1040A. Include any overpayment from 2010 that you had credited to your 2011 estimated tax. You must use Form 1040 or Form 1040A if you paid estimated tax. You cannot use Form 1040EZ.

Name changed. If you changed your name, and you made estimated tax payments using your old name, attach a brief statement to the front of your tax return indicating:
- When you made the payments,
- The amount of each payment,
- The IRS address to which you sent the payments,
- Your name when you made the payments, and
- Your social security number.

The statement should cover payments you made jointly with your spouse as well as any you made separately.

Separate Returns

If you and your spouse made separate estimated tax payments for 2011 and you file separate returns, you can take credit only for your own payments.

If you made joint estimated tax payments, you must decide how to divide the payments between your returns. One of you can claim all of the estimated tax paid and the other none, or you can divide it in any other way you agree on. If you cannot agree, you must divide the payments in proportion to each spouse's individual tax as shown on your separate returns for 2011.

Divorced Taxpayers

If you made joint estimated tax payments for 2011, and you were divorced during the year, either you or your former spouse can claim all of the joint payments, or you each can claim part of them. If you cannot agree on how to divide the payments, you must divide them in proportion to each spouse's individual tax as shown on your separate returns for 2011.

If you claim any of the joint payments on your tax return, enter your former spouse's social security number (SSN) in the space provided on the front of Form 1040 or Form 1040A. If you divorced and remarried in 2011, enter your present spouse's SSN in that space and write your former spouse's SSN, followed by "DIV," to the left of Form 1040, line <u>63</u>, or Form 1040A, line <u>37</u>.

Underpayment Penalty for 2011

If you did not pay enough tax, either through withholding or by making timely estimated tax payments, you will have an underpayment of estimated tax and you may have to pay a penalty.

Generally, you will not have to pay a penalty for 2011 if any of the following situations applies.
- The total of your withholding and estimated tax payments was at least as much as your 2010 tax (or 110% of your 2010 tax if your AGI was more than $150,000, $75,000 if your 2011 filing status is married filing separately) and you paid all required estimated tax payments on time.
- The tax balance due on your 2011 return is no more than 10% of your total 2011 tax, and you paid all required estimated tax payments on time.
- Your total 2011 tax minus your withholding and refundable credits is less than $1,000.
- You did not have a tax liability for 2010 and your 2010 tax year was 12 months.
- You did not have any withholding taxes and your current year tax less any household employment taxes is less than $1,000.

See Publication 505, chapter 4, for a definition of "total tax" for 2010 and 2011.

Farmers and fishermen. Special rules apply if you are a farmer or fisherman. See *Farmers and Fishermen* in chapter 4 of Publication 505 for more information.

IRS can figure the penalty for you. If you think you owe the penalty but you do not want to figure it yourself when you file your tax return, you may not have to. Generally, the IRS will figure the penalty for you and send you a bill. However, if you think you are able to lower or eliminate your penalty, you must complete Form 2210 or Form 2210-F and attach it to your return. See chapter 4 of Publication 505.

TAXPLANNER

The safest method of paying enough estimated tax and withholding, and thereby avoiding underpayment penalties, is to use last year's tax. The tax shown on your previous year's tax return less the tax that is expected to be withheld during the current year must be paid in estimated installments throughout the year.

Example

Elizabeth West's 2011 tax return indicates that her 2011 tax liability (including self-employment tax and alternative minimum tax) was $14,000. In 2012, Elizabeth estimates that her tax liability will jump to $24,000 due to several contemplated stock sales that should result in a substantial capital gain. Elizabeth's withholding on her 2012 salary is expected to be $13,000.

Because her withholding of $13,000 during 2012 is not expected to exceed her 2011 tax of $14,000, she should increase her withholding by $1,000 during the year. Even though she will have paid less than 90% of her tax liability for 2012, she will avoid an underpayment penalty because she has paid an amount at least equal to her 2011 tax. If she made this determination early enough in the year, she could accomplish the same result by making four quarterly estimated tax payments of $250.

However, Elizabeth will have to pay an additional $10,000 ($24,000 − $14,000) when she files her 2012 tax return by April 15, 2013. Nevertheless, she will have had the use of this money from the time she sold her stock until the time she filed her 2012 tax return.

Explanation

Underpayment penalties. You may be penalized for not paying enough tax for a particular installment period. The amount subject to the penalty is the amount by which the required installment, defined as the lesser of items 1 or 2 below, exceeds the amount paid for the quarterly period:

1. 90% of the tax shown on the return (after certain adjustments), allocated evenly to each of the quarterly periods; or
2. 100% of the 2011 tax, allocated evenly to each of the quarterly periods (provided the prior year comprised 12 months and a return was filed for such year); if your 2011 adjusted gross income exceeded $150,000, you must have paid 110% of the 2011 tax liability to avoid underpayment penalties for 2012. Note: 100% of prior year tax is the tax liability as shown on the 2011 original return. The tax liability on an amended return is not used for purposes of quarterly estimated payments.

Example

Ms. Green's adjusted gross income in 2010 was $175,000, while her 2010 tax liability was $40,000. Her 2011 income tax liability is $55,000. Ms. Green will avoid an underpayment penalty in 2011 if the total amount of tax withheld and estimated tax payments exceeds 110% of her 2010 tax liability, or $44,000. To avoid a penalty in 2012, she would have to pay in $60,500 (110% of $55,000), since her adjusted gross income also exceeded $150,000 in 2011.

The underpayment penalty may also be avoided by using a special rule based on your annualized income. Under the special rule, no penalty is imposed for a quarter if the cumulative amount paid by the installment date equals or exceeds 90% of the cumulative estimated tax as computed on annualized income.

In general, the annualized method allows you to calculate your quarterly payment based on taxable income received up to the end of the latest quarter, annualized to a 12-month period. You can usually benefit from the annualized method if you do not receive your taxable income evenly throughout the year (e.g., if you are the owner of a ski shop that receives most of its revenue during the winter months).

The use of the methods for determining the underpaid amount, described previously, may vary from quarter to quarter to provide the minimum underpayment amount by quarter. Remember, however, that if you pay the annualized income installment, you must add the difference between the amount you pay and the required installment to the required installment for the next period if the annualized income method is not used for the next period.

The tax computed for purposes of determining the quarterly payment required to avoid the underpayment penalty includes the self-employment tax and all other taxes (including the alternative minimum tax), minus any allowable credits.

If the amount paid for a quarterly period is greater than the amount required to avoid penalty, the excess is applied first against underpayments in prior quarters, and then against subsequent underpayments. Any penalty is assessed from the installment due date to the date paid or the original due date of the return, whichever is earlier. The rate of the penalty is the same as the rate of interest for underpayments of tax. However, the penalty is not compounded daily, whereas the interest is.

Special requirements and exceptions are provided for farmers, fishermen, and nonresident aliens

TAXALERT

The underpayment of estimated tax penalty is not imposed where the total tax liability for the year, reduced by any withheld tax and estimated tax payments, is less than $1,000.

TAXPLANNER

You may avoid an underpayment penalty before the end of the year by taking a distribution from your IRA account and having enough taxes withheld to cover your underpayment. It is important to remember to repay the entire amount of the distribution, including taxes withheld, within 60 days after the distribution. Otherwise, the distribution is subject to taxes as well as a 10% early withdrawal penalty if you are under age 59½.

Part 2
Income

The eight chapters in this part discuss many kinds of income. They explain which type of income is and is not taxed. The chart on the following page lists some of the topics covered in this part. It is divided into (1) items you generally must include in income and (2) items you generally do not include in income.

See _Part 3_ for information on gains and losses you report on Schedule D (Form 1040) and for information on selling your home.

INCOME

INCOME GENERALLY INCLUDES:

Alimony (chapter 18, *Alimony*)

Bartering income (chapter 12, *Other income*)

Canceled debt income (chapter 12, *Other income*)

Dividends (chapter 8, *Dividends and other corporate distributions*)

Gain on the sale of personal items, such as a car (chapter 12, *Other income*)

Gambling winnings (chapter 12, *Other income*)

Income from an activity not for profit (chapter 12, *Other income*)

Interest (chapter 7, *Interest income*)

Part of social security benefits and equivalent railroad retirement benefits (chapter 11, *Social security and equivalent railroad retirement benefits*)

Pensions and annuities (chapter 10, *Retirement plans, pensions, and annuities*)

Recoveries of amounts previously deducted (chapter 12, *Other income*)

Rental income (chapter 9, *Rental income and expenses*)

Royalties (chapter 12, *Other income*)
Tips (chapter 6, *Tip income*)

Wages, salaries, and other earnings (chapter 5, *Wages, salaries, and other earnings*)

Your share of estate and trust income (chapter 12, *Other income*)

Your share of partnership and S Corporation income (chapter 12, *Other income*)

INCOME GENERALLY DOES NOT INCLUDE:

Accident and health insurance proceeds (chapter 12, *Other income*)

Gifts and inheritances (chapter 12, *Other income*)

Housing allowance for members of the clergy (chapter 5, *Wages, salaries, and other earnings*)

Interest on state and local government obligations (chapter 7, *Interest income*)

Life insurance proceeds (chapter 12, *Other income*)

Military allowances (chapter 5, *Wages, salaries, and other earnings*)

Part of scholarship and fellowship grants (chapter 12, *Other income*)

Part of social security benefits and equivalent railroad retirement benefits (chapter 11, *Social security and equivalent railroad retirement benefits*)

Veterans' benefits (chapter 5, *Wages, salaries, and other earnings*)

Welfare and other public assistance benefits (chapter 12, *Other income*)

Workers' compensation and similar payments for sickness and injury (chapter 12, *Other income*)

Chapter 5
Wages, salaries, and other earnings

Note

IRS Publication 17 (*Your Federal Income Tax*) has been updated by Ernst & Young LLP for 2011. Dates and dollar amounts shown are for 2011. Underlined type is used to indicate where IRS text has been updated. Places where text has been removed are indicated by the sentence: *Text intentionally omitted.*

ey.com/EYTaxGuide

Ernst & Young LLP will update the *Ernst & Young Tax Guide 2012* website with relevant taxpayer information as it becomes available. You can also sign up for email alerts to let you know when changes have been made.

Introduction

Ask most people how much they get paid, and, if they are willing to admit anything, they'll tell you what their salary is. Usually, there's more to income than that.

The way the IRS sees it, "gross income means all income from whatever source derived." That means not only is your salary subject to tax, but so are many of the fringe benefits provided by your employer that you might receive—everything from country club membership and employer-provided discounts to a company car. This chapter spells out in greater detail items of compensation that are taxable.

Some fringe benefits you receive from your employer are tax-free. For example, the cost of the first $50,000 of coverage in a group-term life insurance plan will be tax-free if all employees in the plan are treated in the same way. But, if your employer, in a moment of detached and disinterested generosity, presents you with a Rolls-Royce as a gift, you will probably have to pay taxes on it. This chapter prepares you—in a tax sense—for whatever lies ahead.

TAXALERT

Limit on elective deferrals. The maximum amount of elective deferrals under a salary reduction agreement that can be contributed to a qualified plan (such as a section 401(k) or 403(b) plan) in 2011 is $16,500 ($22,000 if you were age 50 or older). For more information, see the TaxPlanner regarding elective deferrals in chapter 10, *Retirement plans, pensions, and annuities.*

What's New

Temporary decrease in employee's share of payroll tax. For 2011, social security will be withheld from an employee's wages at the rate of 4.2% (down from 6.2%) up to the social security wage limit of $106,800. There will be no change to Medicare withholding.

Increase in additional tax on certain distributions not used for qualified medical expenses. The tax on distributions from health savings accounts (HSAs) and Archer MSAs made after December 31, 2010, that are not used for qualified medical expenses, is increased to 20%.

Withholding on Wages. If you're getting a very large refund when you file your return, remember that you can claim withholding allowances based on your expected deductions for 2012. Claiming more allowances will increase the amount of your take home pay. For more details, see *Getting the Right Amount of Tax Withheld* in chapter 4, *Tax withholding and estimated tax.*

Health Flexible Spending Arrangements (FSAs). If your employer provides you with an FSA (also known as a cafeteria plan), consider taking advantage of it. You can contribute part of your salary to the arrangement on a pre-tax basis (not subject to income, social security, or Medicare taxes). You can then pay for qualified health care expenses (including prescription medication and insurance co-payments) tax-free. FSA coverage and reimbursement are now allowed for your children who are under age 27 as of the end of your tax year. For more details, see *Cafeteria Plans* in chapter 22, *Medical and dental expenses.*

401(k) and 403(b) Plan Contributions. You can reduce your taxable wages (and your tax bill) by contributing on a pre-tax basis to a 401(k) or 403(b) plan sponsored by your employer. In 2011, you can contribute up to $16,500 ($22,000 if you are 50 or older by the end of the year). For more details, see chapter 10, *Retirement plans, pensions, and annuities.*

Disability Income. If you become disabled, any benefits paid to you while you can't work are usually taxable income. But if an in-

Nonprescription, over-the-counter drugs not reimburseable from health reimbursement arrangements. Effective January 1, 2011, the cost of an over-the-counter medicine or drug cannot be reimbursed from Flexible Savings Accounts (FSAs), Health Reimbursement Arrangements (HRAs), and Archer Medical Savings Accounts (Archer MSAs) unless a prescription is obtained. The change does not affect insulin, even if purchased without a prescription, or other health care expenses such as medical devices, eyeglasses, contact lenses, co-pays and deductibles.

Exclusion from income of benefits provided to volunteer firefighters and emergency medical responders. This exclusion from income is not available for benefits received in 2011.

Reminder

Foreign income. If you are a U.S. citizen or resident alien, you must report income from sources outside the United States (foreign income) on your tax return unless it is exempt by U.S. law. This is true whether you reside inside or outside the United States and whether or not you receive a Form W-2, Wage and Tax Statement, or Form 1099 from the foreign payer. This applies to earned income (such as wages and tips) as well as unearned income (such as interest, dividends, capital gains, pensions, rents, and royalties).

If you reside outside the United States, you may be able to exclude part or all of your foreign source earned income. For details, see Publication 54, *Tax Guide for U.S. Citizens and Resident Aliens Abroad.*

This chapter discusses compensation received for services as an employee, such as wages, salaries, and fringe benefits. The following topics are included.

- Bonuses and awards.
- Special rules for certain employees.
- Sickness and injury benefits.

The chapter explains what income is included in the employee's gross income and what is not included.

EXPLANATION

One of the most important decisions you have to make in determining your correct taxable income is what payments to include. A taxable payment is not limited to cash. It may be property, stock, or other assets. Also, you must include in your gross income the fair market value of payments in kind.

Example 1
Your employer provides you with a car that is used for both personal and business purposes. The value of the personal use of the car is included in earnings and it is taxable to you.

Example 2
You assist a group of investors in purchasing a piece of real estate. In consideration of your services, the investors award you an unconditional percentage of ownership in the acquired asset. You have invested none of your personal funds. The fair market value of your ownership interest is considered as wages taxable to you in the year the transfer is completed.

Example 3
A farmer receives 50 bushels of wheat as a payment in kind. Unless specifically excluded under a government program, the farmer has income to the extent of the fair market value of the wheat.

Useful Items

You may want to see:

Publication

- ☐ **463** Travel, Entertainment, Gift, and Car Expenses
- ☐ **503** Child and Dependent Care Expenses
- ☐ **505** Tax Withholding and Estimated Tax
- ☐ **525** Taxable and Nontaxable Income

EXPLANATION

Other useful publications and references include:
- ☐ **Publication 15, Circular E,** *Employer's Tax Guide*; chapter 5, *Wages and Other Compensation*
- ☐ **Publication 15-B,** *Employer's Tax Guide to Fringe Benefits*; chapter 1, *Fringe Benefit Overview*

These and other IRS publications are available online at *www.irs.gov.*

Employee Compensation

This section discusses various types of employee compensation including fringe benefits, retirement plan contributions, stock options, and restricted property.

EXPLANATION

All compensation for personal services, no matter what the form of payment, must be included in gross income. Such compensation is subject to taxes in the year received, unless the taxpayer reports income on the accrual basis.

If you perform services and decide that payment for them should be made to another person, the monies remitted to the third party are taxable to you. The IRS and the courts have long held that "fruits" of a taxpayer's labor are attributable to the "tree" that grew them. Furthermore, you may not render services and then ask your employer to hold the funds in an attempt to control artificially when the wages will be included in your taxable income.

Example

You are due compensation for work you performed. You advise the payer to hold the money because you will not require the funds immediately. The payer credits the payment due you on the company books. You do not request the money until after the close of the tax year in which the services were rendered.

The IRS may hold that you were in **constructive receipt** of the funds before year's end. The compensation may have to be included in your income for the year in which the payment could have been received, even though you were not actually paid until later.

TAXPLANNER

You will have a problem with the IRS if you ask your employer after you have performed the work to withhold funds in an attempt to artificially control when the wages will be included in your taxable income. If you make arrangements to defer receipt of income prior to commencing work, you may not have a problem as long as the arrangement meets the requirements of the law.

However, if your employer forces you to take your bonus in a later year, then it is not taxable to you until the year in which you receive it.

EXAMPLE

If you arrange to have your employer pay your year-end bonus over a 5-year period, the IRS will not claim that you were in **constructive receipt** of the entire bonus at the end of the first year, if the deferral of your bonus is within the strict nonqualified deferred compensation rules. (These rules are complex. Your employer will likely provide you with guidelines if you are eligible to participate in such a plan. Also, consider consulting with your tax advisor.) You may even arrange to have your employer add interest to your deferred bonus. You must make these arrangements prior to performance of the work for which the bonus will be paid. Keep in mind these types of arrangements must meet a complicated set of requirements, which have been in place since 2004. (You should consider consulting your tax advisor for specific guidance.)

Form W-2. If you are an employee, you should receive Form W-2 from your employer showing the pay you received for your services. Include your pay on line 7 of Form 1040 or Form 1040A, or on line 1 of Form 1040EZ, even if you do not receive a Form W-2.

If you performed services, other than as an independent contractor, and your employer did not withhold social security and Medicare taxes from your pay, you must file Form 8919, Uncollected Social Security and Medicare Tax on Wages, with your Form 1040. These wages must be included on line 7 of Form 1040. See Form 8919 for more information.

EXPLANATION

For 2011, your employer is required to furnish your W-2 to you no later than January 31, 2012. If a Form W-2 is not received from your employer by the tax filing deadline, Form 4852, the substitute for W-2, should be attached to the return. If you leave your job prior to December 31, 2011, and are not expecting to return to it prior to the calendar year-end, you can request a copy of your W-2 in writing from your employer and they are required to provide a copy to you within 30 days of the request if the 30-day period ends before January 31, 2012.

surance company pays the benefits, and the premium payments were originally taxable to you, those benefits will not be taxable. Check to see how your employer treats those premium payments. For more details, see *Disability Pensions* in chapter 10, *Retirement plans, pensions, and annuities.*

Health Savings Accounts (HSAs). If you are covered by a health plan with a high deductible amount (HDHP) and meet other certain requirements, you may want to consider establishing a health savings account (HSA). Contributions made by you would be a deduction from your adjusted gross income and contributions by your employer are excluded from your income and are **not** subject to employment taxes. Similar to FSAs, HSAs coverage and reimbursement are now allowed for your children under age 27 as of the end of your tax year. For frequently asked questions related to HSAs, see Publication 969, *Health Savings Accounts and Other Tax-Favored Health Plans*, and additional information included in this chapter.

Childcare providers. If you provide childcare, either in the child's home or in your home or other place of business, the pay you receive must be included in your income. If you are not an employee, you are probably self-employed and must include payments for your services on Schedule C (Form 1040), Profit or Loss From Business, or Schedule C-EZ (Form 1040), Net Profit From Business. You generally are not an employee unless you are subject to the will and control of the person who employs you as to what you are to do and how you are to do it.

Babysitting. If you babysit for relatives or neighborhood children, whether on a regular basis or only periodically, the rules for childcare providers apply to you.

Miscellaneous Compensation

This section discusses different types of employee compensation.

Advance commissions and other earnings. If you receive advance commissions or other amounts for services to be performed in the future and you are a cash-method taxpayer, you must include these amounts in your income in the year you receive them.

If you repay unearned commissions or other amounts in the same year you receive them, reduce the amount included in your income by the repayment. If you repay them in a later tax year, you can deduct the repayment as an itemized deduction on your Schedule A (Form 1040), or you may be able to take a credit for that year. See *Repayments* in chapter 12.

EXPLANATION

In some cases, an advance payment of a commission or salary may be considered a loan, thus permitting you to delay paying tax on that amount. If the loan is repaid, you will not have to recognize any taxable income. If the loan is forgiven, you will recognize the amount of the loan as compensation in the year in which it was forgiven. See *Canceled Debts* in chapter 12, *Other income*, for a complete discussion. Commissions and salaries are considered to be income when they are paid to you or when they are applied as a reduction to your loan account.

The key question is: When may a payment be characterized as a loan? Generally, for a transaction to be considered a loan, a debtor-creditor relationship must exist from the beginning. In other words, the lending party expects and will eventually receive monetary repayment. Payment in return for a future obligation to render services is not a loan. Thus, an advance on your wages is not a loan. Whether a payment is or is not a loan is usually a question of fact, requiring a review of each case's unique circumstances.

Example

If you receive an advance of your January 2012 salary on December 31, 2011, you will have taxable income in 2011.

TAXSAVER

Generally, you should take advantage of your employer's 401(k) plan or 403(b) plan. Your contribution to the plan will not be included in your taxable wages. See chapter 10, *Retirement plans, pensions, and annuities,* for more information about these plans.

TAXPLANNER

You may wish to consider a loan from your employer's qualified pension or annuity plan rather than an advance on your next year's salary. Loans are not considered taxable income to the borrower under most circumstances. See chapter 10, *Retirement plans, pensions, and annuities,* for rules regarding loans from an employer's qualified pension or annuity plan.

TAXALERT

Owner-employees, such as S corporation shareholders, partners, and sole proprietors, are able to borrow from their pension plans without being subject to a penalty tax.

Allowances and reimbursements. If you receive travel, transportation, or other business expense allowances or reimbursements from your employer, see Publication 463. If you are reimbursed for moving expenses, see Publication 521, *Moving Expenses.*

Back pay awards. Include in income amounts you are awarded in a settlement or judgment for back pay. These include payments made to you for damages, unpaid life insurance premiums, and unpaid health insurance premiums. They should be reported to you by your employer on Form W-2.

> ### EXPLANATION
> If you received an amount in settlement or judgment for back wages and liquidated damages (e.g., under Title VII as amended by the 1991 Civil Rights Act), see *Court Awards and Damages* in chapter 12, *Other income*. Generally, awards intended to replace lost wages are included in your taxable income.

> ### TAXPLANNER
> Prior to entering any settlement agreement, you should consult with a tax advisor to ensure that you negotiate the most tax-favorable terms.

Bonuses and awards. Bonuses or awards you receive for outstanding work are included in your income and should be shown on your Form W-2. These include prizes such as vacation trips for meeting sales goals. If the prize or award you receive is goods or services, you must include the fair market value of the goods or services in your income. However, if your employer merely promises to pay you a bonus or award at some future time, it is not taxable until you receive it or it is made available to you.

Employee achievement award. If you receive tangible personal property (other than cash, a gift certificate, or an equivalent item) as an award for length of service or safety achievement, you generally can exclude its value from your income. However, the amount you can exclude is limited to your employer's cost and cannot be more than $1,600 ($400 for awards that are not qualified plan awards) for all such awards you receive during the year. Your employer can tell you whether your award is a qualified plan award. Your employer must make the award as part of a meaningful presentation, under conditions and circumstances that do not create a significant likelihood of it being disguised pay.

However, the exclusion does not apply to the following awards.

- A length-of-service award if you received it for less than 5 years of service or if you received another length-of-service award during the year or the previous 4 years.
- A safety achievement award if you are a manager, administrator, clerical employee, or other professional employee or if more than 10% of eligible employees previously received safety achievement awards during the year.

Example. Ben Green received three employee achievement awards during the year: a nonqualified plan award of a watch valued at $250, and two qualified plan awards of a stereo valued at $1,000 and a set of golf clubs valued at $500. Assuming that the requirements for qualified plan awards are otherwise satisfied, each award by itself would be excluded from income. However, because the $1,750 total value of the awards is more than $1,600, Ben must include $150 ($1,750 − $1,600) in his income.

Differential wage payments. This is any payment made to you by an employer for any period during which you are, for a period of more than 30 days, an active duty member of the uniformed services and represents all or a portion of the wages you would have received from the employer during that period. These payments are treated as wages and are subject to income tax withholding, but not FICA or FUTA taxes. The payments are reported as wages on Form W-2.

Government cost-of-living allowances. Cost-of-living allowances generally are included in your income. However, cost-of-living allowances are not included in your income if you were a federal civilian employee or a federal court employee who was stationed in Alaska, Hawaii, or outside the United States. Beginning January 1, 2010, these federal employees are being transitioned from a nontaxable cost-of-living adjustment to a taxable locality-based comparability payment.

Allowances and differentials that increase your basic pay as an incentive for taking a less desirable post of duty are part of your compensation and must be included in income. For example, your compensation includes Foreign Post, Foreign Service, and Overseas Tropical differentials. For more information, see Publication 516, *U.S. Government Civilian Employees Stationed Abroad.*

Nonqualified deferred compensation plans. Your employer will report to you the total amount of deferrals for the year under a nonqualified deferred compensation plan. This amount is shown on Form W-2, box 12, using code Y. This amount is not included in your income.

However, if at any time during the tax year, the plan fails to meet certain requirements, or is not operated under those requirements, all amounts deferred under the plan for the tax year and all preceding tax years are included in your income for the current year. This amount is included in your wages shown on Form W-2, box 1. It is also shown on Form W-2, box 12, using code Z.

Note received for services. If your employer gives you a secured note as payment for your services, you must include the fair market value (usually the discount value) of the note in your income for the year you receive it. When you later receive payments on the note, a proportionate part of each payment is the recovery of the fair market value that you previously included in your income. Do not include that part again in your income. Include the rest of the payment in your income in the year of payment.

If your employer gives you a nonnegotiable unsecured note as payment for your services, payments on the note that are credited toward the principal amount of the note are compensation income when you receive them.

Severance pay. You must include in income amounts you receive as severance pay and any payment for the cancellation of your employment contract.

Accrued leave payment. If you are a federal employee and receive a lump-sum payment for accrued annual leave when you retire or resign, this amount will be included as wages on your Form W-2.

If you resign from one agency and are reemployed by another agency, you may have to repay part of your lump-sum annual leave payment to the second agency. You can reduce gross wages by the amount you repaid in the same tax year in which you received it. Attach to your tax return a copy of the receipt or statement given to you by the agency you repaid to explain the difference between the wages on the return and the wages on your Forms W-2.

Outplacement services. If you choose to accept a reduced amount of severance pay so that you can receive outplacement services (such as training in resume writing and interview techniques), you must include the unreduced amount of the severance pay in income.

However, you can deduct the value of these outplacement services (up to the difference between the severance pay included in income and the amount actually received) as a miscellaneous deduction (subject to the 2%-of-adjusted-gross-income (AGI) limit) on Schedule A (Form 1040).

Sick pay. Pay you receive from your employer while you are sick or injured is part of your salary or wages. In addition, you must include in your income sick pay benefits received from any of the following payers.
- A welfare fund.
- A state sickness or disability fund.
- An association of employers or employees.
- An insurance company, if your employer paid for the plan.

However, if you paid the premiums on an accident or health insurance policy, the benefits you receive under the policy are not taxable. For more information, see Publication 525.

Social security and Medicare taxes paid by employer. If you and your employer have an agreement that your employer pays your social security and Medicare taxes without deducting them from your gross wages, you must report the amount of tax paid for you as taxable wages on your tax return. The payment also is treated as wages for figuring your social security and Medicare taxes and your social security and Medicare benefits. However, these payments are not treated as social security and Medicare wages if you are a household worker or a farm worker.

TAXALERT

Temporary decrease in employee's share of payroll tax. For 2011, Social security will be withheld from an employee's wages at the rate of 4.2% (down from 6.2%) up to the social security wage limit of $106,800. There will be no change to Medicare withholding.

The same reduction applies to the self-employment tax rate applied to net earnings from self-employment—the temporary rate will be 10.4% (down from 12.4%) up to the social security wage limit of $106,800. For more information about self-employment tax, see chapter 38, *Self-employment income: How to file Schedule C.*

Stock appreciation rights. Do not include a stock appreciation right granted by your employer in income until you exercise (use) the right. When you use the right, you are entitled to a cash payment equal to the fair market value of the corporation's stock on the date of use minus the fair market value on the date the right was granted. You include the cash payment in your income in the year you use the right.

EXPLANATION

Stock appreciation rights (SARs) are rights awarded to an employee by a corporation that enable the employee to benefit over a certain period of time from the appreciation in value of the employer's stock without the employee actually owning the stock.

Example

In January 2011, you were given 10 SARs when your company's stock was valued at $25 per share. You may exercise your SARs at any time during a 24-month period. In the first 6 months after the SARs are awarded, the company's stock rises to $50 per share. However, you do not exercise your SARs because you expect the stock to continue to appreciate in value. Even though you have an unrealized gain of $250 [($50 less $25) x 10 SARs], you do not include it in gross income because the SARs have not been exercised.

Eighteen months after the SARs are issued, the company stock is selling for $85 per share. You exercise your SARs, and the company pays you $600 [($85 less $25) x 10 SARs]. The $600 gain must now be included in your gross income as compensation.

TAXALERT

SARs that vest after 2004 must meet certain requirements in order to defer taxation until exercise:
1. The value of the stock used in the SAR can't be less than the value on the date the SAR was granted, and
2. The SAR's spread can't be further deferred. Similar rules apply to the grant of non-statutory options, discussed later.

Fringe Benefits

Fringe benefits received in connection with the performance of your services are included in your income as compensation unless you pay fair market value for them or they are specifically excluded by law. Abstaining from the performance of services (for example, under a covenant not to compete) is treated as the performance of services for purposes of these rules.

Accounting period. You must use the same accounting period your employer uses to report your taxable noncash fringe benefits. Your employer has the option to report taxable noncash fringe benefits by using either of the following rules.

- The general rule: benefits are reported for a full calendar year (January 1 – December 31).
- The special accounting period rule: benefits provided during the last 2 months of the calendar year (or any shorter period) are treated as paid during the following calendar year. For example, each year your employer reports the value of benefits provided during the last 2 months of the prior year and the first 10 months of the current year.

Your employer does not have to use the same accounting period for each fringe benefit, but must use the same period for all employees who receive a particular benefit.

You must use the same accounting period that you use to report the benefit to claim an employee business deduction (for use of a car, for example).

Form W-2. Your employer reports your taxable fringe benefits in box 1 (Wages, tips, other compensation) of Form W-2. The total value of your fringe benefits also may be noted in box 14. The value of your fringe benefits may be added to your other compensation on one Form W-2, or you may receive a separate Form W-2 showing just the value of your fringe benefits in box 1 with a notation in box 14.

TAXALERT

Starting with 2012 Form W-2's (optional for 2011), your employer will be required to provide in Form W-2, box 12, code DD, the "aggregate cost of employer-sponsored health coverage."

Accident or Health Plan

Generally, the value of accident or health plan coverage provided to you by your employer is not included in your income. Benefits you receive from the plan may be taxable, as explained later under *Sickness and Injury Benefits*.

For information on the items covered in this section, other than *Long-term care coverage*, see Publication 969, *Health Savings Accounts and Other Tax-Favored Health Plans*.

EXPLANATION

This exclusion applies to coverage provided to the taxpayer and the taxpayer's spouse, dependents, and children under age 27 as of the calendar year-end.

Long-term care coverage. Contributions by your employer to provide coverage for long-term care services generally are not included in your income. However, contributions made through a flexible spending or similar arrangement (such as a cafeteria plan) must be included in your income. This amount will be reported as wages in box 1 of your Form W-2.

Contributions you make to the plan are discussed in Publication 502, *Medical and Dental Expenses*.

Archer MSA contributions. Contributions by your employer to your Archer MSA generally are not included in your income. Their total will be reported in box 12 of Form W-2 with code R. You must report this amount on Form 8853, Archer MSAs and Long-Term Care Insurance Contracts. File the form with your return.

Health flexible spending arrangement (health FSA). If your employer provides a health FSA that qualifies as an accident or health plan, the amount of your salary reduction, and reimbursements of your medical care expenses, generally are not included in your income.

Qualified HSA distribution. A health FSA can make a qualified HSA distribution. This distribution is a direct transfer to your HSA trustee by your employer. Generally, the distribution is not included in your income and is not deductible. See Publication 969 for the requirements for these qualified HSA distributions.

Health reimbursement arrangement (HRA). If your employer provides an HRA that qualifies as an accident or health plan, coverage and reimbursements of your medical care expenses generally are not included in your income.

Qualified HSA distribution. An HRA can make a qualified HSA distribution. This distribution is a direct transfer to your HSA trustee by your employer. Generally, the distribution is not included in your income and is not deductible. See Publication 969 for the requirements for these qualified HSA distributions.

Health savings accounts (HSA). If you are an eligible individual, you and any other person, including your employer or a family member, can make contributions to your HSA. Contributions, other than employer contributions, are deductible on your return whether or not you itemize deductions. Contributions made by your employer are not included in your income. Distributions from your HSA that are used to pay qualified medical expenses are not included in your income. Distributions not used for qualified medical expenses are included in your income. See Publication 969 for the requirements of an HSA.

EXPLANATION

The contributions you make to your HSA grow tax-free. The funds in the HSA account are used to pay qualified medical expenses. Only eligible individuals can qualify for an HSA. Some of the requirements for eligibility are that you must be covered under a high deductible health plan, you cannot be enrolled in Medicare, and you cannot be claimed as a dependent on someone else's tax return. HSAs offer both tax and non-tax benefits:

- Your current year taxable income is reduced when you make pretax contributions through payroll deductions to your HSA.
- If you or your family members make contributions to your HSA, you can deduct them on your federal income tax return, even if you do not itemize your deductions.
- If your employer contributes to your HSA, the funds contributed are not taxable income to you.
- Contributions do not have to be distributed from your HSA. The funds remain in your account until used for the payment of your medical expenses.
- The earnings on your account grow tax-free.
- Distributions from your HSA are tax-free if used to pay qualified medical expenses.

TAXALERT

In 2011, the maximum amount that can be contributed to an HSA is $3,050 for self-only coverage and $6,150 for family coverage. In 2012, the maximum contribution amounts increase to $3,100 for self-only coverage and $6,250 for family coverage.

Beginning in 2011, qualified medical expenses no longer include over-the-counter medications unless they are prescribed. Doctor-prescribed drugs and insulin are qualified medical expenses.

Also beginning in 2011, distributions not used for qualified medical expenses that are included in your income are also subject to an additional 20% tax (increased from 10% for pre-2011 nonqualified distributions) with certain exceptions.

TAXALERT

File Form 8889, Health Savings Accounts, with your income tax return to report contributions to the HSA, even if only your employer made the contributions. In addition to contributions, the form is used to report distributions from your HSA, the calculation of your HSA deduction, and the calculation of any income that is taxable to you if you are no longer an eligible individual.

Contributions by a partnership to a *bona fide* partner's HSA are not contributions by an employer. The contributions are treated as a distribution of money and are not included in the partner's gross income. Contributions by a partnership to a partner's HSA for services rendered are treated as guaranteed payments that are includible in the partner's gross income. In both situations, the partner can deduct the contribution made to the partner's HSA.

Contributions by an S corporation to a 2% shareholder-employee's HSA for services rendered are treated as guaranteed payments and are includible in the shareholder-employee's gross income. The shareholder-employee can deduct the contribution made to the shareholder-employee's HSA.

Qualified HSA funding distribution. You can make a one-time distribution from your individual retirement account (IRA) to an HSA and you generally will not include any of the distribution in your income. See Publication 969 for the requirements for these qualified HSA funding distributions.

Failure to maintain eligibility. If your HSA received qualified HSA distributions from a health FSA or HRA (discussed earlier) or a qualified HSA funding distribution, you must be an eligible individual for HSA purposes for the period beginning with the month in which the qualified distribution was made and ending on the last day of the 12th month following that month. If you fail to be an eligible individual during this period, other than because of death or disability, you must include the distribution in your income for the tax year in which you become ineligible. This income is also subject to an additional 10% tax.

TAXALERT

Your employer can make a one-time direct transfer of the balance of a Health Reimbursement Arrangement (HRA) or health Flexible Spending Account (FSA) to your Health Savings Account (HSA) without violating the requirements of those arrangements if the transfer is made before January 1, 2012. The maximum allowable transfer is the smaller of the HRA or health FSA balance on September 21, 2006, or on the date of transfer. The amount transferred is not included in your gross income, is not taken into account in applying the HSA contribution limitation, and is not deductible. However, if you are not an eligible individual, for any reason other than death or becoming disabled, for the 12 months following the month of the transfer, the amount transferred is included in your income and is subject to an additional 10% tax. The income and additional 10% tax are reported for the tax year in which you cease to be an eligible individual.

If the employer makes a transfer available to any employee, all employees who are covered under a High Deductible Health Plan (HDHP) of the employer must be allowed to make a transfer. Otherwise, the employer is subject to an excise tax.

Generally, you are not an eligible individual for an HSA if you have health coverage other than an HDHP. For tax years beginning after 2006, coverage under an FSA for the period immediately following the health FSA's plan year during which unused benefits or contributions remaining at the end of the year may be paid or reimbursed to you for qualifying expenses incurred during that period does not disqualify you from being an eligible individual. The coverage does not disqualify you if the balance in the health FSA at the end of the plan year is zero or the entire remaining balance in the health FSA is transferred to your HSA as described previously.

Adoption Assistance

You may be able to exclude from your income amounts paid or expenses incurred by your employer for qualified adoption expenses in connection with your adoption of an eligible child. See the Instructions for Form 8839 for more information.

Adoption benefits are reported by your employer in box 12 of Form W-2 with code T. They also are included as social security and Medicare wages in boxes 3 and 5. However, they are not included as wages in box 1. To determine the taxable and nontaxable amounts, you must complete Part III of Form 8839, Qualified Adoption Expenses. File the form with your return.

EXPLANATION

Employer-provided adoption benefits are amounts your employer paid directly to either you or a third party for qualified adoption expenses under a qualified adoption assistance program. Generally, a qualified adoption assistance program is a separate written plan set up by an employer to provide adoption assistance to its employees. For more details, see Publication 15-B, *Employer's Tax Guide to Fringe Benefits*.

Qualified adoption expenses are reasonable and necessary expenses directly related to, and for the principal purpose of, the legal adoption of an eligible child. Such expenses include:
• Adoption fees;
• Attorney costs;
• Court costs;
• Travel expenses (including meals and lodging) while away from home; and,
• Re-adoption expenses relating to the adoption of a foreign child.
Qualified adoption expenses do not include expenses:
• For which you received funds under any state, local, or federal program;
• That violate state or federal law;
• For carrying out a surrogate parenting arrangement;
• For the adoption of your spouse's child;
• Paid or reimbursed by your employer or any other person or organization;
• Paid before 1997; or,
• Allowed as a credit or deduction under any other provision of federal income tax law.

De Minimis (Minimal) Benefits

If your employer provides you with a product or service and the cost of it is so small that it would be unreasonable for the employer to account for it, the value is not included in your income. Generally, the value of benefits such as discounts at company cafeterias, cab fares home when working overtime, and company picnics are not included in your income.

Holiday gifts. If your employer gives you a turkey, ham, or other item of nominal value at Christmas or other holidays, do not include the value of the gift in your income. However, if your employer gives you cash, a gift certificate, or a similar item that you can easily exchange for cash, you include the value of that gift as extra salary or wages regardless of the amount involved.

Educational Assistance

You can exclude from your income up to $5,250 of qualified employer-provided educational assistance. For more information, see Publication 970, *Tax Benefits for Education*.

Group-Term Life Insurance

Generally, the cost of up to $50,000 of group-term life insurance coverage provided to you by your employer (or former employer) is not included in your income. However, you must include in income the cost of employer-provided insurance that is more than the cost of $50,000 of coverage reduced by any amount you pay toward the purchase of the insurance.

For exceptions, see *Entire cost excluded* and *Entire cost taxed*, later.

If your employer provided more than $50,000 of coverage, the amount included in your income is reported as part of your wages in box 1 of your Form W-2. Also, it is shown separately in box 12 with code C.

EXAMPLE

Your employer, ABC Company, pays the premiums on your $150,000 group-term life insurance policy. You are 40 years old. Every $1,000 worth of coverage costs $0.10 per month. Because under the law only $50,000 worth of coverage may be excluded from your income, the cost of the additional $100,000 of life insurance, or $120 [($0.10 x 12 months) x $100], has to be included in your income, even though your employer covers the cost.

If you pay any amount of the $120 directly, you may reduce, dollar for dollar, the amount of the premium that would otherwise be included in your income. Thus, if you paid $50, only $70 ($120 − $50) of the premium would be included in your income.

Group-term life insurance. This insurance is term life insurance protection (insurance for a fixed period of time) that:

- Provides a general death benefit,
- Is provided to a group of employees,
- Is provided under a policy carried by the employer, and
- Provides an amount of insurance to each employee based on a formula that prevents individual selection.

Permanent benefits. If your group-term life insurance policy includes permanent benefits, such as a paid-up or cash surrender value, you must include in your income, as wages, the cost of the permanent benefits minus the amount you pay for them. Your employer should be able to tell you the amount to include in your income.

Accidental death benefits. Insurance that provides accidental or other death benefits but does not provide general death benefits (travel insurance, for example) is not group-term life insurance.

Former employer. If your former employer provided more than $50,000 of group-term life insurance coverage during the year, the amount included in your income is reported as wages in box 1 of Form W-2. Also, it is shown separately in box 12 with code C. Box 12 also will show the amount of uncollected social security and Medicare taxes on the excess coverage, with codes M and N. You must pay these taxes with your income tax return. Include them in your total tax on line 60, Form 1040, and enter "UT" and the amount of the taxes on the dotted line next to line 60.

Two or more employers. Your exclusion for employer-provided group-term life insurance coverage cannot exceed the cost of $50,000 of coverage, whether the insurance is provided by a single employer or multiple employers. If two or more employers provide insurance coverage that totals more than $50,000, the amounts reported as wages on your Forms W-2 will not be correct. You must figure how much to include in your income. Reduce the amount you figure by any amount reported with code C in box 12 of your Forms W-2, add the result to the wages reported in box 1, and report the total on your return.

Figuring the taxable cost. Use the following worksheet to figure the amount to include in your income.

Worksheet 5-1. Figuring the Cost of Group-Term Life Insurance To Include in Income

1.	Enter the total amount of your insurance coverage from your employer(s)	1.	
2.	Limit on exclusion for employer-provided group-term life insurance coverage	2.	50,000
3.	Subtract line 2 from line 1	3.	
4.	Divide line 3 by $1,000. Figure to the nearest tenth	4.	
5.	Go to Table 5-1. Using your age on the last day of the tax year, find your age group in the left column, and enter the cost from the column on the right for your age group	5.	
6.	Multiply line 4 by line 5	6.	
7.	Enter the number of full months of coverage at this cost	7.	
8.	Multiply line 6 by line 7	8.	
9.	Enter the premiums you paid per month	9.	
10.	Enter the number of months you paid the premiums	10.	
11.	Multiply line 9 by line 10	11.	
12.	Subtract line 11 from line 8. **Include this amount in your income as wages**	12.	

Worksheet 5-1. Figuring the Cost of Group-Term Life Insurance To Include in Income—Illustrated

1.	Enter the total amount of your insurance coverage from your employer(s)	1.	80,000
2.	Limit on exclusion for employer-provided group-term life insurance coverage	2.	50,000
3.	Subtract line 2 from line 1	3.	30,000
4.	Divide line 3 by $1,000. Figure to the nearest tenth	4.	30.0
5.	Go to Table 5-1. Using your age on the last day of the tax year, find your age group in the left column, and enter the cost from the column on the right for your age group	5.	.23
6.	Multiply line 4 by line 5	6.	6.90
7.	Enter the number of full months of coverage at this cost	7.	12
8.	Multiply line 6 by line 7	8.	82.80
9.	Enter the premiums you paid per month	9.	4.15
10.	Enter the number of months you paid the premiums	10.	12
11.	Multiply line 9 by line 10	11.	49.80
12.	Subtract line 11 from line 8. **Include this amount in your income as wages**	12.	33.00

Example. You are 51 years old and work for employers A and B. Both employers provide group-term life insurance coverage for you for the entire year. Your coverage is $35,000 with employer A and $45,000 with employer B. You pay premiums of $4.15 a month under the employer B group plan. You figure the amount to include in your income as shown in <u>Worksheet 5-1. Figuring the Cost of Group-Term Life Insurance to Include in Income—Illustrated</u>, earlier.

Table 5-1. **Cost of $1,000 of Group-Term Life Insurance for One Month**

Age	Cost
Under 25	$.05
25 through 29	.06
30 through 34	.08
35 through 39	.09
40 through 44	.10
45 through 49	.15
50 through 54	.23
55 through 59	.43
60 through 64	.66
65 through 69	1.27
70 and older	2.06

Entire cost excluded. You are not taxed on the cost of group-term life insurance if any of the following circumstances apply.
1. You are permanently and totally disabled and have ended your employment.
2. Your employer is the beneficiary of the policy for the entire period the insurance is in force during the tax year.
3. A charitable organization (defined in <u>chapter 25</u>) to which contributions are deductible is the only beneficiary of the policy for the entire period the insurance is in force during the tax year. (You are not entitled to a deduction for a charitable contribution for naming a charitable organization as the beneficiary of your policy.)
4. The plan existed on January 1, 1984, and
   a. You retired before January 2, 1984, and were covered by the plan when you retired, or
   b. You reached age 55 before January 2, 1984, and were employed by the employer or its predecessor in 1983.

Entire cost taxed. You are taxed on the entire cost of group-term life insurance if either of the following circumstances apply.
- The insurance is provided by your employer through a qualified employees' trust, such as a pension trust or a qualified annuity plan.
- You are a key employee and your employer's plan discriminates in favor of key employees.

Retirement Planning Services
If your employer has a qualified retirement plan, qualified retirement planning services provided to you (and your spouse) by your employer are not included in your income. Qualified services include retirement planning advice, information about your employer's retirement plan, and information about how the plan may fit into your overall individual retirement income plan. You cannot exclude the value of any tax preparation, accounting, legal, or brokerage services provided by your employer.

Transportation
If your employer provides you with a qualified transportation fringe benefit, it can be excluded from your income, up to certain limits. A qualified transportation fringe benefit is:
- Transportation in a commuter highway vehicle (such as a van) between your home and work place,
- A transit pass,
- Qualified parking, or
- Qualified bicycle commuting reimbursement.

Cash reimbursement by your employer for these expenses under a *bona fide* reimbursement arrangement also is excludable. However, cash reimbursement for a transit pass is excludable only if a voucher or similar item that can be exchanged only for a transit pass is not readily available for direct distribution to you.

Exclusion limit. The exclusion for commuter vehicle transportation and transit pass fringe benefits cannot be more than $230 a month.

The exclusion for the qualified parking fringe benefit cannot be more than $230 a month.

The exclusion for qualified bicycle commuting in a calendar year is $20 multiplied by the number of qualified bicycle commuting months that year.

If the benefits have a value that is more than these limits, the excess must be included in your income. You are not entitled to these exclusions if the reimbursements are made under a compensation reduction agreement.

TAXALERT

An exclusion from gross income is allowed for an employee whose employer offers the choice between cash or employer-provided parking, and the employee chooses parking. If you choose cash, the amount offered is includable in your income.

Commuter highway vehicle. This is a highway vehicle that seats at least six adults (not including the driver). At least 80% of the vehicle's mileage must reasonably be expected to be:

- For transporting employees between their homes and work place, and
- On trips during which employees occupy at least half of the vehicle's adult seating capacity (not including the driver).

Transit pass. This is any pass, token, fare-card, voucher, or similar item entitling a person to ride mass transit (whether public or private) free or at a reduced rate or to ride in a commuter highway vehicle operated by a person in the business of transporting persons for compensation.

Qualified parking. This is parking provided to an employee at or near the employer's place of business. It also includes parking provided on or near a location from which the employee commutes to work by mass transit, in a commuter highway vehicle, or by carpool. It does not include parking at or near the employee's home.

Qualified bicycle commuting. This is reimbursement based on the number of qualified bicycle commuting months for the year. A qualified bicycle commuting month is any month you use the bicycle regularly for a substantial portion of the travel between your home and place of employment and you do not receive any of the other qualified transportation fringe benefits. The reimbursement can be for expenses you incurred during the year for the purchase of a bicycle and bicycle improvements, repair, and storage.

EXPLANATION
Employer-Provided Vehicles

If your employer provides a car (or other highway motor vehicle) to you, your personal use of the car is usually a taxable noncash fringe benefit.

Your employer must determine the actual value of this fringe benefit to include in your income.

Note: Certain employer-provided transportation can be excluded from gross income.

Tip

For information on distributions from retirement plans, see Publication 575, Pension and Annuity Income (or Publication 721, Tax Guide to U.S. Civil Service Retirement Benefits, if you are a federal employee or retiree).

Retirement Plan Contributions

Your employer's contributions to a qualified retirement plan for you are not included in income at the time contributed. (Your employer can tell you whether your retirement plan is qualified.) However, the cost of life insurance coverage included in the plan may have to be included. See *Group-Term Life Insurance*, earlier, under *Fringe Benefits*.

If your employer pays into a nonqualified plan for you, you generally must include the contributions in your income as wages for the tax year in which the contributions are made. However, if your interest in the plan is not transferable or is subject to a substantial risk of forfeiture (you have a good chance of losing it) at the time of the contribution, you do not have to include the value of your interest in your income until it is transferable or is no longer subject to a substantial risk of forfeiture.

EXPLANATION

Under a *qualified plan*, participating employees may defer taxation on an employer's contributions into their individual accounts or for their vested benefits in qualified plans until some future date of distribution. Additionally, the tax on the income the account generates may be deferred until the money is distributed to the employee. The same deferred taxation is allowed under a *nonqualified plan* as long as the employee's interest in the plan is simply an unfunded promise to pay by the employer and meets requirements under a 2004 tax law change. (Whether a plan is qualified or nonqualified depends on whether or not certain statutory requirements are satisfied.) See chapter 10, *Retirement plans, pensions, and annuities*, for suggestions about what to do when you receive distributions from qualified plans.

Elective deferrals. If you are covered by certain kinds of retirement plans, you can choose to have part of your compensation contributed by your employer to a retirement fund, rather than have it paid to you. The amount you set aside (called an elective deferral) is treated as an employer contribution to a qualified plan. An elective deferral, other than a designated Roth contribution (discussed later), is not included in wages subject to income tax at the time contributed. However, it is included in wages subject to social security and Medicare taxes.

Elective deferrals include elective contributions to the following retirement plans.

1. Cash or deferred arrangements (section 401(k) plans).
2. The Thrift Savings Plan for federal employees.
3. Salary reduction simplified employee pension plans (SARSEP).
4. Savings incentive match plans for employees (SIMPLE plans).
5. Tax-sheltered annuity plans (403(b) plans).
6. Section 501(c)(18)(D) plans.
7. Section 457 plans.

Qualified automatic contribution arrangements. Under a qualified automatic contribution arrangement, your employer can treat you as having elected to have a part of your compensation contributed to a section 401(k) plan. You are to receive written notice of your rights and obligations under the qualified automatic contribution arrangement. The notice must explain

- Your rights to elect not to have elective contributions made, or to have contributions made at a different percentage, and
- How contributions made will be invested in the absence of any investment decision by you.

You must be given a reasonable period of time after receipt of the notice and before the first elective contribution is made to make an election with respect to the contributions.

Overall limit on deferrals. For 2011, you generally should not have deferred more than a total of $16,500 of contributions to the plans listed in (1) through (3) and (5) above. The limit for SIMPLE plans is $11,500. The limit for section 501(c)(18)(D) plans is the lesser of $7,000 or 25% of your compensation. The limit for section 457 plans is the lesser of your includible compensation or $16,500.

Designated Roth contributions. Employers with section 401(k) and section 403(b) plans can create qualified Roth contribution programs so that you may elect to have part or all of your elective deferrals to the plan designated as after-tax Roth contributions. Designated Roth contributions are treated as elective deferrals, except that they are included in income.

TAXALERT

Since 2007, the limit on contributions to 401(k) plans has been indexed annually for inflation, based on the cost-of-living index for the quarter ending on September 30th of each year. If the cost-of-living index drops, as it did for the quarter ending September 30, 2009, compared to the quarter ending September 30, 2008, the limit on contributions is not reduced, but instead stays the same as the previous tax year. For the quarter ended September 30, 2010, although the cost-of-living index was greater than the quarter ended September 30, 2009, it was actually less than the cost-of-living index for the quarter ended September 30, 2008. Therefore, the limit on contributions to 401(k) for 2011 stayed at the same amount—$16,500—as it was for 2010.

Excess deferrals. Your employer or plan administrator should apply the proper annual limit when figuring your plan contributions. However, you are responsible for monitoring the total you defer to ensure that the deferrals are not more than the overall limit.

If you set aside more than the limit, the excess generally must be included in your income for that year, unless you have an excess deferral of a designated Roth contribution. See Publication 525 for a discussion of the tax treatment of excess deferrals.

Catch-up contributions. You may be allowed catch-up contributions (additional elective deferral) if you are age 50 or older by the end of your tax year.

Stock Options

If you receive a nonstatutory option to buy or sell stock or other property as payment for your services, you usually will have income when you receive the option, when you exercise the option (use it to buy or sell the stock or other property), or when you sell or otherwise dispose of the option. However, if your option is a statutory stock option, you will not have any income until you sell or exchange your stock. Your employer can tell you which kind of option you hold. For more information, see Publication 525.

Incentive stock options (ISOs). Generally, incentive stock options let you take advantage of a specific provision of the Internal Revenue Code that gives favorable tax treatment to this type of stock option.

Incentive stock options are not taxable to you at the time the option is granted, nor do you pay tax when the option is exercised. Furthermore, if you do not dispose of the stock within 2 years after the option is granted, and you hold the stock for over 12 months after you exercise the option, any gain will be taxed as a long-term capital gain.

However, if you sell the stock within 1 year after the date you exercised the option, or 2 years from the date of grant, the option loses its preferential treatment and the difference between the exercise price and the value at date of exercise is taxed to you as ordinary income.

The spread between the option price and the fair market value of the stock upon exercise of the incentive stock option may be taxed indirectly if you are subject to alternative minimum tax. For a discussion of the alternative minimum tax, see chapter 31, *How to figure your tax.* For a further discussion of stock options, see chapter 13, *Basis of property.*

TAXALERT

The top individual rate on net capital gains of assets held more than 1 year is 15% (zero percent for taxpayers with net capital gains taxed in the lower tax brackets). These lower rates apply to both the regular tax and the alternative minimum tax. For taxpayers with net capital gains taxed in the lower tax brackets, the zero percent rate is applicable in 2011.

TAXPLANNER

Some employers allow you to use employer stock already owned to finance the exercise of stock options. This exercise method is called a stock swap and allows you to use the stock value without recognizing the gain that would result if you sold the stock and used the proceeds to exercise the stock options. Certain stock holding periods and other restrictions can apply, which should be stipulated in your employer's stock option plan.

TAXSAVER

Employee stock purchase plans. Many companies have stock purchase plans that offer participating employees the opportunity to buy company stock at a discount. Employees usually contribute to the plan by authorizing payroll deductions, which are not excludable from gross income.

As an employee, you do not have to pay any tax when the plan's trustee exercises the option and purchases company stock. The stock is credited to your account within the plan.

At a future time, you may request to receive the stock purchased for your account. On distribution, if you immediately sell the stock, any gain will be taxed as ordinary income. The gain will generally be determined by the sale price less the amount you contributed to the plan to buy the stock. Your company should be able to provide you with all relevant information.

However, if after exercising the option you hold it for 2 years from the grant date and over 1 year from the purchase date, any gain will typically be treated as a long-term capital gain (except for the original discount). If you have a capital loss carryover, the fact that the gain is characterized as a capital gain could result in a tax benefit for you.

Restricted Property

Generally, if you receive property for your services, you must include its fair market value in your income in the year you receive the property. However, if you receive stock or other property that has certain restrictions that affect its value, you do not include the value of the property in your income until it has substantially vested. (You can choose to include the value of the property in your income in the year it is transferred to you.) For more information, see *Restricted Property* in Publication 525.

Dividends received on restricted stock. Dividends you receive on restricted stock are treated as compensation and not as dividend income. Your employer should include these payments on your Form W-2.

Stock you chose to include in income. Dividends you receive on restricted stock you chose to include in your income in the year transferred are treated the same as any other dividends. Report them on your return as dividends. For a discussion of dividends, see chapter 8.

For information on how to treat dividends reported on both your Form W-2 and Form 1099-DIV, see *Dividends received on restricted stock* in Publication 525.

Special Rules for Certain Employees

This section deals with special rules for people in certain types of employment: members of the clergy, members of religious orders, people working for foreign employers, military personnel, and volunteers.

Clergy

If you are a member of the clergy, you must include in your income offerings and fees you receive for marriages, baptisms, funerals, masses, etc., in addition to your salary. If the offering is made to the religious institution, it is not taxable to you.

If you are a member of a religious organization and you give your outside earnings to the organization, you still must include the earnings in your income. However, you may be entitled to a charitable contribution deduction for the amount paid to the organization. See chapter 25.

Pension. A pension or retirement pay for a member of the clergy usually is treated as any other pension or annuity. It must be reported on lines 16a and 16b of Form 1040 or on lines 12a and 12b of Form 1040A.

Housing. Special rules for housing apply to members of the clergy. Under these rules, you do not include in your income the rental value of a home (including utilities) or a designated housing allowance provided to you as part of your pay. However, the exclusion cannot be more than the reasonable pay for your service. If you pay for the utilities, you can exclude any allowance designated for utility cost, up to your actual cost. The home or allowance must be provided as compensation for your services as an ordained, licensed, or commissioned minister. However, you must include the rental value of the home or the housing allowance as earnings from self-employment on Schedule SE (Form 1040) if you are subject to the self-employment tax. For more information, see Publication 517, *Social Security and Other Information for Members of the Clergy and Religious Workers*.

> ### EXPLANATION
> To qualify for the exclusions from gross income, you must be appropriately ordained, commissioned, or licensed as a minister or other member of the clergy and you must be employed by a religious organization to perform ministerial functions. You qualify as a member of the clergy if you have been appropriately ordained according to the customs of your faith. The exclusion also applies to retired ministers, but not their widows.
>
> #### Exception
> An ordained minister may not claim the exclusions from gross income when the crux of his or her ministry consists of preachings against communism for a nonreligious, tax-exempt organization. Such a message is not religious because anticommunism is not an adopted tenet of his or her faith.
>
> **Sham churches.** The IRS has been cracking down on individuals who declare themselves clergy of newly established churches, arrange to have all their income paid to the church, and then have the church pay their living expenses. The object of such individuals is to take advantage of a church's tax-exempt status and shield income from taxation. Individuals who set up sham churches may be subject to criminal sanctions.

> ### EXPLANATION
> **Designation requirement.** The church or organization that employs you must officially designate the payment as a housing allowance before the payment is made. A definite amount must be designated; the amount of the housing allowance cannot be determined at a later date.
>
> If you are employed and paid by a local congregation, a resolution by a national church agency of your denomination does not effectively designate a housing allowance for you. The local congregation must officially designate the part of your salary that is to be a housing allowance. However, a resolution of a national church agency can designate your housing allowance if you are directly employed by the agency. If no part has been officially designated, you must include your total salary in your income.
>
> **Homeownership.** If you own your home or are buying it, you can exclude your housing allowance from your income if you spend it for the down payment on the home, for mortgage payments, or for interest, taxes, utilities, repairs, etc. However, you cannot exclude more than the fair rental value of the home plus the cost of utilities, even if a larger amount is designated as a housing allowance. The fair rental value of a home includes the fair rental value of the furnishings in it.

You can deduct on Schedule A (Form 1040) the qualified mortgage interest and real estate taxes you pay on your home even if you use nontaxable housing allowance funds to make the payments. See chapter 23, *Taxes you may deduct*, and chapter 24, *Interest expense*.

Teachers or administrators. If you are a minister employed as a teacher or administrator by a church school, college, or university, you are performing ministerial services for purposes of the housing exclusion.

However, if you perform services as a teacher or administrator on the faculty of a nonchurch college, you cannot exclude from your income a housing allowance or the value of a home that is provided to you.

If you serve as a minister of music or minister of education or serve in an administrative or other function of your religious organization, but are not authorized to perform substantially all of the religious duties of an ordained minister in your church (even if you are commissioned as a minister of the gospel), the housing exclusion does not apply to you.

Theological students. The housing exclusion does not apply if you are a theological student serving a required internship as an assistant pastor, unless you are ordained, commissioned, or licensed as a minister.

Traveling evangelists. If you are an ordained minister and are providing evangelistic services, you can exclude amounts received from out-of-town churches that are designated as a housing allowance, provided you actually use them to maintain your permanent home.

Retired members of the clergy. The rental value of a home provided rent free by your church for your past services is not income if you are a retired minister. In addition, the amount of your housing allowance that you spend for utilities, maintenance, repairs, and similar expenses that are directly related to providing a home is not income to you. These amounts are also not included in net earnings from self-employment.

The general convention of a national religious denomination can designate a housing allowance for retired ministers that can be excluded from income. This applies if the local congregations authorize the general convention to establish and maintain a unified pension system for all retired clergy members of the denomination for their past services to the local churches. A surviving spouse of a retired minister cannot exclude a housing allowance from income.

Members of Religious Orders

If you are a member of a religious order who has taken a vow of poverty, how you treat earnings that you renounce and turn over to the order depends on whether your services are performed for the order.

Services performed for the order. If you are performing the services as an agent of the order in the exercise of duties required by the order, do not include in your income the amounts turned over to the order.

If your order directs you to perform services for another agency of the supervising church or an associated institution, you are considered to be performing the services as an agent of the order. Any wages you earn as an agent of an order that you turn over to the order are not included in your income.

Example. You are a member of a church order and have taken a vow of poverty. You renounce any claims to your earnings and turn over to the order any salaries or wages you earn. You are a registered nurse, so your order assigns you to work in a hospital that is an associated institution of the church. However, you remain under the general direction and control of the order. You are considered to be an agent of the order and any wages you earn at the hospital that you turn over to your order are not included in your income.

Services performed outside the order. If you are directed to work outside the order, your services are not an exercise of duties required by the order unless they meet both of the following requirements.

- They are the kind of services that are ordinarily the duties of members of the order.
- They are part of the duties that you must exercise for, or on behalf of, the religious order as its agent.

If you are an employee of a third party, the services you perform for the third party will not be considered directed or required of you by the order. Amounts you receive for these services are included in your income, even if you have taken a vow of poverty.

Example. Mark Brown is a member of a religious order and has taken a vow of poverty. He renounces all claims to his earnings and turns over his earnings to the order.

Mark is a schoolteacher. He was instructed by the superiors of the order to get a job with a private tax-exempt school. Mark became an employee of the school, and, at his request, the school made the salary payments directly to the order.

Because Mark is an employee of the school, he is performing services for the school rather than as an agent of the order. The wages Mark earns working for the school are included in his income.

Foreign Employer
Special rules apply if you work for a foreign employer.

U.S. citizen. If you are a U.S. citizen who works in the United States for a foreign government, an international organization, a foreign embassy, or any foreign employer, you must include your salary in your income.

Social security and Medicare taxes. You are exempt from social security and Medicare employee taxes if you are employed in the United States by an international organization or a foreign government. However, you must pay self-employment tax on your earnings from services performed in the United States, even though you are not self-employed. This rule also applies if you are an employee of a qualifying wholly owned instrumentality of a foreign government.

Employees of international organizations or foreign governments. Your compensation for official services to an international organization is exempt from federal income tax if you are not a citizen of the United States or you are a citizen of the Philippines (whether or not you are a citizen of the United States).

Your compensation for official services to a foreign government is exempt from federal income tax if all of the following are true.
- You are not a citizen of the United States or you are a citizen of the Philippines (whether or not you are a citizen of the United States).
- Your work is like the work done by employees of the United States in foreign countries.
- The foreign government gives an equal exemption to employees of the United States in its country.

Waiver of alien status. If you are an alien who works for a foreign government or international organization and you file a waiver under section 247(b) of the Immigration and Nationality Act to keep your immigrant status, different rules may apply. See *Foreign Employer* in Publication 525.

Employment abroad. For information on the tax treatment of income earned abroad, see Publication 54.

Military
Payments you receive as a member of a military service generally are taxed as wages except for retirement pay, which is taxed as a pension. Allowances generally are not taxed. For more information on the tax treatment of military allowances and benefits, see Publication 3, *Armed Forces' Tax Guide*.

Differential wage payments. Any payments made to you by an employer during the time you are performing service in the uniformed services are treated as compensation. These wages are subject to income tax withholding and are reported on a Form W-2. See the discussion under *Miscellaneous Compensation*, earlier.

Military retirement pay. If your retirement pay is based on age or length of service, it is taxable and must be included in your income as a pension on lines 16a and 16b of Form 1040 or on lines 12a and 12b of Form 1040A. Do not include in your income the amount of any reduction in retirement or retainer pay to provide a survivor annuity for your spouse or children under the Retired Serviceman's Family Protection Plan or the Survivor Benefit Plan.

For more detailed discussion of survivor annuities, see chapter 10.

Disability. If you are retired on disability, see *Military and Government Disability Pensions* under *Sickness and Injury Benefits*, later.

Veterans' benefits. Do not include in your income any veterans' benefits paid under any law, regulation, or administrative practice administered by the Department of Veterans Affairs (VA). The following amounts paid to veterans or their families are not taxable.
- Education, training, and subsistence allowances.
- Disability compensation and pension payments for disabilities paid either to veterans or their families.
- Grants for homes designed for wheelchair living.
- Grants for motor vehicles for veterans who lost their sight or the use of their limbs.
- Veterans' insurance proceeds and dividends paid either to veterans or their beneficiaries, including the proceeds of a veteran's endowment policy paid before death.

- Interest on insurance dividends you leave on deposit with the VA.
- Benefits under a dependent-care assistance program.
- The death gratuity paid to a survivor of a member of the Armed Forces who died after September 10, 2001.
- Payments made under the compensated work therapy program.
- Any bonus payment by a state or political subdivision because of service in a combat zone.

Volunteers

The tax treatment of amounts you receive as a volunteer worker for the Peace Corps or similar agency is covered in the following discussions.

Peace Corps. Living allowances you receive as a Peace Corps volunteer or volunteer leader for housing, utilities, household supplies, food, and clothing are exempt from tax.

Taxable allowances. The following allowances must be included in your income and reported as wages.

- Allowances paid to your spouse and minor children while you are a volunteer leader training in the United States.
- Living allowances designated by the Director of the Peace Corps as basic compensation. These are allowances for personal items such as domestic help, laundry and clothing maintenance, entertainment and recreation, transportation, and other miscellaneous expenses.
- Leave allowances.
- Readjustment allowances or termination payments. These are considered received by you when credited to your account.

Example. Gary Carpenter, a Peace Corps volunteer, gets $175 a month as a readjustment allowance during his period of service, to be paid to him in a lump sum at the end of his tour of duty. Although the allowance is not available to him until the end of his service, Gary must include it in his income on a monthly basis as it is credited to his account.

Volunteers in Service to America (VISTA). If you are a VISTA volunteer, you must include meal and lodging allowances paid to you in your income as wages.

EXPLANATION
VISTA volunteers do not benefit from the same gross income exclusions as do members of the Peace Corps.

National Senior Services Corps programs. Do not include in your income amounts you receive for supportive services or reimbursements for out-of-pocket expenses from the following programs.

- Retired Senior Volunteer Program (RSVP).
- Foster Grandparent Program.
- Senior Companion Program.

Service Corps of Retired Executives (SCORE). If you receive amounts for supportive services or reimbursements for out-of-pocket expenses from SCORE, do not include these amounts in income.

Volunteer tax counseling. Do not include in your income any reimbursements you receive for transportation, meals, and other expenses you have in training for, or actually providing, volunteer federal income tax counseling for the elderly (TCE).

You can deduct as a charitable contribution your unreimbursed out-of-pocket expenses in taking part in the volunteer income tax assistance (VITA) program. See chapter 25.

Text intentionally omitted.

Sickness and Injury Benefits

This section discusses sickness and injury benefits including disability pensions, long-term care insurance contracts, workers' compensation, and other benefits.

TAXALERT
Holocaust restitution payments paid to eligible individuals or their heirs are exempt from taxable income. The restitution payments are also not considered in computations that include tax-exempt income (e.g., the calculation of taxable social security payments).

Generally, you must report as income any amount you receive for personal injury or sickness through an accident or health plan that is paid for by your employer. If both you and your employer pay for the plan, only the amount you receive that is due to your employer's payments is reported as income. However, certain payments may not be taxable to you. Your employer should be able to give you specific details about your pension plan and tell you the amount you paid for your disability pension. In addition to disability pensions and annuities, you may be receiving other payments for sickness and injury.

Cost paid by you. If you pay the entire cost of a health or accident insurance plan, do not include any amounts you receive from the plan for personal injury or sickness as income on your tax return. If your plan reimbursed you for medical expenses you deducted in an earlier year, you may have to include some, or all, of the reimbursement in your income. See *Reimbursement in a later year* in chapter 22.

Cafeteria plans. Generally, if you are covered by an accident or health insurance plan through a cafeteria plan, and the amount of the insurance premiums was not included in your income, you are not considered to have paid the premiums and you must include any benefits you receive in your income. If the amount of the premiums was included in your income, you are considered to have paid the premiums, and any benefits you receive are not taxable.

Do not report as income any amounts paid to reimburse you for medical expenses you incurred after the plan was established.

> ### EXPLANATION
> If you paid disability premiums with after-tax dollars, the value of any disability benefits you receive will not be taxable. If you paid the premiums with pre-tax dollars or your employer paid the premiums and you did not elect to treat these premiums as taxable, the value of benefits you receive will be taxable.

Disability Pensions

If you retired on disability, you must include in income any disability pension you receive under a plan that is paid for by your employer. You must report your taxable disability payments as wages on line 7 of Form 1040 or Form 1040A, until you reach minimum retirement age. Minimum retirement age generally is the age at which you can first receive a pension or annuity if you are not disabled.

Beginning on the day after you reach minimum retirement age, payments you receive are taxable as a pension or annuity. Report the payments on lines 16a and 16b of Form 1040 or on lines 12a and 12b of Form 1040A. The rules for reporting pensions are explained in *How To Report* in chapter 10.

For information on disability payments from a governmental program provided as a substitute for unemployment compensation, see chapter 12.

Tip

You may be entitled to a tax credit if you were permanently and totally disabled when you retired. For information on this credit and the definition of permanent and total disability, see chapter 34.

Retirement and profit-sharing plans. If you receive payments from a retirement or profit-sharing plan that does not provide for disability retirement, do not treat the payments as a disability pension. The payments must be reported as a pension or annuity. For more information on pensions, see chapter 10.

Accrued leave payment. If you retire on disability, any lump-sum payment you receive for accrued annual leave is a salary payment. The payment is not a disability payment. Include it in your income in the tax year you receive it.

Military and Government Disability Pensions
Certain military and government disability pensions are not taxable.

Service-connected disability. You may be able to exclude from income amounts you receive as a pension, annuity, or similar allowance for personal injury or sickness resulting from active service in one of the following government services.
- The armed forces of any country.
- The National Oceanic and Atmospheric Administration.
- The Public Health Service.
- The Foreign Service.

Conditions for exclusion. Do not include the disability payments in your income if any of the following conditions apply.
1. You were entitled to receive a disability payment before September 25, 1975.
2. You were a member of a listed government service or its reserve component, or were under a binding written commitment to become a member, on September 24, 1975.

3. You receive the disability payments for a combat-related injury. This is a personal injury or sickness that
    a. Results directly from armed conflict,
    b. Takes place while you are engaged in extra-hazardous service,
    c. Takes place under conditions simulating war, including training exercises such as maneuvers, or
    d. Is caused by an instrumentality of war.
4. You would be entitled to receive disability compensation from the Department of Veterans Affairs (VA) if you filed an application for it. Your exclusion under this condition is equal to the amount you would be entitled to receive from the VA.

Pension based on years of service. If you receive a disability pension based on years of service, you generally must include it in your income. However, if the pension qualifies for the exclusion for a service-connected disability (discussed earlier), do not include in income the part of your pension that you would have received if the pension had been based on a percentage of disability. You must include the rest of your pension in your income.

Retroactive VA determination. If you retire from the armed services based on years of service and are later given a retroactive service-connected disability rating by the VA, your retirement pay for the retroactive period is excluded from income up to the amount of VA disability benefits you would have been entitled to receive. You can claim a refund of any tax paid on the excludable amount (subject to the statute of limitations) by filing an amended return on Form 1040X for each previous year during the retroactive period.

If you receive a lump-sum disability severance payment and are later awarded VA disability benefits, exclude 100% of the severance benefit from your income. However, you must include in your income any lump-sum readjustment or other nondisability severance payment you received on release from active duty, even if you are later given a retroactive disability rating by the VA.

Special statute of limitations. Generally, under the statute of limitations a claim for credit or refund must be filed within 3 years from the time a return was filed. However, if you receive a retroactive service-connected disability rating determination, the statute of limitations is extended by a 1-year period beginning on the date of the determination. This 1-year extended period applies to claims for credit or refund filed after June 17, 2008, and does not apply to any tax year that began more than 5 years before the date of the determination.

Example. You retired in 2005 and receive a pension based on your years of service. On August 6, 2011, you receive a determination of service-connected disability retroactive to 2005. Generally, you could claim a refund for the taxes paid on your pension for 2008, 2009, and 2010. However, under the special limitation period, you can also file a claim for 2007 as long as you file the claim by August 8, 2012. You cannot file a claim for 2005 and 2006 because those tax years began more than 5 years before the determination.

Terrorist attack or military action. Do not include in your income disability payments you receive for injuries resulting directly from a terrorist or military action.

Long-Term Care Insurance Contracts

Long-term care insurance contracts generally are treated as accident and health insurance contracts. Amounts you receive from them (other than policyholder dividends or premium refunds) generally are excludable from income as amounts received for personal injury or sickness. To claim an exclusion for payments made on a *per diem* or other periodic basis under a long-term care insurance contract, you must file Form 8853 with your return.

A long-term care insurance contract is an insurance contract that only provides coverage for qualified long-term care services. The contract must:
- Be guaranteed renewable,
- Not provide for a cash surrender value or other money that can be paid, assigned, pledged, or borrowed,
- Provide that refunds, other than refunds on the death of the insured or complete surrender or cancellation of the contract, and dividends under the contract may be used only to reduce future premiums or increase future benefits, and
- Generally not pay or reimburse expenses incurred for services or items that would be reimbursed under Medicare, except where Medicare is a secondary payer or the contract makes *per diem* or other periodic payments without regard to expenses.

Qualified long-term care services. Qualified long-term care services are:
- Necessary diagnostic, preventive, therapeutic, curing, treating, mitigating, and rehabilitative services, and maintenance and personal care services, and
- Required by a chronically ill individual and provided pursuant to a plan of care as prescribed by a licensed health care practitioner.

Chronically ill individual. A chronically ill individual is one who has been certified by a licensed health care practitioner within the previous 12 months as one of the following.
- An individual who, for at least 90 days, is unable to perform at least two activities of daily living without substantial assistance due to loss of functional capacity. Activities of daily living are eating, toileting, transferring, bathing, dressing, and continence.
- An individual who requires substantial supervision to be protected from threats to health and safety due to severe cognitive impairment.

Limit on exclusion. You generally can exclude from gross income up to $300 a day for 2011. See *Limit on exclusion*, under *Long-Term Care Insurance Contracts*, under *Sickness and Injury Benefits* in Publication 525 for more information.

Workers' Compensation

Amounts you receive as workers' compensation for an occupational sickness or injury are fully exempt from tax if they are paid under a workers' compensation act or a statute in the nature of a workers' compensation act. The exemption also applies to your survivors. The exemption, however, does not apply to retirement plan benefits you receive based on your age, length of service, or prior contributions to the plan, even if you retired because of an occupational sickness or injury.

Return to work. If you return to work after qualifying for workers' compensation, salary payments you receive for performing light duties are taxable as wages.

Other Sickness and Injury Benefits

In addition to disability pensions and annuities, you may receive other payments for sickness or injury.

Railroad sick pay. Payments you receive as sick pay under the Railroad Unemployment Insurance Act are taxable and you must include them in your income. However, do not include them in your income if they are for an on-the-job injury.

If you received income because of a disability, see *Disability Pensions*, earlier.

Federal Employees' Compensation Act (FECA). Payments received under this Act for personal injury or sickness, including payments to beneficiaries in case of death, are not taxable. However, you are taxed on amounts you receive under this Act as continuation of pay for up to 45 days while a claim is being decided. Report this income on line 7 of Form 1040 or Form 1040A or on line 1 of Form 1040-EZ. Also, pay for sick leave while a claim is being processed is taxable and must be included in your income as wages.

You can deduct the amount you spend to buy back sick leave for an earlier year to be eligible for nontaxable FECA benefits for that period. It is a miscellaneous deduction subject to the 2%-of-AGI limit on Schedule A (Form 1040). If you buy back sick leave in the same year you used it, the amount reduces your taxable sick leave pay. Do not deduct it separately.

Other compensation. Many other amounts you receive as compensation for sickness or injury are not taxable. These include the following amounts.
- Compensatory damages you receive for physical injury or physical sickness, whether paid in a lump sum or in periodic payments.
- Benefits you receive under an accident or health insurance policy on which either you paid the premiums or your employer paid the premiums but you had to include them in your income.
- Disability benefits you receive for loss of income or earning capacity as a result of injuries under a no-fault car insurance policy.
- Compensation you receive for permanent loss or loss of use of a part or function of your body, or for your permanent disfigurement. This compensation must be based only on the injury and not on the period of your absence from work. These benefits are not taxable even if your employer pays for the accident and health plan that provides these benefits.

Reimbursement for medical care. A reimbursement for medical care is generally not taxable. However, it may reduce your medical expense deduction. For more information, see chapter 22.

Caution

If part of your workers' compensation reduces your social security or equivalent railroad retirement benefits received, that part is considered social security (or equivalent railroad retirement) benefits and may be taxable. For more information, see Publication 915, Social Security and Equivalent Railroad Retirement Benefits.

Caution

If part of the payments you receive under FECA reduces your social security or equivalent railroad retirement benefits received, that part is considered social security (or equivalent railroad retirement) benefits and may be taxable. For a discussion of the taxability of these benefits, see Social security and equivalent railroad retirement benefits under Other Income, in Publication 525.

Chapter 6
Tip income

Keeping a Daily Tip Record 141
Reporting Tips to Your Employer 142
   Reporting Tips on Your Tax Return 145
Allocated Tips 147

Note

IRS Publication 17 (*Your Federal Income Tax*) has been updated by Ernst & Young LLP for 2011. Dates and dollar amounts shown are for 2011. Underlined type is used to indicate where IRS text has been updated. Places where text has been removed are indicated by the sentence: *Text intentionally omitted.*

ey.com/EYTaxGuide

Ernst & Young LLP will update the *Ernst & Young Tax Guide 2012* website with relevant taxpayer information as it becomes available. You can also sign up for email alerts to let you know when changes have been made.

Introduction

Tips are one of the least-reported types of income and the IRS has been trying to do something about that. Since 2000, it has been undertaking a controversial audit program under which it conducts employer-only tip examinations and assessments for FICA in cases of "flagrant violations" of tip reporting rules. This audit program focuses on cases of serious noncompliance at businesses in which tipping is customary. As an alternative to audit examinations, the IRS also established voluntary compliance agreements for industries, such as the restaurant industry, where tipping is customary. These agreements are designed to enhance tax compliance among tipped employees through taxpayer education, instead of through traditional enforcement actions, such as tip examinations. Nevertheless, employee reporting requirements and employer withholding requirements have not changed. This chapter spells out the details of reporting tip income.

This chapter is for employees who receive tips.

All tips you receive are income and are subject to federal income tax. You must include in gross income all tips you receive directly, charged tips paid to you by your employer, and your share of any tips you receive under a tip-splitting or tip-pooling arrangement.

The value of noncash tips, such as tickets, passes, or other items of value, are also income and subject to tax.

EXPLANATION

Self-employed individuals may receive cash tips or other income from clients. This additional income is not considered income from tips. It is, however, considered self-employment income and must be reported to the IRS on Schedule C. See chapter 38, *Self-Employment Income: How to File Schedule C,* for more information.

Reporting your tip income correctly is not difficult. You must do three things.
1. Keep a daily tip record.
2. Report tips to your employer.
3. Report all your tips on your income tax return.

This chapter will explain these three things and show you what to do on your tax return if you have not done the first two. This chapter will also show you how to treat allocated tips.

For information on special tip programs and agreements, see Publication 531.

Useful Items

You may want to see:

Publication
- ☐ **531**   Reporting Tip Income
- ☐ **1244** Employee's Daily Record of Tips and Report to Employer
- ☐ **4902** Tax Tips for the Cosmetology and Barber Industry

Form (and Instructions)

- ☐ **4137**   Social Security and Medicare Tax on Unreported Tip Income
- ☐ **4070**   Employee's Report of Tips to Employer
- ☐ **<u>4070A</u>**   <u>Employee's Daily Record of Tips</u>

Keeping a Daily Tip Record

Why keep a daily tip record. You must keep a daily tip record so you can:

- Report your tips accurately to your employer,
- Report your tips accurately on your tax return, and
- Prove your tip income if your return is ever questioned.

How to keep a daily tip record. There are two ways to keep a daily tip record. You can either:

- Write information about your tips in a tip diary, or
- Keep copies of documents that show your tips, such as restaurant bills and credit or debit card charge slips.

You should keep your daily tip record with your tax or other personal records. You must keep your records for as long as they are important for administration of the federal tax law. For information on how long to keep records, see Publication 552, Recordkeeping for Individuals.

If you keep a tip diary, you can use Form 4070A, Employee's Daily Record of Tips. To get Form 4070A, ask the Internal Revenue Service (IRS) or your employer for Publication 1244. Publication 1244 includes a 1-year supply of Form 4070A. Each day, write in the information asked for on the form.

In addition to the information asked for on Form 4070A, you also need to keep a record of the date and value of any noncash tips you get, such as tickets, passes, or other items of value. Although you do not report these tips to your employer, you must report them on your tax return.

TAXPLANNER

You are not required to complete Form 4070A as long as you have an alternative method of recording your tips. The IRS issues the form merely to help employees keep track of their income from tips.

Complete written records are essential, particularly if you must later substantiate a claim that you did not receive all the tips your employer alleges were allocated to you.

Examples of documentary evidence are copies of restaurant bills, credit card charges, or charges under any other arrangement containing amounts added by the customer as a tip.

If you do not use Form 4070A, start your records by writing your name, your employer's name, and the name of the business (if it is different from your employer's name). Then, each workday, write the date and the following information.

- Cash tips you get directly from customers or from other employees.
- Tips from credit and debit card charge customers that your employer pays you.
- The value of any noncash tips you get, such as tickets, passes, or other items of value.
- The amount of tips you paid out to other employees through tip pools or tip splitting, or other arrangements, and the names of the employees to whom you paid the tips.

EXPLANATION

An arbitrary fixed charge that your employer adds to the customer's bill is not a tip or gratuity subject to tip reporting and withholding requirements. Even if it is called a tip, the amount an employee is guaranteed from his or her employer is additional wage compensation.

Example

A club does not permit its members to tip its employees but adds 10% to each member's restaurant charges. This additional amount is set aside in a fund and is disbursed monthly to all employees. Because the employer controls the allocation of the funds, they are additional wages, not tips.

However, if a headwaiter receives one lump-sum payment to be distributed to all waiters and waitresses, then the payments are income from tips. The headwaiter would include in his income only the amount he retained, not the total he distributed.

Tax Breaks and Deductions You Can Use Checklist

Tip Income. If you work in a business where tips are common, make sure you read this chapter. Tips must be reported as income but there are special rules on how much tip income you must report and what records you must keep. Keeping good records will keep you from having to pay more tax than required.

Electronic tip record. You can use an electronic system provided by your employer to record your daily tips. If you do, you must receive and keep a paper copy of this record.

Mandatory service charges. Do not write in your tip diary the amount of any mandatory service charge that your employer adds to a customer's bill and then pays to you and treats as wages. This is part of your wages, not a tip. See examples below.

Example 1. Good Food Restaurant adds an 18% charge to the bill for parties of 6 or more customers. Jane's bill for food and beverages for her party of 8 includes an amount on the tip line equal to 18% of the charges for food and beverages, and the total includes this amount. Since Jane did not have an unrestricted right to determine the amount of the tip, the 18% charge is considered a mandatory service charge. Do not include the 18% charge in your tip diary. Mandatory service charges that are paid to you are considered wages, not tips.

Example 2. Good Food Restaurant also includes sample calculations of tip amounts at the bottom of its bills for food and beverages provided to customers. David's bill includes a blank "tip line," with sample tip calculations of 15%, 18%, and 20% of his charges for food and beverages at the bottom of the bill beneath the signature line. Since David was free to enter any amount on the "tip line" or leave it blank, any amount he includes is considered a tip. Be sure to include this amount in your tip diary.

Reporting Tips to Your Employer

Why report tips to your employer. You must report tips to your employer so that:

- Your employer can withhold federal income tax and social security and Medicare taxes or railroad retirement tax,
- Your employer can report the correct amount of your earnings to the Social Security Administration or Railroad Retirement Board (which affects your benefits when you retire or if you become disabled, or your family's benefits if you die), and
- You can avoid the *penalty for not reporting tips* to your employer (explained later).

TAXSAVER

Your employer usually deducts the withholding due on tips from your regular wages. However, you do not have to have income tax withheld if you can claim exemption from withholding. You can claim exemption only if you had no income tax liability last year and expect none this year. See *Exemption from Withholding* in chapter 4, *Tax withholding and estimated tax*, for more information.

Example

Many students and retired persons who expect to have no federal income tax liability work part-time in occupations in which they receive tips. To avoid unnecessary income tax withholding, you may file a Form W-4 with your employer, certifying that you had no federal income tax liability last year and expect to have none this year as well.

What tips to report. Report to your employer only cash, check, and debit and credit card tips you receive.

If your total tips for any 1 month from any one job are less than $20, do not report the tips for that month to that employer.

If you participate in a tip-splitting or tip-pooling arrangement, report only the tips you receive and retain. Do not report to your employer any portion of the tips you receive that you pass on to other employees. However, you must report tips you receive from other employees.

Do not report the value of any noncash tips, such as tickets or passes, to your employer. You do not pay social security and Medicare taxes or railroad retirement tax on these tips.

EXAMPLE

If you earn only $15 in tips in October, you do not have to report anything to your employer. However, you must still pay federal income tax on the tips when you report them on your tax return. The $15 is never subject to social security and Medicare taxes.

How to report. If your employer does not give you any other way to report tips, you can use Form 4070. Fill in the information asked for on the form, sign and date the form, and give it to your employer. To get a 1-year supply of the form, ask the IRS or your employer for Publication 1244.

If you do not use Form 4070, give your employer a statement with the following information.
- Your name, address, and social security number.
- Your employer's name, address, and business name (if it is different from your employer's name).
- The month (or the dates of any shorter period) in which you received tips.
- The total tips required to be reported for that period.

You must sign and date the statement. Be sure to keep a copy with your tax or other personal records.

Your employer may require you to report your tips more than once a month. However, the statement cannot cover a period of more than 1 calendar month.

Electronic tip statement. Your employer can have you furnish your tip statements electronically.

When to report. Give your report for each month to your employer by the 10th of the next month. If the 10th falls on a Saturday, Sunday, or legal holiday, give your employer the report by the next day that is not a Saturday, Sunday, or legal holiday.

Example 1. You must report your tips received in October 2012 by November 12, 2012. November 10 is a Saturday, and the 12th is the next day that is not a Saturday, Sunday, or legal holiday.

Example 2. You must report your tips received in November 2012 by December 10, 2012.

Final report. If your employment ends during the month, you can report your tips when your employment ends.

Penalty for not reporting tips. If you do not report tips to your employer as required, you may be subject to a penalty equal to 50% of the social security and Medicare taxes or railroad retirement tax you owe on the unreported tips. (For information about these taxes, see _Reporting social security and Medicare taxes on tips not reported to your employer_ under *Reporting Tips on Your Tax Return*, later.) The penalty amount is in addition to the taxes you owe.

You can avoid this penalty if you can show reasonable cause for not reporting the tips to your employer. To do so, attach a statement to your return explaining why you did not report them.

Giving your employer money for taxes. Your regular pay may not be enough for your employer to withhold all the taxes you owe on your regular pay plus your reported tips. If this happens, you can give your employer money until the close of the calendar year to pay the rest of the taxes.

If you do not give your employer enough money, your employer will apply your regular pay and any money you give to the taxes in the following order.

1. All taxes on your regular pay.
2. Social security and Medicare taxes or railroad retirement tax on your reported tips.
3. Federal, state, and local income taxes on your reported tips.

Any taxes that remain unpaid can be collected by your employer from your next paycheck. If withholding taxes remain uncollected at the end of the year, you may be subject to a penalty for underpayment of estimated taxes. See Publication 505, *Tax Withholding and Estimated Tax*, for more information.

Reporting Tips on Your Tax Return

How to report tips. Report your tips with your wages on Form 1040, line 7; Form 1040A, line 7; or Form 1040EZ, line 1.

What tips to report. You must report all tips you received in 2011 on your tax return, including both cash tips and noncash tips. Any tips you reported to your employer for 2011 are included in the wages shown in box 1 of your Form W-2. Add to the amount in box 1 only the tips you did not report to your employer.

Caution

If you did not keep a daily tip record as required and an amount is shown in box 8 of your Form W-2, see Allocated Tips, *later.*

EXPLANATION

All voluntary payments received from customers are taxable to the employee. This includes the fair market value of any noncash items given to employees.

Example

Tokens given to blackjack dealers in gambling casinos are taxable as income from tips to the dealers.

If you kept a daily tip record and reported tips to your employer as required under the rules explained earlier, add the following tips to the amount in box 1 of your Form W-2.

- Cash and charge tips you received that totaled less than $20 for any month.
- The value of noncash tips, such as tickets, passes, or other items of value.

Example. Ben Smith began working at the Blue Ocean Restaurant (his only employer in 2011) on June 30 and received $10,000 in wages during the year. Ben kept a daily tip record showing that his tips for June were $18 and his tips for the rest of the year totaled $7,000. He was not required to report his June tips to his employer, but he reported all of the rest of his tips to his employer as required.

Ben's Form W-2 from Blue Ocean Restaurant shows $17,000 ($10,000 wages plus $7,000 reported tips) in box 1. He adds the $18 unreported tips to that amount and reports $17,018 as wages on his tax return.

Reporting social security and Medicare taxes on tips not reported to your employer. If you received $20 or more in cash and charge tips in a month from any one job and did not report all of those tips to your employer, you must report the social security and Medicare taxes on the unreported tips as additional tax on your return. To report these taxes, you must file a return even if you would not otherwise have to file. You must use Form 1040. (You cannot file Form 1040EZ or Form 1040A.)

TAXSAVER

Limit on social security and railroad retirement tax. There are limits on the amount of social security and railroad retirement tax that your employer withholds from your wages and reported tips. If you worked for two or more employers in 2011, you may have overpaid one or more of these taxes. You may be eligible for a credit for excess social security tax or railroad retirement tax, discussed in chapter 37, *Other credits including the earned income credit.*

TAXALERT

There is currently no limit on the amount of wages and reported tips subject to Medicare tax. The Medicare tax rate is 1.45%. However, only the first $106,800 of wages and tips are subject to social security tax in 2011. In 2011, the employer social security tax rate is 6.2%, and the employee rate is 4.2%. (For self-employed individuals, the tax rate is 10.4% on their self-employment income for 2011.) Under current law, the employee social security tax rates will revert to 6.2% on January 1, 2012 (12.4% for self-employed individuals).

Caution

If you are subject to the Railroad Retirement Tax Act, you cannot use Form 4137 to pay railroad retirement tax on unreported tips. To get railroad retirement credit, you must report tips to your employer.

Use Form 4137 to figure these taxes. Enter the tax on your return as instructed, and attach the completed Form 4137 to your return.

Reporting uncollected social security and Medicare taxes on tips reported to your employer. You may have uncollected taxes if your regular pay was not enough for your employer to withhold all the taxes you owe and you did not give your employer enough money to pay the rest of the taxes. For more information, see *Giving your employer money for taxes*, under *Reporting Tips to Your Employer*, earlier.

If your employer could not collect all the social security and Medicare taxes or railroad retirement tax you owe on tips reported for 2011, the uncollected taxes will be shown in box 12 of your Form W-2 (codes A and B). You must report these amounts as additional tax on your return.

To report these uncollected taxes, you must file a return even if you would not otherwise have to file. Include the taxes in your total tax amount on Form 1040, line 60, and write "UT" and the total of the uncollected taxes on the dotted line next to line 60. (You cannot file Form 1040EZ or Form 1040A.)

Allocated Tips

If your employer allocated tips to you, they are shown separately in box 8 of your Form W-2. They are not included in box 1 with your wages and reported tips. If box 8 is blank, this discussion does not apply to you.

What are allocated tips? These are tips that your employer assigned to you in addition to the tips you reported to your employer for the year. Your employer will have done this only if:

- You worked in an establishment (restaurant, cocktail lounge, or similar business) that must allocate tips to employees,
- The tips you reported to your employer were less than your share of 8% of food and drink sales, and
- You did not participate in your employer's Attributed Tip Income Program (ATIP).

No income, social security, or Medicare taxes are withheld on allocated tips.

How were your allocated tips figured? The tips allocated to you are your share of an amount figured by subtracting the reported tips of all employees from 8% (or an approved lower rate) of food and drink sales (other than carryout sales and sales with a service charge of 10% or more). Your share of that amount was figured using either a method provided by an employer-employee agreement or a method provided by IRS regulations based on employees' sales or hours worked. For information about the exact allocation method used, ask your employer.

The allocation computations would be as follows:
1. Total tips to be allocated: $100,000 (gross receipts) × 0.08 = $8,000.
2. Tips reported by indirectly tipped employees = $500.
3. Tips to be allocated to directly tipped employees: $8,000 − $500 (indirect employees' tips) = $7,500.
4. Allocation of tips to directly tipped employees:

	Directly tipped employees' share of 8% gross	×	Gross receipts ratio	=	Employee share of 8% gross
Amos	$7,500	×	18,000/100,000	=	$1,350
Mitchell	7,500	×	16,000/100,000	=	1,200
Charlie	7,500	×	23,000/100,000	=	1,725
Nelson	7,500	×	17,000/100,000	=	1,275
Ed	7,500	×	12,000/100,000	=	900
Allan	7,500	×	14,000/100,000	=	1,050
					$7,500

5. Calculation of tip shortfall of directly tipped employees:

	Employee share of 8% gross	−	Tips reported	=	Employees' shortfall
Amos	$1,350	−	$1,080	=	$270
Mitchell	1,200	−	880	=	320
Charlie	1,725	−	1,810	=	−
Nelson	1,275	−	800	=	475
Ed	900	−	450	=	450
Allan	1,050	−	680	=	370
			Total Shortfall		$1,885

Because Charlie has no reporting shortfall, there is no allocation to him.
6. Total tips reported, including reported tips of indirectly tipped employees: $8,000 − $6,200 (total tips reported) = $1,800 (amount allocable among shortfall employees).
7. Allocation of tip shortfall among directly tipped employees:

	Allocable amount	×	Shortfall ratio	=	Amount of allocation
Amos	$1,800	×	270/1,885	=	$258
Mitchell	1,800	×	320/1,885	=	305
Nelson	1,800	×	475/1,885	=	454
Ed	1,800	×	450/1,885	=	430
Allan	1,800	×	370/1,885	=	353
			Total		$1,800

These allocated amounts must be reported by the employer on the employees' W-2s in box 8. For example, Amos would have allocated tip income of $258.

TAXPLANNER
The reporting requirements for employers are only guidelines and apply only to large food or beverage establishments. Nevertheless, the courts have imposed industry averages on taxpayers who had no records or inadequate records.

TAXPLANNER

If the employee or employer would like to request a tip rate lower than 8%, he or she must file a petition with the district director for the IRS district in which the business is located. The petition must include specific information to justify the lower rate. An employee petition can only be filed with the consent of the majority of the directly tipped employees. The petition must state the total number of directly tipped employees and the number of employees consenting to the petition. The employer must also be notified immediately, and the employer must promptly give the district director a copy of any Form 8027, Employer's Annual Information Return of Tip Income and Allocated Tips, filed by the employer for the prior 3 years.

Must you report your allocated tips on your return. You must report allocated tips on your tax return unless either of the following exceptions applies.

- You kept a daily tip record, or other evidence that is as credible and reliable as a daily tip record, as required under rules explained earlier.
- Your tip record is incomplete, but it shows that your actual tips were more than the tips you reported to your employer plus the allocated tips.

If either exception applies, report your actual tips on your return. Do not report the allocated tips. See *What tips to report* under *Reporting Tips on Your Tax Return*, earlier.

How to report allocated tips. If you do not meet either of the exceptions above, report the total of box 1 and box 8 of your Forms(s) W-2 as wages on Form 1040, line 7. (You cannot file Form 1040A or Form 1040EZ.)

Because social security and Medicare taxes were not withheld from the allocated tips, you must report those taxes as additional tax on your return. Complete Form 4137, and include the allocated tips on line 1 of the form. See *Reporting social security and Medicare taxes on tips not reported to your employer* under *Reporting Tips on Your Tax Return*, earlier.

TAXORGANIZER

Records you should keep:
- Daily tip record/journal
- Copies of bills and credit card charge slips
- Copies of reports provided to employers related to tip income
- Summary of money given to employers to pay any of your taxes on tips not covered by withholding, and receipts from your employer or canceled checks to evidence these payments

Chapter 7
Interest income

Note

IRS Publication 17 (*Your Federal Income Tax*) has been updated by Ernst & Young LLP for 2011. Dates and dollar amounts shown are for 2011. Underlined type is used to indicate where IRS text has been updated. Places where text has been removed are indicated by the sentence: *Text intentionally omitted.*

ey.com/EYTaxGuide
Ernst & Young LLP will update the *Ernst & Young Tax Guide 2012* website with relevant taxpayer information as it becomes available. You can also sign up for email alerts to let you know when changes have been made.

Introduction

Interest income is a significant portion of all income earned by many Americans. The government takes pains to make sure that all such income is reported by taxpayers. That's why payers of interest, like banks, are required to report to the government the amounts of interest they pay out and to whom. If you do not supply your proper tax identification number—usually your social security number—to a payer of interest, tax will automatically be withheld.

Some investments permit you to defer reporting interest income. Such investments may boost the after-tax rate of return on your money, because you may pay tax on the income in a year—a retirement year, for example—when your tax rate is lower. This chapter outlines several tax planning ideas for deferring taxes on interest income.

TAXALERT

Tax on child's investment income. Form 8615, Tax for Certain Children Who Have Investment Income of More than $1,900, is required to figure the tax for a child with investment income of more than $1,900 if the child:

1. Was under age 18 at the end of 2011,
2. Was age 18 at the end of 2011 and did not have earned income that was more than half of the child's support, or
3. Was a full-time student over age 18 and under age 24 at the end of 2011 and did not have earned income that was more than half of the child's support.

The election to report a child's investment income on a parent's return and the special rule for when a child must file Form 6251, Alternative Minimum Tax-Individuals, also applies to the children listed above. For more information, see *Tax on investment income of certain children* under *General Information*, later.

Reminder

Foreign-source income. If you are a U.S. citizen with interest income from sources outside the United States (foreign income), you must report that income on your tax return unless it is exempt by U.S. law. This is true whether you reside inside or outside the United States and whether or not you receive a Form 1099 from the foreign payer.

This chapter discusses the following topics.
- **Different types of interest income.**
- **What interest is taxable and what interest is nontaxable.**
- **When to report interest income.**
- **How to report interest income on your tax return.**

In general, any interest you receive or that is credited to your account and can be withdrawn is taxable income. Exceptions to this rule are discussed later in this chapter.

You may be able to deduct expenses you have in earning this income on Schedule A (Form 1040) if you itemize your deductions. See chapter 29.

Useful Items

You may want to see:

Publication
- ☐ **537**   Installment Sales
- ☐ **550**   Investment Income and Expenses
- ☐ **1212**   Guide to Original Issue Discount (OID) Instruments

Form (and Instructions)
- ☐ **Schedule B (Form 1040A or 1040)**   Interest and Ordinary Dividends
- ☐ **8815**   Exclusion of Interest From Series EE and I U.S. Savings Bonds Issued After 1989
- ☐ **8818**   Optional Form To Record Redemption of Series EE and I U.S. Savings Bonds Issued After 1989

General Information

A few items of general interest are covered here.

Recordkeeping. You should keep a list showing sources and interest amounts received during the year. Also, keep the forms you receive showing your interest income (Forms 1099-INT, for example) as an important part of your records.

Tax Breaks and Deductions You Can Use Checklist

Interest Income. Interest income that is subject to federal tax is taxed as ordinary income and is subject to tax at your highest tax rate (currently as high as 35%). (Interest paid on most municipal bonds is exempt from federal income tax. See *Government Bond Interest*, discussed later.) You should compare federally taxable interest income to qualified dividend income, which is currently subject to a maximum tax rate of 15%. Although you may think that some items are dividend income they may actually be interest—such as interest paid on a bank money market account. (Dividends on money market funds, like those sold by mutual fund companies, are dividends but are not qualified dividends.)

Withholding on Interest Income. Interest income is usually not subject to income-tax withholding. But the payer may be required to withhold tax and you may be subject to a penalty if you don't provide your correct social security number. So make sure you provide the correct information when you open an account or buy a bond.

Government Bond Interest. Interest on federal bonds is subject to federal taxation but not to state and local tax. Although the interest on most municipal bonds is not subject to federal income taxation, the amount of that interest earned must be reported on page 1, Line 8b, of your Form 1040. Interest on municipal "private activity" bonds is not subject to regular federal income tax but is subject to the alternative minimum tax.

Family Loans. If you make a loan to a member of your family (or anyone else) without charging interest, you may have to recognize interest income anyway. There are exceptions based on the size of the loan and other factors, so make sure you check out the discussion in this chapter before you make such a loan.

Series E, Series EE, and Series I Bonds. If you own these bonds, and are a cash method taxpayer, you can choose whether or not to report the increase in value of the bonds as income each year or instead report the interest income when the bonds are cashed in or when they reach final maturity (whichever is earlier). This enables you to control when the income is recognized. If you decide to hold off on recognizing interest earned until you redeem your bonds, consider cashing them in a year when you are subject to a low tax rate in order to minimize the tax you'll need to pay on the bonds.

Tax on investment income of certain children. Part of a child's 2011 investment income may be taxed at the parent's tax rate. If so, Form 8615, Tax for Certain Children Who Have Investment Income of More Than $1,900, must be completed and attached to the child's tax return. If not, Form 8615 is not required and the child's income is taxed at his or her own tax rate.

TAXALERT

The investment income of a child under age 19 (or under age 24 if the child is a full-time student) may be taxed at the parent's rate if the child does not have earned income that is more than one-half of his support. These rules for taxing a child's investment income at their parent's rate are commonly known as the "kiddie tax." Children whose earned income exceeds one-half of the amount of support they receive are not subject to the kiddie tax under this provision. For more information, see chapter 32, *Tax on investment income of certain children*.

TAXPLANNER

To avoid paying the "kiddie tax," you should consider investments for your child that generate little or no taxable income until your child "grows out" of the reach of the kiddie tax.

Some parents can choose to include the child's interest and dividends on the parent's return. If you can, use Form 8814, Parents' Election To Report Child's Interest and Dividends, for this purpose.

EXPLANATION

You may elect to include your child's income on your return only if (1) your child's income consists solely of interest and dividends, including capital gain distributions and Alaska Permanent Fund dividends, and is between $950 and $9,500 in 2011, (2) your child made no estimated tax payments, (3) your child had no backup withholding, (4) your child did not have any overpayment of tax shown on his or her 2010 return applied to the 2011 return, and (5) your child is not required to file his or her own return. You may still need to file a state income tax return for your child.

For more information about the tax on investment income of children and the parents' election, see chapter 32.

Beneficiary of an estate or trust. Interest you receive as a beneficiary of an estate or trust is generally taxable income. You should receive a Schedule K-1 (Form 1041), Beneficiary's Share of Income, Deductions, Credits, etc., from the fiduciary. Your copy of Schedule K-1 and its instructions will tell you where to report the income on your Form 1040.

Social security number (SSN). You must give your name and SSN to any person required by federal tax law to make a return, statement, or other document that relates to you. This includes payers of interest.

SSN for joint account. If the funds in a joint account belong to one person, list that person's name first on the account and give that person's SSN to the payer. (For information on who owns the funds in a joint account, see *Joint accounts*, later.) If the joint account contains combined funds, give the SSN of the person whose name is listed first on the account. This is because only one name and SSN can be shown on Form 1099.

These rules apply both to joint ownership by a married couple and to joint ownership by other individuals. For example, if you open a joint savings account with your child using funds belonging to the child, list the child's name first on the account and give the child's SSN.

Custodian account for your child. If your child is the actual owner of an account that is recorded in your name as custodian for the child, give the child's SSN to the payer. For example, you must give your child's SSN to the payer of interest on an account owned by your child, even though the interest is paid to you as custodian.

Penalty for failure to supply SSN. If you do not give your SSN to the payer of interest, you may have to pay a penalty. See *Failure to supply social security number* under *Penalties* in chapter 1. Backup withholding also may apply.

Backup withholding. Your interest income is generally not subject to regular withholding. However, it may be subject to backup withholding to ensure that income tax is collected on the income. Under backup withholding, the payer of interest must withhold, as income tax, 28% of the amount you are paid.

Backup withholding may also be required if the IRS has determined that you underreported your interest or dividend income. For more information, see _Backup Withholding_ in chapter 4.

Reporting backup withholding. If backup withholding is deducted from your interest income, the payer must give you a Form 1099-INT for the year indicating the amount withheld. The Form 1099-INT will show any backup withholding as "Federal income tax withheld."

Joint accounts. If two or more persons hold property (such as a savings account or bond) as joint tenants, tenants by the entirety, or tenants in common, each person's share of any interest from the property is determined by local law.

Income from property given to a child. Property you give as a parent to your child under the Model Gifts of Securities to Minors Act, the Uniform Gifts to Minors Act, or any similar law becomes the child's property.

Income from the property is taxable to the child, except that any part used to satisfy a legal obligation to support the child is taxable to the parent or guardian having that legal obligation.

Savings account with parent as trustee. Interest income from a savings account opened for a minor child but placed in the name and subject to the order of the parents as trustees, is taxable to the child if, under the law of the state in which the child resides, both of the following are true.

- The savings account legally belongs to the child.
- The parents are not legally permitted to use any of the funds to support the child.

Form 1099-INT. Interest income is generally reported to you on Form 1099-INT, or a similar statement, by banks, savings and loans, and other payers of interest. This form shows you the interest you received during the year. Keep this form for your records. You do not have to attach it to your tax return.

Report on your tax return the total interest income you receive for the tax year.

Interest not reported on Form 1099-INT. Even if you do not receive Form 1099-INT, you must still report all of your taxable interest income. For example, you may receive distributive shares of interest from partnerships or S corporations. This interest is reported to you on Schedule K-1 (Form 1065) or Schedule K-1 (Form 1120S).

Nominees. Generally, if someone receives interest as a nominee for you, that person will give you a Form 1099-INT showing the interest received on your behalf.

If you receive a Form 1099-INT that includes amounts belonging to another person, see the discussion on nominee distributions under *How To Report Interest Income* in chapter 1 of Publication 550, or Schedule B (Form 1040A or 1040) instructions.

Incorrect amount. If you receive a Form 1099-INT that shows an incorrect amount (or other incorrect information), you should ask the issuer for a corrected form. The new Form 1099-INT you receive will be marked "Corrected."

Form 1099-OID. Reportable interest income also may be shown on Form 1099-OID, Original Issue Discount. For more information about amounts shown on this form, see *Original Issue Discount (OID)*, later in this chapter.

Exempt-interest dividends. Exempt-interest dividends you receive from a mutual fund or other regulated investment company are not included in your taxable income. (However, see *Information-reporting requirement*, next.) Exempt-interest dividends should be shown in box 8 of Form 1099-INT. You do not reduce your basis for distributions that are exempt-interest dividends.

Information-reporting requirement. Although exempt-interest dividends are not taxable, you must show them on your tax return if you have to file. This is an information-reporting requirement and does not change the exempt-interest dividends into taxable income.

Note. Exempt-interest dividends paid from specified private activity bonds may be subject to the alternative minimum tax. See *Alternative Minimum Tax* in chapter 31 for more information. Chapter 1 of Publication 550 contains a discussion on private activity bonds under *State or Local Government Obligations.*

Interest on VA dividends. Interest on insurance dividends left on deposit with the Department of Veterans Affairs (VA) is not taxable. This includes interest paid on dividends on converted United States Government Life Insurance and on National Service Life Insurance policies.

Individual retirement arrangements (IRAs). Interest on a Roth IRA generally is not taxable. Interest on a traditional IRA is tax deferred. You generally do not include it in your income until you make withdrawals from the IRA. See chapter 17.

Taxable Interest

Taxable interest includes interest you receive from bank accounts, loans you make to others, and other sources. The following are some sources of taxable interest.

Dividends that are actually interest. Certain distributions commonly called dividends are actually interest. You must report as interest so-called "dividends" on deposits or on share accounts in:

- Cooperative banks,
- Credit unions,
- Domestic building and loan associations,
- Domestic savings and loan associations,
- Federal savings and loan associations, and
- Mutual savings banks.

The "dividends" will be shown as interest income on Form 1099-INT.

Money market funds. Money market funds pay dividends and are offered by nonbank financial institutions, such as mutual funds and stock brokerage houses. Generally, amounts you receive from money market funds should be reported as dividends, not as interest.

Certificates of deposit and other deferred interest accounts. If you open any of these accounts, interest may be paid at fixed intervals of 1 year or less during the term of the account. You generally must include this interest in your income when you actually receive it or are entitled to receive it without paying a substantial penalty. The same is true for accounts that mature in 1 year or less and pay interest in a single payment at maturity. If interest is deferred for more than 1 year, see *Original Issue Discount (OID)*, later.

Interest subject to penalty for early withdrawal. If you withdraw funds from a deferred interest account before maturity, you may have to pay a penalty. You must report the total amount of interest paid or credited to your account during the year, without subtracting the penalty. See *Penalty on early withdrawal of savings* in chapter 1 of Publication 550 for more information on how to report the interest and deduct the penalty.

Money borrowed to invest in certificate of deposit. The interest you pay on money borrowed from a bank or savings institution to meet the minimum deposit required for a certificate of deposit from the institution and the interest you earn on the certificate are two separate items. You must report the total interest you earn on the certificate in your income. If you itemize deductions, you can deduct the interest you pay as investment interest, up to the amount of your net investment income. See *Interest Expenses* in chapter 3 of Publication 550.

Example. You deposited $5,000 with a bank and borrowed $5,000 from the bank to make up the $10,000 minimum deposit required to buy a 6-month certificate of deposit. The certificate earned $575 at maturity in 2011, but you received only $265, which represented the $575 you earned minus $310 interest charged on your $5,000 loan. The bank gives you a Form 1099-INT for 2011 showing the $575 interest you earned. The bank also gives you a statement showing that you paid $310 interest for 2011. You must include the $575 in your income. If you itemize your deductions on Schedule A (Form 1040), you can deduct $310, subject to the net investment income limit.

TAXPLANNER

Note in the previous example, the $310 of interest is deductible only if you itemize your deductions and may be further limited if you do not have net investment income (see chapter 24, *Interest expense*). If you are not able to fully deduct the interest you pay, you may want to reconsider the investment arrangement.

Example

Assuming the same facts as in the previous example, if you are in the top tax bracket, paying 35%, $201 of the $575 interest you earned will go to the IRS, leaving you with only $374. Since you paid $310 in interest charges (for which you receive no tax benefit if you do not itemize) to earn that $374, you have only $64 of after-tax gain on your $5,000 investment, for an after-tax rate of return of 1.28% on this investment.

TAXSAVER

You should be very interested in the after-tax rate of return on your investments. If your interest income is fully taxable, you may determine your after-tax rate of return in the following manner. First, determine from the Tax Rate Schedules (see chapter 48) what you expect your highest marginal tax rate to be by calculating your total taxable income and then determining the highest rate at which it will be taxed. If the rate is, say, 33%, then the IRS gets 33% of your interest income on any investment, and you keep 67%. Thus, if you earn 10% on a bank deposit, your after-tax rate of return is really 6.7% (10% × 67%). See the chart later in this chapter in the *State or Local Government Obligations* section for a comparison of after-tax yields with the yield of municipal bonds. As the chart indicates, you should remember to include your state and local taxes when computing your marginal tax rate.

Gift for opening account. If you receive non-cash gifts or services for making deposits or for opening an account in a savings institution, you may have to report the value as interest.

For deposits of less than $5,000, gifts or services valued at more than $10 must be reported as interest. For deposits of $5,000 or more, gifts or services valued at more than $20 must be reported as interest. The value is determined by the cost to the financial institution.

Example. You open a savings account at your local bank and deposit $800. The account earns $20 interest. You also receive a $15 calculator. If no other interest is credited to your account during the year, the Form 1099-INT you receive will show $35 interest for the year. You must report $35 interest income on your tax return.

Interest on insurance dividends. Interest on insurance dividends left on deposit with an insurance company that can be withdrawn annually is taxable to you in the year it is credited to your account. However, if you can withdraw it only on the anniversary date of the policy (or other specified date), the interest is taxable in the year that date occurs.

Prepaid insurance premiums. Any increase in the value of prepaid insurance premiums, advance premiums, or premium deposit funds is interest if it is applied to the payment of premiums due on insurance policies or made available for you to withdraw.

U.S. obligations. Interest on U.S. obligations, such as U.S. Treasury bills, notes, and bonds, issued by any agency or instrumentality of the United States is taxable for federal income tax purposes.

Interest on tax refunds. Interest you receive on tax refunds is taxable income.

Interest on condemnation award. If the condemning authority pays you interest to compensate you for a delay in payment of an award, the interest is taxable.

Installment sale payments. If a contract for the sale or exchange of property provides for deferred payments, it also usually provides for interest payable with the deferred payments. That interest is taxable when you receive it. If little or no interest is provided for in a deferred payment contract, part of each payment may be treated as interest. See *Unstated Interest and Original Issue Discount* in Publication 537, *Installment Sales*.

Interest on annuity contract. Accumulated interest on an annuity contract you sell before its maturity date is taxable.

Usurious interest. Usurious interest is interest charged at an illegal rate. This is taxable as interest unless state law automatically changes it to a payment on the principal.

Interest income on frozen deposits. Exclude from your gross income interest on frozen deposits. A deposit is frozen if, at the end of the year, you cannot withdraw any part of the deposit because:
  • The financial institution is bankrupt or insolvent, or
  • The state where the institution is located has placed limits on withdrawals because other financial institutions in the state are bankrupt or insolvent.
The amount of interest you must exclude is the interest that was credited on the frozen deposits minus the sum of:
  • The net amount you withdrew from these deposits during the year, and
  • The amount you could have withdrawn as of the end of the year (not reduced by any penalty for premature withdrawals of a time deposit).
If you receive a Form 1099-INT for interest income on deposits that were frozen at the end of 2011, see *Frozen deposits* under *How To Report Interest Income* in chapter 1 of Publication 550, for information about reporting this interest income exclusion on your tax return.

The interest you exclude is treated as credited to your account in the following year. You must include it in income in the year you can withdraw it.

Example. $100 of interest was credited on your frozen deposit during the year. You withdrew $80 but could not withdraw any more as of the end of the year. You must include $80 in your income and exclude $20 from your income for the year. You must include the $20 in your income for the year you can withdraw it.

Bonds traded flat. If you buy a bond at a discount when interest has been defaulted or when the interest has accrued but has not been paid, the transaction is described as trading a bond flat. The defaulted or unpaid interest is not income and is not taxable as interest if paid later. When you receive a payment of that interest, it is a return of capital that reduces the remaining cost basis of your bond. Interest that accrues after the date of purchase, however, is taxable interest income for the year it is received or accrued. See *Bonds Sold Between Interest Dates*, later, for more information.

Below-market loans. In general, a below-market loan is a loan on which no interest is charged or on which interest is charged at a rate below the applicable federal rate. See *Below-Market Loans* in chapter 1 of Publication 550 for more information.

EXPLANATION

If you make a below-market loan, you must report as interest income any forgone interest (defined next) arising from that loan. How you should report the income as well as the application of the below-market loan rules and exceptions are described in this section.

If you receive a below-market loan, you may be able to claim a deduction for interest expense in excess of the interest that you actually paid—but only if you use the funds to buy investment property.

Forgone interest. For any period, forgone interest is:
1. The amount of interest that would be payable for that period if interest accrued on the loan at the applicable federal rate and was payable annually on December 31, *minus*
2. Any interest actually payable on the loan for the period.

The applicable federal rate is set by the IRS each month and is published in the *Internal Revenue Bulletin*. You can also contact an IRS office to get these rates.

Below-market loans. A below-market loan is a loan on which no interest is charged or on which interest is charged at a rate below the applicable federal rate. A below-market loan is generally recharacterized as an arm's length transaction in which the lender is treated as having made:
1. A loan to the borrower in exchange for a note that requires the payment of interest at the applicable federal rate, and
2. An additional payment to the borrower.

The lender's additional payment to the borrower is treated as a gift, dividend, contribution to capital, payment of compensation, or other payment, depending on the substance of the transaction. The borrower may have to report this payment as taxable income depending on its classification.

Loans subject to the rules. The rules for below-market loans apply to:
- Gift loans
- Compensation-related loans
- Corporation-shareholder loans
- Tax avoidance loans
- Certain loans to qualified continuing care facilities (made after October 11, 1985)
- Certain other below-market loans

Exceptions

The rules for below-market loans do not apply to certain loans on days on which the total outstanding amount of loans between the borrower and lender is $10,000 or less. The rules do not apply on those days to:
1. Gift loans between individuals if the gift loan is not directly used to purchase or carry income-producing assets
2. Compensation-related loans or corporation-shareholder loans if the avoidance of federal tax is not a principal purpose of the loan

A compensation-related loan is any below-market loan between an employer and an employee or between an independent contractor and a person for whom the contractor provided services.

Other loans not subject to the rules. Other loans are excluded from the below-market rules, including:
1. Loans made available by the lender to the general public on the same terms and conditions and that are consistent with the lender's customary business practice.
2. Loans subsidized by a federal, state, or municipal government that are made available under a program of general application to the public.
3. Certain employee-relocation loans.
4. Loans to or from a foreign person, unless the interest income would be effectively connected with the conduct of a U.S. trade or business and would not be exempt from U.S. tax under an income tax treaty.
5. Other loans on which the interest arrangement can be shown to have no significant effect on the federal tax liability of the lender or the borrower.
6. Certain refundable loans to a qualified continuing care facility under a continuing care contract. The reporting of interest income from loans to continuing care facilities is subject to the rules for below-market loans unless certain requirements are met. However, there is no dollar limit on the total outstanding loan balance for these loans if the lender or the lender's spouse is at least 62 years old and is to receive services under the continuing care service contract. It is important to understand the definition of a qualified continuing care facility and the type of services allowed for purposes of this

loan type. Facilities which are of a type traditionally considered as nursing homes are not considered continuing care facilities. A continuing care facility which falls under this exception must: (1) provide service under a continuing care contract, (2) include an independent living unit, plus an assisted living or nursing facility, or both, and (3) substantially all of the independent living unit residents living there must be covered by continuing care contracts. For more information, see Publication 550, *Investment Income and Expenses*, and consult your tax advisor.

If a taxpayer structures a transaction to be a loan not subject to the below-market loan rules, and one of the principal purposes of structuring the transaction in such a way is to avoid federal tax, then the IRS may consider the loan to be a tax-avoidance scheme and, as such, subject the loan to the rules for below-market loans.

All the facts and circumstances are used to determine if the interest arrangement of a loan has a significant effect on the federal tax liability of the lender or borrower. Some factors to be considered are:

- Whether income and deduction items generated by the loan offset each other
- The amount of such items
- The cost to the taxpayer of complying with the below-market loan provisions, if they applied
- Any reasons other than tax avoidance purposes for structuring the transaction as a below-market loan

Gift and demand loans. A gift loan is any below-market loan where the forgone interest is in the nature of a gift. A demand loan is a loan payable in full at any time upon demand by the lender. A lender who makes a gift loan or demand loan is treated as transferring an additional payment to the borrower (as a gift, dividend, etc.) in an amount equal to the forgone interest. The borrower is treated as transferring the forgone interest to the lender and may be entitled to an interest expense deduction depending on the use of the monies borrowed. The lender must report that amount as interest income. These transfers are considered to occur annually, generally on December 31.

Example 1
Jill's grandmother makes an interest-free loan to Jill on July 1 for $50,000. Jill has net investment income from outside sources of $5,000. The applicable federal interest rate is 5% at this time. This loan will be treated as a gift loan. On December 31, Jill will be treated as having paid her grandmother $1,250 in interest and her grandmother must report $1,250 of interest income and as a gift, even though no money has changed hands.

Special rules for gift loans between individuals that do not exceed $100,000. For gift loans that do not exceed $100,000, the amount of forgone interest that is treated as transferred by the borrower to the lender is limited. This limit is the borrower's net investment income for the year, unless one of the principal purposes of the loan is the avoidance of federal tax. Also, if a borrower has net investment income of $1,000 or less for the year, the borrower's net investment income is considered to be zero and the borrower will have no interest expense deduction.

Example 2
Using the same facts in Example 1, assume Jill has $1,100 in net investment income for the year. On December 31, Jill will be treated as having paid her grandmother $1,100 in interest (not $1,250) because of the net investment income limitation. Jill's grandmother would include the $1,100 as interest income.

Term loans. A lender who makes a below-market term loan (a loan that is not a demand loan) is treated as transferring, as a gift, dividend, etc., an additional lump-sum cash payment to the borrower on the date the loan is made. The amount of this payment is the amount of the loan minus the present value of all payments due under the loan. An amount equal to this excess is treated as an original issue discount (OID). Accordingly, the OID rules of Section 1272 of the Internal Revenue Code apply. The lender must report the annual part of the OID as interest income. The borrower may be able to deduct some or all of the excess as interest expense depending on the use of the monies borrowed. The OID rules are discussed in greater detail later in this chapter.

Effective dates. These rules apply to term loans made after June 6, 1984, and to demand loans outstanding after that date.

U.S. Savings Bonds

This section provides tax information on U.S. savings bonds. It explains how to report the interest income on these bonds and how to treat transfers of these bonds.

For other information on U.S. savings bonds, write to:

For series EE and I:
Bureau of the Public Debt
Division of Customer Assistance

P.O. Box 7012
Parkersburg, WV 26106-7012

For series HH/H:
Bureau of the Public Debt
Division of Customer Assistance
P.O. Box 2186
Parkersburg, WV 26106-2186

Or, on the Internet, visit: *www.treasurydirect.gov/indiv/products/products. htm/.*

Accrual method taxpayers. If you use an accrual method of accounting, you must report interest on U.S. savings bonds each year as it accrues. You cannot postpone reporting interest until you receive it or until the bonds mature. Accrual methods of accounting are explained in chapter 1 under *Accounting Methods.*

Cash method taxpayers. If you use the cash method of accounting, as most individual taxpayers do, you generally report the interest on U.S. savings bonds when you receive it. The cash method of accounting is explained in chapter 1 under *Accounting Methods.* But see *Reporting options for cash method taxpayers,* later.

Series HH bonds. These bonds were issued at face value. Interest is paid twice a year by direct deposit to your bank account. If you are a cash method taxpayer, you must report interest on these bonds as income in the year you receive it.

Series HH bonds were first offered in 1980 and last offered in August 2004. Before 1980, series H bonds were issued. Series H bonds are treated the same as series HH bonds. If you are a cash method taxpayer, you must report the interest when you receive it.

Series H bonds have a maturity period of 30 years. Series HH bonds mature in 20 years.

Series EE and series I bonds. Interest on these bonds is payable when you redeem the bonds. The difference between the purchase price and the redemption value is taxable interest.

Series EE bonds. Series EE bonds were first offered in January 1980 and have a maturity period of 30 years.

Before July 1980, series E bonds were issued. The original 10-year maturity period of series E bonds has been extended to 40 years for bonds issued before December 1965 and 30 years for bonds issued after November 1965. Paper series EE and series E bonds are issued at a discount. The face value is payable to you at maturity. Electronic series EE bonds are issued at their face value. The face value plus accrued interest is payable to you at maturity.

Owners of paper series E and EE bonds can convert them to electronic bonds. These converted bonds do not retain the denomination listed on the paper certificate but are posted at their purchase price (with accrued interest).

Series I bonds. Series I bonds were first offered in 1998. These are inflation-indexed bonds issued at their face amount with a maturity period of 30 years. The face value plus all accrued interest is payable to you at maturity.

Reporting options for cash method taxpayers. If you use the cash method of reporting income, you can report the interest on series EE, series E, and series I bonds in either of the following ways.
1. *Method 1.* Postpone reporting the interest until the earlier of the year you cash or dispose of the bonds or the year they mature. (However, see *Savings bonds traded,* later.)
   Note. Series E and EE bonds issued in 1981 matured in 2011. If you have used method 1, you generally must report the interest on these bonds on your 2011 return.
2. *Method 2.* Choose to report the increase in redemption value as interest each year.

You must use the same method for all series EE, series E, and series I bonds you own. If you do not choose method 2 by reporting the increase in redemption value as interest each year, you must use method 1.

Change from method 1. If you want to change your method of reporting the interest from method 1 to method 2, you can do so without permission from the IRS. In the year of change you must report all interest accrued to date and not previously reported for all your bonds.

Once you choose to report the interest each year, you must continue to do so for all series EE, series E, and series I bonds you own and for any you get later, unless you request permission to change, as explained next.

Change from method 2. To change from method 2 to method 1, you must request permission from the IRS. Permission for the change is automatically granted if you send the IRS a statement that meets all the following requirements.

Tip

If you plan to cash your bonds in the same year you will pay for higher education expenses, you may want to use method 1 because you may be able to exclude the interest from your income. To learn how, see Education Savings Bond Program, *later.*

1. You have typed or printed the following number at the top: "131."
2. It includes your name and social security number under "131."
3. It includes the year of change (both the beginning and ending dates).
4. It identifies the savings bonds for which you are requesting this change.
5. It includes your agreement to:
    a. Report all interest on any bonds acquired during or after the year of change when the interest is realized upon disposition, redemption, or final maturity, whichever is earliest, and
    b. Report all interest on the bonds acquired before the year of change when the interest is realized upon disposition, redemption, or final maturity, whichever is earliest, with the exception of the interest reported in prior tax years.

You must attach this statement to your tax return for the year of change, which you must file by the due date (including extensions).

You can have an automatic extension of 6 months from the due date of your return for the year of change (excluding extensions) to file the statement with an amended return. On the statement, type or print "Filed pursuant to section 301.9100-2." To get this extension, you must have filed your original return for the year of the change by the due date (including extensions).

By the date you file the original statement with your return, you must also send a signed copy to the address below.

> Internal Revenue Service
> Attention: CC:IT&A (Automatic Rulings Branch)
> P.O. Box 7604
> Benjamin Franklin Station
> Washington, DC 20044

If you use a private delivery service, send the signed copy to the address below.

> Internal Revenue Service
> Attention: CC:IT&A (Automatic Rulings Branch)
> Room 5336
> 1111 Constitution Avenue, NW
> Washington, DC 20224

Instead of filing this statement, you can request permission to change from method 2 to method 1 by filing Form 3115, Application for Change in Accounting Method. In that case, follow the form instructions for an automatic change. No user fee is required.

EXPLANATION

Series E, Series EE, and Series I bonds are unique investments from a tax viewpoint. Since you, as a cash method taxpayer, may decide not to report the increase in value of the bonds as income each year and instead may decide to report the interest income when the bonds are cashed in or when they reach final maturity (whichever is earlier), you can—to an unusual extent—control when the income is recognized. The best time to redeem the bonds is a year in which you have low taxable income and a low tax rate.

Few people choose to report income annually rather than at sale or maturity, but if you do, you would report as income the increase in the redemption value of each bond each year. All you must do is report the income on your tax return. It would be advantageous to report the income annually only if you had an income so low that your personal exemption and itemized deductions or standard deduction might otherwise be wasted. The most likely people to choose this option are retired people and children over 18 years old in 2011 (or, if a full-time student, over age 23), both of whom may have low taxable income. (Income received by children under age 19 or, if a full-time student, under age 24, may be taxed at their parents' rate.) Remember, once you choose to report the income each year, you must obtain permission from the IRS to change your reporting method.

Example

A 70-year-old unmarried man with only $1,500 of other income might wish to report his savings bond interest each year, since his first $10,950 of income (his standard deduction and exemption) is tax-free in 2011. If he holds the bonds and reports all the income in the year they mature, his taxable income in that year might be more than $10,950, and he would therefore pay taxes he could have otherwise avoided by reporting a smaller amount of interest each year over the life of the bond.

The interest rate on Series EE bonds varies depending upon when the bonds were purchased. The method of calculating the interest rate is different for bonds purchased prior to May 1, 1995, between May 1, 1995, and April 30, 1997, and after May 1, 1997. The interest rate on Series I bonds, the value of which is adjusted with inflation, also changes periodically. The Treasury site at *www.publicdebt.treas.gov* has more details.

Millions of Series E and H bonds continue to be held by the public. Most are still earning interest due to extended maturity rates. Some, however, have reached their final maturity and should be exchanged or redeemed.

Prior to September 1, 2004, Series HH bonds could be obtained in exchange for outstanding eligible Series EE bonds and Series E bonds having a combined redemption value of $500 or more. Owners who deferred reporting interest earned on the bonds that they exchange can continue to defer the interest until the year in which the Series HH bonds received in the exchange are redeemed, reach final maturity, or are otherwise disposed of.

Although Series H bonds cannot be exchanged for Series HH bonds (nor can Series E bonds be exchanged for Series EE bonds), the redemption proceeds can be reinvested in new series bonds. However, any previously tax-deferred interest must be reported for federal income tax purposes in the year of redemption.

TAXPLANNER

For most bonds issued prior to May 1997, interest is credited to U.S. savings bonds at specified dates (i.e., there is no proration of interest for bonds cashed during the middle of an interest period). Thus, you should plan ahead to cash in your bonds just after (versus just before) an interest credit date.

Co-owners. If a U.S. savings bond is issued in the names of co-owners, such as you and your child or you and your spouse, interest on the bond is generally taxable to the co-owner who bought the bond.

One co-owner's funds used. If you used your funds to buy the bond, you must pay the tax on the interest. This is true even if you let the other co-owner redeem the bond and keep all the proceeds. Under these circumstances, the co-owner who redeemed the bond will receive a Form 1099-INT at the time of redemption and must provide you with another Form 1099-INT showing the amount of interest from the bond taxable to you. The co-owner who redeemed the bond is a "nominee." See *Nominee distributions* under *How To Report Interest Income* in chapter 1 of Publication 550 for more information about how a person who is a nominee reports interest income belonging to another person.

Both co-owners' funds used. If you and the other co-owner each contribute part of the bond's purchase price, the interest is generally taxable to each of you, in proportion to the amount each of you paid.

Community property. If you and your spouse live in a community property state and hold bonds as community property, one-half of the interest is considered received by each of you. If you file separate returns, each of you generally must report one-half of the bond interest. For more information about community property, see Publication 555, *Community Property.*

Table 7-1. These rules are also shown in Table 7-1.

Table 7-1. **Who Pays the Tax on U.S. Savings Bond Interest**

IF...	THEN the interest must be reported by...
you buy a bond in your name and the name of another person as co-owners, using only your own funds	you.
you buy a bond in the name of another person, who is the sole owner of the bond	the person for whom you bought the bond.
you and another person buy a bond as co-owners, each contributing part of the purchase price	both you and the other co-owner, in proportion to the amount each paid for the bond.
you and your spouse, who live in a community property state, buy a bond that is community property	you and your spouse. If you file separate returns, both you and your spouse generally report one-half of the interest.

Ownership transferred. If you bought series E, series EE, or series I bonds entirely with your own funds and had them reissued in your co-owner's name or beneficiary's name alone, you must include in your gross income for the year of reissue all interest that you earned on these bonds and have not previously reported. But, if the bonds were reissued in your name alone, you do not have to report the interest accrued at that time.

This same rule applies when bonds (other than bonds held as community property) are transferred between spouses or incident to divorce.

> ### EXPLANATION
> If you make a gift of Series E, Series EE, or Series I bonds to a child, remember that it is not possible to transfer the obligation of reporting the interest income that has already accumulated. The interest that has accumulated through the date of the gift must be reported by the donor in the year of the gift. Interest that accumulates from the date of the gift until maturity is reported by the individual receiving the gift.

Purchased jointly. If you and a co-owner each contributed funds to buy series E, series EE, or series I bonds jointly and later have the bonds reissued in the co-owner's name alone, you must include in your gross income for the year of reissue your share of all the interest earned on the bonds that you have not previously reported. The former co-owner does not have to include in gross income at the time of reissue his or her share of the interest earned that was not reported before the transfer. This interest, however, as well as all interest earned after the reissue, is income to the former co-owner.

This income-reporting rule also applies when the bonds are reissued in the name of your former co-owner and a new co-owner. But the new co-owner will report only his or her share of the interest earned after the transfer.

If bonds that you and a co-owner bought jointly are reissued to each of you separately in the same proportion as your contribution to the purchase price, neither you nor your co-owner has to report at that time the interest earned before the bonds were reissued.

Example 1. You and your spouse each spent an equal amount to buy a $1,000 series EE savings bond. The bond was issued to you and your spouse as co-owners. You both postpone reporting interest on the bond. You later have the bond reissued as two $500 bonds, one in your name and one in your spouse's name. At that time neither you nor your spouse has to report the interest earned to the date of reissue.

Example 2. You bought a $1,000 series EE savings bond entirely with your own funds. The bond was issued to you and your spouse as co-owners. You both postpone reporting interest on the bond. You later have the bond reissued as two $500 bonds, one in your name and one in your spouse's name. You must report half the interest earned to the date of reissue.

Transfer to a trust. If you own series E, series EE, or series I bonds and transfer them to a trust, giving up all rights of ownership, you must include in your income for that year the interest earned to the date of transfer if you have not already reported it. However, if you are considered the owner of the trust and if the increase in value both before and after the transfer continues to be taxable to you, you can continue to defer reporting the interest earned each year. You must include the total interest in your income in the year you cash or dispose of the bonds or the year the bonds finally mature, whichever is earlier.

> ### TAXSAVER
> If you transfer the bonds to a revocable trust, of which you are considered the owner, you may continue to defer reporting the income. Many individuals use a revocable trust as a substitute for a will. A revocable trust is not required to pay federal income tax on income earned in the trust. Instead, all income (and deductions) is reported on your individual tax return, as if the revocable trust did not exist. In essence, you are treated as if you owned the assets outright. For more details, consult your tax advisor.

The same rules apply to previously unreported interest on series EE or series E bonds if the transfer to a trust consisted of series HH or series H bonds you acquired in a trade for the series EE or series E bonds. See *Savings bonds traded*, later.

Decedents. The manner of reporting interest income on series E, series EE, or series I bonds, after the death of the owner, depends on the accounting and income-reporting methods previously used by the decedent. This is explained in chapter 1 of Publication 550.

Income that the decedent had a right to receive at the time of death, but which is included on another's tax return (or the estate tax return), is called "income in respect of the decedent." See chapter 43, *Decedents: Dealing with the death of a family member*, for more information.

TAXPLANNER

If the final income tax return of the decedent shows a low amount of taxable income, it would be better to include the interest income from the date of purchase of the bonds through the date of death, the choice described in Example 1. Otherwise, the IRS says that the interest income must be reported by the person who receives the bonds, the choice described in Example 2.

However, there is a third option. If the bonds are in the name of the decedent alone, their ownership passes to the estate. The estate is a separate taxable entity that files its own income tax return. If the estate has a low amount of taxable income, it might be advisable for the executor to redeem the bonds.

A point to remember is this: The unique method by which interest from U.S. savings bonds are taxed gives you an opportunity to reduce income tax by selecting the person or entity with the lowest tax rate to receive the income.

Example 1

Your uncle, a cash method taxpayer, died near the end of 2010 and left you a $1,000 Series E bond. He bought the bond for $750 and chose not to report the interest each year. At the date of death, interest of $200 had accrued on the bond and its value of $950 was included in your uncle's estate. Your uncle's executor did not choose to include the $200 accrued interest in your uncle's final income tax return.

You are a cash method taxpayer and do not choose to report the interest each year as it is earned. If you cash the bond when it reaches its maturity value of $1,000, you will report $250 of interest income—the difference between the maturity value of $1,000 and the original cost of $750. Also, you may deduct (as a miscellaneous deduction not subject to the 2% AGI limit) in that year any federal estate tax that was paid on the $200 of interest that was included in your uncle's estate. For more information on this subject, see chapter 43, *Decedents: Dealing with the death of a family member.*

Example 2

If, in Example 1, the executor had chosen to include the $200 accrued interest in your uncle's final tax return, you would report only $50 as interest when you cashed the bond at maturity. This $50 is the interest earned after your uncle's death.

Example 3

Your aunt died owning Series H bonds that she got in a trade for Series E bonds. (See *Savings bonds traded*, in the next section.) You were the beneficiary of these bonds. Your aunt used the cash method and did not choose to report the interest on the Series E bonds each year as it accrued. Your aunt's executor did not choose to include on her final tax return any interest earned before her death.

The income in respect of a decedent is the sum of the unreported interest on the Series E bonds and the interest, if any, payable on the Series H bonds but not received as of the date of your aunt's death. You must report any interest received during the year as income on your return. The part of the interest that was payable but not received before your aunt's death is income in respect of the decedent and may qualify for the estate tax deduction. For when to report the interest on the Series E bonds traded, see *Savings bonds traded*, in the next section.

TAXPLANNER

There is an annual limitation on the purchase of Series EE and Series I bonds. An individual may purchase a total of up to $20,000 (face amount) per year. Because bonds are sold for one-half their face value, this means you can spend no more than $10,000 on Series EE bonds per year ($5,000 in paper bonds and $5,000 electronically). In addition, you can only buy up to $10,000 of Series I bonds each year, as well ($5,000 in paper bonds and $5,000 electronically).

Savings bonds traded. If you postponed reporting the interest on your series EE or series E bonds, you did not recognize taxable income when you traded the bonds for series HH or series H bonds, unless you received cash in the trade. (You cannot trade series I bonds for series HH bonds. After

August 31, 2004, you cannot trade any other series of bonds for series HH bonds.) Any cash you received is income up to the amount of the interest earned on the bonds traded. When your series HH or series H bonds mature, or if you dispose of them before maturity, you report as interest the difference between their redemption value and your cost. Your cost is the sum of the amount you paid for the traded series EE or series E bonds plus any amount you had to pay at the time of the trade.

Example. In 2004, you traded series EE bonds (on which you postponed reporting the interest) for $2,500 in series HH bonds and $223 in cash. You reported the $223 as taxable income in 2004, the year of the trade. At the time of the trade, the series EE bonds had accrued interest of $523 and a redemption value of $2,723. You hold the series HH bonds until maturity, when you receive $2,500. You must report $300 as interest income in the year of maturity. This is the difference between their redemption value, $2,500, and your cost, $2,200 (the amount you paid for the series EE bonds). (It is also the difference between the accrued interest of $523 on the series EE bonds and the $223 cash received on the trade.)

Choice to report interest in year of trade. You could have chosen to treat all of the previously unreported accrued interest on the series EE or series E bonds traded for series HH bonds as income in the year of the trade. If you made this choice, it is treated as a change from method 1. See *Change from method 1* under *Series EE and series I bonds,* earlier.

Form 1099-INT for U.S. savings bonds interest. When you cash a bond, the bank or other payer that redeems it must give you a Form 1099-INT if the interest part of the payment you receive is $10 or more. Box 3 of your Form 1099-INT should show the interest as the difference between the amount you received and the amount paid for the bond. However, your Form 1099-INT may show more interest than you have to include on your income tax return. For example, this may happen if any of the following are true.

- You chose to report the increase in the redemption value of the bond each year. The interest shown on your Form 1099-INT will not be reduced by amounts previously included in income.
- You received the bond from a decedent. The interest shown on your Form 1099-INT will not be reduced by any interest reported by the decedent before death, or on the decedent's final return, or by the estate on the estate's income tax return.
- Ownership of the bond was transferred. The interest shown on your Form 1099-INT will not be reduced by interest that accrued before the transfer.
- You were named as a co-owner, and the other co-owner contributed funds to buy the bond. The interest shown on your Form 1099-INT will not be reduced by the amount you received as nominee for the other co-owner. (See *Co-owners*, earlier in this chapter, for more information about the reporting requirements.)
- You received the bond in a taxable distribution from a retirement or profit-sharing plan. The interest shown on your Form 1099-INT will not be reduced by the interest portion of the amount taxable as a distribution from the plan and not taxable as interest. (This amount is generally shown on Form 1099-R, Distributions From Pensions, Annuities, Retirement or Profit-Sharing Plans, IRAs, Insurance Contracts, etc., for the year of distribution.)

For more information on including the correct amount of interest on your return, see *How To Report Interest Income*, later. Publication 550 includes examples showing how to report these amounts.

Tip

Interest on U.S. savings bonds is exempt from state and local taxes. The Form 1099-INT you receive will indicate the amount that is for U.S. savings bond interest in box 3.

EXPLANATION

When you redeem U.S. savings bonds, the government assumes that the difference between the issue price and the redemption amount is interest paid to you entirely at that time, even though some of the interest may already have been reported by you or someone else. The government will therefore issue a Form 1099-INT to you for the full amount.

If you should not be taxed on the full amount of interest, you should show the full amount as reported on the Form 1099-INT issued by the government on Schedule B (Form 1040 or Form 1040A) and also show a subtraction for the amount that is not taxable to you. This will help you to avoid IRS deficiency notices.

Education Savings Bond Program

You may be able to exclude from income all or part of the interest you receive on the redemption of qualified U.S. savings bonds during the year if you pay qualified higher educational expenses during the same year. This exclusion is known as the Education Savings Bond Program.

You do not qualify for this exclusion if your filing status is married filing separately.

Form 8815. Use Form 8815 to figure your exclusion. Attach the form to your Form 1040 or Form 1040A.

Qualified U.S. savings bonds. A qualified U.S. savings bond is a series EE bond issued after 1989 or a series I bond. The bond must be issued either in your name (sole owner) or in your and your spouse's names (co-owners). You must be at least 24 years old before the bond's issue date. For example, a bond bought by a parent and issued in the name of his or her child under age 24 does not qualify for the exclusion by the parent or child.

Beneficiary. You can designate any individual (including a child) as a beneficiary of the bond.

Verification by IRS. If you claim the exclusion, the IRS will check it by using bond redemption information from the Department of the Treasury.

Qualified expenses. Qualified higher educational expenses are tuition and fees required for you, your spouse, or your dependent (for whom you claim an exemption) to attend an eligible educational institution.

Qualified expenses include any contribution you make to a qualified tuition program or to a Coverdell education savings account.

Qualified expenses do not include expenses for room and board or for courses involving sports, games, or hobbies that are not part of a degree or certificate granting program.

Eligible educational institutions. These institutions include most public, private, and nonprofit universities, colleges, and vocational schools that are accredited and eligible to participate in student aid programs run by the U.S. Department of Education.

Reduction for certain benefits. You must reduce your qualified higher educational expenses by all of the following tax-free benefits.

1. Tax-free part of scholarships and fellowships (see *Scholarships and fellowships* in chapter 12).
2. Expenses used to figure the tax-free portion of distributions from a Coverdell ESA.
3. Expenses used to figure the tax-free portion of distributions from a qualified tuition program.
4. Any tax-free payments (other than gifts or inheritances) received for educational expenses, such as
   a. Veterans' educational assistance benefits,
   b. Qualified tuition reductions, or
   c. Employer-provided educational assistance.
5. Any expense used in figuring the American opportunity and lifetime learning credits.

Amount excludable. If the total proceeds (interest and principal) from the qualified U.S. savings bonds you redeem during the year are not more than your adjusted qualified higher educational expenses for the year, you may be able to exclude all of the interest. If the proceeds are more than the expenses, you may be able to exclude only part of the interest.

To determine the excludable amount, multiply the interest part of the proceeds by a fraction. The numerator of the fraction is the qualified higher educational expenses you paid during the year. The denominator of the fraction is the total proceeds you received during the year.

Example. In February 2011, Mark and Joan, a married couple with 2011 MAGI of $100,000, cashed a qualified series EE U.S. savings bond they bought in April 1996. They received proceeds of $8,124 representing principal of $5,000 and interest of $3,124. In 2011, they paid $4,000 of their daughter's college tuition. They are not claiming an education credit for that amount, and their daughter does not have any tax-free educational assistance. They can exclude $1,538 ($3,124 × ($4,000 ÷ $8,124)) of interest in 2011. They must pay tax on the remaining $1,586 ($3,124 − $1,538) interest.

Caution

The issue date of a bond may be earlier than the date the bond is purchased because the issue date assigned to a bond is the first day of the month in which it is purchased.

Modified adjusted gross income limit. The interest exclusion is limited if your modified adjusted gross income (modified AGI) is:

- $71,100 to $86,100 for taxpayers filing single or head of household, and
- $106,650 to $136,650 for married taxpayers filing jointly or for a qualifying widow(er) with dependent child.

You do not qualify for the interest exclusion if your modified AGI is equal to or more than the upper limit for your filing status.

Modified AGI, for purposes of this exclusion, is adjusted gross income (Form 1040A, line 21, or Form 1040, line 37) figured before the interest exclusion, and modified by adding back any:

1. Foreign earned income exclusion,
2. Foreign housing exclusion and deduction,
3. Exclusion of income for *bona fide* residents of American Samoa,
4. Exclusion for income from Puerto Rico,
5. Exclusion for adoption benefits received under an employer's adoption assistance program,
6. Deduction for student loan interest,
7. Deduction for tuition and fees, and
8. Deduction for domestic production activities.

Text intentionally omitted.

Use the worksheet in the instructions for line 9, Form 8815, to figure your modified AGI. If you claim any of the exclusion or deduction items listed above (except items 6–8), add the amount of the exclusion or deduction (except any deduction for student loan interest, tuition and fees or domestic production activities) to the amount on line 5 of the worksheet, and enter the total on Form 8815, line 9, as your modified AGI.

If you have investment interest expense incurred to earn royalties and other investment income, see *Education Savings Bond Program* in chapter 1 of Publication 550.

Recordkeeping. If you claim the interest exclusion, you must keep a written record of the qualified U.S. savings bonds you redeem. Your record must include the serial number, issue date, face value, and total redemption proceeds (principal and interest) of each bond. You can use Form 8818 to record this information. You should also keep bills, receipts, canceled checks, or other documentation that shows you paid qualified higher educational expenses during the year.

U.S. Treasury Bills, Notes, and Bonds

Treasury bills, notes, and bonds are direct debts (obligations) of the U.S. Government.

Taxation of interest. Interest income from Treasury bills, notes, and bonds is subject to federal income tax but is exempt from all state and local income taxes. You should receive Form 1099-INT showing the interest (in box 3) paid to you for the year.

Payments of principal and interest generally will be credited to your designated checking or savings account by direct deposit through the Treasury Direct® system.

Treasury bills. These bills generally have a 4-week, 13-week, 26-week, or 52-week maturity period. They are issued at a discount in the amount of $100 and multiples of $100. The difference between the discounted price you pay for the bills and the face value you receive at maturity is interest income. Generally, you report this interest income when the bill is paid at maturity.

Treasury notes and bonds. Treasury notes have maturity periods of more than 1 year, ranging up to 10 years. Maturity periods for Treasury bonds are longer than 10 years. Both generally are issued in denominations of $100 to $1 million and generally pay interest every 6 months. Generally, you report this interest for the year paid. For more information, see *U.S. Treasury Bills, Notes, and Bonds* in chapter 1 of Publication 550.

For other information on Treasury notes or bonds, write to:

Bureau of The Public Debt
P.O. Box 7015
Parkersburg, WV 26106-7015

Or, on the Internet, visit: *www. treasury direct.gov/write htm*.

For information on series EE, series I, and series HH savings bonds, see *U.S. Savings Bonds*, earlier.

Treasury inflation-protected securities (TIPS). These securities pay interest twice a year at a fixed rate, based on a principal amount adjusted to take into account inflation and deflation. For the tax treatment of these securities, see *Inflation-Indexed Debt Instruments* under *Original Issue Discount (OID)*, in Publication 550.

EXPLANATION

The paragraph above discusses interest income only when a Treasury bill is held until maturity. When a Treasury bill is sold before maturity, the difference between the purchase price and the selling price may be part interest and part short-term capital gain or loss.

Example

You buy a $10,000 Treasury bill for $9,760 exactly 100 days before maturity. Thirty days later, you sell the bill for $9,850.

For tax purposes, you have earned a pro rata portion of the discount as interest income for the time you held the bill: 30/100 × ($10,000 − $9,760) = $72. The other $18 you receive over and above the purchase price is a short-term capital gain.

TAXSAVER

U.S. Treasury bills are relatively short-term investments. Their maturity dates vary from a few days to 26 weeks. Since the interest income in most cases is reported at maturity (unless the bill is sold beforehand) purchasing Treasury bills with a maturity date falling in the following year offers cash basis taxpayers an opportunity to postpone interest income from one year to the next. However, if you borrow money to acquire Treasury bills, your interest expense deduction may also be deferred. See chapter 24, *Interest expense*, for an explanation.

Bonds Sold Between Interest Dates

If you sell a bond between interest payment dates, part of the sales price represents interest accrued to the date of sale. You must report that part of the sales price as interest income for the year of sale.

If you buy a bond between interest payment dates, part of the purchase price represents interest accrued before the date of purchase. When that interest is paid to you, treat it as a return of your capital investment, rather than interest income, by reducing your basis in the bond. See *Accrued interest on bonds* under *How To Report Interest Income* in chapter 1 of Publication 550 for information on reporting the payment.

EXPLANATION

Usually, interest on a bond is paid every 6 months. When a bond is sold between interest payment dates, the seller is entitled to payment from the buyer for the interest earned since the issuer's last interest payment, in addition to payment for the bond itself. This extra payment—often called "purchased interest" on a broker's statement—is interest income to the seller of the bond, reportable for tax purposes as of the date of the sale. The buyer of the bond should record the purchased interest separately from the price of the bond in his or her records. The purchased interest partially offsets the first interest payment made to the buyer.

If the purchased interest is paid in 2011 but the first interest payment is not received until 2012, the buyer should report the purchased interest as an adjustment to interest income in 2012, not in 2011.

Example 1

On April 1, 2011, Cindy bought from Michelle a $10,000 bond yielding 10%. Interest on the bond is paid on January 1 and July 1 of each year. Cindy paid $10,250, representing $10,000 in principal plus $250 for interest earned from January 1 to April 1. Thus, Michelle received $250 of interest income on April 1, 2011. Cindy received her first interest check on July 1, 2011. Half of the $500 Cindy received on July 1 represented a payment of purchased interest, and the other half represented interest income. In order to avoid any IRS notices, Cindy should report the full $500 on Schedule B (Form 1040 or Form 1040A) and also show a subtraction for $250 of interest that she purchased.

Insurance

Life insurance proceeds paid to you as beneficiary of the insured person are usually not taxable. But if you receive the proceeds in installments, you must usually report a part of each installment payment as interest income.

For more information about insurance proceeds received in installments, see Publication 525, *Taxable and Nontaxable Income.*

Annuity. If you buy an annuity with life insurance proceeds, the annuity payments you receive are taxed as pension and annuity income from a nonqualified plan, not as interest income. See chapter 10 for information on pension and annuity income from nonqualified plans.

State or Local Government Obligations

Interest on a bond used to finance government operations generally is not taxable if the bond is issued by a state, the District of Columbia, a possession of the United States, or any of their political subdivisions.

Bonds issued after 1982 (including tribal economic development bonds issued after February 17, 2009) by an Indian tribal government are treated as issued by a state. Interest on these bonds is generally tax exempt if the bonds are part of an issue of which substantially all proceeds are to be used in the exercise of any essential government function.

Similarly, a $12,000, 10-year tax-exempt municipal bond with a 5.2% coupon ($624 interest per year) purchased on May 1, 2001, at $10,000 will yield a total of $8,240 over the life of the bond: $624 of tax-free interest each year plus $200 of taxable interest income each year if the bond is held to maturity. The $200 represents the annual market discount accretion. But the taxable interest income will be subject to tax of up to 35%, so the net earnings for the 10 years may be reduced to $7,540.

TAXPLANNER

When you are determining whether to invest in tax-exempt securities, compare the net after-tax income from a tax-exempt investment with a similar taxable investment.

Equivalent Yield Needed from a Taxable Bond

Tax-Exempt Yield	Based on Your Combined Federal and State Marginal Tax Bracket						
	27%	30%	33%	35%	38.6%	42%	44%
3.50	4.79	5.00	5.22	5.38	5.70	6.03	6.25
4.00	5.48	5.71	5.97	6.15	6.51	6.90	7.14
4.50	6.16	6.43	6.72	6.92	7.33	7.76	8.04
5.00	6.85	7.14	7.46	7.69	8.14	8.62	8.93
5.50	7.53	7.86	8.21	8.46	8.96	9.48	9.82
6.00	8.22	8.57	8.96	9.23	9.77	10.34	10.71
6.50	8.90	9.29	9.70	10.00	10.59	11.21	11.61
7.00	9.59	10.00	10.45	10.77	12.0	12.07	12.50

For information on federally guaranteed bonds, mortgage revenue bonds, arbitrage bonds, private activity bonds, qualified tax credit bonds, and Build America bonds, see *State or Local Government Obligations* in chapter 1 of Publication 550.

Information reporting requirement. If you must file a tax return, you are required to show any tax-exempt interest you received on your return. This is an information-reporting requirement only. It does not change tax-exempt interest to taxable interest.

EXPLANATION

Payers of tax-exempt interest are required to report those payments to you and the IRS.

Original Issue Discount (OID)

Original issue discount (OID) is a form of interest. You generally include OID in your income as it accrues over the term of the debt instrument, whether or not you receive any payments from the issuer.

A debt instrument generally has OID when the instrument is issued for a price that is less than its stated redemption price at maturity. OID is the difference between the stated redemption price at maturity and the issue price.

All debt instruments that pay no interest before maturity are presumed to be issued at a discount. Zero coupon bonds are one example of these instruments.

The OID accrual rules generally do not apply to short-term obligations (those with a fixed maturity date of 1 year or less from date of issue). See *Discount on Short-Term Obligations* in chapter 1 of Publication 550.

De minimis **OID.** You can treat the discount as zero if it is less than one-fourth of 1% (.0025) of the stated redemption price at maturity multiplied by the number of full years from the date of original issue to maturity. This small discount is known as *"de minimis"* OID.

Example 1. You bought a 10-year bond with a stated redemption price at maturity of $1,000, issued at $980 with OID of $20. One-fourth of 1% of $1,000 (stated redemption price) times 10 (the number of full years from the date of original issue to maturity) equals $25. Because the $20 discount is less than $25, the OID is treated as zero. (If you hold the bond at maturity, you will recognize $20 ($1,000 − $980) of capital gain.)

Example 2. The facts are the same as in *Example 1*, except that the bond was issued at $950. The OID is $50. Because the $50 discount is more than the $25 figured in *Example 1*, you must include the OID in income as it accrues over the term of the bond.

Debt instrument bought after original issue. If you buy a debt instrument with *de minimis* OID at a premium, the discount is not includible in income. If you buy a debt instrument with *de minimis* OID at a discount, the discount is reported under the market discount rules. See *Market Discount Bonds* in chapter 1 of Publication 550.

Exceptions to reporting OID. The OID rules discussed in this chapter do not apply to the following debt instruments.

1. Tax-exempt obligations. (However, see *Stripped tax-exempt obligations* under *Stripped Bonds and Coupons* in chapter 1 of Publication 550).
2. U.S. savings bonds.
3. Short-term debt instruments (those with a fixed maturity date of not more than 1 year from the date of issue).
4. Obligations issued by an individual before March 2, 1984.
5. Loans between individuals, if all the following are true.
   a. The lender is not in the business of lending money.
   b. The amount of the loan, plus the amount of any outstanding prior loans between the same individuals, is $10,000 or less.
   c. Avoiding any federal tax is not one of the principal purposes of the loan.

EXPLANATION

The IRS interpretation is misleading with respect to tax-exempt obligations issued after September 3, 1982, and acquired after March 1, 1984. Even though interest on such obligations is tax-free, the OID rules will apply in determining the basis of the security in the event of sale, exchange, or maturity. (See the discussion later in this chapter.)

In addition, the original issue discount on a stripped tax-exempt bond may be treated as taxable interest if the stripped bond is sold at a discount rate that is higher than the original issue.

Form 1099-OID. The issuer of the debt instrument (or your broker, if you held the instrument through a broker) should give you Form 1099-OID, Original Issue Discount, or a similar statement, if the total OID for the calendar year is $10 or more. Form 1099-OID will show, in box 1, the amount of OID for the part of the year that you held the bond. It also will show, in box 2, the stated interest you must include in your income. A copy of Form 1099-OID will be sent to the IRS. Do not file your copy with your return. Keep it for your records.

In most cases, you must report the entire amount in boxes 1 and 2 of Form 1099-OID as interest income. But see *Refiguring OID shown on Form 1099-OID*, later in this discussion, for more information.

Form 1099-OID not received. If you had OID for the year but did not receive a Form 1099-OID you can find tables on *www.irs.gov* that list total OID on certain debt instruments and have information that will help you figure OID. The tables are available at *www.irs.gov/formspubs/article/0,,id=213465,00.html*. If your debt instrument is not listed, consult the issuer for further information about the accrued OID for the year.

Nominee. If someone else is the holder of record (the registered owner) of an OID instrument belonging to you and receives a Form 1099-OID on your behalf, that person must give you a Form 1099-OID.

Refiguring OID shown on Form 1099-OID. You must refigure the OID shown in box 1 or box 6 of Form 1099-OID if either of the following apply.

- You bought the debt instrument after its original issue and paid a premium or an acquisition premium.
- The debt instrument is a stripped bond or a stripped coupon (including certain zero coupon instruments).

For information about figuring the correct amount of OID to include in your income, see *Figuring OID on Long-Term Debt Instruments* in Publication 1212.

EXPLANATION

Stripped coupon bonds are coupon bonds that have been separated into component parts. The coupons represent claims for interest payments, which are paid on a periodic basis. The bond itself represents the claim for the repayment of the principal, which occurs at some future time.

Example

A 10-year $10,000, 9% bond (interest paid semiannually) was issued on January 1, 2011, for $10,000. On April 1, 2011, when the bond had a market price of $9,900, the coupons were stripped from the bond so that they and the bond became separate assets that could be bought and sold in the marketplace. In other words, the holder could have sold the right to receive $450 semiannually for the next 9¾ years and could have independently sold the right to receive the $10,000 on January 1, 2021.

Assume that the right to receive 20 semiannual payments is worth $4,100 and the right to receive $10,000 on January 1, 2021, is worth $5,800. The tax treatment to buyer and to seller is as follows:

The seller:

1. Include the accrued interest income of $225 from January 1, 2011, through April 1, 2011, in income.
2. Increase your basis by the $225 to $10,225.
3. Allocate the basis, using fair market value, to the coupons [($4,100 ÷ $9,900) × $10,225 = $4,235] and the bond [($5,800 ÷ $9,900) × $10,225 = $5,990].
4. Compare the proceeds for what you sell—either the coupons or the bond—with the basis figured above to determine if you've had a gain or a loss.
5. The difference between the basis of what is not sold and the amount that will be received over time is considered an original issue discount (OID). That amount is treated as earned over the life of the asset. Thus, if the coupons were retained, the difference between their basis ($4,235) and the amount that will be received over time ($450 semiannually for 10 years, or $9,000) would be the original issue discount.

In this example, $4,765 in interest income must be included on your returns over the 10 years. The amount to be included in your income for each year is figured by performing a complicated computation, for which you will probably require professional assistance.

Similarly, if the bond were retained, the difference between its basis ($5,990) and the proceeds ($10,000) would be its original issue discount. Again, complicated computations are required to determine the amount included in your income each year.

The buyer: The difference between what you pay and what you will receive over time is the original issue discount. A special computation is necessary to figure how much you should include in income each year.

Refiguring periodic interest shown on Form 1099-OID. If you disposed of a debt instrument or acquired it from another holder during the year, see *Bonds Sold Between Interest Dates*, earlier, for information about the treatment of periodic interest that may be shown in box 2 of Form 1099-OID for that instrument.

EXPLANATION

These rules also apply to debt instruments issued by individuals after March 1, 1984. This will affect individuals who borrow and lend at a discounted rate.

The current law also makes original issue discount the general rule with regard to obligations issued after July 18, 1984, and purchased in the open market. (This law also applies to bonds issued before July 19, 1984, and purchased after April 30, 1993.) If you sell property after December 31, 1984, or buy a bond in the marketplace that was issued after July 18, 1984, or a bond issued prior to July 19, 1984, and purchased after April 30, 1993, you must determine whether there is original issue discount and, if so, how much. Some of that amount will be included in your ordinary income each year. You will likely need professional help to make this calculation. For more information, see *Market discount bonds*, later in this chapter.

Example

Assume that Jorge purchases a publicly traded 6% $1 million bond that was issued after December 31, 1984, for $900,000. The bond has a maturity of 10 years at the time of purchase. Jorge will also receive $60,000 in interest each year.

The computation of the amount of original issue discount to be included is as follows:

		Face value	$1,000,000		
		Purchase price	$900,000		
		Length of term	10		
		Coupon rate	6%		

Period	Beginning basis	Total interest income	OID portion	Interest portion	Ending basis
1	$900,000	$69,533	9,533	$60,000	$909,533
2	909,533	69,634	9,634	60,000	919,166
3	919,166	69,736	9,736	60,000	928,902
4	928,902	69,839	9,839	60,000	938,740
5	938,740	69,943	9,943	60,000	948,683
6	948,683	70,048	10,048	60,000	958,732
7	958,732	70,155	10,155	60,000	968,866
8	968,886	70,262	10,262	60,000	979,148
9	979,148	70,371	70,371	60,000	989,519
10	989,519	70,481	70,481	60,000	1,000,000
		$700,000	$100,000	$600,000	

The total interest income recognized for the first year will be $69,533 ($60,000 interest and $9,533 of OID). Further special computations will be required if the obligation is sold prior to maturity. Professional advice is absolutely essential for anyone who needs to make special OID computations.

TAXPLANNER

A zero-coupon bond is one that is purchased at a substantial discount and pays no interest during its life.

If you buy a zero-coupon bond, you do not bear the investment risk entailed in reinvesting interest payments received over the life of the bond because there are no such payments. Moreover, since the issue price and the maturity value have been derived from compound interest tables, you may figure what the precise return on your investment will be if the bond is held until it matures. This is true only of zero-coupon bonds.

Note: Because you do not receive the interest until a zero-coupon bond matures, the market value of the bond during the holding period can be very volatile as market interest rates change. The longer the maturity is, the more volatile is the price.

Even though the interest on a zero-coupon bond is not paid until maturity, it is included in income each year. Consequently, an individual must pay tax on income that he or she has not yet received. However, if the bonds are owned in your IRA or Keogh plan, this income is not currently taxable. (See chapter 17, *Individual retirement arrangements [IRAs].*) The advantage, however, is that you lock in an interest rate.

On the other hand, nontaxable zero-coupon bonds, such as zero-coupon municipal bonds, may be attractive to individuals in a high tax bracket for the obvious reasons that interest rates are locked in and the increase in value each year is not taxable. In this case, you increase your cost basis on the bonds each year by the amount of the original issue discount applicable to that year, even though you don't pay any federal tax on the income. You may, however, have to pay state income taxes. You will need to check your state tax rules.

Example 1

Assume that Jennifer purchases a 10-year $100,000, non-taxable zero-coupon bond on June 30, 2011, for $50,000. The chart below and on the next page illustrates how the basis of the bond increases over the life of the bond.

Face value		$100,000
Purchase price		$50,000
Length of term		10

Period	Beginning basis	OID	Ending basis
1	$50,000	$3,589	$53,589
2	53,589	3,846	57,435
3	57,435	4,122	61,557
4	61,557	4,418	65,975
5	65,975	4,735	70,711
6	70,711	5,075	75,786
7	75,786	5,439	81,225
8	81,225	5,830	87,055
9	87,055	6,248	93,303
10	93,303	6,697	100,000
		$50,000	

The method for determining original issue discount illustrated in this example is applicable to tax-exempt bonds. The annual increase in basis is determined accordingly. However, the original issue discount computation is not the method used for a tax-exempt bond issued before September 4, 1982, and acquired before March 2, 1984. Instead, a rule is used that allocates the discount proportionately over the life of the bond.

Certificates of deposit (CDs). If you buy a CD with a maturity of more than 1 year, you must include in income each year a part of the total interest due and report it in the same manner as other OID.

This also applies to similar deposit arrangements with banks, building and loan associations, etc., including:
- Time deposits,
- Bonus plans,
- Savings certificates,
- Deferred income certificates,
- Bonus savings certificates, and
- Growth savings certificates.

TAXPLANNER

A time deposit with a penalty for early withdrawal is one of the few investments that permits you to defer the recognition of income to a subsequent year when the investment matures rather than in the year when the interest accrues. Other examples are U.S. savings bonds and U.S. Treasury bills.

Bearer CDs. CDs issued after 1982 generally must be in registered form. Bearer CDs are CDs not in registered form. They are not issued in the depositor's name and are transferable from one individual to another.

Banks must provide the IRS and the person redeeming a bearer CD with a Form 1099-INT.

EXPLANATION

Market discount bonds. A market discount bond is any bond having market discount except:
1. Short-term obligations (those with fixed maturity dates of up to 1 year from the date of issue)
2. Tax-exempt obligations that you bought before May 1, 1993
3. U.S. savings bonds
4. Certain installment obligations

Market discount arises when the value of a debt obligation decreases after its issue date, generally because of an increase in interest rates. If you buy a bond on the secondary market, it may have market discount.

If you dispose of a market discount bond, you generally must recognize the gain as taxable interest income up to the amount of the bond's **accrued market discount**, if:
1. The bond was issued after July 18, 1984, or
2. You purchased the bond after April 30, 1993.

The rest of the gain is capital gain if the bond was a capital asset.

More information. See chapter 1 of Publication 550 for more information about OID and related topics, such as market discount bonds.

When To Report Interest Income

When to report your interest income depends on whether you use the cash method or an accrual method to report income.

Cash method. Most individual taxpayers use the cash method. If you use this method, you generally report your interest income in the year in which you actually or constructively receive it. However, there are special rules for reporting the discount on certain debt instruments. See *U.S. Savings Bonds* and *Original Issue Discount*, earlier.

Example. On September 1, 2009, you loaned another individual $2,000 at 12%, compounded annually. You are not in the business of lending money. The note stated that principal and interest would be due on August 31, 2011. In 2011, you received $2,508.80 ($2,000 principal and $508.80 interest). If you use the cash method, you must include in income on your 2011 return the $508.80 interest you received in that year.

Constructive receipt. You constructively receive income when it is credited to your account or made available to you. You do not need to have physical possession of it. For example, you are considered to receive interest, dividends, or other earnings on any deposit or account in a bank, savings and loan, or similar financial institution, or interest on life insurance policy dividends left to accumulate, when they are credited to your account and subject to your withdrawal. This is true even if they are not yet entered in your passbook.

You constructively receive income on the deposit or account even if you must:
• Make withdrawals in multiples of even amounts,
• Give a notice to withdraw before making the withdrawal,
• Withdraw all or part of the account to withdraw the earnings, or
• Pay a penalty on early withdrawals, unless the interest you are to receive on an early withdrawal or redemption is substantially less than the interest payable at maturity.

Accrual method. If you use an accrual method, you report your interest income when you earn it, whether or not you have received it. Interest is earned over the term of the debt instrument.

Example. If, in the previous example, you use an accrual method, you must include the interest in your income as you earn it. You would report the interest as follows: 2009, $80; 2010, $249.60; and 2011, $179.20.

Coupon bonds. Interest on coupon bonds is taxable in the year the coupon becomes due and payable. It does not matter when you mail the coupon for payment.

How To Report Interest Income

Generally, you report all your taxable interest income on Form 1040, line 8a; Form 1040A, line 8a; or Form 1040EZ, line 2.

You cannot use Form 1040EZ if your interest income is more than $1,500. Instead, you must use Form 1040A or Form 1040.

Form 1040A. You must complete Schedule B (Form 1040A or 1040) if you file Form 1040A and any of the following are true.
1. Your taxable interest income is more than $1,500.
2. You are claiming the interest exclusion under the *Education Savings Bond Program* (discussed earlier).
3. You received interest from a seller-financed mortgage, and the buyer used the property as a home.
4. You received a Form 1099-INT for U.S. savings bond interest that includes amounts you reported before 2011.

5. You received, as a nominee, interest that actually belongs to someone else.
6. You received a Form 1099-INT for interest on frozen deposits.
7. You are reporting OID in an amount less than the amount shown on Form 1099-OID.
8. You received a Form 1099-INT for interest on a bond you bought between interest payment dates.
9. You acquired taxable bonds after 1987 and choose to reduce interest income from the bonds by any amortizable bond premium (see *Bond Premium Amortization* in chapter 3 of Publication 550).

List each payer's name and the amount of interest income received from each payer on line 1. If you received a Form 1099-INT or Form 1099-OID from a brokerage firm, list the brokerage firm as the payer.

You cannot use Form 1040A if you must use Form 1040, as described next.

Form 1040. You must use Form 1040 instead of Form 1040A or Form 1040EZ if:
1. You forfeited interest income because of the early withdrawal of a time deposit;
2. You acquired taxable bonds after 1987, you choose to reduce interest income from the bonds by any amortizable bond premium, and you are deducting the excess of bond premium amortization for the accrual period over the qualified stated interest for the period (see *Bond Premium Amortization* in chapter 3 of Publication 550); or
3. You received tax-exempt interest from private activity bonds issued after August 7, 1986.

Schedule B. You must complete Schedule B (Form 1040A or 1040), if you file Form 1040 and any of the following apply.
1. Your taxable interest income is more than $1,500.
2. You are claiming the interest exclusion under the _Education Savings Bond Program_ (discussed earlier).
3. You received interest from a seller-financed mortgage, and the buyer used the property as a home.
4. You received a Form 1099-INT for U.S. savings bond interest that includes amounts you reported before 2011.
5. You received, as a nominee, interest that actually belongs to someone else.
6. You received a Form 1099-INT for interest on frozen deposits.
7. You received a Form 1099-INT for interest on a bond you bought between interest payment dates.
8. You are reporting OID in an amount less than the amount shown on Form 1099-OID.
9. Statement (2) in the preceding list under Form 1040 is true.

In Part I, line 1, list each payer's name and the amount received from each. If you received a Form 1099-INT or Form 1099-OID from a brokerage firm, list the brokerage firm as the payer.

Reporting tax-exempt interest. Total your tax-exempt interest (such as interest or accrued OID on certain state and municipal bonds) and exempt-interest dividends from a mutual fund as shown in box 8 of Form 1099-INT. Add this amount to any other tax-exempt interest you received. Report the total on line 8b of Form 1040A or 1040. If you file Form 1040EZ, enter "TEI" and the amount in the space to the left of line 2. Do not add tax-exempt interest in the total on Form 1040EZ, line 2.

Box 9 shows the tax-exempt interest subject to the alternative minimum tax on Form 6251, Alternative Minimum Tax—Individuals. It is already included in the amount in box 8. Do not add the amount in box 9 to, or subtract from, the amount in box 8.

Caution

Do not report interest from an individual retirement account (IRA) as tax-exempt interest.

Form 1099-INT. Your taxable interest income, except for interest from U.S. savings bonds and Treasury obligations, is shown in box 1 of Form 1099-INT. Add this amount to any other taxable interest income you received. You must report all of your taxable interest income even if you do not receive a Form 1099-INT. Contact your financial institution if you do not receive a Form 1099-INT by February 15.

If you forfeited interest income because of the early withdrawal of a time deposit, the deductible amount will be shown on Form 1099-INT in box 2. See *Penalty on early withdrawal of savings* in chapter 1 of Publication 550.

Box 3 of Form 1099-INT shows the interest income you received from U.S. savings bonds, Treasury bills, Treasury notes, and Treasury bonds. Add the amount shown in box 3 to any other taxable interest income you received, unless part of the amount in box 3 was previously included in your interest income. If part of the amount shown in box 3 was previously included in your interest income, see _U.S. savings bond interest previously reported_, later.

Box 4 of Form 1099-INT (federal income tax withheld) will contain an amount if you were subject to backup withholding. Report the amount from box 4 on Form 1040EZ, line 7; on Form 1040A, line 36; or on Form 1040, line 62 (federal income tax withheld).

Box 5 of Form 1099-INT shows investment expenses you may be able to deduct as an itemized deduction. See chapter 29 for more information about investment expenses.

If there are entries in boxes 6 and 7 of Form 1099-INT, you must file Form 1040. You may be able to take a credit for the amount shown in box 6 (foreign tax paid) unless you deduct this amount on Schedule A of Form 1040 as "Other taxes." To take the credit, you may have to file Form 1116, Foreign Tax Credit. For more information, see Publication 514, *Foreign Tax Credit for Individuals*.

TAXALERT

If you receive a Form 1099-INT that includes an amount of foreign tax paid in box 6, it is likely that the interest was generated by some foreign asset you owned during the year. As noted previously in this chapter, starting in 2011, Form 8938, Statement of Specified Foreign Financial Assets, must be filed with your income tax return if you have an interest in foreign financial assets with an aggregate value of over $50,000. Because the measurement of account value is based on the combined total of the highest value of each of your foreign assets and financial accounts during the calendar year, it is important to consider all of your assets that are invested outside of the United States when determining whether you are required to file Form 8938. Even small accounts may be subject to reporting if the total of all account "maximum balances" exceeds $50,000 at any time during the calendar year. As of the date this book went to press, the instructions for this Form 8938 had not yet been published. Please access the *Ernst & Young Tax Guide 2012* website at *ey.com/EYTaxGuide* for updated information on this topic.

U.S. savings bond interest previously reported. If you received a Form 1099-INT for U.S. savings bond interest, the form may show interest you do not have to report. See *Form 1099-INT for U.S. savings bonds interest*, earlier, under *U.S. Savings Bonds*.

On Schedule B (Form 1040A or 1040), Part I, line 1, report all the interest shown on your Form 1099-INT. Then follow these steps.

1. Several lines above line 2, enter a subtotal of all interest listed on line 1.
2. Below the subtotal enter "U.S. Savings Bond Interest Previously Reported" and enter amounts previously reported or interest accrued before you received the bond.
3. Subtract these amounts from the subtotal and enter the result on line 2.

More information. For more information about how to report interest income, see chapter 1 of Publication 550 or the instructions for the form you must file.

TAXORGANIZER
Records you should keep:
Keep a list of the sources and amounts of interest income received during the year. In particular, keep the following forms that report interest you received for at least 3 years:
• Form 1099-INT
• Form 1099-OID
• Any substitute 1099, such as a broker statement or year-end account summary
You should also keep a written record of Series EE and Series I U.S. savings bonds issued after 1989. Include the serial number, issue date, face value, and amount of redemption proceeds of each bond. You may also use Form 8818.

Chapter 8
Dividends and other corporate distributions

ey.com/EYTaxGuide

Note

IRS Publication 17 (*Your Federal Income Tax*) has been updated by Ernst & Young LLP for 2011. Dates and dollar amounts shown are for 2011. Underlined type is used to indicate where IRS text has been updated. Places where text has been removed are indicated by the sentence: *Text intentionally omitted*.

ey.com/EYTaxGuide

Ernst & Young LLP will update the *Ernst & Young Tax Guide 2012* website with relevant taxpayer information as it becomes available. You can also sign up for email alerts to let you know when changes have been made.

Introduction

Most people think they know what dividends are. The problem is that the term is commonly used to describe a large number of items that the IRS does not consider to be dividends. "Dividends" paid by an insurance company to its policyholders are considered by the IRS to be a return of premiums, not dividends. "Dividends" paid by a savings and loan association to its depositors are considered to be interest, not dividends.

So what is a dividend? A dividend is a share of a corporation's profits that is distributed to shareholders. This chapter discusses how these distributions, as well as other corporate distributions, are taxed.

If you own stock in a company or shares in a mutual fund or real estate investment trust (REIT), you may receive dividend distributions. The distributing company or mutual fund will send you a Form 1099-DIV just after year-end with the total amount of dividends you must report to the IRS on your income tax return. This chapter explains the difference between the various tax forms you may receive and which forms to keep in your records or attach to your income tax return.

This chapter also discusses dividend reinvestment plans (DRPs) that reinvest the dividends in the stock generating them. These plans are provided by companies for all their shareholders and should not be confused with retirement plans run by employers for the benefit of their employees.

Certain dividend income, referred to as "qualified dividend income," is taxed at a maximum rate of 15%. This lower rate on qualified dividend income (but not interest income) applies to both the regular tax and the alternative minimum tax. For taxpayers in the 10% and 15% tax brackets, qualified dividends are subject to no tax in 2011. The reduced rate on qualified dividends is scheduled to expire at the end of 2012, with dividends being once again subject to tax at ordinary income tax rates, unless Congress acts to further extend the reduced rate. For updated information on this and any other tax law changes that occur after this book is published, see our website, *ey.com/EYTaxGuide*.

TAXALERT

Tax on child's investment income. Form 8615, Tax for Certain Children Who Have Investment Income of More than $1,900, is required to figure the tax for a child with investment income of more than $1,900 if the child:

1. Was under age 18 at the end of 2011,
2. Was age 18 at the end of 2011 and did not have earned income that was more than half of the child's support, or
3. Was a full-time student over age 18 and under age 24 at the end of 2011 and did not have earned income that was more than half of the child's support.

Tax Breaks and Deductions You Can Use Checklist

Qualified Dividend Income. Qualified dividend income is currently subject to a maximum tax rate of 15%, the same as that on long-term capital gains. However, taxpayers who are in the 10% and 15% tax brackets have a zero percent tax rate applied to qualified dividend income (and to long-term capital gains. See chapter 16, *Reporting gains and losses*) in 2011. The twist is that not all dividend income is "qualified," so look carefully before you invest. For example, most income from money market funds is not qualified dividend income. Dividends from foreign corporations, on the other hand, may be qualified. Although the tax rates on dividends are scheduled to remain constant through 2012, you may want to evaluate whether those dividend-producing investments you intend to hold beyond 2012 will be appropriate for you in later years.

Foreign Dividends. If you received dividends on foreign corporation stock that you own, it's likely that the corporation withheld foreign tax on those payments. Don't report the net amount on your tax return. Instead, you should report the full amount of the dividend (before withholding) and claim the foreign tax withheld either as a credit or as a deduction on your return. See chapter 23, *Taxes you may deduct*, and chapter 37, *Other credits including the earned income credit*.

Life Insurance Dividends. "Dividends" paid out on life insurance policies are not taxable income. They are actually considered to be a return of your premiums. You should not report them on your return unless their total is more than your accumulated premiums.

The election to report a child's investment income on a parent's return and the special rule for when a child must file Form 6251, Alternative Minimum Tax–Individuals, also applies to the children listed above. For more information, see *Tax on investment income of certain children* under *General Information*, later.

Reminder

Foreign income. If you are a U.S. citizen with dividend income from sources outside the United States (foreign income), you must report that income on your tax return unless it is exempt by U.S. law. This is true whether you reside inside or outside the United States and whether or not you receive a Form 1099 from the foreign payer.

TAXSAVER

Foreign dividends. Foreign governments often withhold tax on dividends from foreign corporations before you receive them. For example, if you are a stockholder in a Canadian company that declares a $100 dividend, you might receive only $85 because of a $15 Canadian withholding tax. Nevertheless, the $100 must be reported on your U.S. income tax return. The $15 of foreign taxes may be claimed either as a foreign tax credit using Form 1116 or as an itemized deduction on Schedule A (Form 1040). It is generally preferable to take the tax credit. For more on this subject, see chapter 23, *Taxes you may deduct*, and chapter 37, *Other credits including the earned income credit*.

TAXSAVER

Individuals with $300 or less of foreign taxes paid ($600 for joint filers) are able to take a foreign tax credit for that entire amount. This is an exemption from the limitation of offsetting foreign tax credits against U.S. tax liability, which applies to taxes paid in excess of $300 ($600 married filing joint). The exemption must be elected each year and is only available if all foreign source income is qualified passive income.

Example

You are a single individual who invests in a mutual fund that holds foreign securities. During 2011, your share of foreign taxes paid by this mutual fund is $250. When you prepare your 2011 tax return, you can claim an exemption from the foreign tax credit limitation and credit the full $250 against your U.S. tax liability.

TAXALERT

Dividends paid on foreign corporation stocks that are readily tradable on U.S. securities markets are eligible for the preferential 15% federal tax rate applicable to qualified dividend income. For this purpose, a share will be treated as so traded if an American Depository Receipt (ADR) backed by such a share is readily tradable on an established securities market in the United States. Moreover, dividends from corporations incorporated in a U.S. possession, or those eligible for benefits under a comprehensive income tax treaty with the United States, are generally eligible for the lower rate. Dividends paid by foreign personal holding companies, foreign investment companies, and passive foreign investment companies do not qualify for the reduced tax rates.

TAXALERT

In 2011, dividends received by an individual shareholder from domestic corporations and "qualified foreign corporations" are eligible for the same reduced federal tax rate as net capital gain income. These reduced rates apply for both the regular tax and the alternative minimum tax.

Thus, dividends are taxed at a maximum rate of 15%. Dividends received by taxpayers subject to tax brackets of 15% or lower are taxed at 0% in 2011.

This reduced tax rate only applies to dividends from common shares held for more than 60 days during the 121-day period beginning 60 days before the ex-dividend period. (The ex-dividend date is the date that determines whether the seller, rather than the buyer, receives the announced dividend.) Hence, this provision combined with the 15% top rate on long-term capital gains makes short-term investing less tax-efficient.

These lower rates on qualified dividends are scheduled to expire after 2012, after which time dividends will be subject to tax at ordinary income tax rates unless Congress acts to further extend the reduced rate. Many commentators expect income tax rates, including those applicable to dividend income, to rise for 2013 and beyond, but as of the publication date of this guide, we are far from knowing the ultimate result of today's tax reform debate. For updated information on this and any other tax law changes that occur after this book is published, see our website, *ey.com/EYTaxGuide*.

Example

You purchase dividend-paying common stock on February 1 and sell it November 1. The company declares dividends on March 31, June 30, and September 30. The lower tax rates apply to all dividends because you held the stock for more than 60 days out of the 121-day period that began 60 days in advance of each ex-dividend date. If you purchase stock on March 1 and sell it on April 15, a March 31 dividend would not qualify for the lower tax rates because you did not hold it for more than 60 days.

Dividends Used to Buy More Stock. If you invest in stock and choose to have the dividends reinvested to purchase additional stock, your basis in the stock is increased by the amount of dividends reinvested. The dividends are taxable to you even though you did not receive the cash, but the basis of your stock is increased by the amount of the dividends reinvested. When the stock is sold, don't forget to increase your basis by the amount of the dividends reinvested.

TAXALERT

You only need to attach Schedule B and report individual dividends if your total dividend income exceeds $1,500.

This chapter discusses the tax treatment of:
- **Ordinary dividends,**
- **Capital gain distributions,**
- **Nondividend distributions, and**
- **Other distributions you may receive from a corporation or a mutual fund.**

This chapter also explains how to report dividend income on your tax return.

Dividends are distributions of money, stock, or other property paid to you by a corporation or by a mutual fund. You also may receive dividends through a partnership, an estate, a trust, or an association that is taxed as a corporation. However, some amounts you receive that are called dividends are actually interest income. (See *Dividends that are actually interest* under *Taxable Interest* in chapter 7.)

EXPLANATION

There are generally two different types of corporations: S corporations and C corporations. The treatment of distributions from S corporations to shareholders differs from that of C corporations to their shareholders.

In this chapter, the IRS is referring to C corporations only, because S corporations do not technically pay dividends. See chapter 12, *Other income*, for information on distributions from S corporations.

Most distributions are paid in cash (or check). However, distributions can consist of more stock, stock rights, other property, or services.

EXPLANATION

Any distribution to a shareholder from earnings and profits is generally a dividend. However, a distribution is not a taxable dividend if it is a return of capital to the shareholder. Most distributions are in the form of money, but they may also be in stock or other property.

An interest-free loan or below-market rate loan by a corporation to a stockholder may result in taxable dividend income to the stockholder.

Additionally, if you are a stockholder who uses company property for personal use, you are considered to be in constructive receipt of a dividend that will be taxable to you and disallowed as a tax deduction to the company. The value of a constructive dividend is the fair market value of the benefit provided to the shareholder.

TAXPLANNER

All personal loans from corporations should have written documentation and charge market interest rates. If the corporation does not charge appropriate interest on the personal loans, and if the corporation has sufficient earnings and profits, the unpaid interest will be treated as a constructive dividend of ordinary income to the borrower (individual taxpayer). Failure to correctly report this transaction may subject the borrower to penalties and interest on the underpaid tax.

Useful Items

You may want to see:

Publication

- ☐ **514**   Foreign Tax Credit for Individuals
- ☐ **550**   Investment Income and Expenses

TAXORGANIZER

Records you should keep. The following is a list of records that you should keep to substantiate your dividend figures in the event of an IRS or state examination. Generally, we recommend that you retain these records for at least 6 years. However, you should keep records related to dividend reinvestment programs for 6 years after you fully exit the program.
- 1099-DIV, Dividends and Distributions
- Dividend Reinvestment Plan Records
- Form 2439, Notice to Shareholders of Undistributed Long-Term Capital Gains
- 1099s with backup withholding for attachment to your tax return
- Form 1096, Annual Summary and Transmittal of U.S. Information Returns
- Schedule K-1 (Form 1041), Beneficiary's Share of Income, Deductions, Credits, etc.
- Schedule K-1 (Form 1065), Partner's Share of Income, Credits, Deductions, etc.
- Schedule K-1 (Form 1120S), Shareholder's Share of Income, Credits, Deductions, etc.

Form (and Instructions)

- ☐ **Schedule B**   (Form 1040A or 1040) Interest and Ordinary Dividends

General Information

This section discusses general rules for dividend income.

Tax on investment income of certain children. Part of a child's 2011 investment income may be taxed at the parent's tax rate. If it is, Form 8615, Tax for Certain Children Who Have Investment Income of More Than $1,900, must be completed and attached to the child's tax return. If not, Form 8615 is not required and the child's income is taxed at his or her own tax rate.

Some parents can choose to include the child's interest and dividends on the parent's return if certain requirements are met. If you can, use Form 8814, Parents' Election To Report Child's Interest and Dividends, for this purpose.

For more information about the tax on investment income of children and the parents' election, see chapter 32.

Beneficiary of an estate or trust. Dividends and other distributions you receive as a beneficiary of an estate or trust are generally taxable income. You should receive a Schedule K-1 (Form 1041), Beneficiary's Share of Income, Deductions, Credits, etc., from the fiduciary. Your copy of Schedule K-1 and its instructions will tell you where to report the income on your Form 1040.

Social security number (SSN). You must give your name and SSN (or individual taxpayer identification number (ITIN)) to any person required by federal tax law to make a return, statement, or other document that relates to you. This includes payers of dividends. If you do not give your SSN or ITIN to the payer of dividends, you may have to pay a penalty.

For more information on SSNs and ITINs, see *Social security number (SSN)* in chapter 17.

TAXALERT

The age at which a child's investment income may be taxed at the parent's rate is under age 19 (or under age 24 if the child is a full-time student) if they did not have earned income that was more than one-half of the support. These rules for taxing a child's investment income at their parent's rate are commonly known as the "kiddie tax" rules. Children whose earned income exceeds one-half of the amount of the support they receive are not subject to the kiddie tax under this provision. For more information, see chapter 32, *Tax on investment income of certain children.*

TAXPLANNER

To avoid paying the "kiddie tax," you should consider investments for your child that generate little or no taxable income until your child "grows out" of the reach of the kiddie tax.

Explanation

A parent may elect on Form 8814 to include on his or her return the unearned income of a child under the age of 19 whose income is less than $9,500 in 2011 and consists solely of interest, dividends, or Alaska Permanent Fund dividends. The election cannot be made if estimated payments were made in your child's name, if your child had an overpayment on his or her 2010 tax return which was applied to 2011, or if your child is subject to backup withholding. (See explanation of backup withholding, later.) The election must be made by the due date (including extensions) of the parent's tax return. A separate election must be made for each child whose income the parents choose to report.

If a child (under age 19) had income in 2011 over $1,900, it would be taxed on Form 8814 as follows: the first $950 would be tax-free, the next $950 would be taxed at 10% (0% for qualified dividends), and the amount of income over $1,900 would be taxed at the parent's tax rate. Note that the same overall tax result is achieved if the election is not made and the child files his or her own tax return. However, the child is required to attach Form 8615 to his or her return, which can be complicated if there is more than one child under age 19 required to file a return.

Explanation

In addition to dividends that may be reported on Schedule K-1 (Form 1041) for beneficiaries of estates and trusts, dividends may also be reported to you on a Schedule K-1 (Form 1065) if you are a partner in a partnership or a Schedule K-1 (Form 1120S) if you are a shareholder in an S corporation. Generally, dividends reported on a Schedule K-1 should be entered on Schedule B, Part II, line 5, of Form 1040.

Backup withholding. Your dividend income is generally not subject to regular withholding. However, it may be subject to backup withholding to ensure that income tax is collected on the income. Under backup withholding, the payer of dividends must withhold, as income tax, 28% of the amount you are paid.

Backup withholding may also be required if the IRS has determined that you underreported your interest or dividend income. For more information, see *Backup Withholding* in chapter 4.

Stock certificate in two or more names. If two or more persons hold stock as joint tenants, tenants by the entirety, or tenants in common, each person's share of any dividends from the stock is determined by local law.

Form 1099-DIV. Most corporations and mutual funds use Form 1099-DIV, Dividends and Distributions, to show you the distributions you received from them during the year. Keep this form with your records. You do not have to attach it to your tax return.

Dividends not reported on Form 1099-DIV. Even if you do not receive Form 1099-DIV, you must still report all your taxable dividend income. For example, you may receive distributive shares of dividends from partnerships or S corporations. These dividends are reported to you on Schedule K-1 (Form 1065) and Schedule K-1 (Form 1120S).

Reporting tax withheld. If tax is withheld from your dividend income, the payer must give you a Form 1099-DIV that indicates the amount withheld.

Nominees. If someone receives distributions as a nominee for you, that person will give you a Form 1099-DIV, which will show distributions received on your behalf.

If you receive a Form 1099 from a nominee, you should cite the source of that income on your tax return as the nominee, not the original payer of the income. If you receive a Form 1099 as a nominee for another person, see the section on _Nominees_ under _How to Report Dividend Income_, toward the end of this chapter, for a complete discussion on the filing and reporting requirements of a nominee.

Example

Brokerage Firm A collects your dividend from XYZ Corporation and reports the income to you on Form 1099. You should show the dividend as being received from Brokerage Firm A, not from XYZ Corporation.

Form 1099-MISC. Certain substitute payments in lieu of dividends or tax-exempt interest received by a broker on your behalf must be reported to you on Form 1099-MISC, Miscellaneous Income, or a similar statement. See _Reporting Substitute Payments_ under _Short Sales_ in chapter 4 of Publication 550 for more information about reporting these payments.

Incorrect amount shown on a Form 1099. If you receive a Form 1099 that shows an incorrect amount (or other incorrect information), you should ask the issuer for a corrected form. The new Form 1099 you receive will be marked "Corrected."

Dividends on stock sold. If stock is sold, exchanged, or otherwise disposed of after a dividend is declared but before it is paid, the owner of record (usually the payee shown on the dividend check) must include the dividend in income.

TAXALERT

If stock is sold, exchanged, or otherwise disposed of after a dividend is declared, but before it is paid, the owner of record (usually the payee shown on the dividend check) must report the dividend. Even if the purchase price of the stock goes up because of the amount of the anticipated dividend, the owner of record must report the dividend.

Explanation

Dividends on stock sold. The owner of record on the "record date" for the dividend, not the owner on the date of payment, receives the dividend.

The following timeline illustrates when you are entitled to receive dividend payments:

Declaration Date	Ex-Dividend Date	Record Date	Payment Date
The company decides to pay a dividend at some point in the future.	On or after this date, the stock trades without its dividend. If you sell your stock prior to this date, the new owner will generally receive the dividend; if you sell on or after this date, you will generally receive the dividend.	The owner as of the record date is entitled to the declared dividend.	The owner as of the record date receives payment of the dividend whether or not he or she still owns the stock.

TAXPLANNER

If you buy stock on or near the date a dividend is declared, make sure you receive all amounts due. The transaction of the sale may not be recorded in time by the corporation paying the dividend, and the former stock owner may receive payment. If you do not receive a dividend due to you, check with your broker as soon as possible.

If you receive a dividend to which you were not entitled in one year and pay it back in another, it is counted as income in the year received and a deduction in the year repaid. Show the deduction as a negative amount of dividend income on Schedule B (Form 1040 or Form 1040A). If the repayment is greater than $3,000, see the calculations for lowering your tax under *Repayments* in chapter 12, *Other Iincome*, and the further information on this topic in IRS Publication 525, *Taxable and Nontaxable iIncome*. Consult your tax advisor.

Dividends received in January. If a mutual fund (or other regulated investment company) or real estate investment trust (REIT) declares a dividend (including any exempt-interest dividend or capital gain distribution) in October, November, or December payable to shareholders of record on a date in one of those months but actually pays the dividend during January of the next calendar year, you are considered to have received the dividend on December 31. You report the dividend in the year it was declared.

TAXSAVER

You should pay close attention to the timing of your purchase of a mutual fund. For example, if you invest in a fund near the end of the year and the fund shortly thereafter makes a year-end distribution, you will have to pay tax on the distribution even though from your point of view you are simply getting back the capital you just invested in the fund. In effect, all you've done is "bought" taxable income that the fund earned earlier in the year but had not yet paid out to shareholders. Typically, the fund's share price drops by the amount of the distribution. However, your cost basis in the mutual fund will be the predistribution price you paid for the shares.

There is one consolation: Your higher basis will reduce any capital gain on a later sale, or if you sell the fund at a loss, it will increase your capital loss. If you want to limit your tax liability and lower your basis in the shares, you should delay your purchase of fund shares until after the record date for the distribution. Usually a fund can tell you when distributions, if any, for the year are expected. Alternatively, you can consult investment publications or websites, which indicate distribution dates for the previous year. They are usually a pretty good guide to future distribution dates.

Example

ABC Fund declares and distributes a $1 dividend on November 1. If you purchased 1,000 shares at $10 per share on October 31, you will have to report $1,000 of income for 2011. If you bought the shares on November 2, after the record date, you will pay $9 per share and have no taxable income to report. Of course, for the shares bought on October 31, your basis would be $10 per share instead of $9.

TAXPLANNER

If you are thinking of selling shares in a mutual fund, particularly near the end of the year when many funds pay dividends, you should consider redeeming your shares before any upcoming dividend payments are made by the fund. If your shares are worth more than you paid, you can maximize your capital gains on the redemption and avoid paying the higher tax rate due if the dividend is not a qualified dividend. (A dividend generally will qualify for the 15% reduced tax rate if you own the underlying common stock for more than 60 days during the 121-day period beginning 60 days before the "ex-dividend date," the day on which the stock starts trading without its next dividend.) If your shares are worth less than you paid for them, you can minimize your capital losses by selling before the dividend. Remember, the net asset value per share of the fund (that is, the amount you would receive on the redemption of your shares) decreases by the amount of the dividend. For more about mutual funds, see chapter 39, *Mutual funds*.

Ordinary Dividends

Ordinary (taxable) dividends are the most common type of distribution from a corporation or a mutual fund. They are paid out of earnings and profits and are ordinary income to you. This means they are not capital gains. You can assume that any dividend you receive on common or preferred stock is an ordinary dividend unless the paying corporation or mutual fund tells you otherwise. Ordinary dividends will be shown in box 1a of the Form 1099-DIV you receive.

Qualified Dividends

Qualified dividends are the ordinary dividends subject to the same 0% or 15% maximum tax rate that applies to net capital gain. They should be shown in box 1b of the Form 1099-DIV you receive.

Qualified dividends are subject to the 15% rate if the regular tax rate that would apply is 25% or higher. If the regular tax rate that would apply is lower than 25%, qualified dividends are subject to the 0% rate.

To qualify for the 0% or 15% maximum rate, all of the following requirements must be met.
- The dividends must have been paid by a U.S. corporation or a qualified foreign corporation. (See *Qualified foreign corporation* later.)
- The dividends are not of the type listed later under *Dividends that are not qualified dividends*.
- You meet the holding period (discussed next).

Holding period. You must have held the stock for more than 60 days during the 121-day period that begins 60 days before the ex-dividend date. The ex-dividend date is the first date following the declaration of a dividend on which the buyer of a stock is not entitled to receive the next dividend payment. Instead, the seller will get the dividend.

When counting the number of days you held the stock, include the day you disposed of the stock, but not the day you acquired it. See the examples later.

Exception for preferred stock. In the case of preferred stock, you must have held the stock more than 90 days during the 181-day period that begins 90 days before the ex-dividend date if the dividends are due to periods totaling more than 366 days. If the preferred dividends are due to periods totaling less than 367 days, the holding period in the previous paragraph applies.

Example 1. You bought 5,000 shares of XYZ Corp. common stock on July 8, 2011. XYZ Corp. paid a cash dividend of 10 cents per share. The ex-dividend date was July 16, 2011. Your Form 1099-DIV from XYZ Corp. shows $500 in box 1a (ordinary dividends) and in box 1b (qualified dividends). However, you sold the 5,000 shares on August 11, 2011. You held your shares of XYZ Corp. for only 34 days of the 121-day period (from July 9, 2011, through August 11, 2011). The 121-day period began on May 17, 2011 (60 days before the ex-dividend date), and ended on September 14, 2011. You have no qualified dividends from XYZ Corp. because you held the XYZ stock for less than 61 days.

Example 2. Assume the same facts as in Example 1 except that you bought the stock on July 15, 2011 (the day before the ex-dividend date), and you sold the stock on September 16, 2011. You held the stock for 63 days (from July 16, 2011, through September 16, 2011). The $500 of qualified dividends shown in box 1b of your Form 1099-DIV are all qualified dividends because you held the stock for 61 days of the 121-day period (from July 16, 2011, through September 14, 2011).

Example 3. You bought 10,000 shares of ABC Mutual Fund common stock on July 8, 2011. ABC Mutual Fund paid a cash dividend of 10 cents a share. The ex-dividend date was July 16, 2011. The ABC Mutual Fund advises you that the portion of the dividend eligible to be treated as qualified dividends equals 2 cents per share. Your Form 1099-DIV from ABC Mutual Fund shows total ordinary dividends of $1,000 and qualified dividends of $200. However, you sold the 10,000 shares on August 11, 2011. You have no qualified dividends from ABC Mutual Fund because you held the ABC Mutual Fund stock for less than 61 days.

Holding period reduced where risk of loss is diminished. When determining whether you met the minimum holding period discussed earlier, you cannot count any day during which you meet any of the following conditions.
1. You had an option to sell, were under a contractual obligation to sell, or had made (and not closed) a short sale of substantially identical stock or securities.
2. You were grantor (writer) of an option to buy substantially identical stock or securities.
3. Your risk of loss is diminished by holding one or more other positions in substantially similar or related property.

For information about how to apply condition (3), see Regulations section 1.246-5.

Qualified foreign corporation. A foreign corporation is a qualified foreign corporation if it meets any of the following conditions.
1. The corporation is incorporated in a U.S. possession.
2. The corporation is eligible for the benefits of a comprehensive income tax treaty with the United States that the Treasury Department determines is satisfactory for this purpose and that includes an exchange of information program. For a list of those treaties, see Table 8-1.
3. The corporation does not meet (1) or (2) above, but the stock for which the dividend is paid is readily tradable on an established securities market in the United States. See *Readily tradable stock*, later.

Table 8-1. **Income Tax Treaties**

Income tax treaties the United States has with the following countries satisfy requirement (2) under *Qualified foreign corporation*.		
Australia	India	Philippines
Austria	Indonesia	Poland
Bangladesh	Ireland	Portugal
Barbados	Israel	Romania
Belgium	Italy	Russian Federation
Bulgaria	Jamaica	Slovak Republic
Canada	Japan	Slovenia
China	Kazakhstan	South Africa
Cyprus	Korea	Spain
Czech Republic	Latvia	Sri Lanka
Denmark	Lithuania	Sweden
Egypt	Luxembourg	Switzerland
Estonia	Malta	Thailand
Finland	Mexico	Trinidad and Tobago
France	Morocco	Tunisia
Germany	Netherlands	Turkey
Greece	New Zealand	Ukraine
Hungary	Norway	United Kingdom
Iceland	Pakistan	Venezuela

Exception. A corporation is not a qualified foreign corporation if it is a passive foreign investment company during its tax year in which the dividends are paid or during its previous tax year.

Readily tradable stock. Any stock (such as common, ordinary stock, or preferred stock) or an American depositary receipt in respect of that stock is considered to satisfy requirement (3) if it is listed on one of the following securities markets: the New York Stock Exchange, the NASDAQ Stock Market, the American Stock Exchange, the Boston Stock Exchange, the Cincinnati Stock Exchange, the Chicago Stock Exchange, the Philadelphia Stock Exchange, or the Pacific Exchange, Inc.

Dividends that are not qualified dividends. The following dividends are not qualified dividends. They are not qualified dividends even if they are shown in box 1b of Form 1099-DIV.
- Capital gain distributions.
- Dividends paid on deposits with mutual savings banks, cooperative banks, credit unions, U.S. building and loan associations, U.S. savings and loan associations, federal savings and loan associations, and similar financial institutions. (Report these amounts as interest income.)
- Dividends from a corporation that is a tax-exempt organization or farmer's cooperative during the corporation's tax year in which the dividends were paid or during the corporation's previous tax year.
- Dividends paid by a corporation on employer securities held on the date of record by an employee stock ownership plan (ESOP) maintained by that corporation.
- Dividends on any share of stock to the extent you are obligated (whether under a short sale or otherwise) to make related payments for positions in substantially similar or related property.
- Payments in lieu of dividends, but only if you know or have reason to know the payments are not qualified dividends.
- Payments shown in Form 1099-DIV, box 1b, from a foreign corporation to the extent you know or have reason to know the payments are not qualified dividends.

TAXPLANNER
When purchasing stock, you should consider whether the dividends received will be qualified dividends that are taxed at a maximum rate of 15% or ordinary dividends taxed at the higher maximum rate of 35%.

Dividends Used to Buy More Stock

The corporation in which you own stock may have a dividend reinvestment plan. This plan lets you choose to use your dividends to buy (through an agent) more shares of stock in the corporation instead of receiving the dividends in cash. Most mutual funds also permit shareholders to automatically reinvest distributions in more shares in the fund, instead of receiving cash. If you use your dividends to buy more stock at a price equal to its fair market value, you still must report the dividends as income.

If you are a member of a dividend reinvestment plan that lets you buy more stock at a price less than its fair market value, you must report as dividend income the fair market value of the additional stock on the dividend payment date.

You also must report as dividend income any service charge subtracted from your cash dividends before the dividends are used to buy the additional stock. But you may be able to deduct the service charge. See chapter 29 for more information about deducting expenses of producing income.

In some dividend reinvestment plans, you can invest more cash to buy shares of stock at a price less than fair market value. If you choose to do this, you must report as dividend income the difference between the cash you invest and the fair market value of the stock you buy. When figuring this amount, use the fair market value of the stock on the dividend payment date.

When you sell shares acquired in a dividend reinvestment plan, you compute the gain or loss in the same way that you normally would by subtracting your cost from the proceeds of the sale. Your cost includes the amount of dividends that have been reinvested. Usually your only record of the shares' cost is the annual statement issued by the administrator of the dividend reinvestment plan. It is imperative to keep these statements as a permanent part of your records. If you don't have this information, you can contact the transfer agent who handles the company's dividend reinvestment plan. You can obtain the name from the company's investor relations office. However, some dividend reinvestment plans charge a fee for re-creating records. Alternatively, you can look up a company's dividend history in Standard & Poor's.

Example

You have accumulated 14 shares of ABC Mutual Fund through a purchase and dividend reinvestments.

Method	Shares	Cost Basis	Date
Purchase	10 shares	$100	4/30/08
Dividend			
Reinvestments	1 share	$10	12/30/09
	1 share	$15	12/28/10
	2 shares	$25	12/30/11
	14 shares	$150	

If you sold all 14 shares in 2011 for $15 per share, your gain would be $60 ($210 proceeds less $150 basis). Without proof of your dividend reinvestments, however, the IRS could argue that your basis was only the original $100 and your gain was actually $110 ($210 proceeds less $100 cost of original purchase).

Note that a portion of your $60 gain would be long-term, but the gain attributable to the 2 shares purchased on December 30, 2011, through the DRP would be short-term, because you would not have owned these shares for more than 12 months. The short-term gain would be $5 of the total gain ($30 proceeds on 2 shares less $25 cost).

See chapter 16, *Reporting gains and losses*, to determine how to calculate your gain or loss if you did not sell all 14 shares of ABC Mutual Fund at once.

Dividend reinvestment plans that permit you to invest at less than market price (e.g., whether by discount or reduction in commissions on purchase) may be a very good deal. In effect, you earn a higher yield because you are receiving "extra" shares.

Money Market Funds

Report amounts you receive from money market funds as dividend income. Money market funds are a type of mutual fund and should not be confused with bank money market accounts that pay interest.

Dividends paid from money market funds are reported as dividends—not interest—even though they represent income the money market fund received on certificates of deposit and other interest-bearing investments. Dividends from money market funds are not eligible for the lower dividend rate. These dividends must be shown in the dividend section of Schedule B (Form 1040). If they are not, you're likely to receive a notice from the IRS requesting an explanation.

However, dividends paid or credited by a mutual savings bank, building and loan association, savings and loan association, cooperative bank, or credit union are considered *interest*—not dividends—for income tax reporting purposes. The Form 1099 that you receive from these organizations tells you which type of income to report and generally instructs you on how to report the income.

Capital Gain Distributions

Capital gain distributions (also called capital gain dividends) are paid to you or credited to your account by mutual funds (or other regulated investment companies) and real estate investment trusts (REITs). They will be shown in box 2a of the Form 1099-DIV you receive from the mutual fund or REIT.

Report capital gain distributions as long-term capital gains regardless of how long you owned your shares in the mutual fund or REIT.

> ### EXPLANATION
> For 2011, capital gain distributions are reported on Schedule D, line 13. For more information, see chapter 16, *Reporting gains and losses.*

> ### TAXALERT
> Although qualifying dividends are taxed at the same rate as capital gains, a taxpayer who has net capital losses and dividend income may not offset those losses against dividends. Net capital losses can be offset against capital gain distributions, however.

Undistributed capital gains of mutual funds and REITs. Some mutual funds and REITs keep their long-term capital gains and pay tax on them. You must treat your share of these gains as distributions, even though you did not actually receive them. However, they are not included on Form 1099-DIV. Instead, they are reported to you in box 1a of Form 2439, Notice to Shareholder of Undistributed Long-Term Capital Gains.

Report undistributed capital gains (box 1a of Form 2439) as long-term capital gains on Schedule D (Form 1040), column (h), line 11.

The tax paid on these gains by the mutual fund or REIT is shown in box 2 of Form 2439. You take credit for this tax by including it on Form 1040, line 71, and checking box a on that line. Attach Copy B of Form 2439 to your return, and keep Copy C for your records.

Basis adjustment. Increase your basis in your mutual fund, or your interest in a REIT, by the difference between the gain you report and the credit you claim for the tax paid.

Additional information. For more information on the treatment of distributions from mutual funds, see Publication 550.

> ### EXPLANATION
> An investment company or mutual fund that realizes capital gains during the year has the option of whether or not to distribute the capital gains to shareholders of the mutual fund. The two different treatments are reported by shareholders as follows:
>
> *Distributed capital gains* are reported to shareholders on Form 1099-DIV box 2a. You will receive this amount in cash and must include the entire amount of the distributed capital gains in your calculation of taxable income.
>
> *Undistributed capital gains* are reported to shareholders on Form 2439. You will not receive this amount in cash. Rather, the mutual fund or real estate investment trust (REIT) has retained the capital gains and paid your proportionate share of the tax due. You will include the entire amount of the undistributed capital gains in your calculation of taxable income, but you will also be credited for the tax that the mutual fund paid on your behalf. In addition, you will increase your basis in the stock by the net amount not distributed to you.
>
> #### Example 1
> ABC Mutual Fund elects to distribute all of its 2011 capital gain. Each *shareholder will receive a pro rata share of the distribution in cash.* Each shareholder reports this distribution and pays the appropriate tax. The fund will provide each shareholder with Form 1099-DIV, which contains the amounts to be reported.
>
> #### Example 2
> ABC Mutual Fund elects to treat all of its 2011 capital gain as an undistributed capital gain. *The shareholders receive no cash distribution.* Each shareholder reports his or her share of capital gain and tax paid on his or her behalf by ABC Mutual Fund. These amounts are shown on the Form 2439 that each shareholder receives.

Nondividend Distributions

A nondividend distribution is a distribution that is not paid out of the earnings and profits of a corporation or a mutual fund. You should receive a Form 1099-DIV or other statement showing the nondividend distribution. On Form 1099-DIV, a nondividend distribution will be shown in box 3. If you do not receive such a statement, you report the distribution as an ordinary dividend.

Basis adjustment. A nondividend distribution reduces the basis of your stock. It is not taxed until your basis in the stock is fully recovered. This nontaxable portion is also called a return of capital. It is a return of your investment in the stock of the company. If you buy stock in a corporation in different lots at different times, and you cannot definitely identify the shares subject to the nondividend distribution, reduce the basis of your earliest purchases first.

When the basis of your stock has been reduced to zero, report any additional nondividend distribution you receive as a capital gain. Whether you report it as a long-term or short-term capital gain depends on how long you have held the stock. See *Holding Period* in chapter 14.

Example. You bought stock in 1997 for $100. In 2000, you received a nondividend distribution of $80. You did not include this amount in your income, but you reduced the basis of your stock to $20. You received a nondividend distribution of $30 in 2011. The first $20 of this amount reduced your basis to zero. You report the other $10 as a long-term capital gain for 2011. You must report as a long-term capital gain any nondividend distribution you receive on this stock in later years.

EXPLANATION

Some mutual fund dividends may be treated as a tax-free return of capital. This occurs when the mutual fund does not have enough current or accumulated earnings and profits to cover the distribution. In this situation, the distribution is considered to be a "return of capital" (the amount you originally invested) and is nontaxable to the extent of the basis in your shares. (Your basis is generally the price at which you bought the shares plus or minus any adjustments. See chapter 13, *Basis of property*.) This amount will be shown in box 3 of Form 1099-DIV.

Although the distribution is tax-free, it will reduce your basis in the mutual fund shares. To the extent the distribution is greater than your basis in your shares, you will be treated as having a gain from the sale or exchange of the shares. This gain must be reported on Schedule D (Form 1040). (See the IRS example directly preceding this explanation.)

TAXORGANIZER

It is extremely important to keep accurate records of nontaxable dividends. Most people do not realize that a nontaxable dividend is usually considered a return of purchase price and then a capital gain once your cost has been recovered. Keep in mind that even nontaxable dividends can become subject to tax at some point.

Liquidating Distributions

Liquidating distributions, sometimes called liquidating dividends, are distributions you receive during a partial or complete liquidation of a corporation. These distributions are, at least in part, one form of a return of capital. They may be paid in one or more installments. You will receive a Form 1099-DIV from the corporation showing you the amount of the liquidating distribution in box 8 or 9.

For more information on liquidating distributions, see chapter 1 of Publication 550.

Distributions of Stock and Stock Rights

Distributions by a corporation of its own stock are commonly known as stock dividends. Stock rights (also known as "stock options") are distributions by a corporation of rights to acquire the corporation's stock. Generally, stock dividends and stock rights are not taxable to you, and you do not report them on your return.

Taxable stock dividends and stock rights. Distributions of stock dividends and stock rights are taxable to you if any of the following apply.

1. You or any other shareholder has the choice to receive cash or other property instead of stock or stock rights.
2. The distribution gives cash or other property to some shareholders and an increase in the percentage interest in the corporation's assets or earnings and profits to other shareholders.
3. The distribution is in convertible preferred stock and has the same result as in (2).
4. The distribution gives preferred stock to some common stock shareholders and common stock to other common stock shareholders.
5. The distribution is on preferred stock. (The distribution, however, is not taxable if it is an increase in the conversion ratio of convertible preferred stock made solely to take into account a stock dividend, stock split, or similar event that would otherwise result in reducing the conversion right.)

The term "stock" includes rights to acquire stock, and the term "shareholder" includes a holder of rights or of convertible securities.

If you receive taxable stock dividends or stock rights, include their fair market value at the time of distribution in your income.

Preferred stock redeemable at a premium. If you hold preferred stock having a redemption price higher than its issue price, the difference (the redemption premium) generally is taxable as a constructive distribution of additional stock on the preferred stock. For more information, see chapter 1 of Publication 550.

Basis. Your basis in stock or stock rights received in a taxable distribution is their fair market value when distributed. If you receive stock or stock rights that are not taxable to you, see *Stocks and Bonds* under *Basis of Investment Property* in chapter 4 of Publication 550 for information on how to figure their basis.

Fractional shares. You may not own enough stock in a corporation to receive a full share of stock if the corporation declares a stock dividend. However, with the approval of the shareholders, the corporation may set up a plan in which fractional shares are not issued but instead are sold, and the cash proceeds are given to the shareholders. Any cash you receive for fractional shares under such a plan is treated as an amount realized on the sale of the fractional shares. You must determine your gain or loss and report it as a capital gain or loss on Schedule D (Form 1040). Your gain or loss is the difference between the cash you receive and the basis of the fractional shares sold.

   Example. You own one share of common stock that you bought on January 3, 2001, for $100. The corporation declared a common stock dividend of 5% on June 30, 2011. The fair market value of the stock at the time the stock dividend was declared was $200. You were paid $10 for the fractional-share stock dividend under a plan described in the above paragraph. You figure your gain or loss as follows:

Fair market value of old stock	$200.00
Fair market value of stock dividend (cash received)	+ 10.00
Fair market value of old stock and stock dividend	$210.00
Basis (cost) of old stock after the stock dividend (($200 ÷ $210) × $100)	$95.24
Basis (cost) of stock dividend (($10 ÷ $210) × $100)	+ 4.76
Total	$100.00
Cash received	$10.00
Basis (cost) of stock dividend	− 4.76
Gain	$5.24

   Because you had held the share of stock for more than 1 year at the time the stock dividend was declared, your gain on the stock dividend is a long-term capital gain.

EXPLANATION

It is *not* true that all amounts received with regard to fractional shares are treated as capital gains, as described in the IRS text.

   A distinction is made when shareholders have the *option* of receiving cash or other property instead of fractional shares. If shareholders have this option and receive cash in lieu of fractional shares, the value received is treated as dividend income. If the corporation issues cash in lieu of fractional shares of stock for the purpose of saving the trouble, expense, and inconvenience of issuing fractional shares, then the capital gain treatment described earlier applies. The transaction will be treated as though fractional shares had been received by the shareholders and were then redeemed by the corporation.

   Scrip dividends. A corporation that declares a stock dividend may issue you a scrip certificate that entitles you to a fractional share. The certificate is generally nontaxable when you receive it. If you choose to have the corporation sell the certificate for you and give you the proceeds, your gain or loss is the difference between the proceeds and the portion of your basis in the corporation's stock allocated to the certificate.

   However, if you receive a scrip certificate that you can choose to redeem for cash instead of stock, the certificate is taxable when you receive it. You must include its fair market value in income on the date you receive it.

Other Distributions

You may receive any of the following distributions during the year.

Exempt-interest dividends. Exempt-interest dividends you receive from a mutual fund or other regulated investment company are not included in your taxable income. Exempt-interest dividends should be shown in box 8 of Form 1099-INT.

Information reporting requirement. Although exempt-interest dividends are not taxable, you must show them on your tax return if you have to file a return. This is an information reporting requirement and does not change the exempt-interest dividends to taxable income.

Alternative minimum tax treatment. Exempt-interest dividends paid from specified private activity bonds may be subject to the alternative minimum tax. See *Alternative Minimum Tax* in chapter 31 for more information.

Dividends on insurance policies. Insurance policy dividends the insurer keeps and uses to pay your premiums are not taxable. However, you must report as taxable interest income the interest that is paid or credited on dividends left with the insurance company.

If dividends on an insurance contract (other than a modified endowment contract) are distributed to you, they are a partial return of the premiums you paid. Do not include them in your gross income until they are more than the total of all net premiums you paid for the contract. Report any taxable distributions on insurance policies on Form 1040, line 21.

Dividends on veterans' insurance. Dividends you receive on veterans' insurance policies are not taxable. In addition, interest on dividends left with the Department of Veterans Affairs is not taxable.

Patronage dividends. Generally, patronage dividends you receive in money from a cooperative organization are included in your income.

Do not include in your income patronage dividends you receive on:
- Property bought for your personal use, or
- Capital assets or depreciable property bought for use in your business. But you must reduce the basis (cost) of the items bought. If the dividend is more than the adjusted basis of the assets, you must report the excess as income.

These rules are the same whether the cooperative paying the dividend is a taxable or tax-exempt cooperative.

Alaska Permanent Fund dividends. Do not report these amounts as dividends. Instead, report these amounts on Form 1040, line 21; Form 1040A, line 13; or Form 1040EZ, line 3.

TAXPLANNER

Election. You can choose to include in gross income the value of restricted stock as pay for services in the year you receive the stock. See chapter 5, *Wages, salaries, and other earnings*, for more information on this election. Consult with your tax advisor if you are considering this election. If you make this choice, the dividends are treated as any other dividends.

If you elect to include in gross income the value of the restricted stock you have received, you must notify your employer so that dividend payments on the stock are no longer included in your W-2 wages.

How To Report Dividend Income

Generally, you can use either Form 1040 or Form 1040A to report your dividend income. Report the total of your ordinary dividends on line 9a of Form 1040 or Form 1040A. Report qualified dividends on line 9b of Form 1040 or Form 1040A.

If you receive capital gain distributions, you may be able to use Form 1040A or you may have to use Form 1040. See *Capital gain distributions only* in chapter 16. If you receive nondividend distributions required to be reported as capital gains, you must use Form 1040. You cannot use Form 1040EZ if you receive any dividend income.

Form 1099-DIV. If you owned stock on which you received $10 or more in dividends and other distributions, you should receive a Form 1099-DIV. Even if you do not receive Form 1099-DIV, you must report all your taxable dividend income.

See Form 1099-DIV for more information on how to report dividend income.

TAXORGANIZER

You should make sure you keep a copy of all Forms 1099-DIV that you received.

Form 1040A or 1040. You must complete Schedule B (Form 1040A or 1040), Part II, and attach it to your Form 1040A or 1040, if:

- Your ordinary dividends (Form 1099-DIV, box 1a) are more than $1,500, or
- You received, as a nominee, dividends that actually belong to someone else.

If your ordinary dividends are more than $1,500, you must also complete Schedule B, Part III.

List on Schedule B, Part II, line 5, each payer's name and the ordinary dividends you received. If your securities are held by a brokerage firm (in "street name"), list the name of the brokerage firm shown on Form 1099-DIV as the payer. If your stock is held by a nominee who is the owner of record, and the nominee credited or paid you dividends on the stock, show the name of the nominee and the dividends you received or for which you were credited.

Enter on line 6 the total of the amounts listed on line 5. Also enter this total on Form 1040, line 9a.

EXPLANATION

Exempt-interest dividends, which are treated as interest, should not be reported on Schedule B of Form 1040A. The amount should be included on line 8b of page 1. See *How to Report Interest Income* in chapter 7, *Interest income*.

EXPLANATION

Even if your dividends are less than $1,500, you must report them and, to the extent that they are taxable, pay tax on them. The $1,500 test determines whether or not you must list each dividend payer separately on Schedule B. If your dividends total less than $1,500, you can include a single amount on line 9a of page 1, Form 1040, and avoid completing Schedule B, Part II.

Qualified dividends. Report qualified dividends (Form 1099-DIV, box 1b) on line 9b of Form 1040 or Form 1040A. The amount in box 1b is already included in box 1a. Do not add the amount in box 1b to, or substract it from, the amount in box 1a.

Do not include any of the following on line 9b.

- Qualified dividends you received as a nominee. See *Nominees* under *How to Report Dividend Income* in chapter 1 of Publication 550.
- Dividends on stock for which you did not meet the holding period. See _Holding period_ earlier under *Qualified Dividends*.
- Dividends on any share of stock to the extent you are obligated (whether under a short sale or otherwise) to make related payments for positions in substantially similar or related property.
- Payments in lieu of dividends, but only if you know or have reason to know the payments are not qualified dividends.
- Payments shown in Form 1099-DIV, box 1b, from a foreign corporation to the extent you know or have reason to know the payments are not qualified dividends.

If you have qualified dividends, you must figure your tax by completing the Qualified Dividends and Capital Gain Tax Worksheet in the Form 1040 or 1040A instructions or the Schedule D Tax Worksheet in the Schedule D instructions, whichever applies. Enter qualified dividends on line 2 of the worksheet.

Investment interest deducted. If you claim a deduction for investment interest, you may have to reduce the amount of your qualified dividends that are eligible for the 0% or 15% tax rate. Reduce it by the qualified dividends you choose to include in investment income when figuring the limit on your investment interest deduction. This is done on the Qualified Dividends and Capital Gain Tax Worksheet or the Schedule D Tax Worksheet. For more information about the limit on investment interest, see _Investment expenses_ in chapter 24.

Expenses related to dividend income. You may be able to deduct expenses related to dividend income if you itemize your deductions on Schedule A (Form 1040). See chapter 29 for general information about deducting expenses of producing income.

EXPLANATION

Expenses that may be deducted include custody fees, investment advisory fees, depository fees (which are usually applicable to foreign dividends), and service charges relating to dividend income. A more complete discussion of these items appears in *chapter 29*, *Miscellaneous deductions*.

Explanation

Stock sold short. If you borrow stock to make a short sale, you may have to pay the lender an amount to replace the dividends distributed while you maintain your short position. Your treatment of the payment depends on the kind of distribution for which you are reimbursing the lender of the stock.

TAXALERT

Owners whose shares are lent in short sales do not receive the lower capital gains rate on "payments in lieu of dividends," which are often called "substitute" dividends. Brokerages commonly lend stock held in margin accounts to short sellers, but may need to accommodate investors who do not want to receive the unfavorable dividend treatment. If this pertains to your investments, your Form 1099-DIV should indicate the status of your dividends.

See chapter 14, *Sale of property*, for an explanation of a short sale.

TAXPLANNER

If you borrow stock to make a short sale, and you pay the lender in lieu of the dividends distributed while you maintain your short position, you can deduct these payments provided you hold the short sale open at least 46 days (more than 1 year in the case of an extraordinary dividend as defined later) and you itemize your deductions. You deduct these expenses as investment interest on Schedule A (Form 1040).

If you close the short sale on or before the 45th day after the date of the short sale (1 year or less in the case of an extraordinary dividend), you cannot deduct the payments made. Instead you must increase the basis of the stock used to close the short sale by that amount.

Exception

The IRS allows a deduction for amounts you pay in place of dividends to the extent of ordinary income received from the lender of the stock for the use of collateral with the short sale. However, this special rule does not apply to payments in place of extraordinary dividends, discussed next.

Explanation

Extraordinary dividends. If the amount of any dividend you receive on a share of preferred stock equals or exceeds 5% (10% in the case of other stock) of the amount realized on the short sale, the dividend you receive is an extraordinary dividend.

If your payment is made for a liquidating distribution or nontaxable stock distribution, or if you buy more shares equal to a stock distribution issued on the borrowed stock during your short position, you have a capital expense. You must add the payment to the cost of the stock sold short.

See *Short Sales* in Publication 550 for more information about the tax treatment of short sales.

If an individual receives an extraordinary dividend eligible for the capital gain rates with respect to any share of stock, any loss on the sale of the stock is treated as a long-term capital loss to the extent of the dividend. A dividend is treated as investment income for purposes of determining the amount of deductible investment interest only if the taxpayer elects to treat the dividend as not eligible for the capital gain rates.

Example

Ben feels that the market value of XYZ Corporation stock is going to decline, so he sells XYZ stock to Sally. However, Ben does not hold any XYZ stock so, to effect the transaction, Ben's broker borrows XYZ stock from another customer, Robert, to deliver to Sally. Sally is now the stockholder of record.

XYZ Corporation will pay any and all dividends on this stock directly to Sally. However, Robert is entitled to the money, because he merely lent his shares to Ben. Ben, not XYZ Corporation, will pay Robert the amount of the dividend. Ben may deduct the payment as an itemized deduction on Schedule A if he borrows the stock for more than 45 days and has not diminished his risk of loss by, for example, holding an option to buy substantially similar stock. Robert enters that amount on page 1 (Form 1040) as income from Ben.

If Ben returns the stock within 45 days, he will not be able to claim a deduction. The amount paid to Robert increases the basis of the stock sold.

More information. For more information about how to report dividend income, see chapter 1 of Publication 550 or the instructions for the form you must file.

> ### *TAXORGANIZER*
> **Records you should keep:**
> - Annual statements from brokerage accounts and mutual funds
> - All Forms 1099
> - All Forms K-1 (partnership, trust, S corporation)
> - All information on purchase of investments and sale of investments
> - All Forms 2439

Chapter 9

Rental income and expenses

ey.com/EYTaxGuide

Note

IRS Publication 17 (*Your Federal Income Tax*) has been updated by Ernst & Young LLP for 2011. Dates and dollar amounts shown are for 2011. Underlined type is used to indicate where IRS text has been updated. Places where text has been removed are indicated by the sentence: *Text intentionally omitted.*

ey.com/EYTaxGuide
Ernst & Young LLP will update the *Ernst & Young Tax Guide 2012* website with relevant taxpayer information as it becomes available. You can also sign up for email alerts to let you know when changes have been made.

Introduction

Rent is the income received for allowing another person to use property that you own. This income is customarily received in cash. If, in lieu of paying all or part of the rent in cash, a tenant provides you with certain services, the value of those services is rental income to you.

You may deduct any expenses incurred to repair or to maintain your rental property. However, certain other expenses may not be deducted in the year in which you pay for them; rather, they must be *capitalized* and deducted over a period of years. You may also deduct any *depreciation* taken on your rental property. Depreciation is a noncash expense claimed in order to deduct each year a small part of what you originally paid for the property. There are a variety of methods by which you may depreciate property and calculate your tax deduction. These methods are explained in this chapter.

Rental real estate activities are generally considered passive activities, and the amount of any loss you can deduct is limited unless you have income from other passive activities or you "materially" or "actively" participate in your rental activity. This chapter explains the rules for figuring rental income, expenses, depreciation, and allowable losses.

What's New for 2011

Special depreciation allowance. For qualified property acquired after September 8, 2010, and placed in service before December 31, 2011, the additional first year depreciation is 100% of the depreciable basis of the property instead of 50%. See Publication 946, *How To Depreciate Property*, for more information.

TAXPLANNER

Residential rental property that may qualify for the special depreciation allowance includes properties placed into service in a federally declared disaster area in which the disaster occurred before January 1, 2010 (a list of the federally declared disaster areas is available at the FEMA website at *www.fema.gov*) or in specified portions of a Gulf Opportunity (GO) Zone.

For 2012, the bonus depreciation allowed for investments placed into service generally drops from 100% to 50% of the depreciable basis of qualified property.

This chapter discusses **rental income and expenses.** It also covers the following topics.

- Personal use of dwelling unit (including vacation home).
- Depreciation.
- Limits on rental losses.
- How to report your rental income and expenses.

If you sell or otherwise dispose of your rental property, see Publication 544, *Sales and Other Dispositions of Assets*.

If you have a loss from damage to, or theft of, rental property, see Publication 547, *Casualties, Disasters, and Thefts*.

If you rent a condominium or a cooperative apartment, some special rules apply to you even though you receive the same tax treatment as other owners of rental property. See Publication 527, *Residential Rental Property*, for more information.

Useful Items

You may want to see:

Publication

- ☐ **527** Residential Rental Property
- ☐ **534** Depreciating Property Placed in Service Before 1987
- ☐ **535** Business Expenses
- ☐ **925** Passive Activity and At-Risk Rules
- ☐ **946** How To Depreciate Property

Form (and Instructions)

- ☐ **4562** Depreciation and Amortization
- ☐ **6251** Alternative Minimum Tax—Individuals
- ☐ **8582** Passive Activity Loss Limitations
- ☐ **Schedule E (Form 1040)**   Supplemental Income and Loss

Rental Income

Generally, you must include in your gross income all amounts you receive as rent. Rental income is any payment you receive for the use or occupation of property. In addition to amounts you receive as normal rent payments, there are other amounts that may be rental income.

When to report. If you are a cash basis taxpayer, you report rental income on your return for the year you actually or constructively receive it. You are a cash basis taxpayer if you report income in the year you receive it, regardless of when it was earned. You constructively receive income when it is made available to you, for example, by being credited to your bank account.

For more information about when you constructively receive income, see *Accounting Methods* in chapter 1.

Advance rent. Advance rent is any amount you receive before the period that it covers. Include advance rent in your rental income in the year you receive it regardless of the period covered or the method of accounting you use.

Example. You sign a 10-year lease to rent your property. In the first year, you receive $5,000 for the first year's rent and $5,000 as rent for the last year of the lease. You must include $10,000 in your income in the first year.

EXPLANATION

Some taxpayers have attempted to circumvent the rule requiring advance rent to be included in current income by structuring the payment as a "loan." The courts have generally disallowed this technique and follow this type of transaction with close scrutiny. As a general rule, if such a loan is to be repaid out of future rental proceeds, the loan will probably be considered advance rent.

However, the courts have held that an up-front payment for an option to purchase the property is not considered advance rent and, as such, does not have to be included in income where the agreement provides no provision for returning the money to the renter or applying it to the rent.

Even if a promissory note is written to support the "loan," the courts will look to the parties' intent, as well as to other factors such as interest charged, whether the loan is secured, and whether the loan payment and rental dates are identified.

Rental Expenses. You can deduct the cost of rental expenses from your rental income. Expenses include advertising, cleaning and maintenance services, utilities, property insurance, taxes, interest on a loan taken out to buy or improve the rental property, commissions paid to collect rent, ordinary and necessary travel and transportation, repairs, depreciation on amounts paid to acquire the property and to make subsequent improvements, and amortization of points paid to acquire a mortgage on the rental property. For more details, see *Rental Expenses* and *Other Expenses*, later.

Rental Expenses of Vacant Rental Property. You can deduct the expenses of managing and maintaining a rental property during the time it is being marketed for rent for the first time and in between rentals, as long as it is actively being held out for rent. For more details, see *Rental Expenses*, later.

Deducting Repairs and Capitalizing Improvements. You can deduct the full amount of the cost of repairs made to your rental property in the year paid (for a cash-basis taxpayer). On the other hand, the cost of improvements cannot be currently deducted but rather must be capitalized and then recovered over time by taking depreciation. An expense can be considered a repair if it keeps the property in good working condition but does not increase its value nor useful life. An improvement adds to the value of property, prolongs its useful life, or adapts the property to new uses. For more details, see _Repairs and Improvements_, later.

Exclusion of Rental Income from a Home Rented for Less Than 15 Days During the Year. If a dwelling unit is used as a personal home and you rent it for less than 15 days during the year, you can exclude all of the rental income received from your taxable income. You are also not permitted to deduct any rental expenses paid. Note, however, that you can continue to deduct qualified residence interest, real estate taxes, and casualty and theft losses if you itemize deductions. For details, see _Exception for Minimal Rental Use_, later.

Passive Rental Losses Allowed as a Deduction. There is an exception to the general rule that disallows passive rental losses as a deduction. If you actively participate in a passive rental real estate activity (you actively participate if you—and your spouse—owned at least 10% of the rental property and you made significant management decisions—such as approving new tenants, deciding on rental terms, and approving expenditures for the property), you can deduct up to $25,000 of your losses from the activity from your nonpassive income. However, if your modified adjusted gross income is $150,000 or more ($75,000 or more if you are married filing separately), this exception to the passive loss deduction rules is disallowed. For more details, see _Losses From Rental Real Estate Activities_, later.

EXPLANATION

Generally, the distinction between advance rent and security deposits depends on the nature of the rights and obligations that are assumed when the deposit is made. If, for example, the landlord has the option either to refund a security deposit or to apply it to a future year's rent, the courts have held that the landlord has unrestricted use of the money and that it is considered advance rent.

In cases in which the landlord is required by law to pay interest on the security deposit, the deposit generally is not considered advance rent.

TAXPLANNER

Landlords often forget whether they have treated a security deposit as a true security deposit or as advance rent. If this happens, the landlord will not be sure how to treat the refund and/or application of the security deposit at the end of the term of the lease. Be sure to note in your records exactly how you are treating the amount for tax purposes so that the tax returns for the year in which the security deposit is returned and/or applied will be easy to prepare.

TAXSAVER

Advice for landlords. When drawing up a rental agreement, it is helpful to include the following language: "that the security deposit of $xx is not to be used for the last month's rent ..." This helps ensure deferred recognition of the security deposit as income until such time as you determine it should not be refunded.

Payment for canceling a lease. If your tenant pays you to cancel a lease, the amount you receive is rent. Include the payment in your income in the year you receive it regardless of your method of accounting.

EXPLANATION

Additionally, the courts have ruled that any payments you receive as consideration for modifying the terms of an existing lease must be treated as ordinary income. However, certain expenses incurred as a result of the cancellation or modification of a lease may be currently deductible. For example, attorney fees attributable to the lessee's forfeiture and termination of a lease would be currently deductible. On the other hand, if the lessor caused the termination, the expense would usually be amortized over a period of time. You should consult your tax advisor.

TAXSAVER

A payment for cancellation of a lease may be very large, depending on the time left on the lease and the agreement of the parties. As with most types of income to cash basis taxpayers, arranging for the receipt of this payment in a year in which you have a lower **marginal tax rate** may save you taxes.

Expenses paid by tenant. If your tenant pays any of your expenses, the payments are rental income. You must include them in your income. You can deduct the expenses if they are deductible rental expenses. See _Rental Expenses_, later, for more information.

EXPLANATION

When a tenant pays to have capital improvements constructed on the landlord's property and these improvements are not made in lieu of rent or other required payments, the value of these improvements is not income to the landlord, either when made or on termination of the lease, even though the landlord keeps the improvements at the end of the lease. However, the landlord will have no basis in the improvements and, therefore, cannot depreciate the improvements.

TAXPLANNER

It would be unusual for an expense paid by a tenant that is the responsibility of the landlord not to be deductible by the landlord as well. But such expenses do exist. Consider, for example, a building code violation fine incurred for some change made in the tenant's space by the tenant without the landlord's consent. The fine is imposed on the landlord, but the violation is the tenant's fault. The tenant pays the penalty, but the landlord still has to declare that amount as income. Since most penalties are not deductible, the landlord probably will not be able to deduct the amount of the fine as an expense. If this is a possibility, a clause in the lease making the payment of such a penalty the responsibility of the tenant when the tenant is at fault would probably keep the payment by the tenant from being income to the landlord.

Property or services. If you receive property or services, instead of money, as rent, include the fair market value of the property or services in your rental income.

EXAMPLE

Denise rents a home to a licensed contractor for $700 per month. The home needed repairs to the kitchen flooring, and the contractor agreed to make the repairs in exchange for living in the home rent free for 2 months. Denise must report the fair market value of the repairs as rental income (presumably the fair market value would be equal to 2 months' rent, or $1,400). Denise may be able to claim a deduction for the repair of the kitchen floor.

EXPLANATION

Examples of other types of income treated as rental income include the following:
1. Amounts received from an insurance company under a policy that reimburses a property owner for rent lost because of a fire or other casualty affecting the rental property.
2. Amounts received by subletting a property to another individual. If you did receive such income, you would be able to deduct the rent you are paying to the landlord as an expense. However, you are still not the owner and therefore would not be able to depreciate the property.

If the services are provided at an agreed upon or specified price, that price is the fair market value unless there is evidence to the contrary.

Security deposits. Do not include a security deposit in your income when you receive it if you plan to return it to your tenant at the end of the lease. But if you keep part or all of the security deposit during any year because your tenant does not live up to the terms of the lease, include the amount you keep in your income in that year.

If an amount called a security deposit is to be used as a final payment of rent, it is advance rent. Include it in your income when you receive it.

Rental of property also used as a home. If you rent property that you also use as your home and you rent it fewer than 15 days during the tax year, do not include the rent you receive in your income and do not deduct rental expenses. However, you can deduct on Schedule A (Form 1040) the interest, taxes, and casualty and theft losses that are allowed for nonrental property. See *Personal Use of Dwelling Unit (Including Vacation Home)*, later.

> ### TAXALERT
> If you plan to convert your rental property into your principal residence, the amount of gain you may be able to exclude from a future sale of that home may be limited. Generally, you are allowed to exclude up to $250,000 ($500,000 if married filing a joint return) of gain realized on the sale or exchange of a principal residence. The sale of a home will qualify for this exclusion if the home is a taxpayer's principal residence for at least two of the five years ending on the date of the sale or exchange. Under this law, the period of time you rented the residence after 2008 and before you converted it into your principal residence will figure into a formula that reduces the maximum exclusion ($250,000 or $500,000 if married filing a joint return) you can apply to offset gains realized when you ultimately sell that home. See chapter 15, *Selling your home*, for more information.

Part interest. If you own a part interest in rental property, you must report your part of the rental income from the property.

Rental Expenses

This part discusses expenses of renting property that you ordinarily can deduct from your rental income. It includes information on the expenses you can deduct if you rent part of your property, or if you change your property to rental use. *Depreciation*, which you can also deduct from your rental income, is discussed later.

> ### TAXSAVER
> You may deduct expenses on your rental property during a period in which it is not being rented as long as it is actively being held out for rent. This applies to a period between rentals, as well as to the period during which a property is being marketed as a rental property for the first time.
>   The IRS can disallow these deductions if you are unable to show you were actively seeking a profit and had a reasonable expectation of achieving one. The deduction cannot be disallowed just because your property is difficult to rent.

Personal use of rental property. If you sometimes use your rental property for personal purposes, you must divide your expenses between rental and personal use. Also, your rental expense deductions may be limited. See *Personal Use of Dwelling Unit (Including Vacation Home)*, later.

Part interest. If you own a part interest in rental property, you can deduct expenses that you paid according to your percentage of ownership.

When to deduct. You generally deduct your rental expenses in the year you pay them.

Pre-rental expenses. You can deduct your ordinary and necessary expenses for managing, conserving, or maintaining rental property from the time you make it available for rent.

Depreciation. You can begin to depreciate rental property when it is ready and available for rent. See *Placed-in-Service* under *When Does Depreciation Begin and End* in chapter 2 of Publication 527.

Vacant rental property. If you hold property for rental purposes, you may be able to deduct your ordinary and necessary expenses (including depreciation) for managing, conserving, or maintaining the property while the property is vacant. However, you cannot deduct any loss of rental income for the period the property is vacant.

Vacant while listed for sale. If you sell property you held for rental purposes, you can deduct the ordinary and necessary expenses for managing, conserving, or maintaining the property until it is sold.

Uncollected rent. If you are a cash basis taxpayer, do not deduct uncollected rent. Because you do not include it in your income, you cannot deduct it.

If you use an accrual method, you report income when you earn it. If you are unable to collect the rent, you may be able to deduct it as a business bad debt. See chapter 10 of Publication 535 for more information about business bad debts.

Repairs and Improvements

You can deduct the cost of repairs to your rental property. You cannot deduct the cost of improvements. Instead, recover the cost of improvements by taking _depreciation_ (explained later).

Repairs. A repair keeps your property in good operating condition. It does not materially add to the value of your property or substantially prolong its life. Repainting your property inside or out, fixing gutters or floors, fixing leaks, plastering, and replacing broken windows are examples of repairs.

If you make repairs as part of an extensive remodeling or restoration of your property, the whole job is an improvement.

Improvements. An improvement adds to the value of property, prolongs its useful life, or adapts it to new uses. Improvements include the following items.

- Putting a recreation room in an unfinished basement.
- Paneling a den.
- Adding a bathroom or bedroom.
- Putting decorative grillwork on a balcony.
- Putting up a fence.
- Putting in new plumbing or wiring.
- Putting in new cabinets.
- Putting on a new roof.
- Paving a driveway.

If you make an improvement to property, the cost of the improvement must be capitalized. The capitalized cost can generally be depreciated as if the improvement were separate property.

Records

Separate the costs of repairs and improvements, and keep accurate records. You will need to know the cost of improvements when you sell or depreciate your property.

Examples of deductible expenses are as follows:
- Replacing a portion of a wooden bathroom when damage has been caused by water
- Repainting or repapering a room in a rooming house when it is necessary to keep the area clean and serviceable
- Reinforcing sagging floors
- Resurfacing a parking lot
- Making piecemeal repairs to floors

TAXORGANIZER

All records and receipts of your rental expenditures, and what they were specifically for, should be kept for a minimum of three years. This will allow you to substantiate items relating to your rental property if the IRS should have any questions. For improvements that are capitalized, receipts need to be maintained for a minimum of three years after the tax return filing for the year the rental property is sold.

It is extremely important to keep accurate records of expenditures segregated for repairs that are currently deductible and improvements that are capitalized. Generally, IRS agents give close attention to repair and maintenance deductions. Sometimes expenditures have completely been disallowed unless the taxpayer can prove each specific amount of repair.

Other Expenses

Other expenses you can deduct from your rental income include advertising, cleaning and maintenance, utilities, fire and liability insurance, taxes, interest, commissions for the collection of rent, ordinary and necessary travel and transportation, and other expenses, discussed next.

EXPLANATION

Although commissions paid to collect rent are deductible, commissions paid to obtain long-term rentals (greater than a 1-year period) must be capitalized and amortized. Commissions paid to acquire the rental property must be capitalized as part of the basis of that property and recovered when the property is depreciated.

Points paid to acquire a mortgage on the rental property must be amortized over the life of the mortgage.

Other deductible expenses connected to renting include legal costs for dispossessing a tenant, property management fees, and pest control fees.

The "ordinary and necessary travel and transportation" category includes local transportation. It also covers the cost of meals and lodging on trips to inspect rental property located outside the immediate area. However, for the cost of nonlocal transportation and some other expenses to be deductible, the primary purpose of the trip must be to take care of the rental property. (See chapter 27, *Car expenses and other employee business expenses,* for a discussion of how to deduct expenses when you use your personal automobile in your trade or business.) In addition, the expense must be "ordinary" in nature. An ordinary expense is one that is common and accepted for the activity.

Example

If you take a 1-week trip to Florida and spend 1 day inspecting your rental property, no nonlocal transportation expenses are deductible. If, on the other hand, 6 of the 7 days are used to repair and attend to the property, all nonlocal transportation expenses are deductible. In both cases, local transportation expenses incurred traveling to and from the property are deductible. However, if a stretch limousine is rented for the local travel, more than likely the IRS would not consider the expense an "ordinary" expense. Any deduction allowed would be limited to the amount that would be considered "ordinary," such as the cost of a rental car or cab fare.

Insurance premiums paid in advance. If you pay an insurance premium for more than one year in advance, for each year of coverage you can deduct the part of the premium payment that will apply to that year. You cannot deduct the total premium in the year you pay it.

Local benefit taxes. Generally, you cannot deduct charges for local benefits that increase the value of your property, such as charges for putting in streets, sidewalks, or water and sewer systems.

These charges are nondepreciable capital expenditures, and must be added to the basis of your property. However, you can deduct local benefit taxes that are for maintaining, repairing, or paying interest charges for the benefits.

Rental of property. You can deduct the rent you pay for property that you use for rental purposes. If you buy a leasehold for rental purposes, you can deduct an equal part of the cost each year over the term of the lease.

EXAMPLES

Example 1
If you pay $1,100 rent for property and collect $1,200 in rent from a third party for the same property, you may deduct the $1,100 you pay. Your profit from the rental activity is $100.

Example 2
If you buy a 10-year lease on property from someone for $1,000, you have to pay the rent that the former owner of the lease had to pay. In turn, you report as income any rent you receive on the property. You may amortize the cost of the lease over 10 years, deducting $100 each year.

Rental of equipment. You can deduct the rent you pay for equipment that you use for rental purposes. However, in some cases, lease contracts are actually purchase contracts. If so, you cannot deduct these payments. You can recover the cost of purchased equipment through depreciation.

EXPLANATION

A lease with an option to buy may be a purchase contract. Generally, if the sum of the rental payments on a lease with an option to buy amounts to a substantial part of what would be the purchase price, and if the option period is clearly less than the useful life of the property, the transaction is treated as a sale. Income is recognized under the installment sale rules. (See chapter 14, *Sale of property*, for details.)

If the lease is treated as a sale on the date the lease is entered into, rather than the date the option is exercised, there may be unwanted tax consequences for the landlord. The payments that the landlord receives will be proceeds from the sale of property, and he or she will report the gain on the installment method. The landlord may also have to report imputed interest income (see chapter 12, *Other income*). Consequently, the landlord might have more income and fewer deductions than expected.

TAXPLANNER

The rules in this area are complex, but a careful drafting of a property agreement will reduce or eliminate the likelihood that the IRS will consider the lease a sale. Professional help should be obtained.

TAXSAVER

Whether or not you are offering property for rent, it is important to keep a file on the assessments you pay for sewers, streets, and the like. These add to your cost basis in the property and are important in determining your gain or loss if you ever sell the property. In addition, if you do rent the property out, the increase in your cost basis for any special assessment may increase your depreciation deduction, depending on the type of assessment.

Local transportation expenses. You can deduct your ordinary and necessary local transportation expenses if you incur them to collect rental income or to manage, conserve, or maintain your rental property.

Generally, if you use your personal car, pickup truck, or light van for rental activities, you can deduct the expenses using one of two methods: actual expenses or the standard mileage rate. For 2011, the standard mileage rate for each mile of business use is 51 cents a mile through June 30,

Records

To deduct car expenses under either method, you must keep records that follow the rules in chapter 27. In addition, you must complete Form 4562, Part V, and attach it to your tax return.

Records

To deduct travel expenses, you must keep records that follow the rules in chapter 27.

2011, and 55.5 cents per mile from July 1, 2011 through December 31, 2011. For more information, see chapter 27.

Travel expenses. You can deduct the ordinary and necessary expenses of traveling away from home if the primary purpose of the trip was to collect rental income or to manage, conserve, or maintain your rental property. You must properly allocate your expenses between rental and non-rental activities. You cannot deduct the cost of traveling away from home if the primary purpose of the trip was to improve your property. You recover the cost of improvements by taking depreciation. For information on travel expenses, see chapter 27.

Tax return preparation. You can deduct, as a rental expense, the part of tax return preparation fees you paid to prepare Schedule E (Form 1040), Part I. For example, on your 2011 Schedule E, you can deduct fees paid in 2011 to prepare your 2010 Schedule E, Part I. You can also deduct, as a rental expense, any expense (other than federal taxes and penalties) you paid to resolve a tax underpayment related to your rental activities.

TAXORGANIZER

Be sure to keep a detailed diary of expenses for your rental property. Include the following:
- Date and amount paid for maintenance expenses
- Travel expenses to and from rental property (keep track of number of miles driven, including the beginning and ending odometer readings and date of travel, or actual car expenses)
- Amount of tax return preparation fee paid for rental income portion of return (have your tax preparer show the amount separately on his or her invoice)

Not Rented for Profit

If you do not rent your property to make a profit, you can deduct your rental expenses only up to the amount of your rental income. You cannot deduct a loss or carry forward to the next year any rental expenses that are more than your rental income for the year. For more information about the rules for an activity not engaged in for profit, see *Not-for-Profit Activities* in chapter 1 of Publication 535.
Text intentionally omitted.

Where to report. Report your not-for-profit rental income on Form 1040, line 21. You can include your mortgage interest and any qualified mortgage insurance premiums (if you use the property as your main home or second home), real estate taxes, and casualty losses on the appropriate lines of Form 1040, Schedule A, if you itemize your deductions.

If you itemize, claim your other rental expenses, subject to the rules explained in chapter 1 of Publication 535, as miscellaneous itemized deductions on Form 1040, Schedule A, line 23. You can deduct these expenses only if they, together with certain other miscellaneous itemized deductions, total more than 2% of your adjusted gross income.

TAXPLANNER

If you move out of your personal residence and rent it, your deductions for real estate tax and mortgage interest are shifted from itemized deductions on Schedule A to rental deductions on Schedule E of Form 1040. The only additional deductions you become entitled to are those for operating expenses and depreciation. Since the rental income is included in your gross income, and the amount of additional deductions you are entitled to may be small, renting out your personal residence could increase your taxable income. If you rent out your personal residence with the intention of returning to live in it in the future, a special rule governing the deduction of mortgage interest may benefit you. See *Passive Activity Limits* later in this chapter.

Property Changed to Rental Use

If you change your home or other property (or a part of it) to rental use at any time other than the beginning of your tax year, you must divide yearly expenses, such as taxes and insurance, between rental use and personal use.

You can deduct as rental expenses only the part of the expense that is for the part of the year the property was used or held for rental purposes.

Text intentionally omitted.

You cannot deduct depreciation or insurance for the part of the year the property was held for personal use. However, you can include the home mortgage interest, qualified mortgage insurance premiums, and real estate tax expenses for the part of the year the property was held for personal use as an itemized deduction on Schedule A (Form 1040).

Example. Your tax year is the calendar year. You moved from your home in May and started renting it out on June 1. You can deduct as rental expenses seven-twelfths of your yearly expenses, such as taxes and insurance.

Starting with June, you can deduct as rental expenses the amounts you pay for items generally billed monthly, such as utilities.

Renting Part of Property

If you rent part of your property, you must divide certain expenses between the part of the property used for rental purposes and the part of the property used for personal purposes, as though you actually had two separate pieces of property.

You can deduct the expenses related to the part of the property used for rental purposes, such as home mortgage interest, qualified mortgage insurance premiums, and real estate taxes, as rental expenses on Schedule E (Form 1040). You can also deduct as rental expenses a portion of other expenses that normally are nondeductible personal expenses, such as expenses for electricity or painting the outside of your house.

There is no change in the types of expenses deductible for the personal-use part of your property. Generally, these expenses may be deducted only if you itemize your deductions on Schedule A (Form 1040).

You cannot deduct any part of the cost of the first phone line even if your tenants have unlimited use of it.

You do not have to divide the expenses that belong only to the rental part of your property. For example, if you paint a room that you rent, or if you pay premiums for liability insurance in connection with renting a room in your home, your entire cost is a rental expense. If you install a second phone line strictly for your tenants' use, all of the cost of the second line is deductible as a rental expense. You can deduct *depreciation*, discussed later, on the part of the house used for rental purposes as well as on the furniture and equipment you use for rental purposes.

EXAMPLE
Allison rents a room in her house to Gladys. Every year Allison has the house, including Gladys' room, painted for maintenance purposes. The portion of the paint and labor cost for the rented room is deducted on Schedule E. The portion that does not relate to the rented room is not deductible.

Allison pays mortgage interest and property taxes each year on this home. A percentage of the interest and tax that relates to the rental is deductible on Schedule E and the remaining amount is deductible as an itemized deduction on Schedule A.

How to divide expenses. If an expense is for both rental use and personal use, such as mortgage interest or heat for the entire house, you must divide the expense between the rental use and the personal use. You can use any reasonable method for dividing the expense. It may be reasonable to divide the cost of some items (for example, water) based on the number of people using them. The two most common methods for dividing an expense are based on (1) the number of rooms in your home, and (2) the square footage of your home.

TAXPLANNER
As there are various methods of dividing expenses, you should use whichever "reasonable" method provides the best result. For more information, see *How to Divide Expenses*, later in this chapter.

Personal Use of Dwelling Unit (Including Vacation Home)

If you have any personal use of a dwelling unit (including a vacation home) that you rent, you must divide your expenses between rental use and personal use. See *What Is a Day of Personal Use* and *How To Divide Expenses*, later.

If you used a dwelling unit for personal purposes, it may be considered a "dwelling unit used as a home." If it is, you cannot deduct rental expenses that are more than your rental income for that dwelling unit. See *Dwelling Unit Used as Home* and *How To Figure Rental Income and Deductions*, later. If your dwelling unit is not considered a dwelling unit used as a home, you can deduct rental expenses that are more than rental income for the unit subject to certain limits. See *Limits on Rental Losses*, later.

Exception for minimal rental use. If you use the dwelling unit as a home and you rent it fewer than 15 days during the year, that period is not treated as rental activity. Do not include any of the rent in your income and do not deduct any of the rental expenses. To determine if you use a dwelling unit as a home, see *Dwelling Unit Used as Home*, later.

TAXSAVER

This is one of the very few instances in which the IRS considers income to be nontaxable. You should be on the lookout for opportunities to rent property for less than 15 days to take advantage of this tax loophole. Residents of Augusta, Georgia, for example, have an annual opportunity to rent their houses for a short period during the Masters golf tournament.

Explanation

In general, the tax rules governing the rental of vacation homes and other dwelling units are the same as those governing any rental property. The allowable methods of depreciation, the types of deductible expenditures, and the types of expenditures that should be capitalized are all determined in the same way for both categories of rental property. However, if you or a member of your family uses the vacation home or dwelling unit during the year, the amount of deductible expenses may be limited by special rules.

Here's an easy way to figure out whether or not you have to follow the special rules for reporting rental income outlined later:

Step 1. Determine the number of days the property was rented at fair market value during the year. If this number is less than 15, STOP. You may not deduct any rental expenses, and you do not report any rental income. (Note: You may always deduct qualified residence interest, taxes, casualty losses, and theft losses if you itemize deductions. To do so, simply take the deduction for the entire amount of these items on Schedule A of Form 1040.) If the number of days rented is 15 or more, you must report rental income. Proceed to Step 2.

Step 2. Determine the number of days you personally use the property. If this number does not exceed the greater of (a) 14 days or (b) 10% of the number of days for which the property was rented at fair market value, you are not subject to any special rules. After completing Step 3, you determine your rental income or loss in the same way you would for any type of rental property.

If your personal use of the property exceeds the limits described earlier, you are subject to special rules limiting the amount of deductible expenses. After completing Step 3, you determine your rental income or loss using the rules discussed in this section.

Step 3. Allocate all expenses between the rental period and the period in which you use the property personally, using the method described in the following section. Expenses allocated to the period of personal use are not deductible, except for interest, taxes, and casualty and theft losses (see Step 1). Then determine your rental income or loss, using either the general rules for rental property or the special rules regarding the personal use of vacation homes, whichever is appropriate.

Note: See *Days Not Counted as Personal Use*, later, regarding use of a home before or after renting.

Dwelling unit. A dwelling unit includes a house, apartment, condominium, mobile home, boat, vacation home, or similar property. It also includes all structures or other property belonging to the dwelling unit. A dwelling unit has basic living accommodations, such as sleeping space, a toilet, and cooking facilities.

A dwelling unit does not include property used solely as a hotel, motel, inn, or similar establishment. Property is used solely as a hotel, motel, inn, or similar establishment if it is regularly available for occupancy by paying customers and is not used by an owner as a home during the year.

Example. You rent a room in your home that is always available for short-term occupancy by paying customers. You do not use the room yourself, and you allow only paying customers to use the room. The room is used solely as a hotel, motel, inn, or similar establishment and is not a dwelling unit.

Dwelling Unit Used as Home

The tax treatment of rental income and expenses for a dwelling unit that you also use for personal purposes depends on whether you use it as a home. (See *How To Figure Rental Income and Deductions*, later.)

You use a dwelling unit as a home during the tax year if you use it for personal purposes more than the greater of:
1. 14 days, or
2. 10% of the total days it is rented to others at a fair rental price.

See *What Is a Day of Personal Use*, later.

If a dwelling unit is used for personal purposes on a day it is rented at a fair rental price, do not count that day as a day of rental use in applying (2) above. Instead, count it as a day of personal use in applying both (1) and (2) above. However, this rule does not apply when dividing expenses between rental and personal use.

Fair rental price. A fair rental price for your property generally is the amount of rent that a person who is not related to you would be willing to pay. The rent you charge is not a fair rental price if it is substantially less than the rents charged for other properties that are similar to your property in your area.

Examples

The following examples show how to determine whether you used your rental property as a home.

Example 1. You converted the basement of your home into an apartment with a bedroom, a bathroom, and a small kitchen. You rented the basement apartment at a fair rental price to college students during the regular school year. You rented to them on a 9-month lease (273 days). You figured 10% of the total days rented to others at a fair rental price is 27 days.

During June (30 days), your brothers stayed with you and lived in the basement apartment rent free.

Your basement apartment was used as a home because you used it for personal purposes for 30 days. Rent-free use by your brothers is considered personal use. Your personal use (30 days) is more than the greater of 14 days or 10% of the total days it was rented (27 days).

Example 2. You rented the guest bedroom in your home at a fair rental price during the local college's homecoming, commencement, and football weekends (a total of 27 days). Your sister-in-law stayed in the room, rent free, for the last 3 weeks (21 days) in July. You figured 10% of the total days rented to others at a fair rental price is 3 days.

The room was used as a home because you used it for personal purposes for 21 days. That is more than the greater of 14 days or 10% of the 27 days it was rented (3 days).

Example 3. You own a condominium apartment in a resort area. You rented it at a fair rental price for a total of 170 days during the year. For 12 of those days, the tenant was not able to use the apartment and allowed you to use it even though you did not refund any of the rent. Your family actually used the apartment for 10 of those days. Therefore, the apartment is treated as having been rented for 160 (170 − 10) days. You figured 10% of the total days rented to others at a fair rental price is 16 days. Your family also used the apartment for 7 other days during the year.

You used the apartment as a home because you used it for personal purposes for 17 days. That is more than the greater of 14 days or 10% of the 160 days it was rented (16 days).

Use As Main Home Before or After Renting

For purposes of determining whether a dwelling unit was used as a home, you may not have to count days you used the property as your main home before or after renting it or offering it for rent as days of personal use. Do not count them as days of personal use if:

- You rented or tried to rent the property for 12 or more consecutive months.
- You rented or tried to rent the property for a period of less than 12 consecutive months and the period ended because you sold or exchanged the property.

This special rule does not apply when dividing expenses between rental and personal use.

What Is a Day of Personal Use

A day of personal use of a dwelling unit is any day that the unit is used by any of the following persons.

1. You or any other person who has an interest in it, unless you rent it to another owner as his or her main home under a shared equity financing agreement (defined later). However, see *Use as Main Home Before or After Renting* under *Dwelling Unit Used as Home*, earlier.
2. A member of your family or a member of the family of any other person who owns an interest in it, unless the family member uses the dwelling unit as his or her main home and pays a fair rental price. Family includes only your spouse, brothers and sisters, half-brothers and half-sisters, ancestors (parents, grandparents, etc.), and lineal descendants (children, grandchildren, etc.).
3. Anyone under an arrangement that lets you use some other dwelling unit.
4. Anyone at less than a fair rental price.

TAXSAVER

The rule relating to personal use does not apply to use by an in-law of the taxpayer who owns the property. Thus, a son-in-law could lease property at a fair market value to his mother-in-law, and it would not be treated as personal use.

Main home. If the other person or member of the family in (1) or (2) above has more than one home, his or her main home is ordinarily the one he or she lived in most of the time.

Shared equity financing agreement. This is an agreement under which two or more persons acquire undivided interests for more than 50 years in an entire dwelling unit, including the land, and one or more of the co-owners is entitled to occupy the unit as his or her main home upon payment of rent to the other co-owner or owners.

Donation of use of property. You use a dwelling unit for personal purposes if:

- You donate the use of the unit to a charitable organization,
- The organization sells the use of the unit at a fund-raising event, and
- The "purchaser" uses the unit.

TAXPLANNER

Although donating your rental property for a certain time period to a charitable organization is considered personal use, you still may be allowed to deduct certain expenses during that time on Schedule A as a charitable contribution. See chapter 25, *Contributions*, for further details on donating your property. You cannot deduct the value of the personal use, or lost rental income, as a charitable deduction.

Examples

The following examples show how to determine days of personal use.

Example 1. You and your neighbor are co-owners of a condominium at the beach. Last year, you rented the unit to vacationers whenever possible. The unit was not used as a main home by anyone. Your neighbor used the unit for 2 weeks last year; you did not use it at all.

Because your neighbor has an interest in the unit, both of you are considered to have used the unit for personal purposes during those 2 weeks.

Example 2. You and your neighbors are co-owners of a house under a shared equity financing agreement. Your neighbors live in the house and pay you a fair rental price.

Even though your neighbors have an interest in the house, the days your neighbors live there are not counted as days of personal use by you. This is because your neighbors rent the house as their main home under a shared equity financing agreement.

Example 3. You own a rental property that you rent to your son. Your son does not own any interest in this property. He uses it as his main home and pays you a fair rental price.

Your son's use of the property is not personal use by you because your son is using it as his main home, he owns no interest in the property, and he is paying you a fair rental price.

Example 4. You rent your beach house to Joshua. Joshua rents his house in the mountains to you. You each pay a fair rental price.

You are using your house for personal purposes on the days that Joshua uses it because your house is used by Joshua under an arrangement that allows you to use his house.

Days Used for Repairs and Maintenance

Any day that you spend working substantially full time repairing and maintaining (not improving) your property is not counted as a day of personal use. Do not count such a day as a day of personal use even if family members use the property for recreational purposes on the same day.

EXPLANATION

If the dwelling unit is rented and you are a guest of the occupant for a brief visit, this will not constitute personal use. Of course, the longer the visit is, the more likely the IRS is to claim you were an occupant rather than a visitor. Certainly, 1 or 2 days should be no problem.

How To Divide Expenses

If you use a dwelling unit for both rental and personal purposes, divide your expenses between the rental use and the personal use based on the number of days used for each purpose. You can deduct expenses for the rental use of the unit under the rules explained in *How To Figure Rental Income and Deductions*, later.

When dividing your expenses, follow these rules.

- Any day that the unit is rented at a fair rental price is a day of rental use even if you used the unit for personal purposes that day. This rule does not apply when determining whether you used the unit as a home.
- Any day that the unit is available for rent but not actually rented is not a day of rental use.

Example. Your beach cottage was available for rent from June 1 through August 31 (92 days). Your family uses the cottage during the last 2 weeks in May (14 days). You were unable to find a renter for the first week in August (7 days). The person who rented the cottage for July allowed you to use it over a weekend (2 days) without any reduction in or refund of rent. The cottage was not used at all before May 17 or after August 31.

You figure the part of the cottage expenses to treat as rental expenses as follows.

- The cottage was used for rental a total of 85 days (92 − 7). The days it was available for rent but not rented (7 days) are not days of rental use. The July weekend (2 days) you used it is rental use because you received a fair rental price for the weekend.
- You used the cottage for personal purposes for 14 days (the last 2 weeks in May).
- The total use of the cottage was 99 days (14 days personal use + 85 days rental use).
- Your rental expenses are 85/99 (86%) of the cottage expenses.

When determining whether you used the cottage as a home, the July weekend (2 days) you used it is personal use even though you received a fair rental price for the weekend. Therefore, you had 16 days of personal use and 83 days of rental use for this purpose. Because you used the cottage for personal purposes more than 14 days and more than 10% of the days of rental use (8 days), you used it as a home. If you have a net loss, you may not be able to deduct all of the rental expenses. See *Property Used as a Home* in the following discussion.

TAXSAVER

The Tax Court allows you to use a different allocation formula for interest and taxes than the one the IRS describes. Under the Tax Court formula, interest and taxes are allocated in the ratio of days rented to days in the year instead of in the ratio of days rented to days used. Using the Tax Court ratio results in a smaller amount of interest and taxes being allocated to the rental property, which creates the potential for you to deduct a larger amount of your other rental expenses.

Example

You own a cabin, which you rented for June and July, lived in for 1 month, and tried to rent the rest of the year. Your rental income for the 2 months was $2,800. Your total expenses for the cabin were as follows:

Interest	$1,500
Taxes	900
Utilities	750
Maintenance	300
Depreciation	1,200

	IRS method	Tax Court method
1) Gross rental income	$2,800	$2,800
2) Minus:		
a) Part of interest for rental use		
($1,500 × 61/91)	(1,005)	
($1,500 × 61/365)		(251)
b) Part of taxes for rental use		
($900 × 61/91)	(603)	
($900 × 61/365)		(150)
3) Gross rental income that is more than the interest and taxes for rental	$1,192	$2,399
4) Minus:		
a) Part of utilities for rental use (61/91)	(503)	(503)
b) Part of maintenance for rental use (61/91)	(201)	(201)
5) Gross rental income that is more than the interest, taxes, and operating expenses for rental use	$ 488	$1,695
6) Minus: Depreciation limited to the part for rental use ($1,200 × 61/91 = $804) or line 5, whichever is less	(488)	(804)
7) Net rental income	$ -0-	$ 891

Both the IRS method and the Tax Court method allocate interest expense and real estate taxes partly to Schedule E (for determining net rental income) and partly to Schedule A (for personal itemized deductions). But examine how these allocations affect Schedule A.

Total interest paid is $1,500. Since the IRS method allocates $1,005 to the rental activity, the $495 balance is allocated to Schedule A. The Tax Court method allocates only $251 to the rental activity, leaving $1,249 for a deduction on Schedule A. Similarly, the IRS method allocates $603 of the $900 in real estate taxes to the rental activity, leaving $297 for Schedule A.

The Tax Court method allocates only $150 to the rental activity, leaving $750 for Schedule A.

	Schedule A Deduction		Additional itemized per Tax Court method
	Tax Court method	IRS method	
Interest	$1,249	$495	$ 754
Real estate taxes	750	297	453
			$1,207

Under the Tax Court method, you end up with additional deductions of $1,207, but you also have an additional net rental income of $891. The difference is that you reduce your taxable income by $316 more than under the IRS method. This conclusion assumes that you had enough other itemized deductions to make itemizing worthwhile and that your itemized deductions are not being limited.

The concept illustrated here is also important because rental income is considered to be passive income and, as such, can be used to offset passive losses. For more details, see chapter 24, *Interest expense.*

How To Figure Rental Income and Deductions

How you figure your rental income and deductions depends on whether you used the dwelling unit as a home (see *Dwelling Unit Used as Home*, earlier) and, if you used it as a home, how many days the property was rented at a fair rental price.

Property Not Used as a Home

If you do not use a dwelling unit as a home, report all the rental income and deduct all the rental expenses. See *How To Report Rental Income and Expenses*, later.

Your deductible rental expenses can be more than your gross rental income. However, see *Limits on Rental Losses*, later.

Property Used as a Home

If you use a dwelling unit as a home during the year (see *Dwelling Unit Used as Home*, earlier), how you figure your rental income and deductions depends on how many days the unit was rented at a fair rental price.

Rented fewer than 15 days. If you use a dwelling unit as a home and you rent it fewer than 15 days during the year, do not include any rental income in your income. Also, you cannot deduct any expenses as rental expenses.

Rented 15 days or more. If you use a dwelling unit as a home and rent it 15 days or more during the year, include all your rental income in your income. See *How To Report Rental Income and Expenses*, later. If you had a net profit from the rental property for the year (that is, if your rental income is more than the total of your rental expenses, including depreciation), deduct all of your rental expenses. However, if you had a net loss, your deduction for certain rental expenses is limited.

To figure your deductible rental expenses and any carryover to next year, use <u>Worksheet 9-1</u> at the end of this chapter.

EXPLANATION

The IRS explanation is correct as far as it goes. However, four areas require clarification:

1. The starting point in determining your rental income is gross rental income, which is defined by the IRS as the gross rent received less expenses incurred to obtain tenants, such as advertising and real estate agents' fees. This definition is important because it enables you to deduct this type of expense *before* taking deductions for interest, taxes, and casualty losses, which might be enough to reduce your rental income to zero. The result may be a larger total deduction. The key point is: Start with gross rent received, deduct your expenses to obtain tenants, and then proceed through the deduction process described earlier.

2. The total amount of a casualty or theft loss allocated to the rental period is deductible. Ordinarily, a personal casualty or theft loss is deductible only to the extent that it is more than $100 and more than 10% of your **adjusted gross income**, but this is not the case when you are dealing with rental property. Your loss in this case would not be subject to the $100 or 10% floor limitation. (See chapter 26, *Casualty and theft losses*, for further details.)

3. Your basis in the vacation home or other dwelling unit is reduced only by the amount of depreciation actually allowed as a deduction, not by the amount of depreciation allocated to the rental period. This, in effect, decreases any gain you have to recognize if you subsequently sell the property. For more details on sales of **depreciable assets**, see *Depreciation*, later in this chapter.

4. Although the deductions for operating expenses and depreciation may not reduce income below zero, the deductions for interest and real estate taxes may.

TAXSAVER

When you personally use a dwelling unit for more than 14 days or more than 10% of the number of days it is rented at fair market value, it is generally to your advantage to use the Tax Court formula for computing the amount of interest and taxes allocable to the rental period. Doing so usually allows you a greater total deduction, since interest, taxes, and casualty losses may be deducted on Schedule A, even if they are disallowed on Schedule E.

However, when your personal use of the dwelling is less than both 15 days and 10% of the number of days it is rented at fair market value, it is to your advantage to use the IRS method of allocating interest and taxes because the net loss on the rental property will be allowed if your personal use is not substantial. (This assumes that the passive loss rules will not limit your net loss.) In this case, the IRS method does not reduce your total deduction; instead, it decreases your rental income (or increases your rental loss) and hence decreases your adjusted gross income.

Decreasing your adjusted gross income can be important, for the following reasons:

1. The amounts of certain itemized deductions, such as medical expenses, casualty losses, and most miscellaneous itemized deductions, are determined by reference to your adjusted gross income. Decreasing your adjusted gross income potentially increases your itemized deductions for these items.
2. Many states use adjusted gross income as the starting point in computing state taxable income. Using the IRS method may reduce your state tax liability.
3. If you are subject to alternative minimum tax, this method will reduce your alternative minimum taxable income.
4. A reduction in adjusted gross income may reduce the taxable amount of social security payments.
5. If you are a participant in a qualified pension plan, a decrease in your adjusted gross income may allow you to deduct contributions to an IRA.

Depreciation

You recover the cost of income-producing property through yearly tax deductions. You do this by depreciating the property; that is, by deducting some of the cost on the tax return each year.

Three basic factors determine how much depreciation you can deduct. They are: (1) your basis in the property, (2) the recovery period for the property, and (3) the depreciation method used. You cannot simply deduct your mortgage or principal payments, or the cost of furniture, fixtures and equipment, as an expense.

You can deduct depreciation only on the part of your property used for rental purposes. Depreciation reduces your basis for figuring gain or loss on a later sale or exchange.

You may have to use Form 4562 to figure and report your depreciation. See *How To Report Rental Income and Expenses*, later.

EXAMPLE

Barbara makes improvements in the amount of $10,000 to her rental property. These improvements are capitalized and depreciated over time. In the first year the improvements are put in service, Barbara does not deduct the correct amount of depreciation. She deducts $100 and reduces her basis by that amount, when the actual depreciation amount allowable is $200. If Barbara sells the property at the beginning of the next year, her basis in the property would be $9,800 (not $9,900). This is because even though Barbara only deducted $100 as depreciation, she was allowed to take a depreciation deduction of $200 and her adjusted basis should reflect the correct amount of depreciation that should have been taken.

Claiming the correct amount of depreciation. You should claim the correct amount of depreciation each tax year. Even if you did not claim depreciation that you were entitled to deduct, you must still reduce your basis in the property by the full amount of depreciation that you could have deducted.

If you deducted an incorrect amount of depreciation for property in any year, you may be able to make a correction by filing Form 1040X, Amended U.S Individual Income Tax Return. If you are not allowed to make the correction on an amended return, you can change your accounting method to claim the correct amount of depreciation. See *Claiming the correct amount of depreciation* in chapter 2 of Publication 527 for more information.

Changing your accounting method to deduct unclaimed depreciation. To change your accounting method, you generally must file Form 3115, Application for Change in Accounting Method, to get the consent of the IRS. In some instances, that consent is automatic. For more information, see chapter 1 of Publication 946.

Land. You cannot depreciate the cost of land because land generally does not wear out, become obsolete, or get used up. The costs of clearing, grading, planting, and landscaping are usually all part of the cost of land and cannot be depreciated.

> ### EXPLANATION
> When calculating your depreciation expense, be sure to separate out the cost of land from the cost of the building since land is not depreciable. Taxpayers often forget to separate these costs, and, therefore, the true adjusted basis of the building is often not reflected. These amounts are normally not allocated on your purchase agreement so you must get an estimate of the value of the land by a real estate broker or by your county. For further details, consult your tax advisor.

More information. See Publication 527 for more information about depreciating rental property and see Publication 946 for more information about depreciation.

> ### EXPLANATION
> Depreciation may perhaps be best understood as a way of deducting the cost of an expenditure over many years. Depreciation is calculated in the same way whether you report income on the cash or the accrual method.
>
> The period of time over which you depreciate your property has long been the subject of controversy. Different taxpayers, often in the same business, have depreciated the same type of property over widely different periods. Efforts to bring more uniformity to the write-off period resulted in the introduction of the Accelerated Cost Recovery System (ACRS). ACRS was replaced with MACRS (Modified ACRS) by the Tax Reform Act of 1986. Most tangible personal property can be depreciated. Artwork is an exception. It cannot be depreciated because no useful life can be established.

Other Rules About Depreciable Property

In addition to the rules about what methods you can use, there are other rules you should be aware of with respect to depreciable property.

Gain from disposition. If you dispose of depreciable property at a gain, you may have to report, as ordinary income, all or part of the gain. See Publication 544, *Sales and Other Dispositions of Assets*.

> ### EXPLANATION
> When you sell an asset for more than your unrecovered cost, you face the problem of recapture, that is, reporting all or part of your gain as ordinary income as opposed to capital gain. If you sell tangible personal property at a gain, your recapture is the lower of your gain or the previous amount of depreciation.
>
> *Example*
>
> | | Case 1 | Case 2 |
> |---|---|---|
> | 1) Cost | $1,000 | $1,000 |
> | 2) Depreciation previously claimed | (600) | (600) |
> | 3) Unrecovered cost | $ 400 | $ 400 |
> | 4) Selling price | $ 900 | $1,200 |
> | 5) Gain on sale (4 minus 3) | $ 500 | $ 800 |
> | 6) Recapture ordinary income (lower of 2 or 5) | (500) | (600) |
> | 7) Possible capital gain (5 minus 6) | $ -0- | $ 200 |
>
> Note that the recapture rules generally do not apply to real property if straight-line depreciation was used.
>
> However, a 25% capital gains tax rate (as opposed to the more favorable 15% capital gains tax rate) may apply to depreciation recapture on real property.

Alternative minimum tax. If you use accelerated depreciation, you may have to file Form 6251. Accelerated depreciation can be determined under MACRS, ACRS, and any other method that allows you to deduct more depreciation than you could deduct using a straight line method.

Limits on Rental Losses

Rental real estate activities are generally considered passive activities, and the amount of loss you can deduct is limited. Generally, you cannot deduct losses from rental real estate activities unless you have income from other passive activities. However, you may be able to deduct rental losses without regard to whether you have income from other passive activities if you "materially" or "actively" participated in your rental activity. See *Passive Activity Limits*, later.

Losses from passive activities are first subject to the at-risk rules. At-risk rules limit the amount of deductible losses from holding most real property placed in service after 1986.

Exception. If your rental losses are less than $25,000, and you actively participated in the rental activity, the passive activity limits probably do not apply to you. See *Losses From Rental Real Estate Activities*, later.

Property used as a home. If you used the rental property as a home during the year, the passive activity rules do not apply to that home. Instead, you must follow the rules explained under _Personal Use of Dwelling Unit (Including Vacation Home)_, earlier.

At-Risk Rules

The at-risk rules place a limit on the amount you can deduct as losses from activities often described as tax shelters. Losses from holding real property (other than mineral property) placed in service before 1987 are not subject to the at-risk rules.

Generally, any loss from an activity subject to the at-risk rules is allowed only to the extent of the total amount you have at risk in the activity at the end of the tax year. You are considered at risk in an activity to the extent of cash and the adjusted basis of other property you contributed to the activity and certain amounts borrowed for use in the activity. See Publication 925 for more information.

> ### EXAMPLE
> Assume Rob maintains an investment in which he made an initial investment of $20,000. Assuming Rob had a loss of $6,000 the first year, he would be able to take the loss deduction of $6,000, but the total maximum amount of loss deductions Rob could take in future years could not exceed $14,000 ($20,000 − $6,000).

Passive Activity Limits

Generally, all rental real estate activities (except those meeting the exception for real estate professionals, below) are passive activities. For this purpose, a rental activity is an activity from which you receive income mainly for the use of tangible property, rather than for services.

Limits on passive activity deductions and credits. Deductions for losses from passive activities are limited. You generally cannot offset income, other than passive income, with losses from passive activities. Nor can you offset taxes on income, other than passive income, with credits resulting from passive activities. Any excess loss or credit is carried forward to the next tax year.

For a detailed discussion of these rules, see Publication 925.

You may have to complete Form 8582 to figure the amount of any passive activity loss for the current tax year for all activities and the amount of the passive activity loss allowed on your tax return.

> ### TAXSAVER
> Note that any passive losses disallowed and carried forward can generally be taken in the year the property is sold. Any passive loss carryforward that has not been utilized at your death is only deductible to the extent that the carryforward loss exceeds the spread between the cost basis of the property that produced the loss and its fair market value on date of death (or alternate valuation date, if so elected by the executor).

Exception for real estate professionals. Rental activities in which you materially participated during the year are not passive activities if, for that year, you were a real estate professional. For a detailed discussion of the requirements, see Publication 527. For a detailed discussion of material participation, see Publication 925.

> ### EXPLANATION
> A rental activity is considered a passive activity unless you are considered a real estate professional. An activity is a rental activity if:
> 1. Tangible property is used by customers.
> 2. Income received is principally for the use of the property whether or not there is a lease, service contract, or other arrangement.
> An activity is not considered a rental activity if:
> 1. The average time the customer uses the property is 7 days or less.
> 2. The average time the customer uses the property is 30 days or less and personal services have been provided by the owner in connection with the rental.

Losses From Rental Real Estate Activities

If you or your spouse actively participated in a passive rental real estate activity, you can deduct up to $25,000 of loss from the activity from your nonpassive income. This special allowance is an exception to the general rule disallowing losses in excess of income from passive activities. Similarly, you can offset credits from the activity against the tax on up to $25,000 of nonpassive income after taking into account any losses allowed under this exception.

Active participation. You actively participated in a rental real estate activity if you (and your spouse) owned at least 10% of the rental property and you made management decisions or arranged for others to provide services (such as repairs) in a significant and *bona fide* sense. Management decisions include approving new tenants, deciding on rental terms, approving expenditures, and similar decisions.

Maximum special allowance. The maximum special allowance is:
- $25,000 for single individuals and married individuals filing a joint return for the tax year,
- $12,500 for married individuals who file separate returns for the tax year and lived apart from their spouses at all times during the tax year, and
- $25,000 for a qualifying estate reduced by the special allowance for which the surviving spouse qualified.

If your modified adjusted gross income (MAGI) is $100,000 or less ($50,000 or less if married filing separately), you can deduct your loss up to the amount specified above. If your MAGI is more than $100,000 (more than $50,000 if married filing separately), your special allowance is limited to 50% of the difference between $150,000 ($75,000 if married filing separately) and your MAGI.

Generally, if your MAGI is $150,000 or more ($75,000 or more if you are married filing separately), there is no special allowance.

More information. See Publication 925 for more information on the passive loss limits, including information on the treatment of unused disallowed passive losses and credits and the treatment of gains and losses realized on the disposition of a passive activity.

TAXSAVER

If you rent out your personal residence with the intention of returning to it (say, for example, you are transferred overseas for several years), the mortgage interest on the property may not be subject to the passive loss limitation rules. This can result in significant tax savings.

Example

Rental of a dwelling unit

Rent income	$15,000
Mortgage interest	(7,000)
Real estate tax	(3,000)
Other expenses	(1,000)
Depreciation	(9,000)
Net loss subject to passive loss rules	($5,000)

This loss may be deductible on your tax return, under the active participation $25,000 limitation mentioned earlier.

Rental of a personal residence with intention of returning

Rent income	$15,000
Real estate tax	(3,000)
Other expenses	(1,000)
Depreciation	(9,000)
Net rental (passive) income	$2,000
Mortgage interest (loss not subject to passive loss rules)	(7,000)
Net loss from property allowed on tax return	($5,000)

Of this loss, $7,000 (the portion representing qualified residence mortgage interest) may be deductible against nonpassive income. In addition, the $2,000 net passive income may offset passive losses from other passive activities.

Be aware that the depreciation deduction reduces the cost basis of your property, thereby increasing the gain upon sale of the property.

Explanation

You must meet the active participation standards both in the year in which the loss arose and in the year in which the loss is allowed. Losses that exceed $25,000 carried over from an active participation year can be used in a later year if the taxpayer continues to actively participate.

The $25,000 offset rule does not apply to the losses carried over from prior years where the taxpayer did not actively participate in the rental.

TAXALERT

A tax-saving opportunity exists depending upon how personal property and real property are grouped. Under final regulations, a taxpayer could not treat as a single activity the rental of real property and the rental of personal property (other than personal property provided in connection with real property). Further, effective for tax years beginning in January 1993, the regulations allow a taxpayer to treat as a single activity real property provided in connection with personal property.

Example

An individual who leases $10,000 of real property (e.g., a small structure or other fixture) in connection with renting $150,000 of computer equipment could treat as one activity the rental of both the real property and the personal property.

To make an election to treat all real property as a single activity, a taxpayer must file a statement with his or her original tax return for the tax year the taxpayer is making the election.

TAXPLANNER

It may not be beneficial for you to group all of your rental real estate interests together if you have interests in nonrental activities that are also passive. Consult your tax advisor for further details.

TAXALERT

A regulation has tightened the "partial disposition" rule, requiring a taxpayer to dispose of "substantially all" of an activity rather than a "substantial part" in order to deduct associated carryover suspended losses, that is, losses from this activity that did not get deducted in prior years. You should consult your tax advisor.

How To Report Rental Income and Expenses

If you rent buildings, rooms, or apartments, and provide only heat and light, trash collection, etc., you normally report your rental income and expenses on Schedule E, Part I. However, do not use that schedule to report a not-for-profit activity. See *Not Rented for Profit*, earlier.

Providing substantial services. If you provide substantial services that are primarily for your tenant's convenience, such as regular cleaning, changing linen, or maid service, report your rental income and expenses on Schedule C (Form 1040), Profit or Loss From Business, or Schedule C-EZ, Net Profit From Business (Sole Proprietorship). Use Form 1065, U.S. Return of Partnership Income, if your rental activity is a partnership (including a partnership with your spouse unless it is a qualified joint venture). Substantial services do not include the furnishing of heat and light, cleaning of public areas, trash collection, etc. For information, see Publication 334, *Tax Guide for Small Business*. You also may have to pay self-employment tax on your rental income using Schedule SE (Form 1040), Self-Employment Tax.

Form 1098, Mortgage Interest Statement. If you paid $600 or more of mortgage interest on your rental property to any one person, you should receive a Form 1098, or similar statement showing the interest you paid for the year. If you and at least one other person (other than your spouse if you file a joint return) were liable for, and paid interest on the mortgage, and the other person received the Form 1098, report your share of the interest on Schedule E (Form 1040), line 13. Attach a statement to your return showing the name and address of the other person. In the left margin of Schedule E, next to line 13, enter "See attached."

Schedule E (Form 1040)

Use Schedule E (Form 1040), Part I, to report your rental income and expenses. List your total income, expenses, and depreciation for each rental property. Be sure to answer the question on line 2.

If you have more than three rental or royalty properties, complete and attach as many Schedules E as are needed to list the properties. Complete lines 1 and 2 for each property. However, fill in the "Totals" column on only one Schedule E. The figures in the "Totals" column on that Schedule E should be the combined totals of all Schedules E.

Page 2 of Schedule E is used to report income or loss from partnerships, S corporations, estates, trusts, and real estate mortgage investment conduits. If you need to use Schedule E, page 2, use page 2 of the same Schedule E you used to enter the combined totals in Part I. Also, include the amount from line 26 (Part I) in the "Total income or (loss)" on line 41 (Part V).

On Schedule E, page 1, line 19, enter the depreciation you are claiming for each property. You must complete and attach Form 4562 for rental activities only if you are claiming:

- Depreciation, including the special depreciation allowance, on property placed in service during 2011,
- Depreciation on listed property (such as a car), regardless of when it was placed in service, or
- Any other car expenses, including the standard mileage rate or lease expenses.

Otherwise, figure your depreciation on your own worksheet. You do not have to attach these computations to your return, but you should keep them in your records for future reference.

TAXORGANIZER
Records you should keep:
- Rental agreement
- Records of tenant-paid improvements, real estate taxes, mortgage payments, etc.
- A log of how many days a property is rented, used for personal purposes, or vacant
- Proof of advertising vacant properties in newspapers, magazines, websites, etc.
- Lists distinguishing the nature of each repair or improvement
- Receipts for each repair and improvement including date and amount paid
- A log of travel expenses allocating between rental and nonrental purposes
- A schedule showing method of division of expenses if part of property is rented
- Schedule listing depreciable assets with respect to the rental property including amount, date purchased, life of asset, method of depreciation, and depreciation already taken
- Carryforward of passive activity losses not utilized in prior years
- Carryforward of rental losses in excess of $25,000 when actively participating in rental activity
- Form 1098 or other form indicating mortgage interest paid
- Property tax forms and receipts
- Proof of tax preparation fees paid in relation to rental property
- Security deposit information

Worksheet for Figuring Rental Deductions for a Dwelling Unit Used as a Home *Keep for Your Records*

Use this worksheet only if you answer "yes" to all of the following questions.
- Did you use the dwelling unit as a home this year? (See *Dwelling Unit Used as Home*.)
- Did you rent the dwelling unit at a fair rental price 15 days or more this year?
- Is the total of your rental expenses and depreciation more than your rental income?

PART I. Rental Use Percentage

A.	Total days available for rent at fair rental price..	**A.**_____
B.	Total days available for rent (line A) but not rented..	**B.**_____
C.	**Total days of rental use.** Subtract line B from line A	**C.**_____
D.	**Total days of personal use** (including days rented at less than fair rental price)	**D.**_____
E.	**Total days of rental and personal use.** Add lines C and D	**E.**_____
F.	**Percentage of expenses allowed for rental.** Divide line C by line E	**F.**_____

PART II. Allowable Rental Expenses

1.	Enter rents received	**1.**_____
2a.	Enter the rental portion of deductible home mortgage interest and qualified mortgage insurance premiums (see instructions)	**2a.**_____
b.	Enter the rental portion of real estate taxes...	**b.**_____
c.	Enter the rental portion of deductible casualty and theft losses (see instructions).............................	**c.**_____
d.	Enter direct rental expenses (see instructions)	**d.**_____
e.	**Fully deductible rental expenses.** Add lines 2a–2d. Enter here and on the appropriate lines on Schedule E (see instructions)	**2e.**_____
3.	Subtract line 2e from line 1. If zero or less, enter -0-	**3.**_____
4a.	Enter the rental portion of expenses directly related to operating or maintaining the dwelling unit (such as repairs, insurance, and utilities)	**4a.**_____
b.	Enter the rental portion of excess mortgage interest and qualified mortgage insurance premiums (see instructions)	**b.**_____
c.	Carryover of operating expenses from 2010 worksheet................................	**c.**_____
d.	Add lines 4a–4c..	**d.**_____
e.	**Allowable expenses.** Enter the **smaller** of line 3 or line 4d (see instructions)	**4e.**_____
5.	Subtract line 4e from line 3. If zero or less, enter -0-	**5.**_____
6a.	Enter the rental portion of excess casualty and theft losses (see instructions).................	**6a.**_____
b.	Enter the depreciation for the rental portion of the dwelling unit.....................	**b.**_____
c.	Carryover of excess casualty losses and depreciation from 2009 worksheet...............	**c.**_____
d.	Add lines 6a–6c..	**d.**_____
e.	**Allowable excess casualty and theft losses and depreciation.** Enter the **smaller** of line 5 or line 6d (see instructions)	**6e.**_____

PART III. Carryover of Unallowed Expenses to Next Year

7a.	**Operating expenses to be carried over to next year.** Subtract line 4e from line 4d	**7a.**_____
b.	**Excess casualty and theft losses and depreciation to be carried over to next year.** Subtract line 6e from line 6d	**b.**_____

Worksheet 9-1 Instructions.   **Worksheet for Figuring Rental Deductions for a Dwelling Unit Used as a Home**

Caution. Use the percentage determined in Part I, line F, to figure the rental portions to enter on lines 2a–2c, 4a–4b, and 6a–6b of Part II.

Line 2a.   Figure the mortgage interest on the dwelling unit that you could deduct on Schedule A (as if you were itemizing your deductions) if you had not rented the unit. Do not include interest on a loan that did not benefit the dwelling unit. For example, do not include interest on a home equity loan used to pay off credit cards or other personal loans, buy a car, or pay college tuition. Include interest on a loan used to buy, build, or improve the dwelling unit, or to refinance such a loan. Include the rental portion of this interest in the total you enter on line 2a of the worksheet.

Figure the qualified mortgage insurance premiums on the dwelling unit that you could deduct on line 13 of Schedule A, if you had not rented the unit. See page A-7 of the Schedule A instructions. However, figure your adjusted gross income (Form 1040, line 38) without your rental income and expenses from the dwelling unit. See *Line 4b* below to deduct the part of the qualified mortgage insurance premiums not allowed because of the adjusted gross income limit. Include the rental portion of the amount from Schedule A, line 13, in the total you enter on line 2a of the worksheet.

Note. Do not file this Schedule A or use it to figure the amount to deduct on line 13 of that schedule. Instead, figure the personal portion on a separate Schedule A. If you have deducted mortgage interest or qualified mortgage insurance premiums on the dwelling unit on other forms, such as Schedule C or F, remember to reduce your Schedule A deduction by that amount.

Line 2c.   Figure the casualty and theft losses related to the dwelling unit that you could deduct on Schedule A if you had not rented the dwelling unit. To do this, complete Section A of Form 4684, Casualties and Thefts, treating the losses as personal losses. If any of the loss is due to a federally declared disaster, see the Instructions for Form 4684. On Form 4684, line 20, enter 10% of your adjusted gross income figured without your rental income and expenses from the dwelling unit. Enter the rental portion of the result from Form 4684, line 22, on line 2c of this worksheet.

Note. Do not file this Form 4684 or use it to figure your personal losses on Schedule A. Instead, figure the personal portion on a separate Form 4684.

Line 2d.   Enter the total of your rental expenses that are directly related only to the rental activity. These include interest on loans used for rental activities other than to buy, build, or improve the dwelling unit. Also include rental agency fees, advertising, office supplies, and depreciation on office equipment used in your rental activity.

Line 2e.   You can deduct the amounts on lines 2a, 2b, 2c, and 2d as rental expenses on Schedule E even if your rental expenses are more than your rental income. Enter the amounts on lines 2a, 2b, 2c, and 2d on the appropriate lines of Schedule E.

Line 4b.   On line 2a, you entered the rental portion of the mortgage interest and qualified mortgage insurance premiums you could deduct on Schedule A if you had not rented the dwelling unit. If you had additional mortgage interest and qualified mortgage insurance premiums that would not be deductible on Schedule A because of limits imposed on them, enter on line 4b of this worksheet the rental portion of those excess amounts. Do not include interest on a loan that did not benefit the dwelling unit (as explained in the line 2a instructions).

Line 4e.   You can deduct the amounts on lines 4a, 4b, and 4c as rental expenses on Schedule E only to the extent they are not more than the amount on line 4e.*

Line 6a.   To find the rental portion of excess casualty and theft losses, use the Form 4684 you prepared for line 2c of this worksheet.

   A.   Enter the amount from Form 4684, line 10

   B.   Enter the rental portion of line A

   C.   Enter the amount from line 2c of this worksheet

   D.   Subtract line C from line B. Enter the result here and on line 6a of this worksheet

Line 6e.   You can deduct the amounts on lines 6a, 6b, and 6c as rental expenses on Schedule E only to the extent they are not more than the amount on line 6e.*

*Allocating the limited deduction. If you cannot deduct all of the amount on line 4d or 6d this year, you can allocate the allowable deduction in any way you wish among the expenses included on line 4d or 6d. Enter the amount you allocate to each expense on the appropriate line of Schedule E, Part I.

Chapter 10

Retirement plans, pensions, and annuities

ey.com/EYTaxGuide

Note

IRS Publication 17 (*Your Federal Income Tax*) has been updated by Ernst & Young LLP for 2011. Dates and dollar amounts shown are for 2011. Underlined type is used to indicate where IRS text has been updated. Places where text has been removed are indicated by the sentence: *Text intentionally omitted.*

ey.com/EYTaxGuide

Ernst & Young LLP will update the *Ernst & Young Tax Guide 2012* website with relevant taxpayer information as it becomes available. You can also sign up for email alerts to let you know when changes have been made.

Introduction

No matter how welcome retirement may be, you're liable to encounter a host of challenging tax dilemmas that you've never before faced. For starters, chances are good that you will have some difficulty projecting your tax liabilities. Your income will most likely be different from what it has been, and the way in which you calculate your tax will be different, too. You'll have to puzzle over the complicated withdrawal requirements from 401(k) and other retirement accounts. You may also be faced with the decision of whether to withdraw certain funds as an annuity, or in one lump-sum distribution. If you are entitled to any lump-sum distributions, you will have to make the difficultdecision as to whether to roll over the funds and defer the tax or to pay the tax currently. If your pension payments are not subject to mandatory withholding rules, you may have to start making estimated tax payments or elect to have income taxes withheld from your pension payments. This chapter helps guide you through this maze of complicated decisions.

What's New for 2011

Rollovers to Roth IRAs. If you roll over amounts from a qualified retirement plan to a Roth IRA in 2011, any taxable amounts that you are required to include in income are taxable in 2011. For more information, see *2011 rollovers to Roth IRAs* later.

Text intentionally omitted.

TAXALERT

AGI limitation for Roth conversions lifted. Beginning in 2010, any taxpayer with a traditional IRA account or a 401(k) or other deferral plan from a former employer can elect to convert the plan to a Roth IRA. Prior to 2010, only taxpayers with AGI less than $100,000 were eligible to convert traditional accounts to Roth IRAs. Also, before 2010, taxpayers who were married filing separately could not make a conversion to a Roth IRA. After 2010, they can. Roth conversions are discussed in greater detail later in this chapter, as well as in chapter 17, *Individual retirement arrangements (IRAs)*.

In-plan rollovers to designated Roth accounts allowed for governmental 457(b) plans. Beginning in 2011, if you are a plan participant in a governmental 457(b) plan, your plan may permit you to roll over amounts in that plan to a designated Roth account within the same plan (in-plan Roth rollover). The rollover of any untaxed amounts must be included in income. You must report in-plan Roth rollovers on Form 8606. See Publication 575 for more information.

Text intentionally omitted.

Excluding a Rollover Distribution from Current Taxes. If you withdraw all or a part of your balance in a qualified plan or tax-sheltered annuity arrangement, and such distribution is eligible to be rolled over to the qualified retirement plan of an employer or an IRA, you can defer tax on the distribution by contributing it to an eligible retirement plan. For more information, see *Rollovers*, later.

Avoiding Mandatory 20% Withholding on Eligible Rollover Distributions. Payers of benefits from your pension, profit-sharing, annuity, stock bonus, or other qualified deferred compensation plans are generally required to withhold 20% of distributions from such plans. However, withholding is not required on an eligible rollover distribution if you elect to have it paid directly to an IRA or qualified retirement plan of an employer. For more information, see *Withholding and Estimated Tax*, later.

401(k) and 403(b) Plan Contributions. You can reduce your taxable wages (and your tax bill) by contributing on a pre-tax basis to a 401(k) or 403(b) plan sponsored by your employer. In 2011, you could contribute up to $16,500 ($22,000 if you were 50 or older by the end of 2011). For more details, see *Elective deferrals*, later.

Roth 401(k) Plans. If your employer plan allows it, you may be able to designate part or all of your contributions to your employer's 401(k) plan as "Roth 401(k)" contributions.

TAXALERT
401(k) and 403(b) plans were allowed to offer participants an in-plan Roth rollover option after September 27, 2010.

TAXPLANNER
In fall 2010, Congress passed the Small Business Jobs Act of 2010, which contains a provision that allows 401(k), 403(b), and governmental 457(b) plans to permit participants to roll their pre-tax account balances into a designated Roth account within the same plan. Under prior law, these distributions could only be rolled over (after taxation) to a Roth IRA. (For more details, see Tax Alert below.) This provision offers eligible taxpayers another option for converting pre-tax amounts held inside their 401(k), 403(b), and/or 457(b) plans to a Roth account.

Reminder

Disaster-related tax relief. Special rules apply to retirement funds received by qualified individuals who suffered an economic loss as a result of:
- The storms that began on May 4, 2007, in the Kansas disaster area, or
- The severe storms in the Midwestern disaster areas in 2008.

For more information on these special rules, see *Relief for Kansas Disaster Area* and *Relief for Midwestern Disaster Areas* in Publication 575, *Pension and Annuity Income*.

This chapter discusses the tax treatment of distributions you receive from:
- **An employee pension or annuity from a qualified plan,**
- **A disability retirement, and**
- **A purchased commercial annuity.**

What is not covered in this chapter. The following topics are not discussed in this chapter.

The General Rule. This is the method generally used to determine the tax treatment of pension and annuity income from nonqualified plans (including commercial annuities). For a qualified plan, you generally cannot use the General Rule unless your annuity starting date is before November 19, 1996. For more information about the General Rule, see Publication 939, *General Rule for Pensions and Annuities*.

Individual retirement arrangements (IRAs). Information on the tax treatment of amounts you receive from an IRA is in chapter 17.

Civil service retirement benefits. If you are retired from the federal government (either regular or disability retirement), see Publication 721, *Tax Guide to U.S. Civil Service Retirement Benefits*. Publication 721 also covers the information that you need if you are the survivor or beneficiary of a federal employee or retiree who died.

Useful Items

You may want to see:

Publication
- ☐ **575** Pension and Annuity Income
- ☐ **721** Tax Guide to U.S. Civil Service Retirement Benefits
- ☐ **939** General Rule for Pensions and Annuities

Form (and Instructions)
- ☐ **W-4P** Withholding Certificate for Pension or Annuity Payments
- ☐ **1099-R** Distributions From Pensions, Annuities, Retirement or Profit-Sharing Plans, IRAs, Insurance Contracts, etc.
- ☐ **4972** Tax on Lump-Sum Distributions
- ☐ **5329** Additional Taxes on Qualified Plans (Including IRAs) and Other Tax-Favored Accounts

General Information

Designated Roth accounts. A designated Roth account is a separate account created under a qualified Roth contribution program to which participants may elect to have part or all of their elective deferrals to a 401(k) or 403(b) plan designated as Roth contributions. Elective deferrals that are designated as Roth contributions are included in your income. However, qualified distributions are not included in your income. See Publication 575 for more information.

> ### TAXPLANNER
> Your contributions to a Roth 401(k) are nondeductible, but all of the income in the plan will be tax-free to you when distributed if you meet the same requirements that apply to Roth IRAs: 5 years of participation and distribution after age 59½, death, disability, or up to $10,000 for a first-time home purchase. Unlike Roth IRAs, the ability to contribute to a Roth 401(k) is not limited by the amount of your income.

In-plan rollovers to designated Roth accounts. After September 27, 2010, if you are a participant in a 401(k) or 403(b) plan, your plan may permit you to roll over amounts in those plans to a designated Roth account within the same plan. Governmental 457(b) plans are allowed to offer this rollover option beginning in 2011. The rollover of any untaxed money must be included in income. *Text intentionally omitted.* You must report in-plan Roth rollovers on Form 8606. See Publication 575 for more information.

> ### TAXALERT
> In fall 2010, Congress passed the Small Business Jobs Act of 2010, which contains a provision that allows 401(k), 403(b), and governmental 457(b) plans to permit participants to roll their pre-tax account balances into a designated Roth account within the same plan. Under prior law, these distributions could only be rolled over (after taxation) to a Roth IRA. Rollovers to a designated Roth account are only allowed, however, in the event of a permitted distributable event such as separation from service or attaining age 59½.
>
> Just like a conversion to a Roth IRA, the amount rolled over is includible in taxable income except to the extent it includes a return of after-tax contributions. This new provision offers eligible taxpayers another option for converting pre-tax amounts held inside their 401(k), 403(b), and/or 457(b) plans to a Roth account.

More than one program. If you receive benefits from more than one program under a single trust or plan of your employer, such as a pension plan and a profit-sharing plan, you may have to figure the taxable part of each pension or annuity contract separately. Your former employer or the plan administrator should be able to tell you if you have more than one pension or annuity contract.

Section 457 deferred compensation plans. If you work for a state or local government or for a tax-exempt organization, you may be able to participate in a section 457 deferred compensation plan. If your plan is an eligible plan, you are not taxed currently on pay that is deferred under the plan or on any earnings from the plan's investment of the deferred pay. You are generally taxed on amounts deferred in an eligible state or local government plan only when they are distributed from the plan. You are taxed on amounts deferred in an eligible tax-exempt organization plan when they are distributed or otherwise made available to you.

This chapter covers the tax treatment of benefits under eligible section 457 plans, but it does not cover the treatment of deferrals. For information on deferrals under section 457 plans, see *Retirement Plan Contributions* under *Employee Compensation* in Publication 525, *Taxable and Nontaxable Income.*

For general information on these deferred compensation plans, see *Section 457 Deferred Compensation Plans* in Publication 575.

Disability pensions. If you retired on disability, you generally must include in income any disability pension you receive under a plan that is paid for by your employer. You must report your taxable disability payments as wages on line 7 of Form 1040 or Form 1040A until you reach minimum retirement age. Minimum retirement age generally is the age at which you can first receive a pension or annuity if you are not disabled.

Unlike contributions made to a "traditional" 401(k) plan that reduce your taxable wages, contributions to a Roth 401(k) do not reduce the amount of your earnings currently subject to tax. However, if certain requirements are met, your entire plan account can be distributed to you completely tax-free. For more details, see *General Information.* left.

Taxation of Appreciated Employer Securities Received as Part of a Lump-Sum Distribution. If a lump-sum distribution includes shares of stock in your employer that have appreciated in value, this "net unrealized appreciation" (NUA), which is determined upon the distribution, will not be subject to tax until you subsequently sell the shares. If the shares are sold, then the gain will be taxed as a long-term capital gain up to the amount of the NUA. Any gain in excess of the NUA will be taxed as long-term capital gain only if you hold the stock after distribution for at least 12 months prior to selling it. Alternatively, you can elect to treat the NUA as part of the lump-sum distribution subject to immediate tax. This may be desirable if you otherwise have tax losses that can offset the amount of the NUA. For more information, see *Net Unrealized Appreciation (NUA),* later.

Beginning on the day after you reach minimum retirement age, payments you receive are taxable as a pension or annuity. Report the payments on Form 1040, lines 16a and 16b, or on Form 1040A, lines 12a and 12b.

For more information on how to report disability pensions, including military and certain government disability pensions, see chapter 5.

Retired public safety officers. An eligible retired public safety officer can elect to exclude from income distributions of up to $3,000 made directly from a government retirement plan to the provider of accident, health, or long-term disability insurance. See *Insurance Premiums for Retired Public Safety Officers* in Publication 575 for more information.

Railroad retirement benefits. Part of any railroad retirement benefits you receive is treated for tax purposes like social security benefits, and part is treated like an employee pension. For information about railroad retirement benefits treated as social security benefits, see Publication 915, *Social Security and Equivalent Railroad Retirement Benefits*. For information about railroad retirement benefits treated as an employee pension, see *Railroad Retirement Benefits* in Publication 575.

EXPLANATION

Unless you elect to have your distribution paid *directly* to an eligible retirement plan, the payer of benefits from your pension, profit-sharing, stock bonus, annuity, or other qualified deferred compensation plan is required to withhold an amount equal to 20% of any designated distribution that is an eligible rollover distribution. An eligible rollover distribution is any distribution of all or a portion of an employee's balance in a qualified plan or tax-sheltered annuity arrangement other than (1) any distribution that is one of a series of substantially equal periodic payments made over the life or life expectancy of the employee (or the joint lives or joint life expectancies of the employee and the employee's designated beneficiary) or made over a period of 10 years or more, (2) required minimum distributions, and (3) certain corrective and deemed distributions. An eligible retirement plan is generally another qualified retirement plan, an individual retirement account, an individual retirement annuity, a governmental Section 457 plan, or a 403(b) tax-sheltered annuity.

If the payment made to you is not an eligible rollover distribution, the payer will withhold income tax on the taxable amounts paid to you. However, withholding from these payments is not mandatory and you can tell the payer how to withhold by filing Form W-4P, Withholding Certificate for Pension or Annuity Payments. If you choose not to have tax withheld, you may have to pay estimated tax.

Withholding and estimated tax. The payer of your pension, profit-sharing, stock bonus, annuity, or deferred compensation plan will withhold income tax on the taxable parts of amounts paid to you. You can tell the payer how much to withhold, or not to withhold, by filing Form W-4P. If you choose not to have tax withheld, or you do not have enough tax withheld, you may have to pay estimated tax.

If you receive an eligible rollover distribution, you cannot choose not to have tax withheld. 20% will generally be withheld, but no tax will be withheld on a direct rollover of an eligible rollover distribution. See *Direct rollover option* under *Rollovers*, later.

For more information, see *Pensions and Annuities* under *Tax Withholding for 2012* in chapter 4.

Qualified plans for self-employed individuals. Qualified plans set up by self-employed individuals are sometimes called Keogh or H.R. 10 plans. Qualified plans can be set up by sole proprietors, partnerships (but not a partner), and corporations. They can cover self-employed persons, such as the sole proprietor or partners, as well as regular (common-law) employees.

Distributions from a qualified plan are usually fully taxable because most recipients have no cost basis. If you have an investment (cost) in the plan, however, your pension or annuity payments from a qualified plan are taxed under the Simplified Method. For more information about qualified plans, see Publication 560, *Retirement Plans for Small Business*.

Purchased annuities. If you receive pension or annuity payments from a privately purchased annuity contract from a commercial organization, such as an insurance company, you generally must use the General Rule to figure the tax-free part of each annuity payment. For more information about the General Rule, get Publication 939. Also, see *Variable Annuities* in Publication 575 for the special provisions that apply to these annuity contracts.

Loans. If you borrow money from your retirement plan, you must treat the loan as a nonperiodic distribution from the plan unless certain exceptions apply. This treatment also applies to any loan under a contract purchased under your retirement plan, and to the value of any part of your interest in the plan or contract that you pledge or assign. This means that you must include in income all or part of the amount borrowed. Even if you do not have to treat the loan as a nonperiodic distribution, you may not be able to deduct the interest on the loan in some situations. For details, see *Loans Treated as Distributions* in Publication 575. For information on the deductibility of interest, see chapter 24.

EXCEPTION

A loan will not be considered a distribution to the extent that the loan (when added to the outstanding balance of all other loans maintained by the employer) does not exceed the lesser of (1) $50,000 or (2) the greater of either $10,000 or one-half of the participant's vested accrued benefits under the plan. The $50,000 limit is reduced by the excess of the participant's highest outstanding loan balance during the preceding 12-month period, over the outstanding balance at the date of the new loan.

In addition, the exception does not apply unless the loan by its terms must be repaid within 5 years and requires level repayments made not less frequently than quarterly over the term of the loan.

The 5-year rule does not generally apply to loans made in connection with the purchase of a principal residence of a participant.

TAXALERT

Interest on a loan from an employee plan is only deductible under the general loan interest rules (discussed in chapter 24, *Interest expense*). Even if the interest is otherwise deductible under the general rules, it will not be deductible if the loan was made to a key employee or secured by amounts attributable to an employee's salary reduction amounts. It should also be noted that personal loan interest is not deductible.

TAXPLANNER

Loans from a retirement plan may be an option to provide for your children's college expenses, a housing down payment, or any other family need. The interest you pay on the loan helps your account grow at an attractive rate if the plan credits interest paid on the loan to your account. But there are some significant risks to consider before taking such a loan. One downside is that you may earn less in your plan from this interest than you would have had you left the money in other investments. Another drawback is that any loan that is not paid back within 5 years is subject to income tax and penalties, and perhaps above all, your retirement plan is depleted. Saving for education through a 529 plan and even taking out student loans may be preferable.

Elective deferrals. Some retirement plans allow you to elect to have your employer contribute part of your compensation to a retirement fund, rather than have it paid to you. You do not pay income tax on this money until you receive it in a distribution from the plan. Generally, you may not defer more than a total of $16,500 ($22,000 for individuals who have attained at least age 50 by year-end) for all qualified plans by which you are covered in 2011.

Elective deferrals generally include elective contributions to cash or deferred arrangements [known as *401(k) plans*] and elective contributions to Section 501(c)(18)(D) plans, salary reduction simplified employee pension (SARSEP) plans, SIMPLE plans, and 403(b) tax-sheltered annuities. Some employers offer a Roth 401(k) account as an alternative to the traditional 401(k) plan. The difference is that instead of your elective contributions being excluded from taxable wages up front and earnings on the 401(k) account being taxed upon withdrawal, your contributions to the Roth 401(k) are included as part of your taxable wages but distributions—if certain requirements are met—of both your contributions and all future earnings thereon are completely tax-free.

Certain deferrals (such as cafeteria plan contributions and qualified transportation fringe benefits) that are not included in your gross income are still included in your compensation for purposes of determining your base amount for your 401(k) contributions. For example, the amounts contributed to a cafeteria plan will not decrease the tax-deferred amount that can be contributed by the employer at the election of the employee to his or her 401(k) plan.

TAXPLANNER

There are several special rules used to determine the limit on employee elective deferrals. If the deferrals are otherwise permitted under these special rules, there is an annual limit on elective deferrals–$16,500 for 2011 (plus an additional $5,500 for persons who have attained at least age 50 by the end of the year). This is an aggregate limit for each individual. It takes into consideration all deferrals by that individual during the year to all 401(k) plans (including Roth 401(k) accounts), 403(b) tax-sheltered annuities, SIMPLE plans, and salary reduction simplified employee pension (SARSEPs) plans. (Employers that established SEPS were prohibited in 1996 from establishing any new SARSEPS–which are salary reduction SEPS–after December 31, 1996). An SEP is a special type of IRA established by an employer for all its employees.

The limit on contributions to a SIMPLE plan is $11,500; so if the employee has access only to a SIMPLE plan, the employee can only defer $11,500 because the SIMPLE limit cuts off the permissible $16,500. However, if the employee moves mid-year to another employer that has a 401(k) plan, then the combined $16,500 limit applies (as long as not more than $11,500 was deferred to the SIMPLE). The limit applies even if the employee makes deferrals to plans sponsored by different employers or to different types of plans (elective contributions to Section 457 plans for government and non-profit employees are not included in this aggregation). Note that this limit is an elective contribution limit. There is also a limit on total employer contributions to qualified defined contribution plans of $49,000 in 2011; for this limit, elective deferrals are treated as employer contributions. Thus, if you are under age 50 and make the maximum deferral of $16,500 in 2011, you only have $32,500 left for other employer contributions.

The dollar limit is indexed annually for inflation in $500 increments.

Example

Assume Steve works for Employer A from January 2011 to April 2011 and defers $5,000 to Employer A's 401(k) plan during this time. If Steve leaves in May 2011 to work for Employer B for the remainder of the year, the most Steve could defer to Employer B's 401(k) plan for the remainder of 2011 is $11,500.

Alternatively, assume Steve works for Employer A from January 2011 to August 2011 and defers $7,500 to Employer A's 401(k) plan. In September, Steve leaves to work for Employer B, which sponsors a SIMPLE IRA for its employees. Steve will only be allowed to defer $8,500 to the SIMPLE IRA for 2011–$16,500 aggregate limit less $7,500 already deferred to Employer A's 401(k) plan. If instead Steve had deferred only $2,500 in Employer A's 401(k) plan, then because the elective deferral limit for a SIMPLE is $11,500, Steve would only be able to defer an additional $11,500 even though the total amount of elective deferrals for the year is only $14,000.

TAXALERT

If you are at least 50 years old by the end of the taxable year, you can elect to defer even more to a 401(k) plan, a 403(b) tax-sheltered annuity, a SARSEP, a SIMPLE plan, or a governmental Section 457 plan. The additional amount of elective contributions that may be made is the lesser of (1) the applicable dollar amount (as described) or (2) your compensation for the year reduced by any other elective deferrals you made for the year. The applicable dollar amount for age 50 catch-up contributions under a 401(k) plan, a 403(b) tax-sheltered annuity, a SARSEP, or a governmental Section 457 plan is $5,500 for 2011. The applicable dollar amount for the age 50 catch-up contributions under a SIMPLE plan is $2,500 for 2011.

TAXALERT

If you realize that you made excess elective deferrals (the limit is $16,500 or, if you have attained age 50, $22,000 for 2011) in any given calendar year, be certain to notify your plan administrator(s) as soon as possible. The excess deferral amount will be taxable to you in the year of the deferral. In addition, if this excess deferral (plus earnings for the year) is not distributed to you by the following April 15, the excess deferral amount will again be taxed to you when it is ultimately distributed to you upon your retirement or separation from your employer. If the excess deferral is distributed to you by the following April 15, however, it will not be taxed a second time when distributed (although the income attributable to the excess deferral will be taxed to you in the year of distribution). Excess deferrals (with earnings or losses attributable to such excess deferrals) in 2011 must be distributed by April 17, 2012. (The due date is April 17, 2012, instead of April 15, because April 15, 2012, falls on Sunday, and the following day, April 16, is the Emancipation Day holiday in the District of Columbia, which is observed as a legal holiday.)

Any earnings or losses on the excess deferral occurring after December 31 of the deferral year do not impact the amount of the distribution if the excess is distributed by April 15 of the following year; only earnings or losses on the excess deferral through December 31 of the year of deferral are distributed at this time.

TAXPLANNER

The benefits of 401(k) plans are substantial. The elective deferrals are not subject to federal, most state, and most local income taxes until they are withdrawn. (They are subject to social security and Medicare taxes at the time of deferral, though.) Earnings on elective deferrals are also not subject to income tax until they are withdrawn. An employer matching contribution program (which is deductible to the employer within certain limits and not taxable to the employee until distributed) can encourage employees to make elective deferrals. Finally, on withdrawal, a lump-sum distribution can escape immediate income tax or excise tax if it is deposited into a rollover account. For more information, see *Rollovers* later in this chapter.

Since 2006, the law also allows employers to offer "Roth 401(k)" plans to their employees. Under a Roth 401(k), contributions are nondeductible but all the income in the plan is tax-free if certain requirements are met at distribution. (The regular 401(k) dollar limitation applies to the combination of regular and Roth 401(k) contributions.) These requirements are similar to those that apply to Roth IRAs, which are discussed in chapter 17, *Individual retirement arrangements (IRAs)*. However, unlike with Roth IRAs, the ability to contribute to a Roth 401(k) is not limited to those with income below certain limits.

TAXPLANNER

403(b) plans (tax-sheltered annuity, or TSA plans), which are available to employees of certain tax-exempt organizations, to employees of educational organizations and of state and local governments, and to certain church employees, offer many of the same benefits that 401(k) plans offer. The elective deferrals are not subject to federal income tax, most state income taxes, and most local income taxes, until they are withdrawn. Earnings on elective deferrals are also not subject to income tax until they are withdrawn. Rollovers are permitted for qualifying distributions, which avoid immediate income tax or excise taxes, if applicable. Effective for distributions made after December 31, 2001, eligible rollover distributions from a TSA plan can be rolled over into a qualified retirement plan, another TSA plan, or an IRA, including a Roth IRA. Under a 2010 tax law, if the TSA has a designated Roth contribution program, amounts held inside a pre-tax account can be rolled over to a designated Roth account within the plan. (Distributions rolled over to either a designated Roth account within the TSA or to a Roth IRA are subject to special rules for rollovers to Roth IRAs from non-Roth accounts.)

State and local governments (other than rural cooperative plans and, for certain employees, Indian tribal governments) cannot provide 401(k) plans to their employees, although they may offer a TSA plan for employees of certain educational organizations and they may offer Section 457 plans.

For information about tax-sheltered annuities, see Publication 571, *Tax-Sheltered Annuity Programs for Employees of Public Schools and Certain Tax-Exempt Organizations*. For information on Section 457 plans, see Publication 4484, *Choose a Retirement Plan for Employees of Tax Exempt and Government Entities*.

TAXSAVER

Individuals earning limited amounts of self-employment income may be able to shelter all or a substantial portion of their income by utilizing a SIMPLE IRA. (Note: Unless you are self-employed, other than as a partner, SIMPLE IRAs may only be established by your employer.) Although an individual may only defer $11,500 in 2011 to a SIMPLE IRA, these deferrals are not limited to a certain percentage of an individual's compensation as is the case with other plans. For example, in 2011 an individual with $12,500 in self-employment income (e.g., director's fees) could defer $11,500 (or 84%) of the income into a SIMPLE IRA. In addition to the $11,500 employee deferral, either a 3% matching contribution or a 2% employer contribution would be required to satisfy the SIMPLE IRA rules. On the other hand, the same individual could only contribute 25% of the income (after reduction for the 25% contribution itself) into an SEP, or $2,500. (An even better alternative would be a Keogh/401(k) plan combination. Under that type of plan, you could contribute up to the full 401(k) limit of $16,500.) See the discussion in chapter 17, *Individual retirement arrangements (IRAs)*, for more details on the requirements for SIMPLE IRAs.

Tax-free exchange. No gain or loss is recognized on an exchange of an annuity contract for another annuity contract if the insured or annuitant remains the same. However, if an annuity contract is exchanged for a life insurance or endowment contract, any gain due to interest accumulated on the contract is ordinary income. See *Transfers of Annuity Contracts* in Publication 575 for more information about exchanges of annuity contracts.

How To Report

If you file Form 1040, report your total annuity on line 16a and the taxable part on line 16b. If your pension or annuity is fully taxable, enter it on line 16b; do not make an entry on line 16a.

If you file Form 1040A, report your total annuity on line 12a and the taxable part on line 12b. If your pension or annuity is fully taxable, enter it on line 12b; do not make an entry on line 12a.

More than one annuity. If you receive more than one annuity and at least one of them is not fully taxable, enter the total amount received from all annuities on Form 1040, line 16a, or Form 1040A, line 12a, and enter the taxable part on Form 1040, line 16b, or Form 1040A, line 12b. If all the annuities you receive are fully taxable, enter the total of all of them on Form 1040, line 16b, or Form 1040A, line 12b.

Joint return. If you file a joint return and you and your spouse each receive one or more pensions or annuities, report the total of the pensions and annuities on Form 1040, line 16a, or Form 1040A, line 12a, and report the taxable part on Form 1040, line 16b, or Form 1040A, line 12b.

Cost (Investment in the Contract)

Before you can figure how much, if any, of a distribution from your pension or annuity plan is taxable, you must determine your cost (your investment in the contract) in the pension or annuity. Your total cost in the plan includes the total premiums, contributions, or other amounts you paid. This includes the amounts your employer contributed that were taxable to you when paid. Cost does not include any amounts you deducted or that were excluded from your income.

From this total cost, subtract any refunds of premiums, rebates, dividends, unpaid loans that were not included in your income, or other tax-free amounts that you received by the later of the annuity starting date or the date on which you received your first payment.

Your annuity starting date is the later of the first day of the first period for which you received a payment, or the date the plan's obligations became fixed.

Designated Roth accounts. Your cost in these accounts is your designated Roth contributions that were included in your income as wages subject to applicable withholding requirements.

Foreign employment contributions. If you worked in a foreign country and contributions were made to your retirement plan, special rules apply in determining your cost. See Publication 575.

Taxation of Periodic Payments

Fully taxable payments. Generally, if you did not pay any part of the cost of your employee pension or annuity and your employer did not withhold part of the cost from your pay while you worked, the amounts you receive each year are fully taxable. You must report them on your income tax return.

Partly taxable payments. If you paid part of the cost of your pension or annuity, you are not taxed on the part of the pension or annuity you receive that represents a return of your cost. The rest of the amount you receive is generally taxable. You figure the tax-free part of the payment using either the Simplified Method or the General Rule. Your annuity starting date and whether or not your plan is qualified determine which method you must or may use.

If your annuity starting date is after November 18, 1996, and your payments are from a qualified plan, you must use the Simplified Method. Generally, you must use the General Rule if your annuity is paid under a nonqualified plan, and you cannot use this method if your annuity is paid under a qualified plan.

If you had more than one partly taxable pension or annuity, figure the tax-free part and the taxable part of each separately.

If your annuity is paid under a qualified plan and your annuity starting date is after July 1, 1986, and before November 19, 1996, you could have chosen to use either the General Rule or the Simplified Method.

Exclusion limit. Your annuity starting date determines the total amount of annuity payments that you can exclude from your taxable income over the years. Once your annuity starting date is determined, it does not change. If you calculate the taxable portion of your annuity payments using the simplified method worksheet, the annuity starting date determines the recovery period for your cost. That recovery period begins on your annuity starting date and is not affected by the date you first complete the worksheet.

Exclusion limited to cost. If your annuity starting date is after 1986, the total amount of annuity income that you can exclude over the years as a recovery of the cost cannot exceed your total cost. Any unrecovered cost at your (or the last annuitant's) death is allowed as a miscellaneous itemized deduction on the final return of the decedent. This deduction is not subject to the 2%-of-adjusted-gross-income limit.

Exclusion not limited to cost. If your annuity starting date is before 1987, you can continue to take your monthly exclusion for as long as you receive your annuity. If you chose a joint and survivor annuity, your survivor can continue to take the survivor's exclusion figured as of the annuity starting date. The total exclusion may be more than your cost.

TAXALERT

Your cost includes contributions by your employer if you were required to include the amounts in your gross income.

For distributions on or after October 22, 2004, your cost will include only amounts that have been taxed in the U.S. or in a foreign jurisdiction.

Simplified Method

Under the Simplified Method, you figure the tax-free part of each annuity payment by dividing your cost by the total number of anticipated monthly payments. For an annuity that is payable for the lives of the annuitants, this number is based on the annuitants' ages on the annuity starting date and is determined from a table. For any other annuity, this number is the number of monthly annuity payments under the contract.

Who must use the Simplified Method. You must use the Simplified Method if your annuity starting date is after November 18, 1996, and you both:

1. Receive pension or annuity payments from a qualified employee plan, qualified employee annuity, or a tax-sheltered annuity (403(b)) plan, and
2. On your annuity starting date, you were either under age 75, or entitled to less than 5 years of guaranteed payments.

TAXALERT

If your annuity starting date is after November 18, 1996, you must use the Simplified Method for payments from a qualified plan unless you have attained age 75 and your annuity payments are guaranteed for at least 5 years.

Guaranteed payments. Your annuity contract provides guaranteed payments if a minimum number of payments or a minimum amount (for example, the amount of your investment) is payable even if you and any survivor annuitant do not live to receive the minimum. If the minimum amount is less than the total amount of the payments you are to receive, barring death, during the first 5 years after payments begin (figured by ignoring any payment increases), you are entitled to less than 5 years of guaranteed payments.

How to use the Simplified Method. Complete the Simplified Method Worksheet in Publication 575 to figure your taxable annuity for 2011.

Single-life annuity. If your annuity is payable for your life alone, use Table 1 at the bottom of the worksheet to determine the total number of expected monthly payments. Enter on line 3 the number shown for your age at the annuity starting date.

Multiple-lives annuity. If your annuity is payable for the lives of more than one annuitant, use Table 2 at the bottom of the worksheet to determine the total number of expected monthly payments. Enter on line 3 the number shown for the combined ages of you and the youngest survivor annuitant at the annuity starting date.

However, if your annuity starting date is before January 1, 1998, do not use Table 2 and do not combine the annuitants' ages. Instead you must use Table 1 and enter on line 3 the number shown for the primary annuitant's age on the annuity starting date.

Example. Bill Smith, age 65, began receiving retirement benefits in 2011, under a joint and survivor annuity. Bill's annuity starting date is January 1, 2011. The benefits are to be paid for the joint lives of Bill and his wife Kathy, age 65. Bill had contributed $31,000 to a qualified plan and had received no distributions before the annuity starting date. Bill is to receive a retirement benefit of $1,200 a month, and Kathy is to receive a monthly survivor benefit of $600 upon Bill's death.

Bill must use the Simplified Method to figure his taxable annuity because his payments are from a qualified plan and he is under age 75. Because his annuity is payable over the lives of more than one annuitant, he uses his and Kathy's combined ages and Table 2 at the bottom of the worksheet in completing line 3 of the worksheet. His completed worksheet is shown in Worksheet 10-A.

Bill's tax-free monthly amount is $100 ($31,000 ÷ 310) as shown on line 4 of the worksheet. Upon Bill's death, if Bill has not recovered the full $31,000 investment, Kathy will also exclude $100 from her $600 monthly payment. The full amount of any annuity payments received after 310 payments are paid must be included in gross income.

If Bill and Kathy die before 310 payments are made, a miscellaneous itemized deduction will be allowed for the unrecovered cost on the final income tax return of the last to die. This deduction is not subject to the 2%-of-adjusted-gross-income limit.

Who must use the General Rule. You must use the General Rule if you receive pension or annuity payments from:

*   A nonqualified plan (such as a private annuity, a purchased commercial annuity, or a nonqualified employee plan), or
*   A qualified plan if you are age 75 or older on your annuity starting date and your annuity payments are guaranteed for at least 5 years.

Annuity starting before November 19, 1996. If your annuity starting date is after July 1, 1986, and before November 19, 1996, you had to use the General Rule for either circumstance just described. You also had to use it for any fixed-period annuity. If you did not have to use the General Rule, you could have chosen to use it. If your annuity starting date is before July 2, 1986, you had to use the General Rule unless you could use the Three-Year Rule.

Records

Be sure to keep a copy of the completed worksheet; it will help you figure your taxable annuity next year.

Worksheet 10-A.   **Simplified Method Worksheet for Bill Smith**

1.	Enter the total pension or annuity payments received this year. Also, add this amount to the total for Form 1040, line 16a, or Form 1040A, line 12a	**1.**	14,400
2.	Enter your cost in the plan (contract) at the annuity starting date plus any death benefit exclusion*. See _Cost (Investment in the Contract)_, earlier	**2.**	31,000

Note: _If your annuity starting date was **before** this year and you completed this worksheet last year, skip line 3 and enter the amount from line 4 of last year's worksheet on line 4 below (even if the amount of your pension or annuity has changed). Otherwise, go to line 3._

3.	Enter the appropriate number from Table 1 below. **But** if your annuity starting date was **after** 1997 **and** the payments are for your life and that of your beneficiary, enter the appropriate number from Table 2 below	**3.**	310
4.	Divide line 2 by the number on line 3	**4.**	100
5.	Multiply line 4 by the number of months for which this year's payments were made. If your annuity starting date was **before** 1987, enter this amount on line 8 below and skip lines 6, 7, 10, and 11. Otherwise, go to line 6	**5.**	1,200
6.	Enter any amounts previously recovered tax free in years after 1986. This is the amount shown on line 10 of your worksheet for last year	**6.**	-0-
7.	Subtract line 6 from line 2	**7.**	31,000
8.	Enter the _smaller_ of line 5 or line 7	**8.**	1,200
9.	**Taxable amount for year.** Subtract line 8 from line 1. Enter the result, but not less than zero. Also, add this amount to the total for Form 1040, line 16b, or Form 1040A, line 12b	**9.**	13,200

Note: _If your Form 1099-R shows a larger taxable amount, use the amount figured on this line instead. If you are a retired public safety officer, see Insurance Premiums for Retired Public Safety Officers in Publication 575 before entering an amount on your tax return._

10.	Was your annuity starting date before 1987? ☐ Yes. **STOP.** Do not complete the rest of this worksheet. ☒ No. Add lines 6 and 8. This is the amount you have recovered tax free through 2010. You will need this number if you need to fill out this worksheet next year	**10.**	1,200
11.	**Balance of cost to be recovered.** Subtract line 10 from line 2. If zero, you will not have to complete this worksheet next year. The payments you receive next year will generally be fully taxable	**11.**	29,800

TABLE 1 FOR LINE 3 ABOVE
AND your annuity starting date was–

IF the age at annuity starting date was...	before November 19, 1996, enter on line 3...	after November 18, 1996, enter on line 3...
55 or under	300	360
56-60	260	310
61-65	240	260
66-70	170	210
71 or older	120	160

TABLE 2 FOR LINE 3 ABOVE

IF the combined ages at annuity starting date were...	THEN enter on line 3...
110 or under	410
111-120	360
121-130	310
131-140	260
141 or older	210

* A death benefit exclusion (up to $5,000) applied to certain benefits received by employees who died before August 21, 1996.

If you had to use the General Rule (or chose to use it), you must continue to use it each year that you recover your cost.

Who cannot use the General Rule. You cannot use the General Rule if you receive your pension or annuity from a qualified plan and none of the circumstances described in the preceding discussions apply to you. See *Who must use the Simplified Method*, earlier.

More information. For complete information on using the General Rule, including the actuarial tables you need, see Publication 939.

Taxation of Nonperiodic Payments

Nonperiodic distributions are also known as amounts not received as an annuity. They include all payments other than periodic payments and corrective distributions. Examples of nonperiodic payments are cash withdrawals, distributions of current earnings, certain loans, and the value of annuity contracts transferred without full and adequate consideration.

Corrective distributions of excess plan contributions. Generally, if the contributions made for you during the year to certain retirement plans exceed certain limits, the excess is taxable to you. To correct an excess, your plan may distribute it to you (along with any income earned on the excess). For information on plan contribution limits and how to report corrective distributions of excess contributions, see *Retirement Plan Contributions* under *Employee Compensation* in Publication 525.

Figuring the taxable amount of nonperiodic payments. How you figure the taxable amount of a nonperiodic distribution depends on whether it is made before the annuity starting date or on or after the annuity starting date. If it is made before the annuity starting date, its tax treatment also depends on whether it is made under a qualified or nonqualified plan and, if it is made under a nonqualified plan, whether it fully discharges the contract, is received under certain life insurance or endowment contracts, or is allocable to an investment you made before August 14, 1982.

Annuity starting date. The annuity starting date is either the first day of the first period for which you receive an annuity payment under the contract or the date on which the obligation under the contract becomes fixed, whichever is later.

Distribution on or after annuity starting date. If you receive a nonperiodic payment from your annuity contract on or after the annuity starting date, you generally must include all of the payment in gross income.

Distribution before annuity starting date. If you receive a nonperiodic distribution before the annuity starting date from a qualified retirement plan, you generally can allocate only part of it to the cost of the contract. You exclude from your gross income the part that you allocate to the cost. You include the remainder in your gross income.

If you receive a nonperiodic distribution before the annuity starting date from a plan other than a qualified retirement plan, it is allocated first to earnings (the taxable part) and then to the cost of the contract (the tax-free part). This allocation rule applies, for example, to a commercial annuity contract you bought directly from the issuer.

For more information, see *Figuring the Taxable Amount*, under *Taxation of Nonperiodic Payments*, in Publication 575.

EXPLANATION
If you receive a distribution and, to avoid the current tax, decide to roll it over into another retirement vehicle such as an IRA, you still are required to show the total amount received on line 16a (or line 12a, Form 1040A). However, on line 16b (or line 12b, Form 1040A) you would show the taxable amount as zero. Also, enter "Rollover" next to line 16b (or line 12b, Form 1040A).

Lump-Sum Distributions

A lump-sum distribution is the distribution or payment in one tax year of a plan participant's entire balance from all of the employer's qualified plans of one kind (for example, pension, profit-sharing, or stock bonus plans). A distribution from a nonqualified plan (such as a privately purchased commercial annuity or a section 457 deferred compensation plan of a state or local government or tax-exempt organization) cannot qualify as a lump-sum distribution.

The participant's entire balance from a plan does not include certain forfeited amounts. It also does not include any deductible voluntary employee contributions allowed by the plan after 1981 and before 1987. For more information about distributions that do not qualify as lump-sum distributions, see *Distributions that do not qualify* under *Lump-Sum Distributions* in Publication 575.

> ### TAXALERT
> Involuntary distribution requirements. A plan may not distribute your vested accrued benefit to you without your consent (and the consent of your spouse if the qualified joint and survivor annuity rules apply) unless the present value of your accrued benefit is $5,000 or less. Effective for distributions made after December 31, 2001, in determining your accrued benefit for purposes of the $5,000 limitation on involuntary distributions, employers may disregard benefits and related earnings, which are attributable to rollover contributions. Involuntary distributions that exceed $1,000 must be rolled over automatically to a designated IRA, unless you affirmatively elect to have the distribution transferred to a different IRA or qualified plan, or to receive it directly.

> ### TAXPLANNER
> If you change jobs and plan to participate in your new employer's plan, you may want to consider a "plan-to-plan" transfer to the new plan, if your new employer allows. If an amount is transferred from one qualified plan to another, no amount will be required to be withheld on the amount transferred from your old employer's plan. While there is nothing in the law that requires your new employer to accept transferred amounts, some employers may do this as an accommodation to new employees.
>
> Plan-to-plan transfers have certain advantages over rollovers. See *Rollovers*, later in this chapter.

If you receive a lump-sum distribution from a qualified employee plan or qualified employee annuity and the plan participant was born before January 2, 1936, you may be able to elect optional methods of figuring the tax on the distribution. The part from active participation in the plan before 1974 may qualify as capital gain subject to a 20% tax rate. The part from participation after 1973 (and any part from participation before 1974 that you do not report as capital gain) is ordinary income. You may be able to use the *10-year tax option*, discussed later, to figure tax on the ordinary income part.

Use Form 4972 to figure the separate tax on a lump-sum distribution using the optional methods. The tax figured on Form 4972 is added to the regular tax figured on your other income. This may result in a smaller tax than you would pay by including the taxable amount of the distribution as ordinary income in figuring your regular tax.

How to treat the distribution. If you receive a lump-sum distribution, you may have the following options for how you treat the taxable part.
- Report the part of the distribution from participation before 1974 as a capital gain (if you qualify) and the part from participation after 1973 as ordinary income.
- Report the part of the distribution from participation before 1974 as a capital gain (if you qualify) and use the 10-year tax option to figure the tax on the part from participation after 1973 (if you qualify).
- Use the 10-year tax option to figure the tax on the total taxable amount (if you qualify).
- Roll over all or part of the distribution. See *Rollovers*, later. No tax is currently due on the part rolled over. Report any part not rolled over as ordinary income.
- Report the entire taxable part of the distribution as ordinary income on your tax return.

The first three options are explained in the following discussions.

Electing optional lump-sum treatment. You can choose to use the 10-year tax option or capital gain treatment only once after 1986 for any plan participant. If you make this choice, you cannot use either of these optional treatments for any future distributions for the participant.

Taxable and tax-free parts of the distribution. The taxable part of a lump-sum distribution is the employer's contributions and income earned on your account. You may recover your cost in the lump sum and any net unrealized appreciation (NUA) in employer securities tax free.

Cost. In general, your cost is the total of:
- The plan participant's nondeductible contributions to the plan,
- The plan participant's taxable costs of any life insurance contract distributed,
- Any employer contributions that were taxable to the plan participant, and
- Repayments of any loans that were taxable to the plan participant.

You must reduce this cost by amounts previously distributed tax free.

Net unrealized appreciation (NUA). The NUA in employer securities (box 6 of Form 1099-R) received as part of a lump-sum distribution is generally tax free until you sell or exchange the securities. (For more information, see *Distributions of employer securities* under *Taxation of Nonperiodic Payments* in Publication 575.)

EXPLANATION

Employer securities distributed as part of a lump-sum distribution may have increased in value after they were purchased by the trust that is making the distribution. This increase is called "net unrealized appreciation." It is not taxed at the time of the lump-sum distribution.

If you later sell these securities, any gain is taxed as a long-term capital gain (i.e., as if held for more than 12 months)—up to the amount of your net unrealized appreciation (NUA). Any gain above this amount is a long-term capital gain only if the employee holds the stock after distribution for more than 12 months prior to selling it.

You may also elect not to use this treatment on your tax return and instead treat the NUA as part of your lump-sum distribution. This may be desirable if you have tax losses that can offset the amount of NUA.

You may not claim a loss if you receive stock that is worth less than your total contributions to the plan. You may claim a loss when you sell the stock if it is sold for less than the amount of your own after-tax employee contributions allocated to the shares of stock sold.

Example

Assume that Widget Company's pension trust used the company's contribution for Sarah Jones to purchase 100 shares of Widget Company common stock at $10 per share on January 10, 2001. These securities were given to Sarah Jones as part of a lump-sum distribution on January 4, 2011, when their value had risen to $15 per share. Sarah is taxed on the $10 per share that was contributed by Widget, but she is not taxed on the NUA of $5 per share on January 4, 2011.

If Sarah sold the 100 shares of Widget Company stock on January 11, 2011, for $25 per share, $500 of the gain [($15 − $10) × 100 shares] attributed to NUA would be taxed as long-term capital gain. The balance of the gain, $1,000 [($25 − $5 − $10) × 100 shares], would be taxed as a short-term capital gain, since Sarah did not hold the securities for more than 12 months from the distribution date.

If Sarah had made her own after-tax contributions of $1,700 to the pension trust and received Widget Company stock valued at only $1,000 at the time of the lump-sum distribution, she could not have claimed a loss at that time. However, if she later sold the stock, she would compare her proceeds with $1,700 to determine if she had a gain or a loss on the sale.

TAXPLANNER

If you receive only employer securities in an eligible rollover distribution (or employer securities and less than $200 in cash), there is no mandatory 20% withholding requirement. See *Rollovers*, later in this chapter. Therefore, it may be beneficial under some circumstances for you to receive an eligible rollover distribution consisting solely of employer securities and up to $200 in cash rather than all cash or a mix of cash (greater than $200) and employer securities.

Capital Gain Treatment

Capital gain treatment applies only to the taxable part of a lump-sum distribution resulting from participation in the plan before 1974. The amount treated as capital gain is taxed at a 20% rate. You can elect this treatment only once for any plan participant, and only if the plan participant was born before January 2, 1936.

Complete Part II of Form 4972 to choose the 20% capital gain election. For more information, see *Capital Gain Treatment* under *Lump-Sum Distributions* in Publication 575.

10-Year Tax Option

The 10-year tax option is a special formula used to figure a separate tax on the ordinary income part of a lump-sum distribution. You pay the tax only once, for the year in which you receive the distribution, not over the next 10 years. You can elect this treatment only once for any plan participant, and only if the plan participant was born before January 2, 1936.

The ordinary income part of the distribution is the amount shown in box 2a of the Form 1099-R given to you by the payer, minus the amount, if any, shown in box 3. You also can treat the capital gain part of the distribution (box 3 of Form 1099-R) as ordinary income for the 10-year tax option if you do not choose capital gain treatment for that part.

Complete Part III of Form 4972 to choose the 10-year tax option. You must use the special Tax Rate Schedule shown in the instructions for Part III to figure the tax. Publication 575 illustrates how to complete Form 4972 to figure the separate tax.

Rollovers

If you withdraw cash or other assets from a qualified retirement plan in an eligible rollover distribution, you can defer tax on the distribution by rolling it over to another qualified retirement plan or a traditional IRA.

For this purpose, the following plans are qualified retirement plans.
- A qualified employee plan.
- A qualified employee annuity.
- A tax-sheltered annuity plan (403(b) plan).
- An eligible state or local government section 457 deferred compensation plan.

TAXSAVER
The distribution from a qualified plan is includible in the taxpayer's gross income subject to tax, except to the extent the distribution consists of a return of after-tax contributions or is rolled over. (See *Can You Move Amounts Into a Roth IRA?* in chapter 17, *Individual retirement arrangements (IRAs),* for more information.)

TAXALERT
Starting in 2010, distributions from a qualified retirement plan can be rolled over directly to a Roth IRA regardless of the taxpayer's adjusted gross income. Also, a 2010 tax law allows 401(k), 403(b), and governmental 457(b) plans to permit participants to roll their pre-tax account balances into a designated Roth account within the same plan.

TAXSAVER
If you want to roll over the taxable portion of your income to a traditional IRA (so it is not currently taxed) and your basis to a Roth IRA so the earnings on the basis won't be taxed when eventually distributed, the safest way to do that is to have the plan distribute the full amount to you (withholding the necessary 20%). Then within 60 days of the distribution, (in this order) roll over the taxable amount plus other funds equal to the amount withheld to a traditional IRA, and then on the next day (or after the first rollover and before 60 days from the date of the distribution), roll the remaining amount (all basis) to the Roth IRA. In this way, you will pay no tax on the distribution now and the earnings on the basis will not be taxed on eventual distribution.

Eligible rollover distributions. Generally, an eligible rollover distribution is any distribution of all or any part of the balance to your credit in a qualified retirement plan. For information about exceptions to eligible rollover distributions, see Publication 575.

Rollover of nontaxable amounts. You may be able to roll over the nontaxable part of a distribution (such as your after-tax contributions) made to another qualified retirement plan that is a qualified employee plan or a 403(b) plan, or to a traditional or Roth IRA. The transfer must be made either through a direct rollover to a qualified plan or 403(b) plan that separately accounts for the taxable and nontaxable parts of the rollover or through a rollover to a traditional or Roth IRA.

If you roll over only part of a distribution that includes both taxable and nontaxable amounts, the amount you roll over is treated as coming first from the taxable part of the distribution.

Any after-tax contributions that you roll over into your traditional IRA become part of your basis (cost) in your IRAs. To recover your basis when you take distributions from your IRA, you must complete Form 8606 for the year of the distribution. For more information, see the Form 8606 instructions.

Direct rollover option. You can choose to have any part or all of an eligible rollover distribution paid directly to another qualified retirement plan that accepts rollover distributions, or to a traditional or Roth IRA. If you choose the direct rollover option, or have an automatic rollover, no tax will be withheld from any part of the distribution that is directly paid to the trustee of the other plan.

Payment to you option. If an eligible rollover distribution is paid to you, 20% generally will be withheld for income tax. However, the full amount is treated as distributed to you even though you actually receive only 80%. You generally must include in income any part (including the part withheld) that you do not roll over within 60 days to another qualified retirement plan or to a traditional or Roth IRA. (See *Pensions and Annuities* under *Tax Withholding for 2012* in chapter 4.)

Caution

If you decide to roll over an amount equal to the distribution before withholding, your contribution to the new plan or IRA must include other money (for example, from savings or amounts borrowed) to replace the amount withheld.

Time for making rollover. You generally must complete the rollover of an eligible rollover distribution paid to you by the 60th day following the day on which you receive the distribution from your employer's plan. (If an amount distributed to you becomes a frozen deposit in a financial institution during the 60-day period after you receive it, the rollover period is extended for the period during which the distribution is in a frozen deposit in a financial institution.)

The IRS may waive the 60-day requirement where the failure to do so would be against equity or good conscience, such as in the event of a casualty, disaster, or other event beyond your reasonable control.

The administrator of a qualified plan must give you a written explanation of your distribution options within a reasonable period of time before making an eligible rollover distribution.

Qualified domestic relations order (QDRO). You may be able to roll over tax free all or part of a distribution from a qualified retirement plan that you receive under a QDRO. If you receive the distribution as an employee's spouse or former spouse (not as a nonspousal beneficiary), the rollover rules apply to you as if you were the employee. You can roll over the distribution from the plan into a traditional IRA or to another eligible retirement plan. See Publication 575 for more information on benefits received under a QDRO.

Rollover by surviving spouse. You may be able to roll over tax free all or part of a distribution from a qualified retirement plan you receive as the surviving spouse of a deceased employee. The rollover rules apply to you as if you were the employee. You can roll over a distribution into a qualified retirement plan or a traditional or Roth IRA. For a rollover to a Roth IRA, see *Rollovers to Roth IRAs*, later.

A distribution paid to a beneficiary other than the employee's surviving spouse is generally not an eligible rollover distribution. However, see *Rollovers by nonspouse beneficiary*, next.

Rollovers by nonspouse beneficiary. If you are a designated beneficiary (other than a surviving spouse) of a deceased employee, you may be able to roll over tax free all or a portion of a distribution you receive from an eligible retirement plan of the employee. The distribution must be a direct trustee-to-trustee transfer to your traditional or Roth IRA that was set up to receive the distribution. The transfer will be treated as an eligible rollover distribution and the receiving plan will be treated as an inherited IRA. For information on inherited IRAs, see Publication 590, *Individual Retirement Arrangements (IRAs)*.

EXPLANATION
An inherited IRA is still subject to the minimum required distribution rules (MRD) that would have otherwise applied. See chapter 17, *Individual retirement arrangements (IRAs)*, for more details on MRDs.

Explanation
Any distribution attributable to an employee that is paid to the employee's surviving spouse is treated in the same manner as if the spouse were the employee. The same rule applies if any distribution attributable to an employee is paid to a spouse or a former spouse as an "alternate payee" under a QDRO. A distribution made to the surviving spouse of an employee (or an alternate payee under a QDRO) is an eligible rollover distribution if it meets the requirements explained earlier. For further details, consult your tax advisor.

Retirement bonds. If you redeem retirement bonds purchased under a qualified bond purchase plan, you can roll over the proceeds that exceed your basis tax free into an IRA as discussed in Publication 590 or a qualified employer plan.

Designated Roth accounts. You can roll over an eligible rollover distribution from a designated Roth account only into another designated Roth account or a Roth IRA. If you want to roll over the part of the distribution that is not included in income, you must make a direct rollover of the entire distribution or you can roll over the entire amount (or any portion) to a Roth IRA. For more information on rollovers from designated Roth accounts, see Publication 575.

In-plan rollovers to designated Roth accounts. After September 27, 2010, if you are a participant in a 401(k) or 403(b) plan, your plan may permit you to roll over amounts in those plans to a designated Roth account within the same plan. Governmental 457(b) plans are allowed to offer this rollover option beginning in 2011. The rollover of any untaxed money must be included in income. *Text intentionally omitted.* You must report in-plan Roth rollovers on Form 8606. See Publication 575 for more information.

Text intentionally omitted.

Rollovers to Roth IRAs. You can roll over distributions directly from a qualified retirement plan (other than a designated Roth account) to a Roth IRA .

You must include in your gross income distributions from a qualified retirement plan (other than a designated Roth account) that you would have had to include in income if you had not rolled them over into a Roth IRA. You do not include in gross income any part of a distribution from a qualified retirement plan that is a return of contributions to the plan that were taxable to you when paid. In addition, the 10% tax on early distributions does not apply.

Text intentionally omitted.

Form 8606. You must file Form 8606 with your tax return to report 2011 rollovers from qualified retirement plans (other than designated Roth accounts) to Roth IRAs (unless you recharacterized the entire amount), and to figure the amount to include in income. See the Instructions for Form 8606 for more information.

More information. For more information on the rules for rolling over distributions, see Publication 575.

TAXALERT

Distributions of after-tax contributions from a qualified retirement plan can be rolled over to either a defined contribution or defined benefit plan or to a tax-sheltered annuity that accepts such rollovers of after-tax contributions. A rollover must be done directly from the trustee of the old plan to the trustee of the new plan, and the plan to which the rollover is made must separately account for the after-tax contributions and earnings thereon. (There is no requirement that a plan accept rollovers of after-tax contributions.)

TAXPLANNER

Hardship distributions are not considered eligible rollover distributions. While they are subject to withholding, they are not subject to the mandatory 20% withholding rules that apply to eligible rollover distributions. If you are receiving a hardship distribution, you can elect to reduce the amount withheld from the distribution and retain more cash to satisfy the need giving rise to the hardship by filing a Form W-4P with your plan administrator. See the earlier discussion in this chapter on *Withholding and Estimated Tax*.

TAXPLANNER

If you receive a hardship distribution and another event occurs, such as separation from your employer or attainment of age 59½, so that the distribution is permitted without regard to hardship, you should consult your plan administrator to determine proper treatment of the distribution under your plan. Plans have two alternatives. First, the amount distributed after that event may be treated as eligible for rollover treatment. Alternatively, the distribution may be treated as *ineligible* for rollover even though another event, such as termination of employment, has occurred which could entitle the recipient to a distribution without regard to hardship. Plans must be consistent in the treatment of all distributions.

Plans also have alternatives with respect to allocation of basis. If a segment of a distribution that includes a hardship distribution is not includible in gross income (e.g., after-tax contributions), that piece may be allocated to either the portion ineligible for rollover or the portion eligible for rollover (or between the two portions) using any reasonable method. Again, plans must be consistent in the treatment of the distributions. Consult your plan administrator for additional information.

TAXPLANNER

Remember, if you receive property (such as stock) as part of a rollover distribution, you cannot roll over cash in place of the property received unless the actual property is sold first. The proceeds from the bona fide sale may then be included in the rollover.

Explanation

Generally, an eligible rollover distribution means any distribution of all or any portion of an employee's balance in a qualified plan. Eligible rollover distributions do not include the following:

- Required minimum distributions (e.g., distributions at the later of age 70½ or retirement from the employer maintaining the plan—except 5% owners do not have the retirement-delay option). Distributions that are part of a series of substantially equal payments received at least annually over the life or life expectancy of the employee (or the joint lives or joint life expectancies of the employee and the employee's designated beneficiary), or over a period of at least 10 years;
- Certain corrective distributions made because of the plan's violation of the Internal Revenue Code's limitations. For example, excess contributions returned to highly compensated employees, because the plan fails the 401(k) nondiscrimination (ADP) test for a year;
- Loans treated as distributions because they violate the Internal Revenue Code's plan loan rules;
- Certain dividends paid on employer securities;
- Hardship distributions;
- The cost of life insurance

Eligible rollover distributions can be rolled over in one of two ways. First, you can transfer funds in a direct rollover where the plan trustee transfers some or all of your eligible rollover distribution directly to the trustee of an eligible retirement plan. Second, you can actually receive the distribution and put the money or assets into another qualified plan or IRA within 60 days.

TAXPLANNER

One of the most difficult decisions you have to make when you near retirement is what to do with the amounts held in your qualified pension or profit-sharing plan. There are usually four choices:

1. **Lump-sum distribution.** While virtually all defined contribution plans offer lump-sum payments of benefits, many defined benefit pension plans do not offer lump-sum payments. Other defined benefit pension plans pay lump sums only if the value of benefits is de minimis ($5,000 or less). If you receive a lump-sum from either type of plan, the tax rules are the same. You must roll the distribution over to another qualified plan or to an IRA within 60 days, or the lump-sum distribution (other than the return of after-tax contributions) generally will be taxed to you as ordinary income; the after-tax balance will not be taxed. If you were born before 1936, you may be eligible to pay tax based on 10-year income averaging (discussed earlier).

2. **Annuity.** Defined benefit pension plans and money purchase plans must provide benefits in the form of a joint and survivor annuity. However, an employee, with spousal consent if the employee is married, may agree to receive the money as a lump sum (if the plan so provides). In a defined benefit pension plan, the normal form of payment is described as a single life annuity and is converted into a joint and survivor annuity. You will receive that amount (generally monthly) while you survive and your spouse usually will receive a reduced benefit monthly if he or she survives you. Larger plans pay the annuity from their assets; smaller plans will normally buy the annuity from an insurance company. In the case of a money purchase plan or other individual account plan, the participant has an account and the monthly annuity will be dependent on the annuity the account can purchase from the insurance company when you commence payments.

    Annuities directly from a plan typically pay more than annuities purchased in the individual insurance market. This is because of "adverse selection," the idea that only the healthiest persons with the best genetic history will choose to use their lump sum to purchase an annuity. Income paid from an annuity is treated as ordinary regardless of whether the earnings actually resulted from qualified dividends and/or long-term capital gains.

3. **Rollover to an IRA or other eligible retirement plan.** There is no income tax required to be withheld on any portion of an eligible rollover distribution that is rolled over directly to a traditional IRA or other eligible retirement plan. The principal continues to earn income without tax until it is withdrawn. Withdrawals are taxed at ordinary income rates and are required to begin not later than April 1 of the calendar year following the calendar year in which the employee attains age 70½, or following the calendar year of retirement in the case of an employer plan where the employee is not a 5% owner. Withdrawals from the plan or IRA are required to be made over the life of such employee or over the lives of such employee and a designated beneficiary (or over a period not extending beyond the life expectancy of such employee or the joint life expectancy of such employee and a designated beneficiary). If the rollover is to a Roth IRA, discussed in the next paragraph, there are no required mandatory distributions while the participant is alive.

Beginning in 2010, taxpayers at all income levels, including those who are married filing separately, are now permitted to roll over ("convert") a distribution from an employer qualified retirement plan and/or a traditional IRA into a Roth IRA. Also, a new 2010 tax law allows 401(k), 403(b), and governmental 457(b) plans to permit participants to roll their pre-tax account balances into a designated Roth account within the same plan. The amount distributed is taxable income at the time of the distribution, except to the extent it includes nontaxable amounts (e.g., after-tax contributions). Contributions and earnings in an employer qualified retirement plan or traditional IRA grow tax-free. However, when funds are ultimately withdrawn, they are taxable to the participant. Contributions to a Roth IRA or designated Roth account have already been taxed, but grow tax-free and future withdrawals are not taxed, provided the funds are not withdrawn prematurely (until age 59½ and five years from the date of conversion; however, tax-free distributions may also be made under other circumstances such as disability). For more information, see the section on _Roth IRAs_ in chapter 17, _Individual retirement arrangements (IRAs)._

TAXSAVER

If you want to roll over the taxable portion of a distribution to a traditional IRA (so it is not currently taxed), and your basis to a Roth IRA so the earnings on the basis won't be taxed when eventually distributed, the safest way to do it is to have the plan distribute the full amount to you (withholding the necessary 20%). Within 60 days of the distribution, (in this order) roll over the taxable amount plus other funds equal to the amount withheld to a traditional IRA, and then on the next day (or after the first rollover and before 60 days from the date of the distribution), roll the remaining amount (all basis) to the Roth IRA. In this way, you will pay no tax on the distribution now, and the earnings on the basis will not be taxed on eventual distribution. If you are considering rolling over only your basis amount to a Roth IRA, you should consult with your tax advisor, as this is a complicated area.

5. **Retention in the plan.** If you have more than $5,000 vested in the plan when you terminate employment, the plan must permit you to leave your accrued benefit or account balance in the qualified plan until you reach the later of age 62 or the plan's normal retirement age. (If you have $5,000 or less vested in the plan, the plan may require that you receive your account balance in a lump sum whether or not you consent. However, the $5,000 just affects whether you have a choice about getting a distribution. It neither limits the tax consequences, such as the 10% excise tax on premature distribution, nor affects your ability to roll over the money to a traditional or Roth IRA.)

Examples

Example 1—401(k) Plan. You have $100,000 in the company's 401(k) plan and you will be retiring shortly at age 65. You may have the following options, depending on the plan's distribution and other provisions:

Option 1—*Leave the $100,000 in the Plan.* Some plans require terminated participants to begin benefit payments at normal retirement age. However, many plans have the option of not requiring payments until April 1 of the year following the year the participant attains age 70½. Leaving amounts in the 401(k) plan as long as possible has some advantages, especially if you can direct the investments and are happy with the investment choices. A significant advantage is that you do not have to pay IRA administrative fees. It is also quite possible that the 401(k) plan allows investing in "wholesale" funds, which have lower fees than the "retail" funds you would have available for an IRA.

Option 2—*Take the $100,000 in the Form of a Lump-Sum Payment.* Taking the lump-sum payment is only the first of your decisions. Remember, other than social security, this money may be the only money you have to live on for a long retirement. Consider other sources of income, such as savings, other plans, benefits from a prior employer, existing IRAs, and continued employment. All of these factors go into what decisions you make.

Option 3—*Roll the $100,000 into an IRA.* Assuming you do not intend to spend the money immediately, another option is to directly roll it over to an IRA. (If you receive the distribution yourself and then roll it, the plan must withhold 20%–$20,000–for federal withholding, and to roll the entire distribution you will need to find that $20,000 from other resources.) Since you are older than 59½, you face no early distribution penalty, even if you take it all out the next day (if you've rolled it to a new Roth IRA, the rules are slightly different). Once you decide to directly roll it to an IRA, you will have to determine what investments you want to make with the money. Different IRAs may have different investment options and/or different fee structures. You should examine these before investing. Another alternative is to invest in an annuity through the IRA. An annuity pays a set monthly benefit for your life and the life of your spouse (if you elect). Individual annuities—even through an IRA—can be costly because only a select group of healthy people with good family health histories are inclined to purchase them.

Option 4—*If Available, Have the Plan Purchase an Annuity.* The example involves a 401(k) plan. Generally, such plans are not required to provide an annuity. However, some do. In that case the plan administrator would take your account balance and purchase an annuity from an insurance company. Such an annuity may be expensive because of the unique nature of persons wanting an annuity. The annuity must be in the form of a joint and at least 50% survivor benefit unless you and, where appropriate, your spouse, waive that form for another form such as a single life annuity or a lump sum.

Example 2—Defined Benefit Plan. Assume you are a participant in a defined benefit plan and the plan would pay you a joint and 50% annuity of $12,000 per year while you are alive and pay your spouse $6,000 a year after you die. Also assume the plan offers you the alternative of electing, with spousal consent, either an actuarially equivalent single life annuity of, say, $14,000 a year (not actuarially precise) or a one-time lump-sum payment of $100,000 (not actuarially precise).

Option 1—*Joint and 50% Annuity Starting Immediately.* All defined benefit pension plans and money purchase plans must offer you a joint and 50% survivor annuity (they generally also have to offer at least a joint and 75% survivor annuity; other offerings are possible). Typically, a defined benefit plan of any size will pay you the annuity directly from the plan. Employers maintaining such plans fund the plan on an aggregate employee basis over time and your benefit is determined in the form of an annuity then converted to other forms on an actuarial basis.

Option 2–*Single Life Annuity.* A joint and survivor annuity protects your spouse if you die before her/him. The greater the percentage, for example 75% vs. 50%, the greater the survivor benefit and generally the lower the joint benefit (i.e., the benefit when you are alive). Whether a joint and survivor benefit is best and, if so, what size, depends on individual circumstances. Generally, if the other spouse has an annuity of his/her own of similar size, the joint and survivor benefit is unnecessary. Otherwise, it could be critical. There are downsides to an annuity. With an annuity, there is generally no money left if you die early and you cannot tap a larger monthly payment if you have needs for more money, for example because of medical costs. You also usually will not be able to leave any money for your heirs.

Option 3–*Lump Sum.* An annuity form avoids you running out of money if you live a long time (although inflation will cut into the value of those monthly payments). However, in many instances, an annuity results in your survivors not receiving the value of your unpaid benefits if you die early. You could have a lump sum transferred directly to an IRA, where you can manage the investments and the flow of funds. However, in such situations, you have to worry about not overspending early. You can try to take the money out over your life expectancy, but what "life expectancy" means is that half the people die before it and half live past it. If you are one of those fortunate to live beyond life expectancy (or your spouse is) you could find yourself with no money left in the IRA.

Example 3–Self-Employed or New Employer. If you will be self-employed during the year in which you retire, you can transfer your qualified pension plan account into a Keogh plan. The virtue of transferring your pension into a Keogh plan instead of an IRA is that, if you were born before January 2, 1936, you can be taxed using the 10-year averaging method (discussed earlier), if you withdraw the money from the Keogh in a lump-sum distribution. You cannot use the 10-year averaging method if you transfer your qualified pension plan account into an IRA. Many people find it easy to arrange to be self-employed in the year in which they retire. If the plan-to-plan transfer is done properly, you can preserve your pre-transfer service from the old plan for purposes of the 5-year minimum participation requirement. If you go to work for another employer immediately, you can directly transfer your balance to that employer's plan and preserve the 10-year averaging option. Remember, 10-year averaging is only available to those born before January 2, 1936.

The choices are tricky and require analysis under various assumptions of interest rates, life expectancy, medical expenses, current needs, and tax rates. Professional help is necessary; you should consult your tax advisor.

If you are a public safety officer (e.g., police, firefighters, and emergency medical technicians) who retires or becomes disabled, there is a special provision allowing you to withdraw up to $3,000 per year tax-free from your governmental retirement plan, if the distribution is used to purchase health, accident, or long-term insurance covering yourself, your spouse, or your dependents.

Special Additional Taxes

To discourage the use of pension funds for purposes other than normal retirement, the law imposes additional taxes on early distributions of those funds and on failures to withdraw the funds timely. Ordinarily, you will not be subject to these taxes if you roll over all early distributions you receive, as explained earlier, and begin drawing out the funds at a normal retirement age, in reasonable amounts over your life expectancy. These special additional taxes are the taxes on:

- Early distributions, and
- Excess accumulation (not receiving minimum distributions).

These taxes are discussed in the following sections.

If you must pay either of these taxes, report them on Form 5329. However, you do not have to file Form 5329 if you owe only the tax on early distributions and your Form 1099-R correctly shows a "1" in box 7. Instead, enter 10% of the taxable part of the distribution on Form 1040, line 58, and write "No" under the heading "Other Taxes" to the left of line 58.

Even if you do not owe any of these taxes, you may have to complete Form 5329 and attach it to your Form 1040. This applies if you meet an exception to the tax on early distributions but box 7 of your Form 1099-R does not indicate an exception.

Tax on Early Distributions

Most distributions (both periodic and nonperiodic) from qualified retirement plans and nonqualified annuity contracts made to you before you reach age 59½ are subject to an additional tax of 10%. This tax applies to the part of the distribution that you must include in gross income.

For this purpose, a qualified retirement plan is:

- A qualified employee plan,
- A qualified employee annuity plan,
- A tax-sheltered annuity plan, or
- An eligible state or local government section 457 deferred compensation plan (to the extent that any distribution is attributable to amounts the plan received in a direct transfer or rollover from one of the other plans listed here or an IRA).

5% rate on certain early distributions from deferred annuity contracts. If an early withdrawal from a deferred annuity is otherwise subject to the 10% additional tax, a 5% rate may apply instead. A 5% rate applies to distributions under a written election providing a specific schedule for the distribution of your interest in the contract if, as of March 1, 1986, you had begun receiving payments under the election. On line 4 of Form 5329, multiply the line 3 amount by 5% instead of 10%. Attach an explanation to your return.

Distributions from rollovers to Roth IRAs from eligible retirement plans within the 5-year period. If, within the 5-year period starting with the first day of your tax year in which you rolled over an amount from an eligible retirement plan to a Roth IRA, you take a distribution from the Roth IRA, you may have to pay the additional 10% tax on early distributions. You generally must pay the 10% additional tax on any amount attributable to the part of the rollover that you had to include in income. The additional tax is figured on Form 5329. For more information, see Form 5329 and its instructions. For information on qualified distributions from Roth IRAs, see *Additional Tax on Early Distributions* in chapter 2 of Publication 590.

Distributions from in-plan rollovers to designated Roth accounts within the 5-year period. If, within the 5-year period starting with the first day of your tax year in which you rolled over an amount from a 401(k) or 403(b) plan to a designated Roth account, you take a distribution from the designated Roth account, you may have to pay the additional 10% tax on early distributions. You generally must pay the 10% additional tax on any amount attributable to the part of the in-plan rollover that you had to include in income. The additional tax is figured on Form 5329. For more information, see Form 5329 and its instructions. For information on qualified distributions from designated Roth accounts, see *Designated Roth accounts* under *Taxation of Periodic Payments* in Publication 575.

Exceptions to tax. Certain early distributions are excepted from the early distribution tax. If the payer knows that an exception applies to your early distribution, distribution code "2," "3," or "4" should be shown in box 7 of your Form 1099-R and you do not have to report the distribution on Form 5329. If an exception applies but distribution code "1" (early distribution, no known exception) is shown in box 7, you must file Form 5329. Enter the taxable amount of the distribution shown in box 2a of your Form 1099-R on line 1 of Form 5329. On line 2, enter the amount that can be excluded and the exception number shown in the Form 5329 instructions.

General exceptions. The tax does not apply to distributions that are:

- Made as part of a series of substantially equal periodic payments (made at least annually) for your life (or life expectancy) or the joint lives (or joint life expectancies) of you and your designated beneficiary (if from a qualified retirement plan, the payments must begin after your separation from service),
- Made because you are totally and permanently disabled, or
- Made on or after the death of the plan participant or contract holder.

TAXPLANNER

You should carefully consider whether substantially equal periodic distributions commencing before you attain age 59½ would be sufficient to satisfy your income needs. Although these distributions are not subject to the 10% early distribution tax they will be subject to this tax if the amount of the distribution is modified (other than by reason of death, disability, or a change in method described later) either before you attain age 59½ or before the end of the calendar 5-year period beginning with the date of the first distribution and after you attain age 59½. In the year the distributions are modified, you will have to pay the 10% penalty tax on all of the distributions you have received to date, plus interest. For example, if you start receiving substantially equal periodic payments over your life expectancy in 2011 when you are age 58, and when you are age 62 in 2015 you take a larger distribution, you will have to pay the 10% penalty tax on all distributions received to date, plus interest. However, if you wait until the 5-year period ends, that is until 2016, there is no penalty if you modify the life expectancy distributions.

Payments are considered to be substantially equal periodic payments if they are made in accordance with one of three calculations: (1) the required minimum distribution method, (2) the fixed amortization method, or (3) the fixed annuitization method. Because of the rule against modification of substantially equal periodic payments, described earlier, individuals who chose annuitization or amortization (which require a fixed amount to be withdrawn each year) would have to pay a retroactive penalty on all of the distributions made, if they wanted to reduce the amount of money they received in order to keep their account from being dissipated. The IRS allows individuals who started distributions using the fixed amortization method or the fixed annuitization method to change to the required minimum distribution method once without incurring that penalty.

Additional exceptions for qualified retirement plans. The tax does not apply to distributions that are:

- From a qualified retirement plan (other than an IRA) after your separation from service in or after the year you reached age 55 (age 50 for qualified public safety employees),
- From a qualified retirement plan (other than an IRA) to an alternate payee under a qualified domestic relations order,
- From a qualified retirement plan to the extent you have deductible medical expenses (medical expenses that exceed 7.5% of your adjusted gross income), whether or not you itemize your deductions for the year,
- From an employer plan under a written election that provides a specific schedule for distribution of your entire interest if, as of March 1, 1986, you had separated from service and had begun receiving payments under the election,
- From an employee stock ownership plan for dividends on employer securities held by the plan,
- From a qualified retirement plan due to an IRS levy of the plan, or
- From elective deferral accounts under 401(k) or 403(b) plans or similar arrangements that are qualified reservist distributions.

Qualified public safety employees. If you are a qualified public safety employee, distributions made from a governmental defined benefit pension plan are not subject to the additional tax on early distributions. You are a qualified public safety employee if you provide police protection, firefighting services, or emergency medical services for a state or municipality, and you separated from service in or after the year you attained age 50.

Qualified reservist distributions. A qualified reservist distribution is not subject to the additional tax on early distributions. A qualified reservist distribution is a distribution (a) from elective deferrals under a section 401(k) or 403(b) plan, or a similar arrangement, (b) to an individual ordered or called to active duty (because he or she is a member of a reserve component) for a period of more than 179 days or for an indefinite period, and (c) made during the period beginning on the date of the order or call and ending at the close of the active duty period. You must have been ordered or called to active duty after September 11, 2001. For more information, see Publication 575.

TAXPLANNER
Withdrawals from a 401(k), 403(b), or similar plan by members of the National Guard or Reserves while on active duty for at least 179 days after September 11, 2001, are not subject to the 10% additional tax on early withdrawals. (This exception to the 10% additional penalty tax is also available for similar distributions from an IRA. See *Exemption from Additional 10% Tax for Distributions Received by National Guard or Reservists Called to Active Duty* in chapter 17, *Individual retirement arrangements (IRAs)*.) A refund or credit of the 10% early withdrawal tax previously paid on distributions that qualify for exemption from this penalty tax may be obtained.

The distribution received may otherwise be subject to ordinary income tax in the year received. See *Taxation of Nonperiodic Payments*, earlier.

The distribution received may otherwise be subject to ordinary income tax in the year received. See *Taxation of Nonperiodic Payments*, earlier.

The law also permits any portion of such distributions to be contributed back into an IRA anytime within the 2-year period following the end of the period of active duty. Although amounts contributed are not eligible for an IRA deduction, you may obtain a refund of the regular income tax you previously paid on the distribution by filing an amended return. Distributions that are contributed into an IRA do not reduce the maximum amount that you can otherwise contribute to an IRA based on compensation you earned during the year.

Additional exceptions for nonqualified annuity contracts. The tax does not apply to distributions from:

- A deferred annuity contract to the extent allocable to investment in the contract before August 14, 1982,
- A deferred annuity contract under a qualified personal injury settlement,
- A deferred annuity contract purchased by your employer upon termination of a qualified employee plan or qualified employee annuity plan and held by your employer until your separation from service, or
- An immediate annuity contract (a single premium contract providing substantially equal annuity payments that start within one year from the date of purchase and are paid at least annually).

TAXPLANNER

Early distributions from IRAs are also subject to the 10% excise tax. The earlier list for qualified plans indicates those that do not apply to IRAs. IRAs also have some additional exceptions if they are:

- Made after separation from employment if, among other requirements, the individual received unemployment compensation for 12 consecutive weeks by reason of the separation, but only to the extent the distributions do not exceed the amount paid for medical insurance or qualified long-term care insurance during the year,
- Distributions to pay for certain higher education expenses, or
- Distributions of $10,000 or less used within 120 days to pay qualified acquisition costs on the principal residence of a first-time homebuyer who is the IRA owner, or the spouse, child, grandchild, or ancestor of the IRA owner or spouse.

For more information, see *Early Distributions* in chapter 17, *Individual retirement arrangements (IRAs)*.

TAXSAVER

Note that the 10% excise tax also does not apply in the year of distribution if you roll over a qualifying distribution (including a direct rollover of an eligible rollover distribution). This is because the tax is applied only to taxable distributions. This helps to make rollovers an even more attractive alternative.

TAXORGANIZER

On Form 1099-R, distributions should be coded by the payer without regard to whether a rollover is made or anticipated (except for a direct rollover). Thus, for purposes of Form 1099-R reporting, a rollover that is planned or has already occurred should not be considered an exception to the early distribution penalty.

Example

If Ben Jones withdraws the total balance in his qualified plan, informs the plan administrator that the funds will be rolled over, is under age 59½, and meets no other exception under the early distribution rules, the Form 1099-R should contain a code "1" in box 7, "Early distribution, no known exception." If Mr. Jones then rolls over his distribution, he should properly report the rollover on his federal income tax return to avoid the early distribution penalty.

Tax on Excess Accumulation

To make sure that most of your retirement benefits are paid to you during your lifetime, rather than to your beneficiaries after your death, the payments that you receive from qualified retirement plans must begin no later than your required beginning date (defined later). The payments each year cannot be less than the required minimum distribution.

Required distributions not made. If the actual distributions to you in any year are less than the minimum required distribution for that year, you are subject to an additional tax. The tax equals 50% of the part of the required minimum distribution that was not distributed.

For this purpose, a qualified retirement plan includes:

- A qualified employee plan,
- A qualified employee annuity plan,
- An eligible section 457 deferred compensation plan, or
- A tax-sheltered annuity plan (for benefits accruing after 1986).

Waiver. The tax may be waived if you establish that the shortfall in distributions was due to reasonable error and that reasonable steps are being taken to remedy the shortfall. See the instructions for Form 5329 for the procedure to follow if you believe you qualify for a waiver of this tax.

State insurer delinquency proceedings. You might not receive the minimum distribution because assets are invested in a contract issued by an insurance company in state insurer delinquency proceedings. If your payments are reduced below the minimum due to these proceedings, you should contact your plan administrator. Under certain conditions, you will not have to pay the 50% excise tax.

Required beginning date. Unless the rule for 5% owners applies, you generally must begin to receive distributions from your qualified retirement plan by April 1 of the year that follows the later of:

- The calendar year in which you reach age 70½, or
- The calendar year in which you retire from employment with the employer maintaining the plan.

However, your plan may require you to begin to receive distributions by April 1 of the year that follows the year in which you reach age 70½, even if you have not retired.

5% owners. If you are a 5% owner, you must begin to receive distributions by April 1 of the year that follows the calendar year in which you reach age 70½.

Age 70½. You reach age 70½ on the date that is 6 calendar months after the date of your 70th birthday.

For example, if you are retired and your 70th birthday was on June 30, 2010, you were age 70½ on December 30, 2010. If your 70th birthday was on July 1, 2010, you reached age 70½ on January 1, 2011.

Required distributions. By the required beginning date, as explained earlier, you must either:

- Receive your entire interest in the plan (for a tax-sheltered annuity, your entire benefit accruing after 1986), or
- Begin receiving periodic distributions in annual amounts calculated to distribute your entire interest (for a tax-sheltered annuity, your entire benefit accruing after 1986) over your life or life expectancy or over the joint lives or joint life expectancies of you and a designated beneficiary (or over a shorter period).

TAXALERT

The IRS has issued final regulations that provide the life expectancy and distribution period tables to be used for determining required minimum distributions (see Table 10-1).

Table 10-1. **Uniform Lifetime Table**

The following table is used for determining the distribution period for lifetime distributions to an employee (or IRA owner) in situations in which the employee's (or IRA owner's) spouse is either not the sole designated beneficiary or is the sole designated beneficiary but is not more than 10 years younger than the employee (or IRA owner).

Age	Distribution Period	Age	Distribution Period
70	27.4	93	9.6
71	26.5	94	9.1
72	25.6	95	8.6
73	24.7	96	8.1
74	23.8	97	7.6
75	22.9	98	7.1
76	22.0	99	6.7
77	21.2	100	6.3
78	20.3	101	5.9
79	19.5	102	5.5
80	18.7	103	5.2
81	17.9	104	4.9
82	17.1	105	4.5
83	16.3	106	4.2
84	15.5	107	3.9
85	14.8	108	3.7
86	14.1	109	3.4
87	13.4	110	3.1
88	12.7	111	2.9
89	12.0	112	2.6
90	11.4	113	2.4
91	10.8	114	2.1
92	10.2	115 and older	1.9

Explanation

Retirement plans must begin to make minimum distributions to you no later than April 1 of the calendar year following the later of:
1. The calendar year in which you reach age 70½, or
2. The calendar year in which you retire (not applicable to 5% owners or to any employee with respect to an IRA).

Roth IRAs do not have to satisfy any minimum distribution requirement while the participant is alive.

Explanation

Although plans must begin making minimum distributions by the later of the calendar year after you retire or the year after you turn 70½, they are not required to wait until you actually retire. They may begin making minimum distributions in the year after you reach retirement age under the plan. Your plan administrator can provide details on the provisions of your plan.

TAXPLANNER

If you work beyond age 70½ and are not a 5% owner, it may be advantageous to delay the minimum distributions (if your plan allows) and allow the amounts in the retirement plan to grow on a tax-deferred basis. You may also be able to defer the minimum distributions from your IRA, if you are still working, by transferring your IRA balance to an employer plan sponsored by the employer for whom you are working as long as you're not a 5% or more owner of that employer. Consult your plan administrator or tax advisor for more information on the decision to delay minimum distributions.

Additional information. For more information on this rule, see *Tax on Excess Accumulation* in Publication 575.

Form 5329. You must file Form 5329 if you owe tax because you did not receive a minimum required distribution from your qualified retirement plan.

Survivors

Generally, a survivor or beneficiary reports pension or annuity income in the same way the plan participant would have. However, some special rules apply.

Survivors of employees. If you are entitled to receive a survivor annuity on the death of an employee, who died before becoming entitled to any annuity payments, you can exclude part of each annuity payment as a tax-free recovery of the employee's investment in the contract. You must figure the taxable and tax-free parts of your annuity payments using the method that applies as if you were the employee.

Survivors of retirees. If you receive benefits as a survivor under a joint and survivor annuity, include those benefits in income in the same way the retiree would have included them in income. If you receive a survivor annuity because of the death of a retiree who had reported the annuity under the Three-Year Rule and recovered all of the cost tax free, your survivor payments are fully taxable.

If the retiree was reporting the annuity payments under the General Rule, you must apply the same exclusion percentage to your initial survivor annuity payment called for in the contract. The resulting tax-free amount will then remain fixed. Any increases in the survivor annuity are fully taxable.

If the retiree was reporting the annuity payments under the Simplified Method, the part of each payment that is tax free is the same as the tax-free amount figured by the retiree at the annuity starting date. This amount remains fixed even if the annuity payments are increased or decreased. See *Simplified Method*, earlier.

In any case, if the annuity starting date is after 1986, the total exclusion over the years cannot be more than the cost.

Estate tax deduction. If your annuity was a joint and survivor annuity that was included in the decedent's estate, an estate tax may have been paid on it. You can deduct the part of the total estate tax that was based on the annuity. The deceased annuitant must have died after the annuity starting date. (For details, see section 1.691 (d)-1 of the regulations.) Deduct it in equal amounts over your remaining life expectancy.

If the decedent died before the annuity starting date of a deferred annuity contract and you receive a death benefit under that contract, the amount you receive (either in a lump sum or as periodic payments) in excess of the decedent's cost is included in your gross income as income in respect of a decedent for which you may be able to claim an estate tax deduction.

You can take the estate tax deduction as an itemized deduction on Schedule A, Form 1040. This deduction is not subject to the 2%-of-adjusted-gross-income limit on miscellaneous deductions. See Publication 559, *Survivors, Executors, and Administrators*, for more information on the estate tax deduction.

EXPLANATION

Example

Alexander dies while receiving an annuity worth $10,000. Alexander's beneficiary will receive $1,000 per year for the next 15 years. The estate tax figured with the annuity included is $4,500 more than when figured without the annuity.

The recipient may claim an itemized deduction (not subject to the 2%-of-adjusted-gross-income limitation) each year of $300 ($1,000/$15,000 × $4,500). In this computation, the $15,000 represents the total dollars that will be received over the 15-year period.

Chapter 11

Social security and equivalent railroad retirement benefits

ey.com/EYTaxGuide

Note

IRS Publication 17 (*Your Federal Income Tax*) has been updated by Ernst & Young LLP for 2011. Dates and dollar amounts shown are for 2011. Underlined type is used to indicate where IRS text has been updated. Places where text has been removed are indicated by the sentence: *Text intentionally omitted.*

ey.com/EYTaxGuide

Ernst & Young LLP will update the *Ernst & Young Tax Guide 2012* website with relevant taxpayer information as it becomes available. You can also sign up for email alerts to let you know when changes have been made.

Introduction

Social security income and equivalent railroad retirement benefits once were tax-free. But that hasn't been the case since 1984. Potentially, up to 85% of the benefits you receive may be subject to income tax, depending on your filing status and total income for the year. Figuring out whether the benefits you receive are taxable is not an easy task. It requires navigating through complicated rules and numerous computations. This chapter will aid in simplifying your task. Among other things, it includes worksheets to help you make the necessary calculations.

This chapter explains the federal income tax rules for social security benefits and equivalent tier 1 railroad retirement benefits. It explains the following topics.

- How to figure whether your benefits are taxable.
- How to use the social security benefits worksheet (with examples).
- How to report your taxable benefits.
- How to treat repayments that are more than the benefits you received during the year.

Social security benefits include monthly retirement, survivor, and disability benefits. They do not include supplemental security income (SSI) payments, which are not taxable.

Equivalent tier 1 railroad retirement benefits are the part of tier 1 benefits that a railroad employee or beneficiary would have been entitled to receive under the social security system. They are commonly called the social security equivalent benefit (SSEB) portion of tier 1 benefits.

If you received these benefits during 2011, you should have received a Form SSA-1099, Social Security Benefit Statement, or Form RRB-1099, Payments by the Railroad Retirement Board (Form SSA-1042S, Social Security Benefit Statement, or Form RRB-1042S, Statement for Nonresident Alien Recipients of: Payments by the Railroad Retirement Board, if you are a nonresident alien). These forms show the amounts received and repaid, and taxes withheld for the year. You may receive more than one of these forms for the same year. You should add the amounts shown on all forms you receive for the year to determine the total amounts received and repaid, and taxes withheld for that year. See the *Appendix* at the end of Publication 915 for more information.

Note. When the term "benefits" is used in this chapter, it applies to both social security benefits and the SSEB portion of tier 1 railroad retirement benefits.

What is not covered in this chapter. This chapter does not cover the tax rules for the following railroad retirement benefits.

- Non-social security equivalent benefit (NSSEB) portion of tier 1 benefits.
- Tier 2 benefits.
- Vested dual benefits.
- Supplemental annuity benefits.

For information on these benefits, see Publication 575, *Pension and Annuity Income*.

This chapter also does not cover the tax rules for foreign social security benefits. These benefits are taxable as annuities, unless they are exempt from U.S. tax or treated as a U.S. social security benefit under a tax treaty.

Useful Items

You may want to see:

Publication

- ☐ **575** Pension and Annuity Income
- ☐ **590** Individual Retirement Arrangements (IRAs)
- ☐ **915** Social Security and Equivalent Railroad Retirement Benefits

Form (and Instructions)

- ☐ **1040-ES** Estimated Tax for Individuals
- ☐ **W-4V** Voluntary Withholding Request

> **TAXPLANNER**
>
> For additional social security and retirement information, you may want to consult the following websites: *www.ssa.gov*, *www.rrb.gov*, and *www.seniors.gov*.

Are Any of Your Benefits Taxable?

To find out whether any of your benefits may be taxable, compare the base amount for your filing status with the total of:

1. One-half of your benefits, plus
2. All your other income, including tax-exempt interest.

When making this comparison, do not reduce your other income by any exclusions for:

- Interest from qualified U.S. savings bonds,
- Employer-provided adoption benefits,
- Foreign earned income or foreign housing, or
- Income earned by bona fide residents of American Samoa or Puerto Rico.

Children's benefits. The rules in this chapter apply to benefits received by children. See *Who is taxed*, later.

> **TAXPLANNER**
>
> If you want to plan ahead, you can request an estimate of your social security benefits by filing Form SSA-7004, Your Social Security Statement. Copies of the form can be obtained from your local social security office, by calling (800) 772-1213, or by visiting *www.ssa.gov*.
>
> **Explanation**
>
> **Taxation of benefits.** In figuring if any of your benefits are taxable, use the amount shown in box 5 of the Form SSA-1099 or Form RRB-1099 you received. If you received more than one form, add together the amount in box 5 of each form.
>
> **SSI payments.** If you received any SSI payments during the year, do not include these payments in your social security benefits received. SSI payments are made under Title XVI of the Social Security Act. They are not taxable for federal income tax purposes.
>
> **Form SSA-1099.** If you received or repaid social security benefits during 2011, you will receive Form SSA-1099, Social Security Benefit Statement. An IRS Notice 703 will be enclosed with your Form SSA-1099. This notice includes a worksheet you can use to determine if any of your benefits may be taxable. Keep this notice for your own records. Do **not** mail it to either the Internal Revenue Service or the SSA.
>
> Every person who received social security benefits will receive a Form SSA-1099, even if the benefit is combined with another person's in a single check. If you receive benefits on more than one social security record, you may get more than one Form SSA-1099.

Figuring total income. To figure the total of one-half of your benefits plus your other income, use Worksheet 11-1 later in this discussion. If the total is more than your base amount, part of your benefits may be taxable.

If you are married and file a joint return for 2011, you and your spouse must combine your incomes and your benefits to figure whether any of your combined benefits are taxable. Even if your spouse did not receive any benefits, you must add your spouse's income to yours to figure whether any of your benefits are taxable.

Tax Breaks and Deductions You Can Use Checklist

Deduction for Repaid Disability Benefits. If you received disability payments from your employer or an insurance company in an earlier year that you included in your taxable income and have since repaid these benefits due to the receipt of a lump-sum payment from the Social Security Administration (SSA) or Railroad Retirement Board (RRB), you can take an itemized deduction for the part of those repaid benefits that had been previously included in your income. If you repay more than $3,000, you may be able to claim a tax credit instead. For more information, see *Repayment of benefits received in an earlier year*, later.

Reducing Your Taxable Social Security Income. Social security and railroad retirement benefits are partially taxable if your total income (defined later in this chapter) is more than $32,000 for married taxpayers filing jointly and $25,000 for single filers. If you expect your total income will be in excess of these amounts, consider the income reduction strategies discussed later in this chapter to reduce your income and the taxability of your social security benefits.

Base amount. Your base amount is:
- $25,000 if you are single, head of household, or qualifying widow(er),
- $25,000 if you are married filing separately and lived apart from your spouse for all of 2011,
- $32,000 if you are married filing jointly, or
- $-0- if you are married filing separately and lived with your spouse at any time during 2011.

EXPLANATION

The filing requirements for individuals are based on income, age, and filing status (e.g., married filing jointly, single). See chapter 1, *Filing information*.

EXPLANATION

Social security and railroad retirement benefits are partially taxable if your *total income* (defined later in this paragraph) is more than $32,000 for married taxpayers filing jointly and $25,000 for single filers. If you are married filing separately and you lived with your spouse at any time during the year, your base amount is $0, which means that your social security retirement benefits are partially taxable regardless of your income level. Your *total income* is the sum of your adjusted gross income, tax-exempt income, excluded employer-provided adoption benefits, excluded foreign source income, excluded interest from U.S. savings bonds (interest excluded in connection with the payment of qualified education expenses), and one-half of your social security retirement benefits.

Tax-exempt income is *not taxable* for federal purposes, even if you receive social security benefits. However, it is one of the items taken into consideration in determining whether or not your income exceeds the threshold amount so that your social security benefits are taxable.

TAXSAVER

If you expect your total income (defined in the preceding explanation) to exceed the base amount ($32,000 if you are filing a joint return, $25,000 if you are filing single), you may wish to consider the following strategies:
- Defer the recognition of income by investing in U.S. savings bonds. Generally, the increase in value of the bonds issued at a discount (Series E and EE) is not taxable until you surrender the bonds. Additionally, if you hold the bonds until death, your heirs will recognize the income (assuming you did not elect to include in income the annual increase in the value of the bond).
- Purchase a certificate of deposit that matures in 2012. None of the interest earned will be subject to tax in 2011, as long as any interest received this year would be penalized by the issuer of the CD.
- Offset capital gains in 2011 by selling property in which you have unrealized capital losses.
- Stagger the recognition of income so that you have alternating years of higher income. Depending on your income level, you could structure income so that your social security benefits are taxed every other year. For example, when considering sources of cash flow, you could surrender U.S. savings bonds and sell appreciated property in alternate years. You could also schedule the maturity dates of U.S. Treasury notes and bills to ensure that your income is under the base amount in certain years.
- If you have earned income, consider contributing to your company's 401(k) plan, your not-for-profit 403(b) plan, or a deductible Individual Retirement Arrangement (IRA) account (see chapter 17, *Individual retirement arrangements (IRAs)*, to determine if you qualify) to decrease your adjusted gross income and also reduce the taxable portion of your social security benefits.

TAXPLANNER

Tax-exempt income is added to your adjusted gross income for purposes of calculating how much, if any, of your social security benefits will be subject to tax. Keep this in mind when evaluating the after-tax rate of return of tax-exempt investments vs. taxable investments.

Worksheet 11-1. You can use Worksheet 11-1 to figure the amount of income to compare with your base amount. This is a quick way to check whether some of your benefits may be taxable.

Worksheet 11-1. A Quick Way To Check If Your Benefits May Be Taxable

A.	Enter the amount from box 5 of all your Forms SSA-1099 and RRB-1099. Include the full amount of any lump-sum benefit payments received in 2011, for 2011 and earlier years. (If you received more than one form, combine the amounts from box 5 and enter the total.)	A._____

Note. If the amount on line A is zero or less, stop here; none of your benefits are taxable this year.

B.	Enter one-half of the amount on line A...	B._____
C.	Enter your taxable pensions, wages, interest, dividends, and other taxable income	C._____
D.	Enter any tax-exempt interest income (such as interest on municipal bonds) plus any exclusions from income (listed earlier)	D._____
E.	Add lines B, C, and D	E._____

Note. Compare the amount on line E to your base amount for your filing status. If the amount on line E equals or is less than the base amount for your filing status, none of your benefits are taxable this year. If the amount on line E is more than your base amount, some of your benefits may be taxable. You need to complete Worksheet 1 in Publication 915 (or the Social Security Benefits Worksheet in your tax form instruction booklet). If none of your benefits are taxable, but you otherwise must file a tax return, see <u>Benefits not taxable</u>, later, under How To Report Your Benefits.

Example. You and your spouse (both over 65) are filing a joint return for 2011 and you both received social security benefits during the year. In January 2012, you received a Form SSA-1099 showing net benefits of $7,500 in box 5. Your spouse received a Form SSA-1099 showing net benefits of $3,500 in box 5. You also received a taxable pension of $22,000 and interest income of $500. You did not have any tax-exempt interest income. Your benefits are not taxable for 2011 because your income, as figured in <u>Worksheet 11-1</u> on this page, is not more than your base amount ($32,000) for married filing jointly.

Even though none of your benefits are taxable, you must file a return for 2011 because your taxable gross income ($22,500) exceeds the minimum filing requirement amount for your filing status.

Filled-in Worksheet 11-1. A Quick Way To Check If Your Benefits May Be Taxable

A.	Enter the amount from box 5 of all your Forms SSA-1099 and RRB-1099. Include the full amount of any lump-sum benefit payments received in 2011, for 2011 and earlier years. (If you received more than one form, combine the amounts from box 5 and enter the total.)	A. $11,000

Note. If the amount on line A is zero or less, stop here; none of your benefits are taxable this year.

B.	Enter one-half of the amount on line A...	B. 5,500
C.	Enter your taxable pensions, wages, interest, dividends, and other taxable income	C. 22,500
D.	Enter any tax-exempt interest income (such as interest on municipal bonds) plus any exclusions from income (listed earlier)	D. -0-
E.	Add lines B, C, and D	E. $28,000

Note. Compare the amount on line E to your base amount for your filing status. If the amount on line E equals or is less than the base amount for your filing status, none of your benefits are taxable this year. If the amount on line E is more than your base amount, some of your benefits may be taxable. You need to complete Worksheet 1 in Publication 915 (or the Social Security Benefits Worksheet in your tax form instruction booklet). If none of your benefits are taxable, but you otherwise must file a tax return, see <u>Benefits not taxable</u>, later, under How To Report Your Benefits.

Who is taxed. Benefits are included in the taxable income (to the extent they are taxable) of the person who has the legal right to receive the benefits. For example, if you and your child receive benefits, but the check for your child is made out in your name, you must use only your part of the benefits to see whether any benefits are taxable to you. One-half of the part that belongs to your child must be added to your child's other income to see whether any of those benefits are taxable to your child.

> ### TAXORGANIZER
> You should maintain a copy of Forms SSA-1099, RRB-1099, and 1042S for 3 years following the due date (including extensions) of your income tax return.

Repayment of benefits. Any repayment of benefits you made during 2011 must be subtracted from the gross benefits you received in 2011. It does not matter whether the repayment was for a benefit you received in 2011 or in an earlier year. If you repaid more than the gross benefits you received in 2011, see _Repayments More Than Gross Benefits_, later.

Your gross benefits are shown in box 3 of Form SSA-1099 or RRB-1099. Your repayments are shown in box 4. The amount in box 5 shows your net benefits for 2011 (box 3 minus box 4). Use the amount in box 5 to figure whether any of your benefits are taxable.

> ### EXAMPLE
> Assume that in 2010 you received $13,000 in social security benefits, and in 2011 you received $12,700. In March 2011, SSA notified you that you should have received only $12,500 in benefits in 2010. During 2011, you repaid $500 to SSA. The Form SSA-1099 you will receive for 2011 will show $12,700 in box 3 (gross amount) and $500 in box 4 (repayment). The amount in box 5 will show your net benefits of $12,200 ($12,700 minus $500). The amount in box 5 (the $12,200) will be the amount you will use to figure whether any of your benefits are taxable.

Tax withholding and estimated tax. You can choose to have federal income tax withheld from your social security benefits and/or the SSEB portion of your tier 1 railroad retirement benefits. If you choose to do this, you must complete a Form W-4V.

If you do not choose to have income tax withheld, you may have to request additional withholding from other income or pay estimated tax during the year. For details, see Publication 505, _Tax Withholding and Estimated Tax_, or the instructions for Form 1040-ES.

How To Report Your Benefits

If part of your benefits are taxable, you must use Form 1040 or Form 1040A. You cannot use Form 1040EZ.

Reporting on Form 1040. Report your net benefits (the amount in box 5 of your Form SSA-1099 or Form RRB-1099) on line 20a and the taxable part on line 20b. If you are married filing separately and you lived apart from your spouse for all of 2011, also enter "D" to the right of the word "benefits" on line 20a.

Reporting on Form 1040A. Report your net benefits (the amount in box 5 of your Form SSA-1099 or Form RRB-1099) on line 14a and the taxable part on line 14b. If you are married filing separately and you lived apart from your spouse for all of 2011, also enter "D" to the right of the word "benefits" on line 14a.

Benefits not taxable. If you are filing Form 1040EZ, do not report any benefits on your tax return. If you are filing Form 1040 or Form 1040A, report your net benefits (the amount in box 5 of your Form SSA-1099 or Form RRB-1099) on Form 1040, line 20a, or Form 1040A, line 14a. Enter -0- on Form 1040, line 20b, or Form 1040A, line 14b. If you are married filing separately and you lived apart from your spouse for all of 2011, also enter "D" to the right of the word "benefits" on Form 1040, line 20a, or Form 1040A, line 14a.

Summary of How to Report Your Benefits

	Form 1040	Form 1040A	Form 1040EZ
Net benefits	Line 20a	Line 14a	Cannot use form
Taxable benefits	Line 20b	Line 14b	Cannot use form

If none of your benefits are taxable, you may file using Form 1040EZ.

How Much Is Taxable?

If part of your benefits are taxable, how much is taxable depends on the total amount of your benefits and other income. Generally, the higher that total amount, the greater the taxable part of your benefits.

Maximum taxable part. Generally, up to 50% of your benefits will be taxable. However, up to 85% of your benefits can be taxable if either of the following situations applies to you.

- The total of one-half of your benefits and all your other income is more than $34,000 ($44,000 if you are married filing jointly).
- You are married filing separately and lived with your spouse at any time during 2011.

EXPLANATION

After determining whether or not your social security retirement benefits are taxable, you must then determine what percentage (either 50% or 85%) of the total benefit is taxable. If you are filing a joint return and your *total income* (adjusted gross income + tax-exempt income + excluded foreign source income + excluded interest income from U.S. savings bonds + one-half of your social security retirement benefits) is less than $44,000 but greater than $32,000, a maximum of 50% of your social security retirement benefits is subject to federal tax. If, however, your total income exceeds $44,000, up to 85% of your social security retirement benefits will be included in income and taxed accordingly.

TAXSAVER

Many states allow a deduction for the amount of social security retirement benefits taxed at the federal level. Consult your tax advisor or state income tax authority for details.

Which worksheet to use. A worksheet you can use to figure your taxable benefits is in the instructions for your Form 1040 or Form 1040A. You can use either that worksheet or Worksheet 1 in Publication 915, unless any of the following situations applies to you.

1. You contributed to a traditional individual retirement arrangement (IRA) and you or your spouse is covered by a retirement plan at work. In this situation, you must use the special worksheets in *Appendix B* of Publication 590 to figure both your IRA deduction and your taxable benefits.
2. Situation (1) does not apply and you take an exclusion for interest from qualified U.S. savings bonds (Form 8815), for adoption benefits (Form 8839), for foreign earned income or housing (Form 2555 or Form 2555-EZ), or for income earned in American Samoa (Form 4563) or Puerto Rico by bona fide residents. In this situation, you must use Worksheet 1 in Publication 915 to figure your taxable benefits.
3. You received a lump-sum payment for an earlier year. In this situation, also complete Worksheet 2 or 3 and Worksheet 4 in Publication 915. See *Lump-sum election* next.

Lump-sum election. You must include the taxable part of a lump-sum (retroactive) payment of benefits received in 2011 in your 2011 income, even if the payment includes benefits for an earlier year.

Generally, you use your 2011 income to figure the taxable part of the total benefits received in 2011. However, you may be able to figure the taxable part of a lump-sum payment for an earlier year separately, using your income for the earlier year. You can elect this method if it lowers your taxable benefits.

Making the election. If you received a lump-sum benefit payment in 2011 that includes benefits for one or more earlier years, follow the instructions in Publication 915 under *Lump-Sum Election*

Tip

This type of lump-sum benefit payment should not be confused with the lump-sum death benefit that both the SSA and RRB pay to many of their beneficiaries. No part of the lump-sum death benefit is subject to tax.

to see whether making the election will lower your taxable benefits. That discussion also explains how to make the election.

> **TAXPLANNER**
>
> **Estimated tax.** Generally, tax is not withheld on social security benefits. This means that you may have to pay estimated tax during the year if these benefits are taxable and you do not have enough taxes withheld from other income. However, you may request to have federal income tax withheld from your benefits at 7%, 10%, 15%, or 25%, but no other percentage or amount is allowed. This request is made by completing Form W-4V, Voluntary Withholding Request, and giving it to the agency making the payments. See chapter 4, *Tax withholding and estimated tax*, for more information on estimated tax.

Examples

The following are a few examples you can use as a guide to figure the taxable part of your benefits.

Example 1. George White is single and files Form 1040 for 2011. He received the following income in 2011:

Fully taxable pension	$18,600
Wages from part-time job	9,400
Taxable interest income	990
Total	$28,990

George also received social security benefits during 2011. The Form SSA-1099 he received in January 2012 shows $5,980 in box 5. To figure his taxable benefits, George completes the worksheet shown here.

Worksheet 1. **Figuring Your Taxable Benefits**

1.	Enter the total amount from box 5 of ALL your Forms SSA-1099 and RRB-1099. Also enter this amount on Form 1040, line 20a, or Form 1040A, line 14a..	$5,980
2.	Enter one-half of line 1	2,990
3.	Combine the amounts from:	
	Form 1040: Lines 7, 8a, 9a, 10 through 14, 15b, 16b, 17 through 19, and 21.	
	Form 1040A: Lines 7, 8a, 9a, 10, 11b, 12b, and 13	28,990
4.	Enter the amount, if any, from Form 1040 or 1040A, line 8b	-0-
5.	Enter the total of any exclusions/adjustments for:	
	• Adoption benefits (Form 8839, line 24),	
	• Foreign earned income or housing (Form 2555, lines 45 and 50, or Form 2555-EZ, line 18), and	
	• Certain income of bona fide residents of American Samoa (Form 4563, line 15) or Puerto Rico...	-0-
6.	Combine lines 2, 3, 4, and 5	31,980
7.	*Form 1040 filers:* Enter the amount from Form 1040, lines 23 through 32, and any write-in adjustments you entered on the dotted line next to line 36	
	Form 1040A filers: Enter the amount from Form 1040A, lines 16 and 17..	-0-
8.	Is the amount on line 7 less than the amount on line 6?	
	No. 🛑 None of your social security benefits are taxable. Enter -0- on Form 1040, line 20b, or Form 1040A, line 14b.	
	Yes. Subtract line 7 from line 6	31,980

9. If you are:
    - Married filing jointly, enter $32,000
    - Single, head of household, qualifying widow(er), or married filing separately and you **lived apart** from your spouse for all of 2011, enter $25,000 .... <u>25,000</u>

    Note. *If you are married filing separately and you lived with your spouse at any time in 2011, skip lines 9 through 16; multiply line 8 by 85% (.85) and enter the result on line 17. Then go to line 18.*

10. Is the amount on line 9 less than the amount on line 8?

    No. 🛑 None of your benefits are taxable. Enter -0- on Form 1040, line 20b, or on Form 1040A, line 14b. If you are married filing separately and you **lived apart** from your spouse for all of 2011, be sure you entered "D" to the right of the word "benefits" on Form 1040, line 20a, or on Form 1040A, line 14a.

    Yes. Subtract line 9 from line 8 .... <u>6,980</u>

11. Enter $12,000 if married filing jointly; $9,000 if single, head of household, qualifying widow(er), or married filing separately and you **lived apart** from your spouse for all of 2011 .... <u>9,000</u>

12. Subtract line 11 from line 10. If zero or less, enter -0- .... <u>-0-</u>

13. Enter the **smaller** of line 10 or line 11 .... <u>6,980</u>

14. Enter one-half of line 13 .... <u>3,490</u>

15. Enter the **smaller** of line 2 or line 14 .... <u>2,990</u>

16. Multiply line 12 by 85% (.85). If line 12 is zero, enter -0- .... <u>-0-</u>

17. Add lines 15 and 16 .... <u>2,990</u>

18. Multiply line 1 by 85% (.85) .... <u>5,083</u>

19. **Taxable benefits.** Enter the **smaller** of line 17 or line 18. Also enter this amount on Form 1040, line 20b, or Form 1040A, line 14b .... <u>$2,990</u>

The amount on line 19 of George's worksheet shows that $2,990 of his social security benefits is taxable. On line 20a of his Form 1040, George enters his net benefits of $5,980. On line 20b, he enters his taxable benefits of $2,990.

Example 2. Ray and Alice Hopkins file a joint return on Form 1040A for 2011. Ray is retired and received a fully taxable pension of $15,500. He also received social security benefits, and his Form SSA-1099 for 2011 shows net benefits of $5,600 in box 5. Alice worked during the year and had wages of $14,000. She made a deductible payment to her IRA account of $1,000. Ray and Alice have two savings accounts with a total of $250 in taxable interest income. They complete Worksheet 1 and find that none of Ray's social security benefits are taxable. On line 3 of the worksheet, they enter $29,750 ($15,500 + $14,000 + $250). On Form 1040A, they enter $5,600 on line 14a and -0- on line 14b.

Worksheet 1. **Figuring Your Taxable Benefits**

1. Enter the total amount from box 5 of ALL your Forms SSA-1099 and RRB-1099. Also enter this amount on Form 1040, line 20a, or Form 1040A, line 14a .... <u>$5,600</u>

2. Enter one-half of line 1 .... <u>2,800</u>

3. Combine the amounts from:

    Form 1040: Lines 7, 8a, 9a, 10 through 14, 15b, 16b, 17 through 19, and 21.

    Form 1040A: Lines 7, 8a, 9a, 10, 11b, 12b, and 13 .... <u>29,750</u>

4.	Enter the amount, if any, from Form 1040 or 1040A, line 8b	-0-
5.	Enter the total of any exclusions/adjustments for:	
	• Adoption benefits (Form 8839, line 24), • Foreign earned income or housing (Form 2555, lines 45 and 50, or Form 2555-EZ, line 18), and • Certain income of bona fide residents of American Samoa (Form 4563, line 15) or Puerto Rico..	-0-
6.	Combine lines 2, 3, 4, and 5	32,550
7.	**Form 1040 filers:** Enter the amount from Form 1040, lines 23 through 32, and any write-in adjustments you entered on the dotted line next to line 36. **Form 1040A filers:** Enter the amount from Form 1040A, lines 16 and 17	1,000
8.	Is the amount on line 7 less than the amount on line 6?	
	No. 🛑 None of your benefits are taxable. Enter -0- on Form 1040, line 20b, or Form 1040A, line 14b.	
	Yes. Subtract line 7 from line 6	31,550
9.	If you are: • Married filing jointly, enter $32,000 • Single, head of household, qualifying widow(er), or married filing separately and you **lived apart** from your spouse for all of 2011, enter $25,000...	32,000
	Note. If you are married filing separately and you lived with your spouse at any time in 2011, skip lines 9 through 16; multiply line 8 by 85% (.85) and enter the result on line 17. Then go to line 18.	
10.	Is the amount on line 9 less than the amount on line 8?	
	No. 🛑 None of your benefits are taxable. Enter -0- on Form 1040, line 20b, or on Form 1040A, line 14b. If you are married filing separately and you **lived apart** from your spouse for all of 2011, be sure you entered "D" to the right of the word "benefits" on Form 1040, line 20a, or on Form 1040A, line 14a.	
	Yes. Subtract line 9 from line 8	_____
11.	Enter $12,000 if married filing jointly; $9,000 if single, head of household, qualifying widow(er), or married filing separately and you **lived apart** from your spouse for all of 2011	_____
12.	Subtract line 11 from line 10. If zero or less, enter -0-	_____
13.	Enter the **smaller** of line 10 or line 11	_____
14.	Enter one-half of line 13	_____
15.	Enter the **smaller** of line 2 or line 14	_____
16.	Multiply line 12 by 85% (.85). If line 12 is zero, enter -0-	_____
17.	Add lines 15 and 16	_____
18.	Multiply line 1 by 85% (.85)	_____
19.	**Taxable benefits.** Enter the **smaller** of line 17 or line 18. Also enter this amount on Form 1040, line 20b, or Form 1040A, line 14b	_____

Example 3. Joe and Betty Johnson file a joint return on Form 1040 for 2011. Joe is a retired railroad worker and in 2011 received the social security equivalent benefit (SSEB) portion of tier 1 railroad retirement benefits. Joe's Form RRB-1099 shows $10,000 in box 5. Betty is a retired government worker and receives a fully taxable pension of $38,000. They had $2,300 in taxable interest income plus interest of $200 on a qualified U.S. savings bond. The savings bond interest

qualified for the exclusion. They figure their taxable benefits by completing Worksheet 1. Because they have qualified U.S. savings bond interest, they follow the note at the beginning of the worksheet and use the amount from line 2 of their Schedule B (Form 1040A or 1040) on line 3 of the worksheet instead of the amount from line 8a of their Form 1040. On line 3 of the worksheet, they enter $40,500 ($38,000 + $2,500).

Worksheet 1.   Figuring Your Taxable Benefits

Before you begin:	
• If you are married filing separately and you lived apart from your spouse for all of 2011, enter "D" to the right of the word "benefits" on Form 1040, line 20a, or Form 1040A, line 14a.	
• Do not use this worksheet if you repaid benefits in 2011 and your total repayments (box 4 of Forms SSA-1099 and RRB-1099) were more than your gross benefits for 2011 (box 3 of Forms SSA-1099 and RRB-1099). None of your benefits are taxable for 2011. For more information, see _Repayments More Than Gross Benefits_.	
• If you are filing Form 8815, Exclusion of Interest From Series EE and I U.S. Savings Bonds Issued After 1989, do not include the amount from line 8a of Form 1040 or Form 1040A on line 3 of this worksheet. Instead, include the amount from Schedule B (Form 1040A or 1040), line 2.	

1.	Enter the total amount from box 5 of ALL your Forms SSA-1099 and RRB-1099. Also enter this amount on Form 1040, line 20a, or Form 1040A, line 14a	$10,000
2.	Enter one-half of line 1	5,000
3.	Combine the amounts from:	
	Form 1040: Lines 7, 8a, 9a, 10 through 14, 15b, 16b, 17 through 19, and 21.	
	Form 1040A: Lines 7, 8a, 9a, 10, 11b, 12b, and 13	40,500
4.	Enter the amount, if any, from Form 1040 or 1040A, line 8b	-0-
5.	Enter the total of any exclusions/adjustments for:	
	• Adoption benefits (Form 8839, line 24),	
	• Foreign earned income or housing (Form 2555, lines 45 and 50, or Form 2555-EZ, line 18), and	
	• Certain income of bona fide residents of American Samoa (Form 4563, line 15) or Puerto Rico	-0-
6.	Combine lines 2, 3, 4, and 5	45,500
7.	**Form 1040 filers:** Enter the amount from Form 1040, lines 23 through 32, and any write-in adjustments you entered on the dotted line next to line 36.	
	Form 1040A filers: Enter the amount from Form 1040A, lines 16 and 17	-0-
8.	Is the amount on line 7 less than the amount on line 6?	
	No. (STOP) None of your benefits are taxable. Enter -0- on Form 1040, line 20b, or Form 1040A, line 14b.	
	Yes. Subtract line 7 from line 6	45,500
9.	If you are:	
	• Married filing jointly, enter $32,000	
	• Single, head of household, qualifying widow(er), or married filing separately and you **lived apart** from your spouse for all of 2011, enter $25,000	32,000

10.	Is the amount on line 9 less than the amount on line 8?	
	No. (STOP) None of your benefits are taxable. Enter -0- on Form 1040, line 20b, or on Form 1040A, line 14b. If you are married filing separately and you **lived apart** from your spouse for all of 2011, be sure you entered "D" to the right of the word "benefits" on Form 1040, line 20a, or on Form 1040A, line 14a.	
	Yes. Subtract line 9 from line 8	13,500
11.	Enter $12,000 if married filing jointly; $9,000 if single, head of household, qualifying widow(er), or married filing separately and you **lived apart** from your spouse for all of 2011	12,000
12.	Subtract line 11 from line 10. If zero or less, enter -0-	1,500
13.	Enter the **smaller** of line 10 or line 11	12,000
14.	Enter one-half of line 13	6,000
15.	Enter the **smaller** of line 2 or line 14	5,000
16.	Multiply line 12 by 85% (.85). If line 12 is zero, enter -0-	1,275
17.	Add lines 15 and 16	6,275
18.	Multiply line 1 by 85% (.85)	8,500
19.	**Taxable benefits.** Enter the **smaller** of line 17 or line 18. Also enter this amount on Form 1040, line 20b, or Form 1040A, line 14b	$6,275

More than 50% of Joe's net benefits are taxable because the income on line 8 of the worksheet ($45,500) is more than $44,000. Joe and Betty enter $10,000 on Form 1040, line 20a, and $6,275 on Form 1040, line 20b.

Deductions Related to Your Benefits

You may be entitled to deduct certain amounts related to the benefits you receive.

Disability payments. You may have received disability payments from your employer or an insurance company that you included as income on your tax return in an earlier year. If you received a lump-sum payment from SSA or RRB, and you had to repay the employer or insurance company for the disability payments, you can take an itemized deduction for the part of the payments you included in gross income in the earlier year. If the amount you repay is more than $3,000, you may be able to claim a tax credit instead. Claim the deduction or credit in the same way explained under *Repayments More Than Gross Benefits*, later.

Legal expenses. You can usually deduct legal expenses that you pay or incur to produce or collect taxable income or in connection with the determination, collection, or refund of any tax.

Legal expenses for collecting the taxable part of your benefits are deductible as a miscellaneous itemized deduction on Schedule A (Form 1040), line 23.

Repayments More Than Gross Benefits

In some situations, your Form SSA-1099 or Form RRB-1099 will show that the total benefits you repaid (box 4) are more than the gross benefits (box 3) you received. If this occurred, your net benefits in box 5 will be a negative figure (a figure in parentheses) and none of your benefits will be taxable. Do not use a worksheet in this case. If you receive more than one form, a negative figure in box 5 of one form is used to offset a positive figure in box 5 of another form for that same year.

If you have any questions about this negative figure, contact your local SSA office or your local RRB field office.

Joint return. If you and your spouse file a joint return, and your Form SSA-1099 or RRB-1099 has a negative figure in box 5, but your spouse's does not, subtract the amount in box 5 of your form from the amount in box 5 of your spouse's form. You do this to get your net benefits when figuring if your combined benefits are taxable.

Example. John and Mary file a joint return for 2011. John received Form SSA-1099 showing $3,000 in box 5. Mary also received Form SSA-1099 and the amount in box 5 was ($500). John and Mary will use $2,500 ($3,000 minus $500) as the amount of their net benefits when figuring if any of their combined benefits are taxable.

> ### EXPLANATION
> Social security benefits are determined on a cash basis, just like most other income of individuals. Accordingly, repayments of prior-year amounts reduce current-year benefits.

Repayment of benefits received in an earlier year. If the total amount shown in box 5 of all of your Forms SSA-1099 and RRB-1099 is a negative figure, you can take an itemized deduction for the part of this negative figure that represents benefits you included in gross income in an earlier year.

Deduction $3,000 or less. If this deduction is $3,000 or less, it is subject to the 2%-of-adjusted-gross-income limit that applies to certain miscellaneous itemized deductions. Claim it on Schedule A (Form 1040), line 23.

Deduction more than $3,000. If this deduction is more than $3,000, you should figure your tax two ways:
1. Figure your tax for 2011 with the itemized deduction included on Schedule A, line 28.
2. Figure your tax for 2011 in the following steps.
   a. Figure the tax without the itemized deduction included on Schedule A, line 28.
   b. For each year after 1983 for which part of the negative figure represents a repayment of benefits, refigure your taxable benefits as if your total benefits for the year were reduced by that part of the negative figure. Then refigure the tax for that year.
   c. Subtract the total of the refigured tax amounts in (b) from the total of your actual tax amounts.
   d. Subtract the result in (c) from the result in (a).

Compare the tax figured in methods (1) and (2). Your tax for 2011 is the smaller of the two amounts. If method (1) results in less tax, take the itemized deduction on Schedule A (Form 1040), line 28. If method (2) results in less tax, claim a credit for the amount from step 2(c) above on Form 1040, line 71, and enter "I.R.C. 1341" in the margin to the left of line 71. If both methods produce the same tax, deduct the repayment on Schedule A (Form 1040), line 28.

> ### EXPLANATION
> This confusing computation allows you to reduce your current tax by the greater of two amounts: 1) the amount of tax you would save by taking the deduction this year or 2) the net increase in tax in the prior year as a result of including the amount in income.

> ### TAXSAVER
> The Social Security Administration (SSA) can reduce your monthly benefits if you have earned income in excess of the threshold amounts and are under full retirement age. The retirement earnings test has been eliminated for individuals attaining full retirement. However, a test remains in effect for individuals ages 62 through full retirement age. For the year in which an individual reaches full retirement age, each $3 of income earned in 2011 over $37,680 will reduce your social security benefits by $1. The $37,680 threshold applies only for the year in which you reach full retirement age, up to the actual month you attain full retirement age. There is no limit on earnings beginning the month an individual attains full retirement age. For individuals between the ages of 62 and the year full retirement age is reached, each $2 of income earned in 2011 over $14,160 will reduce your social security benefits by $1. Other exceptions apply during the initial year you receive social security retirement benefits. Consult the SSA for further explanation.

Earned Income Threshold for Early Recipients of Social Security Benefits

	Self-Employed	Not Self-Employed
Included as income	Net earnings	Wages
Excluded as income	Government benefits	Government benefits
	Investment earnings	Investment earnings
	Interest	Interest
	Pensions	Pensions
	Annuities	Annuities
	Capital gains	Capital gains
	IRA distributions	IRA distributions
	Inheritance payments	Inheritance payments

TAXALERT

If you were born after 1937, your "full retirement age" occurs later than age 65. Full retirement age is the age at which full (100%) social security retirement benefits are available. Beginning with individuals who attained age 62 in the year 2000 (born in 1938), the full retirement age increases over the next 22 years, leveling off at age 67 for individuals who were born in 1960 or later. In other words, the full retirement age for individuals born between 1955 and 1969 will be age 66, plus 2 months for every year after 1954. Refer to the chart below entitled *"Scheduled Increases in Social Security Normal Retirement Age"* for the scheduled increases in the normal retirement age for those born in 1945 and thereafter.

Scheduled Increases in Social Security Normal Retirement Age

Birth Year	Year Worker Attains Age 62	Normal Retirement Age
1945	2007	66
1946	2008	66
1947	2009	66
1948	2010	66
1949	2011	66
1950	2012	66
1951	2013	66
1952	2014	66
1953	2015	66
1954	2016	66
1955	2017	66 + 2 months
1956	2018	66 + 4 months
1957	2019	66 + 6 months
1958	2020	66 + 8 months
1959	2021	66 + 10 months
1960	2022	67
1961 and subsequent years	2023 and later	67

TAXORGANIZER

Records you should keep:
- Copy of Forms SSA-1099, RRB-1099, and 1042S for 3 years following the due date (including extensions) of your income tax return
- Copies of all worksheets used to determine taxability of benefits

Chapter 12
Other income

Note

IRS Publication 17 (*Your Federal Income Tax*) has been updated by Ernst & Young LLP for 2011. Dates and dollar amounts shown are for 2011. Underlined type is used to indicate where IRS text has been updated. Places where text has been removed are indicated by the sentence: *Text intentionally omitted*.

ey.com/EYTaxGuide
Ernst & Young LLP will update the *Ernst & Young Tax Guide 2012* website with relevant taxpayer information as it becomes available. You can also sign up for email alerts to let you know when changes have been made.

Introduction

Your salary, interest you earn, dividends received, a gain from the sale of securities–all of these, of course, are taxable income.

Unfortunately, so are a lot of other things: a debt forgiven by a friend, jury pay, a free trip you receive from a travel agency for organizing a group of tourists, lottery and gambling winnings, and royalties you earn on a book.

The general rule is that anything that enriches you should be included in your gross income, unless it is specifically excluded by the tax law.

Indeed, some things are excluded from taxation. Generally, you don't have to pay income tax on life insurance proceeds that you receive because of the death of the insured. Most gifts and inheritances are excluded from income tax. The value of the vegetables you grow in your garden and eat yourself is not taxable. This chapter tells you what kind of income is not taxable, and how you can tell the difference.

This chapter includes a discussion on passive activity losses. Passive investments include all rental activities, investments in limited partnerships, and those other businesses in which the taxpayer is not involved in the operations on a regular, continuous, and substantial basis.

You must include on your return all items of income you receive in the form of money, property, and services unless the tax law states that you do not include them. Some items, however, are only partly excluded from income. This chapter discusses many kinds of income and explains whether they are taxable or nontaxable.

- Income that is taxable must be reported on your tax return and is subject to tax.
- Income that is nontaxable may have to be shown on your tax return but is not taxable.

This chapter begins with discussions of the following income items.

- Bartering.
- Canceled debts.
- Sales parties at which you are the host or hostess.
- Life insurance proceeds.
- Partnership income.
- S Corporation income.
- Recoveries (including state income tax refunds).
- Rents from personal property.
- Repayments.
- Royalties.
- Unemployment benefits.
- Welfare and other public assistance benefits.

These discussions are followed by brief discussions of other income items.

Useful Items

You may want to see:

Publication

- ☐ **525** Taxable and Nontaxable Income
- ☐ **544** Sales and Other Dispositions of Assets
- ☐ **550** Investment Income and Expenses, Including Capital Gains and Losses
- ☐ **925** Passive Activity and At-Risk Rules
- ☐ **3920** Tax Relief for Victims of Terrorist Attacks
- ☐ **4681** Canceled Debts, Foreclosures, Repossessions, and Abandonments (for Individuals)

Bartering

Bartering is an exchange of property or services. You must include in your income, at the time received, the fair market value of property or services you receive in bartering. If you exchange services with another person and you both have agreed ahead of time on the value of the services, that value will be accepted as fair market value unless the value can be shown to be otherwise.

Generally, you report this income on Schedule C (Form 1040), Profit or Loss from Business, or Schedule C-EZ (Form 1040), Net Profit From Business. However, if the barter involves an exchange of something other than services, such as in *Example 3* below, you may have to use another form or schedule instead.

EXPLANATION

The IRS explanation is correct in stating that if you exchange your property and/or services for the property and/or services of another, you have taxable income. However, when you exchange property for property, you generally recognize income only to the extent that the fair market value of the property you receive exceeds your adjusted basis in the property you give up (note that an exception to this general rule is for like-kind exchanges). The proper way of determining gain on exchanges of property and your basis in the property you receive are discussed in chapter 13, *Basis of property*, and chapter 14, *Sale of property*.

Example 1. You are a self-employed attorney who performs legal services for a client, a small corporation. The corporation gives you shares of its stock as payment for your services. You must include the fair market value of the shares in your income on Schedule C (Form 1040) or Schedule C-EZ (Form 1040) in the year you receive them.

Example 2. You are self-employed and a member of a barter club. The club uses "credit units" as a means of exchange. It adds credit units to your account for goods or services you provide to members, which you can use to purchase goods or services offered by other members of the barter club. The club subtracts credit units from your account when you receive goods or services from other members. You must include in your income the value of the credit units that are added to your account, even though you may not actually receive goods or services from other members until a later tax year.

Example 3. You own a small apartment building. In return for 6 months rent-free use of an apartment, an artist gives you a work of art she created. You must report as rental income on Schedule E (Form 1040), Supplemental Income and Loss, the fair market value of the artwork, and the artist must report as income on Schedule C (Form 1040) or Schedule C-EZ (Form 1040) the fair rental value of the apartment.

Form 1099-B from barter exchange. If you exchanged property or services through a barter exchange, Form 1099-B, Proceeds from Broker and Barter Exchange Transactions, or a similar statement from the barter exchange should be sent to you by February 15, 2012. It should show the value of cash, property, services, credits, or scrip you received from exchanges during 2011. The IRS also will receive a copy of Form 1099-B.

Canceled Debts

Generally, if a debt you owe is canceled or forgiven, other than as a gift or bequest, you must include the canceled amount in your income. You have no income from the canceled debt if it is intended as a gift to you. A debt includes any indebtedness for which you are liable or which attaches to property you hold.

If the debt is a nonbusiness debt, report the canceled amount on Form 1040, line 21. If it is a business debt, report the amount on Schedule C (Form 1040) or Schedule C-EZ (Form 1040) (or on Schedule F (Form 1040), Profit or Loss From Farming, if the debt is farm debt and you are a farmer).

You may be able to elect to recognize a canceled business debt in income over a 5-tax-year period if the income is realized in a reacquisition in 2009 or 2010. For information on this election, see Revenue Procedure 2009-37 available at *www.irs.gov/irb/2009-36_IRB/ar07.html*.

> **TAXPLANNER**
> Family members often make interest-free or below-market interest rate loans to one another. The IRS may recharacterize these loans as arm's-length transactions and impute interest income to the lender and interest expense to the borrower, which are then reported on their respective tax returns. See chapter 7, *Interest income*, for further discussion of below-market loans. You should consult your tax advisor about how to report any below-market loan transactions.

Form 1099-C. If a Federal Government agency, financial institution, or credit union cancels or forgives a debt you owe of $600 or more, you will receive a Form 1099-C, Cancellation of Debt. The amount of the canceled debt is shown in box 2.

Interest included in canceled debt. If any interest is forgiven and included in the amount of canceled debt in box 2, the amount of interest also will be shown in box 3. Whether or not you must include the interest portion of the canceled debt in your income depends on whether the interest would be deductible if you paid it. See *Deductible debt* under *Exceptions*, later.

If the interest would not be deductible (such as interest on a personal loan), include in your income the amount from Form 1099-C, box 2. If the interest would be deductible (such as on a business loan), include in your income the net amount of the canceled debt (the amount shown in box 2 less the interest amount shown in box 3).

Discounted mortgage loan. If your financial institution offers a discount for the early payment of your mortgage loan, the amount of the discount is canceled debt. You must include the canceled amount in your income.

> **TAXSAVER**
> Proceed cautiously if the financial institution that holds your mortgage offers you a substantial discount on your loan balance in exchange for a prepayment on it. Although this might at first appear very attractive, remember that you will have to pay ordinary income tax on the amount of the discount offered, which may considerably reduce any advantage to you. Your money might be put to better use in investments with a high after-tax yield or in paying off expensive consumer credit debt.

Mortgage relief upon sale or other disposition. If you are personally liable for a mortgage (recourse debt), and you are relieved of the mortgage when you dispose of the property, you may realize gain or loss up to the fair market value of the property. To the extent the mortgage discharge exceeds the fair market value of the property, it is income from discharge of indebtedness unless it qualifies for exclusion under *Excluded debt*, later. Report any income from discharge of indebtedness on nonbusiness debt that does not qualify for exclusion as other income on Form 1040, line 21.

Unlawful Discrimination Claims. If you receive damages from a settlement or judgment in a lawsuit for unlawful discrimination that was settled or decided after October 22, 2004, you may be able to deduct attorney fees and court costs paid after that date. Your deduction is limited to the amount of the settlement or judgment you included in income. For more information, see *Court awards and damages* and *Deduction for costs involved in unlawful discrimination suits*, later, and Publication 525.

Tip

You may be able to exclude part of the mortgage relief on your principal residence. See Excluded debt, later.

If you are not personally liable for a mortgage (nonrecourse debt), and you are relieved of the mortgage when you dispose of the property (such as through foreclosure or repossession), that relief is included in the amount you realize. You may have a taxable gain if the amount you realize exceeds your adjusted basis in the property. Report any gain on nonbusiness property as a capital gain.

See Publication 4681 for more information.

> ### TAXALERT
> **Exclusion from gross income of certain discharged mortgage debt.** Tax laws enacted in 2007 and 2008 allow you to exclude from gross income up to $2 million (up to $1 million if married filing separately) in forgiven or canceled mortgage debt on your qualified principal residence. This exclusion applies to a mortgage that has been discharged after 2006 and before 2013. For more information, see *Discharges of qualified principal residence indebtedness* in chapter 15, *Selling your home.*

Stockholder debt. If you are a stockholder in a corporation and the corporation cancels or forgives your debt to it, the canceled debt is a constructive distribution that is generally dividend income to you. For more information, see Publication 542, *Corporations*.

If you are a stockholder in a corporation and you cancel a debt owed to you by the corporation, you generally do not realize income. This is because the canceled debt is considered as a contribution to the capital of the corporation equal to the amount of debt principal that you canceled.

Repayment of canceled debt. If you included a canceled amount in your income and later pay the debt, you may be able to file a claim for refund for the year the amount was included in income. You can file a claim on Form 1040X if the statute of limitations for filing a claim is still open. The statute of limitations generally does not end until 3 years after the due date of your original return.

Exceptions
There are several exceptions to the inclusion of canceled debt in income. These are explained next.

Student loans. Certain student loans contain a provision that all or part of the debt incurred to attend the qualified educational institution will be canceled if you work for a certain period of time in certain professions for any of a broad class of employers.

You do not have income if your student loan is canceled after you agreed to this provision and then performed the services required. To qualify, the loan must have been made by:
1. The Federal Government, a state or local government, or an instrumentality, agency, or subdivision thereof,
2. A tax-exempt public benefit corporation that has assumed control of a state, county, or municipal hospital, and whose employees are considered public employees under state law, or
3. An educational institution
   a. Under an agreement with an entity described in (1) or (2) that provided the funds to the institution to make the loan, or
   b. As part of a program of the institution designed to encourage students to serve in occupations or areas with unmet needs and under which the services provided are for or under the direction of a governmental unit or a tax-exempt section 501(c)(3) organization. Section 501(c)(3) organizations are defined in chapter 25.

A loan to refinance a qualified student loan also will qualify if it was made by an educational institution or a tax-exempt 501(a) organization under its program designed as described in (3)(b) above.

Education loan repayment assistance. Education loan repayments made to you by the National Health Service Corps Loan Repayment Program (NHSC Loan Repayment Program), a state education loan repayment program eligible for funds under the Public Health Service Act, or any other state loan repayment or loan forgiveness program that is intended to provide for the increased availability of health services in underserved or health professional shortage areas are not taxable.

Deductible debt. You do not have income from the cancellation of a debt if your payment of the debt would be deductible. This exception applies only if you use the cash method of accounting. For more information, see chapter 5 of Publication 334, *Tax Guide for Small Business*.

Price reduced after purchase. Generally, if the seller reduces the amount of debt you owe for property you purchased, you do not have income from the reduction. The reduction of the debt is treated as a purchase price adjustment and reduces your basis in the property.

Tip

The provision relating to the "other state loan repayment or loan forgiveness program" was added to this exclusion for amounts received in tax years beginning after December 31, 2008. If you included these amounts in income in 2009 or 2010, you should file an amended tax return to exclude this income. See Form 1040X, Amended U.S. Individual Income Tax Return, and its instructions for details on filing.

Excluded debt. Do not include a canceled debt in your gross income in the following situations.

- The debt is canceled in a bankruptcy case under title 11 of the U.S. Code. See Publication 908, *Bankruptcy Tax Guide.*
- The debt is canceled when you are insolvent. However, you cannot exclude any amount of canceled debt that is more than the amount by which you are insolvent. See Publication 908.
- The debt is qualified farm debt and is canceled by a qualified person. See chapter 3 of Publication 225, *Farmer's Tax Guide.*
- The debt is qualified real property business debt. See chapter 5 of Publication 334.
- The cancellation is intended as a gift.
- The debt is qualified principal residence indebtedness. See Publication 525 for additional information.

TAXPLANNER
To claim the exclusions listed above, Form 982 should be completed and attached to your federal income tax return. Also see the worksheet on page 6 of Publication 4681 to determine the extent of your insolvency immediately prior to the debt forgiveness.

TAXALERT
You cannot exclude from your gross income debt you owe to your employer that is forgiven even if it was incurred for purchasing stock.

Host or Hostess
If you host a party or event at which sales are made, any gift or gratuity you receive for giving the event is a payment for helping a direct seller make sales. You must report this item as income at its fair market value.

Your out-of-pocket party expenses are subject to the 50% limit for meal and entertainment expenses. These expenses are deductible as miscellaneous itemized deductions subject to the 2%-of-AGI limit on Schedule A (Form 1040), but only up to the amount of income you receive for giving the party.

For more information about the 50% limit for meal and entertainment expenses, see chapter 27.

Life Insurance Proceeds
Life insurance proceeds paid to you because of the death of the insured person are not taxable unless the policy was turned over to you for a price. This is true even if the proceeds were paid under an accident or health insurance policy or an endowment contract. However, interest income received as a result of life insurance proceeds may be taxable.

Proceeds not received in installments. If death benefits are paid to you in a lump sum or other than at regular intervals, include in your income only the benefits that are more than the amount payable to you at the time of the insured person's death. If the benefit payable at death is not specified, you include in your income the benefit payments that are more than the present value of the payments at the time of death.

Proceeds received in installments. If you receive life insurance proceeds in installments, you can exclude part of each installment from your income.

To determine the excluded part, divide the amount held by the insurance company (generally the total lump sum payable at the death of the insured person) by the number of installments to be paid. Include anything over this excluded part in your income as interest.

EXAMPLE
Suppose you receive a $100,000 life insurance death benefit that you elect to receive over 10 annual installments. Any amount that you receive in excess of $10,000 each year will be considered taxable interest income to you.

Surviving spouse. If your spouse died before October 23, 1986, and insurance proceeds paid to you because of the death of your spouse are received in installments, you can exclude up to

$1,000 a year of the interest included in the installments. If you remarry, you can continue to take the exclusion.

Surrender of policy for cash. If you surrender a life insurance policy for cash, you must include in income any proceeds that are more than the cost of the life insurance policy. In general, your cost (or investment in the contract) is the total of premiums that you paid for the life insurance policy, less any refunded premiums, rebates, dividends, or unrepaid loans that were not included in your income.

You should receive a Form 1099-R showing the total proceeds and the taxable part. Report these amounts on lines 16a and 16b of Form 1040 or lines 12a and 12b of Form 1040A.

More information. For more information, see *Life Insurance Proceeds* in Publication 525.

Endowment Contract Proceeds
An endowment contract is a policy under which you are paid a specified amount of money on a certain date unless you die before that date, in which case, the money is paid to your designated beneficiary. Endowment proceeds paid in a lump sum to you at maturity are taxable only if the proceeds are more than the cost of the policy. To determine your cost, subtract any amount that you previously received under the contract and excluded from your income from the total premiums (or other consideration) paid for the contract. Include the part of the lump sum payment that is more than your cost in your income.

However, if you agree to take the proceeds as an annuity within 60 days after the lump-sum payment becomes available and before you receive any cash, you are not considered to have received the lump sum for tax purposes. The lump sum is taxed as an annuity; that is, you are taxed on the amounts as you receive them each year.

For certain contracts entered into or materially changed after June 21, 1988, you may be required to treat distributions first as income and then as recovery of investment. Distributions are defined for this purpose to include a loan. In certain circumstances, an additional 10% tax will be imposed on the amount that is includible in gross income. Consult your tax advisor to determine if you are subject to this provision.

Accelerated Death Benefits
Certain amounts paid as accelerated death benefits under a life insurance contract or viatical settlement before the insured's death are excluded from income if the insured is terminally or chronically ill.

Viatical settlement. This is the sale or assignment of any part of the death benefit under a life insurance contract to a viatical settlement provider. A viatical settlement provider is a person who regularly engages in the business of buying or taking assignment of life insurance contracts on the lives of insured individuals who are terminally or chronically ill and who meet the requirements of section 101(g)(2)(B) of the Internal Revenue Code.

Exclusion for terminal illness. Accelerated death benefits are fully excludable if the insured is a terminally ill individual. This is a person who has been certified by a physician as having an illness or physical condition that can reasonably be expected to result in death within 24 months from the date of the certification.

Exclusion for chronic illness. If the insured is a chronically ill individual who is not terminally ill, accelerated death benefits paid on the basis of costs incurred for qualified long-term care services are fully excludable. Accelerated death benefits paid on a *per diem* or other periodic basis are excludable up to a limit. This limit applies to the total of the accelerated death benefits and any periodic payments received from long-term care insurance contracts. For information on the limit and the definitions of chronically ill individual, qualified long-term care services, and long-term care insurance contracts, see *Long-Term Care Insurance Contracts* under *Sickness and Injury Benefits* in Publication 525.

Exception. The exclusion does not apply to any amount paid to a person (other than the insured) who has an insurable interest in the life of the insured because the insured:
- Is a director, officer, or employee of the person, or
- Has a financial interest in the person's business.

Form 8853. To claim an exclusion for accelerated death benefits made on a *per diem* or other periodic basis, you must file Form 8853, Archer MSAs and Long-term Care Insurance Contracts, with your return. You do not have to file Form 8853 to exclude accelerated death benefits paid on the basis of actual expenses incurred.

Public Safety Officer Killed in the Line of Duty
If you are a survivor of a public safety officer who was killed in the line of duty, you may be able to exclude from income certain amounts you receive.

For this purpose, the term public safety officer includes law enforcement officers, firefighters, chaplains, and rescue squad and ambulance crew members. For more information, see Publication 559, *Survivors, Executors, and Administrators*.

Partnership Income
A partnership generally is not a taxable entity. The income, gains, losses, deductions, and credits of a partnership are passed through to the partners based on each partner's distributive share of these items.

Schedule K-1 (Form 1065). Although a partnership generally pays no tax, it must file an information return on Form 1065, U.S. Return of Partnership Income, and send Schedule K-1 (Form 1065) to each partner. In addition, the partnership will send each partner a copy of the Partner's Instructions for Schedule K-1 (Form 1065) to help each partner report his or her share of the partnership's income, deductions, credits, and tax preference items.

For more information on partnerships, see Publication 541, *Partnerships*.

EXPLANATION

General. A partnership includes a group, pool, joint venture, or other unincorporated organization that carries on a business or financial operation. Most entities that qualify for partnership treatment can elect out of partnership treatment under the "check-the-box" regulations. See your tax advisor for more information.

Limited liability companies. All states permit the formation of limited liability companies (LLCs). In an LLC, members and designated managers are not personally liable for any debts of the company. Absent an election to the contrary the entity will generally be treated as a partnership and, as a result, enjoy the same federal income tax benefits that apply to partnerships. If the entity is appropriately established, LLCs combine the benefits of corporate limited liability with the advantages of partnership taxation. In addition to LLCs, one may consider the formation of a limited liability partnership (LLP). Consult your tax advisor or attorney to find out if these are options for your business in the state you live in.

Reporting income. Because a partnership is not a taxable entity, all tax items are passed through to the partners. A partnership is required to give you a Schedule K-1, Partner's Share of Income, Credits, Deductions, etc. A Schedule K-1 will list your distributive share of income, gains, losses, deductions, and credits that is required to be included in your individual tax return. If, for example, the Schedule K-1 indicates interest income of $100, you will need to include $100 as interest income on your Schedule B, Form 1040 or 1040A. (See chapter 7, *Interest income*.)

Basis. Because the partnership's income and losses flow directly through to you, that income or loss will affect your tax basis in the partnership. It is important that you maintain and update this tax-basis calculation every year for two reasons. First, your distributive share of the partnership losses is limited to the adjusted basis of your interest in the partnership at the end of the partnership year in which the losses took place. Second, in the year you sell your partnership interest, you will need to know your tax basis in order to calculate your gain or loss. To determine the adjusted basis of your interest in the partnership, begin with your initial investment and your initial share of the partnership's liabilities and make the following adjustments.

Additions to basis

1. Your distributive share of the partnership's taxable income
2. Your share of any tax-exempt income earned by the partnership
3. Your share of the excess of partnership deductions for depletion over the basis of partnership property subject to depletion
4. Any additional capital you contribute
5. Your share of any increase in partnership liabilities

Subtractions from basis

1. Any cash distributions you receive
2. The basis that you take in any property distributed to you by the partnership
3. Your share of oil and gas depletion claimed by the partnership
4. Your distributive share of partnership losses
5. Your share of nondeductible, noncapital expenditures made by the partnership
6. Your share of any decrease in partnership liabilities

The partnership agreement usually covers the distribution of profits, losses, and other items. However, if there is no agreement for sharing a specific item of gain or loss, generally, each partner's distributive share is figured according to the partner's interest in the partnership.

In addition, special "at-risk" rules apply to a partnership engaged in any activity.

You may deduct your share of a partnership loss from any activity only up to the total amount that you are at risk in the activity at the end of the partnership's tax year.

The amount you are at risk in an activity is the cash and the adjusted basis of other property you contributed to the activity. Also, you are at risk for any amounts borrowed for use in the activity for which you either are personally liable or have pledged property, except property used in the activity, as security.

Generally, you are not at risk for:

1. Any nonrecourse loans used to finance the activity, to acquire property used in the activity, or to acquire your interest in the activity, unless they are secured by property not used in the activity;
2. Amounts for which you are protected against loss by guarantees, stop-loss agreements, or other similar arrangements; or

3. Amounts borrowed from interested or related parties if your partnership is engaged in certain activities.

For more information on the at-risk rules, see Publication 925, *Passive Activity and At-Risk Rules.*

In addition to the factors discussed above, your amount at risk is affected by the operating results of the activity itself. Income from the activity increases the amount you are at risk. Losses from the activity decrease the amount you are at risk. The at-risk amount is determined at the end of each tax year. Any loss in excess of that amount is disallowed for that year. It may, however, be carried over to future years, and to the extent that you subsequently have amounts at risk, it may be deducted in those years.

Under prior law, a partnership engaged in real estate activity was not subject to the at-risk rules. The Tax Reform Act of 1986 extended the at-risk rules to include real estate activities placed in service after December 31, 1986, but makes exceptions for third-party nonrecourse debt from commercial lenders and certain other parties.

In addition to the at-risk rules, the income from real estate partnerships is also subject to the passive activity rules. See *Passive Activity Limitations* and *At-Risk Limitations*, at the end of this chapter. Also, consult your tax advisor for further information.

When to report partnership income. Generally, partnership income is treated as paid to you on the last day of the partnership year. (See chapter 43, *Decedents: Dealing with the death of a family member*, for exceptions relating to partnership interests held by a decedent.) Generally, you must include your distributive share of partnership items on your return for the tax year in which the last day of the partnership year falls. If you receive income from a partnership other than in your capacity as a partner, however, you must report the income in the year in which it was received. For instance, if you sell property to your partnership at a gain, the gain is generally included in income when you receive the sale proceeds, regardless of when your partnership's tax year ends.

Estimated tax payments. A partner must take into account his or her share of the partnership's income or deductions to date at each estimated tax payment date. Often, this information is not readily available. If you are a member of a partnership you may protect yourself from underpayment penalties by basing your payments on one of the exceptions described in chapter 4, *Tax withholding and estimated tax*.

However, if a partner moves from one state to another, and if the states involved follow federal rules, the partnership income or loss should be reported in the state income tax return for the state in which the partner resides when the partnership's year ends.

Sale of partnership interest. If you have a gain or a loss from the sale or exchange of a partnership interest, it is treated as a gain or a loss from the sale of a capital asset. The gain or loss is the difference between the amount you receive and the adjusted basis of your interest in the partnership. If you are relieved of any debts of the partnership, you must include these debts in the amount you receive.

However, you may have ordinary income as well as capital gain or loss on the sale of your partnership interest if the sale involves uncollected accounts receivable or inventory items that have increased in value. Consult your tax advisor for further help.

Qualified joint venture. If you and your spouse each materially participate as the only members of a jointly owned and operated business, and you file a joint return for the tax year, you can make a joint election to be treated as a qualified joint venture instead of a partnership. To make this election, you must divide all items of income, gain, loss, deduction, and credit attributable to the business between you and your spouse in accordance with your respective interests in the venture. Each of you must file a separate Schedule C or Schedule C-EZ (Form 1040).

S Corporation Income

In general, an S corporation does not pay tax on its income. Instead, the income, losses, deductions, and credits of the corporation are passed through to the shareholders based on each shareholder's *pro rata* share.

Schedule K-1 (Form 1120S). An S corporation must file a return on Form 1120S, U.S. Income Tax Return for an S Corporation, and send Schedule K-1 (Form 1120S) to each shareholder. In addition, the S corporation will send each shareholder a copy of the Shareholder's Instructions for Schedule K-1 (Form 1120S) to help each shareholder report his or her share of the S corporation's income, losses, credits, and deductions.

Records

Keep Schedule K-1 (Form 1120S) for your records. Do not attach it to your Form 1040.

EXPLANATION

Shareholder's return. Generally, S corporation distributions are considered a nontaxable return of your basis in the corporation's stock. However, in certain cases, part of the distributions may be taxable as a dividend or as a long-term or short-term capital gain, or as both. The corporation's distributions may be in the form of cash or property.

All current-year income or loss and other tax items are taxed to you at the corporation's year-end. Generally, the items that are passed through to you as a shareholder will increase or decrease the basis of your S corporation stock as appropriate. Dividends are paid only from prior-year earnings (generally retained earnings from years prior to becoming an S corporation). Generally, property (including cash) distributions, except dividend distributions, are considered a return of capital to the extent of your basis in the stock of the corporation. Distributions in excess of basis are treated as a gain from the sale or exchange of property.

You should receive from the S corporation in which you are a shareholder a copy of the Shareholder's Instructions for Schedule K-1 (Form 1120S), together with a copy of Schedule K-1 (Form 1120S), showing your share of the income, credits, and deductions of the S corporation for the tax year. Your distributive share of the items of income, gain, loss, deduction, or credit of the S corporation must be shown separately on your Form 1040 or 1040A. The tax treatment of these items generally is the same as if you had realized or incurred them personally.

Individuals form an S corporation to get the legal benefits of a corporation, such as limited liability, while retaining the tax benefits of an individual. Usually, an S corporation does not pay federal income tax. One exception is a tax on net passive investment income that is paid by the S corporation, but normally, the individual owners of the corporation pay tax or accrue tax benefits on their personal returns based on the corporation's profits and losses. Income from an S corporation is included in an individual's return as if the S corporation did not exist. Dividends that the S corporation receives are included as dividends on your return on Schedule B (Form 1040). Capital gains are included on Schedule D (Form 1040). Types of income from an S corporation that are not treated specially on an individual's return are combined and included on Schedule E (Form 1040). If you have losses from an S corporation when you are not an active participant in the corporation's business activities, your losses will be subject to the passive activity loss limitations. See the section on *Passive Activity Losses* at the end of this chapter.

Estimated tax payments. A shareholder must take into account his or her share of the S corporation's income or deductions to date at each estimated tax payment date. Often, this information is not readily available. If you are a member of an S corporation, you may protect yourself from underpayment penalties by basing your payments on one of the exceptions described in chapter 4, *Tax withholding and estimated tax*.

Generally, an S corporation must have its tax year-end on December 31. However, under certain circumstances, an S corporation may operate on a fiscal year; that is, its tax year may end on a date other than December 31. Your return should include all S corporation income for its operating year that ends within your tax year.

Example

If your S corporation's year ends on October 31, your return for 2011 will include the income items for the corporation's entire year that ended October 31, 2011, even though that means including 2 months of 2010.

Deducting losses. You may deduct any losses of the S corporation for the year up to the amount of your basis.

Basis in an S corporation. Your basis in an S corporation at the end of a year is your investment (basis of stock owned plus loans made directly by you to the S corporation), with the following adjustments.

Additions to basis

1. Your distributive share of the S corporation's separately and non-separately stated taxable income
2. Your share of tax-exempt income earned by the S corporation
3. Any additional capital that you contribute
4. Deductions for depletion in excess of the basis of the property
5. A loan to the corporation directly from the shareholder; however, a guarantee of a third-party loan by a shareholder does not qualify as an addition to basis

Subtractions from basis

1. Generally, any cash distributed and the fair market value of property distributed (other than taxable dividends), but not below zero
2. Your distributive share of the S corporation's separately and non-separately stated items of loss and deduction

3. Your share of nondeductible, noncapital expenditures made by the S corporation
4. Your share of the deductions for depletion for any oil and gas property held by the S corporation to the extent that the deduction does not exceed the proportionate share of the property's adjusted basis allocated to you

Example 1
Your basis in an S corporation is $20,000. The corporation makes a distribution to you of $30,000 in cash or property. You would have to recognize income of $10,000 due to a distribution in excess of basis.

Example 2
Your basis in an S corporation is $20,000. If it reports losses of $30,000, you may deduct only $20,000 for the year. The other $10,000 of losses is carried over until you have more basis.

All you need to prepare your individual tax return is the Form K-1 provided by the S corporation. It tells you what the numbers are and where to put them on your Form 1040.

TAXPLANNER
An S corporation is just one of several alternatives to consider as a vehicle to conduct business activities, but it does offer some of the best features of a regular corporation, a partnership, and a sole proprietorship.
1. As in a regular corporation, the stockholders of an S corporation are normally immune from liabilities in excess of their investment.
2. Like a regular corporation, the S corporation structure is convenient for transferring equity to heirs as part of your estate planning and the gradual transition of management and control to your heirs or successors. As shareholders, the heirs then report their proportionate share of S corporation income and losses on their respective tax returns.
3. Like a partnership or sole proprietorship, the S corporation permits the investors to deduct operating losses. Just as important, profits are not taxed twice, as they are in a regular corporation. A regular corporation itself pays taxes, and so do the individuals who receive a share of those profits when dividends are paid. An S corporation is, except in certain circumstances, exempt from taxes—at least at the federal level.

Recoveries

A recovery is a return of an amount you deducted or took a credit for in an earlier year. The most common recoveries are refunds, reimbursements, and rebates of deductions itemized on Schedule A (Form 1040). You also may have recoveries of non-itemized deductions (such as payments on previously deducted bad debts) and recoveries of items for which you previously claimed a tax credit.

Tax benefit rule. You must include a recovery in your income in the year you receive it up to the amount by which the deduction or credit you took for the recovered amount reduced your tax in the earlier year. For this purpose, any increase to an amount carried over to the current year that resulted from the deduction or credit is considered to have reduced your tax in the earlier year. For more information, see Publication 525.

Federal income tax refund. Refunds of federal income taxes are not included in your income because they are never allowed as a deduction from income.

State tax refund. If you received a state or local income tax refund (or credit or offset) in 2011, you generally must include it in income if you deducted the tax in an earlier year. The payer should send Form 1099-G, Certain Government Payments, to you by January 31, 2012. The IRS also will receive a copy of the Form 1099-G. If you file Form 1040, use the State and Local Income Tax Refund worksheet in the 2011 Form 1040 instructions for line 10 to figure the amount (if any) to include in your income. See Publication 525 for when you must use another worksheet.

EXPLANATION
The State and Local Income Tax worksheet can be used to determine the taxable amount of your state and local income tax refund.

If you could choose to deduct for a tax year either:
- State and local income taxes, or
- State and local general sales taxes, then the maximum refund that you may have to include in income is limited to the excess of the tax you chose to deduct for that year over the tax you did not choose to deduct for that year. For examples, see Publication 525.

Mortgage interest refund. If you received a refund or credit in 2011 of mortgage interest paid in an earlier year, the amount should be shown in box 3 of your Form 1098, Mortgage Interest Statement. Do not subtract the refund amount from the interest you paid in 2011. You may have to include it in your income under the rules explained in the following discussions.

Interest on recovery. Interest on any of the amounts you recover must be reported as interest income in the year received. For example, report any interest you received on state or local income tax refunds on Form 1040, line 8a.

EXPLANATION
Although the amount of a state tax refund may not be included in gross income, any interest you receive on federal or state tax refunds is taxable.

Recovery and expense in same year. If the refund or other recovery and the expense occur in the same year, the recovery reduces the deduction or credit and is not reported as income.

Recovery for 2 or more years. If you receive a refund or other recovery that is for amounts you paid in 2 or more separate years, you must allocate, on a *pro rata* basis, the recovered amount between the years in which you paid it. This allocation is necessary to determine the amount of recovery from any earlier years and to determine the amount, if any, of your allowable deduction for this item for the current year. For information on how to compute the allocation, see *Recoveries* in Publication 525.

Itemized Deduction Recoveries
If you recover any amount that you deducted in an earlier year on Schedule A (Form 1040), you generally must include the full amount of the recovery in your income in the year you receive it.

Where to report. Enter your state or local income tax refund on Form 1040, line 10, and the total of all other recoveries as other income on Form 1040, line 21. You cannot use Form 1040A or Form 1040EZ.

Standard deduction limit. You generally are allowed to claim the standard deduction if you do not itemize your deductions. Only your itemized deductions that are more than your standard deduction are subject to the recovery rule (unless you are required to itemize your deductions). If your total deductions on the earlier year return were not more than your income for that year, include in your income this year the lesser of:
- Your recoveries, or
- The amount by which your itemized deductions exceeded the standard deduction.

Example. For 2010, you filed a joint return. Your taxable income was $60,000 and you were not entitled to any tax credits. Your standard deduction was $11,400, and you had itemized deductions of $13,000. In 2011, you received the following recoveries for amounts deducted on your 2010 return:

Medical expenses	$200
State and local income tax refund	400
Refund of mortgage interest	325
Total recoveries	**$925**

None of the recoveries were more than the deductions taken for 2010. The difference between the state and local income tax you deducted and your local general sales tax was more than $400.

Your total recoveries are less than the amount by which your itemized deductions exceeded the standard deduction ($13,000 − 11,400 = $1,600), so you must include your total recoveries in your income for 2011. Report the state and local income tax refund of $400 on Form 1040, line 10, and the balance of your recoveries, $525, on Form 1040, line 21.

Standard deduction for earlier years. To determine if amounts recovered in 2011 must be included in your income, you must know the standard deduction for your filing status for the year the deduction was claimed. Standard deduction amounts for 2010, 2009, and 2008, are in Publication 525.

Example. You filed a joint return on Form 1040 for 2010 with taxable income of $45,000. Your itemized deductions were $12,050. The standard deduction that you could have claimed was $11,400. In 2011, you recovered $2,100 of your 2010 itemized deductions. None of the recoveries were more than the actual deductions for 2010. Include $650 of the recoveries in your 2011 income. This is the smaller of your recoveries ($2,100) or the amount by which your itemized deductions were more than the standard deduction ($12,050 − $11,400 = $650).

Recovery limited to deduction. You do not include in your income any amount of your recovery that is more than the amount you deducted in the earlier year. The amount you include in your income is limited to the smaller of:
- The amount deducted on Schedule A (Form 1040), or
- The amount recovered.

Example. During 2010 you paid $1,700 for medical expenses. From this amount you subtracted $1,500, which was 7.5% of your adjusted gross income. Your actual medical expense deduction was $200. In 2011, you received a $500 reimbursement from your medical insurance for your 2010 expenses. The only amount of the $500 reimbursement that must be included in your income for 2011 is $200—the amount actually deducted.

Other recoveries. See *Recoveries* in Publication 525 if:
- You have recoveries of items other than itemized deductions, or
- You received a recovery for an item for which you claimed a tax credit (other than investment credit or foreign tax credit) in a prior year.

Rents from Personal Property

If you rent out personal property, such as equipment or vehicles, how you report your income and expenses is generally determined by:
- Whether or not the rental activity is a business, and
- Whether or not the rental activity is conducted for profit.

Generally, if your primary purpose is income or profit and you are involved in the rental activity with continuity and regularity, your rental activity is a business. See Publication 535, *Business Expenses*, for details on deducting expenses for both business and not-for-profit activities.

Reporting business income and expenses. If you are in the business of renting personal property, report your income and expenses on Schedule C or Schedule C-EZ (Form 1040). The form instructions have information on how to complete them.

Reporting nonbusiness income. If you are not in the business of renting personal property, report your rental income on Form 1040, line 21. List the type and amount of the income on the dotted line next to line 21.

Reporting nonbusiness expenses. If you rent personal property for profit, include your rental expenses in the total amount you enter on Form 1040, line 36. Also enter the amount and "PPR" on the dotted line next to line 36.

If you do not rent personal property for profit, your deductions are limited and you cannot report a loss to offset other income. See *Activity not for profit* under *Other Income*, later.

Repayments

If you had to repay an amount that you included in your income in an earlier year, you may be able to deduct the amount repaid from your income for the year in which you repaid it. Or, if the amount you repaid is more than $3,000, you may be able to take a credit against your tax for the year in which you repaid it. Generally, you can claim a deduction or credit only if the repayment qualifies as an expense or loss incurred in your trade or business or in a for-profit transaction.

Type of deduction. The type of deduction you are allowed in the year of repayment depends on the type of income you included in the earlier year. You generally deduct the repayment on the same form or schedule on which you previously reported it as income. For example, if you reported it as self-employment income, deduct it as a business expense on Schedule C or Schedule C-EZ (Form 1040) or Schedule F (Form 1040). If you reported it as a capital gain, deduct it as a capital loss on Schedule D (Form 1040). If you reported it as wages, unemployment compensation, or other nonbusiness income, deduct it as a miscellaneous itemized deduction on Schedule A (Form 1040).

Repaid social security benefits. If you repaid social security benefits or equivalent railroad retirement benefits, see *Repayment of benefits* in chapter 11.

Repayment of $3,000 or less. If the amount you repaid was $3,000 or less, deduct it from your income in the year you repaid it. If you must deduct it as a miscellaneous itemized deduction, enter it on Schedule A (Form 1040), line 23.

Repayment over $3,000. If the amount you repaid was more than $3,000, you can deduct the repayment (as explained under *Type of deduction*, earlier). However, you can choose instead to take a tax credit for the year of repayment if you included the income under a claim of right. This means that at the time you included the income, it appeared that you had an unrestricted right to it. If you qualify for this choice, figure your tax under both methods and compare the results. Use the method (deduction or credit) that results in less tax.

Method 1. Figure your tax for 2011 claiming a deduction for the repaid amount. If you must deduct it as a miscellaneous itemized deduction, enter it on Schedule A (Form 1040), line 28.

Method 2. Figure your tax for 2011 claiming a credit for the repaid amount. Follow these steps.

1. Figure your tax for 2011 without deducting the repaid amount.
2. Refigure your tax from the earlier year without including in income the amount you repaid in 2011.
3. Subtract the tax in (2) from the tax shown on your return for the earlier year. This is the credit.
4. Subtract the answer in (3) from the tax for 2011 figured without the deduction (Step 1).

If method 1 results in less tax, deduct the amount repaid. If method 2 results in less tax, claim the credit figured in (3) above on Form 1040, line 72, and enter "I.R.C. 1341" in the column to the right of line 72.

An example of this computation can be found in Publication 525.

EXAMPLE

For tax year 2010, you were married with no dependents. You filed a joint return with your spouse and reported taxable income of $90,000 (after all deductions and exemptions). Your return showed a tax liability of $14,875, which you paid. In 2011, you had to return $5,000 that you had received and had included in your 2010 gross income. Your marital and filing statuses were the same in 2011 as in 2010, and your taxable income for 2011 is $140,000 (after all deductions and exemptions).

To determine how to treat the repayment on your 2011 return, the following calculations must be performed.

Method 1

2011 taxable income	$140,000
Less: Deduction for repayment	(5,000)
Revised 2011 taxable income	$135,000
Tax using method 1	**$26,113**

Method 2

	2011 taxable income	$140,000
	Recomputed 2011 tax liability	$27,444
(a)	2010 taxable income as previously reported	$90,000
	Less: Deduction for repayment	(5,000)
	2010 taxable income w/out repayment	$85,000
	Recomputed 2010 tax liability	$13,625
(b)	2010 tax as reported	$14,875
	Recomputed 2010 tax liability (w/out repayment)	(13,625)
	Difference	$ 1,250
(c)	Recomputed 2011 tax liability	$27,444
	Difference from (b)	(1,250)
	Tax using method 2	**$26,194**

To determine which method should be used to account for your repayment in 2011, you must now compare the two methods and choose the one that generates the lower tax liability. In the example, method 1 generates the lesser tax liability; therefore, you would claim a deduction for the amount repaid by you in 2011 on your 2011 tax return.

Note that these two methods will only result in different tax liabilities if you fall into different marginal tax brackets in each year (e.g., in 2010, you are in the 25% marginal tax bracket, and in 2011, you are in the 28% marginal tax bracket).

Royalties

Royalties from copyrights, patents, and oil, gas, and mineral properties are taxable as ordinary income.

You generally report royalties in Part I of Schedule E (Form 1040). However, if you hold an operating oil, gas, or mineral interest or are in business as a self-employed writer, inventor, artist, etc., report your income and expenses on Schedule C or Schedule C-EZ (Form 1040).

Copyrights and patents. Royalties from copyrights on literary, musical, or artistic works, and similar property, or from patents on inventions, are amounts paid to you for the right to use your work over a specified period of time. Royalties generally are based on the number of units sold, such as the number of books, tickets to a performance, or machines sold.

Oil, gas, and minerals. Royalty income from oil, gas, and mineral properties is the amount you receive when natural resources are extracted from your property. The royalties are based on units, such as barrels, tons, etc., and are paid to you by a person or company who leases the property from you.

Depletion. If you are the owner of an economic interest in mineral deposits or oil and gas wells, you can recover your investment through the depletion allowance. For information on this subject, see chapter 9 of Publication 535.

Coal and iron ore. Under certain circumstances, you can treat amounts you receive from the disposal of coal and iron ore as payments from the sale of a capital asset, rather than as royalty income. For information about gain or loss from the sale of coal and iron ore, see Publication 544.

Sale of property interest. If you sell your complete interest in oil, gas, or mineral rights, the amount you receive is considered payment for the sale of section 1231 property, not royalty income. Under certain circumstances, the sale is subject to capital gain or loss treatment on Schedule D (Form 1040). For more information on selling section 1231 property, see chapter 3 of Publication 544.

If you retain a royalty, an overriding royalty, or a net profit interest in a mineral property for the life of the property, you have made a lease or a sublease, and any cash you receive for the assignment of other interests in the property is ordinary income subject to a depletion allowance.

Part of future production sold. If you own mineral property but sell part of the future production, you generally treat the money you receive from the buyer at the time of the sale as a loan from the buyer. Do not include it in your income or take depletion based on it.

When production begins, you include all the proceeds in your income, deduct all the production expenses, and deduct depletion from that amount to arrive at your taxable income from the property.

Unemployment Benefits

The tax treatment of unemployment benefits you receive depends on the type of program paying the benefits.

Unemployment compensation. You must include in income all unemployment compensation you receive. You should receive a Form 1099-G showing in box 1 the total unemployment compensation paid to you. Generally, you enter unemployment compensation on line 19 of Form 1040, line 13 of Form 1040A, or line 3 of Form 1040EZ.

Types of unemployment compensation. Unemployment compensation generally includes any amount received under an unemployment compensation law of the United States or of a state. It includes the following benefits.

- Benefits paid by a state or the District of Columbia from the Federal Unemployment Trust Fund.
- State unemployment insurance benefits.
- Railroad unemployment compensation benefits.
- Disability payments from a government program paid as a substitute for unemployment compensation. (Amounts received as workers' compensation for injuries or illness are not unemployment compensation. See chapter 5 for more information.)
- Trade readjustment allowances under the Trade Act of 1974.
- Unemployment assistance under the Disaster Relief and Emergency Assistance Act.

Governmental program. If you contribute to a governmental unemployment compensation program and your contributions are not deductible, amounts you receive under the program are not included as unemployment compensation until you recover your contributions. If you deducted all of your contributions to the program, the entire amount you receive under the program is included in your income.

Repayment of unemployment compensation. If you repaid in 2011 unemployment compensation you received in 2011, subtract the amount you repaid from the total amount you received and enter the difference on line 19 of Form 1040, line 13 of Form 1040A, or line 3 of Form 1040EZ. On the dotted line next to your entry enter "Repaid" and the amount you repaid. If you repaid unemployment compensation in 2011 that you included in income in an earlier year, you can deduct the amount repaid on Schedule A (Form 1040), line 23, if you itemize deductions. If the amount is more than $3,000, see *Repayments*, earlier.

Tax withholding. You can choose to have federal income tax withheld from your unemployment compensation. To make this choice, complete Form W-4V, Voluntary Withholding Request, and give it to the paying office. Tax will be withheld at 10% of your payment.

Supplemental unemployment benefits. Benefits received from an employer-financed fund (to which the employees did not contribute) are not unemployment compensation. They are taxable as wages and are subject to withholding for income tax. They may be subject to social security and Medicare taxes. For more information, see *Supplemental Unemployment Benefits* in section 5 of Publication 15-A, *Employer's Supplemental Tax Guide*. Report these payments on line 7 of Form 1040 or Form 1040A or on line 1 of Form 1040EZ.

Repayment of benefits. You may have to repay some of your supplemental unemployment benefits to qualify for trade readjustment allowances under the Trade Act of 1974. If you repay supplemental unemployment benefits in the same year you receive them, reduce the total benefits by the amount you repay. If you repay the benefits in a later year, you must include the full amount of the benefits received in your income for the year you received them.

Deduct the repayment in the later year as an adjustment to gross income on Form 1040. (You cannot use Form 1040A or Form 1040EZ.) Include the repayment on Form 1040, line 36, and enter "Sub-Pay TRA" and the amount on the dotted line next to line 36. If the amount you repay in a later year is more than $3,000, you may be able to take a credit against your tax for the later year instead of deducting the amount repaid. For more information on this, see *Repayments*, earlier.

Private unemployment fund. Unemployment benefit payments from a private (nonunion) fund to which you voluntarily contribute are taxable only if the amounts you receive are more than your total payments into the fund. Report the taxable amount on Form 1040, line 21.

Payments by a union. Benefits paid to you as an unemployed member of a union from regular union dues are included in your income on Form 1040, line 21. However, if you contribute to a special union fund and your payments to the fund are not deductible, the unemployment benefits you receive from the fund are includible in your income only to the extent they are more than your contributions.

Caution

If you do not choose to have tax withheld from your unemployment compensation, you may be liable for estimated tax. If you do not pay enough tax, either through withholding or estimated tax, or a combination of both, you may have to pay a penalty. For more information on estimated tax, see chapter 4.

Guaranteed annual wage. Payments you receive from your employer during periods of unemployment, under a union agreement that guarantees you full pay during the year, are taxable as wages. Include them on line 7 of Form 1040 or Form 1040A or on line 1 of Form 1040EZ.

State employees. Payments similar to a state's unemployment compensation may be made by the state to its employees who are not covered by the state's unemployment compensation law. Although the payments are fully taxable, do not report them as unemployment compensation. Report these payments on Form 1040, line 21.

Welfare and Other Public Assistance Benefits

Do not include in your income governmental benefit payments from a public welfare fund based upon need, such as payments due to blindness. Payments from a state fund for the victims of crime should not be included in the victims' incomes if they are in the nature of welfare payments. Do not deduct medical expenses that are reimbursed by such a fund. You must include in your income any welfare payments that are compensation for services or that are obtained fraudulently.

Alternative trade adjustment assistance (ATAA) payments. Payments you receive from a state agency under the Demonstration Project for Alternative Trade Adjustment Assistance for Older Workers (ATAA) must be included in your income. The state must send you Form 1099-G to advise you of the amount you should include in income. The amount should be reported on Form 1040, line 21.

Persons with disabilities. If you have a disability, you must include in income compensation you receive for services you perform unless the compensation is otherwise excluded. However, you do not include in income the value of goods, services, and cash that you receive, not in return for your services, but for your training and rehabilitation because you have a disability. Excludable amounts include payments for transportation and attendant care, such as interpreter services for the deaf, reader services for the blind, and services to help mentally retarded persons do their work.

Disaster relief grants. Do not include post-disaster grants received under the Disaster Relief and Emergency Assistance Act in your income if the grant payments are made to help you meet necessary expenses or serious needs for medical, dental, housing, personal property, transportation, or funeral expenses. Do not deduct casualty losses or medical expenses that are specifically reimbursed by these disaster relief grants. If you have deducted a casualty loss for the loss of your personal residence and you later receive a disaster relief grant for the loss of the same residence, you may have to include part or all of the grant in your taxable income. See *Recoveries*, earlier. Unemployment assistance payments under the Act are taxable unemployment compensation. See *Unemployment compensation* under *Unemployment Benefits*, earlier.

Disaster relief payments. You can exclude from income any amount you receive that is a qualified disaster relief payment. A qualified disaster relief payment is an amount paid to you:
1. To reimburse or pay reasonable and necessary personal, family, living, or funeral expenses that result from a qualified disaster;
2. To reimburse or pay reasonable and necessary expenses incurred for the repair or rehabilitation of your home or repair or replacement of its contents to the extent it is due to a qualified disaster;
3. By a person engaged in the furnishing or sale of transportation as a common carrier because of the death or personal physical injuries incurred as a result of a qualified disaster; or
4. By a federal, state, or local government, or agency, or instrumentality in connection with a qualified disaster in order to promote the general welfare.

You can exclude this amount only to the extent any expense it pays for is not paid for by insurance or otherwise. The exclusion does not apply if you were a participant or conspirator in a terrorist action or his or her representative.

A qualified disaster is:
- A disaster which results from a terrorist or military action;
- A federally declared disaster; or
- A disaster which results from an accident involving a common carrier, or from any other event, which is determined to be catastrophic by the Secretary of the Treasury or his or her delegate.

For amounts paid under item (4), a disaster is qualified if it is determined by an applicable federal, state, or local authority to warrant assistance from the federal, state, or local government, agency, or instrumentality.

Disaster mitigation payments. You also can exclude from income any amount you receive that is a qualified disaster mitigation payment. Like qualified disaster relief payments, qualified disaster mitigation payments are also most commonly paid to you in the period immediately following damage to property as a result of a natural disaster. However, disaster mitigation payments are grants you use to mitigate (reduce the severity of) potential damage from future natural disasters. They are paid to you through state and local governments based on the provisions of the Robert T. Stafford Disaster Relief and Emergency Assistance Act or the National Flood Insurance Act.

You cannot increase the basis or adjusted basis of your property for improvements made with nontaxable disaster mitigation payments.

Home Affordable Modification Program (HAMP). If you benefit from Pay-for-Performance Success Payments under HAMP, the payments are not taxable.

Mortgage assistance payments. Payments made under section 235 of the National Housing Act for mortgage assistance are not included in the homeowner's income. Interest paid for the homeowner under the mortgage assistance program cannot be deducted.

Medicare. Medicare benefits received under title XVIII of the Social Security Act are not includible in the gross income of the individuals for whom they are paid. This includes basic (part A (Hospital Insurance Benefits for the Aged)) and supplementary (part B (Supplementary Medical Insurance Benefits for the Aged)).

Old-age, survivors, and disability insurance benefits (OASDI). OASDI payments under section 202 of title II of the Social Security Act are not includible in the gross income of the individuals to whom they are paid. This applies to old-age insurance benefits, and insurance benefits for wives, husbands, children, widows, widowers, mothers and fathers, and parents, as well as the lump-sum death payment.

Nutrition Program for the Elderly. Food benefits you receive under the Nutrition Program for the Elderly are not taxable. If you prepare and serve free meals for the program, include in your income as wages the cash pay you receive, even if you are also eligible for food benefits.

Other Sickness and Injury Benefits

In addition to welfare or insurance benefits, you may receive other payments for sickness or injury.

Workers' compensation. Amounts you receive as workers' compensation for an occupational sickness or injury are fully exempt from tax if they are paid under a workers' compensation act or a statute in the nature of a workers' compensation act. The exemption also applies to your survivor(s). The exemption from tax, however, does not apply to retirement benefits you receive based on your age, length of service, or prior contributions to the plan, even if you retired because of occupational sickness or injury.

Note: If part of your workers' compensation reduces your social security or equivalent railroad retirement benefits received, that part is considered social security (or equivalent railroad retirement) benefits and may be taxable. For more information, see Publication 915, *Social Security and Equivalent Railroad Retirement Benefits.*

Return to work. If you return to work after qualifying for workers' compensation, payments you continue to receive while assigned to light duties are taxable. Report these payments as wages on line 7 of Form 1040 or Form 1040A or on line 1 of Form 1040EZ.

Federal Employees' Compensation Act (FECA). Payments received under this Act for personal injury or sickness, including payments to beneficiaries in case of death, are not taxable. However, you are taxed on amounts you receive under this Act as "continuation of pay" for up to 45 days while a claim is being decided. Report this income on line 7 of Form 1040 or Form 1040A or on line 1 of Form 1040EZ. Also, pay for sick leave while a claim is being processed is taxable and must be included in your income as wages.

The IRS has ruled that the subsidized portion of health benefits provided by an employer to an employee's domestic partner, who does not qualify as a spouse or a dependent, will be taxable as wages to the employee.

You can deduct the amount you spend to "buy back" sick leave for an earlier year to be eligible for nontaxable FECA benefits for that period. It is a miscellaneous deduction subject to the 2% limit on Schedule A (Form 1040). If you buy back sick leave in the same year you use it, the amount reduces your taxable sick leave pay. Do not deduct it separately.

Other compensation. Many other amounts you receive as compensation for injury or illness are not taxable. These include:

- **Compensatory damages** you receive for physical injury or physical illness, whether paid in a lump sum or in periodic payments,
- **Benefits you receive under an accident or health insurance policy** on which either you paid the premiums or your employer paid the premiums but you had to include them in your gross income,
- **Disability benefits** you receive for loss of income or earning capacity as a result of injuries under a "no-fault" car insurance policy, and
- **Compensation you receive for permanent loss or loss of use** of a part or function of your body, or for your permanent disfigurement. This compensation must be based only on the injury and not on the period of your absence from work. These benefits are exempt from tax even if your employer pays for the accident and health plan that provides these benefits.

Only damages received on account of personal physical injury or sickness are nontaxable. Punitive damages will be taxable except those received in a wrongful death action where state law stipulates that they are nontaxable. This law is effective for amounts received after August 20, 1996, unless there was a binding settlement in effect on September 13, 1995.

Reimbursement for medical care. A reimbursement for medical care is generally not taxable. However, this reimbursement may reduce your medical expense deduction. For more information, see Table 22-1 in chapter 22, *Medical and dental expenses.*

Payments to reduce cost of winter energy. Payments made by a state to qualified people to reduce their cost of winter energy use are not taxable.

Other Income

The following brief discussions are arranged in alphabetical order. Income items that are discussed in greater detail in another publication include a reference to that publication.

Activity not for profit. You must include on your return income from an activity from which you do not expect to make a profit. An example of this type of activity is a hobby or a farm you operate mostly for recreation and pleasure. Enter this income on Form 1040, line 21. Deductions for expenses related to the activity are limited. They cannot total more than the income you report and can be taken only if you itemize deductions on Schedule A (Form 1040). See *Not-for-Profit Activities* in chapter 1 of Publication 535 for information on whether an activity is considered carried on for a profit.

EXPLANATION

An activity will be presumed to have been for profit if it results in a profit in at least 3 out of 5 consecutive tax years whether the activity is held individually, in trust, as a partnership, or as an S corporation. However, for the breeding, training, showing, or racing of horses, the activity must result in a profit in at least 2 out of 7 consecutive tax years. If the activity meets this test, it is presumed to be carried on for profit and the limits will not apply.

If you have engaged in an activity for less than 3 years, you can postpone the determination that the activity is not for profit by filing Form 5213, Election to Postpone Determination. Get Publication 535, *Business Expenses*, for more information.

It is possible that the IRS may treat you as engaged in a profit-making activity, even if you do not have a profit for 3 or more years during a period of 5 consecutive tax years. The IRS determines the activity's status—for profit or as a hobby—by considering the facts and circumstances surrounding the case. Some factors that will be considered include the following:

1. The manner in which you carry on the activity. For example, do you conduct your actions in a businesslike manner (records, activity details, separate bank accounts, etc.)?
2. The expertise possessed by you and your advisors
3. The time and effort you expend in carrying on the activity

4. Any expectation you have that assets used in the activity may appreciate in value
5. Prior success in similar or dissimilar activities
6. Your history of income or loss with respect to the activity
7. The amount of occasional profits, if any, that you earn through the activity
8. Your financial status. For example, the fact that you do not have substantial income from other sources may indicate that you are engaging in the activity for profit
9. Elements of personal pleasure or recreation

These factors are not exclusive, and no one factor or number of factors is determinative.

TAXPLANNER

If an activity does show a profit for any 3 of 5 consecutive years (2 of 7 years for horse farms), there is a presumption by law that you are engaged in the activity for profit. The IRS has the burden of proving that the activity is only a hobby. However, if you do not meet the 3-year test and the IRS determines that the activity is a hobby, then you have the burden of proving your profit motive.

You would normally not file Form 5213, Election to Postpone Determination with Respect to the Presumption That an Activity Is Engaged in for Profit, until the IRS has examined records from one of the early years in which you engaged in the activity and has concluded that it is a hobby. Then, to prevent the IRS from assessing a tax on the years under examination, you should file Form 5213.

However, by filing the form, you agree to extend the period for which the IRS may collect additional taxes by disallowing the losses until 2 years after the examination period is over.

Also, by filing, you virtually guarantee that the IRS will carefully examine all years during the period under examination. Because the IRS previously concluded that the activity is a hobby, it is almost certain to reach the same conclusion again.

Alaska Permanent Fund dividend. If you received a payment from Alaska's mineral income fund (Alaska Permanent Fund dividend), report it as income on line 21 of Form 1040, line 13 of Form 1040A, or line 3 of Form 1040EZ. The state of Alaska sends each recipient a document that shows the amount of the payment with the check. The amount also is reported to the IRS.

Alimony. Include in your income on Form 1040, line 11, any alimony payments you receive. Amounts you receive for child support are not income to you. Alimony and child support payments are discussed in chapter 18.

TAXPLANNER

While alimony payments you receive are taxable, property settlements arising out of divorce are not. You should bear this in mind when considering the tax consequences of a divorce. See chapter 18, *Alimony*, for more details.

TAXSAVER

Receipt of alimony payments is considered compensation for purposes of making an IRA contribution. See chapter 17, *Individual retirement arrangements (IRAs)*, for more details.

Bribes. If you receive a bribe, include it in your income.

Campaign contributions. These contributions are not income to a candidate unless they are diverted to his or her personal use. To be exempt from tax, the contributions must be spent for campaign purposes or kept in a fund for use in future campaigns. However, interest earned on bank deposits, dividends received on contributed securities, and net gains realized on sales of contributed securities are taxable and must be reported on Form 1120-POL, U.S. Income Tax Return for Certain Political Organizations. Excess campaign funds transferred to an office account must be included in the officeholder's income on Form 1040, line 21, in the year transferred.

Car pools. Do not include in your income amounts you receive from the passengers for driving a car in a car pool to and from work. These amounts are considered reimbursement for your expenses. However, this rule does not apply if you have developed car pool arrangements into a profit-making business of transporting workers for hire.

Cash rebates. A cash rebate you receive from a dealer or manufacturer of an item you buy is not income, but you must reduce your basis by the amount of the rebate.

Example. You buy a new car for $24,000 cash and receive a $2,000 rebate check from the manufacturer. The $2,000 is not income to you. Your basis in the car is $22,000. This is the basis on which you figure gain or loss if you sell the car and depreciation if you use it for business.

EXPLANATION

The IRS realistically views rebates as another way of offering a price reduction to induce you to buy a product. Similarly, the dividends that a life insurance company pays you are a reduction of your premium rather than an addition to your gross income. The same rule applies to any cash rebates you might receive from your credit card company for using its card.

Casualty insurance and other reimbursements. You generally should not report these reimbursements on your return unless you are figuring gain or loss from the casualty or theft. See chapter 26 for more information.

Child support payments. You should not report these payments on your return. See chapter 18 for more information.

Court awards and damages. To determine if settlement amounts you receive by compromise or judgment must be included in your income, you must consider the item that the settlement replaces. The character of the income as ordinary income or capital gain depends on the nature of the underlying claim. Include the following as ordinary income.

1. Interest on any award.
2. Compensation for lost wages or lost profits in most cases.
3. Punitive damages, in most cases. It does not matter if they relate to a physical injury or physical sickness.
4. Amounts received in settlement of pension rights (if you did not contribute to the plan).
5. Damages for:
   a. Patent or copyright infringement,
   b. Breach of contract, or
   c. Interference with business operations.
6. Back pay and damages for emotional distress received to satisfy a claim under Title VII of the Civil Rights Act of 1964.
7. Attorney fees and costs (including contingent fees) where the underlying recovery is included in gross income.

Do not include in your income compensatory damages for personal physical injury or physical sickness (whether received in a lump sum or installments).

EXPLANATION

Compensation from a discrimination lawsuit and compensation damages awarded from an Employee Retirement and Income Security Act lawsuit are generally included in your income. Legal fees and expenses paid for such awards after October 22, 2004, are deductible in calculating your adjusted gross income.

Emotional distress. Emotional distress itself is not a physical injury or physical sickness, but damages you receive for emotional distress due to a physical injury or sickness are treated as received for the physical injury or sickness. Do not include them in your income.

If the emotional distress is due to a personal injury that is not due to a physical injury or sickness (for example, employment discrimination or injury to reputation), you must include the damages in your income, except for any damages you receive for medical care due to that emotional distress. Emotional distress includes physical symptoms that result from emotional distress, such as headaches, insomnia, and stomach disorders.

Deduction for costs involved in unlawful discrimination suits. You may be able to deduct attorney fees and court costs paid to recover a judgment or settlement for a claim of unlawful discrimination under various provisions of federal, state, and local law listed in Internal Revenue Code section 62(e), a claim against the United States government, or a claim under section 1862(b)(3)(A) of the Social Security Act. For more information, see Publication 525.

Credit card insurance. Generally, if you receive benefits under a credit card disability or unemployment insurance plan, the benefits are taxable to you. These plans make the minimum monthly payment on your credit card account if you cannot make the payment due to injury, illness, disability, or unemployment. Report on Form 1040, line 21, the amount of benefits you received during the year that is more than the amount of the premiums you paid during the year.

Down payment assistance. If you purchase a home and receive assistance from a nonprofit corporation to make the down payment, that assistance is not included in your income. If the corporation qualifies as a tax-exempt charitable organization, the assistance is treated as a gift and is included in your basis of the house. If the corporation does not qualify, the assistance is treated as a rebate or reduction of the purchase price and is not included in your basis.

Text intentionally omitted.

Employment agency fees. If you get a job through an employment agency, and the fee is paid by your employer, the fee is not includible in your income if you are not liable for it. However, if you pay it and your employer reimburses you for it, it is includible in your income.

Energy conservation subsidies. You can exclude from gross income any subsidy provided, either directly or indirectly, by public utilities for the purchase or installation of an energy conservation measure for a dwelling unit.

Energy conservation measure. This includes installations or modifications that are primarily designed to reduce consumption of electricity or natural gas, or improve the management of energy demand.

Dwelling unit. This includes a house, apartment, condominium, mobile home, boat, or similar property. If a building or structure contains both dwelling and other units, any subsidy must be properly allocated.

Estate and trust income. An estate or trust, unlike a partnership, may have to pay federal income tax. If you are a beneficiary of an estate or trust, you may be taxed on your share of its income distributed or required to be distributed to you. However, there is never a double tax. Estates and trusts file their returns on Form 1041, U.S. Income Tax Return for Estates and Trusts, and your share of the income is reported to you on Schedule K-1 (Form 1041).

EXPLANATION

Generally speaking, there are three types of trusts: (1) a trust that is required to distribute all the income it earns during the year (simple trust), (2) a trust that has the choice of whether to distribute all, part, or none of the income (complex trust), and (3) a trust where the person creating the trust is treated as the owner of the trust's assets (grantor trust). The taxability of these trusts varies. A beneficiary of a simple trust must report all the income (though generally not capital gains), whether actually distributed or not, on his or her income tax return (Form 1040). A beneficiary of a complex trust will only report the income of the trust to the extent of distributions actually made by the trust to the beneficiary. The grantor of a grantor trust must report all income, gains, and deductions on his or her individual income tax return, as they are not taxed on the grantor trust return.

Current income required to be distributed. If you are the beneficiary of an estate or trust that must distribute all of its current income, you must report your share of the distributable net income, whether or not you actually received it.

EXAMPLE

A beneficiary of a trust that is required to distribute all of its current income receives a Schedule K-1 reporting $100 of interest income. However, the beneficiary has not received any distributions from the trust. The beneficiary must report the $100 of interest income on Schedule B of Form 1040 even though the beneficiary has not received any distributions.

Current income not required to be distributed. If you are the beneficiary of an estate or trust and the fiduciary has the choice of whether to distribute all or part of the current income, you must report:

• All income that is required to be distributed to you, whether or not it is actually distributed, plus
• All other amounts actually paid or credited to you, up to the amount of your share of distributable net income.

EXPLANATION

When an estate earns income before the assets have all been distributed, it is taxed like a complex trust. Many people find this area of estate taxation very confusing, and for good reason. Gifts and inheritances are not gross income to the recipient. However, money or property that you inherit may earn some interest, dividends, or rent while the estate is being settled. It is that income that must be reported either by you or by the estate. Ordinarily, the executor of the estate files an income tax return for the estate, reporting the income, but he or she may shift the tax burden of that income to the beneficiaries if the property has already been distributed to them. See chapter 43, *Decedents: Dealing with the death of a family member*, for more detail.

TAXALERT

In some instances, adjustments for the alternative minimum tax could flow through a trust to the beneficiary. See chapter 31, *How to figure your tax*, for more details.

How to report. Treat each item of income the same way that the estate or trust would treat it. For example, if a trust's dividend income is distributed to you, you report the distribution as dividend income on your return. The same rule applies to distributions of tax-exempt interest and capital gains.

The fiduciary of the estate or trust must tell you the type of items making up your share of the estate or trust income and any credits you are allowed on your individual income tax return.

Losses. Losses of estates and trusts generally are not deductible by the beneficiaries.

EXCEPTION

There are significant exceptions to the rule that losses of estates and trusts are not deductible by the beneficiaries. When an estate or a trust terminates, the beneficiaries are frequently allowed a deduction for certain expenses that the estate or trust had but was unable to use as a deduction. These items are (1) net operating loss carryovers, (2) certain excess deductions in the year of termination, and (3) capital loss carryovers.

When an estate is terminated, it is not unusual for the attorney's and executor's fees to be paid in the year in which the estate is closed. If these expenses and the net operating loss carryover exceed the estate's income for that year, the excess is deductible by the beneficiaries. This deduction may be claimed only by itemizing deductions on Schedule A (Form 1040). These deductions are subject to the 2% rule on miscellaneous itemized deductions. This means that they are only deductible to the extent that total miscellaneous itemized deductions exceed 2% of AGI.

A capital loss carryover from an estate or a trust may be used in the beneficiaries' current or subsequent returns to reduce capital gains and/or to generate a deduction subject to the limitation that only $3,000 ($1,500 if your filing status is married filing separately) of capital losses in excess of capital gains may be deducted each year.

When to report estate and trust income. You must include your share of the estate or trust income on your return for your tax year in which the last day of the estate or trust tax year falls.

The trustee of the trust or estate will provide you with a Form K-1 that tells you each item of income and deductions, and where they are to be reported on your personal tax return.

TAXSAVER

It may be a good idea if you are the beneficiary of a trust to inform the trustee of your tax situation so that all possible tax-saving alternatives can be explored. Amounts that are not required to be distributed currently, according to the terms of the trust, may sometimes be distributed at the discretion of the trustee. There may be substantial tax planning opportunities relating to the timing, amounts, and methods of such distributions. You and the trustee should consult with a tax professional who specializes in this area.

TAXPLANNER

If you are receiving trust income, you should consider whether it is necessary for you to make estimated tax payments or increase your withholding taxes as a result of this additional income. See chapter 4, *Tax withholding and estimated tax*.

Grantor trust. Income earned by a grantor trust is taxable to the grantor, not the beneficiary, if the grantor keeps certain control over the trust. (The grantor is the one who transferred property to the trust.) This rule applies if the property (or income from the property) put into the trust will or may revert (be returned) to the grantor or the grantor's spouse.

Generally, a trust is a grantor trust if the grantor has a reversionary interest valued (at the date of transfer) at more than 5% of the value of the transferred property.

TAXALERT

Even though the grantor is taxed on the trust income, the trustee of a grantor trust may need to file Form 1041 if the trust income reaches a level that requires a return or if a separate federal identification number has been established by the trust. The items of income, deduction, and credit are treated as owned by the grantor or another person, and are reported on a separate statement (Tax Information Letter) that is attached to Form 1041.

The IRS issued regulations that provide guidance for optional methods of reporting trust income by a grantor trust. For example, alternative methods of reporting include the issuance of a Form 1099 directly from the payer of income to the grantor for inclusion on the grantor's individual income tax return; the issuance of a Form 1099 by the trust to the grantor; or the filing of a Form 1041 by the trustee of the grantor trust.

The rules can get complicated, especially if there is more than one grantor. You should consult with your tax advisor for more information.

Expenses paid by another. If your personal expenses are paid for by another person, such as a corporation, the payment may be taxable to you depending upon your relationship with that person and the nature of the payment. But if the payment makes up for a loss caused by that person, and only restores you to the position you were in before the loss, the payment is not includible in your income.

Fees for services. Include all fees for your services in your income. Examples of these fees are amounts you receive for services you perform as:

- A corporate director,
- An executor, administrator, or personal representative of an estate,
- A manager of a trade or business you operated before declaring Chapter 11 bankruptcy,
- A notary public, or
- An election precinct official.

Nonemployee compensation. If you are not an employee and the fees for your services from the same payer total $600 or more for the year, you may receive a Form 1099-MISC. You may need to report your fees as self-employment income. See *Self-Employed Persons* in chapter 1, for a discussion of when you are considered self-employed.

Corporate director. Corporate director fees are self-employment income. Report these payments on Schedule C or Schedule C-EZ (Form 1040).

Personal representatives. All personal representatives must include in their gross income fees paid to them from an estate. If you are not in the trade or business of being an executor (for instance, you are the executor of a friend's or relative's estate), report these fees on Form 1040, line 21. If you are in the trade or business of being an executor, report these fees as self-employment income on Schedule C or Schedule C-EZ (Form 1040). The fee is not includible in income if it is waived.

Manager of trade or business for bankruptcy estate. Include in your income all payments received from your bankruptcy estate for managing or operating a trade or business that you operated before you filed for bankruptcy. Report this income on Form 1040, line 21.

Notary public. Report payments for these services on Schedule C or Schedule C-EZ (Form 1040). These payments are not subject to self-employment tax. (See the separate instructions for Schedule SE (Form 1040) for details.)

Election precinct official. You should receive a Form W-2 showing payments for services performed as an election official or election worker. Report these payments on line 7 of Form 1040 or Form 1040A or on line 1 of Form 1040EZ.

EXPLANATION

Self-employment income. Chapter 38, *Self-employment income: How to file Schedule C*, includes a more comprehensive discussion of self-employment income.

Corporate director fees and executor fees (if you are in the trade or business of being an executor) are considered self-employment income, and are subject to self-employment tax. For both employees and self-employed individuals, the 2011 wage base is $106,800 for Old Age, Survivor, and Disability Insurance (OASDI) and is unlimited for Medicare. For 2011, the OASDI rate is 10.4% (in 2012, the OASDI rate is scheduled to return to its traditional pre-2011 level of 12.4%) and the Medicare rate is 2.9%. These rates are applied to 92.35% of your self-employment income. Thus, if a person earns self-employment income of $120,000 in 2011, he or she will pay self-employment tax of $14,321–i.e., ($106,800 × 13.3%) plus [($120,000 × 92.35%) – $106,800) × 2.9%; see Schedule SE. However, if your net earnings from self-employment are less than $400, no self-employment tax is payable.

Fees are self-employment income only if you present yourself as being in the trade or business that produces the fees. Therefore, unless you regularly appear as a witness, act as an executor or trustee, or judge elections, the fees earned will not be self-employment income subject to self-employment tax.

Clergy fees. Fees received by clergy for performing funerals, marriages, baptisms, or other services must be included in gross income.

TAXSAVER

A member of the clergy, however, can request to be exempt from the self-employment tax on such income by filing Form 4361, Application for Exemption from Self-Employment Tax for Use by Ministers, Members of Religious Orders, and Christian Science Practitioners.

Foster care providers. Payments you receive from a state, political subdivision, or a qualified foster care placement agency for providing care to qualified foster individuals in your home generally are not included in your income. However, you must include in your income payments received for the care of more than 5 individuals age 19 or older and certain difficulty-of-care payments.

A qualified foster individual is a person who:
1. Is living in a foster family home, and
2. Was placed there by:
   a. An agency of a state or one of its political subdivisions, or
   b. A qualified foster care placement agency.

Difficulty-of-care payments. These are additional payments that are designated by the payer as compensation for providing the additional care that is required for physically, mentally, or emotionally handicapped qualified foster individuals. A state must determine that the additional compensation is needed, and the care for which the payments are made must be provided in your home.

You must include in your income difficulty-of-care payments received for more than:
- 10 qualified foster individuals under age 19, or
- 5 qualified foster individuals age 19 or older.

Maintaining space in home. If you are paid to maintain space in your home for emergency foster care, you must include the payment in your income.

Reporting taxable payments. If you receive payments that you must include in your income, you are in business as a foster care provider and you are self-employed. Report the payments on Schedule C or Schedule C-EZ (Form 1040). See Publication 587, *Business Use of Your Home (Including Use by Daycare Providers)*, to help you determine the amount you can deduct for the use of your home.

Found property. If you find and keep property that does not belong to you that has been lost or abandoned (treasure-trove), it is taxable to you at its fair market value in the first year it is your undisputed possession.

Free tour. If you received a free tour from a travel agency for organizing a group of tourists, you must include its value in your income. Report the fair market value of the tour on Form 1040, line 21, if you are not in the trade or business of organizing tours. You cannot deduct your expenses in serving as the voluntary leader of the group at the group's request. If you organize tours as a trade or business, report the tour's value on Schedule C or Schedule C-EZ (Form 1040).

Gambling winnings. You must include your gambling winnings in income on Form 1040, line 21. If you itemize your deductions on Schedule A (Form 1040), you can deduct gambling losses you had during the year, but only up to the amount of your winnings. See chapter 29 for information on recordkeeping.

Lotteries and raffles. Winnings from lotteries and raffles are gambling winnings. In addition to cash winnings, you must include in your income the fair market value of bonds, cars, houses, and other noncash prizes.

TAXPLANNER
If you win a large lottery, proper financial planning can help you minimize the tax bite. You should consult with a financial planner and/or your tax advisor.

Form W-2G. You may have received a Form W-2G, Certain Gambling Winnings, showing the amount of your gambling winnings and any tax taken out of them. Include the amount from box 1 on Form 1040, line 21. Include the amount shown in box 2 on Form 1040, line 62, as federal income tax withheld.

EXPLANATION
While a winner of the Canadian government lottery does not have to pay Canadian tax on the winnings, a U.S. citizen or resident who wins does have to pay U.S. tax on the amount. Citizens and residents of the United States have to report all income, including foreign income. See chapter 41, *U.S. citizens working abroad: Tax treatment of foreign earned income*, and chapter 42, *Foreign citizens living in the United States*, for more information about worldwide income.

TAXPLANNER
Because you may not win money gambling until late in the year and gambling losses are deductible only up to the amount of your winnings, you should plan ahead by keeping losing racetrack, lottery, and other gambling tickets. In that way, if you do win, you will be able to itemize your gambling losses. It's also a good idea to keep a diary of gambling losses incurred during the entire year. Note that losses from one kind of gambling are deductible against gains from another kind. These losses are claimed as miscellaneous itemized deductions but are not subject to the 2%-of-AGI floor and are reported on Schedule A, line 28. These losses are also allowed for purposes of the alternative minimum tax (AMT).

Gifts and inheritances. Generally, property you receive as a gift, bequest, or inheritance is not included in your income. However, if property you receive this way later produces income such as interest, dividends, or rents, that income is taxable to you. If property is given to a trust and the income from it is paid, credited, or distributed to you, that income is also taxable to you. If the gift, bequest, or inheritance is the income from the property, that income is taxable to you.

EXPLANATION

Items given to you as an incentive to enter into a business transaction are not tax-free gifts. For example, incentive items such as small appliances or dinnerware given to you by a bank as an incentive to open an account are treated as taxable interest income to you and must be reported at their fair market value.

Inherited pension or IRA. If you inherited a pension or an individual retirement arrangement (IRA), you may have to include part of the inherited amount in your income. See chapter 10 if you inherited a pension. See chapter 17 if you inherited an IRA.

Hobby losses. Losses from a hobby are not deductible from other income. A hobby is an activity from which you do not expect to make a profit. See *Activity not for profit*, earlier.

EXPLANATION

While a net loss from the sale of stamps, coins, or other items that you collect for a hobby may not be deducted, a loss from the sale of these items may be offset against a gain from the sale of similar items occurring in the same year.

Example

You sell several stamps at a gain of $1,000. You may offset this gain by up to $1,000 in losses from the sale of other stamps. The result is that there is no net taxable gain to report on your income tax return. Each sale should be listed separately on Schedule D.

TAXSAVER

If you are planning to sell an item in your collection that has appreciated in value and your collection also contains an item that has decreased in value, you may want to sell both in the same year to incur the least amount of tax. In short, clean out the junk to establish losses in a year when you have gains.

Illegal activities. Income from illegal activities, such as money from dealing illegal drugs, must be included in your income on Form 1040, line 21, or on Schedule C or Schedule C-EZ (Form 1040) if from your self-employment activity.

EXPLANATION

It is not necessary for the activity that produces income to be legal for the income to be taxable. Income from illegal activities, such as embezzlement, drug dealing, bookmaking, and bootlegging, is taxable. Al Capone, the notorious Chicago bootlegger during Prohibition, was convicted of income tax evasion because he did not report his illegal income.

Embezzlement income is taxable in the year in which the funds are stolen. If the embezzler pays back the stolen funds in a later year, he or she can claim a deduction in the year of repayment.

Indian fishing rights. If you are a member of a qualified Indian tribe that has fishing rights secured by treaty, executive order, or an Act of Congress as of March 17, 1988, do not include in your income amounts you receive from activities related to those fishing rights. The income is not subject to income tax, self-employment tax, or employment taxes.

TAXALERT

Investment clubs. An investment club is a group of friends, neighbors, business associates, or others who pool limited or stated amounts of funds to invest in stock or other securities. The club may or may not have a written agreement, charter, or bylaws. Usually, the group operates informally with members pledging a regular amount to be paid into the club monthly. Some clubs have a committee that gathers information on securities, selects the most promising, and recommends that the club invest in them. Other clubs rotate the investigatory responsibilities among all their members. Most require all members to vote for or against all investments, sales, exchanges, or other transactions.

How the income from an investment club is reported on your tax return depends on how the club operates. Most clubs operate as partnerships and are treated as such for federal tax purposes. Others operate as corporations, trusts, or associations taxed as corporations.

Members of an investment club organized as a partnership should include their share of each type of the club's income on their returns. For example, dividends are reported on Schedule B, Part II, line 5, and capital gains are reported on Schedule D.

The expenses incurred by the club to produce or to collect income, to manage investment property, or to determine any tax due are also reported separately. You may deduct your share of these items on Schedule A as a miscellaneous deduction if you itemize your deductions.

Note: These expenses—along with some others—must exceed 2% of your AGI to be deductible as miscellaneous itemized deductions.

Depending on how your investment club is organized, it may be required to file a separate partnership, corporation, or trust tax return. More details are explained in IRS Publication 550, *Investment Income and Expenses*, some of which follow.

Tax returns and identifying numbers. Investment clubs must file either Form 1065, U.S. Partnership Return of Income; Form 1041, U.S. Income Tax Return for Estates and Trusts; or Form 1120, U.S. Corporation Income Tax Return. Certain small corporations may be able to file Form 1120-A, U.S. Corporation Short-Form Income Tax Return. See the instructions for Forms 1120 and 1120-A.

Form SS-4. Each club must have an employer identification number (EIN) to use when filing its return. The club's EIN also may have to be given to the payer of dividends. If your club does not have an EIN, use Form SS-4, Application for Employer Identification Number. Mail the completed Form SS-4 to the IRS Center where you file the club's tax return. Form SS-4 can be found on the IRS website at *www.irs.gov.*

Stock in name of club. When stock is recorded in the name of the investment club, the club must give its own EIN to the payer of dividends.

If the club is a partnership or a trust, the dividends distributed to the partners or beneficiaries must be shown on Form 1065 or Form 1041, respectively. The partners' or the beneficiaries' identifying numbers also must be shown on the return.

If the club is an association taxed as a corporation, any distribution it makes that qualifies as a dividend must be reported on Forms 1096 and 1099-DIV if total distributions to the shareholder are $10 or more for the year.

Stock in name of member. When stock is recorded in the name of one club member, this member must give his or her social security number to the payer of dividends. (When stock is held in the names of two or more club members, the social security number of only one member must be given to the payer.) This member is considered as the record owner for the actual owner of the stock, the investment club. This member is a "nominee" and must file Form 1099-DIV showing the club to be the owner of the dividend, his or her social security number, and the EIN of the club.

Example

In order to avoid any matching notices from the IRS, the nominee should report the dividend income on his or her tax return on line 5, Part II, of Form 1040, Schedule B and then subtract out the nominee distribution.

ABC company	$100
Less: Nominee distribution	($100)

No social security coverage for investment club earnings. If an investment club partnership's activities are limited to investing in savings certificates, stock, or securities and collecting interest or dividends for its members' accounts, the members' share of income is not earnings from self-employment. You cannot voluntarily pay the self-employment tax in order to increase your social security coverage and ultimate benefits.

For more information about investment clubs, see Publication 550.

Interest on frozen deposits. In general, you exclude from your income the amount of interest earned on a frozen deposit. See *Interest income on frozen deposits* in chapter 7.

Interest on qualified savings bonds. You may be able to exclude from income the interest from qualified U.S. savings bonds you redeem, if you pay qualified higher educational expenses in the same year. For more information on this exclusion, see *Education Savings Bond Program* under *U.S. Savings Bonds* in chapter 7.

Job interview expenses. If a prospective employer asks you to appear for an interview and either pays you an allowance or reimburses you for your transportation and other travel expenses, the amount you receive is generally not taxable. You include in income only the amount you receive that is more than your actual expenses.

Jury duty. Jury duty pay you receive must be included in your income on Form 1040, line 21. If you must give the pay to your employer because your employer continues to pay your salary while you serve on the jury, you can deduct the amount turned over to your employer as an adjustment to your income. Enter the amount you repay your employer on Form 1040, line 36. Enter "Jury Pay" and the amount on the dotted line next to line 36.

> ### EXPLANATION
> **Jury fees.** This item is often overlooked. Just because a fee is paid by a government body does not mean that it is not subject to tax. However, the Tax Court has ruled that the mileage allowance received by a juror to cover the cost of transportation between the court and his or her home is not included in income. In addition, if you are required to give your jury pay to your employer, you can claim a deduction for the amount paid over. You can claim this deduction whether or not you itemize your deductions. You would report the income on line 21 of Form 1040 and, if you give your jury pay to your employer, report it as an adjustment on line 36 and write "Jury Pay" next to the amount.

Kickbacks. You must include kickbacks, side commissions, push money, or similar payments you receive in your income on Form 1040, line 21, or on Schedule C or Schedule C-EZ (Form 1040), if from your self-employment activity.

Example. You sell cars and help arrange car insurance for buyers. Insurance brokers pay back part of their commissions to you for referring customers to them. You must include the kickbacks in your income.

Medical savings accounts (MSAs). You generally do not include in income amounts you withdraw from your Archer MSA or Medicare Advantage MSA if you use the money to pay for qualified medical expenses. Generally, qualified medical expenses are those you can deduct on Schedule A (Form 1040), Itemized Deductions. For more information about qualified medical expenses, see chapter 22. For more information about Archer MSAs or Medicare Advantage MSAs, see Publication 969, *Health Savings Accounts and Other Tax-Favored Health Plans.*

> ### TAXSAVER
> Contributions to an MSA or HSA can also be deductible. See chapter 22, *Medical and dental expenses*, for details.

Prizes and awards. If you win a prize in a lucky number drawing, television or radio quiz program, beauty contest, or other event, you must include it in your income. For example, if you win a $50 prize in a photography contest, you must report this income on Form 1040, line 21. If you refuse to accept a prize, do not include its value in your income.

> ### EXPLANATION
> An individual wins a prize in a charitable fundraising raffle and refuses to accept the prize, returning the prize to the charity. The individual need not include the value of the prize as income on his or her return. Likewise, the individual is not entitled to a charitable deduction.

Prizes and awards in goods or services must be included in your income at their fair market value.

Employee awards or bonuses. Cash awards or bonuses given to you by your employer for good work or suggestions generally must be included in your income as wages. However, certain non-cash employee achievement awards can be excluded from income. See *Bonuses and awards* in chapter 5.

Pulitzer, Nobel, and similar prizes. If you were awarded a prize in recognition of accomplishments in religious, charitable, scientific, artistic, educational, literary, or civic fields, you generally must include the value of the prize in your income. However, you do not include this prize in your income if you meet all of the following requirements.

- You were selected without any action on your part to enter the contest or proceeding.
- You are not required to perform substantial future services as a condition to receiving the prize or award.
- The prize or award is transferred by the payer directly to a governmental unit or tax-exempt charitable organization as designated by you.

See Publication 525 for more information about the conditions that apply to the transfer.

Qualified tuition programs (QTPs). A qualified tuition program (also known as a 529 program) is a program set up to allow you to either prepay or contribute to an account established for paying a student's qualified higher education expenses at an eligible educational institution. A program can be established and maintained by a state, an agency or instrumentality of a state, or an eligible educational institution.

The part of a distribution representing the amount paid or contributed to a QTP is not included in income. This is a return of the investment in the program.

The beneficiary generally does not include in income any earnings distributed from a QTP if the total distribution is less than or equal to adjusted qualified higher education expenses. See Publication 970 for more information.

Railroad retirement annuities. The following types of payments are treated as pension or annuity income and are taxable under the rules explained in chapter 11.
- Tier 1 railroad retirement benefits that are more than the social security equivalent benefit.
- Tier 2 benefits.
- Vested dual benefits.

Rewards. If you receive a reward for providing information, include it in your income.

Sale of home. You may be able to exclude from income all or part of any gain from the sale or exchange of your main home. See chapter 15.

Sale of personal items. If you sold an item you owned for personal use, such as a car, refrigerator, furniture, stereo, jewelry, or silverware, your gain is taxable as a capital gain. Report it on Schedule D (Form 1040). You cannot deduct a loss.

However, if you sold an item you held for investment, such as gold or silver bullion, coins, or gems, any gain is taxable as a capital gain and any loss is deductible as a capital loss.

Example. You sold a painting on an online auction website for $100. You bought the painting for $20 at a garage sale years ago. Report your gain as a capital gain on Schedule D (Form 1040).

Scholarships and fellowships. A candidate for a degree can exclude amounts received as a qualified scholarship or fellowship. A qualified scholarship or fellowship is any amount you receive that is for:
- Tuition and fees to enroll at or attend an educational institution, or
- Fees, books, supplies, and equipment required for courses at the educational institution.

Amounts used for room and board do not qualify for the exclusion. See Publication 970 for more information on qualified scholarships and fellowship grants.

Payment for services. Generally, you must include in income the part of any scholarship or fellowship that represents payment for past, present, or future teaching, research, or other services. This applies even if all candidates for a degree must perform the services to receive the degree.

For information about the rules that apply to a tax-free qualified tuition reduction provided to employees and their families by an educational institution, see Publication 970.

VA payments. Allowances paid by the Department of Veterans Affairs are not included in your income. These allowances are not considered scholarship or fellowship grants.

Prizes. Scholarship prizes won in a contest are not scholarships or fellowships if you do not have to use the prizes for educational purposes. You must include these amounts in your income on Form 1040, line 21, whether or not you use the amounts for educational purposes.

Stolen property. If you steal property, you must report its fair market value in your income in the year you steal it unless in the same year, you return it to its rightful owner.

Transporting school children. Do not include in your income a school board mileage allowance for taking children to and from school if you are not in the business of taking children to school. You cannot deduct expenses for providing this transportation.

Union benefits and dues. Amounts deducted from your pay for union dues, assessments, contributions, or other payments to a union cannot be excluded from your income.

You may be able to deduct some of these payments as a miscellaneous deduction subject to the 2%-of-AGI limit if they are related to your job and if you itemize deductions on Schedule A (Form 1040). For more information, see *Union Dues and Expenses* in chapter 29.

Strike and lockout benefits. Benefits paid to you by a union as strike or lockout benefits, including both cash and the fair market value of other property, are usually included in your income as compensation. You can exclude these benefits from your income only when the facts clearly show that the union intended them as gifts to you.

Utility rebates. If you are a customer of an electric utility company and you participate in the utility's energy conservation program, you may receive on your monthly electric bill either:
- A reduction in the purchase price of electricity furnished to you (rate reduction), or
- A nonrefundable credit against the purchase price of the electricity.

The amount of the rate reduction or nonrefundable credit is not included in your income.

Passive Activity Limitations and At-Risk Limitations

Explanation

Individuals, estates, trusts, closely held corporations, and personal service corporations are generally prohibited from deducting net losses generated by passive activities. In addition, tax credits from passive activities are generally limited to the tax liability attributable to those activities. Disallowed passive activity losses are suspended and carried forward indefinitely to offset passive activity income generated in future years. Similar carry forward treatment applies to suspended credits.

Note that these rules relate to passive income/losses and do not apply to portfolio income/losses. Portfolio income/losses include interest, dividends, annuities, and royalties, as well as gain or loss from the disposition of income-producing or investment property that is not derived in the ordinary course of a trade or business.

Defining passive activities. A passive activity involves the conduct of any trade or business in which you do not materially participate. You are treated as a material participant only if you are involved in the operations of the activity on a regular, continuous, and substantial basis. If you are not a material participant in an activity but your spouse is, you are treated as being a material participant and the activity is not considered passive.

Seven tests. The IRS has seven tests you can meet to be considered a material participant. If you satisfy one of these tests, you will be considered a material participant in any activity. These tests are:

1. You participate more than 500 hours per taxable year.
2. Your participation during the taxable year constitutes substantially all of the participation of all individuals involved.
3. You participate for more than 100 hours during the taxable year and no one else participates more than you participated.
4. The activity is a significant participation activity (SPA) for the taxable year, and your participation in all SPAs during the taxable year exceeds 500 hours. An SPA is an activity in which an individual participates for more than 100 hours but does not otherwise meet a material participation test.
5. You materially participated in any 5 of the 10 preceding taxable years.
6. The activity is a personal service activity, and you materially participated for any 3 preceding taxable years. A personal service activity involves performance of personal services in the fields of health, law, engineering, architecture, accounting, actuarial sciences, performing arts, consulting, or any other business in which capital is not a material income-producing factor.
7. Based on all the facts and circumstances, your participation is regular, continuous, and substantial during the taxable year.

Defining an activity. The proper grouping of business operations into one or more activities is important in determining the allocation of suspended losses, measuring material participation, separating rental and nonrental activities, and determining when a disposition of an activity has occurred. IRS regulations define an activity as any "appropriate economic unit for measuring gain or loss." What constitutes an "appropriate economic unit" is determined by looking at all facts and circumstances. The regulations list five factors that are to be given the greatest weight. They are:

1. Similarities and differences in types of business
2. The extent of common control
3. The extent of common ownership
4. Geographical location
5. Interdependence between the activities

Generally, taxpayers must be consistent from year to year in determining the business operations that constitute an activity. Consult your tax advisor for more information.

"At-Risk" Limitation Provisions

The deduction for business losses is generally limited to the amount by which you are considered to be "at risk" in the activity. You are considered at risk for the amount of cash you have invested in the venture and the basis of property invested plus certain amounts borrowed for use in the activity.

Borrowed amounts that are considered at risk are (1) loans for which you are personally liable for repayment or (2) loans secured by property, other than that used in the activity. Generally, liabilities that are secured by property within the activity for which you are not otherwise personally liable are not considered to be at risk. An exception: If nonrecourse financing—financing for which you are not personally liable—is secured against real property used in the activity, you may be considered at risk for the amount of financing.

The law provides a broad list of activities (including the holding of real estate acquired after 1986) that are subject to the at-risk provisions. If the "at-risk" provisions apply to you, you should consult with your tax advisor.

Passive Activity Losses

The passive activity rules limit losses and credits from passive trade or business activities. Deductions attributable to passive activities, to the extent they exceed income from passive activities, generally may not be deducted against other income, such as wages, portfolio income, or business income that is not derived from a passive activity. Losses that are suspended under these rules are carried forward indefinitely and are treated as losses from passive activities in succeeding years. Suspended losses from a particular activity are allowed in full when a taxpayer disposes of his or her entire interest in that particular passive activity to an unrelated person. For dispositions made after January 1, 1995, you must dispose of "substantially all" of a passive activity in order to deduct that same portion. You may also be able to deduct suspended losses in a passive activity if your interest is disposed of in other ways, including abandonment and death of the taxpayer. See *Disposition of Passive Activity*, discussed later. Special rules may apply; you should consult your tax advisor.

Rental Real Estate

As previously discussed, generally, a trade or business activity is passive unless the taxpayer materially participates in that activity. Rental real estate activities, however, are passive regardless of the level of the taxpayer's participation. A special rule permits the deduction of up to $25,000 of losses from certain rental real estate activities (even though they are considered passive) if the taxpayer actively participates in them. This special rule is available in full to taxpayers with a modified AGI of $100,000 or less and phases out for taxpayers with a modified AGI between $100,000 and $150,000. For further information about rental real estate passive rules, see chapter 9, *Rental income and expenses*.

Real Estate Professionals

Passive activity limitations for certain real estate professionals are more liberal than they used to be. Taxpayers who satisfy certain eligibility thresholds and materially participate in rental real estate activities may treat any losses as losses from a nonpassive activity and may use these losses against all sources of taxable income.

Eligibility. Only individuals and closely held C corporations can qualify for this special rule. An individual taxpayer will qualify for any tax year if more than one-half of the personal services (with more than 750 hours) performed in trades or businesses by the taxpayer during such a tax year are performed in real property trades or businesses in which the taxpayer materially participates. A real property trade or business includes any real property development, redevelopment, construction, reconstruction, acquisition, conversion, rental, operation, management, leasing, or brokerage trade or business. Personal services performed as an employee are not considered in determining material participation unless the employee has more than a 5% ownership in the business during any part of the tax year. However, independent contractor realtor services would qualify for this purpose. For closely held C corporations, the eligibility requirements are met if more than 50% of the corporation's gross receipts for the tax year are derived from real property trades or businesses in which the corporation materially participates.

Example 1

During 2011, a self-employed real estate developer earned $100,000 in development fees from projects the developer spent 1,200 hours developing. In addition, the developer incurred rental real estate losses of $200,000 from properties that the developer spent over 800 hours managing during 2011. The developer performs no other personal services during the year and has no other items of income or deduction. Because the developer (1) materially participated in the rental real estate activity, (2) performed more than 750 hours in real property trades or businesses, and (3) performed more than 50% of the developer's total personal service hours in real estate trades or businesses in which the developer materially participated, the developer will have a net operating loss of $100,000 to carry back (and the excess to carry forward) to offset any source of income.

This rule for real estate professionals' passive loss relief is a two-step process. First, you must demonstrate eligibility for the relief provision by achieving the required levels of personal services in real estate trades or businesses. Thereafter, you get relief from the passive loss limitations only for your rental real estate activities for which you satisfy the material participation standards.

For spouses filing joint returns, each spouse's personal services are taken into account separately. However, in determining material participation, the participation of the other spouse is taken into account as required under current law.

Example 2

A husband and wife filing a joint return meet the eligibility requirements if, during the tax year, one spouse performs more than 750 hours representing at least half of his or her personal services in a real estate trade or business in which either spouse materially participates.

Aggregation of Activities

Whether a taxpayer *materially participates* in his or her rental real estate activities is determined generally as if each interest of the taxpayer in rental real estate is a separate activity. However, the taxpayer may elect to treat all interest in rental real estate as one activity.

The election permitting a taxpayer to aggregate his or her rental real estate activities for testing for material participation is not intended to alter the rules with respect to material participation through limited partnership interest. Generally, no interest as a limited partner is treated as an interest with respect to which a taxpayer materially participates. However, Treasury regulations provide that a limited partner is considered to materially participate in the activities conducted through the partnership in certain situations where (1) the limited partner is also a general partner at all times during the partnership's tax year, (2) the limited partner materially participates in the activity during any 5 of the preceding 10 years, or (3) the activity is a personal service activity in which the limited partner materially participated for any 3 preceding years.

Losses attributable to limited partnership interests are considered passive, except where regulations provide otherwise. In general, working interests in any oil or gas property held directly or through an entity that does not limit the taxpayer's liability are not considered passive, whether or not the taxpayer is a material participant.

The IRS has issued regulations with regard to the aggregation of activities in order to satisfy the material participation tests for real estate professionals. These rules are very complex and hold potential tax traps for the unwary. We recommend that you consult with your tax advisor if you believe that electing to aggregate activities may be beneficial to you.

Example 1

Three brothers own a hardware store as partners. Two of them consider it their full-time job, because it is their only source of income. The third brother lives 200 miles away and is consulted only on major issues. The two brothers who work at the store meet the material participation test. The third brother has a passive investment.

Example 2

Bonnie owns a one-sixteenth interest in four different racehorses. She does not own the stables where the horses are trained and fed. She is not involved in the daily care of the horses. She pays her fair share of the costs and offers advice regarding when and where the horses are to run. Bonnie has significant salary income from a full-time job and from managing her portfolio. Bonnie is probably not a material participant.

Example 3

Andrea is a limited partner in a partnership. She is not a material participant.

Example 4

Chris owns rental property. He has a passive investment.

Exception

An exception to the general rule that does not allow grouping rental activities with business activity is that, in certain instances, passive rental losses can offset income from business activities. For this exception to apply, you must hold the same proportionate ownership interest in each activity.

Example

Jack and Jill are married and file a joint return. Jack owns and operates a grocery store that generates net income for the current year. Jill owns the building, of which 25% is rented to Jack's grocery store activity (grocery store rental). The building rental activities generate a net loss in the current year.

Because they file a joint return, Jack and Jill are treated as one taxpayer. Therefore, the sole owner of the grocery store activity is also the sole owner of the rental activity. Consequently, each owner of the business activity has the same proportionate ownership interest in the rental activity. Accordingly, both activities may be grouped together; thus, the net income from Jack's grocery store can be offset by the amount of net loss from Jill's building rental activities. See your tax advisor for more information if you think this exception applies to your situation.

You should try to realign your personal finances so that you maximize your interest expense deductions. If you borrowed money to purchase a passive investment, any interest on the loan will be considered part of your passive investment loss. If you are in a real estate limited partnership, you may be able to have all the partners contribute additional capital so that the passive loss is reduced or limited. Your capital contribution could come from your other investments or from a mortgage on a personal residence. If you have untapped appreciation in your personal residence, you can borrow against it and deduct the interest cost subject to certain limitations. Make sure, however, that any mortgage does not exceed the limits applicable to your situation, because such disallowed interest would be considered nondeductible personal interest.

Disposition of Passive Activity

Previously disallowed losses (but not credits) are recognized in full when the taxpayer disposes of his or her entire interest in the passive activity in a fully taxable transaction. However, suspended losses are not deductible when the taxpayer sells the interest to a related party. Rather, the losses remain with the individual (and may offset passive income) until the related purchaser disposes of the interest in a taxable transaction to an unrelated person. Various other types of dispositions trigger suspended losses, including abandonment, death of the taxpayer, gifts, and installment sales of entire interests, although special rules apply.

A sale in a taxable year beginning before January 1, 1987, reported on the installment method and included in income after December 31, 1986, would be considered income from a passive activity.

Example

Bob disposes of rental property in 1986 under the installment sale method and properly reports $2,000 of taxable gain in his 1987 through 2011 tax returns. Bob may treat the 1987 through 2011 gains as income from a passive activity and may offset other passive losses in these years.

Tax Relief for Victims of Terrorism

The following section discusses the tax treatment of certain amounts received by victims injured in a terrorist attack or survivors of victims killed as a result of a terrorist attack.

Qualified disaster relief payments. Qualified disaster relief payments are not included in income. These payments are not subject to income tax, self-employment tax, or employment taxes (social security, Medicare, and federal unemployment taxes). No withholding applies to these payments.

Qualified disaster relief payments include payments you receive (regardless of the source) for the following reasons:

- Reasonable and necessary personal, family, living, or funeral expenses incurred as a result of a terrorist attack.
- Reasonable and necessary expenses incurred for the repair or rehabilitation of a personal residence due to a terrorist attack. (A personal residence can be a rented residence or one you own.)
- Reasonable and necessary expenses incurred for the repair or replacement of the contents of a personal residence due to a terrorist attack.

Qualified disaster relief payments also include the following:

- Payments made by common carriers (for example, American Airlines and United Airlines regarding the September 11 attacks) because of death or physical injury incurred as a result of a terrorist attack.
- Amounts received from a federal, state, or local government in connection with a terrorist at tack by those affected by the attack.

Disability payments. Disability payments received for injuries incurred as a direct result of a terrorist attack directed against the United States (or its allies), whether inside or outside of the United States, are not included in income.

Payments to survivors of public safety officers. If you are the survivor of a public safety officer who died in the line of duty, the following types of payments are not included in your income:

Bureau of Justice Assistance payments. If you are a surviving dependent of a public safety officer (law enforcement officer or firefighter) who died in the line of duty, do not include in your income the death benefit paid to you by the Bureau of Justice Assistance.

Caution

Qualified disaster payments do not include insurance or other reimbursements for expenses, or income replacement payments, such as payments of lost wages, lost business income, or unemployment compensation.

Government plan annuity. If you receive a survivor annuity as the child or spouse (or former spouse) of a public safety officer who was killed in the line of duty, you generally do not have to include it in income. This exclusion applies to the amount of the annuity based upon the officer's service as a public safety officer.

Public safety officer defined. A public safety officer, for the purpose of these exclusions, includes police and law enforcement officers, firefighters, and rescue squads and ambulance crews.

More information. For more information, see Publication 559, *Survivors, Executors, and Administrators*, and Publication 3920, *Tax Relief for Victims of Terrorist Attacks*.

Part 3
Gains and losses

ey.com/EYTaxGuide

The four chapters in this part discuss investment gains and losses, including how to figure your basis in property. A gain from selling or trading stocks, bonds, or other investment property may be taxed or it may be tax-free, at least in part. A loss may or may not be deductible. These chapters also discuss gains from selling property you personally use—including the special rules for selling your home. Nonbusiness casualty and theft losses are discussed in chapter 26, *Casualty and theft losses*, in Part 5.

Chapter 13   Basis of property
Chapter 14   Sale of property
Chapter 15   Selling your home
Chapter 16   Reporting gains and losses

Chapter 13
Basis of property

Note

IRS Publication 17 (*Your Federal Income Tax*) has been updated by Ernst & Young LLP for 2011. Dates and dollar amounts shown are for 2011. Underlined type is used to indicate where IRS text has been updated. Places where text has been removed are indicated by the sentence: *"Text intentionally omitted."*

ey.com/EYTaxGuide

Ernst & Young LLP will update the *Ernst & Young Tax Guide 2012* website with relevant taxpayer information as it becomes available. You can also sign up for email alerts to let you know when changes have been made.

Introduction

The gain or loss you realize on the disposition of property—whether through a sale or exchange—is measured by the difference between the selling price and your basis. In many cases, the basis of an asset is no more than your cost. However, if you acquire property in exchange for services, by inheritance, or in exchange for other property, different factors besides cost are likely to have a crucial bearing on determining your tax basis.

This chapter tells you how to calculate the basis of property. Particular attention is given to some of the more complicated situations that may arise. You'll learn, for instance, how to calculate your basis in a particular piece of property by referring to other assets you already hold. To help you determine which expenditures increase your basis in a piece of property and which do not, comprehensive lists of allowable—but often overlooked—expenditures are provided.

What's New

Property inherited from a decedent who died in 2010. If you acquired property from a decedent who died in 2010, special rules may apply in determining basis, gain, loss, holding period, and character for the property. Tax legislation passed in 2010 allows the executor of the estate of any decedent who died in 2010 to elect not to have the estate tax rules apply and instead to have a modified basis carryover regime apply. This election could impact the amount of tax you owe.

TAXALERT

If you sold property in 2011 that you originally inherited from a person who died (called a decedent) in 2010, you should contact the executor of the decedent's estate to confirm the basis in any property you received. The December 2010 tax law that extended the so-called Bush tax cuts also enacted significant changes to the estate tax rules, including reinstatement of the estate tax to apply to 2010. The new law also allowed the executor of an estate of a decedent who died during 2010 to opt out of having the estate tax apply. If the executor made such an election, then the "modified carryover basis rules" applied to determine your basis in property inherited from a decedent who died during 2010. The modified carryover basis rules are described later in *Property inherited from a decedent who died in 2010*.

Records

Keep accurate records of all items that affect the basis of your property. For more information on keeping records, see chapter 1.

This chapter discusses how to figure your basis in property. It is divided into the following sections.

- Cost basis.
- Adjusted basis.
- Basis other than cost.

Your basis is the amount of your investment in property for tax purposes. Use the basis to figure gain or loss on the sale, exchange, or other disposition of property. Also use it to figure deductions for depreciation, amortization, depletion, and casualty losses.

EXPLANATION

This chapter does not reflect the provisions of the law that deal with bankruptcy. If any of your debts were canceled by a creditor or were discharged because you became bankrupt, the basis of your assets might be affected. For information about the effect these provisions may have on basis, see the *Debt Cancellation* section in Publication 908, *Bankruptcy Tax Guide*. Publication 908 discusses the technical rules related to bankruptcy, but here are several key points to remember:

1. The tax treatment of a forgiven debt depends on how the debt arose. For example, a personal loan from a relative, when it was unrelated to a business or an investment, is not taxed if it is forgiven. Instead, it is considered a gift. If the amount is over $13,000 in 2011, the person forgiving the loan might have to file a gift tax return and pay gift tax.
2. On the other hand, a business loan forgiven for business reasons is taxed. In this case, you may pay the tax on a forgiven loan or opt for a reduction in the basis of your assets by an amount equal to the debt forgiven. The result is that you are not able to deduct as much in depreciating the asset. Thus, if it is sold before it is fully depreciated, you have either a larger gain or a smaller loss on the asset than you would if you paid the tax directly. After 1986, a solvent taxpayer may make this election only if the loan is "purchase money debt," in which case the forgiveness is treated as a purchase price adjustment of the related asset. You cannot make this election for debt forgiven by your employer.
3. If you declare personal bankruptcy, you are not taxed on any debt you owe that is forgiven or canceled. You also are not taxed on any debt you owe that is forgiven or canceled if a business you own goes into bankruptcy. However, you may be required to reduce the net operating loss carryforwards and tax credit carryforwards that otherwise would be available in subsequent years to offset income and reduce your income tax liability. One strategy to avoid losing these tax benefits is to reduce the basis of depreciable property or real property held as inventory by an amount equal to the debt forgiven.

If you use property for both business or investment purposes and for personal purposes, you must allocate the basis based on the use. Only the basis allocated to the business or investment use of the property can be depreciated.

Your original basis in property is adjusted (increased or decreased) by certain events. For example, if you make improvements to the property, increase your basis. If you take deductions for depreciation or casualty losses, or claim certain credits, reduce your basis.

Useful Items

You may want to see:

Publication

- ☐ **15-B** Employer's Tax Guide to Fringe Benefits
- ☐ **525** Taxable and Nontaxable Income
- ☐ **535** Business Expenses
- ☐ **537** Installment Sales
- ☐ **544** Sales and Other Dispositions of Assets
- ☐ **550** Investment Income and Expenses
- ☐ **551** Basis of Assets
- ☐ **564** Mutual Fund Distributions
- ☐ **946** How To Depreciate Property

Cost Basis

The basis of property you buy is usually its cost. The cost is the amount you pay in cash, debt obligations, other property, or services. Your cost also includes amounts you pay for the following items:

- Sales tax,
- Freight,
- Installation and testing,
- Excise taxes,
- Legal and accounting fees (when they must be capitalized),
- Revenue stamps,
- Recording fees, and
- Real estate taxes (if you assume liability for the seller).

In addition, the basis of real estate and business assets may include other items.

TAXPLANNER

If you perform services for an entity, and in exchange receive stock or a partnership capital interest, the fair market value (FMV) of what you receive is treated as compensation. Your basis in the stock or partnership interest is equal to the amount of compensation reported by you, increased by the amount, if any, paid for the stock or partnership interest. For more information, see chapter 5, *Wages, salaries, and other earnings*.

TAXSAVER

If you receive an equity interest in a business in exchange for services rendered, you may be able to discount the value of the equity interest received. You may do this if the shares are restricted, not readily marketable, or if they represent only a minority holding. If you receive stock compensation of this kind, you should consider employing a professional appraiser to value the equity interest received to ensure the valuation discount is properly applied so that you do not have an underpayment of tax and accompanying interest and penalties.

Loans with low or no interest. If you buy property on a time-payment plan that charges little or no interest, the basis of your property is your stated purchase price minus any amount considered to be unstated interest. You generally have unstated interest if your interest rate is less than the applicable federal rate.

For more information, see *Unstated Interest and Original Issue Discount (OID)* in Publication 537.

EXPLANATION

If you buy personal property by contract and the carrying charges are separately stated but the interest you pay cannot be determined, the IRS assumes that interest is being charged at the applicable federal rate applied to the average unpaid balance of the contract during the tax year. Your tax basis is determined by subtracting the interest from the total contract cost of the property. You may deduct the interest in the year in which it is, in effect, being paid. But see chapter 24, *Interest expense*, for possible limitations on your deductions.

Real Property

Real property, also called real estate, is land and generally anything built on, growing on, or attached to land.

If you buy real property, certain fees and other expenses you pay are part of your cost basis in the property.

Lump sum purchase. If you buy buildings and the land on which they stand for a lump sum, allocate the cost basis among the land and the buildings. Allocate the cost basis according to the respective fair market values (FMVs) of the land and buildings at the time of purchase. Figure the basis of each asset by multiplying the lump sum by a fraction. The numerator is the FMV of that asset and the denominator is the FMV of the whole property at the time of purchase.

Tip

If you are not certain of the FMVs of the land and buildings, you can allocate the basis according to their assessed values for real estate tax purposes.

Fair market value (FMV). FMV is the price at which the property would change hands between a willing buyer and a willing seller, neither having to buy or sell, and both having reasonable knowledge of all the necessary facts. Sales of similar property on or about the same date may be helpful in figuring the FMV of the property.

Assumption of mortgage. If you buy property and assume (or buy the property subject to) an existing mortgage on the property, your basis includes the amount you pay for the property plus the amount to be paid on the mortgage.

EXPLANATION
If the real property is used in your trade or business or as a rental, you cannot elect to deduct transfer taxes in lieu of adding them to your basis.

Settlement costs. Your basis includes the settlement fees and closing costs you paid for buying the property. (A fee for buying property is a cost that must be paid even if you buy the property for cash.) Do not include fees and costs for getting a loan on the property in your basis.

The following are some of the settlement fees or closing costs you can include in the basis of your property.
- Abstract fees (abstract of title fees).
- Charges for installing utility services.
- Legal fees (including fees for the title search and preparation of the sales contract and deed).
- Recording fees.
- Survey fees.
- Transfer taxes.
- Owner's title insurance.
- Any amounts the seller owes that you agree to pay, such as back taxes or interest, recording or mortgage fees, charges for improvements or repairs, and sales commissions.

Settlement costs do not include amounts placed in escrow for the future payment of items such as taxes and insurance.

The following are some of the settlement fees and closing costs you cannot include in the basis of property.
- Casualty insurance premiums.
- Rent for occupancy of the property before closing.
- Charges for utilities or other services related to occupancy of the property before closing.
- Charges connected with getting a loan, such as points (discount points, loan origination fees), mortgage insurance premiums, loan assumption fees, cost of a credit report, and fees for an appraisal required by a lender.
- Fees for refinancing a mortgage.

Real estate taxes. If you pay real estate taxes the seller owed on real property you bought, and the seller did not reimburse you, treat those taxes as part of your basis. You cannot deduct them as an expense.

If you reimburse the seller for taxes the seller paid for you, you can usually deduct that amount as an expense in the year of purchase. Do not include that amount in the basis of your property. If you did not reimburse the seller, you must reduce your basis by the amount of those taxes.

Points. If you pay points to get a loan (including a mortgage, second mortgage, line of credit, or a home equity loan), do not add the points to the basis of the related property. Generally, you deduct the points over the term of the loan. For more information on how to deduct points, see chapter 24.

Points on home mortgage. Special rules may apply to points you and the seller pay when you get a mortgage to buy your main home. If certain requirements are met, you can deduct the points in full for the year in which they are paid. Reduce the basis of your home by any seller-paid points.

EXPLANATION
The following costs increase your tax basis:
1. Interest on debt incurred to finance the construction or production of real property, long-lived personal property with a useful life of 20 years or more, and other tangible property requiring more than 2 years (1 year in the case of property costing more than $1 million) to produce, construct, or reach a productive stage. Additionally, interest incurred to finance property produced under a long-term contract increases your tax

basis to the extent that income is not reported under the percentage of completion method. These rules do not apply to interest incurred during the construction of real property to be used as your principal residence or a second home. (For a definition of principal residence, see chapter 15, *Selling your home*. See chapter 24, *Interest expense*, for other rules affecting how much interest you may be able to deduct on a residence.)

2. The costs of defending or perfecting a title, architect's fees, and financing and finder's fees. Points, usually up-front payments on a mortgage charged to purchasers or borrowers, may be deducted as interest. See chapter 24, *Interest expense*, for more information and the timing of the deduction.

3. Certain start-up costs for a business. These include legal fees for the drafting of documents, accounting fees, and other similar expenses directly associated with the organization of a business. The costs of organizing a partnership, such as the expenses incurred in raising capital, putting together a prospectus, and paying commissions on the sale of investment units, also increase your basis, as does the cost of investigating the creation or acquisition of an active trade or business. See chapter 38, *Self-employment income: How to file Schedule C*, for further information.

TAXPLANNER

Some taxpayers who are starting a new business try to deduct the expenses incurred before the business actually begins. The IRS, however, may not accept these as current deductions, and it may either require that you deduct the expenses over a number of years (usually 15) or decide that the expenses should increase your basis in the business. If you started your new business in 2011, you can elect a current deduction of up to $5,000 for start-up expenditures. However, this $5,000 amount is reduced (but not below zero) by the amount by which the cumulative cost of start-up expenditures exceeds $50,000. The remainder of the start-up expenditures can be claimed as a deduction ratably over a 15-year period. If you currently neither deduct nor amortize an expense, the tax benefit is obtained when the entity is sold or ceases operation.

If you wish to amortize start-up or organizational expenditures for a business that started in 2011, you must attach an election statement to your 2011 tax return. Failing to file the election with your 2011 tax return will result in all of your start-up or organizational expenditures being capitalized and recoverable only upon sale or as a loss upon abandonment of the business. See Publication 535, *Business Expenses*, for more information on how to make the election.

Unlike costs of organizing a partnership or starting up its business, costs of selling partnership interests (syndication costs) may not be amortized or deducted. (For further discussion, see *Adjusted Basis*, later.)

TAXSAVER

Increasing your tax basis by as much as possible subsequently reduces the amount of gain or increases the amount of loss realized when you dispose of the property.

TAXALERT

Individuals do not derive any tax benefit from realizing a loss related to the disposition of personal property. Personal property includes any property that is not considered an investment (such as a refrigerator), as well as any property that is not used in a trade or business.

TAXSAVER

If you pay interest, taxes, and other carrying charges on unimproved and unproductive real estate but cannot deduct these expenses because you do not itemize your deductions, consider treating them as capital expenditures, which increase your basis and reduce your gain on sale. This election is made on an annual basis and must be renewed each year that you want to continue capitalizing these costs.

TAXORGANIZER

You should keep a copy of the closing statement you receive when you are either buying or selling real property.

Adjusted Basis

Before figuring gain or loss on a sale, exchange, or other disposition of property or figuring allowable depreciation, depletion, or amortization, you must usually make certain adjustments (increases and decreases) to the cost of the property. The result is the adjusted basis.

EXPLANATION

Note that you may need to make a separate calculation of basis when figuring your alternative minimum tax (AMT). You must take into consideration the impact that AMT adjustments, such as depreciation, have on basis in property. For a discussion of the AMT, see chapter 31, *How to figure your tax.*

Increases to Basis

Increase the basis of any property by all items properly added to a capital account. Examples of items that increase basis are shown in Table 13-1. These include the items discussed below.

Improvements. Add to your basis in property the cost of improvements having a useful life of more than 1 year, that increase the value of the property, lengthen its life, or adapt it to a different use. For example, improvements include putting a recreation room in your unfinished basement, adding another bathroom or bedroom, putting up a fence, putting in new plumbing or wiring, installing a new roof, or paving your driveway.

Table 13-1. **Examples of Adjustments to Basis**

Increases to Basis	Decreases to Basis

• Capital improvements:
  Putting an addition on your home
  Replacing an entire roof
  Paving your driveway
  Installing central air conditioning
  Rewiring your home
• Assessments for local improvements:
  Water connections
  Extending utility service lines to the property
  Sidewalks
  Roads
• Casualty losses:
  Restoring damaged property
• Legal fees:
  Cost of defending and perfecting a title
  Fees for getting a reduction of an assessment
• Zoning costs
	• Exclusion from income of subsidies for energy conservation measures
	• Casualty or theft loss deductions and insurance reimbursements
	• Postponed gain from the sale of a home
	• Alternative motor vehicle credit (Form 8910)
	• Alternative fuel vehicle refueling property credit (Form 8911)
	• Residential energy credits (Form 5695)
	• Depreciation and section 179 deduction
	• Nontaxable corporate distributions
	• Certain canceled debt excluded from income
	• Easements
	• Adoption tax benefits

Assessments for local improvements. Add to the basis of property assessments for improvements such as streets and sidewalks if they increase the value of the property assessed. Do not deduct them as taxes. However, you can deduct as taxes assessments for maintenance or repairs, or for meeting interest charges related to the improvements.

Example. Your city changes the street in front of your store into an enclosed pedestrian mall and assesses you and other affected property owners for the cost of the conversion. Add the assessment to your property's basis. In this example, the assessment is a depreciable asset.

Decreases to Basis

Decrease the basis of any property by all items that represent a return of capital for the period during which you held the property. Examples of items that decrease basis are shown in Table 13-1. These include the items discussed below.

Casualty and theft losses. If you have a casualty or theft loss, decrease the basis in your property by any insurance proceeds or other reimbursement and by any deductible loss not covered by insurance.

You must increase your basis in the property by the amount you spend on repairs that restore the property to its pre-casualty condition.

For more information on casualty and theft losses, see chapter 26.

Depreciation and section 179 deduction. Decrease the basis of your qualifying business property by any section 179 deduction you take and the depreciation you deducted, or could have deducted (including any special depreciation allowance), on your tax returns under the method of depreciation you selected.

For more information about depreciation and the section 179 deduction, see Publication 946 and the Instructions for Form 4562.

Example. You owned a duplex used as rental property that cost you $40,000, of which $35,000 was allocated to the building and $5,000 to the land. You added an improvement to the duplex that cost $10,000. In February last year, the duplex was damaged by fire. Up to that time, you had been allowed depreciation of $23,000. You sold some salvaged material for $1,300 and collected $19,700 from your insurance company. You deducted a casualty loss of $1,000 on your income tax return for last year. You spent $19,000 of the insurance proceeds for restoration of the duplex, which was completed this year. You must use the duplex's adjusted basis after the restoration to determine depreciation for the rest of the property's recovery period. Figure the adjusted basis of the duplex as follows:

Original cost of duplex		$35,000
Addition to duplex		10,000
Total cost of duplex		$45,000
Minus: Depreciation		23,000
Adjusted basis before casualty		$22,000
Minus: Insurance		
proceeds	$19,700	
Deducted casualty loss	1,000	
Salvage proceeds	1,300	22,000
Adjusted basis after casualty		$–0–
Add: Cost of restoring duplex		19,000
Adjusted basis after restoration		**$19,000**

Note. Your basis in the land is its original cost of $5,000.

EXPLANATION

For additional information on the Section 179 deduction, see chapter 38, *Self-employment income: How to file Schedule C.* Also see *How to Depreciate Your Property* in Publication 946.

EXPLANATION

If you discover that you deducted less depreciation than you could have claimed on your prior returns, you should consider filing amended returns to claim a refund if the statute of limitations (generally, 3 years from the date you filed the original return) has not expired. Consult your tax advisor.

Easements. The amount you receive for granting an easement is generally considered to be proceeds from the sale of an interest in real property. It reduces the basis of the affected part of the property. If the amount received is more than the basis of the part of the property affected by the easement, reduce your basis in that part to zero and treat the excess as a recognized gain.

If the gain is on a capital asset, see chapter 16 for information about how to report it. If the gain is on property used in a trade or business, see Publication 544 for information about how to report it.

Exclusion of subsidies for energy conservation measures. You can exclude from gross income any subsidy you received from a public utility company for the purchase or installation of an energy conservation measure for a dwelling unit. Reduce the basis of the property for which you received the subsidy by the excluded amount. For more information about this subsidy, see chapter 12.

Postponed gain from sale of home. If you postponed gain from the sale of your main home under rules in effect before May 7, 1997, you must reduce the basis of the home you acquired as a replacement by the amount of the postponed gain. For more information on the rules for the sale of a home, see chapter 15.

Basis Other Than Cost

There are many times when you cannot use cost as basis. In these cases, the fair market value or the adjusted basis of the property can be used. Fair market value (FMV) and adjusted basis were discussed earlier.

Property Received for Services

If you receive property for your services, include its FMV in income. The amount you include in income becomes your basis. If the services were performed for a price agreed on beforehand, it will be accepted as the FMV of the property if there is no evidence to the contrary.

Restricted property. If you receive property for your services and the property is subject to certain restrictions, your basis in the property is its FMV when it becomes substantially vested. However, this rule does not apply if you make an election to include in income the FMV of the property at the time it is transferred to you, less any amount you paid for it. Property is substantially vested when it is transferable or when it is not subject to a substantial risk of forfeiture (you do not have a good chance of losing it). For more information, see *Restricted Property* in Publication 525.

> ### TAXPLANNER
> Although one of the general rules of tax planning is that it is best to defer income and accelerate deductions, under certain circumstances it may be to your benefit to recognize income sooner rather than later. One such situation in which it may be beneficial to accelerate income is when the tax rate at which the income would be taxed would be lower in that earlier year. If you receive restricted property as compensation for your services you may be able to elect to report that income in the year received. For a full discussion of this subject, see *Property Received for Services* in chapter 5, *Wages, salaries, and other earnings*.

Bargain purchases. A bargain purchase is a purchase of an item for less than its FMV. If, as compensation for services, you buy goods or other property at less than FMV, include the difference between the purchase price and the property's FMV in your income. Your basis in the property is its FMV (your purchase price plus the amount you include in income).

If the difference between your purchase price and the FMV is a qualified employee discount, do not include the difference in income. However, your basis in the property is still its FMV. See *Employee Discounts* in Publication 15-B.

> ### EXAMPLES
> Airline, railroad, and subway employees need not include as income free travel provided by their employer if the employer does not incur any substantial additional cost in providing such travel. Employee clothing discounts, discount brokerage fees, and lodging and meal discounts can also qualify as nontaxable compensation. Employees are eligible for such tax-free benefits only if the merchandise or services are also offered to customers in the ordinary course of the employer's business. The amount of the tax-free discount is subject to specific dollar limitations.
>
> Business use of a company car, parking at or near your business premises, business periodicals, and any other property or service provided by your employer can be excluded from your taxable income if you would be allowed to take a business deduction had you paid for the benefit yourself.
>
> Other nontaxable fringe benefits from employers include medical savings account (MSA) or health savings account (HSA) contributions, free medical services, reimbursement of medical expenses, payments of premiums for up to $50,000 of group term life insurance coverage, tuition given to children of university employees, and meals furnished to employees on the employer's business premises for the convenience of the employer.

Taxable Exchanges

A taxable exchange is one in which the gain is taxable or the loss is deductible. A taxable gain or deductible loss also is known as a recognized gain or loss. If you receive property in exchange for other property in a taxable exchange, the basis of the property you receive is usually its FMV at the time of the exchange.

Involuntary Conversions

If you receive replacement property as a result of an involuntary conversion, such as a casualty, theft, or condemnation, figure the basis of the replacement property using the basis of the converted property.

Similar or related property. If you receive replacement property similar or related in service or use to the converted property, the replacement property's basis is the same as the converted property's basis on the date of the conversion, with the following adjustments.

1. Decrease the basis by the following.
   a. Any loss you recognize on the involuntary conversion.
   b. Any money you receive that you do not spend on similar property.
2. Increase the basis by the following.
   a. Any gain you recognize on the involuntary conversion.
   b. Any cost of acquiring the replacement property.

Money or property not similar or related. If you receive money or property not similar or related in service or use to the converted property, and you buy replacement property similar or related in service or use to the converted property, the basis of the replacement property is its cost decreased by the gain not recognized on the conversion.

TAXSAVER

You can elect to exclude the gain if, within 2 years following the year in which the involuntary gain was realized, you buy new property that is similar or related in service or use to the old property. If this election is made, a gain will be recognized to the extent the gain realized exceeds the difference between the cost of the replacement property and the adjusted basis of the old property. The basis of the new property is the cost of the new property decreased by the amount of gain that is not recognized.

For a principal residence (or its contents) in a federally declared disaster area, the replacement period is extended to 4 years after the close of the first year in which the gain on conversion is realized Check the Federal Emergency Management Agency's (FEMA) website at *www.fema .gov*, to determine if your involuntary gain property is located in a federally declared disaster area.

Example

You are a calendar year taxpayer. A tornado destroyed your home in October 2010. In January 2011, the insurance company paid you $8,000 more than the adjusted basis of your home. The area in which your home is located is not a federally declared disaster area. You first realized a gain from the reimbursement for the casualty in 2011, so you have until December 31, 2013, to replace the property. If your home had been in a federally declared disaster area, you would have until December 31, 2015, to replace the property.

Explanation

Property in the Midwestern, Kansas, or Hurricane Katrina disaster areas. For property located in:

- a Midwestern disaster area that was destroyed, damaged or stolen during the period beginning on or after May 20, 2008, and ending before August 1, 2008, as a result of severe storms, tornadoes, or flooding;
- the Kansas disaster area that was destroyed, damaged, or stolen on or after May 4, 2007, as a result of storms and tornadoes; or,
- the Hurricane Katrina disaster area that was destroyed, damaged, or stolen on or after August 25, 2005,

the replacement period is extended to 5 years. Substantially all of the use of the replacement property must be located in one of the disaster areas listed above.

Example. The state condemned your property. The adjusted basis of the property was $26,000 and the state paid you $31,000 for it. You realized a gain of $5,000 ($31,000 − $26,000). You bought replacement property similar in use to the converted property for $29,000. You recognize a gain of $2,000 ($31,000 − $29,000), the unspent part of the payment from the state. Your unrecognized gain is $3,000, the difference between the $5,000 realized gain and the $2,000 recognized gain. The basis of the replacement property is figured as follows:

Cost of replacement property……...………..………..	$29,000
Minus: Gain not recognized……………………..……….	3,000
Basis of replacement property……………..………..	**$26,000**

Allocating the basis. If you buy more than one piece of replacement property, allocate your basis among the properties based on their respective costs.

TAXPLANNER

When you buy more than one asset for a single amount, such as land with buildings or the operating assets of a business, your costs must be reasonably allocated among the different assets. While the IRS may always question whether you have allocated these costs fairly, the IRS is unlikely to do so if the allocation has been contractually agreed to by the parties involved, particularly if you and the seller have adverse interests. Therefore, it may often be to your advantage to have the allocation spelled out in the purchase agreement.

If you are acquiring a trade, business, or investment asset, a favorable allocation of costs may have tax advantages. For example, raw land may not be depreciated, but buildings may. A favorable allocation between land and buildings enables you to claim more depreciation. The costs of specified intangible assets (such as goodwill, covenant-not-to-compete, franchise, etc.) are amortized over a 15-year period. Thus, while you can amortize costs allocated to certain intangible assets, allocating more cost to operating assets instead may create an income tax advantage because of the more rapid depreciation methods available for equipment. However, while the allocation of purchase price to tangible assets (e.g., equipment) will generally produce a favorable income tax result, this allocation can cause state and local sales and use taxes and business property taxes to be imposed on the tangible assets acquired.

If you dispose of a specified intangible asset that was acquired in a transaction, but you retain other specified intangible assets acquired in the same transaction, you may not claim a loss as a result of the disposition. Instead, the bases of the retained specified intangible assets are increased by the amount of the unrecognized loss.

For information about asset allocations, see chapter 38, *Self-employment income: How to file Schedule C.*

The residual method must be used to allocate the purchase price of acquired assets. Under the residual method, the amount allocated to the value of goodwill and going concern value is the excess of the purchase price over the FMV of the tangible assets and the other identifiable intangible assets.

For certain types of acquisitions of assets used in a trade or a business, the buyer and seller must file Form 8594 with the IRS, showing how the purchase price was allocated among various classes of assets. For more information, consult your tax advisor.

Basis for depreciation. Special rules apply in determining and depreciating the basis of MACRS property acquired in an involuntary conversion. For information, see *What Is the Basis of Your Depreciable Property?* in chapter 1 of Publication 946.

Nontaxable Exchanges

A nontaxable exchange is an exchange in which you are not taxed on any gain and you cannot deduct any loss. If you receive property in a nontaxable exchange, its basis is generally the same as the basis of the property you transferred. See *Nontaxable Trades* in chapter 14.

Like-Kind Exchanges

The exchange of property for the same kind of property is the most common type of nontaxable exchange. To qualify as a like-kind exchange, the property traded and the property received must be both of the following.
• Qualifying property.
• Like-kind property.

The basis of the property you receive is generally the same as the adjusted basis of the property you gave up. If you trade property in a like-kind exchange and also pay money, the basis of the property received is the adjusted basis of the property you gave up increased by the money you paid.

Qualifying property. In a like-kind exchange, you must hold for investment or for productive use in your trade or business both the property you give up and the property you receive.

Like-kind property. There must be an exchange of like-kind property. Like-kind properties are properties of the same nature or character, even if they differ in grade or quality. The exchange of real estate for real estate and personal property for similar personal property are exchanges of like-kind property.

Example. You trade in an old truck used in your business with an adjusted basis of $1,700 for a new one costing $6,800. The dealer allows you $2,000 on the old truck, and you pay $4,800. This is a like-kind exchange. The basis of the new truck is $6,500 (the adjusted basis of the old one, $1,700, plus the amount you paid, $4,800).

If you sell your old truck to a third party for $2,000 instead of trading it in and then buy a new one from the dealer, you have a taxable gain of $300 on the sale (the $2,000 sale price minus the $1,700 adjusted basis). The basis of the new truck is the price you pay the dealer.

EXPLANATION

In general, all gains realized on sales and other dispositions of property are taxable, but an exception is made when business or investment property is traded or exchanged for "like-kind" property. In this case, the newly acquired property is viewed as a continuation of the investment in the original property, so the tax basis does not change. The reason to make tax-free exchanges is not to avoid taxes but to defer them while realizing some other investment aims. (For more details on nontaxable exchanges, see chapter 14, *Sale of property*.)

Partially nontaxable exchanges. A partially nontaxable exchange is an exchange in which you receive unlike property or money in addition to like-kind property. The basis of the property you receive is the same as the adjusted basis of the property you gave up, with the following adjustments.

1. Decrease the basis by the following amounts.
   a. Any money you receive.
   b. Any loss you recognize on the exchange.
2. Increase the basis by the following amounts.
   a. Any additional costs you incur.
   b. Any gain you recognize on the exchange.

If the other party to the exchange assumes your liabilities, treat the debt assumption as money you received in the exchange.

Allocation of basis. If you receive like-kind and unlike properties in the exchange, allocate the basis first to the unlike property, other than money, up to its FMV on the date of the exchange. The rest is the basis of the like-kind property.

More information. See *Like-Kind Exchanges* in chapter 1 of Publication 544 for more information.

Basis for depreciation. Special rules apply in determining and depreciating the basis of MACRS property acquired in a like-kind exchange. For information, see *What Is the Basis of Your Depreciable Property?* in chapter 1 of Publication 946.

Property Transferred From a Spouse

The basis of property transferred to you or transferred in trust for your benefit by your spouse is the same as your spouse's adjusted basis. The same rule applies to a transfer by your former spouse that is incident to divorce. However, for property transferred in trust, adjust your basis for any gain recognized by your spouse or former spouse if the liabilities assumed, plus the liabilities to which the property is subject, are more than the adjusted basis of the property transferred.

If the property transferred to you is a series E, series EE, or series I U.S. savings bond, the transferor must include in income the interest accrued to the date of transfer. Your basis in the bond immediately after the transfer is equal to the transferor's basis increased by the interest income includible in the transferor's income. For more information on these bonds, see chapter 7.

At the time of the transfer, the transferor must give you the records needed to determine the adjusted basis and holding period of the property as of the date of the transfer.

For more information about the transfer of property from a spouse, see chapter 14.

Property Received as a Gift

To figure the basis of property you receive as a gift, you must know its adjusted basis to the donor just before it was given to you, its FMV at the time it was given to you, and any gift tax paid on it.

EXPLANATION

If a gift tax return was filed, you should examine it for information on the donor's tax basis.

FMV less than donor's adjusted basis. If the FMV of the property at the time of the gift is less than the donor's adjusted basis, your basis depends on whether you have a gain or a loss when you dispose of the property. Your basis for figuring gain is the same as the donor's adjusted basis plus or minus any required adjustments to basis while you held the property. Your basis for figuring loss is its FMV when you received the gift plus or minus any required adjustments to basis while you held the property. See *Adjusted Basis*, earlier.

Example. You received an acre of land as a gift. At the time of the gift, the land had an FMV of $8,000. The donor's adjusted basis was $10,000. After you received the property, no events occurred to increase or decrease your basis. If you later sell the property for $12,000, you will have a $2,000 gain because you must use the donor's adjusted basis at the time of the gift ($10,000) as your basis to figure gain. If you sell the property for $7,000, you will have a $1,000 loss because you must use the FMV at the time of the gift ($8,000) as your basis to figure loss.

If the sales price is between $8,000 and $10,000, you have neither gain nor loss.

EXAMPLE

Owen owns a building in which his adjusted basis is $40,000. The fair market value (FMV) of the building, however, is only $30,000. Owen gives the building to Jim. Jim's basis is $40,000–Owen's adjusted basis–for determining depreciation and for computing a gain on the sale of the building. Jim's basis is $30,000–the FMV at the time of the gift–for computing a loss on the sale of the building.

Note: If the FMV of the building increases to $35,000, Jim may sell the property without recognizing a gain or a loss. His proceeds of $35,000 would be greater than the basis used for computing a loss on the sale and less than the basis used for computing a gain on the sale.

TAXPLANNER

If the FMV of property that you intend to give as a gift is less than your adjusted basis in the property, you might want to sell the property and then make a gift of the proceeds. In this way, you recognize a loss on the sale of the property. This could provide you with a tax savings. The recipient of the gift will receive the same amount of value, but in cash rather than property. Had the recipient received property, he or she would not be able to deduct the loss you had on the property when the recipient sold it because the recipient's basis in the property for computing a loss is the property's FMV at the time the gift is made.

Business property. If you hold the gift as business property, your basis for figuring any depreciation, depletion, or amortization deductions is the same as the donor's adjusted basis plus or minus any required adjustments to basis while you hold the property.

FMV equal to or greater than donor's adjusted basis. If the FMV of the property is equal to or greater than the donor's adjusted basis, your basis is the donor's adjusted basis at the time you received the gift. Increase your basis by all or part of any gift tax paid, depending on the date of the gift, explained later.

Also, for figuring gain or loss from a sale or other disposition or for figuring depreciation, depletion, or amortization deductions on business property, you must increase or decrease your basis (the donor's adjusted basis) by any required adjustments to basis while you held the property. See *Adjusted Basis*, earlier.

If you received a gift during the tax year, increase your basis in the gift (the donor's adjusted basis) by the part of the gift tax paid on it due to the net increase in value of the gift. Figure the increase by multiplying the gift tax paid by a fraction. The numerator of the fraction is the net increase in value of the gift and the denominator is the amount of the gift.

The net increase in value of the gift is the FMV of the gift minus the donor's adjusted basis. The amount of the gift is its value for gift tax purposes after reduction by any annual exclusion and marital or charitable deduction that applies to the gift. For information on the gift tax, see Publication 950, *Introduction to Estate and Gift Taxes*.

Example. In 2011, you received a gift of property from your mother that had an FMV of $50,000. Her adjusted basis was $20,000. The amount of the gift for gift tax purposes was $37,000 ($50,000 minus the $13,000 annual exclusion). She paid a gift tax of $7,540 on the property. Your basis is $26,107, figured as follows:

Fair market value..	$50,000
Minus: Adjusted basis...	−20,000
Net increase in value...	$30,000
Gift tax paid...	$7,540
Multiplied by ($30,000 ÷ $37,000).........................	× .81
Gift tax due to net increase in value.........................	$6,107
Adjusted basis of property to your mother..................	+20,000
Your basis in the property..............................	**$26,107**

Note. If you received a gift before 1977, your basis in the gift (the donor's adjusted basis) includes any gift tax paid on it. However, your basis cannot exceed the FMV of the gift at the time it was given to you.

Inherited Property

If you inherited property from a decedent who died in 2011, your basis in property you inherit from a decedent is generally one of the following.

- The FMV of the property at the date of the decedent's death.
- The FMV on the alternate valuation date if the personal representative for the estate elects to use alternate valuation.

TAXALERT

If you inherited property from a person who died during 2010, see *Basis in property inherited from a person (decedent) who died during 2010*, later.

EXPLANATION

The above rules for "stepped up" basis do not apply to appreciated property you receive from a decedent if you or your spouse originally gave the property to the decedent within 1 year before the decedent's death. In such a case, your basis in this property is the same as the decedent's adjusted basis in the property immediately before his or her death, rather than its FMV. Appreciated property is any property whose FMV on the day it was given to the decedent is more than its adjusted basis.

The alternate valuation date is the earlier of the date 6 months after death and the date on which the estate's assets are distributed, sold, exchanged, or disposed of. Alternate valuation may be elected only if it is necessary to file an estate tax return. Furthermore, use of the alternate valuation date must result in a decrease in the estate tax. The election must be made for all property included in the estate and includes only property that is not sold, distributed, or otherwise disposed of within 6 months after the decedent's death.

TAXSAVER

Choosing an alternate valuation date may be helpful in reducing estate tax if the market value of the assets in the estate is declining. However, if this is the case, the tax basis of those assets must also be reduced; this means increased income taxes in the future if the market value of the assets rises and they are then sold. Thus, the decision to elect the alternate valuation date to reduce estate tax should be balanced against a possible increase in future income taxes.

- The value under the special-use valuation method for real property used in farming or a closely held business if elected for estate tax purposes.

EXPLANATION

If a decedent used property that he or she owned for farming, trade, or business purposes at the date of death, the executor of the decedent's estate may, under most conditions, choose the special-use valuation method for that property. This means that the property is included in the decedent's estate at the value based on its *current* use and not at the value based on what its most lucrative use might be. For example, if the land is being used for farming, its value is figured on its worth as farmland and not on what it might be worth if used for industrial purposes.

Certain conditions must be met before you use the special-use valuation method; consult your tax advisor.

The maximum amount that the special-use method can decrease the value of the estate is $1,020,000 in 2011. This amount is increased each year for cost-of-living adjustments.

- The decedent's adjusted basis in land to the extent of the value excluded from the decedent's taxable estate as a qualified conservation easement.

If a federal estate tax return does not have to be filed, your basis in the inherited property is its appraised value at the date of death for state inheritance or transmission taxes.

For more information, see the instructions to Form 706, United States Estate (and Generation-Skipping Transfer) Tax Return.

Community property. In community property states (Arizona, California, Idaho, Louisiana, Nevada, New Mexico, Texas, Washington, and Wisconsin), husband and wife are each usually considered to own half the community property. When either spouse dies, the total value of the community property, even the part belonging to the surviving spouse, generally becomes the basis of the entire property. For this rule to apply, at least half the value of the community property interest must be includible in the decedent's gross estate, whether or not the estate must file a return.

Example. You and your spouse owned community property that had a basis of $80,000. When your spouse died, half the FMV of the community interest was includible in your spouse's estate. The FMV of the community interest was $100,000. The basis of your half of the property after the death of your spouse is $50,000 (half of the $100,000 FMV). The basis of the other half to your spouse's heirs is also $50,000.

For more information about community property, see Publication 555, *Community Property*.

TAXSAVER

In community property states, the basis of the surviving spouse's one-half share of community property assets will also receive a step-up in basis, normally to its FMV, at the date of the decedent spouse's death. Assets held jointly by spouses and not as community property will only receive a step up for the decedent spouse's one-half share of the asset. There are advantages and disadvantages for the various forms of holding title to assets. You should consult your tax advisor for recommendations on how to hold title to property in your state.

Property inherited from a decedent who died in 2010. If you inherited property from a decedent who died in 2010, special rules may apply. For more information, see Publication 4895, *Tax Treatment of a Property Acquired From a Decedent Dying in 2010.*

TAXALERT

For most of 2010, the estate tax was repealed. However, the December 2010 tax law that extended the so-called Bush tax cuts retroactively reinstated the estate tax for 2010. This law also allowed the executor of an estate of a decedent who died during 2010 to opt out of having the estate tax apply. If the estate tax applied to a decedent who died during 2010, then your basis in property you inherited from such decedent is generally the fair market value (FMV) of property at the date of the decedent's death (or alternate valuation date if the executor chose to use the alternate valuation). On the other hand, if the executor chose not to have the estate tax apply to the estate of a decedent who died during 2010, then "modified carryover basis" rules applied to determine your basis in inherited property.

Modified carryover basis rules. Under these rules, you will generally receive a basis equal to the lesser of the fair market value of the property on the decedent's date of death or the decedent's adjusted basis in the property.

Exception. There is one key exception to this new carryover basis rule: A decedent's executor can increase (often referred to as "step up") the basis of assets transferred by a total of $1.3 million plus any unused capital losses, net operating losses, and certain "built-in" losses of the decedent. An additional $3 million basis increase is allowed for property transferred to a surviving spouse, which means that property transferred to a spouse will be allowed a basis increase of $4.3 million. However, certain types of assets are not eligible for this increase in basis. Nonresident aliens would only be allowed increase in basis of $60,000 indexed for inflation after 2010.

The executor can choose to allocate the step up in basis on an asset-by-asset basis. For example, the basis increase can be allocated to a share of stock or a block of stock. However, in no case can the basis of an asset be adjusted above its fair market value. If the amount of basis increase is less than the fair market value of assets whose bases are eligible to be increased under these rules, the executor will determine which assets and to what extent each asset receives a basis increase. This could put the executor in an awkward spot: deciding which family members or other heirs get tax-free assets and which ones get assets with built-in capital gain.

If you report the sale of inherited property on your income tax return and calculate gain using an incorrect basis amount, you risk underpaying tax on the transaction and being subject to additional tax, interest and penalties.

For more information about the estate tax, see chapter 44, *Estate and gift tax planning*.

TAXORGANIZER
If you sold property in 2011 that you originally inherited from a decedent who died during 2010, you should contact the executor of the decedent's estate to confirm the basis in the property you received.

Property Changed From Personal to Business or Rental Use
If you hold property for personal use and then change it to business use or use it to produce rent, you can begin to depreciate the property at the time of the change. To do so, you must figure its basis for depreciation. An example of changing property held for personal use to business or rental use would be renting out your former personal residence.

Basis for depreciation. The basis for depreciation is the lesser of the following amounts.
- The FMV of the property on the date of the change.
- Your adjusted basis on the date of the change.

Example. Several years ago, you paid $160,000 to have your house built on a lot that cost $25,000. You paid $20,000 for permanent improvements to the house and claimed a $2,000 casualty loss deduction for damage to the house before changing the property to rental use last year. Because land is not depreciable, you include only the cost of the house when figuring the basis for depreciation.

Your adjusted basis in the house when you changed its use was $178,000 ($160,000 + $20,000 − $2,000). On the same date, your property had an FMV of $180,000, of which $15,000 was for the land and $165,000 was for the house. The basis for figuring depreciation on the house is its FMV on the date of the change ($165,000) because it is less than your adjusted basis ($178,000).

Sale of property. If you later sell or dispose of property changed to business or rental use, the basis you use will depend on whether you are figuring gain or loss.

Gain. The basis for figuring a gain is your adjusted basis in the property when you sell the property.

Example. Assume the same facts as in the previous example except that you sell the property at a gain after being allowed depreciation deductions of $37,500. Your adjusted basis for figuring gain is $165,500 ($178,000 + $25,000 (land) − $37,500).

Loss. Figure the basis for a loss starting with the smaller of your adjusted basis or the FMV of the property at the time of the change to business or rental use. Then make adjustments (increases and decreases) for the period after the change in the property's use, as discussed earlier under *Adjusted Basis*.

Example. Assume the same facts as in the previous example, except that you sell the property at a loss after being allowed depreciation deductions of $37,500. In this case, you would start with the FMV on the date of the change to rental use ($180,000), because it is less than the adjusted basis of $203,000 ($178,000 + $25,000 (land)) on that date. Reduce that amount ($180,000) by the depreciation deductions ($37,500). The basis for loss is $142,500 ($180,000 − $37,500).

Stocks and Bonds
The basis of stocks or bonds you buy generally is the purchase price plus any costs of purchase, such as commissions and recording or transfer fees. If you get stocks or bonds other than by purchase, your basis is usually determined by the FMV or the previous owner's adjusted basis, as discussed earlier.

You must adjust the basis of stocks for certain events that occur after purchase. For example, if you receive additional stock from nontaxable stock dividends or stock splits, reduce your basis for each share of stock by dividing the adjusted basis of the old stock by the number of shares of old and new stock. This rule applies only when the additional stock received is identical to the stock held. Also reduce your basis when you receive nontaxable distributions. They are a return of capital.

Example. In 2009 you bought 100 shares of XYZ stock for $1,000 or $10 a share. In 2010 you bought 100 shares of XYZ stock for $1,600 or $16 a share. In 2011 XYZ declared a 2-for-1 stock split. You now have 200 shares of stock with a basis of $5 a share and 200 shares with a basis of $8 a share.

Other basis. There are other ways to figure the basis of stocks or bonds depending on how you acquired them. For detailed information, see *Stocks and Bonds* under *Basis of Investment Property* in chapter 4 of Publication 550.

Identifying stocks or bonds sold. If you can adequately identify the shares of stock or the bonds you sold, their basis is the cost or other basis of the particular shares of stocks or bonds. If you buy and sell securities at various times in varying quantities and you cannot adequately identify the shares you sell, the basis of the securities you sell is the basis of the securities you acquired first. For more information about identifying securities you sell, see *Stocks and Bonds* under *Basis of Investment Property* in chapter 4 of Publication 550.

TAXALERT

If you sold property such as stocks, bonds, mutual funds, or certain commodities through a broker during 2011, your broker should send you, for each sale, a Form 1099-B, Proceeds From Broker and Barter Exchange Transactions, or an equivalent statement that will show the gross proceeds from the sale. The broker will also file a copy of Form 1099-B with the IRS.

Starting for 2011, if the stock you sold during the year was acquired after 2010, your broker will also be generally required to report on Form 1099-B your basis in the shares sold and whether any capital gain or loss was short-term or long-term. (For stock purchased and sold during 2011, any gain or loss will be classified as short-term since the securities have been held for less than a year.) The requirements to report basis and holding period (i.e., short- or long-term) will be expanded during 2012 and 2013 to cover other types of securities, such as sales of mutual fund shares, stock acquired in connection with a dividend reinvestment plan, bonds, commodity contracts, and options on securities. On the other hand, brokers are not required to report basis or holding period for any securities acquired before 2011.

TAXALERT

Beginning January 1, 2011, shares acquired through a dividend reinvestment plan (DRP) may use the average method for computing basis provided that the written plan documents require at least 10 % of every dividend is reinvested in identical stock. A DRP may also average the basis of shares acquired through non-dividend distributions such as capital gain distributions, nontaxable returns of capital, and cash in lieu.

TAXPLANNER

If you made multiple purchases of a particular stock during 2011 and sold only a portion of the total shares you acquired, then your broker is required to report your basis in the shares sold on Form 1099-B using the first-in, first-out (FIFO) method; that is, the broker must consider the oldest shares you acquired as the ones sold first. However, your broker does not need to use the FIFO method if you provide him or her with an adequate and timely identification of the specific shares that you want to sell or, if identical shares were sold, request that your broker use the average basis. In order for you to elect specific identification, you must identify the stock to be sold by the earlier of the settlement date or the time for settlement under SEC regulations. You may also issue a standing order to specify a lot selection method.

Mutual fund shares. If you sell mutual fund shares you acquired at various times and prices and left on deposit in an account kept by a custodian or agent, you can elect to use an average basis. For more information, see Publication 564.

Bond premium. If you buy a taxable bond at a premium and elect to amortize the premium, reduce the basis of the bond by the amortized premium you deduct each year. See *Bond Premium Amortization* in chapter 3 of Publication 550 for more information. Although you cannot deduct the premium on a tax-exempt bond, you must amortize the premium each year and reduce your basis in the bond by the amortized amount.

EXAMPLE

On February 16, 2010, Tamera purchases a tax-exempt obligation maturing on February 16, 2015, for $120,000. The bond has a stated principal amount of $100,000, payable at maturity. The obligation provides for unconditional payments of interest of $9,000, payable on February 16 of each year. The interest payments on the obligation are qualified stated interest. The amount of bond premium is $20,000 ($120,000 – $100,000).

Based on the remaining payment schedule of the bond and Tamera's basis in the bond, Tamera's yield is 5.48%, compounded annually (per her broker, who looked up the yield rate). The bond premium amortized annually is equal to the excess of the qualified stated interest payment ($9,000) less the adjusted acquisition price at the beginning of the period ($120,000 for 2011) multiplied by Tamera's yield (5.48%, compounded annually) ($120,000 × 5.48%, or $6,576).

Thus, the bond premium that must be amortized on February 16, 2011, is $2,424 ($9,000 – $6,576). Since the bond is a tax-exempt obligation, Tamera may not claim the amortization as a deduction on her tax return.

Original issue discount (OID) on debt instruments. You must increase your basis in an OID debt instrument by the OID you include in income for that instrument. See *Original Issue Discount (OID)* in chapter 7 and Publication 1212, *Guide To Original Issue Discount (OID) Instruments.*

Tax-exempt obligations. OID on tax-exempt obligations is generally not taxable. However, when you dispose of a tax-exempt obligation issued after September 3, 1982, and acquired after March 1, 1984, you must accrue OID on the obligation to determine its adjusted basis. The accrued OID is added to the basis of the obligation to determine your gain or loss. See chapter 4 of Publication 550.

EXPLANATION

For further discussion of original issue discount, see chapter 7, *Interest income*.

TAXSAVER

Automatic investment service and dividend reinvestment plans. If you take part in an automatic investment service, your cost basis per share of stock, including fractional shares, bought by the bank or other agent is your proportionate share of the agent's cost of all shares purchased at the same time plus the same share of the brokerage commission paid by the agent. If you take part in a dividend reinvestment plan and you receive stock from the corporation at a discount, your cost is the full FMV of the stock on the dividend payment date. You must include the amount of the discount in your income as an additional dividend.

Beginning in 2011, all shares acquired on or after January 1 through a dividend reinvestment plan (DRP) may use the average method for tracking basis provided that the DRP shares are held in plans for which a written document requires at least 10% of every dividend paid is reinvested in identical stock. In 2012, brokers will be required to report basis and holding periods of shares acquired after 2011 through a DRP. If a taxpayer sells DRP shares in 2011 that were also acquired in 2011, the taxpayer may use the average method, but the broker will not be required to report adjusted cost basis or holding period.

Stock dividends. Special rules apply in determining the basis of stock you acquired through a stock dividend or a stock right. Stock dividends are distributions by a corporation of its own stock. Usually, stock dividends are not taxable to the shareholder. However, for exceptions to this rule, see chapter 8, *Dividends and other corporate distributions*. If stock dividends are not taxable, you must allocate your basis for the stock between the old and the new stock in proportion to the FMV of each on the date of the distribution of the new stock. If your stock dividend is taxable on receipt, the original basis of your new stock is its FMV on the date of distribution. Your holding period is determined from the date of distribution.

New and old stock identical. If the new stock you received as a nontaxable dividend is the same as the old stock on which the dividend is declared, both new and old shares probably have equal FMVs and you can divide the adjusted basis of the old stock by the number of shares of old and new stock. The result is your basis for each share of stock.

Example

You owned one share of common stock that you bought for $45. The corporation distributed two new shares of common stock for each share you held. You then had three shares of common stock, each with a basis of $15 ($45 ÷ 3). If you owned two shares before the distribution, one bought for $30 and the other for $45, you would have six shares after the distribution: three with a basis of $10 each and three with a basis of $15 each.

New and old stock not identical. If the new stock you received as a nontaxable dividend is not the same as the old stock on which the dividend was declared, the FMVs of the old stock and the new stock will probably be different, so you should allocate the adjusted basis of your old stock between the old stock and the new stock in proportion to the FMVs of each on the date of the distribution of the new stock.

Example 1

This example shows how to account for stock splits and stock dividends.

	Block 1		
	Shares	**Total Cost**	**Cost per Share**
March 14, 2009	100	$3,000	$30
Nov. 30, 2010			
2 for 1 stock split	100	-0-	
	200	$3,000	$15
Nov. 1, 2011			
10% stock dividend	20		
Dec. 30, 2011	220	$3,000	$13.636

	Block 2		
	Shares	**Total Cost**	**Cost per Share**
Oct. 28, 2011	100	$2,000	$20
10% stock dividend	10		
Dec. 30, 2011	110	$2,000	$18.182

The original cost of each block of stock must be divided by the number of shares on hand at any given date to arrive at basis per share.

Example 2

This example shows how to account for nontaxable stock dividends with an FMV that is different from the value of the original stock held.

	Shares	**Total Cost**	**Cost per Share**	**Total FMV**	**FMV per Share**
Feb. 8, 2011 Purchased common stock	1,000	$14,000	$14	$14,000	$14
Sept. 1, 2011 10% stock dividend of preferred stock	100			$1,000	$10
FMV of original stock is $22 per share.					
1,000 shares ×					
$14 = $14,000	Cost of originating stock				
1,000 shares ×					
$22 = $22,000	Market value of original stock				

100 shares ×

$10 = $1,000	Market value of preferred stock
$22,000/$23,000 ×	
$14,000 =	
$13,391	Cost of original stock apportioned to such stock
$1,000/$23,000 ×	
$14,000 =	
$609	Cost of original stock apportioned to the preferred stock

Example 3

This example shows how to calculate the basis of shares in a DRP using the average basis method election.

On June 1, 2011, Betty acquires 100 shares of stock at $25 per share and enrolls them in the company's DRP plan. On August 15, 2011, the company pays a dividend of $3.00 per share while the shares are trading at $30 per share, and on November 15, 2011, the company pays a dividend of $4.00 per share while the shares are trading at $32.50 per share. Since Betty elects to use the average basis method upon her initial purchase, this election will be effective for identical shares held across all of Betty's accounts through December 31, 2011. For share sales prior to January 1, 2012, the average basis will be computed as follows:

Date	Action	Share Price	No. of Shares	Total Shares Owned
Original shares				
June 1, 2011	Invest $2,500	$25.00	100	100
DRP shares				
Aug. 15, 2011	Reinvest $300 dividend	$30.00	10	10
Nov. 15, 2011	Reinvest $520	$32.50	16	26

AVERAGE BASIS	To figure the basis of the shares, use the basis of all shares acquired in 2011.

cost of 126 shares	$3,320.00
number of shares ÷	126
average basis per share	$26.35

If Betty does not notify her broker of her average basis election, the basis on the first 100 shares sold will be calculated using the FIFO method ($25/share).

For shares purchased after December 31, 2011, the average basis method will only apply on an account-by-account basis. If Betty wishes to continue to use the average basis method with identical shares held across all of her accounts, she should contact her broker to make this election.

Explanation

Stock rights. A stock right is rarely taxable when you receive it. For more information, see chapter 8, *Dividends and other corporate distributions*.

If you receive stock rights that are taxable, the basis of the rights is their FMV at the time of distribution.

If you receive stock rights that are not taxable and you allow them to expire, they have no basis.

If you exercise or sell the nontaxable stock rights and if, at the time of distribution, the rights had an FMV of 15% or more of the FMV of the old stock, you must divide the adjusted basis of the stock between the stock and the stock rights. Use a ratio of the FMV of each to the FMV of both at the time of distribution of the rights. If the FMV of the stock rights is less than 15%, their basis is zero unless you choose to allocate a part of the basis of the old stock to the rights. You make this allocation on your return for the tax year in which the rights are received.

Basis of new stock. If you exercise the stock rights, the basis of the new stock is its cost plus the basis of the stock rights exercised. The holding period of the new stock begins on the date on which you exercised the stock rights.

Example

You own 100 shares of Tan Company stock, which cost you $22 per share. Tan Company gave you 10 nontaxable stock rights that would allow you to buy 10 additional shares of stock at $26 per share. At the time the rights were distributed, the stock had a market value of $30, without the rights, and each right had a market value of $3. The market value of the stock rights is less than 15% of the market value of the stock, but you choose to divide the basis of your stock between the stock and the rights. You figure the basis of the rights and the basis of the old stock as follows:

100 shares × $22 = $2,200, basis of old stock

100 shares × $30 = $3,000, market value of old stock

10 rights × $3 = $30, market value of rights

30/3,030 × $2,200 = $21.78, basis of rights

3,000/3,030 × $2,200 = $2,178.22, new basis of old stock

If you sell the stock rights, the basis for figuring gain or loss is $2.178 per right. If you exercise the stock rights, the basis of the new stock you receive is $28.178 per share, the subscription price paid ($26) plus the basis of the stock rights exercised ($2.178 each). The remaining basis of the 100 shares of old stock for figuring gain or loss on a later sale is $2,178.22, or $21.7822 per share.

Explanation

Other basis rules. There are many other special rules you must follow in determining your basis in certain types of property. Here are some examples.

If you receive stock of one corporation in exchange for stock of another corporation in certain types of corporate reorganizations, your basis in the stock received will be equal to the basis of the stock you exchanged.

Certain types of tax credits may reduce basis in whole or in part. For example, if you claim rehabilitation credits on a building, the basis of the property is reduced by the amount of the credit.

If you lease real property on which the lessee makes improvements and the value of such improvements is excluded from income, your basis in the improvements is zero.

If you sell property to charity in a bargain sale, your basis for determining the gain from the sale is reduced by the ratio of the total basis of the property to its FMV.

For more information, you should consult your tax advisor.

Chapter 14
Sale of property

Note

IRS Publication 17 (*Your Federal Income Tax*) has been updated by Ernst & Young LLP for 2011. Dates and dollar amounts shown are for 2011. Underlined type is used to indicate where IRS text has been updated. Places where text has been removed are indicated by the sentence: *Text intentionally omitted.*

ey.com/EYTaxGuide

Ernst & Young LLP will update the *Ernst & Young Tax Guide 2012* website with relevant taxpayer information as it becomes available. You can also sign up for email alerts to let you know when changes have been made.

Introduction

Anytime you sell or exchange a piece of property at a gain–whether it be your house, a stock you own, or something you use in your trade or business–you usually have to pay taxes on the transaction. That, of course, doesn't mean that sales and exchanges should be avoided, but the manner in which you choose to dispose of an asset may determine how much you will have to pay in taxes. This chapter describes the various options available to you and the tax consequences of each.

Because the amounts involved in sales and exchanges of property are often quite large relative to other items that make up your income, this chapter merits careful attention. It not only spells out how you determine the way in which various transactions are taxed but also offers suggestions about how to minimize or defer the tax burdens that you may incur.

In addition, this chapter discusses bad debts. When a borrower cannot repay a loan, it is known as a bad debt. Some loans are made in connection with a trade or a business, some are made for purely personal reasons, and still others are made to make a profit. All sorts of rules have to be followed, and not every bad debt qualifies for a deduction. This chapter spells out what kind of documentation you need to prove that the money you lost was a bona fide debt and that there is no chance of repayment–the two conditions that must be met for you to take a deduction.

What's New

100% exclusion of gain on qualified small business stock. You may be able to exclude from income up to 100% of your gain from the sale or trade of qualified small business stock you acquired after September 27, 2010, and before January 1, 2012, if you hold the stock for more than 5 years.

TAXALERT

Generally, noncorporate taxpayers may exclude 50% of the gain from the sale of certain small business stock acquired at original issue and held for more than 5 years. For stock acquired after February 17, 2009, and before September 28, 2010, the exclusion was increased to 75%. (At the time of sale, however, 28% of the excluded gain is treated as a tax preference item subject to the alternative minimum tax (AMT).)

Two new tax laws (including the one that extended the Bush tax cuts) enacted in 2010 temporarily increased the amount of the exclusion to 100% of the gain from the sale of qualifying small business stock that is acquired at original issue after September 27, 2010, and before January 1, 2012. There is also no AMT preference item attributable for that sale.

For more information, see *Gain on qualified small business stock*, later in this chapter.

Reminder

Foreign income. If you are a U.S. citizen who sells property located outside the United States, you must report all gains and losses from the sale of that property on your tax return unless it is exempt by U.S. law. This is true whether you reside inside or outside the United States and whether or not you receive a Form 1099 from the payer.

◤ TAXALERT

U.S. citizens are subject to U.S. income tax on their worldwide income, regardless of whether they live in the United States or not. The IRS has significantly increased its scrutiny of offshore income and investments of U.S. citizens. In addition to reporting income from the sale of property located outside of the United States, virtually any kind of income that a U.S. citizen receives or has the right to receive is generally taxable and must be reported on a U.S. tax return. U.S. citizens are also generally required to disclose investments and financial accounts held outside of the United States, even if those assets do not generate current income. If you have overseas income or investments you may be eligible to take a credit on your U.S. return for the related foreign income taxes paid. Furthermore, you may be eligible for benefits under a U.S. tax treaty with the country in which your foreign income arises. Substantial penalties may apply if foreign income and financial interests are not properly reported. If you have foreign income, you should consult your tax advisor to confirm that your foreign interests are reported completely and timely. For more information, see chapter 37, *Other credits including the earned income credit*, and chapter 41, *U.S. citizens working abroad: Tax treatment of foreign earned income*.

This chapter discusses the tax consequences of selling or trading investment property. It explains the following.
- What a sale or trade is.
- Figuring gain or loss.
- Nontaxable trades.
- Related party transactions.
- Capital gains or losses.
- Capital assets and noncapital assets.
- Holding period.
- Rollover of gain from publicly traded securities.

Other property transactions. Certain transfers of property are not discussed here. They are discussed in other IRS publications. These include the following.
- Sales of a main home, covered in chapter 15.
- Installment sales, covered in Publication 537, *Installment Sales*.
- Transactions involving business property, covered in Publication 544, *Sales and Other Dispositions of Assets*.
- Dispositions of an interest in a passive activity, covered in Publication 925, *Passive Activity and At-Risk Rules*.

Publication 550, *Investment Income and Expenses (Including Capital Gains and Losses)*, provides a more detailed discussion about sales and trades of investment property. Publication 550 includes information about the rules covering nonbusiness bad debts, straddles, section 1256 contracts, puts and calls, commodity futures, short sales, and wash sales. It also discusses investment-related expenses.

Useful Items

You may want to see:

Publication

☐ **550** Investment Income and Expenses

Form (and Instructions)

- ☐ **Schedule D (Form 1040)** Capital Gains and Losses
- ☐ **8949** Sales and Other Dispositions of Capital Assets
- ☐ 8824 Like-Kind Exchanges

Sales and Trades

If you sold property such as stocks, bonds, or certain commodities through a broker during the year, you should receive, for each sale, a Form 1099-B, Proceeds From Broker and Barter Exchange Transactions, or an equivalent statement from the broker. You should receive the statement by February 15 of the next year. It will show the gross proceeds from the sale. If shares of corporate stock sold during 2011 were acquired during 2011, the statement will also show the basis and holding period of these shares. The IRS will also get a copy of Form 1099-B from the broker.

Use Form 1099-B (or an equivalent statement received from your broker) to complete Form 8949 and Schedule D (Form 1040).

> ### TAXORGANIZER
> Because of changes made to the rules regarding broker reporting requirements that took effect beginning in 2011, you may receive multiple Forms 1099-B from the same broker for the same account. Generally, you can expect to receive multiple Forms 1099-B if some of the securities you sold were held for more than one year and other securities sold were held for a year or less. Examine carefully the forms you receive. Don't assume that any additional copies of forms received are duplicates or superseded forms. For more information, see chapter 16, *Reporting gains and losses*.

What Is a Sale or Trade?

This section explains what is a sale or trade. It also explains certain transactions and events that are treated as sales or trades.

A sale is generally a transfer of property for money or a mortgage, note, or other promise to pay money.

A trade is a transfer of property for other property or services and may be taxed in the same way as a sale.

Sale and purchase. Ordinarily, a transaction is not a trade when you voluntarily sell property for cash and immediately buy similar property to replace it. The sale and purchase are two separate transactions. But see *Like-kind exchanges* under *Nontaxable Trades*, later.

> ### EXAMPLE
> You sell your car to your brother and buy a new one from a dealer. You have entered into two separate transactions.

Redemption of stock. A redemption of stock is treated as a sale or trade and is subject to the capital gain or loss provisions unless the redemption is a dividend or other distribution on stock.

Dividend versus sale or trade. Whether a redemption is treated as a sale, trade, dividend, or other distribution depends on the circumstances in each case. Both direct and indirect ownership of stock will be considered. The redemption is treated as a sale or trade of stock if:

- The redemption is not essentially equivalent to a dividend (see chapter 8),
- There is a substantially disproportionate redemption of stock,
- There is a complete redemption of all the stock of the corporation owned by the shareholder, or
- The redemption is a distribution in partial liquidation of a corporation.

Redemption or retirement of bonds. A redemption or retirement of bonds or notes at their maturity is generally treated as a sale or trade.

In addition, a significant modification of a bond is treated as a trade of the original bond for a new bond. For details, see Regulations section 1.1001-3.

Nontaxable Exchanges and Like-Kind Exchanges in chapter 13, *Basis of property*.

Installment Sales. Selling property through an installment sale can enable you to spread out the recognition of the tax gain on the sale over a period of years. This may result in a lower overall tax on your realized gain. With an installment sale, you receive part or all of the sales proceeds in one or more years after the year in which you sold the property. You report your gain only as you actually receive the payment, and are taxed only on the portion of each payment that represents your profit from the sale. For more information, see *Installment sales*, later.

Nontaxable Trades: You usually have to pay tax on any gains you realize when you sell or exchange a piece of property. However, the tax law provides a number of specific exceptions to this general rule. Following is a list of exchanges or trades that do not result in a taxable gain (nor trigger a deductible loss):

- *Like-kind exchanges:* an exchange of business or investment property for other business or investment property of a similar nature;
- *Corporate reorganizations:* an exchange of common stock for preferred stock or vice versa, or stock in one corporation for stock in another company as a result of a reorganization of a corporation, such as through a merger, recapitalization, or corporate division or acquisition;
- *Stock for stock of the same corporation:* an exchange of common stock for other common stock or preferred stock for other preferred stock in the same corporation;

- *Convertible stocks and bonds:* a conversion of bonds into stock or preferred stock into common stock of the same corporation in accordance with a conversion privilege that was included in the terms of the bond or the preferred stock certificate; and

- *Property for stock of a controlled corporation:* an exchange of property with a corporation in return for stock in the company, and you control the corporation immediately after the trade.

For more information, see *Nontaxable Trades*, later.

Nontaxable Exchanges of Insurance Policies and Annuities. You will not have to recognize a gain or loss on the exchange of a life insurance contract for another life insurance contract, endowment, or annuity contract, or an annuity contract for another annuity contract, if the insured or annuitant are the same under both contracts. However, starting in 2011, restrictions have changed for certain annuity contract exchanges. For more information, see *Nontaxable Trades: Insurance policies and annuities*, later.

Nonbusiness Bad Debts. If you are owed money, and you can no longer collect on that debt, you may be able to deduct the amount still owed to you as a bad debt. If the debt came about from operating your trade or business, the bad debt deduction is an ordinary loss. A nonbusiness bad debt, on the other hand, can only be deducted as a short-term capital loss. You are entitled to claim a bad debt deduction only in the year the debt becomes totally worthless. That can be tricky to determine. As a result, you should claim the bad debt deduction

Surrender of stock. A surrender of stock by a dominant shareholder who retains ownership of more than half of the corporation's voting shares is treated as a contribution to capital rather than as an immediate loss deductible from taxable income. The surrendering shareholder must reallocate his or her basis in the surrendered shares to the shares he or she retains.

Worthless securities. Stocks, stock rights, and bonds (other than those held for sale by a securities dealer) that became completely worthless during the tax year are treated as though they were sold on the last day of the tax year. This affects whether your capital loss is long term or short term. See *Holding Period*, later.

Worthless securities also include securities that you abandon after March 12, 2008. To abandon a security, you must permanently surrender and relinquish all rights in the security and receive no consideration in exchange for it. All the facts and circumstances determine whether the transaction is properly characterized as an abandonment or other type of transaction, such as an actual sale or exchange, contribution to capital, dividend, or gift.

If you are a cash basis taxpayer and make payments on a negotiable promissory note that you issued for stock that became worthless, you can deduct these payments as losses in the years you actually make the payments. Do not deduct them in the year the stock became worthless.

EXPLANATION
A security is considered worthless when it has no recognizable value. You should be able to establish that the worthless security had value in the year preceding the year in which you take the deduction, and that an identifiable event reduced the value to zero, causing the loss in the year in which you deduct it. A drop in the value of a stock, even though substantial, does not constitute worthlessness. The courts have held that if stock is sold for a very nominal sum (e.g., less than 1 cent per share), that is proof of worthlessness.

TAXPLANNER
The deduction for a worthless security must be taken in the year the security becomes worthless, even if it is sold for a nominal sum in the following year. If you do not learn that a security has become worthless until a later year, you should file an amended return for the year in which it became worthless. Because it may be difficult to determine exactly when a stock becomes worthless, the capital loss deduction should be claimed in the earliest year a claim may be reasonably made.

If you hold securities that seem to be on the verge of worthlessness, it may be easier to sell them now and take your capital loss without waiting for proof of worthlessness. Make sure you sell the securities to an unrelated buyer—otherwise your loss may be disallowed. If you hold shares that are delisted—stock that is removed from a national exchange such as the New York Stock Exchange or NASDAQ (this sometimes happens because the share trading price drops below the minimum price required to continue trading)—you may want to consider abandoning your ownership of the shares, as they may be very difficult to sell. To abandon shares, you must give up your legal right to the shares and receive no remuneration in exchange for giving up that right. You should retain documentation of the shares being removed from your account, as the transaction generates no proceeds and therefore may not be reported on your year-end statements.

When securities are bought on credit, the timing of the deduction for worthlessness depends on the type of debt you have incurred. If the stock is purchased by giving the seller a note and the stock becomes worthless before the note is paid off, you may deduct the loss only as you make the payments on the note. However, if you borrow the funds from a third party, you may deduct the loss in the year in which the stock becomes worthless. In either case, an accrual basis taxpayer takes the deduction in the year the security becomes worthless.

at the earliest time you believe the debt to be worthless. For more information, see _Nonbusiness Bad Debts_, later.

How to report loss. Report worthless securities on Form 8949, Part I, line 1, or Part II, line 3, whichever applies. In columns (d) and (e), enter "Worthless." *Text intentionally omitted.*

Filing a claim for refund. If you do not claim a loss for a worthless security on your original return for the year it becomes worthless, you can file a claim for a credit or refund due to the loss. You must use Form 1040X, *Amended U.S. Individual Income Tax Return*, to amend your return for the year the security became worthless. You must file it within 7 years from the date your original return for that year had to be filed, or 2 years from the date you paid the tax, whichever is later. For more information about filing a claim, see _Amended Returns and Claims for Refund_ in chapter 1.

EXCEPTIONS

While an exchange is generally taxable, the following "exchanges" are not:
- The extension of the maturity date of promissory notes
- The exercise of an option to convert a bond into stock of the issuing corporation, if the conversion privilege is provided for in the bond
- The conversion of security interests to stock in the same corporation subsequent to certain reorganizations (one example: the exchange of common stock for preferred stock)

TAXPLANNER

You may save taxes by carefully planning major sales and exchanges. It may be better to wait until after the end of the year before finalizing a sale so that a gain may be deferred until the next year. Alternatively, you may want to finalize the sale before the end of the year to take advantage of any losses in the current year. Professional advice should be obtained before a major transaction, not after.

Explanation

Estates. The transfer of property of a decedent to the executor or administrator of the estate, or to the heirs or beneficiaries, generally is not a sale or exchange. No taxable gain or deductible loss results from the transfer.

Easements. Granting or selling an easement usually is not a taxable sale of property. Instead, the amount received for the easement is subtracted from the basis of the property. If only a part of an entire tract of property is permanently affected by the easement, only the basis of that part is reduced by the amount received. Any amount received that is more than the basis of the property to be reduced is a taxable gain. The transaction is reported as if it were a sale of the property.

If you transfer a perpetual easement for consideration, the transaction will be treated as a sale of property.

Life estate, etc. The entire amount you realize from disposing of a life interest in property, an interest in property for a set number of years, or an income interest in a trust is a taxable gain if you first got the interest as a gift, inheritance, or transfer in trust. Your basis in the property is considered to be zero. This rule does not apply if all interests in the property are disposed of at the same time.

Example 1

Your father dies, leaving his farm to you for life, with a remainder interest to your younger brother. You decide to sell your life interest in the farm. The entire amount you receive is a taxable gain, and your basis in the farm is disregarded.

Example 2

The facts are the same as in Example 1, except that your younger brother joins you in selling the farm. Because the entire interest in the property is conveyed, your taxable gain is the amount by which your share of the proceeds exceeds your adjusted basis in the farm.

Note: In Example 2, each brother's gain is computed by allocating the tax basis between them. The basis for the entire property—the fair market value at the date of the decedent's death—is adjusted for depreciation and improvements. Then, using actuarial tables, you compute the value of the life interest and of the remainder interest at the date of sale.

The younger brother could sell his remainder interest in the property independently of his brother, using his separate basis in computing his gain or loss on the sale. However, the older brother may not get the benefit of his basis in the property if he sells his life interest separately. The moral of the story is: Sometimes you save on taxes if you get along with your brother.

Sale versus lease. Just because a document says that it is a lease does not necessarily make it a lease for tax purposes. The rules are very complicated and not completely clear. Professional help is advisable. See Publication 544, *Sales and Other Dispositions of Assets*.

Installment sales. Some sales are made under a plan that provides for part or the entire sales price to be paid in a later year. These are called installment sales. If you finance the buyer's purchase of your property instead of the buyer getting a loan or mortgage from a bank, you probably have an installment sale.

You report your gain on an installment sale only as you actually receive payment. You are taxed only on the part of each payment that represents your profit on the sale. In this way, the installment method of reporting income relieves you of paying tax on income that you have not yet collected.

The first step in using the installment method is to find what portion of each installment payment represents a gain. This is determined by calculating the gross profit percentage, which is your gross profit divided by the contract price. Apply this percentage to all payments you receive in a year.

Gross profit is the selling price less the adjusted basis of the property sold. The selling price includes any cash you receive, the fair market value of any property received from the buyer, plus the amount of any existing mortgage on the property that the buyer became subject to or assumed.

Contract price is the selling price less any mortgage encumbrance on the property. However, if the amount of the mortgage is more than the adjusted basis of the property, then the selling price is reduced only by the adjusted basis, so the gross profit percentage is 100%.

Example

In 1991, Martha bought commercial real estate for $100,000. She put $20,000 down and took out a mortgage for $80,000. By 2011, Martha had reduced the mortgage to $40,000 and had an adjusted basis in the real estate of $85,000 (original cost, less depreciation, plus improvements). Martha sold the real estate to Benjamin for $190,000. To pay Martha, Benjamin assumed the rest of the mortgage and made three installment payments of $50,000 each.

Martha figures her gross profit as follows:

Selling price	$190,000
Less: Adjusted tax basis	(85,000)
Gross profit	$105,000
Martha figures her contract price as follows:	
Selling price	$190,000
Less: Mortgage assumed	(40,000)
Contract price	$150,000

Martha's gross profit percentage is 70% (gross profit divided by contract price). Martha must report 70% of all contract-price collections as a taxable gain in the year they are received.

TAXSAVER

Using the installment sale method may spread out your gain over several years and may result in a lower total tax on your gain.

By taking only a portion of the gain into income each year, you may avoid reaching a higher tax bracket. Even if you are already in the highest bracket, use of the installment sale method may still be beneficial, because taxes may be deferred to later years.

A disadvantage of the installment sale method is that if you are the seller, you do not obtain the sale proceeds immediately and therefore cannot reinvest them elsewhere. Also, a special rule applies to installment obligations arising from a sale of real or personal property if you're a non-dealer where the sales price exceeds $150,000. To the extent the total face amount of these obligations arising during any tax year and outstanding at the end of that tax year exceed $5,000,000, interest is payable to the IRS annually on a certain percentage of the deferred tax liability.

TAXSAVER

Installment sale treatment is not obligatory. You may elect not to follow the installment sale rules, in which case your total gain is recognized in the year of the sale.

While it is generally advantageous to defer recognition of a gain or part of a gain by using the installment sale method, under certain circumstances, accelerating recognition may result in overall tax savings. For example, if you expect your income in future years to be much higher than it is now or if you currently have a capital loss that may be offset by a gain, you may want to recognize your gain immediately.

The law limits the ability to defer tax by restricting use of the installment sale method to certain kinds of property. For example, the installment sale method may not be used for sales of publicly traded stocks or securities. However, you may sell other types of property, such as real property used in your business or for rental, under an installment sale and still defer the tax on the gain.

If you decide not to use the installment sale reporting method, indicate this decision by reporting the full transaction sales price on either Form 8949 and Schedule D (Form 1040) or Form 4797 by the date your tax return for the year of the sale is due. (Form 8949 and Schedule D are used to report sales of capital assets. Form 4797 is used to report sales of trade or business property and other noncapital assets.) Once you decide not to use the installment sale method, you may change your decision only with the consent of the IRS.

If you choose not to use the installment method and you are a cash basis taxpayer, remember that you may discount (reduce the stated value of) any installment payments that you are to receive at a later date. Therefore, the total gain on the sale you report should be discounted because you do not receive the total payment at the time of the sale.

TAXALERT

Sales at a loss do not qualify for installment sale reporting. Also, sales by dealers or by persons who regularly sell personal property on the installment basis no longer qualify for the installment method.

Explanation

The gain you have from an installment sale will be treated as capital gain if the property you sold was a capital asset (discussed later). However, if you took depreciation deductions on the assets, including the section 179 deduction, part of your gain may be treated as ordinary income.

Example

On January 31, 2011, Susan sells property for $4,000 on which she has a $1,000 gain. Half of the gain is taxable at ordinary rates.

If Susan receives the initial $2,000 payment in 2011, she is receiving one-half the proceeds and must report one-half of the gain, or $500. Because the ordinary income portion must be reported first, the entire $500 is treated as an ordinary gain. When Susan receives the second $2,000 payment, she reports the second half of the gain, $500, as a capital gain.

Explanation

Any depreciation claimed on personal property must be recaptured as ordinary income in the year of sale, even if there are no payments received in the year of sale. The depreciation recapture for real property is generally limited to the amount by which the depreciation claimed exceeds the amount available under the straight-line method of depreciation. The adjusted basis of the property being sold is increased by the amount of recaptured income that you include in your gross income in the year of sale so that the gain recognized in future years is decreased.

Example

Sam sells tangible personal property to Betty in 2011 for $100,000 to be paid in installments over 5 years, beginning in 2011. Interest is payable at market rates. The property was originally purchased for $30,000. Because of depreciation, it has an adjusted basis of $20,000. There is a gain of $80,000 ($100,000 – $20,000), of which $10,000 is recaptured income to be reported on Sam's 2011 return.

The $10,000 that is included in Sam's income in the year of sale is added to the $20,000 adjusted basis to figure how much income Sam must report using the installment method. Therefore, Sam's gross profit is $70,000 ($100,000 – $30,000). Sam's gross profit percentage is 70%.

On each of the $20,000 payments that Sam receives from 2011 through 2015, $14,000 would be included in his income ($20,000 × 70%).

Explanation

The installment sale rules contain a number of very important limitations.

Sales to a spouse or an 80% controlled entity. If you sell depreciable property to your spouse or to a partnership or corporation of which you own 80% or more, you must report all of the gain in the year of the sale, despite any installment payment schedules set up under the sale agreement. The same rule may also apply to the sale of property to a trust of which you (or your spouse) are a beneficiary.

Sales to other relatives. If you sell property, other than marketable securities, to a related person on an installment basis and that person resells (or makes a gift of) the property within 2 years, you have to recognize any additional gain in the year of the resale.

If you sell marketable securities to a related person and that person resells the property, you have to recognize any additional gain, unless the sale takes place after you have received all the installment payments due to you. There is no 2-year cutoff date as with other kinds of property, noted earlier. See the special rules regarding publicly traded property, below.

A related person includes your spouse, children, grandchildren, brothers and sisters, and parents. A related person is also any partnership in which you are a partner, any estates and trusts of which you are a beneficiary, any grantor trusts of which you are treated as an owner, and any corporation in which you own at least half of the total value of the stock.

The normal 3-year statute of limitations for tax assessments by the IRS is extended for resales of installment property by a related person. In these cases, the statute of limitations will not expire until 2 years after you report to the IRS that a resale took place.

Nontaxable trades. Special rules apply to the exchange of like-kind property, which is tax-free. However, property that is not like-kind included in the exchange is taxable. The installment method may be used for the property that is not like-kind.

Like-kind exchanges. For like-kind exchanges involving related parties, both parties must hold the property for more than 2 years for the original exchange to qualify as tax-free. This rule is applicable to both parties to the transaction, even though only one party avails himself or herself of like-kind treatment. Also, real property located in the United States and real property located outside the United States does not qualify as property of a like kind.

Disposing of installment obligations. If you sell property on an installment basis and then later dispose of the installment note, you may have to report a gain or a loss. Generally, the amount of your gain or loss is equal to the difference between your basis in the installment note and the amount you receive when you dispose of the note.

Example

Toni sells real estate on an installment basis for a $200,000 note receivable and has a $120,000 gross profit from the sale. After she collects $100,000 (and reports a profit of $60,000, half her gross profit), she sells the remaining $100,000 note receivable to a bank for $95,000. Toni reports a $55,000 profit in the year of the sale of the note (the remaining $60,000 of gross profit less the $5,000 loss on the sale of the note).

Explanation

A disposition for this purpose is not limited to a sale of the installment note. For example, if you make a sale of property after December 31, 1988, for more than $150,000, and you assign the installment obligation as collateral security for a loan, the IRS will treat this as a disposition. This is because you would have deferred the gain on the sale while obtaining the use of the money through a loan.

Publicly traded property. The installment method cannot be used for sales of publicly traded property, including stock or securities that are traded on an established securities market.

Repossessing property sold under the installment method. If you sell property on an installment plan, you may have to repossess it if, for example, the buyer defaults on his or her obligation. When repossession takes place, you may have to report a gain or a loss. You follow different rules for determining your gain or loss, depending on whether the property being repossessed is personal property or real property.

Personal property. If you repossess personal property sold under an installment plan, you must compare the fair market value of the property recovered with your basis in the installment notes plus any expenses you had in connection with repossession. Under the installment method, your basis is the face value of the note still outstanding less the amount of unreported profit on the original sale. (If you did not use the installment reporting method, your basis is the value of the property at the time of the original sale less payments of principal received to date.)

Your gain or loss is of the same character (short term or long term) as the gain or loss realized on the original sale if you used the installment method. If you did not, any gain resulting from repossession is treated as **ordinary income**. Any loss is an ordinary loss if the property is business property. If it is nonbusiness property, any loss resulting from repossession is treated as a short-term capital loss.

Real property. If you have to repossess your former residence because the buyer defaults and you excluded the gain (see chapter 15, *Selling your home*, for details), no gain or loss is recognized if you resell the house within 1 year of repossession. If the property is not resold within 1 year, you may have to recognize the gain. The amount of tax you may have to pay on the gain will depend on whether the house you repossessed was originally sold before, on, or after May 6, 1997. For houses sold before May 7, 1997, $125,000 of the gain could have been excluded or the gain could have been deferred by acquiring a replacement home. For houses sold after May 6, 1997, up to $250,000 or $500,000 of the gain may be excluded (see chapter 15, *Selling your home,* for more information). You may never deduct a loss on repossession because you may not deduct losses on property used primarily for personal purposes.

Computing your gain or loss on repossessed real property. Generally, your gain or loss on property that you have repossessed equals (1) the total amount of payments you have received under the installment sale minus (2) the amount of taxable gain you have already reported on the installment sale.

The gain you report on the repossessed property is limited, however, to the gross profit you expected on the installment sale less repossession costs and the amount of taxable gain you have already reported on the installment sale. Your basis in the repossessed property is your adjusted basis at the time of the original sale less deferred gain on repossession.

Example

Linda Smith sold a building that was not her personal residence to Ann Carter in 2006 for $100,000, payable in 10 annual installments. Linda's basis in the building was $70,000, and no mortgage was outstanding. The expected gross profit in the sale was $30,000, and the gross profit percentage was 30%.

In 2011, Ann failed to pay the sixth installment. By then, Linda had recognized $15,000 of gain from the $50,000 in payments received. She repossessed the building, incurring legal fees of $1,000 in the process. Linda's gain is computed as follows:

Gain	
Payments received	$50,000
Less: Taxable gain already reported on sale	(15,000)
Gain subject to limitation	$35,000

Limitation on gain	
Gross profit expected on installment sale	$30,000
Less: Repossession costs	(1,000)
Less: Taxable gain already reported on sale	(15,000)
Limitation	$14,000

Linda must report a $14,000 gain on repossession. Her basis in the reacquired building is $49,000, figured by taking $70,000 (her original adjusted basis) and subtracting $21,000 ($35,000 – $14,000), the amount of gain on repossession unrecognized because of the limitation on gain.

TAXPLANNER

Computing interest on installment sales. Special rules may apply regarding the amount of interest to be recognized on installment sales of more than $3,000.

If the amount of interest is not specifically stated in the sales agreement or if the stated interest is at an unrealistically low rate, you must calculate unstated or imputed interest. In general, you have unstated interest if (1) the sum of all payments due more than 6 months after the date of sale exceeds (2) the present value of such payments and the present value of any interest payment provided for in the contract. Present value is determined by using a so-called testing rate compounded semiannually. If there is unstated interest, you are required to impute interest using the testing rate.

The testing rate is calculated by using the applicable federal rate (AFR). The AFR is based on average market yields of U.S. obligations. The AFR may be the short-, medium-, or long-term rate that U.S. obligations are yielding, depending on the length of the contract. If unstated interest results using the testing rate, then interest must be computed using the testing rate, compounded semiannually.

How To Figure Gain or Loss

You figure gain or loss on a sale or trade of property by comparing the amount you realize with the adjusted basis of the property.

Gain. If the amount you realize from a sale or trade is more than the adjusted basis of the property you transfer, the difference is a gain.

Loss. If the adjusted basis of the property you transfer is more than the amount you realize, the difference is a loss.

Adjusted basis. The adjusted basis of property is your original cost or other original basis properly adjusted (increased or decreased) for certain items. See chapter 13 for more information about determining the adjusted basis of property.

Amount realized. The amount you realize from a sale or trade of property is everything you receive for the property minus your expenses of sale (such as redemption fees, sales commissions, sales charges, or exit fees). Amount realized includes the money you receive plus the fair market value of any property or services you receive. If you received a note or other debt instrument for the property, see *How To Figure Gain or Loss* in chapter 4 of Publication 550 to figure the amount realized.

If you finance the buyer's purchase of your property and the debt instrument does not provide for adequate stated interest, the unstated interest that you must report as ordinary income will reduce the amount realized from the sale. For more information, see Publication 537.

Fair market value. Fair market value is the price at which the property would change hands between a buyer and a seller, neither being forced to buy or sell and both having reasonable knowledge of all the relevant facts.

Example. You trade A Company stock with an adjusted basis of $7,000 for B Company stock with a fair market value of $10,000, which is your amount realized. Your gain is $3,000 ($10,000 − $7,000).

TAXPLANNER

An appraisal by a qualified person is usually accepted by both the courts and the IRS as the fair market value. The appraiser should be familiar with valuation methods accepted in the particular field (real estate, art objects, equipment and machinery, etc.). For real estate, a local appraiser is better qualified than an out-of-towner. In other fields, prior experience in the field is more important. It may be prudent to obtain an appraisal at the date of the transaction, just in case it is needed later. In general, the more unique (like an original piece of artwork) or infrequently sold (like shares of stock in a closely held corporation) an item is, the more important it is to get a professional appraisal at the date of the transaction. It is also important to obtain a professional appraisal if an item is being sold between related parties.

TAXORGANIZER

You should keep a copy of your appraisal report of any property sold in order to verify its value.

Debt paid off. A debt against the property, or against you, that is paid off as a part of the transaction, or that is assumed by the buyer, must be included in the amount realized. This is true even if neither you nor the buyer is personally liable for the debt. For example, if you sell or trade property that is subject to a nonrecourse loan, the amount you realize generally includes the full amount of the note assumed by the buyer even if the amount of the note is more than the fair market value of the property.

Example. You sell stock that you had pledged as security for a bank loan of $8,000. Your basis in the stock is $6,000. The buyer pays off your bank loan and pays you $20,000 in cash. The amount realized is $28,000 ($20,000 + $8,000). Your gain is $22,000 ($28,000 − $6,000).

EXAMPLE

You sell property and the buyer pays you $20,000 cash and assumes an existing mortgage on the property of $8,000. You bought the property for $6,000 and added improvements costing $10,000. Your selling expenses were $1,400. Your gain on the sale is computed:

Amount realized		
Cash	$20,000	
Mortgage assumed by buyer	8,000	$28,000
Minus: Adjusted basis		
Cost	$ 6,000	
Improvements	10,000	
Total	$16,000	
Plus: Selling expenses	1,400	($17,400)
Gain		$10,600

Payment of cash. If you trade property and cash for other property, the amount you realize is the fair market value of the property you receive. Determine your gain or loss by subtracting the cash you pay plus the adjusted basis of the property you trade in from the amount you realize. If the result is a positive number, it is a gain. If the result is a negative number, it is a loss.

No gain or loss. You may have to use a basis for figuring gain that is different from the basis used for figuring loss. In this case, you may have neither a gain nor a loss. See *Basis Other Than Cost* in chapter 13.

Nontaxable Trades

This section discusses trades that generally do not result in a taxable gain or deductible loss. For more information on nontaxable trades, see chapter 1 of Publication 544.

Like-kind exchanges. If you trade business or investment property for other business or investment property of a like kind, you do not pay tax on any gain or deduct any loss until you sell or dispose of the property you receive. To be nontaxable, a trade must meet all six of the following conditions.

1. The property must be business or investment property. You must hold both the property you trade and the property you receive for productive use in your trade or business or for investment. Neither property may be property used for personal purposes, such as your home or family car.

2. The property must not be held primarily for sale. The property you trade and the property you receive must not be property you sell to customers, such as merchandise.
3. The property must not be stocks, bonds, notes, choses in action, certificates of trust or beneficial interest, or other securities or evidences of indebtedness or interest, including partnership interests. However, see *Special rules for mutual ditch, reservoir, or irrigation company stock*, in chapter 4 of Publication 550 for an exception. Also, you can have a non-taxable trade of corporate stocks under a different rule, as discussed later.
4. There must be a trade of like property. The trade of real estate for real estate, or personal property for similar personal property, is a trade of like property. The trade of an apartment house for a store building, or a panel truck for a pickup truck, is a trade of like property. The trade of a piece of machinery for a store building is not a trade of like property. Real property located in the United States and real property located outside the United States are not like property. Also, personal property used predominantly within the United States and personal property used predominantly outside the United States are not like property.
5. The property to be received must be identified in writing within 45 days after the date you transfer the property given up in the trade.
6. The property to be received must be received by the earlier of:
   a. The 180th day after the date on which you transfer the property given up in the trade, or
   b. The due date, including extensions, for your tax return for the year in which the transfer of the property given up occurs.

EXPLANATION
The term *like kind* refers to a property's nature or character, not its grade or quality. With real estate, for example, whether or not it has been improved is a factor that affects only grade or quality, not its nature. Property held for productive use in a trade or a business may be exchanged for property held for investment.

Examples
Like-kind exchanges include the following:
- Improved for unimproved real estate when exchanged by a person who does not deal in real estate
- A used car for a new one to be used for the same purpose.

The following are *not* considered like-kind exchanges:
- Personal property (such as a boat) for real property
- Gold numismatic coins for gold bullion (the IRS ruled that an investment in gold coins was an investment in the coins themselves, while the investment in bullion was an investment in the world gold market)
- Gold bullion for silver bullion
- Male livestock for female livestock

TAXALERT
Depreciable, tangible personal property may be exchanged for either like-kind or like-class property and may qualify for **like-kind exchange treatment**. Like-class properties are depreciable, tangible personal properties within the same "general asset classes" as defined in the Standard Industrial Classification Manual (see Publication 544, *Sales and Other Dispositions of Assets*).
You are not required to make a property-by-property comparison if you:
1. Separate the properties into two or more exchange groups, or
2. Transfer or receive more than one property within a single exchange group.

If you trade property with a related party in a like-kind exchange, a special rule may apply. See *Related Party Transactions*, later in this chapter. Also, see chapter 1 of Publication 544 for more information on exchanges of business property and special rules for exchanges using qualified intermediaries or involving multiple properties.

Partly nontaxable exchange. If you receive money or unlike property in addition to like property, and the above six conditions are met, you have a partly nontaxable trade. You are taxed on any gain you realize, but only up to the amount of the money and the fair market value of the unlike property you receive. You cannot deduct a loss.

Like property and unlike property transferred. If you give up unlike property in addition to the like property, you must recognize gain or loss on the unlike property you give up. The gain or loss is the difference between the adjusted basis of the unlike property and its fair market value.

Like property and money transferred. If conditions (1) – (6) are met, you have a nontaxable trade even if you pay money in addition to the like property.

Basis of property received. To figure the basis of the property received, see *Nontaxable Exchanges* in chapter 13.

How to report. You must report the trade of like property on Form 8824. If you figure a recognized gain or loss on Form 8824, report it on Schedule D (Form 1040), or on Form 4797, Sales of Business Property, whichever applies.

For information on using Form 4797, see chapter 4 of Publication 544.

a. Mortgage, deed of trust, or other security interest in property
   b. Standby letter of credit meeting certain specifications and a guarantee of a third party
2. You may not have an immediate ability or unrestricted right to receive, pledge, borrow, or otherwise obtain the benefits of the cash or cash equivalent held in an escrow account or qualified trust. However, the replacement property may be secured by cash or a cash equivalent if the cash or cash equivalent is held in a qualified escrow account or in a qualified trust.
3. You may not have an immediate ability or unrestricted right to receive, pledge, borrow, or otherwise obtain the benefits of money or other property held by a qualified intermediary. However, you may use a qualified intermediary in a deferred exchange if the qualified intermediary is unrelated to you (see the IRS final regulations for details). A qualified intermediary may be an escrow or title company.

   More than one IRS guideline can be used in the same deferred exchange, but the terms and conditions of each must be separately satisfied. You should consult your tax advisor if you are contemplating a like-kind exchange.

Corporate stocks. The following trades of corporate stocks generally do not result in a taxable gain or a deductible loss.

Corporate reorganizations. In some instances, a company will give you common stock for preferred stock, preferred stock for common stock, or stock in one corporation for stock in another corporation. If this is a result of a merger, recapitalization, transfer to a controlled corporation, bankruptcy, corporate division, corporate acquisition, or other corporate reorganization, you do not recognize gain or loss.

Stock for stock of the same corporation. You can exchange common stock for common stock or preferred stock for preferred stock in the same corporation without having a recognized gain or loss. This is true for a trade between two stockholders as well as a trade between a stockholder and the corporation.

Convertible stocks and bonds. You generally will not have a recognized gain or loss if you convert bonds into stock or preferred stock into common stock of the same corporation according to a conversion privilege in the terms of the bond or the preferred stock certificate.

Property for stock of a controlled corporation. If you transfer property to a corporation solely in exchange for stock in that corporation, and immediately after the trade you are in control of the corporation, you ordinarily will not recognize a gain or loss. This rule applies both to individuals and to groups who transfer property to a corporation. It does not apply if the corporation is an investment company.

For this purpose, to be in control of a corporation, you or your group of transferors must own, immediately after the exchange, at least 80% of the total combined voting power of all classes of stock entitled to vote and at least 80% of the outstanding shares of each class of non-voting stock of the corporation.

If this provision applies to you, you may have to attach to your return a complete statement of all facts pertinent to the exchange. For details, see Regulations section 1.351-3.

Additional information. For more information on trades of stock, see *Nontaxable Trades* in chapter 4 of Publication 550.

EXPLANATION
The statement must include the following information:
- A description of the property transferred, with its cost or other basis
- The kind of stock received, including the number of shares and fair market value
- The principal amount and fair market value of any securities received
- The amount of money received, if any
- A description of any liabilities assumed by the corporation in the transaction, including the corporate business reason for the assumption

Generally, when you transfer property to a corporation that you alone will control in exchange for its stock, no gain or loss is recognized. "Control" means that you or your group of investors owns at least 80% of the outstanding voting stock and at least 80% of the shares of all other classes of outstanding stock. However, if you receive property other than stock, then you may have to recognize a gain equal to that additional property's value. Moreover, if the property you transfer to the corporation has been depreciated, all or a portion of your gain may be ordinary income rather than a capital gain.

Insurance policies and annuities. You will not have a recognized gain or loss if the insured or annuitant is the same under both contracts and you trade:

- A life insurance contract for another life insurance contract or for an endowment or annuity contract or for a qualified long-term care insurance contract,
- An endowment contract for another endowment contract that provides for regular payments beginning at a date no later than the beginning date under the old contract or for an annuity contract or for a qualified long-term insurance contract,
- An annuity contract for annuity contract or for a qualified long-term care insurance contract, or
- A qualified long-term care insurance contract for a qualified long-term care insurance contract.

You also may not have to recognize gain or loss on an exchange of a portion of an annuity contract for another annuity contract. See Revenue Ruling 2003-76 in Internal Revenue Bulletin 2003-33 and Revenue Procedure 2011-38 in Internal Revenue Bulletin 2011-30. Revenue Ruling 2003-76 is available at *www.irs.gov/irb/2003-33_IRB/ar11.html*. Revenue Procedure 2011-38 is available at *http://www.irs.gov/irb/2011-30_IRB/ar09.html*.

Exchanges of contracts not included in this list, such as an annuity contract for an endowment contract, or an annuity or endowment contract for a life insurance contract, are taxable.

Demutualization of life insurance companies. If you received stock in exchange for your equity interest as a policyholder or an annuitant, you generally will not have a recognized gain or loss. See *Demutualization of Life Insurance Companies* in Publication 550.

U.S. Treasury notes or bonds. You can trade certain issues of U.S. Treasury obligations for other issues designated by the Secretary of the Treasury, with no gain or loss recognized on the trade. See the discussion in chapter 1 of Publication 550 for more information.

Transfers Between Spouses

Generally, no gain or loss is recognized on a transfer of property from an individual to (or in trust for the benefit of) a spouse, or if incident to a divorce, a former spouse. This nonrecognition rule does not apply in the following situations.

- The recipient spouse or former spouse is a nonresident alien.
- Property is transferred in trust. Gain must be recognized to the extent the amount of the liabilities assumed by the trust, plus any liabilities on the property, exceed the adjusted basis of the property.

For other situations, see Publication 550, chapter 4.

Any transfer of property to a spouse or former spouse on which gain or loss is not recognized is treated by the recipient as a gift and is not considered a sale or exchange. The recipient's basis in the property will be the same as the adjusted basis of the giver immediately before the transfer. This carryover basis rule applies whether the adjusted basis of the transferred property is less than, equal to, or greater than either its fair market value at the time of transfer or any consideration paid by the recipient. This rule applies for purposes of determining loss as well as gain. Any gain recognized on a transfer in trust increases the basis.

A transfer of property is incident to a divorce if the transfer occurs within 1 year after the date on which the marriage ends, or if the transfer is related to the ending of the marriage.

EXPLANATION

For transfers of property incident to divorce to a former spouse who is a nonresident alien, gain or loss may be recognized to the spouse who transferred the property based on the fair market value of the property transferred.

Related Party Transactions

Special rules apply to the sale or trade of property between related parties.

TAXPLANNER

Special rules are imposed on taxpayers who try to avoid taxation on property gains by passing the property on to a trust. A special tax is imposed on a trust when the trust sells appreciated property within 2 years of having received it. The property may have been acquired by gift, through a bargain purchase, or as a transfer from another trust. The trust's gain is taxed at the highest rate that the donor of the property would have had to pay had he or she reported the gain on the sale in the same year in which the trust did.

Exception

This special tax is not imposed on a sale or an exchange that occurs within 2 years of the transfer of property if the sale or exchange takes place after the death of the donor of the property.

The purpose of the special tax is to prevent the grantor from taking advantage of a lower tax bracket in a trust. The law assumes, except in the case of death, that if the property is sold within 2 years, this was the plan all along.

Gain on sale or trade of depreciable property. Your gain from the sale or trade of property to a related party may be ordinary income, rather than capital gain, if the property can be depreciated by the party receiving it. See chapter 3 of Publication 544 for more information.

Like-kind exchanges. Generally, if you trade business or investment property for other business or investment property of a like kind, no gain or loss is recognized. See *Like-kind exchanges* earlier under *Nontaxable Trades.*

This rule also applies to trades of property between related parties, defined next under *Losses on sales or trades of property.* However, if either you or the related party disposes of the like property within 2 years after the trade, you both must report any gain or loss not recognized on the original trade on your return filed for the year in which the later disposition occurs. See Publication 550, chapter 4, for exceptions.

Losses on sales or trades of property. You cannot deduct a loss on the sale or trade of property, other than a distribution in complete liquidation of a corporation, if the transaction is directly or indirectly between you and the following related parties.
- Members of your family. This includes only your brothers and sisters, half-brothers and half-sisters, spouse, ancestors (parents, grandparents, etc.), and lineal descendants (children, grandchildren, etc.).
- A partnership in which you directly or indirectly own more than 50% of the capital interest or the profits interest.

- A corporation in which you directly or indirectly own more than 50% in value of the outstanding stock. (See *Constructive ownership of stock*, later.)
- A tax-exempt charitable or educational organization directly or indirectly controlled, in any manner or by any method, by you or by a member of your family, whether or not this control is legally enforceable.

In addition, a loss on the sale or trade of property is not deductible if the transaction is directly or indirectly between the following related parties.

- A grantor and fiduciary, or the fiduciary and beneficiary, of any trust.
- Fiduciaries of two different trusts, or the fiduciary and beneficiary of two different trusts, if the same person is the grantor of both trusts.
- A trust fiduciary and a corporation of which more than 50% in value of the outstanding stock is directly or indirectly owned by or for the trust, or by or for the grantor of the trust.
- A corporation and a partnership if the same persons own more than 50% in value of the outstanding stock of the corporation and more than 50% of the capital interest, or the profits interest, in the partnership.
- Two S corporations if the same persons own more than 50% in value of the outstanding stock of each corporation.
- Two corporations, one of which is an S corporation, if the same persons own more than 50% in value of the outstanding stock of each corporation.
- An executor and a beneficiary of an estate (except in the case of a sale or trade to satisfy a pecuniary bequest).
- Two corporations that are members of the same controlled group. (Under certain conditions, however, these losses are not disallowed but must be deferred.)
- Two partnerships if the same persons own, directly or indirectly, more than 50% of the capital interests or the profit interests in both partnerships.

Multiple property sales or trades. If you sell or trade to a related party a number of blocks of stock or pieces of property in a lump sum, you must figure the gain or loss separately for each block of stock or piece of property. The gain on each item may be taxable. However, you cannot deduct the loss on any item. Also, you cannot reduce gains from the sales of any of these items by losses on the sales of any of the other items.

Indirect transactions. You cannot deduct your loss on the sale of stock through your broker if, under a prearranged plan, a related party buys the same stock you had owned. This does not apply to a trade between related parties through an exchange that is purely coincidental and is not prearranged.

Constructive ownership of stock. In determining whether a person directly or indirectly owns any of the outstanding stock of a corporation, the following rules apply.

Rule 1. Stock directly or indirectly owned by or for a corporation, partnership, estate, or trust is considered owned proportionately by or for its shareholders, partners, or beneficiaries.

Rule 2. An individual is considered to own the stock directly or indirectly owned by or for his or her family. Family includes only brothers and sisters, half-brothers and half-sisters, spouse, ancestors, and lineal descendants.

Rule 3. An individual owning, other than by applying rule 2, any stock in a corporation is considered to own the stock directly or indirectly owned by or for his or her partner.

Rule 4. When applying rule 1, 2, or 3, stock constructively owned by a person under rule 1 is treated as actually owned by that person. But stock constructively owned by an individual under rule 2 or rule 3 is not treated as owned by that individual for again applying either rule 2 or rule 3 to make another person the constructive owner of the stock.

Property received from a related party. If you sell or trade at a gain property you acquired from a related party, you recognize the gain only to the extent it is more than the loss previously disallowed to the related party. This rule applies only if you are the original transferee and you acquired the property by purchase or exchange. This rule does not apply if the related party's loss was disallowed because of the wash sale rules described in chapter 4 of Publication 550 under *Wash Sales*.

If you sell or trade at a loss property you acquired from a related party, you cannot recognize the loss that was not allowed to the related party.

Example 1. Your brother sells you stock for $7,600. His cost basis is $10,000. Your brother cannot deduct the loss of $2,400. Later, you sell the same stock to an unrelated party for $10,500, realizing a gain of $2,900. Your reportable gain is $500 (the $2,900 gain minus the $2,400 loss not allowed to your brother).

Example 2. If, in *Example 1*, you sold the stock for $6,900 instead of $10,500, your recognized loss is only $700 (your $7,600 basis minus $6,900). You cannot deduct the loss that was not allowed to your brother.

> ## EXPLANATION
> Transactions between a trust and the relative of a trust beneficiary may be indirect related-party transactions. Similarly, the sale of stock by one spouse followed by the purchase by the other spouse of an equal number of the same corporation's shares is an indirect sale between related parties, even though both spouses deal through brokers on the New York Stock Exchange. However, if there is a significant time lapse between the two transactions—a month or more—the transactions are not considered linked.

Capital Gains and Losses

This section discusses the tax treatment of gains and losses from different types of investment transactions.

Character of gain or loss. You need to classify your gains and losses as either ordinary or capital gains or losses. You then need to classify your capital gains and losses as either short term or long term. If you have long-term gains and losses, you must identify your 28% rate gains and losses. If you have a net capital gain, you must also identify any unrecaptured section 1250 gain.

The correct classification and identification helps you figure the limit on capital losses and the correct tax on capital gains. Reporting capital gains and losses is explained in chapter 16.

Capital or Ordinary Gain or Loss

If you have a taxable gain or a deductible loss from a transaction, it may be either a capital gain or loss or an ordinary gain or loss, depending on the circumstances. Generally, a sale or trade of a capital asset (defined next) results in a capital gain or loss. A sale or trade of a noncapital asset generally results in ordinary gain or loss. Depending on the circumstances, a gain or loss on a sale or trade of property used in a trade or business may be treated as either capital or ordinary, as explained in Publication 544. In some situations, part of your gain or loss may be a capital gain or loss and part may be an ordinary gain or loss.

Capital Assets and Noncapital Assets

For the most part, everything you own and use for personal purposes, pleasure, or investment is a capital asset. Some examples are:
- Stocks or bonds held in your personal account,
- A house owned and used by you and your family,
- Household furnishings,
- A car used for pleasure or commuting,
- Coin or stamp collections,
- Gems and jewelry, and
- Gold, silver, or any other metal.

> ## EXAMPLE
> You bought a car for personal use and later sold it for less than you paid for it. The loss is not deductible. However, if you had sold it for more than you paid for it, the gain would be taxable. A loss would be deductible only if, or to the extent that, the car was used for business. If the car had been stolen, you would have had a theft loss.
> *Note:* In determining the amount of the loss, what you paid for the car would have to be reduced by any depreciation allowed as a deduction. This would reduce the amount of the loss you could claim.
>
> ### Explanation
> While losses on personal property generally are not deductible, losses associated with a trade or a business may be. However, property originally held for personal use may be converted to business use under certain circumstances (and vice versa). There are very few court cases in this area, and those that exist do not provide much guidance about how long property must be rented before it is considered converted to business use. Each case depends on the specific facts and circumstances. In general, if a residence has been rented for a period of years, there is strong evidence that it has been converted to rental property.

Any property you own is a capital asset, except the following noncapital assets.

1. Property held mainly for sale to customers or property that will physically become a part of the merchandise for sale to customers. For an exception, see *Capital Asset Treatment for Self-Created Musical Works* later.
2. Depreciable property used in your trade or business, even if fully depreciated.
3. Real property used in your trade or business.
4. A copyright, a literary, musical, or artistic composition, a letter or memorandum, or similar property that is:
   a. Created by your personal efforts,
   b. Prepared or produced for you (in the case of a letter, memorandum, or similar property), or
   c. Acquired under circumstances (for example, by gift) entitling you to the basis of the person who created the property or for whom it was prepared or produced.

For an exception to this rule, see *Capital Asset Treatment for Self-Created Musical Works* later.

5. Accounts or notes receivable acquired in the ordinary course of a trade or business for services rendered or from the sale of property described in (1).
6. U.S. Government publications that you received from the government free or for less than the normal sales price, or that you acquired under circumstances entitling you to the basis of someone who received the publications free or for less than the normal sales price.
7. Certain commodities derivative financial instruments held by commodities derivatives dealers.
8. Hedging transactions, but only if the transaction is clearly identified as a hedging transaction before the close of the day on which it was acquired, originated, or entered into.
9. Supplies of a type you regularly use or consume in the ordinary course of your trade or business.

Investment Property

Investment property is a capital asset. Any gain or loss from its sale or trade is generally a capital gain or loss.

Gold, silver, stamps, coins, gems, etc. These are capital assets except when they are held for sale by a dealer. Any gain or loss you have from their sale or trade generally is a capital gain or loss.

TAXPLANNER

If you collect gold, silver, stamps, antiques, and the like, you should be aware that losses from the sale or trade of such property generally are not deductible. In order to claim a loss, you must be able to show that your primary purpose in collecting the property was to make a profit. Furthermore, you must show that you were not collecting the items purely as a hobby or for personal enjoyment. Obviously, there may be a very fine line between a hobby and a profit-making activity.

Example

The Tax Court did not allow a taxpayer to deduct a loss on the sale of antiques he used to furnish his home. The taxpayer argued that he was speculating on large increases in the value of the antiques. The Tax Court emphasized his personal use of the antiques and noted that most of the taxpayer's sales of antiques were merely a means of financing the acquisition of more antiques.

Stocks, stock rights, and bonds. All of these (including stock received as a dividend) are capital assets except when held for sale by a securities dealer. However, if you own small business stock, see *Losses on Section 1244 (Small Business) Stock* and *Losses on Small Business Investment Company Stock* in chapter 4 of Publication 550.

Personal Use Property

Property held for personal use only, rather than for investment, is a capital asset, and you must report a gain from its sale as a capital gain. However, you cannot deduct a loss from selling personal use property.

Capital Asset Treatment for Self-Created Musical Works

You can elect to treat musical compositions and copyrights in musical works as capital assets when you sell or exchange them if:

- Your personal efforts created the property, or
- You acquired the property under circumstances (for example, by gift) entitling you to the basis of the person who created the property or for whom it was prepared or produced.

You must make a separate election for each musical composition (or copyright in a musical work) sold or exchanged during the tax year. You must make the election on or before the due date (including extensions) of the income tax return for the tax year of the sale or exchange. You must make the election on Schedule D (Form 1040) by treating the sale or exchange as the sale or exchange of a capital asset, according to Schedule D and its instructions.

You can revoke the election if you have IRS approval. To get IRS approval, you must submit a request for a letter ruling under the appropriate IRS revenue procedure. See, for example, Rev. Proc. 20011-1, 201-1 I.R.B. 1, available at *http://www.irs.gov/irb/2011-01_IRB/ar06.html*. Alternatively, you are granted an automatic 6-month extension from the due date of your income tax return (excluding extensions) to revoke the election, provided you timely file your income tax return, and within this 6-month extension period, you file Form 1040X that treats the sale or exchange as the sale or exchange of property that is not a capital asset.

Discounted Debt Instruments

Treat your gain or loss on the sale, redemption, or retirement of a bond or other debt instrument originally issued at a discount or bought at a discount as capital gain or loss, except as explained in the following discussions.

Short-term government obligations. Treat gains on short-term federal, state, or local government obligations (other than tax-exempt obligations) as ordinary income up to your ratable share of the acquisition discount. This treatment applies to obligations with a fixed maturity date not more than 1 year from the date of issue. Acquisition discount is the stated redemption price at maturity minus your basis in the obligation.

However, do not treat these gains as income to the extent you previously included the discount in income. See *Discount on Short-Term Obligations* in chapter 1 of Publication 550.

Short-term nongovernment obligations. Treat gains on short-term nongovernment obligations as ordinary income up to your ratable share of original issue discount (OID). This treatment applies to obligations with a fixed maturity date of not more than 1 year from the date of issue.

However, to the extent you previously included the discount in income, you do not have to include it in income again. See *Discount on Short-Term Obligations* in chapter 1 of Publication 550.

Tax-exempt state and local government bonds. If these bonds were originally issued at a discount before September 4, 1982, or you acquired them before March 2, 1984, treat your part of OID as tax-exempt interest. To figure your gain or loss on the sale or trade of these bonds, reduce the amount realized by your part of OID.

If the bonds were issued after September 3, 1982, and acquired after March 1, 1984, increase the adjusted basis by your part of OID to figure gain or loss. For more information on the basis of these bonds, see *Discounted Debt Instruments* in chapter 4 of Publication 550.

> ### EXAMPLE
> On March 1, 1997, Kathy bought a $10,000 tax-exempt state government bond for $9,000 that was originally issued at $8,500 on September 1, 1995. Kathy must treat her part of the original issue discount (OID) as tax-exempt interest. The accumulated OID from the date of issue to the date Kathy purchased the bond was $600. On August 16, 2011, Kathy sold the bond for $9,800. Kathy must report a $100 capital gain on the sale. The market discount in the bond is the original issue price ($8,500) plus the accumulated OID from the date of issue that represented interest to any earlier holders ($600) and minus the price Kathy paid for the bond ($9,000). As a result, the market discount is $100 ($9,100 - $9,000). The remaining difference of $700 ($9,800 - $9,100) is treated as tax-exempt interest.

Any gain from market discount is usually taxable on disposition or redemption of tax-exempt bonds. If you bought the bonds before May 1, 1993, the gain from market discount is capital gain. If you bought the bonds after April 30, 1993, the gain is ordinary income.

You figure the market discount by subtracting the price you paid for the bond from the sum of the original issue price of the bond and the amount of accumulated OID from the date of issue that represented interest to any earlier holders. For more information, see *Market Discount Bonds* in chapter 1 of Publication 550.

A loss on the sale or other disposition of a tax-exempt state or local government bond is deductible as a capital loss.

> ### EXPLANATION
> You must accrue OID on tax-exempt state and local government bonds issued after September 3, 1982, and acquired after March 1, 1984. Your adjusted basis at the time of disposition is figured by adding accrued OID to your basis. You must accrue OID on tax-exempt obligations under the same method used for OID on corporate obligations issued after July 1, 1982.
>
> #### Example
> On March 1, 1998, Julie bought a $10,000 tax-exempt state government bond for $9,100 that was originally issued at $8,500 on September 1, 1995. On August 16, 2011, Julie sold the bond for $9,800. Julie previously accrued $500 of OID tax-exempt interest over the period she held the bond. Julie must report a $200 capital gain on the sale of the bond [$9,800 - ($9,100 + $500)].

Redeemed before maturity. If a state or local bond issued before June 9, 1980, is redeemed before it matures, the OID is not taxable to you.

If a state or local bond issued after June 8, 1980, is redeemed before it matures, the part of OID earned while you hold the bond is not taxable to you. However, you must report the unearned part of OID as a capital gain.

Example. On July 1, 2000, the date of issue, you bought a 20-year, 6% municipal bond for $800. The face amount of the bond was $1,000. The $200 discount was OID. At the time the bond was issued, the issuer had no intention of redeeming it before it matured. The bond was callable at its face amount beginning 10 years after the issue date.

The issuer redeemed the bond at the end of 11 years (July 1, 2011) for its face amount of $1,000 plus accrued annual interest of $60. The OID earned during the time you held the bond, $73, is not taxable. The $60 accrued annual interest also is not taxable. However, you must report the unearned part of OID ($127) as a capital gain.

Long-term debt instruments issued after 1954 and before May 28, 1969 (or before July 2, 1982, if a government instrument). If you sell, trade, or redeem for a gain one of these debt instruments, the part of your gain that is not more than your ratable share of the OID at the time of the sale or redemption is ordinary income. The rest of the gain is capital gain. If, however, there was an intention to call the debt instrument before maturity, all of your gain that is not more than the entire OID is treated as ordinary income at the time of the sale. This treatment of taxable gain also applies to corporate instruments issued after May 27, 1969, under a written commitment that was binding on May 27, 1969, and at all times thereafter.

Long-term debt instruments issued after May 27, 1969 (or after July 1, 1982, if a government instrument). If you hold one of these debt instruments, you must include a part of OID in your gross income each year you own the instrument. Your basis in that debt instrument is increased by the amount of OID that you have included in your gross income. See _Original Issue Discount (OID)_ in chapter 7 for information about OID that you must report on your tax return.

If you sell or trade the debt instrument before maturity, your gain is a capital gain. However, if at the time the instrument was originally issued there was an intention to call it before its maturity, your gain generally is ordinary income to the extent of the entire OID reduced by any amounts of OID previously includible in your income. In this case, the rest of the gain is capital gain.

Market discount bonds. If the debt instrument has market discount and you chose to include the discount in income as it accrued, increase your basis in the debt instrument by the accrued discount to figure capital gain or loss on its disposition. If you did not choose to include the discount in income as it accrued, you must report gain as ordinary interest income up to the instrument's accrued market discount. The rest of the gain is capital gain. See _Market Discount Bonds_ in chapter 1 of Publication 550.

A different rule applies to market discount bonds issued before July 19, 1984, and purchased by you before May 1, 1993. See _Market discount bonds_ under _Discounted Debt Instruments_ in chapter 4 of Publication 550.

Retirement of debt instrument. Any amount you receive on the retirement of a debt instrument is treated in the same way as if you had sold or traded that instrument.

Notes of individuals. If you hold an obligation of an individual issued with OID after March 1, 1984, you generally must include the OID in your income currently, and your gain or loss on its sale or retirement is generally capital gain or loss. An exception to this treatment applies if the obligation is a loan between individuals and all the following requirements are met.

- The lender is not in the business of lending money.
- The amount of the loan, plus the amount of any outstanding prior loans, is $10,000 or less.
- Avoiding federal tax is not one of the principal purposes of the loan.

If the exception applies, or the obligation was issued before March 2, 1984, you do not include the OID in your income currently. When you sell or redeem the obligation, the part of your gain that is not more than your accrued share of OID at that time is ordinary income. The rest of the gain, if any, is capital gain. Any loss on the sale or redemption is capital loss.

EXPLANATION
Short Sales, Put Options, Other Kinds of Options, Wash Sales, and Other Types of Sales

There are other kinds of sales or trades that many individuals enter into. Some of these transactions—short sales, put options, and wash sales—are discussed below. The tax rules are very complicated. Professional advice should be obtained if you plan to invest in any of these transactions.

Short sales. A short sale occurs when the seller borrows the property delivered to the buyer and, at a later date, either buys substantially identical property and delivers it to the lender or makes delivery out of such property held by the seller at the time of the sale. The holding period on a short sale is usually determined by the length of time the seller actually holds the property that is eventually delivered to the lender to close the short sale.

Example

Even though you do not own any stock in the Ace Corporation, you contract to sell 100 shares of it, which you borrow from your broker. After 13 months, when the price of the stock has fallen, you buy 100 shares of Ace Corporation stock and immediately deliver them to your broker to close out the short sale. Your gain is treated as a short-term capital gain because your holding period for the delivered property is less than 1 day.

Explanation

Long and short positions. If you have held substantially identical property to the property sold short for 1 year or less on the date of the short sale, the following two rules apply:

1. Any gain on closing a short sale is a short-term gain.
2. The holding period of the substantially identical property begins on the date of the closing of the short sale or on the date of the sale, gift, or other disposition of this property, whichever comes first.

These two rules also apply if you acquire substantially identical property after the originating short sale and before the closing of the short sale.

Example

On February 4, 2010, you bought 100 shares of Able Corporation stock for $1,000. On June 4, 2010, you sold short 100 shares of similar Able stock for $1,600. On November 4, 2010, you purchased 100 more shares of Able stock for $1,800 and used them to close the short sale. On this short sale, you realized a $200 short-term capital loss.

On February 5, 2011, you sold for $1,800 the stock originally bought on February 4, 2010. Although you have actually held this stock for more than 1 year, by using rule 2, the holding period is treated as having begun on November 4, 2010, the date of the closing of the short sale. The $800 gain realized on the sale is therefore a short-term capital gain.

TAXALERT

Short sales take away the tax benefits of long-term holding periods with respect to any substantially identical stock held in a long position, unless you have already met the long-term holding requirement at the time you make the short sale.

TAXALERT

The basis reporting rules which go into effect in 2011 require basis and holding period reporting of short sale transactions on Form 1099-B. Previously, brokers were required to report short sales for the year in which the sale opened. Under the new reporting rules, for all short sales opened on or after January 1, 2011, brokers must report gross proceeds for the year in which the short sale closed. For more information, see chapter 13, *Basis of property*.

Treatment of losses. If, on the date of a short sale of a capital asset, you have held substantially identical property for more than 1 year, any loss you have on the short sale is treated as a long-term capital loss, even though the property used to close the sale was held for 1 year or less.

TAXORGANIZER

You should keep a copy of your broker confirmation statement for the purchase of any securities or options. Also, keep a copy of the Form 1099-B provided by your broker for any sales of securities or options. Remember that the information shown on your Form 1099-B is also provided to the IRS. It is important to ensure that the amounts you report on your tax return match the amounts shown on the Form 1099-B received from your broker. If you are issued an incorrect Form 1099-B, request a corrected form from your broker.

TAXPLANNER

Short sales against the box. Selling short against the box means that you are selling borrowed securities while owning substantially identical securities that you later deliver to close the short sale.

You will generally be required to recognize gain (but not loss) of any appreciated position in stock, a partnership interest, or certain debt instruments that has the effect of eliminating your risk of loss and upside gain potential. You will be treated as making a constructive sale of an appreciated position when you do one of the following: (1) enter into a short sale of the same or substantially identical property; (2) enter into an offsetting contract with respect to the same or substantially identical property (an equity swap, for example); or (3) enter into a futures or forward contract to deliver the same or substantially identical property. In addition, future Treasury regulations are expected to expand these rules to other transactions that have substantially the same effects as the ones described in the Internal Revenue Code.

Exceptions

Certain exceptions apply to these rules. One of the most important is that short sales against the box are effective for tax purposes, so long as the following requirements are met:
1. The transaction is closed within 30 days of the close of the taxable year; and
2. You hold the appreciated financial position throughout the 60-day period beginning on the date such transaction is closed, and you do not enter into certain positions that would diminish the risk of loss during that time.

TAXPLANNER

Purchasing put options. Acquiring a put option means that you are buying an option contract to sell 100 shares of stock at a set price during a specific time period. Investors who own appreciated securities that they are not yet ready to sell because of tax reasons often buy put options as a way of protecting their securities against possible price declines.

If the stock price subsequently increases, you obtain the benefit of the price increase less the cost of the put, which expires as worthless. If the stock price declines, however, you may either sell your shares at the put option price or sell the put option separately.

Example

Jim Smith purchased 100 shares of XYZ stock in July 2010 at $25 per share. The selling price in November 2010 was $55. Jim could have sold his shares in November and realized a $30 per-share gain, but it would have been taxed in 2010. Since Jim believed that the stock still had some upward potential and also wanted to postpone recognizing the gain, he bought a put option with an expiration date in March 2011, giving him the right to sell his stock at $55 per share. He locked in his gain and limited his loss to the cost of the put option.

Tax Treatment of Put Options

1. If you sell the put—in lieu of exercising it—the gain or loss is a short-term or long-term capital gain or loss, depending on how long the put has been held.
2. If you neither sell nor exercise the put, the expiration is treated as a sale or an exchange of the put on the expiration date. Whether the loss you incur is a short-term or long-term capital loss depends on how long the put has been held.
3. If you exercise the put, its cost increases your basis in the underlying securities and thus is included in computing your gain or loss at the time of the securities' sale. Whether the gain or loss is short-term or long-term usually depends on the holding period of the underlying stock at the time the put option was acquired.

TAXPLANNER

Stock index options. Unlike a put option, which is based on shares in a specific company, a stock index option represents a group of stocks. For example, an index option is available that is keyed to Standard & Poor's 500 stock averages. Investors use stock index options to reduce portfolio exposure to general market or industry fluctuations and to improve their return on investment. Stock index options may also be used to protect current paper gains (gains you have on paper but have not yet realized) and to save taxes when a taxpayer owns appreciated stock that has not been held long enough to qualify for long-term capital gain treatment.

If you expect the stock market to go down, you might purchase stock index put options. If the market does go down, the put options gain in value, perhaps offsetting the loss in any appreciated stock you might hold.

TAXPLANNER

Writing covered call options. If you have stock that has appreciated in value but want to (1) defer the gain until the following year and (2) provide yourself with protection from market declines, consider writing a covered call option with an expiration date next year. A covered call is the selling of an option to purchase shares that you own at a specified price within a set time frame. If the purchaser of the call doesn't exercise it until next year (or lets it lapse), both the amount you receive from selling the call and the proceeds from disposition of the stock are not reported until the following year.

One disadvantage is that you give up the opportunity to benefit from a price increase in the stock you own above the option exercise price.

Example

Bill purchased 100 shares of XYZ stock for $20 per share on December 20, 2009. On December 21, 2010, the stock was selling for $50 per share, but Bill wanted to defer the gain until 2011 and protect himself against a market decline. Bill wrote a covered call option, agreeing to sell his 100 shares for $50 per share at any time within the next 3 months. He received $3 per share for selling this call option. Bill has acquired protection against a market decline because he now has $3 per share in the bank. If the person who bought the option does not exercise it, Bill reports the $3 per share as a short-term capital gain in 2011. If the option is exercised, the $3 per share is added to the $50 per-share exercise price.

If the stock had continued to appreciate, Bill could have bought other shares of the stock in the open market to deliver against the call, or he could have chosen to purchase, or buy back, the option. A short-term loss would have been realized when the option position was closed in either of these two ways.

Explanation

Wash sales. A wash sale occurs when you sell stock or securities, and, within 30 days before or after the sale, you buy, acquire in a taxable exchange, or acquire a contract or option to buy substantially identical stock. The substantially identical stock may be acquired by subscription for newly issued stock as well as by buying old stock. However, the unallowable loss is added to the basis of the newly acquired stock or security. For additional information about wash sales, see the section on *Wash Sales* later in this chapter.

Losses from wash sales or exchanges of stocks or securities are not deductible. However, the gain from these sales is taxable. Commodity futures contracts are not stock or securities and are not covered by the wash sale rule. Any position of a straddle acquired after June 23, 1981, however, is covered by the wash sale rule. This includes futures contracts. See Publication 550, *Investment Income and Expenses*.

TAXALERT

Under the new basis reporting rules in effect for 2011, brokers are required to adjust cost basis to reflect wash sales if the acquired securities are identical (instead of substantially equivalent) to the sold securities and purchases and sales occur within the same account. Since brokers are only required to report wash sales for identical securities and sales occurring within an account, taxpayers will need to continue to monitor all sales of substantially identical securities across all of their accounts to ensure wash sales are being appropriately reported. For more information, see chapter 13, *Basis of property*.

Explanation

Options. Gain or loss from the sale or exchange of a purchased option to buy or sell property that is a capital asset in your hands, or would be if you acquired it, is a capital gain or loss.

If you do not exercise an option to buy or sell, and you have a loss, the option is treated as having been sold or exchanged on the date that it expired.

The Capital Asset Treatment Does Not Apply

1. To a gain from the sale or exchange of an option, if the gain from the sale of the property underlying the option would be ordinary income, or
2. To a dealer in options, if the option is part of inventory, or
3. To a loss from failure to exercise a fixed-price option acquired on the same day the property identified in the option was acquired; such loss is not deductible.

If you grant an option on stocks, securities, commodities, or commodity futures and it is not exercised, the amount you receive (if you are not in the business of granting options) is treated as a short-term capital gain reportable on Schedule D (Form 1040), regardless of the classification of the property in your hands. If the option is exercised, you add the option payment to other amounts you receive to figure the amount you realize on the sale of the property. The classification of your gain or loss is then determined by the type of property you sold.

Your holding period for property acquired under an option to purchase begins on the day after the property was acquired, not the day after the option was acquired.

Commodity futures. A commodity future is a contract for the sale or purchase of some fixed amount of a commodity at a future date for a fixed price. The contracts are treated as either (1) hedges to ensure against unfavorable price changes in a commodity bought or sold in the course of business or (2) capital investments.

Gains and losses on hedging contracts for a commodity purchased in the ordinary course of a trade or a business to ensure the price of, and an adequate supply of, the commodity for use in the business are treated as ordinary business gains and losses.

Straddles. A straddle is a position that offsets an interest an investor has in personal property other than stock. It may take the form of a futures contract, an option, or cash. The purpose of a straddle is to reduce an individual's risk of property loss.

Example

Karen bought an option to have 5,000 bushels of wheat delivered to her in June 2011. At the same time, she bought an option to deliver 5,000 bushels of wheat in July 2011. Karen has a straddle.

Explanation

The treatment of straddles is designed to prevent the deferral of income and the conversion of ordinary income to capital gains.

Example 1

ABC stock is selling at $30. Peter purchases two options on ABC. He purchases a call to buy 100 shares of the stock for $25 per share and a put to sell 100 shares of the stock for $35 per share. As long as the stock does not stay at $30, one of the options will produce a gain and the other one will produce a loss.

Assume that by the end of the year the price of ABC is $34. The value of the call should have increased by $400, and the value of the put should have declined by $400.

Peter cannot recognize the loss on the put until he recognizes the offsetting gain on the call.

Example 2

James purchases 100 shares of BCD stock on September 1, 2010, at $40 per share. On November 1, the BCD sells at $46 per share. James sells a call due in February 2011 for $100. In December, the stock is selling for $50, and James repurchases the call for $400. James has a $300 short-term loss, which he cannot yet deduct. When he sells BCD in the following year, he could have a long-term gain. The loss cannot be deducted until the year in which the call is closed. The holding period of BCD stock is also changed. If James sells BCD in February 2011 for $50 per share, he would have a short-term gain of $700 to report (the $1,000 gain on the stock minus the $300 loss on the call).

Note: There are many special terms, rules, and exceptions to learn if you want to try your luck on these investment strategies. You should study the markets and the tax law very carefully.

TAXPLANNER

Specific types of capital gains can be treated as ordinary income for certain additional financial transactions and certain gains from the sale of a conversion transaction can be treated as ordinary income.

Conversion transaction. A conversion transaction occurs when substantially all of the expected return from an investment is attributable to the time value of the net investment. In addition, if the transaction falls within one of the following classifications, it will be considered a conversion transaction:

1. Acquiring property and, on a contemporaneous basis, contracting to sell the same property for a determined price
2. Certain straddles
3. Any transaction that is marketed as or sold as producing capital gains
4. Other transactions that the U.S. Treasury Department will describe in future regulations

A special rule exempts options dealers and commodities traders from these provisions, but anti-abuse rules prevent limited partners or entrepreneurs from unduly profiting by this exception.

The amount of gain that can be considered ordinary income will not exceed the amount of interest that would have accrued on your net investment in the property at a rate equal to 120% of the applicable federal rate for the period of time you held the investment. This amount is then reduced by the amount of ordinary income that was recognized from the conversion transaction and any interest expense in connection with purchasing the property.

Example

Celine acquires stock for $10,000 on April 1, 2009, and on that same day agrees to sell it to Ricardo for $11,500 on April 1, 2011. Assume that the applicable federal rate is 5%. On April 1, 2011, Celine delivers the stock to Ricardo in exchange for $11,500.

This arrangement is a conversion transaction. Thus, $1,236 of Celine's gain is ordinary income (120% of 5% compounded for 2 years, applied to an investment of $10,000).

Computation of ordinary gain	
Investment	$10,000
Applicable rate (120% × 5%)	6%
	$600
Amount after first year ($10,000 + $600)	$10,600
Applicable rate (120% × 5%)	6%
	$636
Amount after second year ($10,600 + $636)	$11,236
Investment	($10,000)
Ordinary income	$1,236

The difference between the ordinary income and the appreciation, $264 ($1,500 - $1,236), is classified as a long-term capital gain.

Additional requirements are imposed on conversion transactions with respect to built-in losses, options dealers, commodities traders, and limited partners and limited entrepreneurs in an entity that deals in options or trades in commodities.

Because the application of these rules is complex, you should consult your tax advisor when considering a potential conversion transaction.

Sale of business. The sale of a business is not usually the sale of one asset. If you sell your business or your interest in a business and need more information, see Publication 544, *Sales and Other Dispositions of Assets.*

Canceling a sale of real property. If you sell real property to an individual and the sales contract gives the buyer the right to return the property to you for the amount paid, you may not have to recognize gain or loss on the sale. You will not recognize gain or loss if the property is returned to you within the same tax year as the sale. However, if the property is returned to you in a future tax year, you must recognize gain or loss in the year of the sale. In the year in which the property is returned to you, your new basis in the property will be equal to the amount of cash, notes, or other property you give back to the buyer.

Lease canceled or sold. If a tenant receives payments for the cancellation of a lease on property used as the tenant's home, a gain is taxed as a capital gain, but any loss is not deductible. If the lease was used in the tenant's trade or business, gain or loss may be capital or ordinary, as explained in Publication 544, *Sales and Other Dispositions of Assets.*

Payments received by a landlord. If a landlord receives payments for cancellation of a lease, they are ordinary income and not capital gains.

Subleases. When you transfer leased property under an arrangement in which the new occupant takes over your monthly lease payments and also pays you an amount each month for relinquishing use of the property, a sublease has been entered into and payments you receive are ordinary income.

Repossession of real property. If real property that is a capital asset in your hands is repossessed by the seller under the terms of the sales contract or by foreclosure of a mortgage, you may have a capital gain or loss. The gain or loss is the difference between your adjusted basis in the property (purchase price with adjustments) and the full amount of your obligation cancelled, plus any money received in exchange for the property. Losses on repossessions of property held for personal use, however, are not deductible. See Publication 537, *Installment Sales.* Also see the discussion of installment sales in this chapter.

Subdivision of land. If you own a tract of land, and, in order to sell or exchange it, you subdivide it into individual lots or parcels, you may receive capital gains treatment on at least a part of the proceeds if you meet the following four conditions:

1. You are not a dealer in real estate.
2. As the owner, you have not made any major improvement on the tract that substantially enhances the value of the lot or parcel sold, and no such improvement will be made as part of the contract of sale with the buyer. A substantial improvement is generally one that increases the value of the property by more than 10%. Some improvements that are considered substantial are: structural work on commercial and residential buildings, laying down hard-surface roads, and installing utility services.
3. You have held the land for at least 5 years, unless you got it by inheritance or devise.
4. You did not previously hold the tract or any lot or parcel on such tract mainly for sale to customers in the ordinary course of your trade or business (unless the tract previously would have qualified for this treatment), and, during the same tax year in which the sale occurred, you were not holding any other land for sale to customers in the ordinary course of trade or business. This treatment also applies to S corporations.

Gain on sale of lots. If your land meets these tests, the gain realized on the sale or exchange will be treated in the following manner:

If you sell less than six lots or parcels from the same tract, the entire gain is a capital gain. In figuring the number of lots or parcels sold, two or more adjoining lots sold to a single buyer in a single sale are counted as only one parcel.

When you sell or exchange the sixth lot or parcel from the same tract, the amount by which 5% of the selling price is more than the expenses of the sale is treated as ordinary income, and the rest of any gain will be a capital gain. Additionally, 5% of the selling price of all lots sold or exchanged from the tract in the tax year in which the sixth lot is sold or exchanged, as well as in later years, is treated as ordinary income.

If you sell the first six lots of a single tract in 1 year, to the extent of gain, the lesser of 5% of the selling price of each lot sold, or the gain is treated as ordinary income. On the other hand, if you sold the first three lots in a single tract in 1 year and the next three lots in the following year, the 5% rule would apply only to the gains realized in the second year.

The selling expenses of the sale must first be deducted from the part of the gain treated as ordinary income, and any remaining expenses must be deducted from the part treated as a capital gain. You may not deduct the selling expenses from other income as ordinary business expenses.

Example 1
You sold five lots from a single tract last year. This year, you sell the sixth lot for $20,000. Your basis for this lot is $10,000, and your selling expenses are $1,500. Your gain is $8,500, all of which is capital gain, figured as follows:

Selling price		$20,000
Less:		
Basis	$10,000	
Expense of sale	1,500	(11,500)
Gain from sale of lot		$8,500
5% of selling price	$1,000	
Less: Expense of sale	1,500	
Gain reported as ordinary income		-0-
Gain reported as capital gain		$8,500

Because the selling expenses are more than 5% of the selling price, none of the gain is treated as ordinary income.

Example 2
Assume in Example 1 that the selling expenses are $800. The amount of gain is $9,200, of which $200 is ordinary income and $9,000 is capital gain, figured as follows:

Selling price		$20,000
Less:		
Basis	$10,000	
Expense of sale	800	(10,800)
Gain from sale of lot		$9,200
5% of selling price	$1,000	
Less: Expense of sale	800	
Gain reported as ordinary income		(200)
Gain reported as capital gain		$9,000

Explanation
Loss on sale of lots. The 5% rule does not apply to losses. If you sell a lot at a loss, it will be treated as a capital loss if you held it for investment.

For more information on subdivision of land, see Publication 544, *Sales and Other Dispositions of Assets.*

Inventions. An invention is usually a capital asset in the hands of the inventor, whether or not a patent has been applied for or has been obtained. The inventor is the individual whose efforts created the property, and who qualifies as the original and first inventor or joint inventor.

If you are an inventor and transfer all substantial rights to patent property, you may get special tax treatment, as described below, if the transfer is not to your employer or to a related person.

If, for a consideration paid to the inventor, you acquire all the substantial rights to patent property before the invention is reduced to practice (tested and operated successfully under operating conditions), you may, when you dispose of your interest, get special tax treatment, if you are not the employer of the inventor or related to the inventor. However, if you buy patent property after it is reduced to practice, it may be treated as either a capital or a noncapital asset, depending on the circumstances.

Special tax treatment. If you are the inventor or an individual who acquired all the substantial rights to the patent property before the invention was reduced to practice, and you transfer all the substantial rights or an undivided interest in all such rights, the transfer will be treated as a sale or an exchange of a long-term capital asset. This rule applies even if you have not held the patent property for more than 1 year and whether or not the payments received are made periodically during the transferee's use of the patent or are contingent on the productivity, use, or disposition of the property transferred.

Courts have enforced the substantial rights requirement very strictly. Generally, a patent seller must be able to show that any rights he or she retains are insubstantial in order to treat the sale of rights in the patent property as a long-term capital gain.

The U.S. Courts of Appeals for the Sixth, Seventh, and Ninth Circuits have overturned lower court rulings that allowed patent owners transferring exclusive rights to impose geographical limitations within the United States on the person purchasing the patent. However, the official IRS position is that a transfer of all substantial rights may be limited to one or more countries.

Payment for the patent may be received by the seller in a lump sum, as an installment sale, as a fixed percentage of all future profits from the patent, or as a fee per item produced. All these methods qualify for capital gains treatment, even if the total amount of payment is uncertain.

Transfers between related parties. The special tax treatment does not apply if the transfer is either directly or indirectly between you and certain related parties. The rules defining related parties are very specific. You should consult your tax advisor for assistance with the interpretation.

Copyrights. Literary, musical, or artistic compositions, or similar property, are not treated as capital assets if your personal efforts created them or if you got the property in such a way that all or part of your basis in the property is determined by reference to a person whose personal efforts created the property (e.g., if you got the property as a gift). The sale of such property, whether or not it is copyrighted, results in ordinary income.

Deposit in Insolvent or Bankrupt Financial Institution

If you lose money you have on deposit in a bank, credit union, or other financial institution that becomes insolvent or bankrupt, you may be able to deduct your loss in one of three ways.

- Ordinary loss.
- Casualty loss.
- Nonbusiness bad debt (short-term capital loss).

For more information, see *Deposit in Insolvent or Bankrupt Financial Institution,* in chapter 4 of Publication 550.

TAXPLANNER

Whether you elect to claim a casualty or an ordinary loss in the year in which the requirements for the election are met will depend on a number of factors. First, you must compare the available casualty loss deduction (after reducing your loss by $100 plus 10% of your adjusted gross income) to your ordinary loss deduction (after adding the loss to other miscellaneous itemized deductions and reducing the total by 2% of adjusted gross income). The ordinary loss election is available on deposits of up to $20,000 ($10,000 if you are married and file a separate return), which are not federally insured. The $20,000 limitation applies to each financial institution, not each deposit or each tax year. This is important if you hold deposits in more than one institution.

The election to claim an ordinary loss, once made, cannot be revoked unless you obtain the consent of the IRS.

You should also consider whether it is better to forgo either election and claim the entire amount as a **capital loss** from a nonbusiness bad debt (see *Nonbusiness Bad Debts*, later). This might be advisable if you have sufficient capital gain income with which to offset the capital loss. Consult with your financial advisor when considering these elections.

Example

Judy Porter estimates that she has incurred a total loss of her $30,000 bank account with an insolvent financial institution. Her account is not federally insured. Judy's adjusted gross income (AGI) is $70,000, and she has no miscellaneous itemized deductions. Judy wants to review the tax consequences of electing to claim the estimated loss as either a casualty loss or an ordinary loss, which is treated as a miscellaneous itemized deduction.

The net deduction available under each method is as follows:

	Casualty loss	Ordinary loss
Estimated loss	$30,000	$20,000*
$100 casualty loss limitation	(100)	n/a
10% AGI limitation	(7,000)	n/a
2% AGI limitation	n/a	(1,400)
Net deduction available	$22,900	$18,600

* Limited to $20,000 per institution.

In addition, if the loss actually sustained by Judy exceeds the amount deducted as an estimated loss, she can claim the excess loss as a bad debt in the year in which that loss is finally determined. Thus, if Judy elects to treat the estimated loss as an ordinary loss and she determines in a subsequent year that her entire balance of $30,000 was lost, she could claim an additional $10,000 deduction for bad debts. This would increase her cumulative deductions under this alternative to a total amount of $28,600.

Sale of Annuity
The part of any gain on the sale of an annuity contract before its maturity date that is based on interest accumulated on the contract is ordinary income.

Losses on Section 1244 (Small Business) Stock
You can deduct as an ordinary loss, rather than as a capital loss, your loss on the sale, trade, or worthlessness of section 1244 stock. Report the loss on Form 4797, line 10.

Any gain on section 1244 stock is a capital gain if the stock is a capital asset in your hands. Report the gain on Schedule D (Form 1040). See *Losses on Section 1244 (Small Business) Stock* in chapter 4 of Publication 550.

Losses on Small Business Investment Company Stock
See *Losses on Small Business Investment Company Stock* in chapter 4 of Publication 550.

EXPLANATION
While individuals who own certain stock in a small business investment company may be allowed to deduct an ordinary loss on the sale, exchange, or worthlessness of their stock, the amount that may be claimed is subject to an annual limit of $50,000 per taxpayer ($100,000 for a married couple filing a joint return).

Ordinary loss treatment is generally available only to the original owner. If you obtain stock in a small business corporation or investment company through purchase, gift, inheritance, or the like, you may not claim ordinary losses. Similarly, if small business stock is owned through a partnership, to claim a loss, you must have been a partner when the stock was issued. If you were not a partner at such time and the partnership later distributed the stock to the partners, you may not take an ordinary loss deduction.

To qualify for ordinary loss treatment, you must own Section 1244 stock. This is the stock of a small business corporation or investment company with total capital of under $1 million that meets a *passive income test*. To meet this test, the aggregate of any gross receipts generated over the last 5 years by royalties, rents, dividends, interest, annuities, and sales of stock or securities must be less than 50% of total gross receipts taken in by the corporation in the 5-year period. In addition, the corporation's stock must have been issued for money or property other than securities. Stock that is convertible into other securities of the corporation is not treated as Section 1244 stock.

TAXPLANNER

The loss limitation of $50,000 per taxpayer is an annual limitation. Therefore, if you are considering a sale of Section 1244 stock that is expected to produce a loss of over $50,000, you should consider structuring the transaction so that stock sales will take place in more than 1 year.

Example

Craig, a bachelor, has owned 10,000 shares of qualified small business stock for several years. The stock has a basis of $150,000. He plans to dispose of the stock but expects to realize only $50,000 on the sale. If he sells all 10,000 shares in 2011, he will recognize a $100,000 loss in 1 year. Only $50,000 will be deductible as an ordinary loss. The other $50,000 will be treated as a long-term capital loss. The long-term capital loss can be offset against other capital gains, but the excess can be deducted at the rate of only $3,000 per year.

If Craig sells 5,000 shares in 2011 and 5,000 shares in 2012 for the same price, he will still have a total loss of $100,000. Yet, because $50,000 of the loss will be recognized in 2011 and the other $50,000 in 2012, Craig may treat both losses as ordinary losses, which makes the total $100,000 loss fully deductible without regard to capital gains from other sources.

Craig should use Form 4797 to report the Section 1244 loss as a sale of a noncapital asset.

TAXSAVER

Gain on sale of qualified small business stock. Generally, noncorporate taxpayers who held qualified small business stock (QSBS) for more than 5 years can exclude from gross income 50% of any gain realized from the sale or exchange of the stock. (The exclusion can be up to 60% for certain empowerment zone business stock and the stock was acquired after December 21, 2000. See Publication 954, *Tax Incentives for Distressed Communities*, for more information.) The gain is taxed at a maximum rate of 28%. Under a 2009 tax law, the exclusion can be up to 75% for stock acquired after February 17, 2009, and held for five years. Two new tax laws (including the one that extended the Bush tax cuts) enacted in 2010 increased the exclusion to 100% for stock acquired at original issue after September 27, 2010, and before January 1, 2012, if the qualified stock has been held at least 5 years.

This exclusion is limited to the greater of:

1. 10 times the taxpayer's basis in the stock; or
2. $10 million in gain from all of the taxpayer's transactions in stock of that corporation (held for more than 5 years); $5 million if married filing separately

The rules for determining whether stock is qualified small business stock can be summarized as follows:

• The stock must be newly issued stock and issued after August 10, 1993.
• The stock cannot be acquired in exchange for other stock.
• The issuing corporation must be a C corporation but may not be a cooperative, domestic international sales corporation (DISC), former DISC, real estate investment trust (REIT), regulated investment company (RIC), real estate mortgage investment conduit (REMIC), or a corporation having a possessions tax credit election in effect or owning a subsidiary that has a possessions tax credit election in effect.
• At least 80% of the corporation's assets must be used in the active conduct of a qualified trade or business or in the start-up of a future qualified trade or business.
• A qualified trade or business is any business other than one involving the performance of services in the fields of health, law, engineering, architecture, accounting, actuarial science, performing arts, consulting, athletics, financial services, brokerage services, or any other trade or business where the principal asset of the business is the reputation or skill of one or more employees. A qualified trade or business also cannot involve the businesses of banking, insurance, financing, leasing, investing or similar businesses, farming or certain businesses involving natural resource extraction or production, or businesses operating a hotel, motel, restaurant, or similar business.
• The corporation may not have greater than $50 million in gross assets (i.e., the sum of cash plus the aggregate fair market value of other corporate property) at the time the qualified

small business stock is issued. If the corporation meets this test at the time of issuance of the stock, a subsequent event that violates this rule will not disqualify stock that previously qualified.
- The following stock redemption or "buy back" tests must be met:
  i. Within the period beginning 2 years before and ending 2 years after the stock was issued, the corporation cannot have bought more than a minimal amount of its stock from you or a related party.
  ii. Within the period beginning 1 year before and ending 1 year after the stock was issued, the corporation cannot have bought more than a de minimis amount of its stock from anyone, unless the total value of the stock it bought is 5% or less of the total value of all its stock.

Note: Under certain circumstances, the gain on the sale of publicly traded securities will not be taxed if the proceeds from the sale are used to acquire common stock in a specialized small business investment company (SSBIC) within a 60-day period. See *Gains on Qualified Small Business Stock* in chapter 4 of Publication 550, *Investment Income and Expenses*, for a detailed description of these additional requirements. Because of the complexity of the rules related to QSBS transactions, you should consult your tax advisor prior to completing any sale transaction to which these rules may apply.

TAXPLANNER

The maximum tax on long-term capital gains for most taxpayers is 15%. This rate applies for both regular and alternative minimum tax purposes.

Although the maximum tax rate on an individual's net long-term capital gains in 2011 is 15%, a 28% rate applies to the sale of qualified small business stock (QSBS). The effective tax rate for regular tax purposes, after the 50% exclusion, is 14%. The effective tax rate is 11% for stock qualifying for the 60% exclusion, 7% for the 75% exclusion, and, of course, zero for the 100% exclusion. However, for alternative minimum tax (AMT) purposes (see chapter 31, *How to figure your tax*), 7% of the amount excluded from gross income is an AMT preference item and is added back to taxable income to arrive at alternative minimum taxable income. For a taxpayer subject to AMT, the effective maximum rate is 14.98% for stock qualifying for the 50% exclusion (the additional 0.98% results from the 7% add back of the excluded gain taxed at a 28% rate) and 12.88% for stock qualifying for the 75% exclusion. This 7% preference applies through December 31, 2011. There is no AMT add back for stock qualifying for the 100% exclusion.

Therefore, you should consider the after-tax benefit of owning QSBS as compared to other long-term investments taxed at 15% before purchasing the stock. *Note:* Gain from the sale of QSBS can be rolled over into other QSBS. Under the rollover rules, a taxpayer other than a corporation may elect to roll over capital gains from the sale of QSBS held for more than 6 months if other small business stock is purchased by the individual during the 60-day period beginning on the date of sale.

Holding Period

If you sold or traded investment property, you must determine your holding period for the property. Your holding period determines whether any capital gain or loss was a short-term or long-term capital gain or loss.

TAXALERT

Beginning in 2011, if the stock you sold during the year was acquired after 2010, your broker will generally be required to report your holding period. (For stock purchased and sold during 2011, any gain or loss will be classified as short-term since the securities have been held for less than a year.) The requirements to report holding period (i.e., short- or long-term) will be expanded during 2012 and 2013 to cover other types of securities, such as sales of mutual fund shares, stock acquired in connection with a dividend reinvestment plan, bonds, commodity contracts, and options on securities. Brokers are not required to report holding period for any securities acquired before 2011.

Long-term or short-term. If you hold investment property more than 1 year, any capital gain or loss is a long-term capital gain or loss. If you hold the property 1 year or less, any capital gain or loss is a short-term capital gain or loss.

To determine how long you held the investment property, begin counting on the date after the day you acquired the property. The day you disposed of the property is part of your holding period.

Example. If you bought investment property on February 5, 2010, and sold it on February 5, 2011, your holding period is not more than 1 year and you have a short-term capital gain or loss. If you sold it on February 6, 2011, your holding period is more than 1 year and you will have a long-term capital gain or loss.

Securities traded on established market. For securities traded on an established securities market, your holding period begins the day after the trade date you bought the securities, and ends on the trade date you sold them.

Example. You are a cash method, calendar year taxpayer. You sold stock at a gain on December 29, 2011. According to the rules of the stock exchange, the sale was closed by delivery of the stock 3 trading days after the sale, on January 4, 2012. You received payment of the sales price on that same day. Report your gain on your 2011 return, even though you received the payment in 2012. The gain is long term or short term depending on whether you held the stock more than 1 year. Your holding period ended on December 29. If you had sold the stock at a loss, you would also report it on your 2011 return.

U.S. Treasury notes and bonds. The holding period of U.S. Treasury notes and bonds sold at auction on the basis of yield starts the day after the Secretary of the Treasury, through news releases, gives notification of acceptance to successful bidders. The holding period of U.S. Treasury notes and bonds sold through an offering on a subscription basis at a specified yield starts the day after the subscription is submitted.

Automatic investment service. In determining your holding period for shares bought by the bank or other agent, full shares are considered bought first and any fractional shares are considered bought last. Your holding period starts on the day after the bank's purchase date. If a share was bought over more than one purchase date, your holding period for that share is a split holding period. A part of the share is considered to have been bought on each date that stock was bought by the bank with the proceeds of available funds.

> ### *TAXSAVER*
> If you sell stock at the end of the year, your December statement from your broker may not reflect the sale. The broker may not record the transaction until the closing date, which could be the following year. To avoid the penalties associated with underreporting, be sure to examine your January statement as well. You should also receive Form 1099-B from your broker. This form should list all your sales for the year based on the trade date.

Nontaxable trades. If you acquire investment property in a trade for other investment property and your basis for the new property is determined, in whole or in part, by your basis in the old property, your holding period for the new property begins on the day following the date you acquired the old property.

Property received as a gift. If you receive a gift of property and your basis is determined by the donor's adjusted basis, your holding period is considered to have started on the same day the donor's holding period started.

If your basis is determined by the fair market value of the property, your holding period starts on the day after the date of the gift.

Inherited property before <u>or after 2010</u>. If you inherited investment property from a decedent who died <u>either before or after</u> 2010, your capital gain or loss on any later disposition of that property is long-term capital gain or loss. This is true regardless of how long you actually held the property.

Inherited property in 2010. If you inherit investment property from a decedent who died in 2010, use Publication 4895, *Tax Treatment of Property Acquired From a Decedent Dying in 2010*, to determine your holding period.

Real property bought. To figure how long you have held real property bought under an unconditional contract, begin counting on the day after you received title to it or on the day after you took possession of it and assumed the burdens and privileges of ownership, whichever happened first. However, taking delivery or possession of real property under an option agreement is not enough to start the holding period. The holding period cannot start until there is an actual contract of sale. The holding period of the seller cannot end before that time.

Real property repossessed. If you sell real property but keep a security interest in it, and then later repossess the property under the terms of the sales contract, your holding period for a later sale includes the period you held the property before the original sale and the period after the repossession. Your holding period does not include the time between the original sale and the repossession. That is, it does not include the period during which the first buyer held the property.

Stock dividends. The holding period for stock you received as a taxable stock dividend begins on the date of distribution.

The holding period for new stock you received as a nontaxable stock dividend begins on the same day as the holding period of the old stock. This rule also applies to stock acquired in a "spin-off," which is a distribution of stock or securities in a controlled corporation.

Nontaxable stock rights. Your holding period for nontaxable stock rights begins on the same day as the holding period of the underlying stock. The holding period for stock acquired through the exercise of stock rights begins on the date the right was exercised.

Nonbusiness Bad Debts

If someone owes you money that you cannot collect, you have a bad debt. You may be able to deduct the amount owed to you when you figure your tax for the year the debt becomes worthless.

Generally, nonbusiness bad debts are bad debts that did not come from operating your trade or business, and are deductible as short-term capital losses. To be deductible, nonbusiness bad debts must be totally worthless. You cannot deduct a partly worthless nonbusiness debt.

If a seller of real property reacquires the property to satisfy a debt that is secured by the property, no debt is considered to become worthless.

If an amount is owed by two or more debtors jointly, inability to collect from one of the debtors does not justify a deduction for a proportionate amount of the debt.

TAXPLANNER
It is important to know when a debt becomes worthless because you may not take a loss in a subsequent year. Because, in many cases, it may be difficult to determine when a debt loses its value, you should claim a deduction at the earliest time you reasonably believe the debt to be worthless. If you discover you have overlooked a bad debt deduction that you should have taken, amend your return for that year. The statute of limitations for bad debts generally runs 7 years from the due date of the tax return filed for the year in which the debt became worthless.

TAXPLANNER
A debt becomes worthless when a prudent person would abandon the effort to collect the debt. This may mean that you expended a lot of effort trying to collect or that you didn't try at all. You have the burden of proving that the debt is worthless.

In most circumstances, it is wise to obtain the opinion of an attorney about whether or not collection efforts are warranted. His or her opinion should be based on objective facts establishing the loss.

Whenever possible, you should also obtain copies of the debtor's financial statements. If they show a positive net worth, then, in order to establish a debt as worthless, you have to demonstrate that the assets are not worth what the statements claim or that another creditor has a claim on those assets that takes precedence over yours.

TAXORGANIZER
You should document any steps you have taken to recover the amount owed to you. Also, you should get a copy of the debtor's financial statements to substantiate the inability to pay back the loan.

Genuine debt required. A debt must be genuine for you to deduct a loss. A debt is genuine if it arises from a debtor-creditor relationship based on a valid and enforceable obligation to repay a fixed or determinable sum of money.

Basis in bad debt required. To deduct a bad debt, you must have a basis in it—that is, you must have already included the amount in your income or loaned out your cash. For example, you cannot claim a bad debt deduction for court-ordered child support not paid to you by your former spouse. If you are a cash method taxpayer (as most individuals are), you generally cannot take a bad debt deduction for unpaid salaries, wages, rents, fees, interest, dividends, and similar items.

EXPLANATION
The distinction between business and nonbusiness bad debts is generally clear. Business bad debts usually occur because of credit transactions with customers, employees, and others closely related to a trade or a business. The dominant motive in these transactions is to support the business activity. Nonbusiness bad debts frequently arise from casual loans, such as those made to friends or acquaintances. But there is often confusion between business and nonbusiness bad debts in the following areas:
1. **You make loans frequently, but making loans is not a full-time business.** The IRS's position is that business bad debt treatment is limited to those situations in which the taxpayer derives his or her main source of income from credit transactions. Whether or not you are in a trade or business is a question of fact. The greater the regularity of the activity, however, the more likely that a trade or business exists.

Example

You occasionally lend money to individuals starting new businesses. That is an investment activity, not a trade or a business.

2. **You make a loan to a corporation in which you are an employee and a stockholder.** You are allowed a business bad debt deduction if the loan was made primarily to protect your salary. If the loan was made primarily to protect your investment, it is considered a nonbusiness loan. The larger your investment is in a company and the smaller your salary is from it, the greater the chance that a court will determine that a loan you make to the company is for nonbusiness purposes.

TAXPLANNER

If you make advances to a corporation you own, the IRS may attempt to recharacterize the advances as equity capital rather than bona fide loans. This might postpone a deduction for a bad debt until the year in which your stock is wholly worthless. Therefore, it is important that you properly document advances you make to the corporation as bona fide loans. Generally, written, interest-bearing instruments with fixed repayment terms will qualify as bona fide debt.

TAXPLANNER

If you want a loan to a family member to be considered a bona fide debt, you should document the transaction so that it is clear that both parties expect and intend repayment of the loan.

A child may borrow money from his or her parents for a business venture. To indicate that the borrowed money is not intended as a gift, the parents should draft a note saying who owes whom money. (The parties might check with a lawyer about the exact form the note should take.) If the note calls for partial payments of the debt, each payment should be made on time. This provides evidence that a legitimate creditor-debtor relationship exists. To further support their status as creditors, parents may consider investigating the business in which the child is investing the borrowed money. An arm's-length lender typically makes such an investigation.

It's also a good idea for the note from the parents to provide that the money be repaid with interest. Charging interest provides another bit of evidence that the loan between parents and child is a valid arm's-length transaction. Failure to charge adequate interest can also have important gift and income tax consequences. For details, see chapter 7, *Interest income*.

Example 1

Gail lends her son $20,000, which the son then invests in a new business venture. Gail draws up a note that provides for a specific repayment schedule and a stated rate of interest. Collateral is also established on the note to provide Gail with some security. Later, before any payments on the note have been made, the son's business venture fails. Despite repeated efforts to collect the debt, Gail is able to recover only a small amount based on the collateral established at the time of the loan.

Gail may take a bad debt deduction of $20,000, less the amount of collateral she recovered. Gail's son may deduct his loss as a business loss.

Example 2

Assume the same facts as in Example 1 except that Gail does not document the loan. No note is drawn up, and no specific provisions are made about when her son will repay the loan. If the son's business venture fails, he may deduct his loss. The mother, however, may not take a bad debt deduction.

Explanation

Loans in your business. If you are in a business or a profession, you may have bad debts that come from loans you make to your clients. If you are not in the business of lending money and the loans have no close relationship to your business or profession, these bad debts are nonbusiness bad debts.

Mechanics' and suppliers' liens. Workers and material suppliers sometimes file liens against property because of debts owed by a builder or a contractor. If you pay off such a lien to avoid foreclosure and loss of your property, you are entitled to repayment from the builder or contractor. If the debt is uncollectible, you may take a deduction for a bad debt.

Insolvency of contractor. You can take a bad debt deduction for the amount you deposit with a contractor if the contractor becomes insolvent and you are unable to recover (collect) your deposit. If the deposit is for work that is not related to your trade or business, it is a nonbusiness bad debt deduction.

Secondary liability on home mortgage. If you sell your home and the purchaser assumes your mortgage, you may remain secondarily liable for repayment of the mortgage loan. If the purchaser defaults on the loan, you may have to make up the difference if the house is then sold for less than the amount outstanding on the mortgage. You can take a bad debt deduction for the amount you pay to satisfy the mortgage if you cannot collect it from the purchaser. **Corporate securities** that become worthless are generally deductible as capital losses. This includes shares of stock, stock rights, bonds, debentures, notes, or certificates, as explained in chapter 16, *Reporting gains and losses.*

TAXPLANNER

Frequently, it is difficult to establish the year in which a corporate security becomes worthless. One guide is a publication called *Capital Changes Reporter*, published by Commerce Clearing House. The section called *Worthless Securities* provides a current list of companies whose securities have lost their value.

It is even more difficult to determine when a closely held business becomes worthless. It is not necessary for the company to declare bankruptcy. If you are aware that a company is insolvent, you may be able to take a loss. If the business continues to operate and has more than nominal assets, however, it may be only temporarily insolvent. If that is the case, you may not be able to take a loss.

Explanation

Recovery of a bad debt. Any amount recovered for a bad debt deducted in a previous year generally must be included in your income in the year in which the amount was recovered. However, you may exclude the amount recovered up to the amount of the deduction that did not reduce your income subject to tax in the year deducted. Recovery of amounts deducted in previous years is discussed in chapter 12, *Other income.*

Example

In 2007, Bill had a $25,000 long-term capital gain and a $25,000 bad debt loss. Bill had no taxable income for 2007.

In 2011, Bill recovered the entire $25,000 debt. To figure how much he should include in his 2011 income, see the calculations below.

	2007 with bad debt	2007 without bad debt
Income:		
Net long-term capital gain	$25,000	$25,000
Bad debt loss	(25,000)	
Adjusted gross income	–0–	$25,000
Less:		
Standard deductions	–0–	($5,000)
Personal exemption	–0–	($3,200)
Taxable income	–0–	$16,800

The calculations show that Bill's 2007 taxable income was reduced by $16,800 by including the bad debt. Therefore, $16,800 is included in Bill's taxable income for 2011, the year in which he collected the $25,000 debt.

Explanation

Business bad debts. There are two crucial differences in the treatment of business bad debts and nonbusiness bad debts:

1. Business bad debts are treated as **ordinary losses**, which may be deducted directly from gross income. Nonbusiness bad debts are short-term capital losses and should be shown on Schedule D, along with your short-term and long-term gains and losses from other sources. The maximum capital loss that you may use to offset your other income each year is $3,000. See chapter 16, *Reporting gains and losses,* for further information.
2. A business bad debt may be just *partially* worthless and still give rise to a tax deduction. A nonbusiness bad debt has to be totally worthless.

Example

Janet Jones, an accrual basis taxpayer, performs some plumbing work for XYZ Corporation and sends them an invoice for $20,000 in 2010. In 2011, Janet learns that XYZ Corporation will not be able to pay the entire amount of the bill. She may claim a bad debt deduction for the amount of the invoice that is worthless.

Explanation

Some businesses use the reserve method of computing bad debt expense in keeping their books. Under this method, an estimate of accounts for services expected to be uncollectible is computed, based on prior years' experience, and the amount is placed in reserve as bad debt expense.

The reserve method is no longer allowed for tax purposes, except for certain financial institutions. A business bad debt will be allowed only if it is specifically charged off the taxpayer's books during the year. Therefore, if you own a business with a large number of accounts receivable, to maximize your allowable tax deduction, you should carefully review old accounts at year-end to make sure all worthless accounts are written off.

A special rule applies to taxpayers using the accrual method of accounting for amounts to be received for the performance of services: You are not required to include in income any portion of accrued income for services performed that, on the basis of experience, will not be collected. This rule does not apply if interest is required to be paid on a receivable amount or if there is any penalty for failure to pay such amount on time.

The IRS guidelines that spell out how a taxpayer estimates uncollectible amounts for services are somewhat complex. You should consult your tax advisor if these special rules apply to your situation.

Guarantees. If you guarantee payment of another person's debt and then have to pay it off, you may be able to take a bad debt deduction for your loss. It does not matter in what capacity you make the guarantee, whether as guarantor, endorser, or indemnitor.

To qualify for a bad debt deduction, the guarantee must either be entered into with a profit motive or be related to your trade or business or employment.

A worthless debt qualifies as a nonbusiness bad debt if you can show that your reason for making the guarantee was to protect your investment or to make a profit. If you make the guarantee as a favor to friends and are not given anything in return, it is considered a gift and you may not take a deduction.

You are justified in taking the deduction if you can show that you expected to receive something in return at a future time. The expectation must be reasonable.

Example 1

A taxpayer who ran a successful car rental operation loaned money to her brother-in-law to assist him in starting his own car rental business. The taxpayer received a promissory note due 1 year after the date of the loan, with a stated rate of interest. The brother-in-law's business venture was a flop, and the taxpayer eventually took a bad debt deduction. The court allowed the deduction, pointing out that at the time the loan was made, the brother-in-law was solvent and there was a reasonable expectation that the rental business would serve as a source of repayment.

Example 2

A taxpayer loaned his brother-in-law about $2,000 over a 2-year period to help him support the taxpayer's sister and her children. During the entire period, the brother-in-law was low on cash and his business was failing. There was no record of the loan or any understanding about how it would be repaid. The court ruled that the taxpayer could not take a bad debt deduction because there was no reasonable expectation that the loan would be repaid. Instead, the court said that the $2,000 "loan" should be considered a gift.

When deductible. You can take a bad debt deduction only in the year the debt becomes worthless. You do not have to wait until a debt is due to determine whether it is worthless. A debt becomes worthless when there is no longer any chance that the amount owed will be paid.

It is not necessary to go to court if you can show that a judgment from the court would be uncollectible. You must only show that you have taken reasonable steps to collect the debt. Bankruptcy of your debtor is generally good evidence of the worthlessness of at least a part of an unsecured and unpreferred debt.

How to report bad debts. Deduct nonbusiness bad debts as short-term capital losses on Form 8949 and Schedule D (Form 1040).

On Form 8949, Part I mark box (C), and enter on line 1 the name of the debtor and "statement attached" in column (a). Enter the amount of the bad debt in parentheses in column (f). Use a separate line for each bad debt. Enter the totals from your Form 8949 on Schedule D, Part I, line 3.

For each bad debt, attach a statement to your return that contains:

- A description of the debt, including the amount, and the date it became due,
- The name of the debtor, and any business or family relationship between you and the debtor,

- The efforts you made to collect the debt, and
- Why you decided the debt was worthless. For example, you could show that the borrower has declared bankruptcy, or that legal action to collect would probably not result in payment of any part of the debt.

Filing a claim for refund. If you do not deduct a bad debt on your original return for the year it becomes worthless, you can file a claim for a credit or refund due to the bad debt. To do this, use Form 1040X to amend your return for the year the debt became worthless. You must file it within 7 years from the date your original return for that year had to be filed, or 2 years from the date you paid the tax, whichever is later. For more information about filing a claim, see *Amended Returns and Claims for Refund* in chapter 1.

Additional information. For more information, see *Nonbusiness Bad Debts* in Publication 550. For information on business bad debts, see chapter 10 of Publication 535, *Business Expenses*.

Wash Sales

You cannot deduct losses from sales or trades of stock or securities in a wash sale.

A wash sale occurs when you sell or trade stock or securities at a loss and within 30 days before or after the sale you:

1. Buy substantially identical stock or securities,
2. Acquire substantially identical stock or securities in a fully taxable trade,
3. Acquire a contract or option to buy substantially identical stock or securities, or
4. Acquire substantially identical stock for your individual retirement account (IRA) or Roth IRA.

If your loss was disallowed because of the wash sale rules, add the disallowed loss to the cost of the new stock or securities (except in (4) above). The result is your basis in the new stock or securities. This adjustment postpones the loss deduction until the disposition of the new stock or securities. Your holding period for the new stock or securities includes the holding period of the stock or securities sold.

EXAMPLE

You buy 100 shares of X stock for $1,000. At a later date, you sell these shares for $750. Then, within 30 days of the sale, you acquire 100 shares of the same stock for $800. Your loss of $250 on the sale is not deductible. However, the disallowed loss ($250) is added to the cost of the new stock ($800) to get the basis of the new stock ($1,050).

Explanation

For purposes of the wash sale rule, a short sale is considered complete on the date the short sale is entered into if on that date:

1. You own (or, on or before that date, you enter into a contract or option to acquire) stock or securities identical to those sold short, and
2. You later deliver such stock or securities to close the short sale.

    Otherwise, a short sale is not considered complete until the property is delivered to close the sale.

Example

On June 3, you buy 100 shares of stock for $1,000. You sell short 100 shares of the stock for $750 on October 7. On October 8, you buy 100 shares of the same stock for $750. You close the short sale on November 18 by delivering the shares bought on June 3. The $250 loss ($1,000 − $750) is not deductible because the date of entering into the short sale (October 7) is deemed to be the date of sale for wash sale purposes and substantially identical stock was purchased within 30 days from the date of the sale. Therefore, the wash sale rule applies, and the loss is not deductible.

TAXALERT

As previously discussed in this chapter, starting in 2011 for securities acquired on or after January 1, 2011, the basis and holding period of short sales and wash sales will be reported by your broker on Form 1099-B. For any securities acquired prior to January 1, 2011, it will remain your responsibility to calculate cost basis and holding period upon the sale or transfer. It is important that you evaluate the information reported on the Form 1099-B and notify your broker immediately if you do not agree with the reported amounts. If you receive an incorrect Form 1099-B, request a corrected copy from your broker prior to filing your income tax return. Because the IRS matches documents filed with the Service to the related income tax returns, it is important that your broker-reported transactions match those on your tax return.

For more information, see *Wash Sales*, in chapter 4 of Publication 550.

Rollover of Gain From Publicly Traded Securities

You may qualify for a tax-free rollover of certain gains from the sale of publicly traded securities. This means that if you buy certain replacement property and make the choice described in this section, you postpone part or all of your gain.

You postpone the gain by adjusting the basis of the replacement property as described in *Basis of replacement property*, later. This postpones your gain until the year you dispose of the replacement property.

You qualify to make this choice if you meet all the following tests.

- You sell publicly traded securities at a gain. Publicly traded securities are securities traded on an established securities market.
- Your gain from the sale is a capital gain.
- During the 60-day period beginning on the date of the sale, you buy replacement property. This replacement property must be either common stock of or a partnership interest in a specialized small business investment company (SSBIC). This is any partnership or corporation licensed by the Small Business Administration under section 301 (d) of the Small Business Investment Act of 1958, as in effect on May 13, 1993.

Amount of gain recognized. If you make the choice described in this section, you must recognize gain only up to the following amount.

- The amount realized on the sale, minus
- The cost of any common stock or partnership interest in an SSBIC that you bought during the 60-day period beginning on the date of sale (and did not previously take into account on an earlier sale of publicly traded securities).

If this amount is less than the amount of your gain, you can postpone the rest of your gain, subject to the limit described next. If this amount is equal to or more than the amount of your gain, you must recognize the full amount of your gain.

Limit on gain postponed. The amount of gain you can postpone each year is limited to the smaller of:

- $50,000 ($25,000 if you are married and file a separate return), or
- $500,000 ($250,000 if you are married and file a separate return), minus the amount of gain you postponed for all earlier years.

Basis of replacement property. You must subtract the amount of postponed gain from the basis of your replacement property.

How to report and postpone gain. See chapter 4 of Publication 550 for details on how to report and postpone the gain.

Chapter 15

Selling your home

ey.com/EYTaxGuide

Note

IRS Publication 17 (*Your Federal Income Tax*) has been updated by Ernst & Young LLP for 2011. Dates and dollar amounts shown are for 2011. Underlined type is used to indicate where IRS text has been updated. Places where text has been removed are indicated by the sentence: *Text intentionally omitted.*

ey.com/EYTaxGuide

Ernst & Young LLP will update the *Ernst & Young Tax Guide 2012* website with relevant taxpayer information as it becomes available. You can also sign up for email alerts to let you know when changes have been made.

Introduction

Even though home prices have been battered over the past few years, your home may still be the most valuable asset you own. If you've owned your home for a number of years, you may have a significant gain—and lots of taxes to pay—when you sell it. On the other hand, with the sharp declines in home values, you may find yourself selling your home at a loss. Unfortunately, a loss on the sale of your home is generally not deductible. This chapter tells you what you should and shouldn't do when you're considering selling your home.

Your home is probably your best tax shelter. The tax system continues to give many breaks to homeowners. You may deduct the cost of real estate taxes and, subject to certain limitations, the cost of interest paid on your mortgage. Subject to certain limitations, premiums paid or accrued on certain "qualified mortgage insurance" may also be deductible. (See chapter 24, *Interest expense*, for an explanation of the limitations on deducting home mortgage interest and the deductibility of mortgage insurance premiums.) You may also be able to completely exclude up to $250,000 of gain ($500,000 if you're married filing jointly) on the sale of your home if you meet certain conditions. In addition, you may qualify for two federal tax credits on your home. The nonbusiness energy property credit and the residential energy efficient property credit are available for making energy-efficient improvements to your home. (See chapter 37, *Other credits including the earned income credit,* for more information.) Some states continue to allow various types of local residential energy conservation and solar energy tax credits against your state income tax liability. Refer to your state's tax return instruction guide to determine if such state tax credits are available.

Any gain you are required to recognize on the sale of a home will be treated as long-term capital gain if the home was held for more than 1 year. The maximum tax rate, currently, applicable to net capital gains is 15% (and may be as low as 0% depending on your tax bracket). This is significantly lower than the top tax rate applicable to ordinary income. See *Capital Gain Tax Computation* in chapter 16, *Reporting gains and losses.*

What's New

First-time homebuyer credit <u>not available for most taxpayers.</u> For most taxpayers, the first-time homebuyer credit is not available for homes purchased in 2011. *Text intentionally omitted.* However, the first-time homebuyer credit is extended until July 1, 2011, for individuals on qualified official extended duty service (as defined by section 121(d)(9)(C)(i)) outside the United States for at least 90 days. You must have entered into a written binding contract before May 1, 2011, and actually bought the home before July 1, 2011. For details, see chapter 37.

Reminders

Home sold with undeducted points. If you have not deducted all the points you paid to secure a mortgage on your old home, you may be able to deduct the remaining points in the year of the sale. See *Mortgage ending early* under *Points* in chapter 24.

Recapturing the first-time homebuyer credit. If you claimed the first-time homebuyer credit in 2009, and you sold the home or the home stopped being your main home in 2011, you generally must repay the credit. You repay the credit by including it as additional tax on the return for the year your home stops being your main home. For details, see chapter 37.

TAXALERT

If you claimed the first-time homebuyer credit for a home you bought after December 31, 2008, and before May 1, 2010 (before October 1, 2010, if you entered into a written binding contract before May 1, 2010), you do not have to repay the credit unless you dispose of the home, or the home otherwise ceases to be your main home within 36 months of purchase. You may qualify for specified exceptions that could reduce or eliminate your obligation to repay the credit.

Home bought in 2008. If you claimed the credit for a home you bought in 2008, you generally must have begun repaying the credit on your 2010 return and continue the repayment for 14 more years. Therefore, you must repay 1/15 of the credit with your 2011 tax return. In addition, if you sold the home in 2011 or the home stopped being your main home in 2011, you generally must repay any remaining credit you claimed unless one of the exceptions to the repayment rule applies.

For more information, see *Repayment of Credit* in chapter 37, *Other credits including the earned income credit.*

TAXPLANNER

Nonqualified use. If you plan to convert a rental property into your principal residence, the amount of gain you may be able to exclude from a future sale of that home will be limited as a result of tax legislation enacted in 2008. Generally, you are allowed to exclude up to $250,000 ($500,000 if married filing a joint return) of gain realized on the sale or exchange of a principal residence. The sale of a home will qualify for this exclusion if the home is a taxpayer's principal residence for at least 2 of the 5 years ending on the date of the sale or exchange. However, the period of time you rented the residence after 2008 and before you converted it into your principal residence will figure into a formula that reduces the amount of gain that qualifies for the exclusion ($250,000 or $500,000 if married filing a joint return) when you ultimately sell that home.

TAXSAVER

You may be able to exclude from your gross income the income realized from the forgiveness or cancellation of up to $2 million of "qualified principal residence indebtedness." This exclusion applies to debt that is forgiven or canceled in 2007 through 2012.

The amount of any canceled debt you can exclude from your income reduces the basis in your principal residence. That will increase the amount of gain (or decrease any loss) you realize when you ultimately sell your home.

This chapter explains the tax rules that apply when you sell your main home. In most cases, your main home is the one in which you live most of the time.

If you sold your main home in 2011, you may be able to exclude from income any gain up to a limit of $250,000 ($500,000 on a joint return in most cases). See *Excluding the Gain*, later. If you can exclude all the gain, you do not need to report the sale on your tax return.

If you have gain that cannot be excluded, it is taxable. Report it on Form 8949, Sales and Other Dispositions of Capital Assets, and Schedule D (Form 1040). You may also have to complete Form 4797, Sales of Business Property. See *Reporting the Sale*, later.

Tax Breaks and Deductions You Can Use Checklist

Excluding Gain Realized from Selling Your Home. You may be able to exclude from your gross income up to $250,000 ($500,000, if you file jointly with your spouse) of the gain from the sale of your main home. For more information, see *Excluding the Gain*, later.

Loss on the Sale of a Home. You cannot deduct any loss realized from the sale of your home. However, if you own a house as an investment—and do not use it for personal purposes—you may be able to deduct the loss. For more information, see *Amount of Gain or Loss: Loss on sale*, later.

Reduced Exclusion Available If You Do Not Meet the Ownership and Use Requirements for the Sale of Your Main Home. Generally, in order to qualify to exclude gain realized from the sale of your main home, you must have owned and occupied the property as your main home for at least 2 years within the 5-year period that preceded the sale. However, you may be able to claim a reduced, prorated exclusion even if you do not meet the ownership or use tests or sold more than one main home during a 2-year period if you sold the home due to:

- A change in your place of employment, and the new place of employment is at least 50 miles farther from the home you sold than was your former place of employment; or
- Health reasons; or
- An unforeseen circumstance

For more information on what constitutes a sale for health reasons or an unforeseen circumstance, and how to calculate the reduced exclusion, see *Reduced Maximum Exclusion*, later.

Exclusion Reduced to Extent Gain Relates to Non-qualified Use. You will not be able to exclude the gain realized from the sale or exchange of a principal residence to the extent that the gain is associated with a period of nonqualified use after December 31, 2008. For this purpose, a period of nonqualified use means any period after December 31, 2008, where the home is not used as a principal residence by you, your spouse, or your former spouse. See *Periods of Nonqualified Use*, later.

Mortgage Debt Forgiveness. You may be able to exclude from your gross income the income realized from the forgiveness or cancellation of up to $2 million of "Qualified principal residence indebtedness." This exclusion applies to debt canceled or forgiven from 2007 through 2012. Note, however, that the amount of any canceled debt you can exclude from your income reduces your basis in your principal residence. That will increase the amount of gain (or decrease any loss) you realize when you ultimately sell your home.

Repayment of First-Time Homebuyer Credit Claimed in 2008. If you claimed the first-time homebuyer credit for a principal residence you purchased in 2008, you should have begun repaying the credit in 2010, and must continue repaying the credit in equal installments through 2024.

If you have a loss on the sale, you cannot deduct it on your return. However, you may need to report it. See *Reporting the Sale*, later.

The following are main topics in this chapter.

- Figuring gain or loss.
- Basis.
- Excluding the gain.
- Ownership and use tests.
- Reporting the sale.

Other topics include the following.

- Business use or rental of home.
- Recapturing a federal mortgage subsidy.

Useful Items

You may want to see:

Publication

- ☐ **523** Selling Your Home
- ☐ **530** Tax Information for Homeowners
- ☐ **547** Casualties, Disasters, and Thefts

Form (and Instructions)

- ☐ **Schedule D (Form 1040)** Capital Gains and Losses
- ☐ **982** Reduction of Tax Attributes Due to Discharge of Indebtedness (and Section 1082 Basis Adjustments)
- ☐ **8828** Recapture of Federal Mortgage Subsidy
- ☐ **8949** Sales and Other Dispositions of Capital Assets

Main Home

This section explains the term "main home." Usually, the home you live in most of the time is your main home and can be a:

- House,
- Houseboat,
- Mobile home,
- Cooperative apartment, or
- Condominium.

To exclude gain under the rules of this chapter, you in most cases must have owned and lived in the property as your main home for at least 2 years during the 5-year period ending on the date of sale.

Land. If you sell the land on which your main home is located, but not the house itself, you cannot exclude any gain you have from the sale of the land. However, if you sell vacant land used as part of your main home and that is adjacent to it, you may be able to exclude the gain from the sale under certain circumstances. See *Vacant land* under *Main Home* in Publication 523 for more information.

Example. You buy a piece of land and move your main home to it. Then you sell the land on which your main home was located. This sale is not considered a sale of your main home, and you cannot exclude any gain on the sale of the land.

More than one home. If you have more than one home, you can exclude gain only from the sale of your main home. You must include in income gain from the sale of any other home. If you have two homes and live in both of them, your main home is ordinarily the one you live in most of the time.

Example 1. You own and live in a house in the city. You also own a beach house you use during summer months. The house in the city is your main home.

Example 2. You own a house, but you live in another house that you rent. The rented house is your main home.

> ### EXPLANATION
> If you own more than one property, it is important to determine which is your principal, or main, residence. The IRS will not issue a ruling on whether or not a home qualifies as a principal residence. The gain on the sale of your principal residence may be excluded, but the gain on the sale of your non-principal residence or rental property is taxed in the year of the sale.

If you use more than one property as a residence, the determination of which property is your principal residence will be based on all the facts and circumstances. The IRS has said that if you alternate between two properties, the one you use for a majority of time during the year will ordinarily be considered your principal residence. However, regulations indicate that other factors are also relevant in determining which property is your principal residence. Those factors include:

- Where you vote,
- The address you use on your tax returns,
- The address you claim to be your residence in other financial dealings,
- Where your children go to school,
- Where you work,
- Where your car is registered,
- Where you belong to social and religious groups.

That the property is currently rented or has been rented in the past does not mean that you may not consider it to be your principal residence. For example, a property that is rented out for a brief period while you are away or while you are trying to sell it should not affect the property's status as your principal residence. In order to exclude the gain, the home's status as your principal residence at the time of sale is no longer relevant as long as it was your principal residence for 2 of the 5 years prior to the date of sale.

Property used partly as your main home. If you use only part of the property as your main home, the rules discussed in this chapter apply only to the gain or loss on the sale of that part of the property. For details, see *Business Use or Rental of Home*, later.

Figuring Gain or Loss

To figure the gain or loss on the sale of your main home, you must know the selling price, the amount realized, and the adjusted basis. Subtract the adjusted basis from the amount realized to get your gain or loss.

	Selling price
−	Selling expenses
	Amount realized

	Amount realized
−	Adjusted basis
	Gain or loss

Selling Price

The selling price is the total amount you receive for your home. It includes money, all notes, mortgages, or other debts assumed by the buyer as part of the sale, and the fair market value of any other property or any services you receive.

Payment by employer. You may have to sell your home because of a job transfer. If your employer pays you for a loss on the sale or for your selling expenses, do not include the payment as part of the selling price. Your employer will include it as wages in box 1 of your Form W-2, and you will include it in your income on Form 1040, line 7, or on Form 1040NR, line 8.

> **TAXSAVER**
> **Selling your home to your employer.** If during 2011 you sold your home directly to your employer at **fair market value**, no portion of the proceeds is treated as additional compensation. Any gain is subject to the regular rules for home sales. However, if your home was sold to your employer at an amount above fair market value, part of the proceeds would be treated as compensation or ordinary income.

Option to buy. If you grant an option to buy your home and the option is exercised, add the amount you receive for the option to the selling price of your home. If the option is not exercised, you must report the amount as ordinary income in the year the option expires. Report this amount on Form 1040, line 21, or on Form 1040NR, line 21.

Form 1099-S. If you received Form 1099-S, Proceeds From Real Estate Transactions, box 2 (gross proceeds) should show the total amount you received for your home.

However, box 2 will not include the fair market value of any services or property other than cash or notes you received or will receive. Instead, box 4 will be checked to indicate your receipt or expected receipt of these items.

If you can exclude the entire gain, the person responsible for closing the sale in most cases will not have to report it on Form 1099-S. If you do not receive Form 1099-S, use sale documents and other records to figure the total amount you received for your home.

Amount Realized

The amount realized is the selling price minus selling expenses.

Selling expenses. Selling expenses include:
- Commissions,
- Advertising fees,
- Legal fees, and
- Loan charges paid by the seller, such as loan placement fees or "points."

> ## EXPLANATION
> **Other selling expenses.** The following items are also considered selling expenses: (1) broker's fees, (2) fees for drafting a contract of sale, (3) fees for drafting the deed, (4) escrow fees, (5) geological surveys, (6) maps, (7) title insurance, (8) recording fees, (9) abstracts of title, (10) title certificate, (11) title opinion, and (12) title registration.

Adjusted Basis

While you owned your home, you may have made adjustments (increases or decreases) to the basis. This adjusted basis must be determined before you can figure gain or loss on the sale of your home. For information on how to figure your home's adjusted basis, see _Determining Basis_, later.

Amount of Gain or Loss

To figure the amount of gain or loss, compare the amount realized to the adjusted basis.

Gain on sale. If the amount realized is more than the adjusted basis, the difference is a gain and, except for any part you can exclude, in most cases is taxable.

Loss on sale. If the amount realized is less than the adjusted basis, the difference is a loss. A loss on the sale of your main home cannot be deducted.

> ## TAXSAVER
> **Loss on sale of a house held for investment.** While you cannot deduct a loss on the sale of your home, if you own a house as an investment (and do not use it for personal purposes), you may be able to deduct any loss realized.
>
> ### Explanation
> If you convert your residence to rental property, your basis for purposes of calculating depreciation and a loss on sale is limited to the lower of your adjusted basis or the value of the residence on the date of conversion. Your basis, however, for calculating a gain is your adjusted basis less allowable depreciation.
>
> ### Example
> Assume you have a residence with a basis of $150,000, which you convert to business use when its fair market value is $125,000. You would use $125,000 as your basis for calculating depreciation. If you subsequently sold the residence for $130,000 after having deducted $4,000 for depreciation, you would not recognize a gain or loss because a loss results on the gain calculation and a gain results on the loss calculation.
>
> | | Gain Calculation | Loss Calculation |
> |---|---|---|
> | Selling price | $130,000 | $130,000 |
> | Less: | | |
> | Adjusted basis | 146,000 | 121,000 |
> | Gain/(loss) | ($16,000) | $9,000 |

Jointly owned home. If you and your spouse sell your jointly owned home and file a joint return, you figure your gain or loss as one taxpayer.

Separate returns. If you file separate returns, each of you must figure your own gain or loss according to your ownership interest in the home. Your ownership interest is determined by state law.

Joint owners not married. If you and a joint owner other than your spouse sell your jointly owned home, each of you must figure your own gain or loss according to your ownership interest in the home. Each of you applies the rules discussed in this chapter on an individual basis.

Dispositions Other Than Sales
Some special rules apply to other dispositions of your main home.

Foreclosure or repossession. If your home was foreclosed on or repossessed, you have a disposition.

In most cases, you figure the gain or loss from the disposition in the same way as gain or loss from a sale. But the selling price of your home used to figure the amount of your gain or loss depends, in part, on whether you were personally liable for repaying the debt secured by the home and whether the debt is qualified principal residence indebtedness. See Publication 523 for more information.

Form 1099-A and Form 1099-C. Generally, you will receive Form 1099-A, Acquisition or Abandonment of Secured Property, from your lender if your home is transferred in a foreclosure. This form will have the information you need to determine the amount of your gain or loss and any ordinary income from cancellation of debt that is not a discharge of qualified principal residence indebtedness. If your debt is canceled, you may receive Form 1099-C, Cancellation of Debt.

Discharges of qualified principal residence indebtedness. You may be able to exclude from gross income a discharge of qualified principal residence indebtedness. This exclusion applies to discharges made after 2006 and before 2013. If you choose to exclude this income, you must reduce (but not below zero) the basis of the principal residence by the amount excluded from your gross income.

File Form 982 with your tax return. See the form's instructions for detailed information.

TAXALERT
You may be able to exclude from your gross income the income realized from the forgiveness or cancellation of up to $2 million of "qualified principal residence indebtedness." This exclusion applies to discharges made in 2007 through 2012.

Qualified principal residence indebtedness means up to $2 million ($1 million if married filing separately) in acquisition indebtedness. Acquisition indebtedness is generally defined as debt you incurred to acquire, construct, or make substantial improvements to your principal residence and such debt is secured by that residence. It also includes refinancing of such acquisition indebtedness to the extent the balance of the new loan does not exceed the amount of the refinanced acquisition debt.

The amount of any discharged debt you can exclude from your income reduces the basis in your principal residence. That will increase the amount of gain (or decrease any loss) you realize when you ultimately sell your home.

Example
Joe purchased his home in 2009 for $300,000 with 100% financing. In 2011, his employer had significant layoffs and Joe lost his job. Also, in 2011 the value of his home dropped significantly. Due to Joe's financial condition and the depressed value of the home, his lender decided to reduce the outstanding balance on the mortgage to $200,000. Joe would not need to include the $100,000 in his income, but instead would file Form 982 and record an adjustment to his basis in the home. His basis in the home following the debt forgiveness would be $200,000.

Principal residence. Your principal residence is the home where you ordinarily live most of the time. You can have only one principal residence at any one time. See *Main Home*, earlier.

Qualified principal residence indebtedness. This indebtedness is a mortgage you took out to buy, build, or substantially improve your principal residence. It also must be secured by your principal residence, and it cannot be more than the cost of your principal residence plus improvements.

Amount eligible for the exclusion. The exclusion applies only to debt discharged after 2006 and before 2013. The maximum amount you can treat as qualified principal residence indebtedness is $2 million ($1 million if married filing separately). You cannot exclude from gross income discharge of qualified principal residence indebtedness if the discharge was for services performed for the lender or on account of any other factor not directly related to a decline in the value of your residence or to your financial condition.

Abandonment. If you abandon your home, you may have ordinary income. If the abandoned home secures a debt for which you are personally liable and the debt is canceled, you have ordinary income equal to the amount of the canceled debt. See Publication 523 for more information.

> ### TAXALERT
> If you abandon property secured by a debt for which you are personally liable and the debt is canceled, you will realize ordinary income equal to the canceled debt. However, there are certain exceptions that may apply. See *Canceled debts* in Publication 4681 for more details. If you were insolvent before the abandonment of the property, you may not need to include the canceled debt in income. Also, review Form 982, which may need to be attached to your tax return.

Trading (exchanging) homes. If you trade your old home for another home, treat the trade as a sale and a purchase.

Example. You owned and lived in a home with an adjusted basis of $41,000. A real estate dealer accepted your old home as a trade-in and allowed you $50,000 toward a new home priced at $80,000. This is treated as a sale of your old home for $50,000 with a gain of $9,000 ($50,000 − $41,000).

If the dealer had allowed you $27,000 and assumed your unpaid mortgage of $23,000 on your old home, your sales price would still be $50,000 (the $27,000 trade-in allowed plus the $23,000 mortgage assumed).

Transfer to spouse. If you transfer your home to your spouse or to your former spouse incident to your divorce, you in most cases have no gain or loss. This is true even if you receive cash or other consideration for the home. As a result, the rules in this chapter do not apply.

More information. If you need more information, see *Transfer to spouse* in Publication 523 and *Property Settlements* in Publication 504, *Divorced or Separated Individuals*.

Involuntary conversion. You have a disposition when your home is destroyed or condemned and you receive other property or money in payment, such as insurance or a condemnation award. This is treated as a sale and you may be able to exclude all or part of any gain from the destruction or condemnation of your home, as explained later under *Special Situations*.

Determining Basis

You need to know your basis in your home to figure any gain or loss when you sell it. Your basis in your home is determined by how you got the home. Your basis is its cost if you bought it or built it. If you got it in some other way (inheritance, gift, etc.), your basis is either its fair market value when you received it or the adjusted basis of the previous owner.

While you owned your home, you may have made adjustments (increases or decreases) to your home's basis. The result of these adjustments is your home's adjusted basis, which is used to figure gain or loss on the sale of your home. See *Adjusted Basis*, later.

You can find more information on basis and adjusted basis in chapter 13 of this publication and in Publication 523.

Cost As Basis

The cost of property is the amount you pay for it in cash, debt obligations, other property, or services.

Purchase. If you buy your home, your basis is its cost to you. This includes the purchase price and certain settlement or closing costs. In most cases, your purchase price includes your down payment and any debt, such as a first or second mortgage or notes you gave the seller in payment for the home. If you build, or contract to build, a new home, your purchase price can include costs of construction, as discussed in Publication 523.

Settlement fees or closing costs. When you bought your home, you may have paid settlement fees or closing costs in addition to the contract price of the property. You can include in your basis some of the settlement fees and closing costs you paid for buying the home, but not the fees and costs for getting a mortgage loan. A fee paid for buying the home is any fee you would have had to pay even if you paid cash for the home (that is, without the need for financing).

Chapter 13 lists some of the settlement fees and closing costs that you can include in the basis of property, including your home. It also lists some settlement costs that cannot be included in basis.

Also see Publication 523 for additional items and a discussion of basis other than cost.

Adjusted Basis

Adjusted basis is your cost or other basis increased or decreased by certain amounts. To figure your adjusted basis, you can use Worksheet 1 in Publication 523.

Increases to basis. These include the following.
- Additions and other improvements that have a useful life of more than 1 year.
- Special assessments for local improvements.
- Amounts you spent after a casualty to restore damaged property.

Improvements. These add to the value of your home, prolong its useful life, or adapt it to new uses. You add the cost of additions and other improvements to the basis of your property.

For example, putting a recreation room or another bathroom in your unfinished basement, putting up a new fence, putting in new plumbing or wiring, putting on a new roof, or paving your unpaved driveway are improvements. An addition to your house, such as a new deck, a sun-room, or a new garage, is also an improvement.

> **TAXSAVER**
> **Shrubs and trees.** The Tax Court has held that shrubbery and trees may qualify as improvements to be added to the basis of your property.

Repairs. These maintain your home in good condition but do not add to its value or prolong its life. You do not add their cost to the basis of your property.

For example, repainting your house inside or outside, fixing your gutters or floors, repairing leaks or plastering, and replacing broken window panes are examples of repairs.

Decreases to basis. These include the following.
- Discharges of qualified principal indebtedness (but do not reduce basis below zero).
- Gain you postponed from the sale of a previous home before May 7, 1997.
- General sales taxes claimed as an itemized deduction on Schedule A (Form 1040) from 2004 through 2011 that were imposed on the purchase of personal property, such as a houseboat used as your home or a mobile home.
- Deductible casualty losses.
- Insurance payments you received or expect to receive for casualty losses.
- Payments you received for granting an easement or right-of-way.
- Depreciation allowed or allowable if you used your home for business or rental purposes.
- Residential energy credit (generally allowed from 1977 through 1987) claimed for the cost of energy improvements that you added to the basis of your home.
- Nonbusiness energy property credit (allowed beginning in 2006 but not for 2008) claimed for making certain energy saving improvements you added to the basis of your home.
- Residential energy efficient property credit (allowed beginning in 2006) claimed for making certain energy saving improvements you added to the basis of your home.
- Adoption credit you claimed for improvements added to the basis of your home.
- Nontaxable payments from an adoption assistance program of your employer you used for improvements you added to the basis of your home.
- Energy conservation subsidy excluded from your gross income because you received it (directly or indirectly) from a public utility after 1992 to buy or install any energy conservation measure. An energy conservation measure is an installation or modification primarily designed either to reduce consumption of electricity or natural gas or to improve the management of energy demand for a home.
- Carry forward of the District of Columbia first-time homebuyer credit (allowed on the purchase of a principal residence in the District of Columbia beginning on August 5, 1997 and ending on December 31, 2011).

Text intentionally omitted.

The records you should keep include:
- Proof of the home's purchase price and purchase expenses,
- Receipts and other records for all improvements, additions, and other items that affect the home's adjusted basis,
- Any worksheets or other computations you used to figure the adjusted basis of the home you sold, the gain or loss on the sale, the exclusion, and the taxable gain,
- Any Form 982 you filed to report any discharge of qualified principal residence indebtedness,

- Any Form 2119, Sale of Your Home, you filed to postpone gain from the sale of a previous home before May 7, 1997, and
- Any worksheets you used to prepare Form 2119, such as the Adjusted Basis of Home Sold Worksheet or the Capital Improvements Worksheet from the Form 2119 instructions, or other source of computations.

TAXORGANIZER

Documenting the basis in your home. The following documentation should be maintained to support the basis in your home upon sale:
- Receipts for all the above listed increases to your cost basis in your house
- Closing statement from purchase of home to support all transfer taxes, attorney's fees, and other fees (survey, inspection, appraisal)
- Annual statements from cooperative housing corporations (co-ops) regarding maintenance payments used to reduce the indebtedness owed by the corporation

TAXPLANNER

Other documents you can use. If you lose your original receipts, other documents may be used to substantiate the cost of improvements to your home. Canceled checks, contracts, before and after photographs, and building permits may be acceptable to the IRS. If all documentation is lost, you should figure your basis by getting estimates of the cost of similar improvements made at the same time you made yours.

For more information on basis and adjusted basis, see chapter 13, *Basis of property.*

Excluding the Gain

You may qualify to exclude from your income all or part of any gain from the sale of your main home. This means that, if you qualify, you will not have to pay tax on the gain up to the limit described under *Maximum Exclusion*, next. To qualify, you must meet the *ownership and use tests* described later.

You can choose not to take the exclusion by including the gain from the sale in your gross income on your tax return for the year of the sale.

You can use Worksheet 2 in Publication 523 to figure the amount of your exclusion and your taxable gain, if any.

Maximum Exclusion

You can exclude up to $250,000 of the gain on the sale of your main home if all of the following are true.
- You meet the ownership test.
- You meet the use test.
- During the 2-year period ending on the date of the sale, you did not exclude gain from the sale of another home.

You may be able to exclude up to $500,000 of the gain on the sale of your main home if you are married and file a joint return and meet the requirements listed in the discussion of the special rules for joint returns, later, under *Married Persons*.

Ownership and Use Tests

To claim the exclusion, you must meet the ownership and use tests. This means that during the 5-year period ending on the date of the sale, you must have:
- Owned the home for at least 2 years (the ownership test), and
- Lived in the home as your main home for at least 2 years (the use test).

Exception. If you owned and lived in the property as your main home for less than 2 years, you can still claim an exclusion in some cases. The maximum amount you may be able to exclude will be reduced. See *Reduced Maximum Exclusion*, later.

Example 1—home owned and occupied for at least 2 years. Selena bought and moved into her main home in September 2008. She sold the home at a gain on September 15, 2011. During the 5-year period ending on the date of sale (September 16, 2006–September 15, 2011), she owned and lived in the home for more than 2 years. She meets the ownership and use tests.

Caution

If you have any taxable gain from the sale of your home, you may have to increase your withholding or make estimated tax payments. See Publication 505, Tax Withholding and Estimated Tax.

Example 2—ownership test met but use test not met. Rajiv bought a home in 2006. After living in it for 6 months, he moved out. He never lived in the home again and sold it at a gain on June 28, 2011. He owned the home during the entire 5-year period ending on the date of sale (June 29, 2006–June 28, 2011). However, he did not live in it for the required 2 years. He meets the ownership test but not the use test. He cannot exclude any part of his gain on the sale unless he qualified for a reduced maximum exclusion (explained later).

Period of Ownership and Use

The required 2 years of ownership and use during the 5-year period ending on the date of the sale do not have to be continuous nor do they have to occur at the same time.

You meet the tests if you can show that you owned and lived in the property as your main home for either 24 full months or 730 days (365 × 2) during the 5-year period ending on the date of sale.

EXPLANATION

The home you sold must have been owned and lived in as a principal residence by you for 2 of the 5 years prior to its sale. The key terms to remember are "owned" and "lived in" for 2 years.

Temporary absence. Short temporary absences for vacations or other seasonal absences, even if you rent out the property during the absences, are counted as periods of use. The following examples assume that the reduced maximum exclusion (discussed later) does not apply to the sales.

Example 1. David Johnson, who is single, bought and moved into his home on February 1, 2009. Each year during 2009 and 2010, David left his home for a 2-month summer vacation. David sold the house on March 1, 2011. Although the total time David used his home is less than 2 years (21 months), he may exclude any gain up to $250,000. The 2-month vacations are short temporary absences and are counted as periods of use in determining whether David used the home for the required 2 years.

Example 2. Professor Paul Beard, who is single, bought and moved into a house on August 28, 2008. He lived in it as his main home continuously until January 5, 2010, when he went abroad for a 1-year sabbatical leave. On February 6, 2011, 1 month after returning from the leave, Paul sold the house at a gain. Because his leave was not a short temporary absence, he cannot include the period of leave to meet the 2-year use test. He cannot exclude any part of his gain, because he did not use the residence for the required 2 years.

EXAMPLE

Maurice and Mavis purchase a home in 2005. In 2006, Maurice is transferred overseas for 5 years, during which time the house is rented. When Maurice and Mavis return in 2011, Maurice's employer sends Maurice to another city in the United States, instead of back to the home purchased in 2005. Maurice and Mavis sell the original house in 2011 without ever reoccupying it. They are generally not eligible for any exclusion as they did not live in the house at any time during the last 5 years prior to sale.

TAXSAVER

Status of your home. The status of the home when you sell it is irrelevant. Even if you haven't lived in it for 3 years at the time of sale, the exclusion is still available if you meet the 2-year rule.

Ownership and use tests met at different times. You can meet the ownership and use tests during different 2-year periods. However, you must meet both tests during the 5-year period ending on the date of the sale.

Example. In 2000, Helen Jones lived in a rented apartment. The apartment building was later converted to condominiums, and she bought her same apartment on December 3, 2008. In 2009, Helen became ill and on April 14 of that year she moved to her daughter's home. On July 12, 2011, while still living in her daughter's home, she sold her condominium.

Helen can exclude gain on the sale of her condominium because she met the ownership and use tests during the 5-year period from July 13, 2006, to July 12, 2011, the date she sold the condominium. She owned her condominium from December 3, 2008, to July 12, 2011 (more than 2 years). She lived in the property from July 13, 2006 (the beginning of the 5-year period), to April 14, 2009 (more than 2 years).

The time Helen lived in her daughter's home during the 5-year period can be counted toward her period of ownership, and the time she lived in her rented apartment during the 5-year period can be counted toward her period of use.

Cooperative apartment. If you sold stock as a tenant-stockholder in a cooperative housing corporation, the ownership and use tests are met if, during the 5-year period ending on the date of sale, you:
- Owned the stock for at least 2 years, and
- Lived in the house or apartment that the stock entitles you to occupy as your main home for at least 2 years.

Exceptions to Ownership and Use Tests
The following sections contain exceptions to the ownership and use tests for certain taxpayers.

Exception for individuals with a disability. There is an exception to the use test if, during the 5-year period before the sale of your home:
- You become physically or mentally unable to care for yourself, and
- You owned and lived in your home as your main home for a total of at least 1 year.

Under this exception, you are considered to live in your home during any time that you own the home and live in a facility (including a nursing home) licensed by a state or political subdivision to care for persons in your condition.

If you meet this exception to the use test, you still have to meet the 2-out-of-5-year ownership test to claim the exclusion.

Previous home destroyed or condemned. For the ownership and use tests, you add the time you owned and lived in a previous home that was destroyed or condemned to the time you owned and lived in the replacement home on whose sale you wish to exclude gain. This rule applies if any part of the basis of the home you sold depended on the basis of the destroyed or condemned home. Otherwise, you must have owned and lived in the same home for 2 of the 5 years before the sale to qualify for the exclusion.

Members of the uniformed services or Foreign Service, employees of the intelligence community, or employees or volunteers of the Peace Corps. You can choose to have the 5-year test period for ownership and use suspended during any period you or your spouse serve on "qualified official extended duty" as a member of the uniformed services or Foreign Service of the United States, as an employee of the intelligence community, or as an employee or volunteer of the Peace Corps. This means that you may be able to meet the 2-year use test even if, because of your service, you did not actually live in your home for at least the required 2 years during the 5-year period ending on the date of sale.

If this helps you qualify to exclude gain, you can choose to have the 5-year test period suspended by filing a return for the year of sale that does not include the gain.

Example. David bought and moved into a home in 2003. He lived in it as his main home for 2½ years. For the next 6 years, he did not live in it because he was on qualified official extended duty with the Army. He then sold the home at a gain in 2011. To meet the use test, David chooses to suspend the 5-year test period for the 6 years he was on qualified official extended duty. This means he can disregard those 6 years. Therefore, David's 5-year test period consists of the 5 years before he went on qualified official extended duty. He meets the ownership and use tests because he owned and lived in the home for 2½ years during this test period.

Period of suspension. The period of suspension cannot last more than 10 years. Together, the 10-year suspension period and the 5-year test period can be as long as, but no more than, 15 years. You cannot suspend the 5-year period for more than one property at a time. You can revoke your choice to suspend the 5-year period at any time.

For more information about the suspension of the 5-year test period, see *Members of the uniformed services or Foreign Service, employees of the intelligence community, or employees or volunteers of the Peace Corps* in Publication 523.

Periods of nonqualified use. In most cases, gain from the sale or exchange of your main home will not qualify for the exclusion to the extent that the gains are allocated to periods of nonqualified use. Nonqualified use is any period after December 31, 2008, during which the property is not used as the main home.

The gain resulting from the sale of the property is allocated between qualified and nonqualified use periods based on the amount of time the property was held for qualified and nonqualified use.

Gain from the sale or exchange of a main home allocable to periods of qualified use will continue to qualify for the exclusion for the sale of your main home. Gain from the sale or exchange of property allocable to nonqualified use will not qualify for the exclusion.

Gain is in most cases allocated to periods of nonqualified use based on the ratio which: (1) the aggregate periods of nonqualified use during the period the property was owned by you over (2) the total period the property was owned by you. You do not incorporate any period before 2009 for the aggregate periods of nonqualified use. Certain exceptions apply. For details, see Publication 523.

Married Persons

If you and your spouse file a joint return for the year of sale and one spouse meets the ownership and use test, you can exclude up to $250,000 of the gain. (But see *Special rules for joint returns*, next.)

Special rules for joint returns. You can exclude up to $500,000 of the gain on the sale of your main home if all of the following are true.
- You are married and file a joint return for the year.
- Either you or your spouse meets the ownership test.
- Both you and your spouse meet the use test.
- During the 2-year period ending on the date of the sale, neither you nor your spouse excluded gain from the sale of another home.

If either spouse does not satisfy all these requirements, the maximum exclusion that can be claimed by the couple is the total of the maximum exclusions that each spouse would qualify for if not married and the amounts were figured separately. For this purpose, each spouse is treated as owning the property during the period that either spouse owned the property.

> ### EXAMPLE
> In December 2010, Karen, who is single, sells the home she has been living in as a principal residence for the past 4 years and has a gain of $75,000 on the sale. The entire $75,000 qualifies for the exclusion. On December 31, 2010, Karen marries Ray. On January 2, 2011, Ray sells the home he has owned and been living in as a principal residence for over 2 years and has a gain of $350,000 on the sale. Ray can only exclude $250,000 of the gain even if he and Karen file a joint tax return. The $500,000 exclusion does not apply for two reasons: First, Karen sold her home within the 2-year period ending on the date Ray sold his home; second, Karen did not use Ray's home as her principal residence for at least 2 of the 5 years before the sale.

Example 1—one spouse sells a home. Emily sells her home in June 2011. She marries Jamie later in the year. She meets the ownership and use tests, but Jamie does not. Emily can exclude up to $250,000 of gain on a separate or joint return for 2011. The $500,000 maximum exclusion for certain joint returns does not apply because Jamie does not meet the use test.

Example 2—each spouse sells a home. The facts are the same as in *Example 1* except that Jamie also sells a home in 2011 before he marries Emily. He meets the ownership and use tests on his home, but Emily does not. Emily and Jamie can each exclude up to $250,000 of gain from the sale of their individual homes. The $500,000 maximum exclusion for certain joint returns does not apply because Emily and Jamie do not jointly meet the use test for the same home.

Sale of main home by surviving spouse. If your spouse died and you did not remarry before the date of sale, you are considered to have owned and lived in the property as your main home during any period of time when your spouse owned and lived in it as a main home.

If you meet all of the following requirements, you may qualify to exclude up to $500,000 of any gain from the sale or exchange of your main home.
- The sale or exchange took place after 2008.
- The sale or exchange took place no more than 2 years after the date of death of your spouse.
- You have not remarried.
- You and your spouse met the use test at the time of your spouse's death.
- You or your spouse met the ownership test at the time of your spouse's death.
- Neither you nor your spouse excluded gain from the sale of another home during the last 2 years.

Example. Harry has owned and used a house as his main home since 2008. Harry and Wilma marry on July 1, 2011, and from that date they use Harry's house as their main home. Harry died on August 15, 2011, and Wilma inherited the property. Wilma sold the property on September 1, 2011, at which time she had not remarried. Although Wilma owned and used the house for less than 2 years, Wilma is considered to have satisfied the ownership and use tests because her period of ownership and use includes the period that Harry owned and used the property before death.

Home transferred from spouse. If your home was transferred to you by your spouse (or former spouse if the transfer was incident to divorce), you are considered to have owned it during any period of time when your spouse owned it.

Use of home after divorce. You are considered to have used property as your main home during any period when:

- You owned it, and
- Your spouse or former spouse is allowed to live in it under a divorce or separation instrument and uses it as his or her main home.

EXPLANATION

This provision removes the old requirement that the home be your residence at the time of sale.

Reduced Maximum Exclusion

If you fail to meet the requirements to qualify for the $250,000 or $500,000 exclusion, you may still qualify for a reduced exclusion. This applies to those who:

- Fail to meet the ownership and use tests, or
- Have used the exclusion within 2 years of selling their current home.

In both cases, to qualify for a reduced exclusion, the sale of your main home must be due to one of the following reasons.

- A change in place of employment.
- Health.
- Unforeseen circumstances.

TAXALERT

In certain cases, you may be able to claim an exclusion from income even though you have not met the ownership and use tests, or if you have sold more than one home during a 2-year period. A reduced maximum exclusion may apply if the sale or exchange is made by reason of a change of place of employment, health, or unforeseen circumstances. The IRS has issued regulations defining when these special exceptions may apply.

If a new place of employment is at least 50 miles farther from the residence sold or exchanged than was the former place of employment, the change of place of employment exception will be deemed to apply.

Example

Steve and Tina purchase a home in Boston in 2010. In 2011, Steve's employer transfers him to Chicago. They owned the home as their principal residence for 13 months. They can exclude up to $270,833 of gain ($500,000 times the ratio of 13 months / 24 months).

Explanation

If the above test is not met, you may still qualify for a reduced maximum exclusion under this exception if the facts and circumstances indicate that a change of place of employment was the primary reason for the sale or exchange.

A sale or exchange is by reason of health if the taxpayer's primary reason for the sale or exchange is:
- To obtain, provide, or facilitate the diagnosis, cure, mitigation, or treatment of disease, illness, or injury, or
- To obtain or provide medical or personal care for a qualified individual suffering from a disease, illness, or injury.

A sale or exchange is not by reason of health if it is merely beneficial to the individual's general health or well-being. However, if a doctor recommends a change of residence for health reasons, the primary reason will be deemed to be for health.

Example

Steve and Cheryl live in an upstate community where it snows or is overcast for most of the year. They have owned their current home for less than 2 years. Steve believes that moving to Hawaii will permit them to exercise more and will make them both much happier. Although the move may be beneficial to the couple's general well-being, a sale of their residence will not qualify for an exception to the 2-year ownership and use requirement for health reasons.

Unforeseen circumstances. The sale of your main home is because of an unforeseen circumstance if your primary reason for the sale is the occurrence of an event that you could not reasonably have anticipated before buying and occupying your main home.

See Publication 523 for more information and to use Worksheet 3 to figure your reduced maximum exclusion.

TAXALERT

Generally, you are allowed to exclude up to $250,000 ($500,000 if married filing a joint return) of gain realized on the sale or exchange of your principal residence. However, effective for sales or exchanges of a principal residence after December 31, 2008, no exclusion of gain is allowed to the extent that the gain is associated with a period of nonqualified use (for example, renting out the home, using it as a vacation home or second residence, or vacancy) that occurs after 2008. For this purpose, a period of nonqualified use means any period beginning after 2008 that precedes using the home as a principal residence by the taxpayer, the taxpayer's spouse, or the taxpayer's former spouse. A period of nonqualified use does not include any period after the home is no longer used as a principal residence, nor any other period of temporary absence, not to exceed an aggregate period of two years, due to change of employment, health conditions, or such other unforeseen circumstances as may be specified.

Any gain taxable because of depreciation claimed on the property after May 6, 1997, is not taken into account in determining the gain allocated to nonqualified use.

Any gain realized from the sale of the home that is not eligible for the exclusion is calculated by multiplying the total gain from the sale of the home by a fraction. The numerator of the fraction is the period of nonqualified use. The denominator of the fraction is the total period of time the property was owned by the taxpayer.

Example 1

Assume that Corrie buys a property on January 1, 2011, for $400,000. She then uses it as rental property for 2 years, claiming $20,000 of depreciation deductions. On January 1, 2013, she converts the property to her principal residence. On January 1, 2015, Corrie moves out, and subsequently sells the property for $700,000 on January 1, 2016.

Corrie's basis in the home sold is $380,000 ($400,000 purchase price less $20,000 in depreciation deductions claimed). Total gain on the sale is $320,000 ($700,000 sales price less $380,000 basis). $20,000 of the total gain is attributable to the depreciation deductions, and is included in income. Of the remaining $300,000 gain, 40% of the gain (2 years divided by 5 years), or $120,000, is allocated to nonqualified use and is not eligible for the exclusion. Since the remaining gain of $180,000 is less than the maximum gain of $250,000 that may be excluded, the remaining gain of $180,000 is excluded from gross income.

Example 2

Assume Todd buys a principal residence on January 1, 2011, for $400,000. Todd then moves out on January 1, 2020, and on December 1, 2022, sells the property for $600,000. The entire $200,000 gain is excluded from gross income because periods after the last qualified use do not constitute nonqualified use.

Business Use or Rental of Home

You may be able to exclude gain from the sale of a home you have used for business or to produce rental income. But you must meet the ownership and use tests.

Example 1. On May 28, 2005, Amy bought a house. She moved in on that date and lived in it until May 31, 2007, when she moved out of the house and put it up for rent. The house was rented from June 1, 2007, to March 31, 2009. Amy moved back into the house on April 1, 2009, and lived there until she sold it on January 29, 2011. During the 5-year period ending on the date of the sale (January 31, 2006–January 29, 2011), Amy owned and lived in the house for more than 2 years as shown in the following table.

Five-Year Period	Used as Home	Used as Rental
1/31/06-5/31/07	16 months	
6/1/07-3/31/09		22 months
4/1/09-1/29/11	22 months	
	38 months	22 months

Amy can exclude gain up to $250,000. However, she cannot exclude the part of the gain equal to the depreciation she claimed or could have claimed for renting the house, as explained later under *Depreciation after May 6, 1997*.

Example 2. William owned and used a house as his main home from 2005 through 2008. On January 1, 2009, he moved to another state. He rented his house from that date until April 30, 2011, when he sold it. During the 5-year period ending on the date of sale (May 1, 2006–April 30, 2011), William owned and lived in the house for 32 months (more than 2 years). He must report the sale on Form 4797 because it was rental property at the time of sale. Because he met the ownership and use tests, he can exclude gain up to $250,000. However, he cannot exclude the part of the gain equal to the depreciation he claimed or could have claimed for renting the house, as explained next.

TAXALERT

The amount of gain you can exclude is reduced to the extent it is attributable to periods of nonqualified use. See the section *Periods of Nonqualified Use* and the accompanying TaxAlert for a description of these rules.

Explanation

In *Example 1* in the IRS text, the period of time Amy rented her home does not become a period of nonqualified use that reduces the amount of gain she can exclude because that rental period occurred entirely before January 1, 2009 (see the section *Periods of Nonqualified Use*, earlier). If, in *Example 1*, Amy rented the house until January 31, 2009, moved back into the house on February 1, 2009, and lived there until she sold it on February 1, 2012, she would not be able to exclude the gain associated with the period of nonqualified use. The period of nonqualified use is the month of January 2009. In this situation, Amy held the house for 92 months (from May 29, 2004 through February 1, 2012). Out of the 92 months, 91 months are deemed to be for qualifying use. If Amy's total gain on the sale of the home was $230,000, only $227,500 of the gain is eligible for the exclusion [$230,000 × (91/92)].

Explanation

In *Example 2* in the IRS text, even though William rented his home after December 31, 2009, and through April 30, 2011, all of his gain will qualify for the exclusion since the rental of the home occurred after the last time he used the home as his principal residence. As described earlier in the section *Periods of Nonqualified Use*, a period of nonqualified use does not include any portion of the 5-year period ending on the date of the sale that is after the last date you (or your spouse) used the property as a main home. William lived in the home from May 1, 2006, through December 31, 2008, and rented it from January 1, 2009, through April 30, 2011. Accordingly, the period of rental occurred within the 5-year period ending on the date of the sale, and was after the last date William used the property as a main home.